SIPRI Yearbook 2018

Armaments, Disarmament and International Security

**STOCKHOLM INTERNATIONAL
PEACE RESEARCH INSTITUTE**

OXFORD UNIVERSITY PRESS
2018

OXFORD
UNIVERSITY PRESS

Great Clarendon Street, Oxford OX2 6DP,
United Kingdom

Oxford University Press is a department of the University of Oxford.
It furthers the University's objective of excellence in research, scholarship,
and education by publishing worldwide. Oxford is a registered trade mark of
Oxford University Press in the UK and in certain other countries

© SIPRI 2018

British Library Cataloguing in Publication Data
Data available

Library of Congress Cataloging in Publication Data
Data available

ISBN 978–0–19–882155–7

Typeset and originated by SIPRI
Printed and bound by
CPI Group (UK) Ltd, Croydon, CR0 4YY

SIPRI Yearbook 2018 is also published online at
<http://www.sipriyearbook.org>

Contents

Introduction

Part I. Armed conflict and conflict management, 2017

Part II. Military spending and armaments, 2017

Part III. Non-proliferation, arms control and disarmament, 2017

Preface

This, the 49th edition of the SIPRI Yearbook, was finalized against the background of a widely perceived deepening of confrontation between Russia and the United States and a commensurate rise in international tensions. These events took place in a context shaped by broader trends that were an important feature of 2017 and that are tracked in this Yearbook. International arms transfers increased and global military spending stabilized at a level higher than it was at the end of the cold war. There were many challenges in 2017 to the smooth functioning and durability of the international system for managing complex armed conflicts. These challenges included escalating rhetoric between North Korea and the USA, deepening rifts in the Middle East and North Africa (MENA; especially between Saudi Arabia and Iran) and significant pressures on major arms control treaties.

In facing these risks for human security and international stability, it is ever more important to base arguments and policies on evidence. The term 'fake news' has gained currency in recent years. Its widespread use both reflects concerns that information can be manipulated and is often a contrivance to advance misinformation. Countering this trend and presenting hard facts remain central purposes of SIPRI and of the Yearbook. Categorising and authenticating key developments in international security, analysing and placing them in context adds up to a formidable but necessary task. Without a common, agreed set of facts, people are unable to make their own informed judgements and governments cannot be sure that their policies and actions are well-grounded.

Peace, security and conflict are broad and multidimensional. Correspondingly, SIPRI research runs the gamut, and this diversity is reflected in the Institute's publications. From reports to briefs, SIPRI's research on the issues that comprise the world's peace and security horizon can be easily found on the SIPRI website (www.sipri.org). As part of this larger body of work, the Yearbook surveys and provides background to important developments in the field of peace, security and conflict in 2017.

The Introduction (chapter 1) reflects on a year in which some risks to global stability and human security have intensified, while others are being effectively managed. Part I of the Yearbook covers armed conflicts and conflict management in 2017. In a new departure, instead of presenting summarized data on all armed conflicts in the year, the aim is to catch key moments and trends in conflict escalation and peacebuilding. Chapter 2 focuses on armed conflicts and peace processes, looking at the multifaceted root causes of both and summarising their latest developments. Multilateral peace operations are featured in chapter 3, which also discusses multilateral 'non-peace operations' for the first time.

Parts II and III focus on issues related to armament and disarmament; much of the Institute's work in these areas is based on original, rigorous data collection—the basis of SIPRI's databases. Part II is devoted to military spending and armaments, including detailed assessment of recent trends in military expenditure (chapter 4), international arms transfers and arms production (chapter 5). Chapter 6 details world nuclear forces and the current nuclear modernization programmes. Part III covers non-proliferation, arms control and disarmament. Chapter 7 looks at the new Treaty on the Prohibition of Nuclear Weapons and Iran's continued implementation the Joint Comprehensive Plan of Action to limit its nuclear programme. Chapter 8 discusses the use of chemical weapons in Syria and Iraq, and other developments in chemical and biological security threats. Chapter 9 includes a round-up of humanitarian arms control initiatives in 2017, including the emerging debate on how to regulate lethal autonomous weapon systems. Chapter 10 reports on efforts to strengthen controls on the trade in conventional arms and dual-use items, with a section on controls on intangible transfers of technology.

Taken together, this compendium addresses some of the most urgent matters confronting humanity today. SIPRI continues to seek ways to make best use of the Yearbook and its contents as a tool of transparency and accountability. To that end, the Yearbook has been translated for many years into Chinese, Russian and Ukrainian, and in 2017 translation into Arabic resumed.

The SIPRI Yearbook depends on many people's work. This year's edition features contributions from 32 authors. Its content is refereed extensively, both internally and externally. A dedicated editorial team ensures that the book conforms to the highest publishing standards. The communications, library, operations and IT staff at SIPRI all contribute in different ways to the book's production and distribution. I would like to take this opportunity to express my gratitude to everybody involved, within SIPRI and beyond.

The SIPRI Yearbook is the starting place for in-depth, authoritative open source information on critical issues of international security, armaments and disarmament. Even in this digital age when 'facts' of all kinds can be found in a half-second's search, SIPRI's commitment to authenticating the facts means this volume remains an indispensable global public good.

Dan Smith
Director, SIPRI
Stockholm, June 2018

Abbreviations and conventions

ABM	Anti-ballistic missile	CFSP	Common Foreign and Security Policy (of the EU)
AG	Australia Group		
ALCM	Air-launched cruise missile	CICA	Conference on Interaction and Confidence-building Measures in Asia
APC	Armoured personnel carrier		
APEC	Asia–Pacific Economic Cooperation		
		CIS	Commonwealth of Independent States
APM	Anti-personnel mine		
APT	ASEAN Plus Three	COPAX	Conseil de Paix et de Sécurité de l'Afrique Centrale (Central Africa Peace and Security Council)
ARF	ASEAN Regional Forum		
ASEAN	Association of Southeast Asian Nations		
ATT	Arms Trade Treaty	CSBM	Confidence- and security-building measure
ATTU	Atlantic-to-the Urals (zone)	CSDP	Common Security and Defence Policy (of the EU)
AU	African Union		
BCC	Bilateral Consultative Commission (of the Russian–US New START treaty)	CSTO	Collective Security Treaty Organization
		CTBT	Comprehensive Nuclear-Test-Ban Treaty
BMD	Ballistic missile defence	CTBTO	Comprehensive Nuclear-Test-Ban Treaty Organization
BSEC	Organization of the Black Sea Economic Cooperation		
BTWC	Biological and Toxin Weapons Convention	CW	Chemical weapon/warfare
		CWC	Chemical Weapons Convention
CAR	Central African Republic		
CBM	Confidence-building measure	DDR	Disarmament, demobilization and reintegration
CBSS	Council of the Baltic Sea States		
		DPKO	UN Department of Peacekeeping Operations
CBW	Chemical and biological weapon/warfare	DPRK	Democratic People's Republic of Korea (North Korea)
CCM	Convention on Cluster Munitions		
CCW	Certain Conventional Weapons (Convention)	DRC	Democratic Republic of the Congo
CD	Conference on Disarmament	EAEC	European Atomic Energy Community (Euratom)
CDS	Consejo de Defensa Suramericano (South American Defence Council)		
		EAPC	Euro-Atlantic Partnership Council
CEEAC	Communauté Economique des Etats de l'Afrique Centrale (Economic Community of Central African States, ECCAS)	ECOWAS	Economic Community of West African States
		EDA	European Defence Agency
		EDA	Excess Defense Articles
		ERW	Explosive remnants of war
CFE	Conventional Armed Forces in Europe (Treaty)	EU	European Union
		FATF	Financial Action Task Force

FMCT	Fissile material cut-off treaty	NGO	Non-governmental organization
FSC	Forum for Security Cooperation (of the OSCE)	NPT	Non-Proliferation Treaty
FY	Financial year	NSG	Nuclear Suppliers Group
FYROM	Former Yugoslav Republic of Macedonia	NWS	Nuclear weapon state
G7	Group of Seven (industrialized states)	OAS	Organization of American States
GCC	Gulf Cooperation Council	OCCAR	Organisation Conjointe de Coopération en matière d'Armement (Organisation for Joint Armament Cooperation)
GDP	Gross domestic product		
GGE	Group of government experts	ODA	Official development assistance
GLCM	Ground-launched cruise missile	OECD	Organisation for Economic Co-operation and Development
GUAM	Georgia, Ukraine, Azerbaijan and Moldova		
HCOC	Hague Code of Conduct	OHCHR	Office of the UN High Commissioner for Human Rights
HEU	Highly enriched uranium		
IAEA	International Atomic Energy Agency	OIC	Organisation of Islamic Cooperation
ICBM	Intercontinental ballistic missile	OPANAL	Organismo para la Proscripción de las Armas Nucleares en la América Latina y el Caribe (Agency for the Prohibition of Nuclear Weapons in Latin America and the Caribbean)
ICC	International Criminal Court		
ICJ	International Court of Justice		
IED	Improvised explosive device		
IGAD	Intergovernmental Authority on Development	OPCW	Organisation for the Prohibition of Chemical Weapons
INF	Intermediate-range Nuclear Forces (Treaty)	OPEC	Organization of the Petroleum Exporting Countries
ISAF	International Security Assistance Force		
JCG	Joint Consultative Group (of the CFE Treaty)	OSCC	Open Skies Consultative Commission
LEU	Low-enriched uranium	OSCE	Organization for Security and Co-operation in Europe
MDGs	Millennium Development Goals (of the UN)	P5	Five permanent members of the UN Security Council
MIRV	Multiple independently targetable re-entry vehicle	PFP	Partnership for Peace
MRBM	Medium-range ballistic missile	PSC	Peace and Security Council (of the African Union)
MTCR	Missile Technology Control Regime	PSI	Proliferation Security Initiative
NAM	Non-Aligned Movement	R&D	Research and development
NATO	North Atlantic Treaty Organization	SADC	Southern African Development Community

SALW	Small arms and light weapons	TLE	Treaty-limited equipment
SAM	Surface-to-air missile	UAE	United Arab Emirates
SCO	Shanghai Cooperation Organisation	UAV	Unmanned aerial vehicle
SDGs	Sustainable Development Goals (of the UN)	UCAV	Unmanned combat air vehicle
SICA	Sistema de la Integración Centroamericana (Central American Integration System)	UN	United Nations
		UNASUR	Unión de Naciones Suramericanas (Union of South American Nations)
SLBM	Submarine-launched ballistic missile	UNDP	UN Development Programme
SLCM	Sea-launched cruise missile	UNHCR	UN High Commissioner for Refugees
SORT	Strategic Offensive Reductions Treaty	UNODA	UN Office for Disarmament Affairs
SRBM	Short-range ballistic missile	UNROCA	UN Register of Conventional Arms
SRCC	Sub-Regional Consultative Commission	WA	Wassenaar Arrangement
START	Strategic Arms Reduction Treaty	WMD	Weapon(s) of mass destruction

Conventions

..	Data not available or not applicable
–	Nil or a negligible figure
( )	Uncertain data
b.	Billion (thousand million)
kg	Kilogram
km	Kilometre (1000 metres)
m.	Million
th.	Thousand
tr.	Trillion (million million)
$	US dollars
€	Euros

Geographical regions and subregions

Africa	Consisting of North Africa (Algeria, Libya, Morocco and Tunisia, but excluding Egypt) and sub-Saharan Africa
Americas	Consisting of North America (Canada and the USA), Central America and the Caribbean (including Mexico), and South America
Asia and Oceania	Consisting of Central Asia, East Asia, Oceania, South Asia (including Afghanistan) and South East Asia
Europe	Consisting of Eastern Europe (Armenia, Azerbaijan, Belarus, Georgia, Moldova, Russia and Ukraine) and Western and Central Europe (with South Eastern Europe)
Middle East	Consisting of Egypt, Iran, Iraq, Israel, Jordan, Kuwait, Lebanon, Syria, Turkey and the states of the Arabian peninsula

SIPRI Yearbook online

www.sipriyearbook.org

The full content of the SIPRI Yearbook is also available online. With the SIPRI Yearbook online you can

- access the complete SIPRI Yearbook on your desktop or handheld device for research on the go
- navigate easily through content using advanced search and browse functionality
- find content easily: search through the whole SIPRI Yearbook and within your results
- save valuable time: use your personal profile to return to saved searches and content again and again
- share content with colleagues and students easily via email and social networking tools
- enhance your research by following clearly linked references and web resources

How to access the SIPRI Yearbook online

Institutional access

The SIPRI Yearbook online is available to institutions worldwide for a one-time fee or by annual subscription. Librarians and central resource coordinators can contact Oxford University Press to receive a price quotation using the details below or register for a free trial at <http://www.oxford online.com/freetrials/>.

Individuals can recommend this resource to their librarians at <http://www.oup.com/library-recommend/>.

Individual subscriptions

The SIPRI Yearbook online is available to individuals worldwide on a 12-month subscription basis. Purchase details can be found at <http://www.oup.com/>.

Contact information

Customers within the Americas

Email: oxfordonline@oup.com
Telephone: +1 (800) 624 0153
Fax: +1 (919) 677 8877

Customers outside the Americas

Email: institutionalsales@oup.com
Telephone: +44 (0) 1865 353705
Fax: +44 (0) 1865 353308

Introduction

Chapter 1. Introduction: International stability and human security in 2017

1. Introduction: International stability and human security in 2017

DAN SMITH

Global security has deteriorated markedly in the past decade. The number of armed conflicts has increased.[1] There has been prolonged and shocking violence in large parts of the Middle East, Africa and South Asia. Russia's annexation of Crimea in 2014 and support to separatist forces in eastern Ukraine form a focal point of disputation amid a general atmosphere of deepening confrontation between Russia and the West. International transfers of major weapons have increased, and global military spending has stabilized at a high plateau—above the level it stood at during the last years of the cold war.[2] Equally, the number of states possessing nuclear weapons has increased, although the number of deployed nuclear warheads has continued to decline.[3] However the measures that achieved these cuts are under threat.

The introductory chapters to the past two editions of the SIPRI Yearbook remarked on the decline in the conditions for international stability and human security in 2015 and 2016.[4] Although violent conflicts and incidents proliferated in much of the Middle East and parts of Africa and South Asia, the framework of multilateral international institutions continued to function well, producing both the 2030 Agenda for Sustainable Development and the Paris Agreement on climate change in 2015.[5] In 2016, while work to implement those global agreements progressed, many global indicators of peace and security continued to regress: military spending, arms transfers and violent conflict all increased. These developments produced discomfiting questions about, for example, whether gains in peaceful relations since the end of the cold war had been reversed, whether the international security architecture is durable, and whether strategic competition between

---

[1] Sollenberg, M. and Melander, E., 'Patterns of organized violence, 2007–16', *SIPRI Yearbook 2017*, pp. 25–46; and chapter 2, section I, in this volume.
[2] See Tian, N. et al., 'Trends in world military expenditure, 2016', SIPRI Fact Sheet, Apr. 2017; and chapter 4, section I, in this volume.
[3] On the stockpiles of those states possessing nuclear weapons see chapter 6, sections I–IX.
[4] Smith, D., 'Introduction: International security, armaments and disarmament', *SIPRI Yearbook 2016*, pp. 1–13; and Smith, D., 'Introduction: International security, armaments and disarmament', *SIPRI Yearbook 2017*, pp. 3–20.
[5] UN General Assembly Resolution 70/1, 'Transforming our world: The 2030 Agenda for Sustainable Development', adopted 25 Sep. 2015, A/RES/70/1, 21 Oct. 2015; and the Paris Agreement under the United Nations Framework Convention on Climate Change (UNFCCC), adopted 12 Dec. 2015, opened for signature 22 Apr. 2016, entered into force 4 Nov. 2016.

major powers could impede the management of increased conflict risk.[6] A further source of unpredictability by the end of 2016 concerned the potential impact of the incoming President of the United States, Donald J. Trump.

In 2017 the previous year's discomfiting questions persisted without receiving decisive answers. While some risks to global stability and human security have intensified, others are being effectively managed. To take an overview of this terrain, this introduction looks first at developments in global stability, focusing on arms control, including the 2017 Treaty on the Prohibition of Nuclear Weapons (TPNW). It moves on to discuss tensions between major powers and then scans some of the world's most pressing issues of human security—focusing on violence, food insecurity and climate change. It concludes with some reflections on prospects for international institutions.

I. Nuclear weapons in international politics

Nuclear arms control

During the cold war, nuclear arms control negotiations were a central feature of Soviet–US detente. When relations deteriorated, arms control stalled and became an irritant. But as change in the Soviet Union unfolded and the cold war ended, arms control and arms reductions made a radical difference on the international scene. On the nuclear front, two Soviet–US treaties set the pace. The 1987 Treaty on the Elimination of Intermediate-Range and Shorter-Range Missiles (INF Treaty) eliminated all ground-launched nuclear and conventional missiles (and their launchers) of any range from 500 to 5500 kilometres.[7] The 1991 Treaty on the Reduction and Limitation of Strategic Offensive Arms (START I) reduced each side to 6000 strategic nuclear warheads on a maximum of 1600 delivery vehicles (bombers and missiles). Further reductions came from the Presidential Nuclear Initiatives of September and October 1991 that substantially reduced the number of tactical (or battlefield) nuclear weapons on both sides.[8] The negotiation of a follow-on treaty took almost two decades. When the USA withdrew from the 1972 Treaty on the Limitation of Anti-Ballistic Missile Systems (ABM Treaty), one of the first achievements of Soviet–US nuclear arms control, Russian reaction was muted in part, perhaps, because of the Treaty on Stra-

---

[6] See Mead, W. R., 'The return of geopolitics', *Foreign Affairs*, May/June 2014; and World Economic Forum (WEF), *The Global Risks Report 2016*, 11th edn (WEF: Geneva, 2016), pp. 24–28.

[7] For a summary and other details of the INF Treaty and other bilateral arms control treaties in this section see annex A, section III, in this volume. On nuclear arms control developments related to the USA and Russia see chapter 7, section II, in this volume.

[8] 'The Presidential Nuclear Initiatives (PNIs) on tactical nuclear weapons at a glance', Arms Control Association, 1 July 2017.

tegic Offensive Reductions (SORT, Moscow Treaty) agreed the same year.[9] In 2010 Russia and the USA signed the Treaty on Measures for the Further Reduction and Limitation of Strategic Offensive Arms (New START), limiting each side to 1550 nuclear warheads deployed on 700 strategic delivery systems. Overall, the number of nuclear weapons worldwide fell from 65 000–70 000 at its peak in the mid-1980s to 14 470 at the end of 2017.

Conventional arms control was equally dramatic. The 1990 Treaty on Conventional Armed Forces in Europe (CFE Treaty) capped at equal levels the number of heavy weapons deployed between the Atlantic and the Urals by the then members of both the North Atlantic Treaty Organization (NATO) and the Warsaw Treaty Organization (WTO).[10] The CFE limits continued to apply to the latter states, even after the WTO itself fell apart and many joined NATO.

Other arms control milestones of the period included the 1993 Chemical Weapons Convention (CWC), the 1996 Comprehensive Nuclear-Test-Ban Treaty (CTBT), the 1997 Anti-Personnel Mines (APM) Convention and, somewhat later, the 2008 Convention on Cluster Munitions and the 2014 Arms Trade Treaty.[11]

Today, the scene is much different. The CTBT has not entered into force.[12] Russia and the USA accuse each other of infringing the INF Treaty and, although New START is being implemented, it expires in February 2021, and there are no current talks on extending or replacing it.[13]

The horizon is also bleak in the case of conventional weapons. Russia suspended its participation in the CFE Treaty in an extended process that concluded in 2015.[14] The core Russian argument was that NATO's enlargement meant that the equity of the original caps had been lost. Furthermore, despite repeated efforts in the Organization for Security and Co-operation in Europe (OSCE), there is no progress in and little active discussion of confidence- and security-building measures.

What some may regard as the biggest recent failure and the biggest recent success of arms control both lie outside the normal negotiating arenas. On

---

[9] Kile, S. N., 'Russian–US nuclear arms control', *SIPRI Yearbook 2003*, pp. 600–605.

[10] For a summary and other details of the CFE Treaty see annex A, section II, in this volume.

[11] For summaries and other details of these arms control agreements see annex A, section I, in this volume.

[12] Although 166 states have ratified the CTBT, it cannot enter into force until it is ratified by China, Egypt, India, Iran, Israel, North Korea, Pakistan and the USA. See annex A, section I, in this volume.

[13] Panda, A., 'The uncertain future of the INF Treaty', Backgrounder, Council on Foreign Relations, 21 Feb. 2018; Russian Ministry of Foreign Affairs, 'The Treaty between the USSR and the US on the Elimination of Their Intermediate-Range and Shorter-Range Missiles (INF Treaty)', 1 Mar. 2018; US Department of State, Bureau of Arms Control, Verification and Compliance, 'INF Treaty: At a glance', Fact sheet, 8 Dec. 2017; and Woolf, A. F., *The New START Treaty: Central Limits and Key Provisions*, Congressional Research Service (CRS) Report for Congress R41219 (US Congress, CRS: Washington, DC, 5 Feb. 2018). See also chapter 7, section II, in this volume.

[14] See Anthony, I., 'A relaunch of conventional arms control in Europe?', *SIPRI Yearbook 2017*, pp. 577.

the one hand, the Democratic People's Republic of Korea (DPRK, or North Korea) has joined the ranks of nuclear weapon-possessing states, despite major international efforts to prevent it. On the other hand, the Joint Comprehensive Plan of Action (JCPOA) agreed with Iran in 2015 has, thus far, been regarded as a success, even though it is under pressure.

Despite sanctions imposed by nine United Nations Security Council resolutions, North Korea's ballistic missile and nuclear weapon development programmes have frustrated a major international non-proliferation effort.[15] North Korea probably has an arsenal of 10–20 deployable nuclear warheads and the capacity to hit regional powers with ballistic missiles.[16] All evidence indicates that it is aiming to have, and will have, nuclear missiles capable of striking targets in the continental USA. Having arrived at this position, North Korea gave some hints of a wish to engage in substantive diplomacy over security issues during a visit by the UN Under Secretary-General for Political Affairs, Jeffrey Feltman, to Pyongyang in December 2017.[17] Then on 1 January 2018 the North Korean leader, Kim Jong Un, made diplomatic overtures to the Republic of Korea (South Korea) in a speech in which he explicitly stated that he now speaks from a position of strength and security.[18] He proposed that the two states take steps to ease the confrontation on the Korean peninsula and improve their relations.

Unlike North Korea, Iran has neither acknowledged having nor ever been proved to have a nuclear weapon development programme. The JCPOA can, nonetheless, be regarded as an arms control measure. In addition to constraining Iran's uranium enrichment programme and potential path towards nuclear weapons until around 2030, the JCPOA introduced increased monitoring and transparency measures that will remain in place long after that date.[19] Despite its successful implementation thus far, the JCPOA began 2018 under pressure from the USA. President Trump threatened to withdraw the USA from the agreement unless what he describes as the deal's 'flaws'— primarily the fact that the JCPOA is not permanent and does not cover Iran's ballistic missile programme—are 'fixed'.[20] Iran has rejected any change to the JCPOA.[21] It may appear paradoxical that, at a time when arms control

---

[15] See chapter 7, section IV, in this volume.

[16] See chapter 6, section IX, in this volume.

[17] 'North Korea crisis: UN political chief in rare visit to Pyongyang', BBC News, 5 Dec. 2017; and Krever, M. and Berlinger, J., 'UN official who visited North Korea sees "high risk" of miscalculation', CNN, 15 Dec. 2017.

[18] 'Kim Jong Un's 2018 new year's address', National Committee of North Korea, 1 Jan. 2018.

[19] The JCPOA is a time-bound agreement with different end dates for different parts of the agreement. See Rauf, T., 'Resolving concerns about Iran's nuclear programme', SIPRI Yearbook 2016, pp. 673–88; Rauf, T., 'Implementation of the Joint Comprehensive Plan of Action in Iran', SIPRI Yearbook 2017, pp. 505–10; and chapter 7, section V, in this volume.

[20] Holland, S., 'Trump issues ultimatum to "fix" Iran nuclear deal', Reuters, 12 Jan. 2018.

[21] 'Iran fulfilling nuclear deal commitments: IAEA chief', Reuters, 30 Oct. 2017; and Dixit, A., 'Iran is implementing nuclear-related JCPOA commitments, Director General Amano Tells IAEA

seems a relatively weak instrument for enhancing global security, one of its achievements—the JCPOA—is undermined by one of its parties for reasons extraneous to it.

The nuclear weapon 'ban': Decisive moment or distraction?

Despite the post-cold war reductions in the global nuclear weapon stockpile, impatience at the retention of nuclear weapons by a handful of states and their continued prominence in military doctrines has been steadily growing for more than a decade among many non-nuclear weapon states (NNWS). An important bargain is central to the 1968 Treaty on the Non-Proliferation of Nuclear Weapons (Non-Proliferation Treaty, NPT): while the NNWS agreed that they would not seek to obtain nuclear weapons, the nuclear weapon states (NWS) agreed under Article VI to take steps to divest themselves of their nuclear weapons.[22] However, major reductions in Russian and US arsenals have not led to signs of readiness for the complete elimination of nuclear arms, except in occasional rhetoric such as the speech made by US President Barack Obama in Prague in 2009.[23] More tersely, President Trump has reiterated the dream of a nuclear-free world but, in the meantime—like his predecessor in the White House and like the leaders of the other NWS— he has opted to remain energetically engaged in the development of nuclear weapons.[24] All the NWS are modernizing their nuclear weapons and their delivery systems and related infrastructure, as well as developing or deploying new weapon systems.[25]

The frustration of the NNWS over the continued possession of nuclear weapons by the NWS was clearly visible at the 2015 NPT Review Conference. There were stark divisions over disarmament. A major issue of contention was the failure to follow through on the plan agreed at the 2010 Review Conference to convene a conference on the establishment of a zone free of weapons of mass destruction in the Middle East. Divisions between the NWS (together with their allies) and the NNWS are in some cases so sharp that the next Review Conference, in 2020, has the potential to be a critical moment for the NPT.

While the slowly progressing crisis of the NPT might not be apparent to most non-experts, public anxieties have been heightened in recent years

---

Board', International Atomic Energy Agency (IAEA), 5 Mar. 2018.

[22] For a summary and other details of the NPT see annex A, section I, in this volume. According to the NPT, only states that manufactured and exploded a nuclear device prior to 1 Jan. 1967 are legally recognized as NWS. By this definition, there are 5 NWS: China, France, Russia, the UK and the USA. The other nuclear weapon-possessing states fall outside this definition of NWS.

[23] White House, Office of the Press Secretary, Remarks by President Barack Obama in Prague as Delivered, 5 Apr. 2009.

[24] Holland, S., 'Trump wants to make sure US arsenal "at top of the pack"', Reuters, 23 Feb. 2017.

[25] See chapter 6 in this volume.

by the increased salience of nuclear risk. In a symbolic expression of the perception of global risk, in early 2018 the Bulletin of the Atomic Scientists moved its Doomsday Clock to 'two minutes to midnight', the closest to 'midnight' that it has been since 1959.[26] While that assessment is informed by more issues than the risk of nuclear war—climate change, most notably—and might in any case be questioned and nuanced in debate, it reflects an apparently growing public concern.[27]

In the context of these combined developments it is arguably no surprise that an opposing trend has gained growing support. The background lies in a humanitarian perspective on nuclear weapons. While the idea of applying the perspective of international humanitarian law to nuclear weapons had been advocated previously by the International Committee of the Red Cross, it was first linked to the NPT at the 2010 Review Conference. This led to a series of three intergovernmental conferences (in Oslo in 2013, in Nayarit, Mexico, in 2014 and in Vienna in 2014) that highlighted the catastrophic consequences of the use of nuclear weapons and the risk of unintentional use. The Vienna conference also produced an Austrian-sponsored 'humanitarian pledge' that called for international cooperation 'to fill the legal gap for the prohibition and elimination of nuclear weapons'.[28] This approach, supported by civil society movements as well as many NNWS, was taken up in the UN, with a working group set up at the end of 2015 to 'address concrete effective legal measures, legal provisions and norms that will need to be concluded to attain and maintain a world without nuclear weapons'.[29] It produced agreement that a prohibition treaty, even without the nuclear weapon-possessing states, was the best way forward.[30] In July 2017 the Treaty on the Prohibition of Nuclear Weapons was adopted by a UN conference, supported by the votes of 122 NNWS. Fifty states signed it on the day it was opened for signature.[31]

The TPNW is the first multilateral treaty to clearly define the possession, use or threatened use of nuclear weapons as illegal under international law. From early on in the international discussions that led to its drafting

---

[26] Science and Security Board, 'It is now two minutes to midnight: 2018 Doomsday Clock statement', *Bulletin of the Atomic Scientists*, 25 Jan. 2018. The clock was set at 2 minutes to midnight in 1953 and remained at that time until 1960, when it was moved to 7 minutes from midnight. 'Timeline', *Bulletin of the Atomic Scientists*.

[27] See e.g. Savitsky, S., '82% of Americans fear nuclear war with North Korea', Axios, 11 Aug. 2017; Murphy, K., 'Australians fear North Korea standoff will lead to war—Guardian Essential poll', *The Guardian*, 9 Oct. 2017; and Badham, V., 'Fear, anxiety and sleepless nights: The cold war terrors have returned', *The Guardian*, 21 Apr. 2017.

[28] UN General Assembly Resolution 70/48, 'Humanitarian pledge for the prohibition and elimination of nuclear weapons', adopted 7 Dec. 2015, A/RES/70/48, 11 Dec. 2015.

[29] UN General Assembly Resolution 70/33, 'Taking forward multilateral nuclear disarmament negotiations', adopted 7 Dec. 2015, A/RES/70/33, 11 Dec. 2015, para. 2.

[30] International Campaign to Abolish Nuclear Weapons (ICAN), 'Majority of UN members declare intention to negotiate ban on nuclear weapons in 2017', Media release, 19 Aug. 2016.

[31] For a summary and other details of the TPNW see annex A, section I, in this volume. On the negotiation of the treaty see chapter 7, section I, in this volume.

and adoption, the aim was to develop an instrument to stigmatize nuclear weapons as a prelude to banning and eliminating them.[32] The logic is that successfully stigmatizing nuclear weapons will eventually compel states 'to take urgent action on disarmament'.[33]

It is likewise no surprise that there has been considerable opposition to the TPNW and the effort at stigmatization. France, the United Kingdom and the USA issued a joint statement declaring their unqualified opposition to the new treaty as soon as it was adopted, arguing that it failed to 'address the security concerns that continue to make nuclear deterrence necessary'.[34] Russia, too, has been clear in its opposition. The Russian Foreign Minister, Sergey Lavrov, described the rise of the movement to ban nuclear weapons as a 'dangerous and delusive trend' that 'disregards the importance of taking stock of all the current factors that influence strategic stability'.[35] Of the five permanent members of the UN Security Council (the P5), China has been the least unsympathetic in its expressed attitude to the TPNW. Instead of voting against the treaty negotiations at the UN General Assembly, China abstained. According to a statement from the Chinese Ministry of Foreign Affairs in March 2017, China's goal of a 'final comprehensive ban on and total destruction of nuclear weapons' is 'fundamentally in line with the purposes of negotiations on the nuclear weapon ban treaty'.[36]

For the supporters of the TPNW, the treaty offers a new way forward, a potentially decisive opportunity to restart progress towards complete nuclear disarmament. For its opponents, it is a distraction that fails to address the realities of global power politics and the strategic role of nuclear weapons. For its supporters, the commitment of the NWS to maintaining the strategic role of nuclear weapons in the current disposition of global politics is precisely the problem that needs to be addressed. For its opponents, that view simply highlights the clash between their own realism and the naive idealism that gave birth to the treaty. Other grounds for concern about the TPNW have also been aired, not least the possibility that adherence to it might undermine the effectiveness of the NPT, despite language

---

[32] International Campaign to Abolish Nuclear Weapons (ICAN), 'Stigmatize, ban and eliminate: A way forward for nuclear disarmament', 1 Oct. 2013.

[33] Beatrice Fihn, Executive Director of the International Campaign to Abolish Nuclear Weapons, quoted in Högsta, D., 'ICAN at the UNGA', Heinrich Böll Stiftung, 16 Nov. 2016.

[34] US Mission to the United Nations, 'Joint press statement from the permanent representatives to the United Nations of the United States, United Kingdom, and France following the adoption of a treaty banning nuclear weapons', 7 July 2017.

[35] Russian Ministry of Foreign Affairs, 'Foreign Minister Sergey Lavrov's remarks at a UN Security Council meeting on the non-proliferation of weapons of mass destruction: Confidence building measures, New York, January 18, 2018', 18 Jan. 2018. See also Russian Ministry of Foreign Affairs, 'Statement by Foreign Minister Sergey Lavrov at the 72nd session of the UN General Assembly, New York, September 21, 2017', 21 Sep. 2017.

[36] Chinese Ministry of Foreign Affairs, 'Foreign Ministry Spokesperson Hua Chunying's regular press conference on March 20', 20 Mar. 2017.

in the TPNW acknowledging and supporting the NPT, as well as a lack of clarity about how to verify compliance with the treaty.[37] At the heart of the discussion about the TPNW's worth, however, are long-standing and deep philosophical differences regarding the relationship between nuclear weapons and international security. Many of the most influential critics of the TPNW regard nuclear weapons as a contribution to their own security and to global stability. This is true not only of the NWS but also other states that base their security policies on the perceived deterrent effect of an ally's nuclear weapons, such as those member states of NATO that do not have nuclear weapons of their own. In contrast, supporters of the TPNW see an ineradicable risk that, as long as nuclear weapons exist, they may be used, whether by design or by accident, and argue that with such destructive consequences, any risk is too high.

The issue will not be settled by the weight of philosophy on either side of the case but by political weight. The problem that supporters of the TPNW face is that, whereas 50 NNWS signed the treaty straightaway, only 6 more had signed by the end of 2017. A movement to challenge the status quo has to maintain momentum or it may peter out. The problem for the nuclear weapon-possessing states, and especially the P5, is that, even when including their allies, they will always be in a minority on this issue in every international forum except the UN Security Council itself.

The treaty will enter force 90 days after the 50th state has ratified it. As signatories go through their ratification processes, and perhaps as additional states sign, arguments about the TPNW will start to connect with preparations for the 2020 NPT Review Conference. Previous review conferences have been the occasion for the NNWS to articulate their frustrations and for the NWS to be defensive and obstructive. It would be refreshing if the 2020 conference were to be an exception in this regard. Steps could be taken to further reduce nuclear warhead numbers and enhance nuclear safety, for example. The opponents and supporters of the TPNW might unexpectedly find themselves sharing the objective of protecting the world's major non-proliferation instrument—the NPT itself—from the risk of being undermined, which each sees the other as posing.

---

[37] Rühle, M., 'The nuclear weapons ban treaty: Reasons for scepticism', *NATO Review*, 19 May 2017; Carlson, J., 'The nuclear weapon ban treaty is significant but flawed', The Interpreter, Lowy Institute, 11 July 2017; and Afina, Y. et al., *Negotiation of a Nuclear Weapons Prohibition Treaty: Nuts and Bolts of the Ban—The New Treaty: Taking Stock* (UN Institute for Disarmament Research: Geneva, 2017).

II. International tensions and shifting dynamics of power

Russia, the United States and the West

The background to the stalling of nuclear arms control since New START was agreed in 2010 includes the ailing relationship between Russia and the USA. The problem developed slowly. Long before Russia annexed Crimea in 2014, the Obama administration had wanted to reset relations with Russia, which had soured after the fighting between Georgia and Russia in August 2008.[38] Even before then, difficulties had been looming for Russian–US arms control. This was partly because Russia was seeking a way back to a position of global strength and saw many of the arms control agreements, by which it was then bound, as products of earlier Russian weakness. There were also problems within the field of armaments and arms control itself. Following the USA's withdrawal from the ABM Treaty in 2002, Russia argued that US development of missile defence systems was a major obstacle to nuclear arms reductions because, if those systems become effective, it would destabilize the deterrence relationship. Russia has raised those concerns particularly since 2007, especially in relation to the INF Treaty, after the announcement of US plans to set up ballistic missile defences in Eastern Europe.[39] Although the discussion in the USA and other NATO members focused on defence against Iranian missile potential, Russian officials repeatedly stated that the development would diminish Russia's nuclear deterrence posture. In 2008 Russia reportedly began testing ground-launched cruise missiles (GLCMs) with a range prohibited by the INF Treaty.[40] In February 2017 the US media reported that Russia had deployed these GLCMs; a senior US officer repeated this claim in a hearing at the US Congress.[41] It is not possible to prove that, in the absence of a US missile defence capability, Russia would not have developed and tested the new GLCM; however, Russian statements of concern and a need to respond have been persistent and clear.

Irritants arising from the development of armaments and the effective stalling of arms control have only been part of the story of rising tensions between Russia and the USA. Concern about close encounters between Russian and NATO forces in the air and at sea go back several years.[42] More

---

[38] 'Obama resets ties to Russia, but work remains', *New York Times*, 7 July 2009; and Zygar, M., 'The Russian reset that never was', *Foreign Policy*, 9 Dec. 2016.

[39] Erastö, T., *Between the Shield and the Sword: NATO's Overlooked Missile Defense Dilemma* (Ploughshares Fund: San Francisco, CA, June 2017).

[40] Gordon, M. R., 'US says Russia tested cruise missile, violating treaty', *New York Times*, 28 July 2014.

[41] Gordon, M. R., 'Russia deploys missile, violating treaty, and challenging Trump', *New York Times*, 14 Feb. 2017; and Ali, I., 'US general says Russia deploys cruise missile, threatens NATO', Reuters, 8 Mar. 2017. See also chapter 7, section II, in this volume.

[42] Sharkov, D., 'NATO: Russian aircraft intercepted 110 times above Baltic in 2016', *Newsweek*, 4 Jan. 2017; Frear, T., 'List of close military encounters between Russia and the West, March

recently there have been allegations of Russian interference in Western domestic politics, especially the 2016 US presidential election.[43] It was, however, Russia's annexation of Crimea and engagement in the conflict in eastern Ukraine that marked the decisive moments in the long deterioration of the relationship.[44] These actions ended any likelihood that Russia could in the medium term become integrated with the West, as it had attempted during the 1990s. The evolution of Russia's grand strategy has instead confirmed an approach aimed at becoming the geopolitical fulcrum of Eurasia.[45] This implies both that Russia is aiming for a balanced relationship with China and that it is taking a leading role in shaping the politico-strategic environment in its neighbourhood, as most dramatically demonstrated by the Russian decision to engage militarily in Syria since September 2015.[46] The US National Security Strategy announced in December 2017 reflects, from the other side, a similar reading that attempting integration with Russia (and likewise with China) has, for the most part, failed.[47]

These tensions between Russia and the West are reminiscent in some ways of the cold war. However, the parallels should not be overdrawn, as much of fundamental importance has changed in the three decades since that confrontation ended. One salient difference is that the difficult relationship between Russia and the US-led group of powers is only one among several important sites of international tensions in contemporary world politics.

The South China Sea, the East China Sea and China–India tensions

A combination of economic growth and military power has enabled China to pursue an increasingly strong international policy, both in regional geopolitics and on the global stage. Unresolved territorial disputes remain key elements of China's relations within its region. Central among these are disputes with several South East Asian states about islets and islands in the

---

2014–March 2015', European Leadership Network, [2015]; and Frear, T., Kulesa, Ł. and Kearns, I., *Dangerous Brinkmanship: Close Military Encounters Between Russia and the West in 2014* (European Leadership Network: London, Nov. 2014).

[43] Gessen, M., 'Russian interference in the 2016 election: A cacophony, not a conspiracy', *New Yorker*, 3 Nov. 2017; 'Russian hacking and influence in the US election', *New York Times*, [n.d.]; and Mason, R., 'Theresa May accuses Russia of interfering in elections and fake news', *The Guardian*, 14 Nov. 2017.

[44] On the deteriorating relationship between Russia and the USA see Smith, *SIPRI Yearbook 2017* (note 4), pp. 10–12. On Russia's estrangement from the European security architecture see Anthony, I., 'Conflict or peace in Europe? Increasing uncertainties, rising insecurities', *SIPRI Yearbook 2017*, pp. 119–39. On the conflicts in the post-Soviet space see Klimenko, E., 'Conflicts in the post-Soviet space: Recent developments', *SIPRI Yearbook 2017*, pp. 140–50.

[45] Trenin, D., 'Russia's evolving grand Eurasia strategy: Will it work?', Carnegie Moscow Center, 20 July 2017.

[46] 'Unlikely partners', *The Economist*, 29 July 2017.

[47] White House, *National Security Strategy of the United States of America* (White House: Washington, DC, Dec. 2017), p. 3.

South China Sea and with Japan about eight uninhabited islets in the East China Sea.[48] Both disputes intensified in 2016: China's claims in the South China Sea were rejected by international arbitration in a case brought by the Philippines; and Japan announced in late 2016 that it would step up its naval deployments in the East China Sea.[49]

In 2017, however, tensions in both disputes eased somewhat. In June China and Japan agreed to launch an air and maritime contact mechanism to prevent clashes in the East China Sea region.[50] Similarly, in November the Association of Southeast Asian Nations (ASEAN) and China agreed to start negotiations on a code of conduct for regional maritime activities in the South China Sea.[51]

In contrast, tensions in the always difficult relationship between China and India surfaced again in mid-2017, apparently triggered by the Chinese People's Liberation Army (PLA) doing road construction work in territory claimed by both China and Bhutan and close to India's Sikkim state.[52] This was not a direct territorial dispute between China and India, but India deployed military units on behalf of Bhutan, the only neighbouring country with which China lacks diplomatic ties. The stand-off lasted over two months before the two sides extricated themselves from it. The chronic mistrust underlying what was essentially a small and localized crisis flared up again in December 2017, when an Indian unmanned aerial vehicle (UAV, drone) crashed on the Chinese side of the Sikkim section of the China–India border.[53]

Reignition of the India–Pakistan conflict over Kashmir

India has an even more uneasy relationship with Pakistan. This unresolved confrontation—punctuated by four wars and a number of smaller clashes—

---

[48] Lin, K.-C. and Villar Gertner, A., *Maritime Security in the Asia-Pacific: China and the Emerging Order in the East and South China Seas* (Chatham House: London, July 2015).

[49] Permanent Court of Arbitration (PCA), 'PCA Case no. 2013-19 in the matter of the South China Sea arbitration before an arbitral tribunal constituted under Annex VII to the 1982 United Nations Convention on the Law of the Sea between the Republic of the Philippines and the People's Republic of China: Award', 12 July 2016; and Associated Press, 'Japan boosts coast guard fleet to defend disputed East China Sea islands', *The Guardian*, 22 Dec. 2016. For a helpful guide to the dispute and the 500-page judgement see Holmes, O. and Phillips, T., 'South China Sea dispute: What you need to know about The Hague court ruling', *The Guardian*, 12 July 2016.

[50] 'China, Japan agree on early launch of air, maritime contact mechanism', Xinhua, 30 June 2017.

[51] It remains to be seen how the code of conduct will differ from the 2002 ASEAN–China Declaration on the Conduct of Parties in the South China Sea. See Lee, Y., 'A South China Sea code of conduct: Is real progress possible?', The Diplomat, 18 Nov. 2017.

[52] Bhutanese Ministry of Foreign Affairs, Press release, 29 June 2017.

[53] Chinese Ministry of Foreign Affairs, 'Foreign Ministry spokesperson Geng Shuang's regular press conference on December 7, 2017', 8 Dec. 2017; and Indian Press Information Bureau, 'In response to the media article of 07 Dec 17 by Xinhua News Agency', 7 Dec. 2017.

has been a defining issue in South Asia.[54] The ongoing territorial dispute over Kashmir, never settled since the two countries' independence in 1947, is at the heart of these tensions. Since the Kargil conflict of 1999 and despite a ceasefire agreed in 2003, there have been numerous clashes across the line of control and casualties on both sides.[55] During 2017, over 200 militants, around 80 security personnel and at least 57 civilians were killed, making it the deadliest year for a decade in the disputed territory.[56]

The geopolitical rivalry between Iran and Saudi Arabia

Iran and Saudi Arabia are locked in a power struggle that has the potential to become as chronic as India's relationships with China and Pakistan. The two are regional heavyweights, facing each other from opposite sides of the armed conflicts in Iraq, Syria and Yemen. Their disputes form one of the key lines of division in the Middle East, and some commentators have described the situation as a new regional cold war.[57] Their rivalry is often interpreted as a product of conflict within Islam between its Sunni and Shia branches. Religion plays an explicitly crucial political role for both states: Iran's constitution ensures that the Supreme Leader will be a Shia Muslim ayatollah; while the ruling family in Saudi Arabia has a long and close relationship with the Wahhabi interpretation of Sunni Islam, and the Saudi kingdom has the role of guardian of Mecca. While the religious element is important, the Iranian–Saudi Arabian relationship is equally a straightforward contestation for regional power, with each state's strategic objectives being determined by its interpretation of national interests. The historical and national features of this relationship are similarly important since it is an issue between Arabs and Persians as much as between Sunni and Shia Islam.

Iran's strategic interests in the region include supporting President Bashar al-Assad's retention of power in Syria; reinforcing allies in Iraq and preserving that country's territorial unity by opposing Kurdish aspirations for independence; sustaining Hezbollah in Lebanon; and assisting the Houthis in Yemen. The Islamic Revolutionary Guard Corps is the principal conduit for supporting these strategic objectives, which Iran seeks to achieve through

---

[54] 'Conflict between India and Pakistan', Council on Foreign Relations, 15 Mar. 2018.

[55] 'Kargil conflict timeline', BBC News, 13 July 1999; Kumar, H., 'Indian and Pakistani forces agree to cease-fire in Kashmir', *New York Times*, 26 Nov. 2003; Raja, A., 'Over 4,500 soldiers killed along LOC in Pak firing since 2001: Army', *Indian Express*, 5 Nov. 2016; and 'Indian Army killed 137 Pak soldiers in 2017: Reports', The Quint, 10 Jan. 2018.

[56] Agence France-Presse, 'Indian troops kill top militant in Kashmir', *The Guardian*, 26 Dec. 2017.

[57] See e.g. Santini, R. H., 'A new regional cold war in the Middle East and North Africa: Regional security complex theory revisited', *International Spectator*, vol. 52, no. 4 (2017), pp. 93–111. On the conflicts in the MENA region see chapter 2, section V, in this volume.

military aid and by recruiting fighters for Shiite militias in both Iraq and Syria.[58]

Saudi Arabia has sought to block further gains in Iranian influence and advance its own with the help of its allies in the region, in particular the United Arab Emirates (UAE), and with the backing of the USA, some European states and, less visibly, Israel. This has led to a series of military and diplomatic battles around the region—in Iraq, Lebanon, Syria and Yemen, and over Qatar—that pitch Iran and Saudi Arabia against each other. When Saudi Arabia, the UAE and Bahrain severed diplomatic and trading relations with Qatar over its alleged support for terrorist groups, Iran was among those countries that stepped in both to support it and to benefit by increasing trade with it.[59]

In Syria, Iran supports the Assad regime, whereas Saudi Arabia tries to undermine it; in Yemen, Saudi Arabia supports the government, while Iran has started to provide some weapons to the rebels. Although Iranian and Saudi Arabian forces have not directly fought each other, they have each fought forces supported by the other, and their proxies have also fought each other. Their engagement in the region's conflicts has, despite proclaimed intentions, not yet led to a peaceful resolution of any.

Intra-NATO tensions with Turkey

Beyond tensions between dyads of rivals or within specific geographic zones, there is a bigger picture of shifting geopolitical and geostrategic relationships and power dynamics. Neither the bipolar global model of the cold war era nor the unipolar model of the first decade or so after the cold war's end is useful for explaining what is happening now. While it is clear that change is under way, it is not clear what the outcome will be. Seen in that light, the growing difficulties in the relationship between most members of NATO and Turkey may be of at least as much long-term significance as shifts in the relationship between Russia and the USA and in the balance of power between China and the USA.

It is not news that Turkey's place in NATO is often uncomfortable, despite more than seven decades as a member state and a strategic bulwark of the alliance's south-eastern flank. For example, the disputes between Greece and Turkey over Cyprus and the Aegean Sea have been part of intra-NATO politics since they joined the alliance in 1952. More broadly, Turkey's complicated relationship with European states and the European

---

[58] Hiltermann, J., *Tackling the MENA Region's Intersecting Conflicts* (International Crisis Group: Brussels, 22 Dec. 2017), pp. 4–5; and Katzman, K., *Iran's Foreign and Defense Policies*, Congressional Research Service (CRS) Report for Congress RL44017 (US Congress, CRS: Washington, DC, 19 Jan. 2018).

[59] Adil, H., 'Turkey, Iran, Pakistan see big trade boost with Qatar', Al Jazeera, 3 Dec. 2017.

Union (EU), not least because of anti-Turkish prejudice in some European political circles, has been made even more uneasy by periods of direct military rule in 1960–65 and 1980–83 and of military domination of politics in 1971–73 and 1997. These periods gave rise to human rights concerns that resurfaced with the attempted military coup against Turkish President Recep Tayyip Erdoğan in July 2016 and, more particularly, the government's response to it. In the aftermath of the attempted coup, there were large-scale dismissals of government officials including many military officers; an estimated 110 000–150 000 officials were sacked and 36 000–50 000 people were arrested, with a large number of trials continuing into 2018.[60] While critics of the Turkish Government have raised concerns about infringements of liberty, its supporters' concerns include the continued residence in the USA of Fethullah Gülen, the alleged mastermind of the coup.[61] Suspicion of US involvement in what Turkey has consistently described as a 'Gülenist coup' surfaced early and never quite seems to have disappeared.[62] Further concerns arose in 2017 surrounding constitutional changes to give the Turkish presidency greater powers.[63]

Two other recent developments have strained relations between Turkey and its NATO allies: those over Syria and those over Russia.

First, for five years from 2011, Turkey's strategic and political objective in Syria was the overthrow of President al-Assad. In the course of 2016, Turkey's objectives shifted and narrowed in focus, aiming to: secure its border; ensure its continued influence within Syria; counter the Kurdistan Workers' Party (Partiya Karkerên Kurdistanê, PKK) and its sister organizations in northern Syria, the Democratic Union Party (Partiya Yekîtiya Demokrat, PYD) and the People's Protection Units (Yekîneyên Parastina Gel, YPG); and defeat the group called the Islamic State. This shift necessarily meant that Turkey began to distance itself from US strategic objectives and operations in Syria. The fissure created by this shift deepened when Turkey joined with Iran and Russia in convening a conference in Astana, Kazakhstan, at the end of 2016. The conference produced a ceasefire in Syria and, in the process,

---

[60] The lower-end estimates are from 'Turkey suspends 291 navy personnel over links to failed coup', Reuters, 13 Nov. 2016. The higher-end estimates are from 'Admirals, others sentenced to life for FETÖ's 2016 coup bid', *Daily Sabah*, 6 Mar. 2018. On the coup attempt see also Sahlin, M., 'Turkey's search for stability and legitimacy in 2016', *SIPRI Yearbook 2017*, pp. 151–62.

[61] The European Parliament passed, with cross-party support, a non-binding resolution condemning 'disproportionate repressive measures' after the attempted coup and urging the EU to freeze the talks on Turkey's membership to the EU. European Parliament, Resolution on EU–Turkey relations, 2016/2993(RSP), 24 Nov. 2016; and Rankin, J. and Shaheen, K., 'Turkey reacts angrily to symbolic EU parliament vote on its membership', *The Guardian*, 24 Nov. 2016.

[62] Arango, T. and Yeginsu, C., 'Turks can agree on one thing: US was behind failed coup', *New York Times*, 2 Aug. 2016; and 'Turkey seeks arrest of ex-CIA officer Fuller over coup plot', BBC News, 1 Dec. 2017.

[63] Srivastava, M., 'Why does Erdogan want a new Turkish constitution?', *Financial Times*, 19 Jan. 2017; and Shaheen, K., 'Erdoğan clinches victory in Turkish constitutional referendum', *The Guardian*, 16 Apr. 2017.

sidelined US diplomatic peacemaking efforts.[64] The Astana talks continued throughout 2017 and, although less productive, they held enough promise to draw the UN into participating in them.[65] The USA remained outside. In August 2016 Turkey had also launched offensives in northern Syria against the Islamic State and against Kurdish groups.[66] While the USA was also targeting Islamic State forces in Syria, it was simultaneously supporting the Kurdish forces that came under attack from Turkey.

Second, at the same time as Turkey's relationship with the USA was deteriorating in Syria, it signed an agreement with Russia to buy the S-400 surface-to-air missile (SAM) defence system.[67] With NATO–Russia tensions having increased, there is concern in NATO at what could be read as an effort by the Turkish Government to stand on both sides of the dividing line. There is also the more technical but, from a NATO perspective, no less important issue that the Russian system is not interoperable with NATO systems now under development.[68] At the same time as it is ordering new SAMs from Russia, Turkey retains its order for F-35 combat aircraft and other new weapon systems from the USA, which remains by far Turkey's most important arms supplier.[69] Turkey is also one of NATO's 'nuclear sharing' countries: although it does not possess nuclear weapons, about 50 US nuclear weapons are stored at the Incirlik air base.[70]

Hitherto in the disagreements and disputes between Turkey and various of its NATO allies, mutually recognized strategic interest in the alliance has trumped all other considerations. There is insufficient evidence on which to reach the conclusion that this will no longer hold true. Yet with other changes in the patterns of world power, a fundamental change in Turkey's strategic positioning is not out of the question. Were it to reorient itself away from NATO, Europe and the USA—perhaps towards a more clearly defined Middle Eastern and Central Asian role, with new allies and new priorities— some key strategic assumptions of NATO, Russia and some Middle Eastern regional powers would all be given a jolt.

[64] Walker, S. and Shaheen, K., 'Syria ceasefire appears to hold after rivals sign Russia-backed deal', *The Guardian*, 30 Dec. 2016; and Osborn, A. and Coskun, O., 'Russia, Turkey, Iran eye dicing Syria into zones of influence', Reuters, 28 Dec. 2016. On Turkey and the Kurds see also chapter 2, section V, in this volume.
[65] Solovyov, D. and Miles, T., 'UN to join Syria talks in Astana, with humanitarian hopes', Reuters, 21 Dec. 2017.
[66] On Turkish assessments and operations in 2016 see Sahlin (note 60).
[67] The size and final value of the purchase are unclear. Gumrukcu, T. and Toksabay, E., 'Turkey, Russia sign deal on supply of S-400 missiles', Reuters, 29 Dec. 2017.
[68] 'Turkey's $2bn arms deal with Russia faces hurdles, and possible sanctions', *The Economist*, 30 Nov. 2017.
[69] See the SIPRI Arms Transfers Database. On the purchase of the F-35s see F-35 Lightning II, 'Turkey: Building on decades of partnership', Lockheed Martin, [n.d.]. Turkey is 1 of 8 US allies that co-funded its development: 'The 11 countries expected to buy F-35 fighter jet', Reuters, 6 June 2014.
[70] Reif, K., 'US nuclear weapons in Turkey raise alarm', Arms Control Association, Nov. 2017.

III. Human security and insecurity

More complex armed conflicts

The broad trend so far this decade is an increase in armed conflicts, with the number each year returning to the levels of the start of the 1990s as the cold war was coming to an end.[71] There has been some progress. In Colombia, for example, the 2016 peace agreement has held, despite concerns in the border areas with Ecuador, Peru and Venezuela.[72] Similarly, peacebuilding has continued in Nepal.[73] But a scan of some of the main armed conflicts reveals both their intractability and their human costs, which fall primarily on civilian populations.[74] During this decade, the number of civilian deaths in violent conflicts has doubled, as has the number of deaths resulting from combat, which are as always compounded by the indirect lethal effects of conflict in the form of malnutrition and famine, contamination of water supplies, and the collapse of health services in conflict countries.[75] The UN High Commissioner for Refugees estimates that 28 300 people each day are forced to flee their homes because of violent conflict and persecution. The world total of forcibly displaced people is over 65 million and has been climbing sharply in recent years, driven primarily by the effects of violent conflict.[76]

In many places, human security is further diminished because of the fluid and often chaotic nature of conflict. The number of armed groups active in each conflict has tended to increase: the average has risen from 8 in each intrastate conflict in 1950 to 14 in 2010.[77] The latter figure is quite modest compared to the proliferation of armed groups in some wars: in Syria over 1000 separate militias have been identified, and in Libya as many as 2000.[78] As the conflicts continue, these militias exhibit shifting allegiances, making and breaking opportunistic alliances with stronger forces. Among these groups are some that export the violence of the conflict in the form of terrorist attacks. Europol recorded a decline from 2014 to 2016 in the number of attempted terrorist attacks in EU countries (down from 226 to 142, of which only one-third were carried out).[79] Most of the 142 fatalities in terrorist

[71] Sollenberg and Melander (note 1).

[72] On the peace agreement in Colombia see Valenzuela, P., 'Out of the darkness? The hope for peace in Colombia', *SIPRI Yearbook 2017*, pp. 47–57; and chapter 2, section II, in this volume.

[73] On peacebuilding in Nepal see chapter 2, section III, in this volume.

[74] See chapter 2, section I, in this volume.

[75] World Bank Group and United Nations, *Pathways for Peace: Inclusive Approaches to Preventing Violent Conflict—Main Messages and Emerging Policy Directions* (World Bank: Washington, DC, Oct. 2017), pp. 6–8.

[76] UN High Commissioner for Refugees, 'Figures at a glance', 17 June 2017.

[77] World Bank Group and United Nations (note 75), p. 6.

[78] World Bank Group and United Nations (note 75), p. 6; and 'Guide to key Libyan militias', BBC News, 11 Jan. 2016.

[79] European Union Agency for Law Enforcement Cooperation (Europol), *European Union Terrorism Situation and Trend Report 2017* (Europol: The Hague, 2017), p. 10.

attacks in EU states during 2016 were the result of actions by groups and individuals claiming allegiance to fighting groups in the Middle East and North Africa, especially the Islamic State.[80]

In many cases, the activities of a multitude of armed groups are overlaid by criminal violence. Studies of the nexus between crime and conflict show that criminal and political organizations often occupy the same strategic and geographic space, sometimes to contest control of it and sometimes to cooperate in exploiting it.[81] Examples of such spaces include the routes along which narcotics, people, weapons and contraband such as tobacco are traded; illicit or unprotected artisanal mining sites; marginalized communities; and areas of a country and functions of government in which central state control is absent, limited or corrupted. In such cases, the distinction between what is criminal and what is political often becomes a matter of arbitrary labelling.

The lethal potential of criminal violence is as great as that seen in intra-state wars. In Mexico some estimates suggest that murders linked to organized crime exceeded 100 000 in 2006–17; 2006 was the year when President Felipe Calderón took office and the Mexican Government began a major campaign against the country's drug trafficking organizations.[82] After a high level of violence in 2007–11, the murder rate declined somewhat but is reported to have started to climb again in 2014 and reached its highest level for 30 years in 2017.[83] The situation in Mexico since 2006 stands out for the scale and reach of the criminal violence; it illustrates how destructive the problem can become.

Further layers of complexity are added by the internationalization of what often start as purely internal conflicts. Just over one-third of current armed conflicts are internationalized, as measured by the involvement of foreign forces in the conflict, sometimes but not always as direct combatants.[84] Four of the armed conflicts in the Middle East and North Africa are fundamentally shaped by the involvement of foreign forces—those in Iraq, Libya, Syria and Yemen. Conflicts can also be internationalized in a broader sense, through external support—political, financial or technical such as training or providing hardware—for one or more of the combatants, as is the case in Egypt

---

[80] European Union Agency for Law Enforcement Cooperation (note 79). On combating terrorism in Europe see also chapter 2, section IV, in this volume.

[81] De Boer, J. and Bossetti, L., *The Crime–Conflict Nexus: Assessing the Threat and Developing Solutions*, Crime–Conflict Nexus Series no. 1 (United Nations University, Centre for Policy Research: Tokyo, May 2017).

[82] Beittel, J. S., *Mexico: Organized Crime and Drug Trafficking Organizations*, Congressional Research Service (CRS) Report for Congress R41576 (US Congress, CRS: Washington, DC, 25 Apr. 2017), p. 2. See also chapter 2, section II, in this volume.

[83] Flannery, N. P., 'Is Mexico really the world's most dangerous war zone?', *Forbes*, 10 May 2017; and Gillespie, P. 'Mexico reports highest murder rate on record', CNN, 22 Jan. 2018.

[84] Sollenberg and Melander (note 1).

and the Israeli–Palestinian conflict.[85] Likewise in Africa, armed conflicts that originate in the internal social, economic, political and, increasingly, environmental conditions of a country have become ineluctably internationalized. One aspect of that internationalization process in Africa is the counterterrorism activities of France, the UK and the USA, which parallel the tendency of some armed groups in Africa to align themselves with al-Qaeda or the Islamic State.[86]

As external actors take on an active role in otherwise internal conflicts, they often develop an interest either in perpetuating the conflict or in shaping the settlement that ends the violence. In virtually all of today's armed conflicts, external interests have to be accounted for in some way if there is to be a viable peace settlement.

The impact of climate change

In the Sahel region, a large area stretching from Mali and the Lake Chad Basin eastwards to Somalia, is now a zone of chronic insecurity. There is armed conflict in Cameroon, the Central African Republic, northern Ethiopia, Mali, northern Nigeria, Somalia and South Sudan. There are, in addition, instances of localized violent conflict in many parts of the Sahel region, in disputes that do not involve an insurgent group attempting to seize state power. These instances generate an endemic situation of insecurity. In March 2017 the UN Security Council focused international attention and policy on the Lake Chad region following a visit to the area at the start of the year. The resulting Security Council resolution was notable for acknowledging the role of climate change alongside other factors in exacerbating human insecurity.[87] However, the subsequent report on the region that the UN Secretary-General was mandated to produce did not make any reference to climate change as a relevant issue.[88] As this shows, it remains difficult to insert climate and other environmental factors into policy discussions and action on security and insecurity. Nonetheless, an increasing body of research is bringing out evidence of the impact of climate change in generating social and political instability, largely via the intervening variables of food and water insecurities.[89]

Just as climate change interacts with other factors—such as social and economic inequities and governance that is ineffective, unaccountable or

---

[85] See chapter 2, section V, in this volume.

[86] See chapter 2, section VI, in this volume.

[87] UN Security Council Resolution 2349, 31 Mar. 2017. On the conflict in the Lake Chad region see also chapter 2, section VI, in this volume.

[88] United Nations, Security Council, Report of the Secretary-General on the situation in the Lake Chad Basin region, S/2017/764, 7 Sep. 2017.

[89] Vivekananda, J. et al., *Action on Climate and Security Risks: Review of Progress 2017* (Clingendael: The Hague, Dec. 2017).

corrupt—to generate the conditions for violent conflict, so it interacts with violence to produce further destructive effects. After a long period in which world hunger steadily eased, it is on the rise again, driven by climate change and conflict. Chronic hunger now affects 815 million people, about 11 per cent of the world population.[90] Some of the areas hardest hit by food insecurity and malnutrition are severely affected by both conflict and climate change. Famine struck in parts of South Sudan for several months in early 2017; as the UN appealed for an urgent increase in humanitarian assistance there, it named north-east Nigeria, Somalia and Yemen—all conflict-affected areas—as also being at serious risk of famine.[91]

The implications of climate change for social and political stability, via the effects on food security, are not simply matters of concern in the areas where the direct effects of climate change are experienced. Global food security increasingly depends on international trade. Grain production is highly concentrated. Most wheat, soybean and maize is grown in three areas: the Midwest USA, the Black Sea region and Brazil.[92] When food prices are volatile, political risks multiply.[93] For example, in Egypt food price rises in 2008 led to riots and in early 2011 to the popular mobilization that ousted President Hosni Mubarak.[94] Further risks are to be found in the trade 'choke points'—the critical junctures on transport routes through which exceptional volumes of trade pass. Fourteen of these points are critical for food security worldwide, and a 2017 study found that climate change increases the risk of their disruption: increasingly frequent severe weather events will cause more frequent closure of the choke points and damage physical infrastructure, while rising sea levels put port operations at risk.[95] Conflict and insecurity would also threaten smooth passage of trade through those 14 critical chokepoints. In short, the issue of food security and its relationship to climate change and conflict, on the one hand, and to human security and political stability, on the other, is a matter of global concern and is not limited to states that are poor, directly and severely affected by climate change, or mired in violent conflict.

[90] Food and Agriculture Organization of the United Nations (FAO), *The State of Food Security and Nutrition in the World 2017: Building Resilience for Peace and Food Security* (FAO: Rome, 2017), p. 2.

[91] 'Famine "largest humanitarian crisis in history of UN"', Al Jazeera, 11 Mar. 2017.

[92] Bailey, R. and Wellesley, L., *Chokepoints and Vulnerabilities in Global Food Trade* (Chatham House: London, June 2017), p. v.

[93] Rüttinger, L. et al., *A New Climate for Peace: Taking Action on Climate and Fragility Risks* (Adelphi: Berlin, 2015), pp. 42–47.

[94] Hendrix, C. S. and Haggard, S., 'Global food prices, regime type, and urban unrest in the developing world', *Journal of Peace Research*, vol. 52, no. 2 (Mar. 2015), pp. 143–57; and Potsdam Institute for Climate Impact Research and Climate Analytics, *Turn Down the Heat: Confronting the New Climate Change Normal* (World Bank: Washington, DC, 2014), pp. 144–47.

[95] Bailey and Wellesley (note 92), p. vi.

IV. The prospects for international institutions

At the start of 2017, two new personalities took over key roles on the world stage: Donald Trump as US President and António Guterres as UN Secretary-General. There is no doubting that the former has the greater practical power, the bigger stage on which to walk and the higher global profile. Statements made by Trump as a presidential candidate (and even earlier) expressed a deep and consistent scepticism about the UN and about the value of international institutions to the USA.[96] This scepticism appeared to be underlined implicitly by his inaugural speech, with its repeated refrain of 'America first'.[97] This seemed to be expressed in action when he announced his intention to withdraw the USA from the Paris Agreement on climate change.[98]

Guterres was elected as the ninth UN Secretary-General, having run on a platform that placed the prevention of violent conflict at the centre of his political vision.[99] As the contents of this introduction (and of the further chapters in this volume) make clear, that is not the direction in which the world has recently been moving. The scale and complexity of the task of prevention are clear and thus also the need for it is underlined. Nonetheless, despite the many evident challenges to the smooth functioning of the international system for managing conflicts and enhancing human security, there is widespread international backing for making the effort. The Paris Agreement has survived despite President Trump's commitment to withdrawing as soon as possible; indeed, every other country in the world remains committed to the Paris obligations.[100] At the same time, the 2030 Agenda and its Sustainable Development Goals (SDGs) remain the targets that motivate global development efforts. They are the expression of a determination to rid the world of extreme poverty and achieve by 2030 a better, more peaceful, more equitable, more sustainable world than today.[101]

---

[96] Begley, S., 'Read Donald Trump's speech to AIPAC', *Time*, 21 Mar. 2016; and Alexander, H., 'Donald Trump and the United Nations: A fight waiting to happen?', *Daily Telegraph*, 19 Jan. 2017.

[97] White House, 'The inaugural address: Remarks of President Donald J. Trump—as prepared for delivery', 20 Jan. 2017.

[98] Shear, M. D., 'Trump will withdraw US from Paris Climate Agreement', *New York Times*, 1 June 2017; and Volcovici, V., 'US submits formal notice of withdrawal from Paris climate pact', Reuters, 4 Aug. 2017.

[99] Guterres, A., 'Challenges and opportunities for the United Nations', Vision statement circulated by the president of the UN General Assembly, 4 Apr. 2016.

[100] Every state that can join the Paris Agreement has either signed, ratified or acceded to it. The earliest that a party to the agreement can deliver notice of withdrawal is 3 years after entry into force. Since the treaty entered into force for the USA on 4 Nov. 2016, it can deliver the notice no earlier than 4 Nov. 2019 and it will take effect 1 year after delivery. The Paris Agreement (note 5), Article 28(1).

[101] On the SDGs, which are listed in UN General Assembly Resolution 70/1 (note 5), see Jang, S. and Milante, G., 'Development in dangerous places', *SIPRI Yearbook 2016*, pp. 345–63.

The widening gap between the rich and the poor both within and between countries is increasingly recognized as both eroding democracy and a potential driver of conflict.[102] According to one study in 2017, based on a new and comprehensive set of indicators of global inequality, between 1980 and 2016 the combined wealth of the richest 1 per cent of the world's population increased by twice as much as the combined wealth of the poorest 50 per cent.[103] The report's authors warned that inequality had increased to 'extreme levels' in some countries—including Brazil, India, Russia and the USA—and was particularly acute in sub-Saharan Africa and the Middle East. The linking of development and peacebuilding goals, as in the SDGs—and especially SDG 16 on achieving peace and justice by building strong institutions—is thus of great importance for global security prospects.

It is too soon to be able to arrive at conclusions about what impact and on what scale either the US president or the UN secretary-general may have over the years of their respective terms of office. There are, besides, other increasingly influential players in global politics as the patterns and dynamics of international power continue to shift. Their actions, influence and preferences will be part of the mix of factors that determine whether in coming years the world will become more or less peaceful, devote more or less resources to military preparations, and make more or less movement in the direction of disarmament. Future editions of the SIPRI Yearbook will have more to say on that score.

---

[102] See e.g. World Bank Group and United Nations (note 75); and African Development Bank, *African Development Report 2015—Growth, Poverty and Inequality Nexus, Overcoming Barriers to Sustainable Development* (African Development Bank Group: Abijan, June 2016). SDG 10 is to 'reduce inequality within and among countries'. See Jang and Milante (note 101).

[103] Alvaredo, F. et al., *World Inequality Report 2018* (World Inequality Lab: Dec. 2017).

Part I. Armed conflict and conflict management, 2017

Chapter 2. Armed conflicts and peace processes

Chapter 3. Peace operations and conflict management

2. Armed conflicts and peace processes

Overview

In 2017, armed conflicts were active in at least 22 states and many involved multiple non-state armed groups and external actors. Likewise, peace processes are complex and multifaceted, but in 2017 there were few visible examples of successful peacebuilding interventions in the main armed conflicts discussed in this chapter. The resulting human costs fell primarily on civilian populations.

In the first 11 months of 2017 the number of civilian deaths caused by explosive weapons was 42 per cent higher than in 2016, at more than 15 000 people, mostly in cities. The number of forcibly displaced people worldwide at the start of 2017 was over 65 million, and it seems likely that these record numbers continued during the year, especially in the light of a new displacement crisis in Myanmar and protracted displacement crises in other places such as Afghanistan, the Democratic Republic of the Congo (DRC), Somalia, South Sudan, Syria and Yemen. Armed conflicts also contributed to increased food insecurity in 2017, with seven countries—Yemen, South Sudan, Syria, Lebanon, the Central African Republic (CAR), Afghanistan and Somalia—recording crisis or emergency levels of food insecurity in at least a quarter of their people.

In the Americas, there were positive signs that the ongoing peace process in Colombia might soon bring the only active armed conflict in the Western hemisphere to a close (see section II). However, in several countries in Central and South America (including El Salvador, Mexico and Paraguay) the levels of political and criminal violence remained high. Indeed, cities in the Americas are some of the world's most dangerous and there is an escalating crisis of forced displacement.

Five countries in Asia and Oceania were involved in active armed conflicts in 2017: Afghanistan, India, Myanmar, Pakistan and the Philippines (see section III). In Myanmar the forced displacement of the Rohingya caused spillover effects in Bangladesh, while in other places, such as the Philippines, state security forces committed widespread violence with impunity. In Afghanistan and the Philippines, the Islamic State group is a growing threat, while other parts of Asia and Oceania continued to be affected by instability from a variety of causes. Most notably, tensions are rising in North East Asia, chiefly due to the nuclear weapon and ballistic missile programmes of North Korea. On a more positive note, ongoing peace processes in Nepal and Sri Lanka contributed to growing stability in those two countries.

Two armed conflicts were active in Europe in 2017: in Nagorno-Karabakh (involving Armenia and Azerbaijan) and in Ukraine (see section IV). At the same time, unresolved conflicts in Cyprus, Georgia (Abkhazia and South Ossetia), Moldova (Trans-Dniester) and Kosovo, although inactive, seemed as intractable as ever. In the background, tensions remained heightened between Russia and the members of the North Atlantic Treaty Organization (NATO) and the West in general, and there were allegations of Russian interference in Western domestic politics. European states also continued to prioritize combating terrorism.

There were seven active armed conflicts in the Middle East and North Africa in 2017: in Egypt, Iraq, Israel and Palestine, Libya, Syria, Turkey and Yemen (see section V). Many of these conflicts are interconnected and involve regional and international powers as well as numerous substate actors. Key regional developments included the continuing fallout from the Arab Spring; the regional rivalry between Iran and Saudi Arabia; and the territorial losses of the Islamic State. Iraq has the daunting tasks of reconstruction in the areas once held by the Islamic State—especially in Mosul, which suffered widespread destruction—and achieving genuine political reconciliation between and within the Kurdish, Shia Arab and Sunni Arab communities. The complex war in Syria involving regional and international powers has led to the displacement of half the population—over 5.4 million refugees and over 6.1 million internally displaced persons—and has left 6.5 million people with acute food insecurity and a further 4 million at risk of the same. Neither the United Nations-mediated peace talks nor the parallel Astana negotiations made much progress. In Yemen the Saudi Arabian-led coalition maintained its partial blockade of Houthi-controlled territories with devastating humanitarian consequences: at least 17 million people, or 60 per cent of the population, faced acute food insecurity.

There were seven active armed conflicts in sub-Saharan Africa: in CAR, the DRC, Ethiopia, Mali, Nigeria, Somalia and South Sudan (see section VI). In addition, a number of other countries experienced post-war conflict and tension or were flashpoints for potential armed conflict, including Burundi, Cameroon, the Gambia, Kenya, Lesotho, Sudan and Zimbabwe. Two broad developments can be identified in sub-Saharan Africa. First, many conflicts overlap across states and regions as a result of transnational activities of violent Islamist groups, other armed groups and criminal networks. In many countries, and especially those in the Sahel and Lake Chad regions, these overlapping conflicts are linked to extreme poverty, instability, economic fragility and low resilience. Second, there also appears to be a growing internationalization of counter-terrorism activities in sub-Saharan Africa, led primarily by two external state actors—France and the United States.

IAN DAVIS

I. Tracking armed conflicts and peace processes in 2017

IAN DAVIS

Some of the main consequences of armed conflict in 2017

Contemporary armed conflicts tend to be concentrated in urban areas and to affect civilians: according to Action on Armed Violence, in the first 11 months of 2017 at least 15 399 civilians were killed by explosive weapons, the vast majority in cities, an increase of 42 per cent compared to 2016.[1] One important and new aspect of that data is that air strikes (and thus states) were responsible for over 50 per cent of the deaths from explosive weapons for the first time since such data has been recorded.[2] The use of explosive weapons in populated areas—especially explosive weapons with a large destructive radius, an inaccurate delivery system or the capacity to deliver multiple munitions over a wide area—is a growing concern and part of ongoing humanitarian arms control efforts.[3] Accounting for civilian casualties in conflict continued to be controversial in 2017, with official estimates often under-reporting casualty numbers.[4]

Sexual violence is widely perpetrated in war and in the case of women is an extension of the violence that they face in the absence of armed conflict. In a 2017 report the United Nations Secretary-General listed the rise of violent extremism, hybrid criminal networks, mass migration and cultures of impunity as critical risk factors contributing to conflict-related sexual violence.[5] The conviction in 2017 in the Democratic Republic of the Congo (DRC) of 12 members of a militia group for sexual violence crimes represented a potential historic milestone in the fight against impunity for such offences (see section VI).

Armed conflict is a major driver of food insecurity and displacement, as civilians are forced to escape violence and persecution.[6] The number of

---

[1] Organization for Economic Cooperation and Development (OECD), *States of Fragility 2016: Understanding Violence* (OECD: Paris, 2016); Anthony I, 'International humanitarian law: ICRC guidance and its application in urban warfare', *SIPRI Yearbook 2017*, pp. 545–53; International Committee of the Red Cross, 'War in cities', [n.d.]; and Action on Armed Violence, 'First 11 months of 2017 sees 42% increase in civilian deaths from explosive weapons compared to 2016', 8 Jan. 2018.

[2] Action on Armed Violence (note 1).

[3] See chapter 9, section I, in this volume.

[4] On casualty recording see Giger, A., 'Casualty recording in armed conflict: Methods and normative issues', *SIPRI Yearbook 2016*, pp. 247–61. See also e.g. Khan, A. and Gopal, A., 'The uncounted', *New York Times Magazine*, 16 Nov. 2017; and Cockburn, P., 'There's no such thing as precise air strikes in modern warfare—just look at the civilian casualties in Iraq and Syria', *The Independent*, 1 Dec. 2017. Khan and Gopal conclude that 1 in 5 air strikes caused civilian deaths, a rate more than 31 times higher than the US-led air coalition in Iraq acknowledged.

[5] United Nations, Security Council, Report of the Secretary-General on Conflict-Related Sexual Violence, S/2017/249, 15 Apr. 2017.

[6] See Grip, L., 'Coping with crises: Forced displacement in fragile contexts', *SIPRI Yearbook 2017*, pp. 253–83.

forcibly displaced people worldwide at the end of 2016 was 65.6 million, and it seems likely that these record numbers continued into 2017.[7] A new displacement crisis occurred when 580 000 Rohingya refugees fled violence in Myanmar (see section III), while protracted displacement crises continued in many other places, including Afghanistan, the DRC, Somalia, South Sudan, Syria and Yemen. Many displaced people crossed international borders in search of protection and assistance as refugees, although the majority were displaced within their own countries.[8]

Finally, armed conflicts contributed to increased food insecurity in 2017, with seven countries recording crisis or emergency levels of food insecurity in at least a quarter of their people. In Yemen 60 per cent of the population (17 million people) faced acute food insecurity, while in South Sudan the proportion was 45 per cent (4.8 million people). The other countries ranked as having the highest proportions of people with food insecurity were Syria, Lebanon, the Central African Republic, Afghanistan and Somalia.[9]

Defining armed conflict

Determining the existence of an 'armed conflict' within the framework of international law differs according to whether the armed violence is fought between two or more states (interstate armed conflict) or between a state and one or more organized non-state armed groups (non-international or intrastate armed conflict). The Uppsala Conflict Data Program (UCDP) has identified 280 distinct armed conflicts in the period 1946–2016.[10] According to UCDP data, a significantly higher number of armed conflicts occurred in 2014–16 (averaging 47 per year) than in any three-year period in 2007–13 (averaging 35 per year); the vast majority of these occurred within states.[11] While intrastate conflicts are by far the most common form of armed conflict today, the threshold that distinguishes situations of internal political violence or tensions from those of intrastate armed conflict is a major polit-

---

[7] 2016 is the most recent year for which figures are available. UN High Commissioner for Refugees (UNHCR), *Global Trends: Forced Displacement in 2016* (UNHCR: Geneva, 2017).

[8] UN High Commissioner for Refugees (note 7).

[9] Food and Agriculture Organization of the UN (FAO) and Word Food Programme (WFP), *Monitoring Food Security in Countries with Conflict Situations*, Report for the UN Security Council, issue no. 3 (FAO/WFP: [Rome], Jan. 2018). On the relationship between conflict and food insecurity see Food and Agriculture Organization of the UN (FAO), International Fund for Agricultural Development (IFAD), UN Children's Fund (UNICEF), World Food Programme (WFP) and World Health Organization (WHO), *The State of Food Security and Nutrition in the World 2017: Building Resilience for Peace and Food Security* (FAO: Rome, 2017).

[10] Sollenberg, M. and Melander, E., 'Patterns of organized violence, 2007–16', *SIPRI Yearbook 2017*, pp. 25–46.

[11] Sollenberg and Melander (note 10).

ical and legal issue, not least since it is the trigger for the implementation of humanitarian law.[12]

Two fundamental criteria normally dictate whether an intrastate armed conflict exists under international law: the intensity of the violence and a minimum level of organization of the parties (such as a command structure for non-state groups). Sylvain Vité, a legal advisor of the International Committee of the Red Cross, argues that these two components cannot be described in abstract terms and must be evaluated on a case-by-case basis by weighing up a range of indicative data. This might include, for example, the duration of the conflict, the frequency of the acts of violence and military operations, the nature of the weapons used, displacement of civilians, territorial control by opposition forces and the number of victims (dead, wounded, displaced persons, etc.).[13]

In addition, intrastate armed conflicts often have significant international dimensions and risk spilling over into bordering states. Hence, many intrastate armed conflicts have become 'internationalized': they involve troops, armed groups or another form of military-related intervention (such as arms transfers and training) from other states (or armed groups or private actors in neighbouring states) on the side of one or more of the warring parties. In 2016 UCDP categorized about a third of the 49 armed conflicts as internationalized.[14]

In short, armed conflicts are increasingly complex with multifaceted actors at various levels and with diverse objectives. Such complexity is a major challenge to the conceptual-legal categorization of armed conflict, as well as thinking on conflict resolution (via peace processes) and prevention.[15] This chapter takes as its starting point the armed conflicts described in the UCDP database and then casts the net a bit wider to include cases of confrontation and criminal violence, both of which are sometimes precursors or products of armed violence. Key examples are selected for discussion based on a combination of relevant literature, reports, media and conflict-related data in 2017.[16]

---

[12] See e.g. Bouchet-Saulnier, F., Medecins Sans Frontieres, *The Practical Guide to Humanitarian Law*, 3rd edn (Rowman and Littlefield: Lanham, MD, Dec. 2013), 'Non-international armed conflict'; and Odermatt, J., 'Between law and reality: "new wars" and internationalised armed conflict', *Amsterdam Law Forum*, vol. 5, no. 3 (summer 2013), pp. 19–32.

[13] Vité, S., 'Typology of armed conflicts in international humanitarian law: Legal concepts and actual situations', *International Review of the Red Cross*, vol. 91, no. 873 (Mar. 2009).

[14] Sollenberg and Melander (note 10).

[15] This complexity is captured in United Nations and World Bank, *Pathways for Peace: Inclusive Approaches to Preventing Violent Conflict* (World Bank, Washington, DC, 2018).

[16] UCDP Georeferenced Event Dataset (GED).

Peace processes and the reversal of peace

Peace processes can involve a wide range of activities—from a ceasefire achieved by negotiations, via signing of peace agreements, to disarmament, demobilization and rehabilitation of former combatants and state-building—designed to bring about a negotiated and lasting settlement between warring or disputing parties.[17] Multilateral peace operations, including those mandated by the UN, may also be part of a peace process.[18]

Peace processes are one of many tools used by local intra- and inter-community actors, non-state armed groups, states and the international community to realise peace.[19] Not all peace processes lead to a sustainable peace, however. Many have produced only a temporary peace or cessation in hostilities, where an inconclusive political settlement, a failure to address the root causes of the conflict, or ongoing insecurity and tensions eventually led to a recurrence of the armed conflict.[20] In Northern Ireland, for example, the peace process involved several key stepping points, including the Downing Street declaration (1993) and a ceasefire by the Irish Republican Army (1994), before the Good Friday Agreement (1998) finally delivered peace—although the situation still remains tense two decades later (see section IV). Similarly, the 2016 Colombia peace agreement has brought many short-term benefits, but considerable challenges remain (see section II).

Since the mid-1990s most armed conflicts have been recurrences of old conflicts rather than new conflicts, and of the 216 peace agreements signed during 1975–2011, 91 were followed by a resumption in violence within five years.[21] Nonetheless, this would indicate that although peace is difficult, and peace processes are complex and multifaceted, more agreements succeed than fail to terminate armed conflicts. The following sections seek to develop a narrative of trends and events in 2017 affecting all the key armed conflicts and peace processes associated with those armed conflicts. Exam-

[17] A peace agreement is a political settlement whose objective is to manage the risks of violence and reach some form of stability. See United Nations and World Bank (note 15), p. 144. For a database of documents that can be understood broadly as peace agreements see the United Nations Peacemaker website.

[18] On peace operations see chapter 3 in this volume.

[19] On various interpretations of the term 'peace' as well as other tools for realizing peace see 'Sustaining peace and sustainable development in dangerous places', *SIPRI Yearbook 2017*, pp. 211–52; and United Nations and World Bank (note 15).

[20] Bell, C. et al., *Navigating Inclusion in Peace Settlements: Human Rights, and the Creation of the Common Good* (British Academy: London, June 2017); and Bell, C. and Pospisil, J., 'Negotiating inclusion in transitions from conflict: The formalised political unsettlement', *Journal of International Development*, vol. 29, no. 5 (July 2017).

[21] Högbladh, S., 'Peace agreements 1975–2011: Updating the UCDP Peace Agreement Dataset', eds T. Pettersson and L. Themnér, *States in Armed Conflict 2011*, Department of Peace and Conflict Research Report 99 (Uppsala University: Uppsala, 2012), pp. 39–56; and von Einsiedel, S. et al., *Civil War Trends and the Changing Nature of Armed Conflict*, UN University Centre for Policy Research, Occasional Paper no. 10 (UN University: Tokyo, Mar. 2017).

ples of lower levels of intrastate violence (i.e. violence that potentially falls below the legal intrastate armed conflict threshold) are also discussed, but mainly in the context of political violence in South America (section II).[22]

To gain the 'bigger picture'—for example, as to whether the trends in armed conflict in recent years have led to a 'reversal of peace'—the developments discussed in the following sections should be read in conjunction with some the data sets on various forms of violence and conflict, including the Armed Conflict Location and Event Data (ACLED) project, the Global Terrorism Database (GTD) and the UCDP Georeferenced Event Dataset (GED).[23]

---

[22] The chapter is complemented by the chronology of events in annex C in this volume.

[23] On whether the trends in armed conflict in recent years indicate a reversal of peace see Melander E. and Svensson I., 'A reversal of peace? The role of foreign involvement in armed conflict: A case study on East Asia', *SIPRI Yearbook 2016*, pp. 220–35. For an overview of the major advances in the collection and availability of armed conflict data see Brzoska, M., 'Progress in the collection of quantitative data on collective violence', *SIPRI Yearbook 2016*, pp. 191–200.

II. Armed conflict in the Americas

MARINA CAPARINI AND JOSÉ ALVARADO CÓBAR

In 2017 there was one active armed conflict in the Americas: in Colombia, between the Government of Colombia and various guerrilla groups. There were positive signs that the ongoing peace process, despite its many problems, might also soon bring the longest armed conflict in the Western hemisphere to a close. However, in several countries in Central and South America the levels of political and criminal violence were high enough to place them on a par with 'traditional' armed conflicts, even though they could not necessarily be defined as such. Militarized efforts to combat criminal gangs involved in drug trafficking—often underwritten by military and security assistance from the United States—have resulted in elevated homicide rates. This has made cities in the Americas some of the world's most dangerous. Alongside this, there has been endemic political corruption, weak judicial systems and low confidence in state institutions. Together, these have led to an escalating crisis of forced displacement.

This section reviews developments in conflicts in the Americas in 2017. Before looking at the conflict in Colombia in detail, it first outlines and reviews some key general developments in the Americas related to criminal violence, with detailed case studies of El Salvador, Mexico and Paraguay.

Key general developments: The dynamics and knock-on effects of conflict and criminal violence

Violence in many countries in the Americas is perpetrated by criminal gangs, cartels, armed groups and militias involved in drug trafficking, guerrillas, as well as by state police and armed forces. Several of these countries have taken a *mano dura* (iron fist) and militarized approach to criminal gangs involved in narcotics trafficking, often underwritten by US military and security assistance. In Honduras, for example, the USA has invested nearly $114 million in security assistance since 2009 to establish elite military and police units, improve border security and carry out counternarcotic operations.[1] A key indicator of growing insecurity is that 43 cities in South and Central America now rank among the world's 50 most dangerous cities based on homicide rates.[2]

---

[1] Kinosian, S., 'Crisis of Honduras democracy has roots in US tacit support for 2009 coup', *The Guardian*, 7 Dec. 2017.

[2] 'The world's most dangerous cities', *The Economist*, 31 Mar. 2017. See also Seguridad, Justicia y Paz, *Metodología del ranking (2016) de las 50 ciudades más violentas del mundo* [Methodology of the ranking (2016) of the 50 most violent cities in the world] (Seguridad, Justicia y Paz: Mexico City, 6 Apr. 2017).

Low confidence in state institutions

Despite socio-economic progress and narrowing inequalities, unmet aspirations of the expanding middle class are weakening relations between citizens and the state. Power grabs by sitting presidents, endemic corruption, elevated levels of violence and weak judicial systems have resulted in impunity and low confidence in public institutions.[3]

Guatemala, Honduras and Venezuela suffered from high levels of criminal violence and political tensions in 2017. In Venezuela, for example, amid extreme political polarization, the country slid into economic and humanitarian crisis, with ongoing anti-government protests and violence from both loyalists and the opposition.[4]

Similarly, in Honduras, in addition to high levels of violence linked to the drugs trade, counter-narcotics and corruption, the results of the presidential election held on 26 November 2017 were delayed and disputed. This sparked the worst political crisis in nearly a decade.[5] Protests occurred throughout the country and 31 people were killed in post-election violence.[6] In December the Organization of American States (OAS) concluded that there were 'irregularities and deficiencies' in the election.[7] Despite this, the USA recognized the incumbent President Juan Orlando Hernández as the winner and his opponent conceded defeat.[8]

Forced displacement

A key symptom of growing insecurity in the Americas is the escalating crisis of forced displacement in Central America and Mexico.[9] US policy continued to influence the region and each country individually in multiple ways. Three key changes in US policy in 2017 were (*a*) the declared intention to

---

[3] Organisation for Economic Co-operation and Development (OECD), Development Bank of Latin America (CAF) and UN Economic Commission for Latin America and the Caribbean (ECLAC), *Latin American Economic Outlook 2018: Rethinking Institutions for Development* (OECD: Paris, 2018), chapter 1.

[4] Semple, K. and Herrero, A. V., 'Antonio Ledezma, Venezuelan opposition leader, flees to Colombia', *New York Times*, 17 Nov. 2017; 'Venezuela's shameless and colossal vote-rigging', *The Economist*, 3 Aug. 2017; Castro, M., 'Maduro acapara todo el poder municipal' [Maduro monopolizes all municipal power], El País (Madrid), 13 Dec. 2017; and Torres, P. and Casey, N., 'Armed civilian bands in Venezuela prop up unpopular president', *New York Times*, 22 Apr. 2017.

[5] Fernández, S. M., 'Do the numbers lie? Mistrust and military lockdown after Honduras' disputed poll', International Crisis Group, 4 Dec. 2017.

[6] Kinosian, S., 'Families fear no justice for victims as 31 die in Honduras post-election violence', *The Guardian*, 2 Jan. 2018.

[7] Organization of American States, 'Statement by the OAS General Secretariat on the elections in Honduras', Press Release E-092/17, 17 Dec. 2017. See also '"Plan B": Is Honduras' ruling party planning to rig an election?', *The Economist*, 25 Nov. 2017; and Palencia, G., 'OAS says Honduran presidential election should be redone', Reuters, 18 Dec. 2017.

[8] Webber, J., 'Honduras opposition's Nasralla concedes defeat after US backs Hernández', *Financial Times*, 22 Dec. 2017.

[9] Muggah, R., 'Organised violence is ravaging Central America and displacing thousands', *The Guardian*, 29 June 2017.

stem irregular immigration; (*b*) an increased number of deportations of undocumented migrants from Central America and the Caribbean and those residing in the USA on a temporary humanitarian basis; and (*c*) the reinforcement of border security with Mexico.[10]

In August 2017, in response to the arrival at the US–Mexico border of tens of thousands of unaccompanied minors and families fleeing violence in El Salvador, Guatemala and Honduras, the USA ended its 2014 Central American Minors programme.[11] A separate programme, Temporary Protected Status (TPS), has come under threat. The TPS has provided visas on a humanitarian basis since 1990 to people from various countries affected by ongoing armed conflict, natural disasters or other extraordinary conditions, allowing them to live and work legally in the USA on a time-limited basis.[12] Over 435 000 people from 10 countries held TPS in 2017.[13] In November the USA announced an end to TPS for over 50 000 Haitians and 2500 Nicaraguans, and a decision to end TPS for 250 000 people from El Salvador followed in early January 2018.[14] A decision on TPS for Hondurans was postponed until July 2018.[15] Paradoxically, it was the USA's anti-immigrant policies—specifically the deportation to Central America in 2010–12 of nearly 100 000 people convicted of crime in the USA—that exacerbated gang- and cartel-related violence in the region, which in turn drove the migratory surge of undocumented minors to the USA.[16]

To further highlight this phenomenon of political and criminal violence, three examples are discussed in more detail below: El Salvador, Mexico and Paraguay.

[10] Miller, G., 'Stop saying "Mexico is not going to pay for the wall," Trump urges Mexican president in leaked transcript', *Washington Post*, 3 Aug. 2017.

[11] Rosenberg, M., 'US ends program for Central American minors fleeing violence', Reuters, 16 Aug. 2017.

[12] Cohn, D. and Passel, J. S., 'More than 100,000 Haitians and Central American immigrants face decision on their status in the US', Pew Research Center, 8 Nov. 2017.

[13] Park, M., 'Trump administration ended protected status for 250,000 Salvadorans. These immigrants might be next', CNN, 10 Jan. 2018.

[14] Washington Office on Latin America (WOLA), 'Trump administration's decision to end TPS for Haitians is misguided, discriminatory and encourages other governments to reject refugees', Press release, 21 Nov. 2017; Miroff, N., 'DHS ends protected immigration status for Nicaraguans, but Hondurans get extension', *Washington Post*, 6 Nov. 2017; and Park (note 13).

[15] Raphelson, S., 'Central American immigrants brace for end of Temporary Protected Status program', National Public Radio, 10 Nov. 2017.

[16] Chardy, A., 'Deportation of criminals blamed for exodus from Central America', *Miami Herald*, 3 Aug. 2014.

Political and criminal violence in Central and South America

El Salvador

The Chapultepec Peace Accords signed in 1992 transformed El Salvador's political landscape, bringing peace following a decade of civil war.[17] Nevertheless, the key developmental and societal issues that affect Salvadorian society are economic stagnation and violence from organized crime and gangs. According to the Salvadoran National Police, the biggest gangs—the Mara Salvatrucha, or MS-13, and Barrio 18—and other small gangs possess more than 600 cells throughout the country and are responsible for a majority of crime.[18] In January 2017 leaders of MS-13 proposed negotiation of a peace agreement with the government. The draft proposal included a provision for the possible disbanding of the gang.[19] However, this posed a challenge for the government since in 2015 the Constitutional Court had designated gangs as terrorist organizations, which would make them subject to legal prosecution for all crimes committed.[20]

In September 2017 human rights groups based in El Salvador presented a report to the OAS's Inter-American Commission on Human Rights (IACHR). The report chronicled alleged extrajudicial killings carried out by elements of the Salvadoran National Police and claimed that the situation resembled a low-intensity conflict, with conflict shifting from gang-on-gang violence to gang-versus-state violence.[21] While the total number of homicides decreased from 5287 in 2016 to 3947 in 2017, El Salvador is still one of the most dangerous countries in the world outside a warzone, with a homicide rate of 60 per 100 000 people.[22]

Despite the negative developments, in 2017 there were two positive developments related to accountability from the civil war. First, in October the government recognized that in 1981, during the civil war, 978 people were executed by the army in the village of El Mozote. However, payment of reparations has been slow: by May 2017 only 172 survivors and families (27 per cent of those entitled to receive compensation) had received their share of the $1.8 million disbursed by the government.[23] Second, on

[17] Wade, C. J., *Captured Peace: Elites and Peacebuilding in El Salvador* (Ohio University Press: Athens, OH, 2016), p. 2.

[18] EFE, 'El Salvador registró 317 homicidios en enero de 2018, 58 más que en 2017' [El Salvador registered 317 homicides in January 2018, 58 more than in 2017], elsalvador.com, 1 Feb. 2018.

[19] 'El Salvador gang calls for ending "war" with government', Telesur, 10 Jan. 2017.

[20] Martínez, C. and Valencia, R., 'MS-13 pide diálogo al gobierno y pone sobre la mesa su propia desarticulación' [MS-13 asks the government for dialogue and puts its proposal on the table], *El Faro* (San Salvador), 9 Jan. 2017.

[21] Clavel, T., 'El Salvador police running clandestine jails: Report', InSight Crime, 20 Sep. 2017.

[22] Clavel, T. 'InSight Crime's 2017 homicide round-up', Insight Crime, 19 Jan. 2018.

[23] Rauda Zablah, N., 'El Estado hace oficial el número de víctimas en El Mozote: 978 ejecutados, 553 niños' [The state releases official number of victims in El Mozote: 978 executed, 553 children], *El Faro* (San Salvador), 4 Dec. 2017.

29 November 2017 Inocente Orlando Montano, a former Salvadoran army colonel, was extradited from the USA to Spain. Montano faces charges related to the 1989 massacre of six Jesuit priests (including five Spaniards), their housekeeper and her teenage daughter.[24] As explained by Almudena Bernabéu, a Spanish human rights lawyer who helped build the case against Montano, 'This trial offers an opportunity for truth and justice, even if taking place in Spain, and is an effective step towards ending impunity in El Salvador'.[25]

Mexico

While Mexico faced numerous challenges in 2017, its most serious conflict trend was the accelerating pace and impact of narcotics-related crime. The history of the drug trade in Mexico is long and complex, and its trajectories of violence and peace have proven to be non-linear.[26]

One of the most violent inter-cartel conflicts has taken place in Ciudad Juárez, Chihuahua state, in the far north of Mexico. In 2010, at the height of the drug war between the Sinaloa and Juárez cartels over control of the lucrative drug trafficking routes to the USA, over 3000 homicides were registered, at a rate of 8 murders per day.[27] Hopes were raised by community-led reforms of the criminal justice system, which led to a (temporary) reduction in violence (down to 543 homicides in 2016), increased support for the police and strengthened local government.[28] However, in 2017 violence again increased, as 770 homicides were registered in Ciudad Juárez.[29]

In 2017 violence across Mexico once again surged and the country registered 29 168 homicides, marking a 30 year high and exceeding the previous record (27 213) during the drug war in 2011.[30] Mexico's overall homicide rate for 2017 stood at 22.5 per 100 000.[31] The increase can be explained as the result of struggles between criminal groups for control of drug production areas and competition over local drug sales and trafficking routes. For exam-

[24] Burgos Viale, R., 'La defensa de Montano peca de inocente' [Montano's defence team pleading innocent is a sin], *El Faro* (San Salvador), 5 Dec. 2017.

[25] 'Former El Salvador colonel extradited to Spain over 1989 murder of Jesuits', *The Guardian*, 29 Nov. 2017.

[26] Fisher, M. and Taub, A., 'Mexico's record violence is a crisis 20 years in the making', *New York Times*, 28 Oct. 2017; and Agren, D., 'Mexico maelstrom: How the drug violence got so bad', *The Guardian*, 26 Dec. 2017.

[27] Downs, R., 'Dozens killed as wave of violence hits Juárez, Chihuahua', UPI, 8 Jan. 2018; and Seguridad, Justicia y Paz, 'San Pedro Sula, la ciudad más violenta del mundo; Juárez, la segunda' [San Pedro Sula, the most violent city in the world; Juarez the second], Press release, 11 Jan. 2012.

[28] Quinones, S., 'Once the world's most dangerous city, Juárez returns to life', *National Geographic*, June 2016.

[29] Downs (note 27).

[30] Stevenson, M., 'Mexico posts highest homicide rate in decades', Associated Press, 21 Jan. 2018.

[31] Torres, N., 'Mexico suffers deadliest month on record, 2017 set to be worst year', Reuters, 22 Nov. 2017; and Clavel (note 22).

ple, violence intensified after January following the arrest and extradition to the USA of the head of the Sinaloa cartel, Joaquín 'El Chapo' Guzmán.[32]

As violence has increased and spread, those who can afford it purchase security, either from the police or from private security companies: an estimated 70 per cent of police are engaged in protecting private interests, while industry officials claim demand for private security is increasing at 40–60 per cent per year.[33] Since 2013 Mexico has also seen the emergence of community self-defence militias. These militias have emerged in towns with high rates of economic inequality and where a weak historic state presence has led to poorer citizens feeling deprived of both private and state security.[34] However, many self-defence militias have been corrupted by cartels and have themselves become vigilante organizations, often acting with de facto impunity.[35]

In addition, opportunistic crime against Central American migrants—robbery, sexual assaults, kidnapping and extortion, and sometimes lethal violence—continues. This is allegedly perpetrated by cartels and criminal groups either working with the complicity of local police and security personnel or by taking advantage of their lack of capacity.[36]

Pervasive corruption among officials of the ruling Institutional Revolutionary Party (Partido Revolucionario Institucional, PRI) and a lack of political will to implement new anti-corruption measures and prosecute offenders have exacerbated tensions in Mexico.[37] While public outrage over his alleged effort to avoid paying taxes on his sports car finally forced the resignation of Mexico's Attorney General, Raúl Cervantes, in October, there is little public confidence in the ability of the state police and justice system to deal with crime.[38] Only 4.5 per cent of reported crimes result in convictions: an impunity rate of 95 per cent, giving Mexico one of the highest rates of impunity in the world. Since only 7 per cent of crimes are reported, if the

---

[32] 'Mexico murder rate reaches record high', Al Jazeera, 22 June 2017; Heinle, K., Rodriguez Ferreira, O. and Shirk, D. A., *Drug Violence in Mexico: Data and Analysis Through 2016* (Justice in Mexico: San Diego: Mar. 2017), p. 3; and de Córdoba, J., 'With "El Chapo" gone, violence soars in fight for control of cartel', *Wall Street Journal*, 17 July 2017.

[33] Fisher, M. and Taub, A., '"The social contract is broken": Inequality becomes deadly in Mexico', *New York Times*, 30 Sep. 2017; and 'Regulating security sector', *The Business Year: Mexico 2017* (The Business Year: Dubai, 2017).

[34] Phillips, B. J., 'Inequality and the emergence of vigilante organizations: The case of Mexican *autodefensas*', *Comparative Political Studies*, vol. 50, no. 10 (Sep. 2017), pp. 1358–89.

[35] Felbab-Brown, V., 'The rise of militias in Mexico: Citizens' security or further conflict escalation?' *PRISM*, vol. 5, no. 4 (2016), p. 184.

[36] *Migración en tránsito por México: Rostro de una crisis humanitaria internacional* [Migration in transit through Mexico: The face of an international humanitarian crisis] (REDODEM: Mexico City, 2016); and Lakhani, N., 'Mexican kidnappers pile misery onto Central Americans fleeing violence', *The Guardian*, 21 Feb. 2017.

[37] Webber, J., 'Mexico arrests fail to satisfy anti-corruption critics', *Financial Times*, 18 Apr. 2017.

[38] Malkin, E., 'Mexico's attorney general resigns under pressure', *New York Times*, 16 Oct. 2017; and Agence France-Presse, 'A Ferrari and a fake address: Mexico's attorney general resigns after "tax dodge" scandal', *South China Morning Post*, 17 Oct. 2017.

figures for conviction were extrapolated to all crimes it would amount to 99 per cent impunity.[39]

In December the Congress passed a law strengthening the military's role in combating organized crime, including authorizing the government to deploy soldiers to areas under the control of drug gangs.[40] The measure was criticized as expanding the president's ability to deploy the military without congressional or judicial oversight, raising concerns of human rights abuses.[41] The unsolved disappearance of 43 teachers and college students from Guerrero state in 2014, apparently perpetrated by local police and drug cartels, and repeated cover-up attempts by government officials, provides a vivid reminder of the abuses perpetrated—largely with impunity—by drug traffickers and by police, soldiers and other state actors. An estimated 33 000 individuals went missing in Mexico between 2006 and 2017.[42]

With presidential and congressional elections due in July 2018, the spectres of violence and electoral fraud cannot be dismissed as organized crime groups are expected to attempt to manipulate outcomes, while assassinations of government officials, activists and journalists continue to go largely unpunished.[43]

Paraguay

Paraguay's fragile democracy weathered violent protests on 31 March 2017 when the Senate voted to allow President Horacio Cartes to stand for election for a second presidential term.[44] The crisis ended in April when the Chamber of Deputies revoked the decision and Cartes announced that he would not seek a second term, seemingly preserving the constitution's strong checks on executive power.

The border region between Paraguay and Brazil continues to be afflicted by drug trafficking and gang violence. Paraguay is the second largest producer of marijuana in South and Central America, 80 per cent of which is sold in Brazil.[45] The triple frontier area that lies at the junction between Paraguay

[39] Le Clercq Ortega, J. A. and Rodríguez Sánchez Lara, G., *Global Impunity Dimensions: Global Impunity Index 2017* (Universidad de las Américas, Puebla: Puebla, Aug. 2017), p. 96; Herrera, R., 'Revelan impunidad de 99% en México' [99% impunity revealed in Mexico], *Reforma* (Mexico City), 28 Aug. 2017; and Zepeda Lecuona, G. R., 'El tamaño de la impunidad en México' [The size of impunity in Mexico], Impunidad Cero, 2017.

[40] Ley de Seguridad Interior [Internal security law], *Diario Oficial de la Federación*, vol. 771, no. 18 (21 Dec. 2017).

[41] Malkin, E., 'Mexico strengthens military's role in drug war, outraging critics', *New York Times*, 15 Dec. 2017.

[42] Ahmed, A., 'In Mexico, not dead. not alive. just gone', *New York Times*, 20 Nov. 2017.

[43] Paterson, K., 'Who and what will the 2018 Mexican elections bring?', NMPolitics.net, 7 Feb. 2018.

[44] Romero, S., 'Protests erupt in Paraguay over efforts to extend president's term', *New York Times*, 31 Mar. 2017.

[45] Carneri, S., 'Los narcos brasileños también matan en Paraguay' [Brazilian drug traffickers also kill in Paraguay], *El País* (Madrid), 4 Dec. 2017.

(near the city of Ciudad del Este), Argentina (near Puerto Iguazú) and Brazil (near Foz do Iguaçu) is also an important transit corridor for cocaine produced in Bolivia, Peru and Colombia. Brazilian gangs are fighting for control of trafficking routes and are also believed to be expanding their presence in Paraguay.[46] While Paraguay's overall homicide rate, at 7.8 per 100 000 in 2017, was relatively low by regional standards, Amambay department on the border with Brazil has historically been the most violent area in the country, reaching 66.7 homicide's per 100 000 in 2014, with the vast majority of these homicides being drug related.[47]

The Paraguayan authorities have also been unable to dismantle the small but resilient left-wing guerrilla group, the Paraguayan People's Army (Ejército del Pueblo Paraguayo, EPP). The EPP has been active since 2008 in rural areas in the northern departments of Concepción, San Pedro and Canindeyú. It focuses on land ownership, agrarian reform and for the rights of farmers, or *campesinos*.[48] Paraguay is one of the most inequitable countries in South and Central America in terms of land distribution: while 30 per cent of Paraguayans live in rural areas, 85.5 per cent of land is owned by just 2.6 per cent of the population.[49] Despite a booming agriculture sector, 40 per cent of the population lives below the poverty line.[50] Current government policies favour large landowners and agribusiness (especially soya production) and ignore small- and medium-sized farmers and indigenous groups, who are displaced to towns and cities.[51]

The EPP, which is estimated to consist of 50–150 members, has targeted police, businesses and wealthy individuals. It has killed approximately 50 people, including members of the security forces, kidnapped individuals for ransom and attacked public utilities including electricity transmission towers.[52] The EPP is financed through 'taxes' on local ranchers and landowners, ransoms and, allegedly, through growing involvement in narcotics trafficking, which stems from training given by the Revolutionary Armed Forces of Colombia (Fuerzas Armadas Revolucionarias de Colombia, FARC),

[46] Clavel, T., 'Commando-style heist plunges Paraguay border town into chaos', InSight Crime, 25 Apr. 2017.

[47] Clavel (note 22); Tabory, S., 'Paraguay homicides drop, but border remains violent', InSight Crime, 23 Sep. 2015; and US Department of State, Overseas Security Advisory Council, 'Paraguay 2016 crime & safety report', 9 May 2016.

[48] 'Paraguayan guerrilla and land conflict: The next Colombia?', Telesur, 8 Oct. 2014. See also US Department of State, *Country Reports on Terrorism 2016* (Department of State: Washington, DC, July 2017), pp. 294–96.

[49] Yorke, O., 'Paraguay's agricultural sector: How much is at risk?', Global Risk Insights, 19 Sep. 2017; and 'Rural Paraguayans renew demand for land reform', EFE, 29 Mar. 2017.

[50] 'Aumenta la pobreza en el país durante era Cartes' [Poverty increased in the country during the Cartes era], ABC Color, 16 June 2017.

[51] Yorke (note 49).

[52] 'Suspected rebels kill eight soldiers in ambush in Paraguay', BBC News, 27 Aug. 2016.

a Colombian guerrilla group.[53] In 2013 the Paraguayan Government created a joint military–police task force to combat the EPP. The Joint Task Force (Fuerza de Tarea Conjunta, FTC) has been criticized for its failure to defeat the EPP, alleged corruption within the unit and its lack of coordination with other Paraguayan security agencies.[54] The head of the FTC was replaced in 2017, leading to the appointment of its seventh head in four years.[55]

Armed conflict in Colombia

Armed conflict in Colombia has continued for over five decades, leaving in its wake more than 220 000 deaths, as well as 6.9 internally displaced persons in a country with a population of 48 million.[56] The armed conflict has involved various armed groups, drug cartels and the government. The main armed conflict in Colombia was ended by the signing of a peace agreement in November 2016 between the government and FARC.[57]

Several steps to implement the peace agreement were made in 2017. In January a Special Electoral Mission was established by the government and FARC to provide recommendations to modernize the Colombian electoral system, not least to legitimize and assure the participation of FARC as a political party.[58] In February the National Commission for Security Guarantees was created and tasked with dismantling criminal organizations and selecting judges who will preside over the Special Jurisdiction for Peace (Jurisdicción Especial para la Paz, JEP). The JEP will be responsible for prosecuting and punishing the most serious crimes carried out during the armed conflict. As a sign of FARC's commitment to the process, on 6 February the government's High Commissioner for Peace reported that around 6000 members of FARC had demobilized throughout the 20 concentration zones and eight demobilization zones designated by the government and managed by the United Nations Mission in Colombia (UNMC).[59]

In March 2017 the governmental registration office issued national identification documents to former FARC members as a means to reintegrate them into society. In April the process was expanded to create a special entity

---

[53] Clavel, T., 'Military commander's firing highlights failures in combating Paraguay rebels', InSight Crime, 31 May 2017.

[54] Economist Intelligence Unit, 'Divisions over anti-guerrilla strategy emerge', 28 Aug. 2015; and Gagne, D., 'Suspected guerrilla ambush leaves 8 Paraguay solders dead', InSight Crime, 29 Aug. 2016.

[55] Clavel (note 53).

[56] Davis, C. and Trinkunas, H., 'Has Colombia achieved peace? 5 things you should know', Order from Chaos, Brookings Institution, 5 Aug. 2016. On the negotiation of the peace process see Valenzuela, P., 'Out of the darkness? The hope for peace in Colombia', SIPRI Yearbook 2017, pp. 47–57.

[57] Final Agreement to End the Armed Conflict and Build Stable and Lasting Peace, 24 Nov. 2016.

[58] 'Cronología de la implementación del acuerdo de paz' [Chronology of the implementation of the peace agreement], Agenda Propia, 15 June 2017.

[59] Goi, L. and McDermott, J., 'Colombia FARC soldiers demobilize, militias remain in field', InSight Crime, 6 Feb. 2017. On UNMC see chapter 3, section II, in this volume.

that would help ensure gender mainstreaming in implementing the peace agreement.[60] There is an inherent risk that former FARC guerrillas will join organized criminal gangs if they are not successfully reintegrated into productive activities that can give them and their families a licit and dignified livelihood.[61] Whether reintegration plans will result in sufficient numbers of jobs for former FARC combatants remains an open question.

On 20 June the UNMC reported that FARC had completed the handover of its weapons ahead of the 27 June deadline.[62] However, dissident FARC groups, calculated to be around 5–15 per cent of the total number of FARC ex-combatants, continued to expand in certain areas, mainly bordering Ecuador, Peru and Venezuela.[63]

On 4 September 2017 the National Liberation Army (Ejército de Liberación Nacional, ELN), Colombia's second largest guerrilla group, signed a temporary ceasefire agreement with the government until January 2018.[64] Despite the agreement, ELN continued to attack public security officers in Arauca department.[65]

With presidential and congressional elections taking place in 2018, FARC will seek to become fully incorporated into the political arena under its new name, the Common Alternative Revolutionary Force (Fuerza Alternativa Revolucionaria del Común, with the same acronym, FARC), and advocate for reforms with its coalition partners. However, it is unclear whether the Congress will approve laws relating to the JEP and other reforms designed to facilitate FARC's formal participation in politics.[66]

---

[60] Office of the High Commissioner for Peace, 'Así marcha el Acuerdo de Paz' [Current state of the peace agreement], 2017.

[61] Labbé, S., Seucharan, C. and Villagas, A., 'Disarmed and dangerous: Can former Farc guerrillas adjust to civilian life?', The Guardian, 24 May 2017.

[62] United Nations, Security Council, Report of the Secretary-General on the United Nations Mission in Colombia, S/2017/539, 23 June 2017, p. 10.

[63] Albaladejo, A., 'Is Colombia underestimating the scale of FARC dissidence?', InSight Crime, 17 Oct. 2017.

[64] Office of the High Commissioner for Peace, 'Acuerdo y comunicado sobre el cese al fuego bilateral y temporal entre el Gobierno y el ELN' [Agreement and communiqué on the bilateral temporary ceasefire between the government and the ELN], 4 Sep. 2017.

[65] 'Escalada de ataques en Arauca deja tres policias heridos' [Escalation of attacks in Arauca results in three wounded police officers], El Tiempo (Bogotá), 24 Sep. 2017.

[66] Bargent, J., 'Time running out for Colombia Congress to pass FARC peace legislation', InSight Crime, 6 Nov. 2017.

III. Armed conflict in Asia and Oceania

IAN DAVIS, RICHARD GHIASY AND FEI SU

Five countries in Asia and Oceania were involved in active armed conflicts in 2017: Afghanistan, India, Myanmar, Pakistan and the Philippines. In Myanmar the Rohingya were forcibly displaced (with spillover effects in Bangladesh); in places such as the Philippines state security forces committed widespread violence with impunity; and the Islamic State group moved into countries such as Afghanistan and the Philippines. Alongside this, parts of Asia and Oceania continued to be affected by instability from a variety of causes, with no single unifying trend: tensions rose in North East Asia, which is one of the world's most militarized regions, chiefly due to the nuclear weapon and ballistic missile programmes of the Democratic People's Republic of Korea (DPRK, or North Korea); interstate competition between China and its neighbours continued in the South China Sea and the East China Sea; and the India–Pakistan conflict over Kashmir reignited; relations between China and India continued to deteriorate after a military stand-off in the border area adjacent to Bhutan.[1] Concerns about human rights violations were also raised in many countries across the region throughout 2017.[2]

This section briefly discusses the background to each of the armed conflicts as well as ongoing peace processes in two countries. It discusses Nepal as an example of a peace process that is continuing despite various challenges and Sri Lanka in the context of a post-conflict peace process focused on the search for truth, justice and reconciliation.

Armed conflict in Afghanistan

Afghanistan has Asia's youngest population: the median age in 2017 was just 18.8 years.[3] Over 70 per cent of the Afghan population was born amid violent conflict, which has raged almost continuously since 1979. For many Afghans, therefore, conflict and insecurity are part of daily life. The security situation remained highly volatile in 2017 and there are no signs that the country's security situation will improve in the short to medium term.

---

[1] On military spending in Asia see chapter 4, section II, in this volume; on interstate competition in the South and East China seas, the conflict in Kashmir and tensions between India and China see chapter 1, section II, in this volume.

[2] See e.g. Al Hussein, Z. R., UN High Commissioner for Human Rights, 'Current development and challenges in the Asia-Pacific region', Statement at the Jakarta Conversation on the 70th year of the Universal Declaration on Human Rights and 25th year of the Vienna Declaration and Programme of Action, 5 Feb. 2018.

[3] US Central Intelligence Agency, 'Country comparison to the world', World Factbook, [n.d.]. Demographic data on Afghanistan has its limitations as there has been no recent census.

The United Nations recorded 23 744 security-related incidents in 2017, 63 per cent of which were attributed to armed clashes.[4] Insurgents made up of the Taliban, the Taliban-affiliated Haqqani network and the Islamic State–Khorasan Province (a local affiliate of the Islamic State) continued their asymmetric attacks on the Afghan National Defense and Security Forces (ANDSF) and major population centres in 2017, and these attacks remained the main cause of civilian casualties. The violence prompted the International Committee of the Red Cross to announce in October 2017 that it was reducing its presence in the country and that it could no longer continue to operate in some provinces.[5]

The UN Assistance Mission in Afghanistan (UNAMA) documented 3438 deaths and 7015 injuries in 2017. It attributed 65 per cent of these casualties to 'anti-government elements' (42 per cent to the Taliban, 10 per cent to the Islamic State–Khorasan Province and 13 per cent to undetermined 'other anti-government elements') and 20 per cent to pro-government forces (16 per cent to the ANDSF, 2 per cent to international military forces and 2 per cent to other pro-government armed groups) and the remaining 15 per cent to various causes, such as unattributed crossfire. Although the number of casualties decreased by 9 per cent between 2016 and 2017, a higher proportion of the casualties in 2017 (22 per cent, compared to 17 per cent in 2016) were caused by suicide bombings and other attacks using improvised explosive devices (IEDs).[6] The deadliest attack in Kabul since the fall of the Taliban in 2001 took place on 31 May 2017, when a large truck bomb killed at least 150 people and injured more than 300, mostly civilians.[7] The attack occurred just six days before the start of the Kabul Process, an Afghan Government-led peace process that includes stakeholders from neighbouring countries and further afield but in which the Taliban chose not to participate.[8] There was, therefore, no tangible progress towards a peace process in 2017.

The Islamic State–Khorasan Province continued to attack the Shia-majority Hazara community throughout 2017 in an apparent attempt to stoke Shia–Sunni sectarian violence, which Afghanistan has mostly avoided throughout the years of conflict.[9] Despite upheavals over its leadership and strategic direction in 2017, the Taliban managed to sustain the resurgence

[4] United Nations, General Assembly and Security Council, 'The situation in Afghanistan and its implications for international peace and security', Report of the Secretary-General, A/72/768–S/2018/165, 27 Feb. 2018, para. 14.

[5] Abed, F. and Najim, R., 'Red Cross reduces presence in Afghanistan after staff is attacked', *New York Times*, 9 Oct. 2017.

[6] UN Assistance Mission in Afghanistan (UNAMA), *Afghanistan Protection of Civilians in Armed Conflict: Annual Report 2017* (UNAMA: Kabul, Feb. 2018).

[7] No group claimed responsibility but the Afghan Government accused the Haqqani network. Nordland, R., 'Death toll in Kabul bombing has hit 150, Afghan President says', *New York Times*, 6 June 2017.

[8] Afghan Ministry of Foreign Affairs, 'The Kabul Process', 6 June 2017.

[9] Comerford, M., 'Islamic State's Khorasan Province, 2 years on', The Diplomat, 26 Jan. 2017.

that it had made since the 'triple transition' in late 2014—the moment it was envisaged that the Afghan Government would be given autonomy by the international community over politics, security and the economy. The Afghan Government has gradually lost territory to the Taliban since that transition. By mid-2017 the Taliban was thought to control or be contesting about 45 per cent of the country—mostly in rural areas.[10]

The conflict appeared to have reached a deadlock in 2017, although there were growing concerns that the ANDSF might be suffering a level of casualties that is unsustainable over the long term.[11] As well as the ANDSF's limited military capacity, the deadlock is also partially sustained by a combination of weak governance, political infighting, geopolitical scheming among external stakeholders and a largely dysfunctional formal economy.

US President Donald J. Trump announced a new US strategy for Afghanistan in August 2017. In its continued focus on the use of military force, the strategy mirrored those of the previous two US administrations. It did, however, propose a shift from a time-based approach to the war to one based on conditions on the ground, and it increased the number of troops deployed by an estimated 4000.[12] This is in addition to the estimated 8300 US soldiers of the total of 13 576 international soldiers deployed with the Resolute Support mission of the North Atlantic Treaty Organization (NATO), which was launched in 2015 to provide further training, advice and assistance to the ANDSF.[13] President Trump underlined that the strategy will focus not on state building, but instead on defeating the Taliban and other militant groups through (a) better training for the ANDSF; (b) training more Afghan special forces; and (c) joint Afghan–US counterterrorism operations.[14] This relaxing of restraints on the use of military power by the USA has the potential to increase the number of civilian casualties, and by the end of the year there was some evidence that this had already happened.[15]

As part of its new strategy, the USA also stated that it would seek to put more diplomatic pressure on Pakistan to prevent cross-border attacks.[16] Afghanistan and Pakistan blame each other for the frequency of such

[10] Roggio, B. and Gutowski, A., 'LWJ map assessment: Taliban controls or contests 45% of Afghan districts', FDD's Long War Journal, Foundation for the Defense of Democracies (FDD), 26 Sep. 2017.
[11] US Special Inspector General for Afghanistan Reconstruction (SIGAR), Quarterly Report to the United States Congress (SIGAR: Arlington, VA, 30 Oct. 2017).
[12] 'Trump rules out Afghan troops withdrawal', BBC News, 22 Aug. 2017.
[13] The USA does not disclose exact US troop numbers for Afghanistan. For figures on Resolute Support see NATO, 'NATO and Afghanistan', 10 Nov. 2017; and NATO, 'Resolute Support mission (RSM): Key facts and figures', May 2017.
[14] Gibbons-Neff, T., 'US-led mission in Afghanistan lacks troops for new strategy', New York Times, 9 Nov. 2017.
[15] See e.g. Rasmussen, S. E., 'Afghan civilians count cost of renewed US air campaign', The Guardian, 5 Sep. 2017; and Rahim, N. and Nordland, R., 'Did airstrikes in Afghanistan last week kill civilians? US and UN disagree', New York Times, 10 Nov. 2017.
[16] Hirschfield Davis, J. and Landler, M., 'Trump outlines new Afghanistan war strategy with few details', New York Times, 21 Aug. 2017.

attacks, and high-level political exchanges between the two countries to try to seek a resolution to the issue continued in 2017. In addition, the two countries initiated a joint crisis-control mechanism for emergency communications, facilitated by China; and joint operations against terrorists along each other's borders, facilitated by the USA.[17] There were allegations throughout 2017 that Russia was financing and arming the Taliban in its fight against the Islamic State–Khorasan Province, with the aim of curbing the Islamic State's influence in Central Asia. However, it is difficult to obtain reliable information on arms supplies to the Taliban.[18]

Armed conflict in India

In addition to its interstate tensions with China and the reignition of the territorial dispute with Pakistan over Kashmir in 2017, India faced a number of continuing internal security threats, such as the long-running Naxalite–Maoist insurgency.[19] The conflict in its present form began after the 2004 merger of the People's War Group (PWG) and the Maoist Communist Centre (MCC) to form the Communist Party of India-Maoist) (CPI-Maoist), also known as the Naxalites. The People's Liberation Guerrilla Army (PLGA) is the armed wing of the CPI-Maoist.[20]

In the mid-2000s the conflict was affecting around half of India's then 28 states. However, the CPI-Maoist presence has decreased in the past decade following the launch of a counterinsurgency operation in 2009 combined with a series of social programmes initiated by the Indian Government since the mid-2000s, including the 2013 Food Security Bill and the 2005 Mahatma Gandhi National Rural Employment Guarantee Scheme (MGNREGS). In the wake of these, the Indian Government has reported a gradual but steady decline in the level of violence since 2010, although casualties have remained in the low hundreds in each year.[21] In 2016, however, 433 people were reported killed in the conflict (244 CPI-Maoists,

[17] Afghan Ministry of Foreign Affairs, 'Joint press release by China, Afghanistan and Pakistan', 25 June 2017; and Gul, A., 'Afghanistan accepts Pakistan's offer of "coordinated" anti-terror operations', Voice of America, 5 July 2017.

[18] Rasmussen, S. E., 'Russia accused of supplying Taliban as power shifts create strange bedfellows', The Guardian, 22 Oct. 2017. On international arms transfers see chapter 5, section I, in this volume.

[19] On India–China tensions and the conflict in Jammu and Kashmir see chapter 1, section II, in this volume.

[20] 'India's Maoist rebels: An explainer', Al Jazeera, 26 Apr. 2017.

[21] 'Indian Parliament passes Food Security Bill', BRICS Post, 26 Aug. 2013, and Reddy, D. N., Reddy, A. A. and Bantilan, M. C. S., 'The impact of Mahatma Gandhi National Rural Employment Guarantee Act (MGNREGA) on rural labor markets and agriculture', India Review, vol. 13, no. 3 (2014), pp. 251–73.

123 civilians and 66 security force personnel), due in large part to one major ambush.[22]

In 2017 the violence centred on Chhattisgarh state, where two attacks by the PLGA, in March and April, killed at least 36 Indian security force personnel, and for the whole year the state suffered a total of 169 fatalities (78 CPI-Maoists, 32 civilians and 59 security force personnel).[23] Overall, in 2017 approximately 333 people were killed in the conflict, which remains deadlocked with no immediate prospects of a peace process or a political resolution—especially since the Indian Government sees its counterinsurgency strategy as effective.[24]

Armed conflict in Myanmar

Between 1962 and 2011 Myanmar was ruled by a military junta that suppressed almost all dissent. The house arrest of Aung San Suu Kyi, leader of the National League for Democracy (NLD), became symbolic of this suppression. A gradual liberalization process that began in 2010 resulted in nationwide, multiparty elections in November 2015 and the election in March 2016 of the NLD's Htin Kyaw as the first non-military president since 1962. Although Aung San Suu Kyi was barred by the constitution from becoming president, she became head of government in the newly created post of state counsellor.[25]

The military retains considerable power. It has long supported the dominance of Myanmar's largest ethnic group, the Bamar, and this has fuelled a series of long-running insurgencies.

In many parts of the country there are serious humanitarian crises linked to large-scale food insecurity, chronic poverty and lack of adequate health care and other services as a result of decades of military rule, communal and ethnic division, structural inequality and protracted conflict.[26] Myanmar's ethnic minorities comprise around 40 per cent of the population and live mainly in the border areas, where many of the insurgent groups are also located. The military junta negotiated agreements with some of these groups, allowing them to administer small enclaves, but was not prepared to

---

[22] South Asia Terrorism Portal (SATP), 'Fatalities in left-wing extremism: 2016'; 'India's Maoist rebels: An explainer' (note 20); and Roy, S., 'Half a century of India's Maoist insurgency', The Diplomat, 21 Sep. 2017.

[23] Drolial, R., '25 jawans killed as Maoists attack CRPF team in Chhattisgarh's Sukma', Times of India, 24 Apr. 2017; and South Asia Terrorism Portal (SATP), 'Fatalities in left-wing extremism: 2017'.

[24] South Asian Terrorism Portal (note 23); Roy (note 22); and Chauhani, N., 'New anti-Maoist strategy delivers results, Red Corridor shrinks to 58 districts', Times of India, 24 Jan. 2018.

[25] On Myanmar's transition from military junta to democracy see Xu, B. and Albert, E., 'Understanding Myanmar', Backgrounder, Council on Foreign Relations, 25 Mar. 2016.

[26] United Nations and Partners, Humanitarian Country Team, 2017 Myanmar Humanitarian Response Plan: January–December 2017 (United Nations: Dec. 2016).

accept a federal solution or address the grievances of ethnic minorities more broadly.[27]

A gradual peace process yielded a draft ceasefire in 2015, known as the Nationwide Ceasefire Agreement (NCA), but only 8 of the at least 20 ethnic armed groups that operate in Myanmar signed. As part of this peace process, a Union Peace Conference must be held every six months. The first of these conferences took place on 31 August to 4 September 2016.[28]

In March 2017 an insurgent group known as the Myanmar National Democratic Alliance Army (MNDAA) launched attacks against civilian, police and army targets in Laukkai in the eastern state of Shan, killing at least 30 people. The MNDAA, which did not participate in the 2015 peace process, is part of a larger uneasy coalition of insurgent groups.[29] The security situation in Shan remained volatile throughout the remainder of the year, as it did in Kachin state to the north, where armed conflict continued between the government and the Kachin Independence Army, the armed wing of the Kachin Independence Organization.[30]

The second Union Peace Conference took place on 24–29 May 2017 and was attended by around 1400 stakeholders, including representatives of the government, the parliament, the military, political parties, ethnic armed groups and civil society groups.[31] The conference was marked by three critical developments in the peace process: (*a*) the refusal of the United Nationalities Federal Council, a powerful group of non-signatories to the NCA, to participate, despite earlier compliance with the process; (*b*) the issue of secession and different understandings of federalism re-emerging as dividing lines among stakeholders; and (*c*) China's growing role in the dialogue process, particularly in terms of mediating the participation of ethnic armed groups based in northern and north-eastern Myanmar.[32]

While the fact that the conference took place at all—after a delay of almost three months—meant that some, albeit limited, progress was made, events in the north of Rakhine state in August 2017 underlined the fragility of the fledgling peace process. The Rohingya, a predominantly Sunni Muslim ethnic group chiefly based in Rakhine in the west of Myanmar, have repeatedly faced discrimination, denial of basic rights, forced displacement and

---

[27] 'Ending Myanmar's insurgencies: A long road', *The Economist*, 10 Sep. 2016.

[28] International Crisis Group (ICG), *Myanmar's Peace Process: Getting to a Political Dialogue*, Crisis Group Asia Briefing no. 149 (ICG: Brussels, 19 Oct. 2016).

[29] Moe, W. and Ives, M., 'Attacks by rebels in Myanmar leave dozens dead', *New York Times*, 7 Mar. 2017; and Davis, A., 'Myanmar's army struggles against a strong rebel alliance', Nikkei Asian Review, 6 Apr. 2017.

[30] Thompson, N., 'Myanmar's unhappy rebels', The Diplomat, 8 Jan. 2018; and Naw, S., 'Myanmar's other ethnic atrocity', Asia Times, 27 Dec. 2017.

[31] Kipgen, N., 'The continuing challenges of Myanmar's peace process', The Diplomat, 6 June 2017.

[32] Choudhury, A., 'Second 21CPC and Myanmar's stuttering peace process', Institute of Peace and Conflict Studies, 28 June 2017; and Kipgen (note 31).

intercommunal violence since the 1980s.[33] The conflict includes intercommunal and political dimensions. Anti-Muslim sentiment is widespread among the armed forces, large sectors of civil society (especially radical Buddhist groups) and even among members of the NLD. Hence, some of the violence against the Rohingya has been committed by communal groups rather than state security forces. On the political level more generally, the NLD remains weak in relation to the armed forces on all security-related matters.

In a serious escalation of this long-standing conflict, on 25 August militants from the Arakan Rohingya Salvation Army (ARSA)—a relatively new ethnic armed group that claims to be defending the rights of the Rohingya—launched coordinated attacks on 30 police posts and an army base.[34] Around 80 militants and 12 members of the security forces were killed. The military responded by carrying out 'clearance operations', during which there is evidence that Rohingya villages were burned, and by evacuating around 4000 non-Muslim civilians from the area.[35] Up to 38 000 Rohingya people subsequently attempted to flee to Bangladesh.[36] By early September it was estimated that over 580 000 Rohingya civilians had fled across the border, prompting one of the fastest-growing refugee crises since World War II.[37]

The Government of Myanmar denied access to the area to a UN fact-finding mission, most international aid agencies and journalists.[38] The UN Human Rights Council accused the Myanmar military of ethnic cleansing, while other observers and agencies made accusations of sexual violence and crimes against humanity.[39] Senior Myanmar officials denied these accusations, but the members of the European Union (EU) and the United States responded by either suspending or restricting defence cooperation with the

---

[33] On discriminatory legislation against the Rohingya see 'Still oppressed: Rohingya policies and restrictions under Myanmar's new government', Joint briefing paper, International Federation for Human Rights (FIDH) and Alternative ASEAN Network on Burma, 26 Oct. 2016.

[34] The Arakan Rohingya Salvation Army was formerly known as the Harakah al-Yaqin (HaY). International Crisis Group (ICG), *Myanmar: A New Muslim Insurgency in Rakhine State*, Asia Report no. 283 (ICG: Brussels, 15 Dec. 2016). On the attacks and the aftermath see e.g. International Crisis Group, 'Myanmar tips into new crisis after Rakhine State attacks', 27 Aug. 2017.

[35] Human Rights Watch, 'Burma: 40 Rohingya villages burned since October', 17 Dec. 2017.

[36] 'Nearly 40,000 Rohingya fled escalating Myanmar fighting: UN sources', Reuters, 1 Sep. 2017.

[37] Ramzy, A., 'Rohingya refugees fleeing Myanmar await entrance to squalid camps', *New York Times*, 18 Oct. 2017.

[38] International Crisis Group, 'The Rakhine State danger to Myanmar's transition', 8 Sep. 2017.

[39] Al Hussein, Z. R., UN High Commissioner for Human Rights, 'Darker and more dangerous: High Commissioner updates the Human Rights Council on human rights issues in 40 countries', Opening Statement, UN Human Rights Council 36th session, 11 Sep. 2017. See also e.g. Amnesty International, 'Myanmar: Crimes against humanity terrorize and drive Rohingya out', 18 Oct. 2017; Human Rights Watch, 'Burma: New satellite images confirm mass destruction', 17 Oct. 2017; and Human Rights Watch (HRW), *'All of My Body Was Pain': Sexual Violence against Rohingya Women and Girls in Burma* (HRW: New York, Nov. 2017).

country.[40] There were also reports that the Myanmar security forces were building fences and placing landmines along the border to deter people from crossing into Bangladesh.[41] Médecins Sans Frontières estimated that 9000–13 700 Rohingya people, including at least 1000 children under the age of five, died between August and September 2017, with about 71 per cent suffering 'violent deaths' and the remainder dying of starvation or other causes as a result of fleeing the violence.[42]

In Bangladesh an estimated 700 000–900 000 Rohingya, including those displaced earlier, required urgent humanitarian assistance. Although the capacity of Bangladesh to respond was limited, it established a camp at Kutupalong to accommodate 800 000 people and coordinated with international humanitarian partners to install basic facilities and obtain medical supplies.[43] In September 2017 the UN Office for the Coordination of Humanitarian Affairs (OCHA) and its partners published a preliminary response plan requesting $77 million in funding for the crisis unfolding in Myanmar and Bangladesh, which was later increased to $434 million.[44] As part of an effort to share the cost of the response, on 23 October 2017 a pledging conference organized by OCHA, the office of the UN High Commissioner for Refugees (UNHCR) and the International Organization for Migration (IOM), and co-hosted by the EU and Kuwait, raised $360 million.[45]

Efforts to facilitate the voluntary and safe return of the displaced Rohingya faced severe problems, not least that Bangladesh and Myanmar disagreed on the terms for repatriation. Bangladesh favoured UN involvement, while Myanmar wanted the repatriation to be managed in accordance with a 1992 agreement between the two countries, which was negotiated following a previous case of mass displacement.[46]

---

[40] Oliphant, R. and Connor, N., 'Britain to stop training Burmese military until Rohingya crisis is resolved', *Daily Telegraph*, 19 Sep. 2017; Agence France-Press, 'European Union to cut ties with Myanmar military chiefs over Rakhine crisis', *Frontier Myanmar*, 12 Oct. 2017; and Martin, M. F., Margesson, R. and Vaughn, B., *The Rohingya Crises in Bangladesh and Burma*, Congressional Research Service (CRS) Report for Congress R45016 (US Congress, CRS: Washington, DC, 8 Nov. 2017).

[41] Das, K. N., 'Bangladesh protests over Myanmar's suspected landmine use near border', Reuters, 5 Sep. 2017. On landmines see also chapter 9, section II, in this volume.

[42] Médecins Sans Frontières, 'Myanmar/Bangladesh: MSF surveys estimate that at least 6,700 Rohingya were killed during the attacks in Myanmar', 12 Dec. 2017.

[43] Arora, M. and Westcott, B., 'Bangladesh to move 800,000 Rohingya into single enormous camp', CNN, 23 Oct. 2017; and World Health Organization, '900,000 vaccines "en route" to Cox's Bazar to prevent cholera', Press Release 1666, 29 Sep. 2017.

[44] UN Office for the Coordination of Humanitarian Affairs (OCHA), *2017 Humanitarian Response Plan: September 2017–February 2018: Rohingya Refugee Crisis* (OCHA: Oct. 2017).

[45] UN Office for the Coordination of Humanitarian Affairs (OCHA), 'Rohingya refugee crisis: Pledging conference', [n.d.]; and Pledging Conference for the Rohingya Refugee Crisis, 'Pledges', 23 Oct. 2017.

[46] Cameron-Moore, S., 'Myanmar warns UN scolding could harm talks with Bangladesh on Rohingya crisis', Reuters, 8 Nov. 2017; and Zaman, S. S., 'Repatriating Rohingya under 1992 agreement "will be difficult"', *Dhaka Tribune*, 5 Oct. 2017.

The day before the August 2017 attacks, a special international commission established by Aung San Suu Kyi and headed by Kofi Annan, a former UN Secretary-General, had made a series of recommendations on how to end ethnic tensions in Rakhine. These included a call for the repeal of a law that restricts the rights of Rohingya to citizenship and better implementation of the rule of law.[47] Aung San Suu Kyi accepted most of those recommendations and on 9 October appointed a committee to implement them, but by the end of the year the extent to which they had been implemented remained unclear.[48] Myanmar and Bangladesh signed a repatriation agreement on 23 November 2017 but at the end of the year UN agencies stated that the conditions for voluntary and safe repatriation of refugees did not yet exist, and most aid agencies were still barred from working in Rakhine.[49]

Addressing the grievances of ethnic minorities is one of the key obstacles to achieving a sustainable peace process in Myanmar, and the Rohingya refugee crisis compounds that challenge. A three-phase peace proposal by China in late November seemed to offer a pragmatic solution to the crisis. However, at the end of 2017, there was little indication that the proposal was being taken up.[50] Moreover, because of the intercommunal and political dimensions of the conflict, there is no domestic political actor, not even among other ethnic minority groups, that is currently willing to play a moderating role within Myanmar.

Armed conflict in Pakistan

Pakistan's disputes with neighbouring India and Afghanistan periodically erupt into violence. It also faces serious internal security threats. Domestic attacks involving disparate armed groups and counteroffensives by the Pakistani military have killed tens of thousands of Pakistanis over the past decade and displaced nearly 1.5 million people.[51] Although the security situation in Pakistan has improved in recent years, significant levels of violence continued throughout 2017, including some of the deadliest attacks since 2014.

In February 2017 a number of attacks by the Islamic State, Tehrik-i-Taliban Pakistan (TTP, the Taliban Movement of Pakistan) and other militants were

---

[47] Advisory Commission on Rakhine State (ACRS), *Towards a Peaceful, Fair and Prosperous Future for the People of Rakhine*, Final Report of the ACRS (ACRS: Yangon, Aug. 2017).

[48] Martin, Margesson and Vaughn (note 40), p. 13.

[49] 'Myanmar Rohingya crisis: Deal to allow return of Muslim refugees', BBC News, 23 Nov. 2017; International Crisis Group (ICG), *Myanmar's Rohingya Crisis Enters a Dangerous New Phase*, Asia Report no. 292 (ICG: Brussels, 7 Dec. 2017); and Cumming-Bruce, N., 'Myanmar's Rohingya actions may be genocide, UN official says', *New York Times*, 5 Dec. 2017.

[50] Ge, H., 'China's pragmatic solution to Rohingya crisis', *Global Times*, 26 Nov. 2017; and Venkatachalam, K. S., 'Can China solve the Rohingya crisis?', The Diplomat, 2 Dec. 2017.

[51] 'The current situation in Pakistan', Fact sheet, United States Institute of Peace, 9 Jan. 2017.

carried out on state, religious and other targets. These included a suicide attack on 16 February on one of the country's most prominent Sufi shrines, in Sindh province, for which the Islamic State claimed responsibility. The attack killed at least 88 people and injured more than 200. The Pakistan military accused 'hostile powers' of directing the attacks and using sanctuaries in Afghanistan.[52] It enforced an indefinite closure of the Pakistan–Afghanistan border and attacked several targets inside Afghanistan. On 22 February Pakistan launched a new nationwide counterterrorism operation, with a focus on Punjab province.[53]

However, the counterterrorism approach had limitations. Despite the launch of a second counterterrorism operation in July in the Rajgal Valley, in the Federally Administered Tribal Areas, close to the border with Afghanistan, attacks by armed groups continued throughout the year.[54] In addition, there were growing concerns over the large number of 'disappearances' of people—largely attributed to the activities of the security services in combating the insurgency in Balochistan province—and about a crackdown on international non-governmental organizations working in the country.[55] The latter was part of a wider backlash against Western donors, and a decision by the Pakistan Government to reduce reliance on them as a result of the new economic and security opportunities opened up by the China–Pakistan Economic Corridor.[56]

Armed conflict in the Philippines

In 2014 the Moro Islamic Liberation Front (MILF) signed a peace agreement with the Philippine Government in an attempt to transform one of Asia's longest and deadliest conflicts.[57] However, ending the insurgency by the New People's Army (NPA)—the armed wing of the Communist Party of the Philippines (CPP) and its political umbrella organization, the National Democratic Front (NDF)—has proved more elusive. The NPA has been waging

[52] Boone, J., 'Pakistan launches crackdown as Isis shrine attack toll rises to 88', *The Guardian*, 17 Feb. 2017; and Khan, M. H., Khushik, Q. A. and Ali, I., 'At least 70 dead as bomb rips through Lal Shahbaz shrine in Sehwan, Sindh', *Dawn*, 22 Feb. 2017.

[53] 'Pakistan's army launches "Operation Radd-ul-Fasaad" across the country', *Dawn*, 22 Feb. 2017.

[54] Gul, A., 'Pakistan unleashes new anti-IS military operation near Afghan border', Voice of America, 16 July 2017; Rasmussen, S. E., 'Dozens killed in two separate attacks in Pakistan on eve of Eid', *The Guardian*, 23 June 2017; and Khan, I., 'Pakistani Taliban dressed in burqas kill students at dormitory', *New York Times*, 1 Dec. 2017.

[55] Stacey, K. and Bokhari, F., 'Pakistan orders expulsion of 29 international NGOs', *Financial Times*, 14 Dec. 2017; and Hadid, D., 'Concern grows in Pakistan over cases of disappearance', National Public Radio, 14 Dec. 2017.

[56] Shafqat, S., 'CPEC and the Baloch insurgency', The Diplomat, 8 Feb. 2017. See also Ghiasy, R. and Zhou, J., *The Silk Road Economic Belt: Considering Security Implications and EU–China Cooperation Prospects*, SIPRI and Friedrich Ebert Stiftung (SIPRI: Stockholm, 2017), p. 37.

[57] On the peace process with MILF see Svensson, I. and Lundgren, M., 'Mediation and peace agreements', *SIPRI Yearbook 2014*, pp. 51–52.

a guerrilla war against the Philippine Government since 1969 and, despite losses, has continued to operate in many provinces.[58] Talks between the NDF and the government have been sporadic over the years.[59]

Rodrigo Duterte was inaugurated as president of the Philippines on 30 June 2016. In office, he restarted the stalled peace talks with the CPP, with Norway acting as a third-party facilitator for two rounds.[60] After four rounds of peace talks in nine months, the suspension of a fifth and the failure of each side's respective unilateral ceasefire—and amid increasingly angry rhetoric between Duterte and leaders of the NDF—the government formally ended the peace talks in November 2017. On 5 December Duterte designated the CPP–NPA as a terrorist group.[61]

Duterte's presidency has been beset with controversy. Among the most contentious of his policies is his anti-drugs campaign, in which he has called on citizens and the police to conduct extrajudicial killings of suspects. Thousands are thought to have died.[62] While aid and trade restrictions have been introduced by the USA and the EU as a result of the human rights implications of this 'war on drugs', other countries—most notably China and Russia—have expressed unconditional support for the policy.[63]

Duterte caused further controversy in May 2017 when he imposed martial law on Mindanao and associated islands in response to an attempt to take over the city of Marawi by armed non-state actors aligned with the Islamic State, such as the Maute Group (which also calls itself the Islamic State of Lanao) and a faction of the Abu Sayyaf Group (ASG).[64] After a five-month siege of the city by government forces, which included the use of air strikes, the Philippine Government retook Marawi in October. An estimated 360 000 people were displaced by the conflict and, according to official government figures, 920 militants, 165 soldiers and 47 civilians were killed in the fighting.[65] However, research by Amnesty International suggests that

---

[58] Cane, P., 'Philippines sees resurgence in communist violence', NYA, 25 Oct. 2017.

[59] On the peace talks see 'Timeline: The peace talks between the government and the CPP–NPA–NDF, 1986–present', GMA, 6 Dec. 2017.

[60] 'Timeline: The peace talks between the government and the CPP–NPA–NDF, 1986–present' (note 59).

[61] Santos, E. P., 'How peace talks with communist rebels failed', CNN Philippines, 31 Dec. 2017; and Punay, E., 'DOJ to seek declaration of CPP-NPA as terrorist group', *Philippine Star*, 26 Dec. 2017.

[62] Holmes, O., 'Rodrigo Duterte pulls Philippine police out of brutal war on drugs', *The Guardian*, 12 Oct. 2017.

[63] Kine, P., 'Philippine President Rodrigo Duterte's "war on drugs"', *Harvard International Review*, 14 Oct. 2017.

[64] 'Rodrigo Duterte has declared martial law in the southern Philippines', *The Economist*, 25 May 2017.

[65] Philippine Department of Social Welfare and Development (DSWD), Disaster Response Assistance and Management Bureau, Disaster Response Operations Monitoring and Information Center (DROMIC), 'DSWD DROMIC Report #93 on the armed conflict in Marawi City', 14 Oct. 2017; and Gomez, J., 'Philippines declares end to 5-month militant siege in Marawi', Associated Press, 23 Oct. 2017.

the civilian death toll is likely to have been much higher, and it called for an investigation into the proportionality of the force used and the resulting destruction of civilian infrastructure and loss of civilian life.[66] On 13 December Duterte extended martial law in Mindanao for another year.[67]

Many of the insurgents involved in the attack on Marawi were thought to be former fighters from MILF or a number of other Islamist armed militant groups, such as the Bangsamoro Islamic Freedom Fighters (BIFF).[68] Their alignment with the Islamic State and willingness to stage large-scale attacks, as in the case of Marawi, pose major threats to the stability of the government's ongoing peace process with MILF—not least because the Islamic State-affiliated groups form a radical alternative to MILF. Reintegrating former fighters and moving the peace process forward therefore remain pressing challenges, not only because of the situation on Mindanao, but also due to opposition within the Philippine armed forces and the Congress. As of July 2017 only 145 combatants had been demobilized under the 2014 peace agreement with MILF, providing other armed groups with ample opportunities for recruitment.[69]

The peace process in Nepal

The long-running 1995–2006 Nepalese Civil War between the Communist Party of Nepal-Maoist (CPN-M) and the Nepalese monarchy, which resulted in the deaths of around 18 000 people, ended with the signing of the Comprehensive Peace Accord (CPA) in 2006.[70] As well as marking the official end to violence, the CPA dealt with issues of social and political transformation and inclusion. The post-conflict political landscape was opened up to new elements, including the CPN-M, which emerged as the largest party in the 2008 election to the first Constituent Assembly. In 2012 the Maoist People's Liberation Army—the armed wing of the CPN-M—which had been confined to cantonments for over six years, was finally disbanded. In elections in 2013

[66] Amnesty International, *'The Battle of Marawi': Death and Destruction in the Philippines* (Amnesty International: London, Nov. 2017).

[67] Rauhala, E., 'Liberated and angry', *Washington Post*, 9 Dec. 2017; and Villamor, F., 'Philippines extends martial law in south for another year', *New York Times*, 13 Dec. 2017.

[68] Postings, R., 'The battle of Marawi: A brief summary', International Review, 24 Dec. 2017; and Reuters, 'Who are the ISIS-linked Maute group militants terrorizing the Philippines?', *Newsweek*, 23 June 2017.

[69] Third Party Monitoring Team, 'Fourth Public Report, March 2016 to June 2017', 28 July 2017, p. 14.

[70] Nepal Institute for Policy Studies (NIPS), *Nepal's Peace Process: A Brief Overview* (NIPS: Kathmandu, July 2013).

to the second Constituent Assembly, the more established political parties regained ascendancy.[71]

Following two devastating earthquakes in 2015, the three largest political parties in the Constituent Assembly—the Nepali Congress, the CPN Unified Marxist–Leninist (CPN-UML) and the Unified CPN-M—along with the largest party representing the Madhesi people, the Madhesi Jana-dhikar Forum-Democratic (MJF-D), decided to fast-track the adoption of a new constitution, which was adopted in September 2015. At least 46 people were killed in weeks of unrest in the run-up and immediately after the prom-ulgation of the new constitution, which was amended in 2016 to ensure a higher degree of inclusion.[72]

While the Nepali state has been fundamentally transformed since the 2006 CPA, Nepal remains one of the world's poorest countries and still relies heavily on remittances (especially from Nepalese workers in India), aid and tourism.[73] At the start of 2017 issues of political inclusion and transitional justice still loomed large.

Sher Bahadur Deuba, leader of the Nepali Congress party, became prime minister in June 2017, in a scheduled transfer of power following the resig-nation of Pushpa Kamal Dahal, leader of the CPN-Maoist Centre (CPN-MC), formerly the Unified CPN-M.[74] The two coalition partners had agreed in August 2016 to rotate the post. In elections to the 275-member House of Representatives held on 26 November and 7 December 2017, the Left Alli-ance—formed in October by the CPN-UML and the CPN-MC—won a near two-thirds majority. The elections were the next step in implementing the new constitution that it is hoped will lead to an era of political stability and economic development.[75]

Although the question of transitional justice for the victims of conflict is yet to be resolved, Nepal's peace process has already had major successes, with the integration of former combatants into the national army and wider society, and implementation of the new constitution.[76] Nepal has also taken concerted steps to reform its security sector and increase the participation

[71] Nepal Institute for Policy Studies (note 70); and Thapa, D. and Ramsbotham, A. (eds), *Two Steps Forward, One Step Back: The Nepal Peace Process*, Accord no. 26 (Conciliation Resources: London, Mar. 2017).

[72] Thapa and Ramsbotham (note 71); and 'Nepal's election may at last bring stability', *The Econo-mist*, 23 Nov. 2017.

[73] Sapkota, C., 'Remittances in Nepal: Boon or bane?', *Journal of Development Studies*, vol. 49, no. 10 (2013), pp. 1316–31; and World Bank, *Nepal Development Update: Remittances at Risk* (World Bank: Washington, DC, May 2016.

[74] 'Sher Bahadur Deuba elected 40th PM of Nepal', *Kathmandu Post*, 6 June 2017.

[75] 'Nepal's election may at last bring stability' (note 72); and Pattisson, P., '"Politics is still a man's game": Can Nepal's elections finally bring stability?', *The Guardian*, 24 Nov. 2017.

[76] Bhandari, C., 'The reintegration of Maoist ex-combatants in Nepal', *Economic and Political Weekly*, 28 Feb. 2015.

of women in the security forces, although barriers to their meaningful participation remain.[77]

The peace process in Sri Lanka

The war between the Sri Lankan Government and the Liberation Tigers of Tamil Eelam (LTTE or Tamil Tigers), which began in 1983, ended when government forces seized the last area controlled by the LTTE in 2009. However, recriminations over abuses by both sides continue. Following the election of President Maithripala Sirisena in 2015, expectations were raised that a formal investigation would be undertaken into war crimes carried out during the conflict. In 2016 the government set up the Office of Missing Persons to trace the more than 20 000 people who disappeared during the conflict. Little progress has been made, however, with finding out the truth of what happened to those who disappeared.[78]

In 2015 President Sirisena agreed to establish a war crimes court as recommended in the comprehensive report on Sri Lanka by the Office of the UN High Commissioner for Human Rights (OHCHR) and in a UN Human Rights Council resolution that was co-sponsored by Sri Lanka.[79] It was intended that the court would be made up of both Sri Lankan and international judges and would put on trial those suspected of committing war crimes and crimes against humanity during the conflict. Again, however, progress with establishing the tribunal has been slow.[80]

The Consultation Task Force on Reconciliation Mechanisms appointed by the Sri Lankan Government in February 2016 released its final report on 3 January 2017.[81] This was the first broad survey of Sri Lankan citizens' aspirations for truth and justice, including their views on the proposed mech-

---

[77] Racovita, M., *Women in State Security Provision in Nepal: Meaningful Participation?* Briefing Paper (Small Arms Survey: Geneva, Mar. 2018). On the wider importance of gender in the peace process see Baniya, J. et al., *Gender and Nepal's Transition from War*, Accord Spotlight (Conciliation Resources: London, Sep. 2017).

[78] Hart, M., 'The long road to justice for Sri Lanka civil war victims', Geopolitical Monitor, 4 Dec. 2017.

[79] United Nations, General Assembly, Human Rights Council, Comprehensive Report of the Office of the United Nations High Commissioner for Human Rights on Sri Lanka, A/HRC/30/61, 28 Sep. 2015; and United Nations, General Assembly, Human Rights Council, Resolution 30/1, 'Promoting reconciliation, accountability and human rights in Sri Lanka', 1 Oct. 2015, A/HRC/RES/30/1, 14 Oct. 2015.

[80] Sirilal, R., 'UN says Sri Lanka's delay in post-war reconciliation involves risks', Reuters, 23 Oct. 2017; and 'Sri Lanka leader to shield general from war crimes case', Al Jazeera, 3 Sep. 2017.

[81] The report was completed in Nov. 2016 but was not released until Jan. 2017. Vol. I of the report contains the task force's observations during the consultation process and its recommendations regarding the 4 transitional justice mechanisms. Vol. II contains the reports of the zonal task forces submitted to the task force after the conclusion of public meetings and focus group discussions in the zones. Consultation Task Force on Reconciliation Mechanisms (CTF), *Final Report of the Consultation Task Force on Reconciliation Mechanisms*, vol. I, and *Consolidated Report: Zonal Task Forces on Reconciliation Mechanisms*, vol. II (CTF: Nov. 2016).

anisms set out in the UN Human Rights Council resolution. In addition to endorsing the proposal for a war crimes court with no time limit on its jurisdiction, among the task force's other recommendations are financial and symbolic reparations, a constitutional and political settlement, resolution of long-standing land disputes, and greater attention to psychosocial needs.[82]

March 2017 was the deadline set for implementing recommendations in the UN Human Rights Council resolution on establishing a war crimes court and reparations for victims. It passed without the commitments being met. Sri Lanka was given a two-year extension by the Human Rights Council to enact the reforms.[83] Although the government has introduced some limited reforms, the longer it delays the implementation of a valid process for establishing the truth of what happened during the conflict and securing justice for those affected, the more likely it is that intercommunal tensions will increase.[84] In May and again in November 2017, for example, there were outbreaks of Buddhist violence and intimidation against Muslims.[85]

[82] Human Rights Watch, 'Sri Lanka: Adopt task force's justice proposals', 12 Jan. 2017.

[83] Aneez, S., 'UN presses Sri Lanka to meet commitments on war crimes investigations, reform', Reuters, 23 Mar. 2017.

[84] Cronin-Furman, K., 'Why a Sri Lankan leader might be tried for war crimes in Brazil', *Washington Post*, 30 Aug. 2017.

[85] 'Militant Buddhist extremism resurfaces in Sri Lanka', Southasian Monitor, 23 May 2017; and 'Sri Lanka violence: 19 held amid Buddhist–Muslim street clashes', BBC News, 18 Nov. 2017.

IV. Armed conflict in Europe

IAN DAVIS AND IAN ANTHONY

Two armed conflicts were active in Europe in 2017: in Nagorno-Karabakh (involving Armenia and Azerbaijan) and in Ukraine. At the same time, some unresolved conflicts, although inactive, seemed as intractable as ever. In the background, tensions remained heightened between Russia and the members of the North Atlantic Treaty Organization (NATO) and the West in general, and there were allegations of Russian interference in Western domestic politics.[1] European states also continued to prioritize combating terrorism. This section reviews developments in European counterterrorism, the unresolved conflicts in Europe and in the two active armed conflicts.

Terrorism in Europe

Compared with other regions, Europe is relatively safe from terrorist attacks.[2] However, while global data on terrorist incidents suggests that the number of incidents and the deaths they cause are falling, Europe has experienced the opposite trend. According to the Global Terrorism Index, fatalities from terrorist attacks in Europe increased from fewer than 20 in 2002 to almost 650 in 2016.[3]

In 2017 European cities such as Barcelona, Istanbul, Manchester and St Petersburg were targets for terrorist attacks, although the attacks were less lethal than comparable attacks in 2016.[4] Since 2014 a significant number of the European citizens who travelled as 'foreign fighters' to countries in conflict in the Middle East and North Africa have returned to Europe. The number returning has been falling, however, and while only 'a fairly small number' of those fighters that are still in the conflict zone are now expected

---

[1] On the deteriorating relationship between Russia and the USA see Smith, D., 'International politics and global security', *SIPRI Yearbook 2017*, pp. 10–12; and chapter 1, section II, in this volume. On Russia's estrangement from the European security architecture see Anthony, I., 'Conflict or peace in Europe? Increasing uncertainties, rising insecurities', *SIPRI Yearbook 2017*, pp. 119–39. On allegations of Russian interference in Western elections see 'Russian hacking and influence in the US election', *New York Times*, [n.d.]; and Mason, R., 'Theresa May accuses Russia of interfering in elections and fake news', *The Guardian*, 14 Nov. 2017.

[2] There is no shared European definition of terrorism, but the Council of Europe is currently discussing the development of one. Council of Europe, 'Council of Europe Counter-Terrorism Committee', [n.d.].

[3] Institute for Economics and Peace, *Global Terrorism Index 2017: Measuring and Understanding the Impact of Terrorism* (Institute for Economics and Peace: Sydney, 2017).

[4] While the Global Terrorism Index data for 2016 includes Istanbul as a part of Europe, this chapter discusses Turkey in section V.

to return, those that do 'will be hardened fighters and present a significant threat upon their return'.[5]

The main European security-building institutions all include finding an effective response to terrorist attacks as part of their agenda. In 2017, alongside its work to promote the implementation of existing counterterrorism agreements and guidelines, the Organization for Security and Co-operation in Europe (OSCE) emphasized two issues: (a) dialogue initiatives with youth groups in the Black Sea region, Central Asia and the western Balkans; and (b) inclusion of terrorism risk reduction as one element of creating inclusive, safe and sustainable cities.[6] The latter was an enhancement to a programme to promote local approaches to global challenges.[7]

An important focus of the Council of Europe in 2017 was the nexus between organized crime and terrorism, with an emphasis on the financing of terrorism.[8] The European Union (EU) also included counterterrorism as a central component of its Renewed Internal Security Strategy for 2015–20. Two key priorities of the EU in 2017 were countering the use of digital technology by terrorists and strengthening border controls.[9] In April 2017, for example, a revision to the Schengen Borders Code obliged participating states to carry out systematic checks that include a security risk assessment of everyone entering or exiting at the external border of the Schengen Area (which includes most EU member states and some EU neighbours).[10]

Unresolved conflicts in Europe

Although most of Europe has seemed peaceful for about two decades, tensions remain linked to the unresolved conflicts in Cyprus, Georgia (Abkhazia and South Ossetia), Moldova (Trans-Dniester) and Kosovo. More positively, the Basque separatist group Euskadi Ta Askatasuna (ETA, Basque Home-

---

[5] United Nations, Security Council, 'Nineteenth report of the Analytical Support and Sanctions Monitoring Team submitted pursuant to Resolution 2253 (2015) concerning ISIL (Da'esh), Al-Qaida and associated individuals and entities', 30 Dec. 2016, S/2017/35, 13 Jan. 2017.

[6] OSCE Secretariat, Transnational Threats Department, *Overview of OSCE Counter-Terrorism Related Commitments* (OSCE: Vienna, Feb. 2017); 'OSCE-wide Counter-terrorism conference 2017: Preventing and countering violent extremism and radicalization that lead to terrorism', Vienna, 23–24 May 2017; and Neumann, P. R., 'Countering violent extremism and radicalisation that lead to terrorism: Ideas, recommendations, and good practices from the OSCE Region', OSCE, 28 Sep. 2017.

[7] OSCE, 'Security Days—Creating inclusive, safe and sustainable cities: Local approaches to global challenges', Vienna, 30–31 Mar. 2017.

[8] Council of Europe, Committee of Experts on Terrorism (CODEXTER), 'Abridged report: List of items discussed and decisions taken', 32nd plenary meeting, 23–24 May 2017, Strasbourg, 24 May 2017.

[9] Council of the European Union, 'Renewed European Union internal security strategy and counter terrorism implementation paper: Report of the first half of 2017 and programme for the second half of 2017', 10827/17, 12 July 2017.

[10] European Commission, Communication from the Commission to the European Parliament and the Council on preserving and strengthening Schengen, COM(2017) 570 final, 27 Sep. 2017.

land and Liberty) gave up its weapons to the French authorities in what was seen as a crucial move towards the final closure of an armed conflict with Spain that lasted from 1959 to 2011.[11]

In Cyprus the United Nations Secretary-General, António Guterres, announced on 7 July that negotiations to reunify the country had collapsed following the ending of talks between Greek and Turkish Cypriot leaders in Switzerland.[12] UN diplomats have been trying to broker an agreement to reunify Cyprus for decades. The collapse was attributed to a failure to reach agreement on security guarantees and power-sharing arrangements in a unified government; each side blamed the other.[13] The exploration of contested gas reserves off the coast of Cyprus is likely to add to tensions.[14]

Kosovo made the Kosovo Specialist Chambers and Specialist Prosecutor's Office operational, but it remained unclear when its first indictments would be filed.[15] It is a domestic court established in The Hague with an international staff to try serious war crimes committed by the Kosovo Liberation Army during the 1998–99 Kosovo war. Tensions between Kosovo Serbs and Kosovo Albanians continued, particularly in the north, and the process of normalizing relations with Serbia made limited progress.[16]

In Moldova the OSCE has been involved in attempts to resolve the conflict with Trans-Dniester, which has controlled Moldovan territory to the east of the Dniester river since 1992.[17] In November 2017 the OSCE reported 'substantial progress' in talks between the leaders of Moldova and the breakaway region. The two sides 'further solidified the agreements on several social and economic issues signed in recent days', including on the reopening of a bridge linking the territories, and committed to swiftly resolve the remaining issues at the beginning of 2018.[18] In early December the OSCE Ministerial Council adopted a statement welcoming these achievements.[19] However, whether these breakthroughs will be sufficient to overcome the

---

[11] 'Eta: Basque separatists begin weapons handover', BBC News, 8 Apr. 2017; and Tremlett, G., 'Eta declares halt to armed conflict', *The Guardian*, 20 Oct. 2011.

[12] United Nations, Secretary-General, 'The Secretary-General remarks at the closure of the Conference on Cyprus', 7 July 2017.

[13] Smith, H., 'Cyprus reunification talks collapse amid angry scenes', *The Guardian*, 7 July 2017; and 'Cyprus may have missed its last chance for reunification', *The Economist*, 9 July 2017.

[14] Orphanides, S., 'Cyprus ready for all outcomes as drilling programme commences', *Business Mail* (Nicosia), 28 Dec. 2017.

[15] Bytyci, F., 'Kosovo war crimes court ready for first indictments: Chief judge', Reuters, 24 Nov. 2017.

[16] Morina, D. and Zivanovic, M., 'Kosovo–Serbia talks fail to defuse tensions', Balkan Insight, 2 Feb. 2017.

[17] Klimenko, E., 'Conflicts in the post-Soviet space: Recent developments', *SIPRI Yearbook 2017*, pp. 140–50.

[18] OSCE, 'Substantial progress in Transdniestrian settlement talks in Vienna, clear commitment to solve remaining issues says OSCE Special Representative', Press release, 28 Nov. 2017.

[19] OSCE, Ministerial Council, 'Ministerial statement on the negotiations on the Transdniestrian settlement process in the "5+2" format', MC.DOC/1/17, 8 Dec. 2017.

deep differences at the root of the 25-year old conflict remained an open question.[20]

Tensions and uncertainty also surfaced in Northern Ireland, where the protracted conflict was largely settled in 1998 through the Good Friday Agreement and the establishment of the consociational Northern Ireland Assembly and Executive. However, the result of the United Kingdom's 2016 referendum on leaving the EU has raised uncertainty about the form of the land border between the UK and Ireland. Demilitarization of the border and ease of passage across it were important components of the Good Friday Agreement. Further, in January 2017 disagreements between the two largest political parties in Northern Ireland led to inconclusive elections in March. As no agreement on the appointment of a new Executive could be made, the Assembly remained idle throughout the year.[21] There continue to be fears about a possible return to violence if it proves impossible, for whatever reason, to sustain the political and constitutional settlement in Northern Ireland.[22]

Armed conflict in Nagorno-Karabakh

The Nagorno-Karabakh conflict is an interstate confrontation between Armenia and Azerbaijan over disputed territory, in which two modern armies in trenches confront each other across the line of contact.[23] Following the ceasefire that ended the 1988–94 Nagorno-Karabakh War, the underlying conflict remained unresolved and periodically escalates into violence as it did in April 2016 and in 2017.[24] Regular peace talks between Armenia and Azerbaijan mediated by the OSCE Minsk Group have failed to resolve a conflict that will enter its fourth decade in 2018.[25] Both sides have increased their military capabilities in recent years and the risk of another large-scale conflict is steadily growing.[26]

[20] Hill, W. H., 'The Moldova–Transdniestria dilemma: Local politics and conflict resolution', Carnegie Moscow Center, 24 Jan. 2018.

[21] 'Northern Ireland notches up a year without a government', The Economist, 24 Jan. 2018.

[22] Kennedy, D., 'Growing gap between Irishness and Britishness is most dangerous', Irish Times, 20 Dec. 2017; and Lyall, S., 'On Irish border, worries that "Brexit" will undo a hard-won peace', New York Times, 5 Aug. 2017.

[23] Although the conflict was previously treated as an internationalized intrastate conflict, it is now generally accepted that it has evolved into an interstate conflict. See e.g. de Waal, T., 'The Karabakh conflict as "project minimum"', Carnegie Moscow Center, 20 Feb. 2018.

[24] On the ceasefire negotiations see Dehdashti-Rasmussen, R., 'The conflict over Nagorno-Karabakh: Causes, the status of negotiations, and prospects', Institute for Peace Research and Security Policy at the University of Hamburg (IFSH), OSCE Yearbook 2006 (Nomos: Baden-Baden, 2007), pp. 189–210.

[25] For a brief description and list of members of the OSCE Minsk Group see annex B, section II, in this volume.

[26] See Klimenko (note 17), pp. 143–46; and de Waal (note 23).

Exchanges of fire between Armenian and Azerbaijani forces around Nagorno-Karabakh intensified in 2017.[27] In December the foreign ministers of the OSCE Minsk Group co-chairs—France, Russia and the United States—issued a joint statement supporting resumed and intensified diplomacy, called for agreement on the expansion of the special representatives' office and urged both sides to 'focus their efforts on finding compromise solutions to the substantive issues of political settlement'.[28] Amid the intensified diplomacy, there were fewer incidents and casualties in December.[29]

Armed conflict in Ukraine

Since gaining independence after the break-up of the Soviet Union in 1991, Ukraine has sought to balance closer integration with Western Europe and cooperation with Russia. Russia, which sees its interests as threatened by a Western-leaning Ukraine, annexed Crimea in March 2014, following the fall of Ukrainian President Viktor Yanukovych. It was also instrumental in provoking a rebellion in Luhansk and Donetsk oblasts in the industrialized Donbas region in eastern Ukraine (see figure 2.1).[30] After three years of war and around 10 000 deaths, Russia's military intervention dominates most aspects of political life in Ukraine.[31] According to the OSCE Special Monitoring Mission to Ukraine (SMM), the peace deal and ceasefire reached in the Minsk II Agreement in February 2015 were violated almost daily in 2017.[32]

Fighting intensified in eastern Ukraine at the end of January. In a press statement, the UN Security Council expressed 'grave concern about the dangerous deterioration of the situation in eastern Ukraine and its severe impact on the local civilian population'.[33] Most of the fighting was carried out from a distance, using artillery. In March 2017 Ukraine imposed an economic

---

[27] See e.g. Sanamyan, E., 'Fighting in Karabakh flares as Azerbaijan marks memorial', Eurasianet, 27 Feb. 2017; and International Crisis Group (ICG), *Nagorno-Karabakh's Gathering War Clouds*, Europe Report no. 244 (ICG: Brussels, 1 June 2017).

[28] OSCE, 'Joint statement by the heads of delegation of the OSCE Minsk Group co-chair countries', Press release, 7 Dec. 2017.

[29] International Crisis Group, 'CrisisWatch: Tracking conflict worldwide', Dec. 2017.

[30] The initial causes of the conflict in Ukraine, and the extent to which it represents a civil war with primarily domestic sources or a foreign intervention by Russia, are hotly contested. See Wilson, A., 'External intervention in the Ukraine conflict: Towards a frozen conflict in the Donbas', *SIPRI Yearbook 2016*, pp. 143–57.

[31] Office of the UN High Commissioner for Human Rights, 'Conflict in Ukraine enters its fourth year with no end in sight—UN report', 13 June 2017.

[32] The SMM makes weekly and ad hoc reports on the crisis in Ukraine. See OSCE, Special Monitoring Mission to Ukraine, [n.d.], 'Daily and spot reports from the Special Monitoring Mission to Ukraine'. On the conflict and crisis management in Ukraine see Anthony (note 1), pp. 137–38; Klimenko (note 17), pp. 146–49; Wilson (note 30), pp. 143–58; and 'The Ukraine conflict and its implications', *SIPRI Yearbook 2015*, pp. 55–98.

[33] United Nations, Security Council, 'Security Council press statement on deterioration of situation in Donetsk region, Ukraine', SC/12700, 31 Jan. 2017; United Nations, Security Council, 'Thousands of civilians risk losing access to basic necessities as fighting escalates in eastern Ukraine,

Figure 2.1. The conflict zone in eastern Ukraine, January 2018

Credit: Hugo Ahlenius, Nordpil.

Source: 'Ukraine', Live Universal Awareness Map (Liveuamap), 1 Jan. 2018.

blockade on territory held by the separatists. The Ukrainian central bank expected this to reduce Ukraine's economic growth to 1.9 per cent in 2017 from an earlier estimate of 2.8 per cent.[34]

Throughout the year, the conflict continued to grow in strength and intensity along the 400-kilometre front line. By the end of October 2017

Security Council told', SC/12704, 2 Feb. 2017; and Grono, M., 'Ukraine flare-up lays bare fears in Europe's east', Commentary, International Crisis Group, 3 Feb. 2017.

[34] Polityuk, P., 'Ukrainian economy to feel the squeeze of economic blockade', Reuters, 21 Mar. 2017.

the UN High Commissioner for Refugees (UNHCR) had identified 1.8 million internally displaced or conflict-affected persons in Ukraine, including 22 000 from Crimea. As a result of the fighting, many moved west, mostly to neighbouring areas within Luhansk and Donetsk oblasts and to Kharkiv oblast. Others moved to Kiev. In addition, nearly 430 000 people had moved east to seek refuge in Russia.[35] Humanitarian agencies reported that 4.4 million people had been directly affected by the conflict, while 3.8 million needed urgent assistance.[36] The SMM reported 411 confirmed civilian fatalities in the first 10 months of 2017.[37]

In September Russia circulated a draft UN Security Council resolution proposing a UN peacekeeping operation in eastern Ukraine, and shortly afterwards Ukraine put forward an alternative proposal.[38] However, further escalation and ceasefire violations occurred in mid-December. By the end of the year, the number of ceasefire violations recorded by the OSCE in 2017 reached almost 400 000 with almost 4000 instances of proscribed weapons being deployed in violation of the agreed withdrawal lines.[39] At the same time, none of the key provisions of the Minsk II Agreement—a ceasefire and special constitutional status for the separatist-held territories of the Donbas region, which would then be reintegrated into Ukraine and hold elections— had taken effect.

[35] UN High Commissioner for Refugees (UNHCR), 'Ukraine', Fact sheet, Oct. 2017; UN High Commissioner for Refugees (UNHCR), 'Ukraine, 01–31 Oct. 2017', Operational update; and Bonenberger, A., 'The war no one notices in Ukraine', *New York Times*, 20 June 2017.

[36] Coman, J., 'On the frontline of Europe's forgotten war in Ukraine', *The Observer*, 12 Nov. 2017.

[37] OSCE, Special Monitoring Mission to Ukraine, 'Status report as of 01 November 2017', 1 Nov. 2017.

[38] Arbatov, A., 'A UN peacekeeping operation is the only way forward in Ukraine', War on the Rocks, University of Texas, 28 Sep. 2017; 'Canada making diplomatic push For Ukraine's UN peacekeeping plan', Radio Free Europe/Radio Liberty, 10 Nov. 2017; and International Crisis Group (ICG), *Can Peacekeepers Break the Deadlock in Ukraine?*, Europe Report no. 246 (ICG: Brussels, 15 Dec. 2017).

[39] 'OSCE SMM: Over 400,000 ceasefire violations recorded in eastern Ukraine this year', Ukraine Crisis Media Center, 22 Dec. 2017. For SMM reports on ceasefire violations see OSCE (note 32).

V. Armed conflict in the Middle East and North Africa

IAN DAVIS

There were seven active armed conflicts in the Middle East and North Africa in 2017: Egypt, Iraq, Israel and Palestine, Libya, Syria, Turkey, and Yemen. Many of these conflicts are interconnected and involve regional and international powers as well as numerous substate actors.[1] Key regional developments in 2017 included the continuing fallout from the Arab Spring; the regional rivalry between Iran and Saudi Arabia; and the territorial losses of the Islamic State group. This section first examines these developments and then gives accounts of each of the armed conflicts in 2017.

Key general developments

Continuing fallout from the Arab Spring

The legacy of the Arab Spring continued to shape events in the Middle East and North Africa in 2017. The uprisings that started in Tunisia in 2010 and rapidly spread across much of the Arab world failed to flower into the establishment of peaceful democracies. Civil discord, violence and war continued in Libya, Syria and Yemen. A fragile state of stability had returned to much of Egypt, but armed conflict persisted in the Sinai peninsula and difficult socio-economic conditions continued for most of the population. The oil-producing Arab states of the Gulf continued to use their financial resources to largely resist the wave of change. In Jordan and Morocco some limited reforms took place without fundamentally altering the status quo.[2] Only in Tunisia have the protests triggered consensual, society-led reforms.[3]

Regional rivalry between Iran and Saudi Arabia

Iran and Saudi Arabia are locked in a power struggle that some commentators have described as a new regional cold war.[4] In 2017 the Iranian–Saudi Arabian proxy confrontation flared in Qatar and Lebanon (but remained confined to diplomacy, sanctions and politics) and continued in the active armed conflicts in Iraq, Syria and Yemen. In June Saudi Arabia led efforts to force Qatar to abandon its alleged support for terrorism and Iran. Together

---

[1] Hiltermann, J., *Tackling the MENA Region's Intersecting Conflicts* (International Crisis Group: Brussels, 22 Dec. 2017).

[2] Delegation of the European Union to Jordan, 'The European Union supports Jordan on political and environmental reforms with €115 million', Press release, 12 Feb. 2017; and Saleh, H., 'Rabat pushes modernity as Morocco's political reforms stall', *Financial Times*, 3 Nov. 2017.

[3] Muasher, M., 'Nascent hopes', IMF, *Finance and Development*, vol. 54, no. 4 (Dec. 2017).

[4] See e.g. Santini, R. H., 'A new regional cold war in the Middle East and North Africa: Regional security complex theory revisited', *International Spectator*, vol. 52, no. 4 (2017), pp. 93–111. See also chapter 1, section II, in this volume.

with Bahrain, Egypt, the United Arab Emirates (UAE) and Yemen, Saudi Arabia broke off diplomatic ties and closed transport links with Qatar.[5] In October Bahrain called for Qatar's membership of the Gulf Cooperation Council (GCC) to be suspended.[6] In December the UAE announced the formation of a new political and military alliance with Saudi Arabia.[7]

Reform initiatives in both Iran and Saudi Arabia and protests in Iran in December introduced new and unpredictable variables.[8] Overall, however, with so many flashpoints and so little diplomacy, the risk of a broader confrontation between a Saudi Arabian-led bloc of predominantly Sunni states and groups and an Iranian-led bloc of predominantly Shia states and groups remained high at the end of 2017.

Territorial losses by the Islamic State

Iraq and Syria both declared victory over the Islamic State in December 2017 after a year in which their national armies, a range of external allies and various local forces drove Islamic State fighters out of all the towns and villages that once made up its self-proclaimed caliphate.[9] According to the United States-led global coalition to defeat Islamic State of Iraq and Syria, fewer than 1000 Islamic State fighters remained in Iraq and Syria at the end of the year.[10] However, the threat from the Islamic State remains, both as a dangerously resilient force in Iraq and Syria (see figure 2.2) and more widely as a result of its geographic refocusing, in particular on its affiliates in Libya, the Philippines, Sinai and West Africa, and greater emphasis on directing, enabling and inspiring acts of terrorism.[11]

In order to prevent another insurgency or state failure, the military victory against the Islamic State will need to be followed up with strategies for polit-

[5] Hiltermann, J., 'Qatar punched above its weight: Now it's paying the price', *New York Times*, 18 June 2017.

[6] Khan, G. A., 'Bahrain calls for suspension of Qatar's GCC membership', Arab News, 31 Oct. 2017. For a brief description of the GCC see annex B, section II, in this volume. Its 6 members are Bahrain, Kuwait, Oman, Qatar, Saudi Arabia and the UAE.

[7] Wintour, P., 'UAE announces new Saudi alliance that could reshape Gulf relations', *The Guardian*, 5 Dec. 2017.

[8] Erdbrink, T., 'Rouhani wins re-election in Iran by a wide margin', *New York Times*, 20 May 2017; 'Iran protests: Violence on third day of demonstrations', BBC News, 30 Dec. 2017; Dehghan, S. K., 'Rouhani acknowledges Iranian discontent as protests continue', *The Guardian*, 31 Dec. 2017; Chulov, M. and Borger, J., 'Saudi king ousts nephew to name son as first in line to throne', *The Guardian*, 21 June 2017; and 'Muhammad bin Salman has swept aside those who challenge his power', *The Economist*, 9 Nov. 2017.

[9] On Islamic State, its goals, operations and affiliates and the international military campaign to defeat the group see Davis, I., 'The aims, objectives and modus operandi of the Islamic State and the international response', *SIPRI Yearbook 2016*, pp. 22–39; and Davis, I., 'The Islamic State in 2016: A failing "caliphate" but a growing transnational threat?', *SIPRI Yearbook 2017*, pp. 89–104.

[10] 'Less than 1,000 IS fighters remain in Iraq and Syria, coalition says', Reuters, 27 Dec. 2017.

[11] Coker, M., Schmitt, E. and Callimachi, R., 'With loss of its Caliphate, ISIS may return to guerrilla roots', *New York Times*, 18 Oct. 2017.

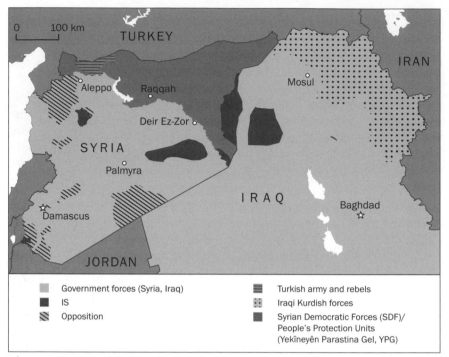

Figure 2.2. Armed factions in Iraq and Syria, January 2018

Credit: Hugo Ahlenius, Nordpil.

Sources: Live Universal Awareness Map (Liveuamap), cited in 'What foreign powers want from the Syrian war', Deutsche Welle, 22 Feb. 2018.

ical and economic reconstruction in both Iraq and Syria.[12] Addressing the problem of the Islamic State's foreign fighters returning to their home countries, both within and beyond the region, will be another key challenge.[13]

Armed conflict in Egypt

Egypt is the most populous Arab country and has played a central role in the politics of the Middle East in modern times. In 2011, after a presidency that lasted almost 30 years, President Hosni Mubarak was toppled by the Arab Spring protests. In July 2013 his successor, President Mohamed Morsi, was

[12] See e.g. Culbertson, S. and Robinson, L., *Making Victory Count After Defeating ISIS: Stabilization Challenges in Mosul and Beyond* (RAND Corporation: Santa Monica, CA, 2017); International Crisis Group (ICG), *Counterterrorism Pitfalls: What the US fight Against ISIS and al-Qaeda Should Avoid*, Special Report no. 3 (ICG: Brussels, 22 Mar. 2017); and Crocker, R. (chair), *Report of the Task Force on the Future of Iraq: Achieving Long-term Stability to Ensure the Defeat of ISIS* (Atlantic Council: Washington, DC, 31 May 2017).

[13] '5,600 "have returned home" from ISIL-held areas', Al Jazeera, 25 Oct. 2017; and Schmitt, E., 'Defeated in Syria, ISIS fighters held in camps still pose a threat', *New York Times*, 24 Jan. 2018.

removed from office in a popularly backed military coup, and Abdel Fattah al-Sisi, a retired field marshal and former defence minister, was elected president in May 2014.[14]

An insurgency erupted in northern Sinai in 2013, with attacks focused on the security forces. However, after the militants in Sinai embraced the Islamic State in 2014 (the local Islamic State affiliate is the Islamic State–Sinai Province), there were large-scale attacks on civilian targets, including the bombing of a Russian airliner in 2015 that killed all 224 passengers and crew.[15] A state of emergency has existed in northern Sinai since October 2014 and at the end of 2016 the insurgency in the region was Egypt's main internal security threat.[16]

In April 2017 the Islamic State increased its attacks, particularly against Coptic Christians. On 9 April, 48 people were killed in two separate attacks on Coptic churches, prompting the government to declare a nationwide state of emergency.[17] The Islamic State attacks on Christians continued in May when the group launched its first major attack in southern Egypt, which left at least 29 dead.[18] The Egyptian Government responded by carrying out air strikes on what it alleged were the training camps of the Islamic State attackers in Libya and by intensifying repression at home.[19] Reports also suggest that anti-Islamic State cooperation between Israel and Egypt in Sinai included Israeli air strikes against the Islamic State inside Egypt.[20]

In April and May 2017 several local tribes in northern Sinai—including the two largest, al-Tarabin and al-Sawarka—announced that they would join the fight against the Islamic State.[21] In July at least 23 soldiers were killed when suicide car bombs claimed by the Islamic State hit two military checkpoints in Sinai.[22] In November, in a further escalation of the conflict, the Islamic State killed more than 300 people in a Sufi mosque in northern Sinai.[23]

[14] 'Egypt country profile', BBC News, 6 Nov. 2017.

[15] 'Russian plane crash: What we know', BBC News, 17 Nov. 2015.

[16] Agence France-Presse, 'Egypt declares state of emergency in Sinai after checkpoint bombing', *The Guardian*, 25 Oct. 2014.

[17] 'Egypt's Coptic churches hit by deadly blasts on Palm Sunday', BBC News, 9 Apr. 2017.

[18] Michaelson, R., 'Egypt launches raids in Libya after attack on Coptic Christians kills 26', *The Guardian*, 26 May 2017.

[19] Aboulenein, A., 'Egypt detains ex-presidential candidate, latest in arrest series', Reuters, 23 May 2017; and El-Shimy, Y. and Dworkin, A., *Egypt on the Edge: How Europe Can Avoid Another Crisis in Egypt*, Policy Brief no. 218 (European Council on Foreign Relations: London, June 2017).

[20] Kirkpatrick, D. D., 'Secret alliance: Israel carries out airstrikes in Egypt, with Cairo's OK', *New York Times*, 3 Feb. 2018.

[21] Mikhail, G., 'Sinai tribes take up arms against IS', Al-Monitor, 15 May 2017.

[22] Associated Press, 'At least 23 Egyptian soldiers killed in attack on Sinai checkpoint', *The Guardian*, 7 July 2017.

[23] Walsh, D. and Kirkpatrick, D. D., 'In Egypt, furious retaliation but failing strategy in Sinai', *New York Times*, 25 Nov. 2017.

Another attack on Coptic Christians outside Cairo killed at least nine people on 29 December.[24]

At the end of the year, Egypt was facing its worst human rights situation in decades and open civil war in Sinai.[25] In advance of the presidential elections due in March 2018, the government had introduced a host of repressive laws, reinstated a state of emergency and repressed all forms of dissent.[26]

Armed conflict in Iraq

The mainly Shia-led governments that have held power in Iraq since 2003 have struggled to provide security amid high levels of sectarian violence. In 2014 the Islamic State seized large parts of Iraq, which it held until it was driven out of most of the country in 2016.[27] The armed conflict to dislodge the Islamic State from its remaining pockets of territory in northern Iraq, especially the cities of Mosul and Tal Afar, continued in 2017 (see figure 2.2). Underlying sectarian tensions in Iraq, especially between Sunni and Shia groups, and the fragmented nature of the anti-Islamic State forces added to this challenge. In addition to the Iraqi Army, supported by the US-led international coalition, other groups involved in fighting to retain territory included the Peshmerga forces of the Kurdistan Regional Government (KRG), the Popular Mobilization Forces (PMF, largely Shia paramilitaries supported by Iran) and local tribal Sunni forces.[28]

The battle for Mosul, Iraq's second largest city, commenced in September 2016 and was estimated to involve 54 000 soldiers in the Iraqi Army, 14 000 PMF fighters, 40 000 Peshmerga and 500 US troops against an estimated 5000–9000 Islamic State fighters.[29] The offensive to recapture western Mosul began on 19 February 2017, but progress was slow as troops encountered fierce resistance.[30] The battle for central Mosul began in June and the city was finally recaptured from the Islamic State in July, and Tal Afar and Hawijah some weeks later.[31]

---

[24] 'Egypt attack: Gunman targets Coptic Christians in church and shop', BBC News, 29 Dec. 2017.
[25] Luther, P., 'Stronger EU–Egypt ties must not disregard human rights', EU Observer, 24 July 2017.
[26] 'Human Rights Watch, Egypt: Untamed repression', 18 Jan. 2018.
[27] On the conflict in Iraq see chapters on the armed conflicts in the Middle East and North Africa in SIPRI Yearbook 2015, SIPRI Yearbook 2016 and SIPRI Yearbook 2017 and on the Islamic State in SIPRI Yearbook 2016 and SIPRI Yearbook 2017.
[28] Mansour, R. and Van Veen, E., 'Iraq's competing security forces after the battle for Mosul', War on the Rocks, 25 Aug. 2017.
[29] Hume, T, 'Battle for Mosul: How ISIS is fighting to keep its Iraqi stronghold', CNN, 25 Oct. 2016; and Wright, R., 'The secret eye inside Mosul', New Yorker, 27 Oct. 2016.
[30] Karimi, F., Alkhshali, H. and Atassi, B., 'Iraq starts operation to drive ISIS out of West Mosul', CNN, 20 Feb. 2017; and 'How the battle for Mosul unfolded', BBC News, 10 July 2017.
[31] Al Ansary, K., Abu-Nasr, D. and Alexander, C., 'Honking horns hail the liberation of Mosul from Islamic State', Bloomberg, 10 July 2017; and 'IS conflict: Iraq launches ground offensive in Tal Afar', BBC News, 20 Aug. 2017.

The UN Assistance Mission for Iraq (UNAMI) and the Office of the UN High Commissioner for Human Rights (OHCHR) reported that at least 2521 civilians were killed in the battle for Mosul. Most of these deaths were attributed to the activities of the Islamic State, including executions of at least 741 people, but the report also attributes 461 civilian deaths to air strikes.[32] Similarly, Amnesty International, while accusing both sides of violating international law in the battle, pointed to the heavy use of explosive weapons with wide-area effects and improvised rocket-assisted munitions by Iraqi forces and the US-led coalition, and the failure of the Iraqi Government to take necessary precautions to prevent the loss of civilian lives.[33] There were also allegations that the Islamic State used chemical weapons in Mosul.[34]

Iraqi forces launched new operations in Anbar governorate in October, and in early December the Iraqi Government formally declared that the Islamic State had been driven from all the territory it had previously held.[35] However, having initially grown out of an insurgent movement, the Islamic State—or new offshoots from it that are yet to emerge—seems likely to continue to be a threat for many years to come. Iraq also has a daunting task of reconstruction and reintegration in the areas once held by the group—especially in Mosul, which suffered widespread destruction—and about 3 million Iraqis were still displaced as of 31 December 2016.[36] After the military defeat of the Islamic State, Iraq's main challenges are to achieve genuine political reconciliation between and within the Kurdish, Shia Arab and Sunni Arab communities, including the dismantlement of all militias, and to build more resilient, independent and inclusive state institutions.[37]

As part of the process of uniting the country against the Islamic State, the central government and the autonomous Kurdistan Regional Government signed an agreement in December 2014 to share the country's oil wealth and military resources. However, some territorial disputes between the KRG and the central government remained unresolved, especially over

[32] UN Assistance Mission for Iraq and Office of the UN High Commissioner for Human Rights, 'Report on the protection of civilians in the context of the Ninewa operations and the retaking of Mosul City, 17 October 2016–10 July 2017', Nov. 2017.

[33] Amnesty International, *At Any Cost: The Civilian Catastrophe in West Mosul, Iraq* (Amnesty International: London, July 2017).

[34] On the allegations see chapter 8, section II, in this volume.

[35] Abdul-Ahad, G., 'After the liberation of Mosul, an orgy of killing', *The Guardian*, 21 Nov. 2017; and Graham-Harrison, E., 'Iraq formally declares end to fight against Islamic State', *The Guardian*, 9 Dec. 2017.

[36] Internal Displacement Monitoring Centre, 'Iraq: Mid-year update 2017 (January–June)', [n.d.], Videmsek, B., 'Mosul was destroyed to "save" it from Islamic State: Can its inhabitants return?', *Sydney Morning Herald*, 9 Dec. 2017; and Westcott, T., 'Donors talk big on Iraq reconstruction, but Mosul residents go it alone', IRIN, 15 Feb. 2018.

[37] Sayigh, Y., 'The crisis of the Iraqi state', Carnegie Middle East Center, 23 Nov. 2017; and Mansour, R., *Iraq after the Fall of ISIS: The Struggle for the State*, Research Paper (Chatham House–Royal Institute of International Affairs: London, July 2017).

areas secured by Kurdish forces during fighting against the Islamic State in 2016, including Kirkuk, adjacent oil fields and parts of Nineveh governorate. Tensions increased at the end of 2016 as the KRG set out plans to negotiate independence for Kurdistan.

The KRG pressed ahead with a referendum on independence from Iraq on 25 September 2017, ignoring requests to delay or cancel it from within the region, the Iraqi Government and, among others, both Iran and Turkey, which have their own Kurdish minorities.[38] Despite the fact that over 92 per cent of the votes were in favour of independence, the Iraqi Government refused to recognize the result and threatened the region with economic and political isolation unless it was annulled. Internationally, only Israel offered unequivocal support, while most of the KRG's other Western allies—most importantly the USA—publicly supported the preservation of Iraq's territorial integrity.[39] Four days after the referendum, the Iraqi Government banned international flights to and from Iraqi Kurdistan and began to prepare a military offensive to forcibly take back Kirkuk and the neighbouring oil fields, as well as other disputed territories.[40] Despite some limited clashes between Iraqi Government and Kurdish forces, most Kurdish forces withdrew to pre-2014 positions without incident.[41]

With few other options, on 25 October 2017 the KRG offered to suspend its push for independence and called for dialogue. Nonetheless, the Iraqi Government continued to insist that the KRG declare the referendum null and void. On 29 October the region's president, Masoud Barzani, resigned.[42] Despite the KRG's statement in mid-November that it would respect a ruling by the Supreme Federal Court that no Iraqi province can secede, the KRG and the Iraqi Government remained deadlocked at the end of the year.[43]

The Israeli–Palestinian conflict

While news of the Israeli–Palestinian conflict has been largely overshadowed in recent years by other conflicts in the Middle East and North Africa, it remained potent and dangerous during 2017. A notable display of Palestinian unity across the Green Line—the internationally recognized border separating Israel from the occupied Palestinian territories—occurred in July

[38] International Institute for Strategic Studies, 'The repercussions of the Iraqi Kurdistan independence referendum', *Strategic Comments*, vol. 23, no. 10 (Nov. 2017), pp. iii–v.

[39] International Institute for Strategic Studies (note 38).

[40] 'Iraq imposes flight ban on Kurdish region after poll', Al Jazeera, 29 Sep. 2017.

[41] 'Iraq takes disputed areas as Kurds "withdraw to 2014 lines"', BBC News, 18 Oct. 2017.

[42] 'Iraqi Kurdish leader Massoud Barzani to step down', BBC News, 29 Oct. 2017; and International Crisis Group (ICG), *Oil and Borders: How to Fix Iraq's Kurdish Crisis*, Crisis Group Middle East Briefing no. 55 (ICG: Brussels, 17 Oct. 2017).

[43] Rasheed, A. and Jalabi, R., 'Abadi says Iraq to act soon over border areas in stand-off with Kurds', Reuters, 14 Nov. 2017.

2017. Following the killing of two Israeli policemen near the Al-Aqsa Mosque in Eastern Jerusalem on the 14 July, the Israeli authorities installed metal detectors at the entrance to the site.[44] However, massive demonstrations by Palestinians led to the removal of the metal detectors on 24 July.[45]

On 6 December 2017 the conflict returned to centre stage when US President Donald J. Trump formally recognized Jerusalem as the capital of Israel and announced that the US embassy would move there from Tel Aviv.[46] All other countries recognize Tel Aviv as the capital, and none recognizes Israel's annexation of East Jerusalem. The declaration triggered protests by Palestinians throughout the West Bank, Gaza and Jerusalem. Four Palestinians were killed in clashes with Israeli security forces, rocket launches from Gaza to Israel increased and the Israeli Air Force carried out air strikes on targets in Gaza.[47]

Israel routinely describes Jerusalem as its 'united and eternal' capital, while the Palestinians insist that East Jerusalem must be the capital of a future independent Palestinian state. The international view, accepted by all previous US administrations, is that the city's status must be resolved through negotiations. On 13 December a meeting of the Organisation of Islamic Cooperation (OIC) in Turkey responded to President Trump's move by formally declaring East Jerusalem the Palestinian capital, while in a speech at the meeting Palestinian President Mahmoud Abbas stated that he no longer accepted any role for the USA in the peace process.[48]

On 18 December the USA used its UN Security Council veto for the first time in six years to block a resolution that would have indirectly criticized the US decision to recognize Jerusalem as the capital of Israel.[49] On 20 December the UN General Assembly voted 128 to 9, with 35 abstentions, for a non-binding (and therefore largely symbolic) resolution demanding that the USA rescind its recognition of Jerusalem as Israel's capital.[50]

---

[44] Zalzberg, O., 'Palestinian activism reawakens in Jerusalem after holy esplanade attack', Commentary, International Crisis Group, 19 July 2017.

[45] Beaumont, P., 'Israel removes metal detectors from holy site in Jerusalem', The Guardian, 25 July 2017.

[46] Landler, M., Halbfinger, D. M. and Kershner, I., 'Did Trump kill-off a two-state solution? He says no, Palestinians say yes', New York Times, 7 Dec. 2017; and Chan, S., 'Nearly every former US ambassador to Israel disagrees with Trump's Jerusalem decision', New York Times, 7 Dec. 2017.

[47] Zalzberg, O. and Thrall, N., 'Counting the costs of US recognition of Jerusalem as Israel's capital', International Crisis Group, 7 Dec. 2017; 'Palestinians killed in protests against Jerusalem move', Al Jazeera, 15 Dec. 2017; and Shehadeh, R., 'The power politics behind Trump's Jerusalem declaration', New Yorker, 26 Dec. 2017.

[48] Bilginsoy, Z. and El Deeb, S., 'Palestinian president says no role for US in peace process', Arab News, 13 Dec. 2017; and Gall, C., 'Muslim leaders declare East Jerusalem the Palestinian capital', New York Times, 13 Dec. 2017.

[49] United Nations, Security Council, 'Permanent member vetoes Security Council draft calling upon states not to establish diplomatic missions in Jerusalem', SC/13125, 18 Dec. 2017.

[50] UN General Assembly Resolution 72/240, 'Permanent sovereignty of the Palestinian people in the Occupied Palestinian Territory, including East Jerusalem, and of the Arab population in the occupied Syrian Golan over their natural resources', 20 Dec. 2017, A/RES/72/240, 18 Jan. 2018; and

Armed conflict in Libya

Libya was led by Muammar Gaddafi for 42 years until he was overthrown in 2011 in an armed rebellion assisted by Western military intervention. The power vacuum, instability and rise of Islamist militancy that followed allowed large-scale migration from Africa and the Middle East through Libya to take place, and many of these migrants were able to reach Europe. Following years of conflict, as part of the 2015 Libyan Political Agreement (LPA) signed in Skhirat, Morocco, in December 2015, a new UN-backed 'unity government', called the Government of National Accord (GNA), was installed in a naval base in Tripoli in 2016. However, the GNA continued to face opposition from two rival governments and many militias. The situation is further complicated by the tense relationship between Fayez Sarraj, prime minister and head of the GNA, and General Khalifa Haftar, head of the self-styled Libyan National Army (LNA)—a mix of military units and tribal or regional-based armed groups—based in eastern Libya.[51]

In early March 2017 the Benghazi Defence Brigade (BDB)—a coalition comprised mainly of fighters from Benghazi opposed to the LNA that includes members of Ansar al-Sharia, a Salafi Islamist militia group—took over key oil terminals at Sidra and Ras Lanuf. Within weeks, however, the LNA had recaptured them and pushed the BDB back to Jufra district to the south-west. In Tripoli, rival armed factions clashed in several neighbourhoods.[52] On 2 May, Sarraj met Haftar for talks in Abu Dhabi for the first time in over a year, and again in Paris in July, but further fighting between various militias in the south and in Tripoli suggested that an agreement on Libya's future was unlikely.[53]

On 20 September the UN Support Mission in Libya (UNSMIL) launched a UN action plan, which was endorsed by the UN Security Council, the African Union, the European Union (EU) and the League of Arab States. UNSMIL facilitated talks that generated some agreement over proposed amendments to the LPA but failed to reach consensus over military command arrangements, the relative powers and mechanisms of governing entities, and other constitutional issues.[54]

Gladstone R. and Landler, M., 'Defying Trump, UN General Assembly condemns US decree on Jerusalem', *New York Times*, 21 Dec. 2017.

[51] 'A quick guide to Libya's main players', European Council on Foreign Relations, Dec. 2016. On the Libyan conflict in 2016 see Smith D., 'The Middle East and North Africa: 2016 in perspective', *SIPRI Yearbook 2017*, pp. 83–84. On the UN arms embargo on Libya see chapter 10, section II, in this volume.

[52] Gazzini, C., 'New Libyan militia's oil strike risks wider conflagration', International Crisis Group, 10 Mar. 2017.

[53] Gazzini, C., 'Libya: No political deal yet', International Crisis Group, 11 May 2017; and International Crisis Group, 'CrisisWatch: Tracking conflict worldwide', May 2017.

[54] Blanchard, C. M., *Libya: Transition and US Policy*, Congressional Research Service (CRS) Report to Congress RL33142 (US Congress, CRS: Washington, DC, 8 Jan. 2018), p. 3.

In early October fighting escalated in the west. The Libyan Revolutionaries Operations Room, an anti-Islamic State militia, said it had taken control of the coastal city of Sabratha, a major hub for irregular migrants crossing the Mediterranean to Europe.[55] Forces sympathetic to the LNA captured other strategic areas in western Libya. Meanwhile, the UN-led talks aimed at renegotiating parts of the LPA faltered.[56] The USA, which had carried out intermittent air strikes against the Islamic State in Libya in August and December 2016, resumed those air strikes in late September 2017 and again on 17 and 19 November. These targeted militants in Fuqaha, south of the former Islamic State stronghold of Sirte.[57]

In 2017 at least 118 064 migrants arrived in Italy by sea, 34 per cent fewer than in 2016. At least 2832 died on the central Mediterranean route from Libya, 39 per cent fewer than in 2016.[58] In November the GNA launched an investigation into an alleged slave trade in Libya, following the broadcast of a video apparently showing migrants from elsewhere in Africa being sold to Libyans as slaves.[59]

On 17 December 2017, the second anniversary of the LPA, General Haftar announced that he considered the agreement to have expired and that related institutions, most notably the GNA and the Presidency Council headed by Serraj, were now 'void'.[60] Haftar said that the LNA was now the 'sole legitimate institution' in Libya and rejected the authority of any government or parliament until new elections. The move raised the prospect of new fighting in the west between his allies and forces aligned with the UN-backed GNA.[61]

[55] Elumami, A. and Lewis, A., 'Armed force claims victory in Libyan migrant smuggling hub', Reuters, 6 Oct. 2017; and Mannocchi, F., 'After Sabratha battle, scramble for Western Libya is on', Middle East Eye, 25 Oct. 2017.

[56] International Crisis Group, 'Restoring UN leadership of Libya's peace process', Statement, 18 Sep. 2017.

[57] Joscelyn, T. and Roggio, B., 'US resumes airstrikes against Islamic State in Libya', FDD's Long War Journal, Foundation for Defense of Democracies (FDD), 30 Sep. 2017; and Babb, C., 'US launches new airstrikes against Islamic State in Libya', Voice of America, 21 Nov. 2017.

[58] International Organization for Migration, 'Mediterranean migrant arrivals reach 168,314 in 2017; deaths reach 3,115', Press release, 19 Dec. 2017; International Organization for Migration, Missing Migrants Project; and Walsh, D. and Horowitz, J., 'Italy, going it alone, stalls the flow of migrants. But at what cost?', New York Times, 17 Sep. 2017.

[59] Cascais, A., 'Slave trade in Libya: Outrage across Africa', Deutsche Welle, 22 Nov. 2017; and Jacobson, S., 'EU–African Union summit to debate alleged Libyan slave trading', The National (Abu Dhabi), 29 Nov. 2017.

[60] 'Haftar: Libya's UN-backed government's mandate obsolete', Al Jazeera, 18 Dec. 2017.

[61] El Amrani, I., 'New risks in Libya as Khalifa Haftar dismisses UN-backed accord', Commentary, International Crisis Group, 21 Dec. 2017.

Armed conflict in Syria

Political power in Syria has long been dominated by an Alawite elite. Since 2011 that power has been contested in a multi-sided armed conflict that, while initially sparked by the Arab Spring, has evolved into a complex war involving regional and international powers. Conflict continued to be the driver of humanitarian needs in Syria. As of 7 December 2017 the war had resulted in the displacement of half the population—over 5.4 million refugees and over 6.1 million internally displaced persons, nearly 3 million of whom were in 'hard-to-reach and besieged areas'.[62] As of November 2017, 13.1 million people, over half the Syrian population, urgently required humanitarian assistance, 6.5 million people had acute food insecurity and a further 4 million were at risk of acute food insecurity.[63] Although there are no reliable casualty statistics, over 400 000 Syrians are thought to have died as a result of the fighting.[64]

Amid the complex array of contending forces in Syria, by the end of 2016 the balance of power had tilted sharply in favour of President Bashar al-Assad.[65] According to Amnesty International, the Syrian Government used local agreements—presented as a 'reconciliation effort'—reached between August 2016 and March 2017 to force the mass displacement of civilians and reclaim control of territory. Amnesty International has claimed that the sieges, unlawful killings and forced displacement carried out by government forces constitute crimes against humanity.[66]

UN-sponsored peace talks on Syria took place in Geneva between 23 February and 3 March 2017, but they failed to make a breakthrough. In April an escalation in violence by Syrian forces and external interventions by Turkey and the USA eroded prospects for a political settlement. On 4 April an attack with chemical weapons on the opposition-held town of Khan Shaykhoun killed at least 80 people. The USA, among others, held the Assad regime responsible for the attack.[67] Three days later the USA launched a cruise mis-

---

[62] UN High Commissioner for Refugees (UNHCR), 'Syria emergency', 7 Dec. 2017.

[63] Food and Agriculture Organization of the UN (FAO), *Global Early Warning—Early Action Report on Food Security and Agriculture January–March 2018* (FAO: Rome, Jan. 2018), p. 18.

[64] Kleinfeld, R., Carnegie Endowment for International Peace, 'Why is it so difficult to count dead people?', BBC News, 12 Oct. 2017; and Humud, C., Margesson, R. and Chesser, S., 'Counting casualties in Syria and Iraq: Process and challenges', CRS Insight, Congressional Research Service (CRS), 12 Apr. 2016.

[65] See Smith (note 51), pp. 77–82. On the threat to impose a UN arms embargo on Syria see chapter 10, section II, in this volume.

[66] Amnesty International, *'We Leave or We Die': Forced Displacement under Syria's 'Reconciliation' Agreements* (Amnesty International: London, 2017).

[67] Chulov, M. and Shaheen, K., 'Syria chemical weapons attack toll rises to 70 as Russian narrative is dismissed', *The Guardian*, 5 Apr. 2017; and 'Syria chemical "attack": What we know', BBC News, 26 Apr. 2017. See also chapter 8, section I, in this volume.

sile strike on the air base it believed to be the source of the attack.[68] In other escalatory developments in late April, Turkey bombed Kurdish fighters of the People's Protection Units (Yekîneyên Parastina Gel, YPG) in north-eastern Syria, while the US-backed Syrian Democratic Forces (SDF), led primarily by the YPG, prepared to attack the city of Raqqah, the last stronghold of the Islamic State.[69]

On 6 May, four 'de-escalation zones' in western Syria were created in an agreement between Iran, Russia, Syria and Turkey.[70] This partial ceasefire allowed the Assad regime to shift resources to the east, where it was competing against the US-led coalition and SDF to capture territory from the Islamic State. In June the US-backed SDF forces began their assault on Raqqah, and on 18 June the USA shot down a Syrian Government Su-22 combat aircraft and carried out several strikes on pro-regime forces that were advancing towards an SDF-controlled town.[71] In addition, Turkey deployed troops to its border with Syria in preparation for an offensive against Kurdish-held Afrin in the north-west.[72]

Russia has supported the Syrian Government since the beginning of the conflict in 2011, both politically and with military aid, and since 30 September 2015 also through direct military participation in the armed conflict.[73] According to the Russian Ministry of Defence, 41 of its troops had been killed in Syria between October 2015 and December 2017.[74] Reports suggest that at least 73 Russian mercenaries have also been killed there.[75] Although Russia announced a drawdown of forces in December, it will keep its naval facility at Tartous (which was first established in 1971) and the Khmeimim airbase in Latakia governorate (which first became operational in September 2015).[76] In a new treaty with Syria signed in January 2017, Russia's lease

[68] Ackerman, S., Pilkington, E., Jacobs, B. and Borger, J., 'Syria missile strikes: US launches first direct military action against Assad', *The Guardian*, 7 Apr. 2017.

[69] International Crisis Group (ICG), *Fighting ISIS: The Road To and Beyond Raqqa*, Crisis Group Middle East Briefing no. 53 (ICG: Brussels, 28 Apr. 2017).

[70] Russian Ministry of Foreign Affairs, 'Memorandum on the creation of de-escalation areas in the Syrian Arab Republic', 6 May 2017.

[71] Binnie, J., 'Tensions increase in Syria after Su-22 shoot-down', *IHS Jane's Defence Weekly*, 26 June 2017.

[72] Bonsey, N., 'The post-Caliphate gauntlet in eastern Syria', War on the Rocks, 3 July 2017.

[73] On Russia's involvement in the conflict see Smith (note 51), pp. 77–82; and Trenin, D., *What is Russia up to in the Middle East?* (Polity Press: Cambridge, 2018).

[74] 'Heroes of war: Casualties among Russian servicemen in Syria', TASS, 7 Mar. 2018; and Vasilyeva, N., 'Thousands of Russian private contractors fighting in Syria', Associated Press, 12 Dec. 2017.

[75] Vasilyeva (note 74); and Tsvetkova, M., 'Death certificate offers clues on Russian casualties in Syria', Reuters, 27 Oct. 2017.

[76] Pinchuk, D., 'Russia will keep bases in Syria to strike at insurgents—Kremlin', Reuters, 12 Dec. 2017; and Roth, A., 'On visit to Syria, Putin lauds victory over ISIS and announces withdrawals', *Washington Post*, 11 Dec. 2017.

for both facilities was extended by 49 years, with the option of extending that arrangement for 25-year periods.[77]

The Islamic State suffered major reversals in eastern Syria with the liberation of Deir Ez-Zor and Raqqah. The SDF captured Raqqah, the symbolic capital of the Islamic State, in October 2017. Raqqah's infrastructure was destroyed during the campaign and the city will have to be demined.[78] The Assad regime retook Deir Ez-Zor in November, but the level of destruction there was severe and most of the population was displaced.[79] Continuing instability and unpredictability in both Deir Ez-Zor and Raqqah governorates is likely to prevent any large-scale return by refugees.[80]

In November President Assad met with Russian President Vladimir Putin in Sochi, Russia. Putin then met with Iranian President Hassan Rouhani and Turkish President Recep Tayyip Erdoğan, who agreed to coordinate their military operations against the Islamic State in Syria.[81] On the sidelines of an Asia-Pacific summit, Russia and the USA also agreed in a joint statement to continue their efforts to fight the Islamic State, while also noting that there was no military solution to the conflict in Syria.[82] Nonetheless, fighting continued even in the de-escalation zones and humanitarian assistance was limited. On 13 November air strikes on a market in Atareb, Aleppo governorate, in northern Syria, which were thought to have been carried out by either the Syrian Government or Russia, killed at least 53 people.[83]

UN-mediated peace talks between the Syrian Government and opposition forces resumed in Geneva in late November, but they made little progress. The UN mediator, Staffan de Mistura, said that he 'did not see . . . the Government really looking to find a way to have a dialogue and negotiate'.[84] Nonetheless, further talks were proposed for January 2018.[85] Parallel negotiations backed by Russia, Iran and Turkey took place periodically in Astana, Kazakhstan. The eighth round of talks in Astana on 21–22 December ended with agreement to hold a peace congress for Syria in Sochi in late January

---

[77] 'Moscow cements deal with Damascus to keep 49-year presence at Syrian naval and air bases', TASS, 20 Jan. 2017.

[78] Barnard, A. and Saad, H., 'Raqqa, ISIS "capital", is captured, US-backed forces say', New York Times, 17 Oct. 2017.

[79] Loveluck, L. and El-Ghobashy, T., 'Syrian army declares victory in Deir al-Zour as Islamic State territory crumbles', Washington Post, 3 Nov. 2017.

[80] Khaddour, K., 'Back to what future? What remains for Syria's displaced people', Brief, Carnegie Endowment for International Peace, Jan. 2018.

[81] Chulkovskaya, Y., 'Have Russia, Turkey reached Syrian simpatico yet?', Al-Monitor, 15 Nov. 2017; and Wintour, P., 'Putin brings Iran and Turkey together in bold Syria peace plan', The Guardian, 22 Nov. 2017.

[82] 'Trump, Putin agree "no military solution" in Syria', Al Jazeera, 11 Nov. 2017.

[83] 'Syria war: Air strikes on Atareb market "kill more than 50"', BBC News, 13 Nov. 2017.

[84] UN Office at Geneva, 'Transcript of press conference by UN special envoy for Syria, Mr Staffan de Mistura', 14 Dec. 2017.

[85] Cumming-Bruce, N., '"Golden opportunity missed": Syria peace talks falter, again', New York Times, 14 Dec. 2017.

2018.[86] Around 40 opposition groups rejected the proposed congress, alleging that Russia was trying to bypass the Geneva process.[87]

The armed conflict between Turkey and the Kurds

Since the start of the armed conflict in Syria in 2011 there have been increased tensions along the border between Turkey and Syria, and a huge influx of refugees into Turkey. An attempted military coup in Turkey in July 2016 led to a further consolidation of power by President Erdoğan and his Justice and Development Party (Adalet ve Kalkınma Partisi, AKP).[88] In August 2016 Turkey launched a military offensive in northern Syria against the Islamic State and Kurdish groups.

While Turkey declared the military offensive to be complete in March 2017, it continued to provide cross-border support to non-Kurdish Syrian opposition forces.[89] In October 2017 Turkey deployed troops in Idlib governorate, one of the four de-escalation zones in Syria announced in May 2017 (see above), and there was regular speculation that Turkey might expand operations into other Kurdish-held parts of Syria.[90] In May 2017 the USA decided to continue military cooperation with the SDF, which is led by the Kurdish YPG, including enhanced training and providing arms. This aggravated tensions between the USA and Turkey that had been brewing since the US administration of President Barack Obama initiated this cooperation in the fight against the Islamic State in 2015.[91]

Turkish military action against Kurdish forces in northern Syria, and Turkey's sensitivity to proposals to strengthen Kurdish forces or support some degree of Kurdish political autonomy in the area, have to be understood in the light of the conflict inside Turkey's predominantly Kurdish south-eastern region. This region has been the focus of an almost relentless armed confrontation between Turkish security forces and the Kurdistan Workers' Party (Partiya Karkerên Kurdistanê, PKK) since 1984, punctuated by occasional ceasefires. The collapse of a 2013 ceasefire agreement in July 2015 led to a new cycle of violence.[92] According to the OHCHR, as well as 2000 people

[86] 'Russia, Turkey and Iran agree Syrian peace talks for January', France 24, 23 Dec. 2017.

[87] Associated Press, 'Syria rebels, opposition reject Russia-proposed talks', Wall Street Journal, 26 Dec. 2017.

[88] On events in Turkey in 2016 see Sahlin, M., 'Turkey's search for stability and legitimacy in 2016', SIPRI Yearbook 2017, pp. 151–62; see also chapter 1, section II, in this volume.

[89] 'Turkey "ends" Euphrates Shield campaign in Syria', BBC News, 30 Mar. 2017.

[90] Lister, C., 'Turkey's Idlib incursion and the HTS question: Understanding the long game in Syria', War on the Rocks, 31 Oct. 2017; and 'Turkish military's Idlib operation almost completed, next is Afrin: Erdoğan', Hürriyet Daily News, 24 Oct. 2017.

[91] Gordon, M. R. and Schmitt, E., 'Trump to arm Syrian Kurds, even as Turkey strongly objects', New York Times, 9 May 2017.

[92] On the role of the Kurds in Turkish politics see Özel, S. and Yilmaz, A., 'The Kurds in the Middle East, 2015', SIPRI Yearbook 2016, pp. 53–71.

killed and potentially thousands more detained, 350 000–500 000 people were displaced by the fighting between July 2015 and December 2016.[93]

The violence continued in 2017. According to Turkish Government figures, which tend to overstate successes against the PKK, over 2500 PKK militants were killed and over 7200 were detained in 2017, while 148 members of the security forces and 32 civilians were killed.[94] Ending the conflict with the PKK in Turkey is inextricably linked to the creation of peaceful relations between Turkey and the YPG in Syria, but at the close of the year there seemed little prospect of peace talks between the parties towards such an end.

Armed conflict in Yemen

The roots of the current conflict and humanitarian crisis in Yemen are complex and contested.[95] The country was created after the People's Democratic Republic of Yemen (South Yemen) and the Yemen Arab Republic (North Yemen) merged in 1990. Ali Abdallah Saleh, who had been president of North Yemen since 1978, served as Yemen's first president. However, tensions continued between north and south. A southern separatist movement was defeated in a short civil war in 1994. The Houthi insurgency began in 2004 when Hussein Badreddin al-Houthi, the leader of the Zaidi sect, launched an uprising against the Yemeni Government. Although he was killed in that uprising, since then the insurgents have been known as the Houthis (although their official name is Ansar Allah). Several years of intermittent warfare in the north, which killed hundreds and displaced more than 250 000 people, was ended by a ceasefire agreement in 2010. However, further protests in 2011 inspired by the Arab Spring and a major armed attack by opposition forces on the presidential compound forced President Saleh to resign. Yemen also become a base for affiliates of al-Qaeda and the Islamic State (al-Qaeda in the Arabian Peninsula, AQAP, and the Islamic State–Yemen Province, respectively), which added to the instability in the country.

In 2014, after several years of growing violence, the country descended into the next phase of a civil war between the internationally recognized government of President Abdo Rabu Mansour al-Hadi and an uneasy alliance of Houthis and forces loyal to former president Saleh, which controlled the capital, Sana'a, and large parts of the country. In March 2015 a Saudi

[93] Office of the UN High Commissioner for Human Rights (OHCHR), *Report on the Human Rights Situation in South-East Turkey: July 2015 to December 2016* (OHCHR: Feb. 2017).

[94] Anadolu Agency, 'Over 2,500 PKK terrorists neutralized in Turkey in 2017', *Yeni Şafak*, 4 Jan. 2018. For an alternative account of casualty figures see Mandıracı, B., 'Turkey's PKK conflict kills almost 3000 in two years', Commentary, International Crisis Group, 20 July 2017.

[95] See e.g. Royal Institute of International Affairs (RIIA), *Yemen: Drivers of Conflict and Peace*, Workshop summary, 7–8 Nov. 2016 (Chatham House–RIIA: London, 2017); and Orkaby, A., 'Yemen's humanitarian nightmare: The real roots of the conflict', *Foreign Affairs*, Nov/Dec. 2017.

Arabian-led coalition intervened militarily on the side of the Hadi government. Officially the intervention was at the request of Hadi, now living in
exile in Saudi Arabia, but by the end of 2016 it was seen by many analysts as
part of a wider proxy war with Iran.[96] Various unsuccessful peace initiatives
and ceasefire attempts failed to stop the fighting and left 1 million people on
the brink of famine.[97]

In January 2017 the Saudi Arabian-led coalition and Yemeni troops loyal to
Hadi launched a new military offensive against the Houthi–Saleh forces in
the south-west and north of the country. The UN estimated that the conflict
had killed more than 10 000 people, mostly civilians, and displaced 3 million since March 2015 and that more than 10 million people needed 'urgent
assistance'.[98] Intensive fighting continued throughout March and escalated
again in July, especially in Ta'iz governorate in the south-west.[99] On 22 July
Houthi forces claimed to have launched a ballistic missile into Saudi Arabia,
the latest of many attempts to hit targets in Saudi Arabia with long-range
ballistic missiles.[100]

On 24 August Saleh conducted a large rally in Sana'a, increasing tensions
within the Saleh–Houthi alliance, and air strikes by the Saudi Arabian-led
coalition increased in the period afterwards.[101] There were 5676 air strikes
in the first six months of 2017, up from 3936 in all of 2016.[102] In response
to a missile fired at Riyadh on 4 November, the Saudi Arabian-led coalition
again stepped up its bombing campaign.[103] In a bid to stop alleged weapon
shipments to the Houthis from Iran, Saudi Arabia also temporarily closed
all entry ports to Yemen. This tightening of the blockade on Houthi–
Saleh-controlled territories aggravated the already severe humanitarian
crisis in the country.[104] The number of suspected cholera cases reached

[96] Blasina, N., 'Saudi Arabia and Iran: Four proxy conflicts explained', *Wall Street Journal*, 8 Dec.
2017.

[97] Duncan, C., 'The conflict in Yemen: A primer', Lawfare, 28 Nov. 2017; and Smith (note 51),
pp 85–87; and 'How Yemen became the most wretched place on earth', *The Economist*, 30 Nov. 2017.
On the UN arms embargo on Yemen see chapter 10, section II, in this volume.

[98] 'Death toll in Yemen conflict passes 10,000', Al Jazeera, 17 Jan. 2017; and UN Children's Fund
(UNICEF), 'Yemen humanitarian situation report', Mar. 2017.

[99] Dearden, L., 'Yemen civil war: 20 civilians including women and children "killed in Saudi-led
air strike," UN says', *The Independent*, 19 July 2017.

[100] Carlino, L., 'Incremental improvements in Houthi militants' ballistic missile campaign
increase risk to assets in central Saudi Arabia', *IHS Jane's Intelligence Weekly*, 26 July 2017. See also
chapter 10, section II, in this volume.

[101] Al-Mujahed, A. and Raghavan, S., 'Tens of thousands rally in support of Yemen's former president amid growing rifts', *Washington Post*, 24 Aug. 2017.

[102] Protection Cluster Yemen, 'Protection cluster: Update', Aug. 2017.

[103] Longley Alley, A., 'A Huthi missile, a Saudi purge and a Lebanese resignation shake the Middle
East', Commentary, International Crisis Group, 10 Nov. 2017; and Carlino, L., 'Houthi missile fired
at Riyadh indicates intent to engage targets deep in Saudi Arabia, despite escalation risk', *IHS Jane's
Country Risk Daily Report*, 6 Nov. 2017.

[104] Erickson, A., 'Saudi Arabia lifted its blockade of Yemen: It's not nearly enough to prevent a
famine', *Washington Post*, 1 Dec. 2017; and Miles, T., 'Famine survey warns of thousands dying daily

1 million in December, in what is the largest and fastest-spreading outbreak of the disease in modern history.[105]

On 30 November armed clashes broke out in Sana'a between Houthi and Saleh forces, culminating in the killing of Saleh on 4 December. Saleh was reportedly seeking dialogue with Saudi Arabia and its allies.[106] His death left the Houthis as the strongest power in northern Yemen and continuing deadlock in the civil war.[107] A second ballistic missile fired at Riyadh on 19 December was reportedly intercepted by Saudi Arabian air defences. Saudi Arabia and the USA claimed that the missile was supplied by Iran.[108] This was followed by a further intensification in the Saudi Arabian-led coalition's air strikes.[109]

On 20 December the USA confirmed that 'multiple ground operations' involving US troops were taking place in Yemen, in addition to the roughly 125 US air strikes in 2017—more than in the previous four years combined—targeting both AQAP and the Islamic State–Yemen Province, mainly in the south of the country.[110]

At the end of the year, the Saudi Arabian-led coalition was maintaining its partial blockade of Houthi-controlled territories with devastating humanitarian consequences. At least 17 million people, or 60 per cent of the population, faced acute food insecurity.[111] In a joint statement on 29 December, on reaching the milestone of 1000 days of war in Yemen, the heads of three UN agencies reiterated calls for parties to the conflict to immediately allow full humanitarian access and to stop the fighting.[112]

in Yemen if ports stay closed', Reuters, 21 Nov. 2017.

[105] International Rescue Committee, 'Yemen hits 1 million cases of cholera as even more preventable diseases wreak havoc on Yemeni children', Press release, 21 Dec. 2017. See also World Health Organization, Regional Office for the Eastern Mediterranean, 'Cholera outbreak response', Weekly cholera bulletins.

[106] Dehghan, S. K., 'Killing of Ali Abdullah Saleh changes dynamics of Yemen's civil war', The Guardian, 5 Dec. 2017.

[107] Longley Alley, A., 'The killing of former President Saleh could worsen Yemen's war', Commentary, International Crisis Group, 6 Dec. 2017.

[108] Hubbard B. and Cumming-Bruce, N., 'Rebels in Yemen fire second ballistic missile at Saudi capital', New York Times, 19 Dec. 2017.

[109] Wintour, P., 'Saudi-led airstrikes kill 68 civilians in one day in Yemen's "absurd" war', The Guardian, 28 Dec. 2017.

[110] Purkiss, J. and Fielding-Smith, A., 'US counter terror air strikes double in Trump's first year', Bureau of Investigative Journalism, 19 Dec. 2017; and Nichols, H. and Gains, M., 'Pentagon confirms US ground operations in Yemen', NBC News, 20 Dec. 2017.

[111] Food and Agriculture Organization of the UN (note 63).

[112] UN Children's Fund (UNICEF), 'Joint statement: WHO, WFP and UNICEF: Yemen's families cannot withstand another day of war, let alone 1,000', 29 Dec. 2017.

VI. Armed conflict in sub-Saharan Africa

IAN DAVIS, FLORIAN KRAMPE, NEIL MELVIN AND ZOË GORMAN

In 2017 there were seven active armed conflicts in sub-Saharan Africa: in Mali, Nigeria, the Central African Republic (CAR), the Democratic Republic of the Congo (DRC), Ethiopia, Somalia and South Sudan.[1] In addition, a number of other countries experienced post-war conflict and tension or were flashpoints for potential armed conflict, including Burundi, Cameroon, the Gambia, Kenya, Lesotho, Sudan and Zimbabwe.

In Cameroon long-standing tensions within the mainly English-speaking provinces worsened in 2017 and turned violent in September, while the far north continued to be affected by the regional Islamist insurgency of Boko Haram (also known as Islamic State in West Africa).[2] The symbolic declaration of independence by militant anglophone secessionist groups on 1 October set the stage for further violence in Cameroon.[3] The conflict is creating a growing refugee crisis, with at least 7500 people fleeing into Nigeria since 1 October.[4] In Kenya, following serious electoral violence, the year ended with major divisions and tensions between President Uhuru Kenyatta and the opposition leader, Raila Odinga.[5] In Zimbabwe political tensions led to a military coup during November and the replacement of President Robert Mugabe, who has ruled the country since its independence in 1980, by his former vice-president, Emmerson Mnangagwa.[6] Burundi, the Gambia, Lesotho and Sudan each hosted a multilateral peace operation in 2017.[7]

This section reviews developments in each of the seven active armed conflicts. Before doing that, it first outlines two general trends that can be identified in armed conflicts in sub-Saharan Africa.

[1] This chapter discusses armed conflicts in North Africa in section V.

[2] Atabong, A. B., 'The crisis in Cameroon's English-speaking regions has turned violent with bombings', Quartz Africa, 22 Sep. 2017; and Amnesty International, 'Cameroon: Seventeen killed following protests in anglophone regions', Press release, 2 Oct. 2017.

[3] Iyare, T. and Essomba, F., 'In Nigeria and Cameroon, secessionist movements gain momentum', New York Times, 8 Oct. 2017; and International Crisis Group (ICG), Cameroon's Anglophone Crisis at the Crossroads, Africa Report no. 250 (ICG: Brussels, 2 Aug. 2017).

[4] 'Cameroon separatists kill four gendarmes as anglophone crisis worsens', Reuters, 18 Dec. 2017.

[5] Kenyatta, U., 'Kenya deserves a strong and credible opposition', Washington Times, 18 Dec. 2017; Chepkwony, M., 'US pushing for Uhuru, Raila talks', The Standard (Nairobi), 20 Dec. 2017; and Kisika, S., 'Ten out of 92 killed in poll chaos were kids–report', The Star (Nairobi), 21 Dec. 2017.

[6] 'Will Zimbabwe's new president make things better?', The Economist, 25 Nov. 2017; and International Crisis Group (ICG), Zimbabwe's 'Military-Assisted Transition' and Prospects for Recovery, Africa Briefing no. 134 (ICG: Brussels, 20 Dec. 2017).

[7] On peacekeeping-related developments in these countries see chapter 3, section II, in this volume.

Key general trends

Given sub-Saharan Africa's complexity and diversity, it is difficult to make generalizations about trends across the region. However, two broad developments can be identified. First, many conflicts overlap across states and regions as a result of transnational activities of violent Islamist groups, other armed groups and criminal networks. In many countries, and especially those in the Sahel and Lake Chad regions, these overlapping conflicts are linked to extreme poverty, instability, economic fragility and low resilience—situations that are further exacerbated by climate change, corruption, inadequate economic policies and mismanagement. Second, there also appears to be a growing internationalization of counterterrorism activities in Africa, led primarily by two external state actors—France and the United States.

Cross-border conflicts: The Sahel and Lake Chad crises

Following the 2012 crisis in Mali, the Sahel has witnessed an escalation in violent extremist activity and a burgeoning of trafficking and migratory networks.[8] Historically, the region has suffered from weak governance, high youth unemployment, porous borders, drought, food insecurity and paltry development progress. The presence of the Islamic State group in Africa has added to instability. Islamic State has an estimated 6000 African foreign fighters in Iraq and Syria and could be looking to the Sahel for its next safe haven.[9] Foreign interventions have failed to provide stability in the region (see below).[10]

The Lake Chad crisis is an example of the increasingly complex relationship between transnational security and climate change. The Lake Chad region lies to the south of the Sahara Desert, bordering Cameroon, Chad, Niger and Nigeria. Multiple factors such as unemployment, poverty and conflict interact with environmental change and degradation in the region around the lake. In the past 40 years Lake Chad has shrunk by 90 per cent.[11] Contributing factors include mismanagement of water

---

[8] De Melo, J., 'Sahel faces poverty and conflict traps: A call for international action', Brookings Institute, 1 Dec. 2016; and Walther, O. J., *Wars and Conflicts in the Sahara-Sahel*, West African Papers no. 10 (OECD: Paris, Sep. 2017).

[9] 'L'Union africaine redoute le retour de 6 000 combattants de l'Etat islamique sur le continent' [The African Union fears the return of 6000 Islamic State combatants to the continent], *Le Monde*, 11 Dec. 2017.

[10] Sieff, K., 'The world's most dangerous UN mission', *Washington Post*, 17 Feb. 2017; G5 Sahel, Permanent Secretariat, Résolution 00-01/2017 relative à la creation d'une force conjointe du G5 Sahel [Resolution on the creation of a joint G5 Sahel force], 6 Feb. 2017; and Hickendorff, A., Tobie, A. and Van der Lijn, J., 'Success of Joint Force Sahel depends on local actor engagement', Commentary, SIPRI, 18 Aug. 2017.

[11] Wirkus, L. and Volker, B., 'Transboundary water management on Africa's international rivers and lakes: Current state and experiences', eds W. Scheumann and S. Neubert, *Transboundary Water Management in Africa: Challenges for Development Cooperation*, Deutsches Institut für Entwick-

resources and prolonged severe droughts. In addition, the ongoing insurgency by Boko Haram in northern Nigeria further reduces both the livelihood and security of communities in the region. These factors have resulted in diminished livelihoods, extreme poverty, and exacerbated tensions between pastoralists, farmers and fishers.[12] As the Boko Haram insurgency spread from Nigeria across the region, the security situation deteriorated causing a massive humanitarian crisis and increasing cross-border displacement of populations.[13]

In March 2017 the United Nations Security Council recognized the significance of the Lake Chad crisis and unanimously adopted a resolution on terrorism and human rights violations in the Lake Chad Basin.[14] In addition to identifying the insurgency by Boko Haram as a destabilizing factor, the resolution accepted the role of climate change in exacerbating human insecurity. However, the subsequent report by the UN Secretary-General was notably silent on climate and environmental change, although it does underscore the enormity of the current crisis in estimating that about 10.7 million people across the Lake Chad region currently need humanitarian assistance. This figure includes 8.5 million people in Nigeria, and 7.2 million people who face severe food insecurity, of which 4.7 million are located in the north-eastern Nigeria.[15]

Internationalized counterterrorism operations in Africa

Several external state actors are building a military presence in sub-Saharan Africa.[16] Djibouti, located in the Horn of Africa, is the epicentre of this external military presence. China, France (which also hosts troops from Germany and Spain), Italy, Japan and the USA each have military bases in Djibouti.[17] However, only a few states—primarily France and the USA—play a direct role in counterterrorism.

The total number of US troops in sub-Saharan Africa is still relatively small compared to other parts of the world—around 6000, of which about two-thirds are based in Djibouti. Although Djibouti was until recently the

---

lungspolitik (DIE) Studies no. 21 (DIE: Bonn, 2006), pp. 11–102; and Gao, H. et al., 'On the causes of the shrinking of Lake Chad', *Environmental Research Letters*, vol. 6, no. 3 (2011).

[12] United Nations, Security Council, Report of the Secretary-General on the situation in the Lake Chad Basin region, S/2017/764, 7 Sep. 2017; and Thébaud, B. and Batterbury, S., 'Sahel pastoralists: Opportunism, struggle, conflict and negotiation. a case study from eastern Niger', *Global Environmental Change*, vol. 11, no. 1 (Apr. 2001), pp. 69–78.

[13] United Nations, S/2017/764 (note 12); and Angerbrandt, H., *Nigeria and the Lake Chad Region beyond Boko Haram*, Nordic Africa Institute (NAI) Policy Note no. 3 (NAI: Uppsala, June 2017).

[14] UN Security Council Resolution 2349, 31 Mar. 2017.

[15] United Nations, S/2017/764 (note 12).

[16] See Sköns, E. and Ismail, O., SIPRI, *Security Activities of External Actors in Africa* (Oxford University Press: Oxford, 2014).

[17] Dahir, A. L., 'How a tiny African country became the world's key military base', *Quartz Africa*, 18 Aug. 2017; and Olsen, G. R., 'Transatlantic cooperation on terrorism and Islamist radicalisation in Africa: The Franco-American axis', *European Security*, vol. 27, no. 1 (2018), pp. 41–57.

only permanent and officially acknowledged US military base in the region, the US presence is more widespread than this suggests, largely as a result of the increased number of 'advise, assist and train' missions. These are low profile and 'small footprint' arrangements.[18] The numbers and global reach of US special forces have grown considerably since the start of the 'global war on terrorism' in 2001, and the most significant increase in deployments in the last decade was in Africa.[19] In 2017, with around 1700 US special forces soldiers operating in at least 33 African states, this was the second largest deployment of US special forces anywhere in the world, after the Middle East.[20] Another aspect of the increased US military presence in sub-Saharan Africa has been the stationing and use of unmanned aerial vehicles (UAVs, drones).[21] At least two serious allegations of human rights violations in 2017 linked to the US military raised questions about oversight and the effectiveness of US counterterrorism efforts in sub-Saharan Africa.[22]

French special forces and other military assets in sub-Saharan Africa are predominately dedicated to Operation Barkhane, which involves an estimated 3500–4000 troops targeting Islamic extremists in five states in the Sahel region: Burkina Faso, Chad, Côte d'Ivoire, Mali and Niger.[23] France also has military personnel stationed in Djibouti (1450 personnel), Côte d'Ivoire (900 personnel), Gabon (350 personnel) and Senegal (350 personnel).[24]

Unlike the USA and France, most external support by other states involves little or no direct engagement on the ground. Instead, these states currently focus on providing counterterrorism or counter-insurgency training and military assistance. The United Kingdom, for example, provides training and military assistance to Kenya, Nigeria and Sierra Leone, including to Kenyan forces combating al-Shabab in Somalia and Nigerian armed forces fighting Boko Haram.[25] China also has a growing security presence in sub-Saharan

---

[18] Sköns, E., 'The United States', eds Sköns and Ismail (note 16); Myre, G., 'The US military in Africa: A discreet presence in many places', National Public Radio, 20 Oct. 2017; and Turse, N., 'The US military is conducting secret missions all over Africa', Vice, 25 Oct. 2017.

[19] US special forces in sub-Saharan Africa fall under the responsibility of US Africa Command (AFRICOM), which also includes all of North Africa except Egypt.

[20] Turse, N., 'The next Niger', Vice, 29 Nov. 2017.

[21] Cooper, H. and Schmitt, E., 'Niger approves armed US drone flights, expanding Pentagon's role in Africa', New York Times, 30 Nov. 2017.

[22] McClaughlin, E. and Martinez, L., 'US military orders new investigation after report that special operations killed Somali civilians', ABC News, 14 Dec. 2017; McLeary, P., 'Pentagon investigating if US troops knew of torture at Cameroonian base', Foreign Policy, 27 July 2017; and Goldbaum, C., 'On the eve of Congressional hearings, new evidence about alleged US massacre in Somalia', Daily Beast, 6 Dec. 2017.

[23] French Ministry of Defence, 'Opération Barkhane' [Operation Barkhane], 28 Dec. 2017.

[24] French Ministry of Defence, 'Forces prépositionnées' [Prepositioned forces], Oct. 2016.

[25] Tossini, J. V., 'The British forces in Africa: The training unit in Kenya', UK Defence Journal, 30 Mar. 2017; Tossini, J. V., 'British forces in Nigeria: A long partnership in West Africa', UK Defence Journal, 29 Aug. 2017; and British Government, 'UK reiterates support to the fight against Boko Haram', News release, 6 Oct. 2017.

Africa, which includes counter-piracy operations in the Gulf of Aden (since 2008), the deployment of 2400 peacekeepers on UN operations, the opening of its first overseas military base, in Djibouti in 2016 (with a naval component added in 2017), and its status as one of the most important suppliers of conventional arms.[26] It also provides military capacity-building programmes, including in counterterrorism.[27]

Armed conflict in the Central African Republic

The Central African Republic has experienced inter-religious and inter-communal violence and hostilities since 2013. Séléka—an armed group which consists mostly of Muslims—seized power in March 2013. It was opposed by the Anti-balaka, an armed group which consists mostly of Christians. In 2014 Séléka gave into international pressure and handed power to a transitional government. However, violence continued and the country was effectively partitioned despite the presence of a French operation (which withdrew in October 2016) and a UN peace operation, the UN Multidimensional Integrated Stabilization Mission in CAR (MINUSCA).[28] Since 2014 the country has been undergoing an internationally supervised transition involving a constitutional referendum as well as presidential and parliamentary elections.[29]

In February 2017 fighting escalated between two rival factions within Séléka—the Popular Front for the Renaissance of CAR (Front Populaire pour la Renaissance de Centrafrique, FPRC) and the Union for Peace in CAR (Union pour la Paix en Centrafrique, UPC)—and a UN attack helicopter fired on a FPRC militia as it approached the town of Bambari.[30] In May violence involving several armed groups from both the Anti-balaka and Séléka increased in the south, east and north-west, leaving at least 300 people dead and an estimated 100 000 displaced. UN peacekeepers were also targeted in some of the attacks.[31]

[26] On China's arms transfers to sub-Saharan Africa see chapter 5, section I, in this volume.

[27] 'Djibouti: Chinese troops depart for first overseas military base', BBC News, 12 July 2017; Duchâtel, M., Gowan, R., and Lafont Rapnouil, M., *Into Africa: China's Global Security Shift*, Policy Brief no. 179 (European Council on Foreign Relations: London, June 2016); and Nantulya, P., 'Pursuing the China dream through Africa: Five elements of China's Africa strategy', Africa Center for Strategoc Studies, 6 Apr. 2017.

[28] On MINUSCA see chapter 3, section II, in this volume.

[29] 'Central African Republic country profile', BBC News, 21 Sep. 2017; and International Crisis Group (ICG), *Central African Republic: The Roots of Violence*, Africa Report no. 230 (ICG: Brussels, 21 Sep. 2015).

[30] 'UN air operation disperses Central African Republic militia', Reuters, 26 Feb. 2017.

[31] International Crisis Group (ICG), *Avoiding the Worst in Central African Republic*, Africa Report no. 253 (ICG: Brussels, 28 Sep. 2017); 'Militia violence in Central African Republic leaves 300 dead', Reuters, 25 May 2017; and 'Armed group attacks civilians, UN in Central African Republic overnight; peacekeeper killed', UN News Centre, 13 May 2017.

Among the peace processes, a series of parallel mediation efforts were launched in 2017 by the African Union (AU), some other African states, including Angola and Chad, and the Community Sant'Egidio, part of the Roman Catholic Church. As part of a merged peace process that combined the earlier parallel efforts, a meeting with armed groups in Rome resulted in a 'political peace agreement' in June 2017 between the government and 13 of the 14 armed groups.[32] However, the agreement was soon disrupted by a resumption of violence.[33] In July the AU and partners (under the merged peace process) produced a new road map for peace and reconciliation in CAR.[34]

In August 2017 violence worsened in the north and east between Anti-balaka militants and the UPC, which had now left Séléka. This violence left over 100 people dead and aid agencies suspended their operations after their workers were targeted by armed groups.[35] The UN Under-Secretary-General for Humanitarian Affairs and Emergency Relief Coordinator, Stephen O'Brien, warned the UN Security Council on 7 August that the situation displayed 'warning signs of genocide' and called for additional troops for MINUSCA.[36] In November MINUSCA's mandate was extended until 15 November 2018 and an extra 900 military personnel were added to the mission.[37]

The conflict continued to deteriorate. By the end of October the number of internally displaced people had increased to over 600 000 and a further 538 000 people were refugees in neighbouring countries—in total about a quarter of the population had been displaced.[38] However, only 40.7 per cent of the $497.3 million humanitarian response plan for CAR agreed by the UN Office for the Coordination of Humanitarian Affairs (OCHA) was funded in

---

[32] Accord politique pour la paix en République centrafricaine [Political agreement for peace in the Central African Republic], Comunità di Sant'Egidio, [19 June 2017]; International Crisis Group (note 31), pp. 14–23; and Reuters, 'Central African Republic foes sign church-mediated peace accord', Voice of America, 19 June 2017.

[33] International Crisis Group (note 31).

[34] 'African Union adopts new crisis resolution roadmap for CAR', Agence de Presse Africaine, 19 July 2017.

[35] Ratcliff, R., '"People are dying": Violence forces aid workers out of Central African Republic', The Guardian, 1 Sep. 2017.

[36] O'Brien, S., UN Under-Secretary-General for Humanitarian Affairs and Emergency Relief Coordinator, 'Statement to member states on his 16–21 July 2017 mission to the Central African Republic and the Democratic Republic of the Congo', UN Office for the Coordination of Humanitarian Affairs, 7 Aug. 2017.

[37] 'Central African Republic: UN mission mandate extended, additional "blue helmets" authorized', UN News Centre, 15 Nov. 2017.

[38] UN High Commissioner for Refugees (UNHCR), 'Refugees from the Central African Republic', UNHCR Operational Data Portal.

2017.[39] By the end of 2017, the possibility of a resumption of a civil war in CAR remained a growing possibility.[40]

Armed conflict in the Democratic Republic of the Congo

The recent history of the Democratic Republic of the Congo is dominated by civil war and corruption, fuelled by competition over the country's vast mineral wealth. The 1998–2003 Second Congo War drew in the armed forces of at least six countries and its death toll has been estimated to be as high as 5.4 million (although that is a controversial statistic), either as a direct result of fighting or because of disease and malnutrition.[41] Since 2003 conflict in the DRC has persisted in the east, where there are still dozens of armed groups, and UN peace operations have been deployed since 2000.[42] Joseph Kabila, who has been president since 2001, won two consecutive elections, in 2006 and 2011.

Elections were due to take place in December 2016, at the end of Kabila's final term. However, as a result of a deal brokered by the Catholic Church in the DRC and signed on 31 December 2016, elections did not take place. Under the Comprehensive and Inclusive Political Agreement (also known as the Saint Sylvester agreement), Kabila remained in office and elections were postponed until late 2017; he was expected to rule in partnership with the opposition in a transitional power-sharing arrangement; and an oversight mechanism and platform for further talks, the National Council for Monitoring the Agreement and the Electoral Process (Conseil National de Suivi de l'Accord et du processus électoral, CNSA), was to be created.[43] The uncertainty that surrounded the implementation of the agreement increased following the death of the main opposition leader, Etienne Tshisekedi, on 1 February 2017.[44] Following the failure of a new round of negotiations between the opposition and the Alliance for the Presidential Majority, the largest party in the National Assembly, in March the Catholic Church

[39] UN Office for the Coordination of Humanitarian Affairs, 'Central African Republic 2017 (humanitarian response plan)', Financial Tracking Service, [n.d.]; and '"Leave no stone unturned" to secure aid funding for Central African Republic, senior UN official urges', UN News Centre, 9 Nov. 2017.

[40] Vinograd, C., 'The Central African Republic could be on the brink of a bloodbath', *Washington Post*, 10 Oct. 2017.

[41] The estimate of 5.4 million was made by the International Rescue Committee (IRC), a humanitarian non-governmental organization. It was later challenged as being "far too high" by the Human Security Report project. International Rescue Committee (IRC), *Mortality in the Democratic Republic of Congo: An Ongoing Crisis* (IRC: New York, 2006), p. 16; and 'DR Congo war deaths "exaggerated"', BBC News, 20 Jan. 2010.

[42] On the peace operation in the DRC see chapter 3, section II, in this volume.

[43] International Crisis Group (ICG), *Time for Concerted Action in DR Congo*, Africa Report no. 257 (ICG: Brussels, 4 Dec. 2017).

[44] Hoebeke, H. and Moncrieff, R., 'What does opposition leader Etienne Tshisekedi's death mean for DR Congo's road to elections', African Arguments, 3 Feb. 2017.

withdrew from its mediating role.[45] Although talks continued, achieving a consensus on critical aspects of governing arrangements seemed unlikely without the involvement of religious leaders.

Security forces clashed with opposition groups in several provinces in February 2017, with the worst violence involving the Kamuina Nsapu militia in Kasai province, where at least 100 people were killed.[46] Violence in Kasai continued in March, with 39 police officers reportedly killed in an ambush.[47] Two UN experts investigating the violence were also killed.[48] The violence in Kasai intensified from March to August. About 5000 people were killed in the conflict in Kasai in the 12 months to the end of August, and roughly 1.5 million people were displaced (out of a total of 4.1 million displaced in the country).[49] By late October almost half of the displaced people had returned home as the violence in Kasai began to wane.[50] However, violence between government forces and militia in the areas near the DRC's eastern borders with Burundi, Rwanda and Uganda began to increase.

In November 2017 it was announced that presidential elections were rescheduled to 23 December 2018.[51] By the end of the year, Kabila's regime had achieved a 'non-consensual' implementation of the Saint Sylvester agreement: it continued to control the government, the CNSA and the electoral commission.[52] In addition to the continuing political impasse, violence was rising in several provinces, resulting in a growing humanitarian crisis.[53] An estimated 3.2 million people continued to suffer from severe food insecurity in Kasai and 762 000 people were internally displaced. An estimated 2 million people were internally displaced in North Kivu, South Kivu and Tanganyika provinces.[54]

[45] Catholic News Service, 'Bishops in Democratic Republic of Congo withdraw from peace talks', *Catholic Herald*, 28 Mar. 2017.

[46] 'Reported killings in DR Congo town could amount to serious rights violations—UN rights arm', UN News Centre, 14 Feb. 2017.

[47] Akwei, I, 'DRC police accuses rebels of killing 39 officers, AU calls for restraint', Africa News, 28 Mar. 2017.

[48] De Freytas-Tamura, K. and Sengupta, S., 'For 2 experts killed in Congo, UN provided little training and no protection', *New York Times*, 20 May 2017.

[49] Burke, J., 'Congo violence fuels fears of return to 90s bloodbath', *The Guardian*, 30 June 2017; International Crisis Group (note 43); and Oxfam, 'Congo's Cinderella crisis: Horrific suffering overlooked in largest displacement crisis of 2017', Press release, 1 Sep. 2017.

[50] 'Half of central Congo's 1.5 million displaced people have returned', Reuters, 23 Oct. 2017.

[51] Congolese National Independent Electoral Commission (Commission Electorale Nationale Indépendante, CENI), Décision no. 065/CENI/BUR/17 du 05 Novembre 2017 portant publication du calendrier des élections présidentielle, législatives, provinciales, urbaines, municipales et locales [Decision no. 065/CENI/BUR/17 of 5 Nov. 2017 on the publication of the calendar of presidential, legislative, provincial, urban, municipal and local elections], 5 Nov. 2017.

[52] International Crisis Group (note 43).

[53] 'The Democratic Republic of Congo (DRC): A dangerous stalemate', Commentary, International Crisis Group, 26 Oct. 2017; and Ataman, D., 'The art of resilience in the Democratic Republic of the Congo', Huffington Post, 6 Oct. 2017.

[54] Emergency Telecommunications Cluster (ETC), 'Democratic Republic of Congo (DRC)—Conflict', ETC Situation Report no. 1, Reporting period 20 Nov. 2017–5 Dec. 2017.

In December, 12 members of a Congolese militia group, including a member of the South Kivu provincial assembly who masterminded the attacks between 2013–16, were convicted of raping young girls in a landmark case in the fight against impunity for sexual violence crimes. The trial lasted just over a month and was held in a mobile military court in Kavumu, South Kivu, where the crimes were committed, so that locals could attend.[55]

Armed conflict in Ethiopia

During 2017 Ethiopia experienced a wave of ethno-political violence, which had first begun in 2014. The immediate source of the violence lies in a deterioration of interethnic relations in the country, most notably involving the largest ethnic communities: the Oromo, the Amhara and the Somali. The violence consists of conflict between these communities and the central government and paramilitary groups linked to the government. The governing Ethiopian Peoples' Revolutionary Democratic Front (EPRDF) is a coalition dominated by the Tigrayan People's Liberation Front (TPLF), which represents the Tigray ethnic community. Violent unrest in Ethiopia may be viewed as a product of ethnic federalism introduced in 1994 by the EPRDF. Over subsequent decades, the new constitutional order promoted a politicization of ethnic identities and fostered territorial competition and disputes and conflicts over resources, water and land.[56]

Oromia region has been the centre of much of this ethnic violence. This reflects the deep-seated grievances and sense of marginalization among the Oromo, the country's largest ethnic group, which is estimated to make up about one-third of the population.[57] The next largest group, the Amhara, makes up about one-quarter of the population.[58]

Protests that started in western Oromia in April 2014 gained momentum and spread, notably to Amhara region in July 2016.[59] The protests also widened to combine local ethnic complaints, grievances about the political domination of the ruling EPRDF and restrictions on the majority ethnic communities.[60] Government security forces responded to the largely peaceful demonstrations with violence, leading to the deaths of an estimated

[55] Maclean, R., 'Congolese fighters convicted of raping young girls in landmark case', The Guardian, 13 Dec. 2017.

[56] International Crisis Group (ICG), Ethiopia: Ethnic Federalism and Its Discontents, Africa Report no. 153 (ICG: Brussels, 4 Sep. 2009).

[57] Woldemariam, Y., 'What is behind the Oromo rebellion in Ethiopia?', Huffington Post, 21 Dec. 2015.

[58] US Central Intelligence Agency, 'Ethiopia', World Factbook, 3 Jan. 2018.

[59] Pinaud, M., Raleigh, C. and Moody, J., 'Popular mobilisation in Ethiopia: An investigation of activity from November 2015 to May 2017', Country Report, Armed Conflict Location & Event Data Project (ACLED), June 2017.

[60] Human Rights Watch, 'Ethiopia', World Report 2017 (Seven Stories Press: New York, 2017), pp. 251–56.

500 people.[61] In October 2016, as clashes escalated, the government imposed a state of emergency.

Early in 2017 the Liyu Police, a paramilitary group affiliated with the government of Somali region in eastern Ethiopia, conducted raids in eastern and southern Oromia, leading to hundreds of people being killed.[62] A government commission estimated that, by mid-2017, a total of 900 people had been killed since the onset of the unrest, but it blamed a lot of the violence on opposition groups.[63] The state of emergency was lifted in July 2017, but protests against continued paramilitary raids led to renewed violence and dozens of deaths.[64] Fighting escalated as ethnic Somali and Oromo communities along the regional administrative border clashed over an unresolved territorial dispute, reportedly leading to hundreds of deaths between October and December.[65]

Tens of thousands fled Somali and Oromia regions in one of Ethiopia's largest internal population displacements.[66] OCHA reported in early 2018 that 1 million people had been displaced due to conflict along the Oromia–Somali border (nearly 700 000 in 2017 alone).[67] Amid the ongoing conflict, there were signs of a growing struggle within the EPRDF over whether to introduce political reforms in the country.[68]

Armed conflict in Mali

The conflict in Mali stems from the pursuit of self-determination by the Tuareg, an ethnic group that principally inhabits the Sahara Desert in a vast area that includes south-western Libya, southern Algeria, the northern Saharan regions of Mali and parts of Niger and Burkina Faso. The Tuareg separatists form part of an armed coalition, the Coordination of Azawad Movements (Coordination des Mouvements de l'Azawad, CMA), which has been involved in regularly uprisings or rebellions against the Platform, an opposing coalition that supports national unity. Rebellions in 2012, fuelled by the post-2011 influx of fighters from Libya, propelled the secular nationalist movement to evolve into an Islamist insurgency. Since then, the conflict

[61] Human Rights Watch (note 60).

[62] 'What is behind clashes in Ethiopia's Oromia and Somali regions?', BBC News, 18 Sep. 2017.

[63] 'Report: 669 killed in Ethiopia violence since August', Al Jazeera, 18 Apr. 2017.

[64] Fuller, B., 'Ethiopia—November 2017 update', Armed Conflict Location & Event Data Project (ACLED), 14 Nov. 2017; and Feleke, L., 'Analysis of rising death toll, displacement & protests in east, south & south east Ethiopia. What lies beneath?', Ethiopia Observatory, 15 Sep. 2017.

[65] Jeffrey, J., 'Ethnic violence in Ethiopia leaves deep wounds', Deutsche Welle, 5 Dec. 2017; and Schemm, P., '"They started to burn our houses": Ethnic strife in Ethiopia threatens a key US ally', Washington Post, 20 Oct. 2017.

[66] 'What is behind clashes in Ethiopia's Oromia and Somali regions?' (note 62).

[67] UN Office for the Coordination of Humanitarian Affairs (OCHA), 'Ethiopia'.

[68] 'Ethiopia's ruling coalition sweats over insecurity as Oromo, Amhara MPs protest', Africa News, 21 Dec. 2017.

has continued to spiral with a proliferation of armed groups in northern and central Mali seeking to pursue the interests of various ethnic, religious or criminal factions.

Operation Serval, a 2013 French military intervention in collaboration with the Malian Government, dispersed the extremist groups to remote desert strongholds. With the creation in April 2013 of the UN Multidimensional Integrated Stabilization Mission in Mali (MINUSMA), the international intervention in Mali was effectively divided between two military missions: the UN peace operation and Operation Serval (which was replaced by Operation Barkhane, a regional French-led counterterrorism effort, in September 2014).[69]

Despite a UN-sponsored ceasefire and peace agreement with some Tuareg separatists in 2015—the fifth between the Malian Government and the Tuareg-led armed movement—significant challenges remained.[70] At the start of 2017 Tuareg rebels remained sporadically active, while in northern and central Mali the Islamist insurgency continued with attacks by al-Qaeda-linked militants. In January 2017 one such group, al-Mourabitoun, killed at least 47 people with a car bomb at a military camp in Gao in northern Mali, which housed government troops and former rebels brought together as part of the 2015 peace agreement.[71]

In February the Follow-Up Committee, an international mediation team led by the Algerian Foreign Minister, Ramtane Lamamra, gave new momentum to the peace process in three key ways. First, the committee launched a joint patrol on 23 February in Gao comprised of government forces, the Platform and the CMA.[72] The latter two armed groups had boycotted the committee in January, citing a lack of inclusiveness. Plans for further joint patrols in Kidal, also in the north, were derailed after violence between the Platform and the CMA broke out again but were then rescheduled after a ceasefire in September.[73]

Second, an agreement was reached on the composition of interim authorities in five regions of northern Mali. These interim authorities were installed in Kidal on 28 February (but without representatives from the Platform), in Gao and Ménaka on 2 March, and in Timbuktu and Taoudenni on 20 April.[74]

---

[69] Charbonneau, B., 'Intervention in Mali: Building peace between peacekeeping and counterterrorism', *Journal of Contemporary African Studies*, vol. 35, no. 4 (Aug. 2017); and Sieff (note 10). On the role of MINUSMA see also chapter 3, sections I and II, in this volume.

[70] For a chronology of the crisis in Mali and the development of the peace process see Sköns, E., 'The implementation of the peace process in Mali: A complex case of peacebuilding', *SIPRI Yearbook 2016*, pp. 159–88.

[71] 'Dozens killed in suicide attack on Gao military camp in northern Mali', France 24, 18 Jan. 2017.

[72] Anara, S. A., 'Mali soldiers, armed groups hold first joint patrol in northern town', Reuters, 23 Feb. 2017.

[73] 'New indefinite ceasefire between CMA and GATIA', GardaWorld, 22 Sep. 2017.

[74] United Nations, Security Council, Report of the Secretary-General on the situation in Mali, S/2017/811, 28 Sep. 2017.

Third, the Conference for National Harmony took place from 27 March to 2 April. Some armed groups and opposition political parties initially announced that they would boycott the conference, but they later decided to participate. The participants contributed to the creation of a charter for peace, unity and national reconciliation, which records some of the key root causes of the crisis and renews commitment towards their resolution.[75]

In June violence in northern Mali continued to hinder the implementation of the peace agreement and ethnic violence erupted again in central Mali. Security concerns had become as fraught as those in the north.[76] During this time, farmers from the Dogon ethnic group and pastoralist Fulani communities clashed in several villages in the Mopti region in central Mali, leaving 30 people dead.[77] In July fighting between the CMA and the Self-Defence Group of Imrad Tuareg and Allies (Groupe Aurodéfense Tuareg Imghad et Alliés, GATIA), a member of the Platform, resumed in Kidal.[78]

In terms of the peace process, on 5 September the UN Security Council established a sanctions regime on Mali consisting of a travel ban and assets freeze on individuals and entities deemed to be impeding the implementation of the 2015 peace agreement.[79] Soon after, on 20 September, the CMA and the Platform came to an agreement that included a ceasefire, the release of prisoners of war and other confidence-building measures. Reconciliation talks that took place on 5–11 October in Anéfis, Kidal region, established additional measures. First, the two parties agreed on a road map for the implementation of the agreement of 20 September and, second, they established reconciliation committees to visit the northern regions to disseminate details of the latest agreement.[80]

At the end of the year, the peace process in Mali remained fragile, with violent Islamist extremists and armed rebel groups continuing to launch attacks on Malian Government forces and UN peacekeepers. Citing an unstable atmosphere, the government decided to postpone local and regional elections originally scheduled for December 2017 until April 2018.[81]

[75] Boutellis, A. and Zahar, M.-J., 'Mali: Two years after Bamako agreement, what peace is there to keep?', IPI Global Observatory, International Peace Institute (IPI), 22 June 2017; and United Nations, Security Council, Report of the Secretary-General on the situation in Mali, S/2017/271, 30 Mar. 2017.

[76] International Crisis Group (ICG), *Central Mali: An Uprising in the Making?*, Africa Report no. 238 (ICG: Brussels, 6 July 2016); and Tobie, A., 'Central Mali: Violence, local perspectives and diverging narratives', SIPRI Insights on Peace and Security no. 2017/5, Dec. 2017.

[77] Agence France-Presse, 'Over 30 killed in ethnic violence in central Mali', *Indian Express*, 20 June 2017.

[78] Diallo, T., 'Tuareg separatists seize north Mali town in battle', Reuters, 12 July 2017.

[79] United Nations, Security Council, 'Security Council imposes sanctions on those derailing Mali peace process, unanimously adopting Resolution 2374 (2017)', SC/12979, 5 Sep. 2017; and UN Security Council Resolution 2374, 5 Sep. 2017.

[80] United Nations, Security Council, Report of the Secretary-General on the situation in Mali, S/2017/1105, 26 Dec. 2017, p. 2.

[81] United Nations, S/2017/1105 (note 80).

Presidential elections are also due to take place in July 2018 and elections to the National Assembly in December.

Armed conflict in Nigeria

After a series of military regimes, Nigeria has had a civilian elected leadership since 1999. However, the country continued to suffer from ethnic and religious divisions. These divisions were exacerbated by the insurgent group Boko Haram, which first emerged in 2002 and began its violent uprising in 2009, and growing separatist aspirations in eastern Nigeria.[82] In addition, Nigeria has suffered from periodic episodes of religious violence between Christians and Muslims since the country's return to democracy.[83]

Throughout 2017 Boko Haram's eight-year-long insurgency continued, despite Nigerian President Muhammadu Buhari's declaration in December 2016 that the group had been defeated.[84] In May 2017, 82 of the 276 schoolgirls abducted by Boko Haram from Chibok, Borno state, in 2014 were freed in a prisoner exchange.[85] With government security forces concentrating their attacks on remaining Boko Haram strongholds, the group has responded by relying more heavily on suicide attacks against security forces and civilians.[86] In November, for example, Boko Haram increased the intensity of attacks in the north-east, causing a spike in civilian casualties, including a suicide attack at a mosque in Kano that killed at least 50 people.[87] Moreover, Boko Haram has increasingly used women and children to carry out suicide attacks. Between January and August 2017, it used 83 children as suicide bombers, a fourfold increase since 2016.[88]

Insecurity in Nigeria is also fuelled by growing economic difficulties. Notably, violent conflicts between nomadic herders and sedentary farming communities have escalated in recent years. Tensions deepened further in 2017 when new legislation was adopted on cattle grazing in Benue and

[82] Obasi, N., 'Nigeria's Biafran separatist upsurge', Commentary, International Crisis Group, 4 Dec. 2015.

[83] Sampson, I. T., 'Religious violence in Nigeria', *African Journal on Conflict Resolution*, vol. 12, no. 1 (1 Apr. 2012).

[84] Gaffey, C., 'Nigeria's president says Boko Haram is finished as a fighting force', *Newsweek*, 7 Dec. 2016.

[85] 'Nigeria Chibok girls: Eighty-two freed by Boko Haram', BBC News, 7 May 2017.

[86] Ola, L. and Kingimi, A., 'Suicide bombers kill 12 in Nigeria's Borno state—police', Reuters, 19 June 2017; and Hickie, S., Abbott, C. and Clarke, M., *Remote Warfare and the Boko Haram Insurgency* (Oxford Research Group: London, Jan. 2018), p. 25.

[87] Maclean, R., 'Nigeria mosque attack: Suicide bomber kills dozens', *The Guardian*, 21 Nov. 2017.

[88] Nebehay, S. and Akwagyiram, A., 'Boko Haram Nigerian child bombings this year are quadruple 2016's: UNICEF', Reuters, 22 Aug. 2017; and ; and 'Women suicide bombers kill 27 in north-east Nigeria', *The Guardian*, 16 Aug. 2017.

Taraba states.[89] This culminated in an attack on 20 November by local vigilantes on herder settlements in Adamawa state that killed about 60 people.[90]

Armed conflict in Somalia

The current phase of civil war in Somalia, which stems from 2009, involves a conflict between the Federal Government of Somalia with the support of an AU peace operation—the AU Mission in Somalia (AMISOM)—and violent Islamist groups, notably al-Shabab.[91] Somalia has also been affected by inter-clan fighting, and violence between competing clans and federal and some state governments, including the breakaway region of Somaliland and the autonomous region of Puntland.[92]

Events in 2017 were dominated by ongoing efforts by the Federal Government and the AU, the European Union, the UN and the USA to stabilize the country politically, to improve security and to resist violent Islamist groups, notably al-Shabab. In January at least 28 people were killed in an al-Shabab attack on a hotel in Mogadishu, and over 50 Kenyan troops were killed in an al-Shabab raid on an AMISOM base in southern Somalia.[93] At least 34 people were killed and about 50 people were injured in early February by a car bomb at a market in Mogadishu. No group claimed responsibility for the attack, although al-Shabab militants were suspected of carrying it out.[94]

Also in February, Mohamed Abdullahi 'Farmajo' Mohamed, a former prime minister, was elected president for a four-year term after defeating the incumbent, Hassan Sheikh Mohamud. The election of Farmajo was perceived as an important step towards stabilizing Somalia politically and tackling the country's security crisis.[95] The presidential elections were held under a new parliamentary electoral college system that was introduced due to concerns about the viability of conducting a safe nationwide poll. In

[89] International Crisis Group, 'Watch List 2017: Second update', 20 July 2017, pp. 3–6. See also Johnson, I. and Olaniyan, A., 'The politics of renewed quest for a Biafra republic in Nigeria', *Defense & Security Analysis*, vol. 33, no. 4 (Oct. 2017), pp. 320–32.

[90] International Crisis Group (ICG), *Herders against Farmers: Nigeria's Expanding Deadly Conflict*, Africa Report no. 252 (ICG: Brussels, 19 Sep. 2017); and Anwar, K. R., '60 Adamawa Fulani killed in suspected ethnic attack', *Daily Trust* (Abuja), 21 Nov. 2017.

[91] On the role of AMISON in Somalia see chapter 3, section II, in this volume. On the UN arms embargo on Somalia see chapter 10, section II, in this volume.

[92] Loubser, H-M. and Solomon, H., 'Responding to state failure in Somalia', *Africa Review*, vol. 6, no. 1 (2014), pp. 1–17; and 'Galkayo and Somalia's dangerous faultlines', International Crisis Group, Commentary, 10 Dec. 2015.

[93] Sheikh, A. and Omar, F., 'Somali militants ram car bomb into hotel, killing 28', Reuters, 25 Jan. 2017; and Burke, J., 'Witnesses say dozens killed in al-Shabaab attack on Kenyan troops', *The Guardian*, 27 Jan. 2017.

[94] 'Somalia Mogadishu car bomb: At least 34 people killed', BBC News, 9 Feb. 2017.

[95] Burke, J., 'Somalis greet "new dawn" as US dual national wins presidency', *The Guardian*, 8 Feb. 2017; and Fantaye, D. (ed.), '2017 elections: Making Somalia great again?', *Horn of Africa Bulletin*, vol. 29, no. 1 (Jan–Feb. 2017).

April Farmajo negotiated an agreement between the Federal Government and Federal Member States on a new security architecture, announced a 60-day amnesty for al-Shabab militants and offered to open discussions with the movement's leadership.[96] While about 50 militants surrendered following the amnesty, the core of al-Shabab's leadership remained united. They responded with a campaign of devastating attacks in south-central Somalia and extended their reach into other regions of the country.[97] In June al-Shabab demonstrated their commitment to expand their presence from southern and central Somalia with an attack on a military base in Puntland that left at least 70 people dead.[98]

President Farmajo's other policies included renewed efforts to establish a Somali National Army (SNA) in order to initiate a staged withdrawal of AMISOM. At a conference convened in London in May 2017, Somalia agreed a security pact with international donors, under which, support would be provided to train Somalia's army and police.[99]

In September Turkey opened a military training base in Mogadishu to provide some of this support. It is Turkey's largest overseas military base and functions to train soldiers from the SNA.[100] By the end of the year, however, the replacement of AMISOM with the SNA was facing severe challenges as a result of political infighting between the federal and regional governments, widespread corruption and increased attacks by al-Shabab.[101] In September an attack on an SNA base left 15 people dead, and al-Shabab also increased attacks in Mogadishu, most notably with a truck bomb attack on 14 October that was estimated to have killed 587 people.[102]

In April the USA deployed an estimated 500 troops to Somalia to support the Somali Government's campaign against al-Shabab. This is the first time since 1994 that US regular forces have been sent to the country.[103] In May a member of US special forces was killed in combat with al-Shabab, marking

[96] 'Al-Shabab fighters offered amnesty as new Somali president declares war', BBC News, 6 Apr. 2017.
[97] Mahmood, O. S., 'Al-Shabaab holds its ground against Somalia's amnesty deal', Institute for Security Studies, 4 Aug. 2017.
[98] 'Al-Shabab attack Puntland army base leaves scores dead', Al Jazeera, 8 June 2017.
[99] British Department for International Development, British Foreign and Commonwealth Office and British Ministry of Defence, 'Security pact', London Somalia Conference, 11 May 2017.
[100] Hussein, A. and Coskun, O., 'Turkey opens military base in Mogadishu to train Somali soldiers', Reuters, 30 Sep. 2017.
[101] Williams, P. D., 'Somalia's African Union mission has a new exit strategy. But can troops actually leave?', Washington Post, 30 Nov. 2017.
[102] Omar, F. and Sheikh A., 'Militants attack Somali military base, kill at least 15', Reuters, 29 Sep. 2017. A Somali committee investigating the 14 Oct. attack initially gave a death toll of 358 before revising it to 512 in Dec. 2017. In the committee's final report the figure was raised to 587. See Sullivan, E., 'Mogadishu truck bomb's death toll now tops 500, probe committee says', National Public Radio, 2 Dec. 2017; and 'Committee: 587 dead in Oct 14 terror attack', Hiiraan Online, 5 Mar. 2018.
[103] 'US troops to help Somalia fight al-Shabab', BBC News, 14 Apr. 2017; and Vandiver, J., 'US escalates Somalia fight while Pentagon downplays buildup', Stars and Stripes, 17 Nov. 2017.

the first US casualty in combat in Somalia since 18 special forces personnel were killed in Mogadishu in 1993.[104] During 2017 the US also intensified its air strikes in Somalia. By early December, 30 air strikes had been carried out, twice as many as in 2016. An air strike in November is reported to have killed over 100 al-Shabab militants.[105] As the USA increased its military activity it assessed that it would take a further two years to defeat al-Shabab.[106]

In March the USA relaxed its combat rules for Somalia. Principally, it identified parts of Somalia as an 'area of active hostilities', which gives US commanders greater latitude to carry out offensive air strikes and raids by ground troops against al-Shabab militants. Where such war zone targeting rules apply there is generally an increased risk of civilian casualties.[107] At the end of 2017 discussions were reported to be under way on further changes to the US combat guidelines as a part of the escalating conflict with al-Shabab.[108] Renewed focus on combat rules occurred as reports emerged of possible civilian causalities as a result of a military raid involving US forces in August.[109] Ongoing concerns regarding corruption within the Somali security forces also led the USA to suspend some of its food and fuel assistance to the military in December.[110]

While al-Shabab posed the largest challenge to the Somali Government, Islamic State was also viewed as a threat to the country due to a potential influx of fighters from Iraq and Syria. During 2017 Islamic State was reported by the UN to be building its operations in Somalia.[111] Most notably, it established a presence within Puntland, where it was first reported to be active in 2016.[112] During the year, Islamic State claimed responsibility for attacks in Somalia as it sought to displace al-Shabab.[113] In November, for the

---

[104] Stewart, P. and Sheikh, A., 'US Navy SEAL killed in Somalia raid on militant compound', Reuters, 5 May 2017.

[105] Starr, B. and Browne, R., 'US airstrike in Somalia kills more than 100 al-Shabaab militants', CNN, 21 Nov. 2017.

[106] Savage, C. and Schmitt, E., 'Pentagon foresees at least two more years of combat in Somalia', *New York Times*, 10 Dec. 2017.

[107] Savage, C. and Schmitt, E., 'Trump eases combat rules in Somalia intended to protect civilians', *New York Times*, 30 Mar. 2017.

[108] Savage and Schmitt (note 107).

[109] Vandiver, J., 'AFRICOM seeks probe into civilian deaths in Somalia raid', *Stars and Stripes*, 13 Dec. 2017; and Kelley, K. J., 'US lawmaker presses Pentagon on reports of civilian massacre in Somalia', *Daily Nation* (Nairobi), 9 Dec. 2017.

[110] Houreld, K., 'US suspends aid to Somalia's battered military over graft', Reuters, 14 Dec. 2017.

[111] 'Islamic State "significantly growing" in Somalia: UN report', The New Arab, 11 Nov. 2017; and United Nations, Security Council, Report on Somalia of the Monitoring Group on Somalia and Eritrea, S/2017/924, 2 Nov. 2017.

[112] 'The Islamic State threat in Somalia's Puntland state', Commentary, International Crisis Group 17 Nov. 2016.

[113] Gaffey, C., 'ISIS claims Somali suicide attack as it vies with al-Shabab for recognition', *Newsweek*, 24 May 2017.

first time, the US military conducted two air strikes against Islamic State in Puntland.[114]

As 2017 came to an end, efforts to stabilize the country were further disrupted by attacks by al-Shabab. In December at least 18 police officers were killed by an assault on the police academy in Mogadishu.[115] As a result of the violence during the year, Somalia was the most conflict-affected country in sub-Saharan Africa in the first nine months of 2017, with twice as many violent incidents as South Sudan, the next most violent state.[116] In December a UN report highlighted the high level of violence towards civilians, mostly from al-Shabab, but also involving AMISOM forces.[117]

Armed conflict in South Sudan

South Sudan gained independence from Sudan on 9 July 2011 after a 2005 agreement that ended one of Africa's longest-running civil wars. A post-independence civil war in 2013–15 displaced 2.2 million people and, despite a 2015 peace agreement, which stipulated a power-sharing government, the legacy of conflict continues to threaten one of the world's newest countries.

The armed conflict is waged primarily between two groups—the Government of South Sudan and its allies, led by Salva Kiir (an ethnic Dinka), and the Sudan People's Liberation Army-in-Opposition (SPLA-IO) and the Nuer White Army, led by former vice-president Riek Machar (an ethnic Nuer). Although the civil war has been fought largely between the Dinka and Nuer ethnic groups, underlying conflict dynamics vary considerably across the country and opposition groups have become more fractured and localized.[118]

In February 2017 the UN declared a famine in South Sudan as a result of the ongoing armed conflict and collapsing economy.[119] As of April 2017 the conflict among the different factions had resulted in over 1.9 million internally displaced people, with 224 000 fleeing to bases of the UN Mission in South Sudan (UNMISS), and 1.6 million refugees in neighbouring countries. This

[114] 'US launches air strikes against Isis fighters in Somalia for first time', *The Independent*, 3 Nov. 2017.
[115] 'Somalia suicide bomber kills police at Mogadishu academy', BBC News, 14 Dec. 2017.
[116] As well as the highest number of organized violent events (1537 events), Somalia had the highest number of fatalities (3287 fatalities) in 2017. South Sudan had 686 organized violent events. Kishi, R., 'Somalia—September 2017 update', Armed Conflict Location & Event Data Project (ACLED), 22 Sep. 2017.
[117] Office of the UN High Commissioner for Human Rights (OHCHR), 'Somalia conflict exacting terrible toll on civilians—UN report Al Shabaab responsible for most civilian casualties', 11 Dec. 2017; and Kelley, K. J., 'Kenya disputes UN claim that KDF killed 40 Somali civilians', *Daily Nation* (Nairobi), 11 Dec. 2017.
[118] Kalpakian, J. V., 'Peace agreements in a near-permanent civil war: Learning from Sudan and South Sudan', *South African Journal of International Affairs*, vol. 24, no. 1 (2017), p. 11; and International Crisis Group, 'Instruments of pain (II): Conflict and famine in South Sudan', Crisis Group Africa Briefing no. 124, 26 Apr. 2017).
[119] Quinn, B., 'Famine declared in South Sudan', *The Guardian*, 20 Feb. 2017.

represents the largest national exodus in sub-Saharan Africa in 20 years.[120] According to Payton Knopf of the United States Institute of Peace, five civil wars are now unfolding within the country's broader conflict: 'a war of resistance against Kiir's regime in Juba by the population of the surrounding Greater Equatoria region; a land contest between the Dinka and the Shilluk in Upper Nile; an intra-Nuer war in Unity; a drive to establish Dinka primacy in Greater Bahr el Ghazal; and diversionary "crises of convenience" in Lakes and Jonglei that have been exploited by Kiir and his allies'.[121]

In May President Kiir declared a unilateral ceasefire and launched a national dialogue process.[122] Nevertheless, in response to continued fighting and harassment of UN peacekeepers and aid workers, in November the USA threatened to place additional sanctions against the country, having already imposed sanctions against three senior South Sudanese officials in September. Within the UN Security Council, however, no agreement could be reached on imposing a UN arms embargo on South Sudan.[123] In October Jean-Pierre Lacroix, the UN Under-Secretary-General for Peacekeeping Operations, warned the UN Security Council that the country was sliding into chaos and escalating violence.[124]

As negotiators convened in Addis Ababa, Ethiopia, for another round of peace talks in December, government forces captured the town of Lasu, Central Equatoria state, which was the southern headquarters of the SPLA-IO. The fall of Lasu further splintered the opposition groups that had lost significant ground to the government in recent months.[125] Despite the continued fighting, the government and opposition armed groups signed a ceasefire agreement in Addis Ababa on 21 December.[126] The UK, Norway and the USA, which form a 'troika' that supported the 2005 agreement that led to the independence of South Sudan, welcomed the agreement. The next phase of the negotiations is expected to focus on a revised power-sharing arrangement in the lead up to new elections.[127]

---

[120] International Crisis Group (note 118). On UNMISS see chapter 3, section II, in this volume.
[121] Knopf, P., 'South Sudan's conflict and famine', Testimony before the US Senate Foreign Relations Subcommittee on Africa and Global Health Policy, United States Institute of Peace, 26 July 2017.
[122] 'South Sudan's Kiir declares unilateral ceasefire, prisoner release', Reuters, 22 May 2017.
[123] Nichols, M., 'US threatens South Sudan action, Russia warns against UN measures', Reuters, 28 Nov. 2017. On threats to impose a UN arms embargo see chapter 10, section II, in this volume.
[124] Gladstone, R., 'UN peacekeeping chief issues warning on South Sudan', New York Times, 17 Oct. 2017.
[125] Patinkin, J. and Moore, J., 'South Sudan army makes push against rebels as peace talks begin', New York Times, 19 Dec. 2017.
[126] Maasho, A., 'South Sudan government, rebel groups sign ceasefire', Reuters, 21 Dec. 2017.
[127] British Foreign and Commonwealth Office, 'The Troika statement on South Sudan', 21 Dec. 2017.

3. Peace operations and conflict management

Overview

In contrast to 2016, 2017 was a hectic year for peace operations, both in the field and at headquarters, particularly for the United Nations. The fall in the total number of personnel deployed in peace operations, which began in 2012 with the drawdown of the International Security Assistance Force (ISAF), continued in 2017. The total number of personnel deployed in the field (145 911) declined by 4.5 per cent compared to 2016. Although UN deployments had been on the rise before 2016, they continued to fall in 2017, by 7.6 per cent, whereas the number of personnel in non-UN operations increased by 2.3 per cent to 47 557 (see section I).

There were 63 peace operations active during 2017, one more than in 2016. Three UN peace operations closed: the UN Operation in Côte d'Ivoire (UNOCI), the UN Mission in Colombia (UNMC) and the UN Stabilization Mission in Haiti (MINUSTAH). The latter two were replaced by smaller missions: the UN Verification Mission in Colombia (UNVMC) and the UN Mission for Justice Support in Haiti (MINUJUSTH). Only one non-UN mission closed during the year—the Regional Assistance Mission to the Solomon Islands (RAMSI)—while three new non-UN operations were established: the Economic Community of West African States (ECOWAS) Mission in the Gambia (ECOMIG); the European Union (EU) Advisory Mission in support of Security Sector Reform in Iraq (EUAM Iraq); and the Southern African Development Community (SADC) Preventive Mission in the Kingdom of Lesotho (SAPMIL) (see section II).

Under the sustaining peace agenda, UN peace operations are giving increased attention to political processes, peace building and conflict prevention. In so doing, they increasingly encounter tensions over national sovereignty and operate on the boundary of host-state consent. This is already evident in Burundi, South Sudan and the Democratic Republic of the Congo, where host governments see UN efforts as an infringement of their sovereignty and respond by obstructing deployment. Outside the UN system, much more has been possible. Host governments have tended to favour predominantly military solutions in support of their authority, such as the Group of Five for the Sahel (G5 Sahel) Joint Force (Force Conjointe des Etats du G5 Sahel, FC-G5S) and the Multinational Joint Task Force (MNJTF) against Boko Haram. In the cases of Gambia and Lesotho, regional organizations were able to intervene in small countries, even though the amount of host government support was debatable in the former.

Although the UN clearly remains the principal actor in peace operations, the two non-UN operations deployed by African regional economic communities show how African actors are claiming an increasing role on the peace operations stage. This is also reflected in the establishment of the FC-G5S, a multilateral non-peace operation that falls into the grey zone outside the SIPRI definition of multilateral peace operations.

Peacekeeping reform, including implementation of the report by the UN High-level Independent Panel on Peace Operations, continued to be discussed in the General Assembly and the Security Council. At times, this discussion was overshadowed by two other developments: the greater insecurity of person-nel deployed in UN peace operations, and the efforts by the administration of United States President Donald J. Trump to drastically reduce the UN peace-keeping budget.

In previous years, peacekeeper fatalities linked to hostile acts had primarily been a challenge for the UN Multidimensional Integrated Stabilization Mission in Mali (MINUSMA). In 2017, however, the UN Multidimensional Integrated Stabilization Mission in the Central African Republic (MINUSCA) and the UN Stabilization Mission in the Democratic Republic of the Congo (MONUSCO) also faced substantial losses. A particular low point was the attack on a MONUSCO Company Operating Base at Semuliki, North Kivu, on 7 December, in which 15 Tanzanian peacekeepers were killed and at least 53 injured. Overall, the UN witnessed a dramatic escalation in fatalities linked to hostile acts—in both absolute terms (from 34 in 2016 to 61 in 2017) and as a ratio of the number of personnel deployed (from 0.31 to 0.61 per 1000). An independent review into the security of peacekeepers, led by Lieutenant General Carlos Alberto dos Santos Cruz, left one main question unanswered: How would the UN generate the agile and mobile forces needed for the more robust and proactive force pos-ture required to deal with these more challenging mission environments?

In 2017, UN peace operations, like African peace operations, could no longer be certain of 'predictable and sustainable funding'. The budget cuts sought by the Trump administration, in particular, meant that the UN had to rethink its strategy in many operations. A number of finance-contributing countries hoped that these budget cuts might be used pragmatically to strengthen peacekeeping reform. However, the effects of 'salami-slicing tactics' on some operations, such as MONUSCO, and of more substantial drawdowns in other operations, such as the African Union/UN Hybrid Operation in Darfur (UNAMID), might put peacekeepers more at risk and leave populations more vulnerable. If so, it raises the question: Is it realistic to expect the UN to continue to do more with less, and is it worth taking the risk?

JAÏR VAN DER LIJN

I. Global trends and developments in peace operations

TIMO SMIT AND JAÏR VAN DER LIJN

Multilateral peace operations in 2017

Sixty-three multilateral peace operations were active during 2017 (see figure 3.1).[1] This was one more than in 2016 and the second-highest number of operations conducted in the period 2008–17.

Among the 63 operations were 5 new missions and 4 that terminated during the year. The remaining 54 missions were active for the entire year. The new missions were, in chronological order, the Economic Community of West African States (ECOWAS) Mission in the Gambia (ECOMIG), the United Nations Verification Mission in Colombia (UNVMC), the UN Mission for Justice Support in Haiti (MINUJUSTH), the European Union (EU) Advisory Mission in support of Security Sector Reform in Iraq (EUAM Iraq) and the Southern African Development Community (SADC) Preventive Mission in the Kingdom of Lesotho (SAPMIL). The missions that terminated during 2017 were, in chronological order, the Regional Assistance Mission to the Solomon Islands (RAMSI), the UN Operation in Côte d'Ivoire (UNOCI), the UN Mission in Colombia (UNMC) and the UN Stabilization Mission in Haiti (MINUSTAH).[2] The closure of these 4 missions meant that there were 59 ongoing multilateral peace operations at the end of the year.

Multilateral peace operations were deployed to 42 countries and territories in 2017.[3] This included two countries—Gambia and Lesotho—that did not host peace operations in the preceding year. The Solomon Islands and Côte d'Ivoire no longer hosted any peace operations following the closure of RAMSI and UNOCI in mid-2017. Nineteen countries hosted more than one peace operation. Mali hosted 4 peace operations in 2017—more than any other country.

---

[1] The quantitative analysis draws on data collected by SIPRI to examine trends in peace operations. According to SIPRI's definition, a multilateral peace operation must have the stated intention of: (a) serving as an instrument to facilitate the implementation of peace agreements already in place; (b) supporting a peace process; or (c) assisting conflict prevention or peacebuilding efforts. Good offices, fact-finding or electoral assistance missions, and missions comprising non-resident individuals or teams of negotiators are not included (see section IV). Since all SIPRI data is reviewed on a continual basis and adjusted when more accurate information becomes available, the statistics in this chapter may not always fully correspond with data found in previous editions of the SIPRI Yearbook or other SIPRI publications.

[2] For a description of the missions that opened and terminated in 2017 see section II.

[3] Including Abyei (Sudan), Western Sahara and the Palestinian Territories.

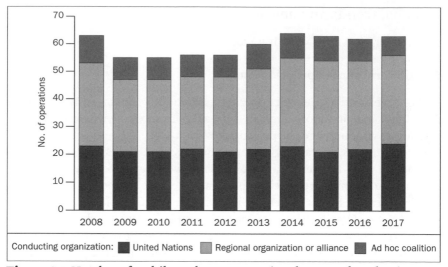

Figure 3.1. Number of multilateral peace operations by type of conducting organization, 2008–17

Trends in personnel deployments

The total number of personnel deployed in all multilateral peace operations decreased by 4.5 per cent over the course of 2017—from 152 822 to 145 911— and fell below 150 000 for the first time in the 2008–17 period (see figure 3.2).[4] This was a continuation of a steady decline that began in 2016, after overall personnel deployments had remained relatively stable during 2015 at around 162 000. Of those deployed in 2017, 94 per cent were uniformed personnel (125 803 military and 11 846 police) while 8262 were international civilian personnel.

Personnel deployments in multilateral peace operations were much higher in the period 2008–14, but this was primarily due to the North Atlantic Treaty Organization (NATO)-led International Security Assistance Force (ISAF) in Afghanistan. ISAF inflated the figures to such an extent— it reached its maximum strength of over 130 000 personnel in 2010—that this disguised underlying trends. The number of personnel deployed in all multilateral peace operations fell sharply as NATO reduced its footprint in Afghanistan to approximately 13 000 between 2012 and the end of 2014,

---

[4] The analyses of personnel levels in this chapter are based on estimates of the number of international personnel (i.e. military, police and international civilian staff) deployed at the end of each month in each of the multilateral peace operations that were active in the period Jan. 2008 to Dec. 2017. In previous editions of the SIPRI Yearbook, similar analyses used annual snapshot data on the number of international personnel in multilateral peace operations at the end of each year or, in the case of an operation terminated during a calendar year, on the number at their closure. Consequently, the data in this chapter does not exactly match data used in previous editions of the SIPRI Yearbook.

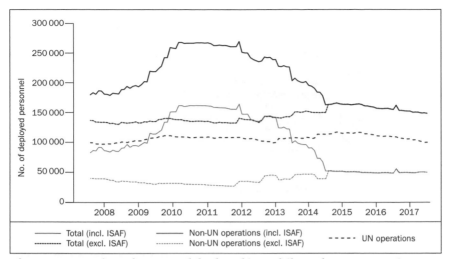

Figure 3.2. Number of personnel deployed in multilateral peace operations, 2008–17

ISAF = International Security Assistance Force.

Note: Year marker indicates monthly data at the mid-year point (June).

when ISAF terminated. However, in the same period the total number of personnel in all other multilateral peace operations increased by 13 per cent, from approximately 130 000 to more than 147 000.

The decrease in the total number of personnel deployed in multilateral peace operations after 2015 was caused primarily by a steady decline in personnel deployments by the UN. The number of personnel in UN peace operations increased quite significantly between 2012 and 2015, from less than 100 000 to nearly 115 000, but subsequently fell to 98 354 by December 2017—approximately the same level as before it began to rise five years earlier. The decrease in the number of personnel in UN peace operations in 2016–17 resulted primarily from reductions in the strength of the UN/African Union (AU) Hybrid Operation in Darfur (UNAMID), the UN Organization Stabilization Mission in the Democratic Republic of the Congo (MONUSCO) and the UN Mission in Liberia (UNMIL), as well as the gradual departure of peacekeepers from Côte d'Ivoire and Haiti prior to the closure of UNOCI and MINUSTAH. Although some of these reductions in mission strength were justified by the conditions on the ground, financial constraints also played a role as significant cuts to the UN peacekeeping budget compelled the UN Secretariat to reduce the number of peacekeepers in the field.

The number of personnel in non-UN peace operations—that is multilateral peace operations conducted by regional organizations and alliances or by ad hoc coalitions of states—remained within the range of

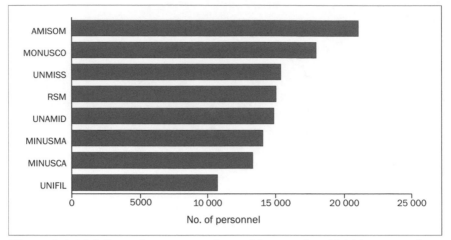

Figure 3.3. Multilateral peace operations with more than 10 000 personnel on 31 December 2017

AMISOM = AU Mission in Somalia; MONUSCO = UN Organization Stabilization Mission in the Democratic Republic of the Congo; UNMISS = UN Mission in South Sudan; RSM = Resolute Support Mission; UNAMID = AU/UN Hybrid Operation in Darfur; MINUSMA = UN Multidimensional Integrated Stabilization Mission in Mali; MINUSCA = UN Multidimensional Integrated Stabilization Mission in the Central African Republic; UNIFIL = UN Interim Force in Lebanon.

45 000–50 000 in 2014–17. Deployments in these operations first decreased somewhat in 2014–15, but increased by 2.3 per cent in 2017 from 46 432 to 47 557. This included a noticeable, albeit brief, peak in January 2017 as a result of the deployment of ECOMIG, which had an initial strength of 7000 before it quickly reconfigured into a much smaller mission of 500 after the post-electoral crisis regarding the succession of the Gambian presidency was resolved.

The AU Mission in Somalia (AMISOM) remained the largest multilateral peace operation throughout 2017. At the end of the year it had a total strength of 21 039 personnel. Besides AMISOM, seven operations fielded more than 10 000 personnel (see figure 3.3). These were, in decreasing order of size, the UN Organization Stabilization Mission in the Democratic Republic of the Congo (MONUSCO), the UN Mission in South Sudan (UNMISS), the NATO-led Resolute Support Mission (RSM), the AU/UN Hybrid Operation in Darfur (UNAMID), the UN Multidimensional Integrated Stabilization Mission in Mali (MINUSMA), the UN Multidimensional Integrated Stabilization Mission in the Central African Republic (MINUSCA), and the UN Interim Force in Lebanon (UNIFIL). During the year, UNMISS and the RSM surpassed UNAMID to become the third- and fourth-largest operations, respectively, while MINUSMA surpassed MINUSCA to become the sixth-largest mission. At the end of 2017, these eight missions alone accounted for 84 per cent of all personnel deployed in multilateral peace operations worldwide.

Organizations conducting peace operations

As in previous years, the UN was the organization that conducted the most multilateral peace operations and deployed the largest number of personnel in 2017. The UN led 24 of the 63 multilateral peace operations active in 2017, which is two more than in 2016. Three of these missions—UNOCI, MINUSTAH and the UNMC—terminated during the year. MINUSTAH and the UNMC were immediately succeeded by the new UN missions, MINUJUSTH and the UNVMC (see section II). Although the number of personnel deployed in UN peace operations fell by 7.6 per cent to 98 354, the UN accounted for two-thirds of all personnel in multilateral peace operations at the end of 2017 (compared to 70 per cent at the end of 2016).

Regional organizations and alliances were responsible for 32 of the 63 multilateral peace operations active in 2017. At the end of 2017, these actors deployed 44 902 personnel in multilateral peace operations, which accounted for 31 per cent of the total number of personnel deployed. The number of personnel in peace operations led by regional organizations and alliances increased by 2.7 per cent during 2017.

African regional organizations conducted seven multilateral peace operations. The AU conducted four and remained the regional organization that deployed the most personnel in its missions. The number of personnel in AU missions decreased by 4.1 per cent during 2017, from 22 004 to 21 104, as a result of the withdrawal of 1000 troops from AMISOM, which continued to account for nearly all the personnel deployed in AU-led peace operations. ECOWAS conducted two peace operations, one more than in 2016. The number of personnel in ECOWAS operations increased during 2017 as a result of the deployment of ECOMIG, from 543 to 977. SADC conducted one peace operation, SAPMIL, which it deployed to Lesotho in December 2017.

The EU, NATO and the Organization for Security and Co-operation in Europe (OSCE) led 23 missions and operations that qualified as multilateral peace operations. The number of personnel deployed in the two NATO-led operations, the RSM and the Kosovo Force (KFOR), increased by 8.3 per cent in 2017, from 17 621 to 19 077. The EU conducted 12 peace operations in the framework of its Common Security and Defence Policy (CSDP). EUAM Iraq was launched in November 2017. The number of personnel in EU peace operations increased by 2.7 per cent in 2017, from 2395 to 2460. The OSCE conducted nine peace operations. At the end of the year it deployed 1000 personnel in these missions, which was almost exactly the same number as one year earlier.

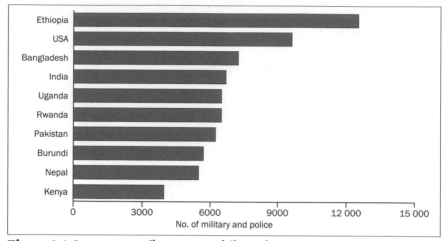

Figure 3.4. Largest contributors to multilateral peace operations on 31 December 2017

The Pacific Islands Forum and the Organization of American States conducted one peace operation each in 2017. These were RAMSI and the Mission to Assist the Peace Process in Colombia (MAPP/OEA), respectively. RAMSI terminated in mid-2017. There were no notable changes in the composition of MAPP/OEA.

Finally, seven multilateral peace operations were conducted by ad hoc coalitions of states—one fewer than in 2016. The number of personnel deployed in peace operations by such non-standing coalitions decreased by 2.5 per cent during 2017, from 2722 to 2655. This decrease resulted primarily from the completion of the reconfiguration of the Multinational Force and Observers (MFO) in the Sinai Peninsula, which was the largest ad hoc peace operation in 2017, even though its force was reduced from 1383 to 1300.

Troop and police contributions

Ethiopia, the United States and Bangladesh were the three largest contributors of uniformed personnel (both military and police) to multilateral peace operations in 2017 (see figure 3.4). The ten largest contributors accounted for approximately half of all uniformed personnel in multilateral peace operations as of 31 December. The same ten countries were also the largest contributors in 2016.

Ethiopia has been the largest contributor of uniformed personnel to multilateral peace operations since it joined AMISOM in 2014. Ethiopia was also the largest contributor of uniformed personnel to UN peace operations. In December 2017, Ethiopia contributed 12 534 uniformed personnel to peace operations: 8420 to UN peace operations and 4114 to AMISOM. It was a major contributor to AMISOM, UNAMID, the UN Interim Security Force for Abyei (UNISFA) and UNMISS, all of which are active in neighbouring countries. Except for one staff officer in MINUSMA, all the Ethiopian troops and police were deployed in these four operations.

As the second-largest contributor of uniformed personnel to multilateral peace operations in 2017, the USA was the only Western country to rank among the 10 largest contributors. The USA deployed 9627 uniformed personnel, an increase of around 1500 on the year before. The increase in US contributions to peace operations resulted from a decision by the US Government to deploy more troops to Afghanistan, among other things to reinforce the NATO-led RSM (see section II). In addition to the RSM, the USA was a major contributor to the NATO-led KFOR and the MFO in the Sinai Peninsula. It contributed only 55 military and police personnel to UN peace operations.

Bangladesh ended 2017 as the third-largest contributor of uniformed personnel to multilateral peace operations. During the year it surpassed India and Pakistan—the third- and fourth-largest contributors in December 2016—by increasing its contribution from 6862 to 7246 uniformed personnel. In the same period, India's contribution decreased from 7710 to 6697 and Pakistan's decreased from 7156 to 6238, which made them the fourth- and seventh-largest contributors of uniformed personnel, respectively. Nepal—the other South Asian country in the top ten—maintained its position as the ninth-largest contributor. Bangladesh, India, Nepal and Pakistan only contributed to UN peace operations.

The other countries in the top ten were Burundi, Kenya, Rwanda and Uganda. Rwanda was the sixth-largest contributor to multilateral peace operations in 2017 and the fourth-largest contributor to UN peace operations. Although Burundi, Kenya and Uganda contributed uniformed personnel to UN missions, their rankings are predominantly the result of their large contingents in AMISOM. The fact that five African countries were ranked among the ten largest contributors to multilateral peace operations illustrates how significant their role has become.[5]

Fatalities among peace operations personnel

Several of the multilateral peace operations active in 2017 were deployed amid ongoing or deteriorating situations of armed conflict in areas where viable peace agreements and state authority were either absent or highly fragile and contested. A number of missions that operated in these

---

[5] Avezov, X., Van der Lijn, J. and Smit, T., *African Directions: Towards an Equitable Partnership in Peace Operations* (SIPRI: Stockholm, Feb. 2017).

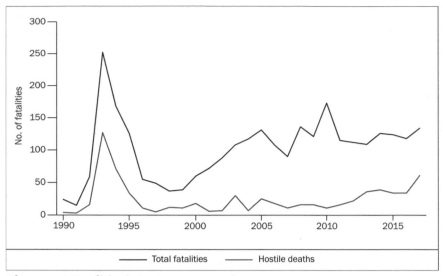

Figure 3.5. Fatalities in UN peace operations, 1990–2017

environments faced sustained threats and deliberate attacks from non-state armed groups and other spoilers (see section II).

It continues to be challenging for UN peace operations to adapt to these new realities on the ground. This has been reflected in the increase in the number of hostile deaths—that is, fatalities resulting from malicious acts—among personnel in UN peace operations in recent years. The number of hostile deaths was significantly higher in the period 2013–17 than in any other period since 1993–95, when the UN suffered exceptional losses in Bosnia and Herzegovina, Cambodia and Somalia (see figure 3.5). The ratio of hostile deaths per 1000 personnel was also markedly higher in 2013–17 than in earlier periods, albeit that similar or even higher ratios were regularly reported in the 1990s and occasionally in the 2000s (see figure 3.6). One caveat is that half of all the UN peacekeepers killed as a result of violent acts in the period 2013–16 were serving in MINUSMA, which since it was established in mid-2013 has suffered more hostile deaths than any other contemporary UN mission. In fact, the ratio of hostile deaths in all UN peace operations excluding MINUSMA in 2013–16 was not unusually high compared to other years—and in 2016 it was even the lowest in the entire 1990–2017 period.

This was clearly not the case in 2017, however, as UN peace operations witnessed a fairly dramatic increase in hostile deaths in both absolute and relative terms. UN peace operations suffered 61 hostile deaths in 2017, of which 58 were of uniformed personnel. The ratio of hostile deaths among uniformed personnel—0.61 per 1000—was twice as high in 2017 as it was in 2016. Both the number and the ratio of hostile deaths were significantly higher in 2017 than in any year since 1994. Excluding MINUSMA, the ratio

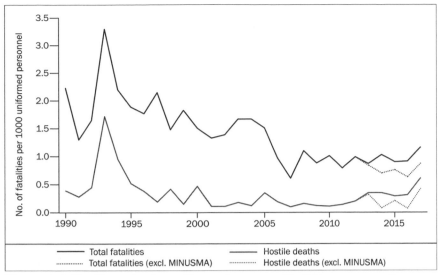

Figure 3.6. Fatality ratios for uniformed personnel in UN peace operations, 1990–2017

MINUSMA = UN Multidimensional Integrated Stabilization Mission in Mali

of hostile deaths rose from 0.07 per 1000 to 0.42 per 1000—the highest since 2000. In addition, for the first time since 1993, hostile deaths made up more than half of all fatalities (52 per cent). All the hostile deaths among personnel in UN peace operations occurred in Africa, and the vast majority of the peacekeepers killed by violent acts were themselves from African countries.[6] All but one of the 61 victims of hostile deaths in 2017 were deployed in MINUSCA, MINUSMA or MONUSCO.

These worrying developments further aggravated concerns about the safety and security of UN peacekeepers and their ability to deliver their mandates in complex security environments. The UN Secretary-General therefore appointed retired Lt General Carlos Alberto dos Santos Cruz of Brazil, in November 2017, to lead an independent review of the hostile deaths and injuries of UN peacekeepers, and suggest measures to reduce them. The review concluded that the increase in hostile deaths in recent years 'is not a spike but rather a rise to a continuing plateau'.[7] The Cruz Report urged the UN and contributors to UN peacekeeping operations to accept and adapt to the changed nature of mission environments in which challenges are multifaceted, complex and fluid, and in which blue helmets can no longer count on their status as an impartial force for protection against the security

---

[6] Dos Santos Cruz, C. A., Phillips, W. R. and Cusimano, S., *Improving Security of United Nations Peacekeepers: We Need to Change the Way we are Doing Business* (United Nations Independent Report: New York, 19 Dec. 2017), p. 5.

[7] Dos Santos Cruz, Phillips and Cusimano (note 6), p. 5.

threats that emanate from this. To face up to these challenges, the report emphasized, among other things, that stronger leadership, less risk-averse strategies and tactics, and a more flexible interpretation of the guiding principles of peacekeeping should allow proactive and pre-emptive use of force by missions against combatants that might otherwise threaten them.[8]

The UN peacekeeping budget

In addition to developments in the field, the year also saw a number of discussions and developments regarding UN peace operations in the Security Council and the General Assembly in New York. These were held under the shadow of the Trump administration's intention to cut its spending on UN peacekeeping by as much as 40 per cent.[9] This was to be achieved by reducing the US share of assessed contributions to the UN peacekeeping budget from 28 per cent to 25 per cent, and by dramatically reducing this budget overall.[10] With this goal, the US Ambassador to the UN, Nikki Haley, called for a review of the 16 UN peacekeeping missions, arguing that some might no longer be useful, while others might need to be reconfigured, shrunk or closed down.[11]

A US concept note argued that: 'The United Nations becomes trapped in these frozen conflicts, and peacekeeping missions that were initially conceived to provide temporary security to allow space for political solutions to take hold instead deploy for years without clear mandates or exit plans'.[12] Haley's call resonated with a number of finance-contributing countries and the Secretary-General, as they perceived it as an opportunity to make UN peacekeeping operations fit for purpose. While they may not favour sudden cuts in the peacekeeping budget, they would like to see the UN focus more on conflict prevention and supporting political processes.[13]

The outcome of the negotiations in 2017 was that the UN peacekeeping budget was reduced from nearly $7.9 billion for the period 2016–17 to around $6.8 billion for the period 2017–18. The share of US assessed contributions determined in 2015 for the period up to 2018 decreased from slightly over to slightly under 28.5 per cent. As a consequence, the US assessed contribution

---

[8] Dos Santos Cruz, Phillips and Cusimano (note 6), section III, pp. 9–17.

[9] Lynch, C., '$1 billion in cuts to UN Peacekeeping', *Foreign Policy*, 23 Mar. 2017.

[10] US Senate Foreign Relations Committee, Hearing Transcript, Hearing on the nomination of Gov. Haley to be US Ambassador to the United Nations, 18 Jan. 2017.

[11] United Nations, Security Council, Seventy-second year, 7918th meeting, United Nations Peacekeeping Operations, S/PV.7918, 6 Apr. 2017.

[12] United Nations, Security Council, Annex to the letter dated 4 April 2017 from the Permanent Representative of the United States of America to the United Nations addressed to the Secretary-General, 'Concept paper: Thematic debate, Peacekeeping operations review', S/2017/287, 5 Apr. 2017.

[13] Gowan, R., 'Why Trump could speed up—and complicate—inevitable UN Peacekeeping reforms', *World Politics Review*, 27 Mar. 2017.

for the budget period 2017–18 decreased by some $300 million, or 14 per cent, compared to the previous budget period.[14] While the Trump administration continues to seek a further reduction in the US contribution to the peace-keeping budget, in practice the result will depend on diplomatic outcomes and it is likely to push less hard for cuts to operational costs than in 2017.[15]

UN peacekeeping reform

The term 'peacekeeping reform' has been used to describe discussions on a variety of adjustments both within the UN Secretariat and in the field, following the 2015 report of the High-level Independent Panel on Peace Operations (HIPPO) and that of the Secretary-General on the implementa-tion of the HIPPO report's recommendations.[16] It encompasses fundamental questions similar to those raised by the US administration, such as how to continue to operate where there is no political process to support, how to guard against mission creep, and how to act when the strategic consent of the host government is absent or weak. In addition there are questions about how to ensure that there is an exit strategy, particularly if the political pro-cess breaks down, and whether there are any alternatives to peacekeeping operations in such cases.[17] Peacekeeping reform also includes more oper-ational areas, such as those suggested by the Permanent Representative of Ethiopia to the UN: (a) assessing the impact of reforms implemented over the past two years on the performance of missions; (b) enhancing the role of the Security Council in ensuring implementation and follow-up; (c) the Secretary-General's efforts to reform the UN peace and security architec-ture; (d) the status of member state commitments in terms of force genera-tion and the deployment of critical capabilities, and remaining gaps; (e) the new strategic partnership between the UN and the AU; and (f) support for AU-led peace support operations.[18] Discussions on all these topics are likely

---

[14] United Nations, General Assembly, Scale of assessments for the apportionment of the expenses of United Nations peacekeeping operations: Implementation of General Assembly resolutions 55/235 and 55/236, Report of the Secretary-General, A/70/331/Add.1, 28 Dec. 2015; United Nations, General Assembly, Fifth Committee, Administrative and budgetary aspects of the financing of the United Nations peacekeeping operations: Approved resources for peacekeeping operations for the period from 1 July 2016 to 30 June 2017, A/C.5/70/24, 22 June 2016; and United Nations, General Assembly, Fifth Committee, Administrative and budgetary aspects of the financing of the United Nations peacekeeping operations: Approved resources for peacekeeping operations for the period from 1 July 2017 to 30 June 2018, A/C.5/71/24, 30 June 2017.

[15] US Department of State, Congressional Budget Justification: Department of State, Foreign Operations, and Related Programs, fiscal year 2019.

[16] See Van der Lijn, J., 'A year of reviews', *SIPRI Yearbook 2016*, pp. 294–304.

[17] United Nations, Security Council, 'Letter dated 4 April 2017 from the Permanent Represent-ative of the United States of America to the United Nations addressed to the Secretary-General', S/2017/287, 5 Apr. 2017.

[18] United Nations, Security Council, 'Letter dated 22 August 2017 from the Permanent Repre-sentative of Ethiopia to the United Nations addressed to the Secretary-General', S/2017/766, 12 Sep.

to continue in the coming years but, given the current momentum, some progress may be expected in 2018.

One of the main items on this agenda, where progress was made in 2017, was the Secretary-General's intention to reform the UN Secretariat to reinforce the peace and security architecture. The internal review team he established on taking office, to study existing proposals and present options for further improvement of structures and working methods, made five core proposals: (*a*) a restructuring of the Department of Political Affairs, the Department of Peacekeeping Operations (DPKO) and the Peacebuilding Support Office, to create a Department of Political and Peacebuilding Affairs and a Department of Peace Operations; (*b*) the creation of a single political-operational structure under Assistant Secretaries-General with regional responsibilities, reporting to the Under-Secretaries-General for Political and Peacebuilding Affairs and for Peace Operations; (*c*) the establishment of a Standing Principals' Group of the Under-Secretary-General for Political and Peacebuilding Affairs and the Under-Secretary-General for Peace Operations; (*d*) enhanced coherence and coordination across the peace and security pillar; and (*e*) the introduction of non-structural changes to the way the peace and security pillar works on a daily basis.[19] The General Assembly supported the Secretary-General's vision of reform and asked him to formulate a comprehensive proposal for its implementation.[20]

Sustaining peace and peace operations

The concept of 'sustaining peace' has its origins in the 2015 report by the Advisory Group of Experts on its review of the UN peacebuilding architecture.[21] It was also used by HIPPO.[22] In 2017, the Security Council gave special attention to the relationship between peace operations and sustaining peace in a presidential statement. The Council broadly understood the concept as 'a goal and a process to build a common vision of a society, ensuring that the needs of all segments of the population are taken into account, which encompasses activities aimed at preventing the outbreak, escalation, continuation and recurrence of conflict, addressing root causes, assisting parties

2017; and UN Security Council Resolution 2378, 20 Sep. 2017.

[19] United Nations, General Assembly, Strengthening of the United Nations system, 'United Nations reform: Measures and proposals', Restructuring of the United Nations peace and security pillar, Report of the Secretary-General, A/72/525, 13 Oct. 2017.

[20] United Nations, General Assembly Resolution 72/199, 19 Jan. 2018.

[21] On sustaining peace see Caparini, M. and Milante, G., 'Sustaining peace: The new overarching United Nations framework', *SIPRI Yearbook 2017*, pp. 220–32.

[22] Advisory Group of Experts, The challenge of sustaining peace: Report of the Advisory Group of Experts for the 2015 review of the United Nations peacebuilding architecture, 29 June 2015; and United Nations, General Assembly and Security Council, 'Identical letters dated 17 June 2015 from the Secretary-General addressed to the President of the General Assembly and the President of the Security Council', A/70/95-S/2015/446, 17 June 2015.

to conflict to end hostilities, ensuring national reconciliation, and moving towards recovery, reconstruction and development'.[23]

The Security Council stressed that sustaining peace requires all three pillars of the UN to be involved and that peacekeeping should grasp the challenges of peacebuilding and sustaining peace at the start of a mission through integrated assessment and planning. It expressed its intention to consider the following elements when mandating peace operations: (*a*) an assessment of mandate implementation in all its dimensions, including when relevant peacebuilding and sustaining peace; (*b*) support for a consultation process within the mission to support national ownership; (*c*) the existence of clear goals and objectives for peacebuilding and sustaining peace; (*d*) periodic strategic integrated analyses of opportunities and challenges for national and local authorities to build and sustain peace; (*e*) progress in the political and operational delivery of mandates in a coherent manner; (*f*) clarity regarding the roles and responsibilities of peace operations and other actors to ensure effective integration of effort and maximum contribution to addressing the root causes of conflict; and (*g*) the existence of an exit strategy that lays the foundations for a long-term and sustainable peace.[24] Similar efforts in the past, however, have shown that many of these elements are difficult to achieve and progress can only be made slowly.

Ecological footprint, cultural heritage and gender mainstreaming

In 2017, the Security Council paid increased attention to three topics in relation to peace operations: (*a*) managing their environmental impact, (*b*) their role in protecting cultural heritage, and (*c*) their contribution to improving gender relations and gender mainstreaming.

With 98 354 UN peace operations personnel in the field, the Security Council has increasingly emphasized the importance of managing the environmental impact of peace operations. The topic was first mentioned in 2013, in the mandates of MINUSMA and UNAMID, and again in 2015 in relation to UN support to AMISOM. In 2017, the topic was stressed in the mandate renewals of the missions in the Central African Republic and the Democratic Republic of the Congo, and the Security Council addressed it in a separate press release.[25] At the same time, however, the USA objected to the inclusion of the term 'climate change' in a resolution on the Lake Chad Basin.[26]

---

[23] United Nations, Security Council, Statement by the President of the Security Council, S/PRST/2017/27, 21 Dec. 2017.

[24] United Nations (note 23).

[25] UN Security Council Resolution 2387, 15 Nov. 2017; UN Security Council Resolution 2348, 31 Mar. 2017; and United Nations, Security Council, Press statement on environmental management of peacekeeping operations, Press Release SC/13134-ENV/DEV/1830-PKO/700, 21 Dec. 2017.

[26] 'Resolution on the Lake Chad Basin', What's in Blue, 31 Mar. 2017.

The first, and so far only, time that the Security Council included the protection of cultural heritage in the mandate of a peace operation was in that of MINUSMA.[27] In a special resolution on the topic in 2017, however, the Council affirmed that UN peace operations can be mandated to assist governments to protect cultural heritage from destruction, illicit excavation, looting and smuggling, and that operations should operate with care in the vicinity of such sites.[28]

Finally gender received greater attention in peace operations' mandates in 2017. The UN Integrated Peacebuilding Office in Guinea-Bissau (UNIOGBIS) and the UN Support Mission in Libya (UNSMIL) were asked to incorporate a gender perspective into their efforts.[29] The Council also reaffirmed the importance of gender mainstreaming when it established MINUJUSTH.[30] However, China and Russia in particular have often resisted such insertions, as they see them as an expansion of the women, peace and security agenda, as a challenge to national sovereignty or as the responsibility of other parts of the UN system.[31]

Moreover, sexual exploitation and abuse (SEA) perpetrated by UN peacekeepers remained high on the agenda. There were 62 allegations of SEA in UN peacekeeping operations and special political missions recorded in 2017, compared to 103 in 2016 and 69 in 2015. Of the 62 allegations in 2017, 41 involved military personnel and implicated 101 alleged perpetrators. The remaining allegations all pertained to single-perpetrator incidents, of which 11 involved civilian personnel and 10 involved police personnel. The allegations in 2017 involved a total of 130 victims, of which 21 were girls and 109 were women. The percentage of allegations of SEA that concerned sexual abuse—as opposed to sexual exploitation—was 32 per cent in 2017, compared to 55 per cent in 2016. This lower percentage is more in line with previous years. The decrease in the number of allegations of SEA in 2017 compared to 2016 is largely linked to a decrease in the number of allegations in MINUSCA. There were 19 reported allegations of SEA by members of MINUSCA in 2017, compared to 52 in 2016. The share of allegations of SEA that involved members of MINUSCA fell accordingly, from about half in 2016 to less than one-third in 2017.[32]

---

[27] UN Security Council Resolution 2100, 25 Apr. 2013.

[28] UN Security Council Resolution 2347, 24 Mar. 2017.

[29] UN Security Council Resolution 2343, 23 Feb. 2017; and UN Security Council Resolution 2376, 14 Sep. 2017.

[30] UN Security Council Resolution 2350, 13 Apr. 2017.

[31] 'Presidential statement on the Liberia Peacebuilding Plan and elections preparation', What's in Blue, 21 July 2017.

[32] United Nations, General Assembly, Report of the Secretary-General, Special measures for protection from sexual exploitation and abuse, A/72/751, 15 Feb. 2018.

II. Regional trends and developments in peace operations

JAÏR VAN DER LIJN AND TIMO SMIT

The 63 multilateral peace operations that were active in 2017 were spread across all the main regions of the world (see table 3.1). There were 25 peace operations in Africa, 18 in Europe, 9 in the Middle East, 6 in Asia and Oceania, and 5 in the Americas. Although the majority of peace operations were located in Africa and Europe—as was the case for the entire 2008–17 period (see figure 3.7)—these two regions hosted very different types of missions. Whereas most of the peace operations in Europe were small civilian missions in post-conflict countries, the peace operations active in Africa included many major missions with significant uniformed components. Six of the missions in Africa, for example, had a strength exceeding 10 000 personnel (see section I). Their combined strength was greater than the total number of personnel deployed in all 18 peace operations in Europe.

Comparisons of the distribution of personnel across the different regions in 2008–17 underscore the degree to which peace operations have become increasingly concentrated in Africa (see figure 3.8). Personnel deployments in Africa increased by nearly 60 per cent in the first eight years of the 2008–17 period, from approximately 75 000 to almost 120 000 in December 2015. Although they fell by 11 per cent in 2016–17, missions in Africa continued to account for the overwhelming majority of all the personnel deployed in multilateral peace operations. At the end of 2017, nearly three-quarters of all personnel were deployed in Africa.

Africa

There were 25 multilateral peace operations in Africa in 2017, one fewer than in 2016. The number of personnel deployed in missions in Africa decreased by 4 per cent during the year, from 110 623 to 106 240. This was the second year in a row that personnel deployments in the region fell, following a period of more or less continuous growth since 2000.

The United Nations–African Union (AU) partnership was further strengthened in 2017. A Joint UN–AU Framework for enhanced cooperation between the UN Secretariat and the AU Commission was signed on 19 April.[1] The UN Secretary-General produced a report outlining different options for planning, mandating and financing AU and AU-mandated peace support operations.[2] Introducing the AU Peace Fund, on the basis of a 0.2 per

---

[1] UN Security Council Resolution 2378, 20 Sep. 2017.
[2] United Nations, Security Council, 'Report of the Secretary-General on options for authorization and support for African Union peace support operations', S/2017/454, 26 May 2017.

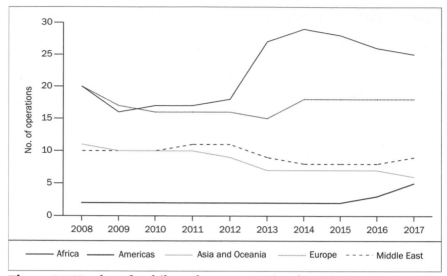

Figure 3.7. Number of multilateral peace operations by region, 2008–17

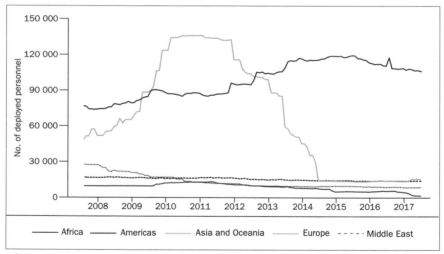

Figure 3.8. Number of personnel in multilateral peace operations by region, 2008–17

Note: Year marker indicates monthly data at the mid-year point (June).

cent import tax on 'eligible imports' into the continent, proved challenging as modalities for implementing it had to be found.[3] By May, 12 per cent of the total target amount of contributions had been collected by 14 AU member

[3] Apiko, P. and Aggad, F., 'Analysis of the implementation of the African Union's 0.2% levy: Progress and challenges', Briefing Note no. 98 (European Centre for Development Policy Management: Maastricht, Nov. 2017).

Table 3.1. Number of peace operations and personnel deployed, by region and type of organization, 2017

Conducting organization	Africa	Americas	Asia and Oceania	Europe	Middle East	World
Operations	25	5	6	18	9	63
United Nations[a]	12	4	2	2	4	24
Regional organization or alliance	12	1	2	14	3	32
Ad hoc coalition	1	–	2	2	2	7
Personnel[b]	**106 240**	**1 606**	**15 467**	**8 597**	**14 001**	**145 911**
United Nations[a]	82 739	1 580	375	1 101	12 559	98 354
Regional organization or alliance	23 404	26	15 046	6 347	79	44 902
Ad hoc coalition	97	–	46	1 149	1 363	2 655

[a] United Nations figures include peace operations led by the UN Department of Peacekeeping Operations, the UN Department of Political Affairs and the UN/African Union Mission in Darfur (UNAMID).

[b] Personnel figures are as of 31 Dec. 2017.

Source: SIPRI Multilateral Peace Operations Database.

states.[4] Discussions continued on predictable funding for AU-led peace support operations under Chapter VIII of the UN Charter. The AU Peace and Security Council, while acknowledging that decisions on the financing of specific missions will be taken on a case-by-case basis, sought to establish the principle that AU-mandated or authorized peace support operations authorized by the UN Security Council should be financed by UN assessed contributions.[5] The Security Council expressed its intention to establish mechanisms for UN funding on a case-by-case basis, and with the necessary strategic and financial oversight and accountability.[6]

West Africa

In 2017, two peace operations were drawn down in West Africa, while the region also hosted a quick and successful intervention in Gambia. On 30 June 2017, after some 13 years, the UN Operation in Côte d'Ivoire (UNOCI) completed its mandate and closed. The UN will remain committed through its Country Team, the personal involvement of the Secretary-General and the UN Office for West Africa and the Sahel (UNOWAS).[7] The UN Mission in Liberia (UNMIL) is moving towards closure on 30 March 2018. After the

[4] 'Briefing and Informal Interactive Dialogue on AU-UN Cooperation', What's in Blue, 14 June 2017.

[5] African Union, Peace and Security Council, 689th Meeting, Communiqué PSC/PR/COMM (DCLXXXIX), 30 May 2017.

[6] UN Security Council Resolution 2378, 20 Sep. 2017.

[7] United Nations, Security Council, Statement by the President of the Security Council, S/PRST/2017/8, 30 June 2017; and UN Security Council Resolution 2284, 28 Apr. 2016.

victory of the former footballer, George Weah, in the presidential election in December 2017, its remaining task is to contribute to the development of national capacities to sustain peace. The UN Country Team and the Peacebuilding Commission will remain involved after UNMIL's departure.[8]

Following a strategic review, and given the continuing political and institutional impasse and deadlocked implementation of the Conakry Agreement, the UN Integrated Peacebuilding Office in Guinea-Bissau (UNIOGBIS) was refocused to create the political space for sustainable peace. Its good offices and political facilitation tasks are now being emphasized over other tasks and its management structure has been streamlined.[9]

The financial difficulties of the Economic Community of West African States (ECOWAS) Mission in Guinea Bissau (ECOMIB) persisted. The mission has been in long-term limbo over its future. The Monrovia Summit of ECOWAS Heads of State and Government extended its mandate by three months beyond its intended end date of 30 June.[10] The Security Council called for a further extension and for international financial support.[11] Although the ECOWAS Heads of State and Government did not prolong the mission at their subsequent summit, ECOMIB continued its efforts in the absence of a formal mandate.

The only new mission in West Africa was the ECOWAS Mission in the Gambia (ECOMIG). President Yahya Jammeh initially conceded defeat following the 1 December 2016 elections, which were won by Adama Barrow, but on 9 December Jammeh claimed that there had been irregularities and rejected the results. Troops were deployed on the streets of Banjul by the Jammeh Government and on 18 January 2017 the Gambian Parliament approved a 90-day state of emergency. Diplomatic pressure on Jammeh to resign was strong and unified from the beginning. ECOWAS, the AU Peace and Security Council and the UN Security Council all recognized Barrow as the new president. The first two warned that the use of force could not be excluded, while the third welcomed and supported the efforts of the first two but added that a solution should be sought 'by political means first'.[12]

On 19 January, Barrow was inaugurated as *de jure* president, while the de facto incumbent government led by Jammeh was still in power.

---

[8] United Nations, Security Council, Statement by the President of the Security Council, S/PRST/2017/11, 24 July 2017; and MacDougall, C. and Cooper, C., 'George Weah wins Liberia election', *New York Times*, 28 Dec. 2017.

[9] UN Security Council Resolution 2343, 23 Feb. 2017.

[10] Economic Community of West African States, Final Communique of the 51st Ordinary Session of the ECOWAS Authority of Heads of States and Government, 4 June 2017.

[11] UN Security Council Resolution 2343, 23 Feb. 2017.

[12] Economic Community of West African States, Final Communique of the 50th Ordinary Session of the ECOWAS Authority of Heads of States and Government, 17 Dec. 2016; African Union, Peace and Security Council, 647th Meeting, Communiqué PSC/PR/COMM (DCXLVII), 13 Jan. 2017; and UN Security Council Resolution 2337, 19 Jan. 2017.

Immediately after Barrow's inauguration as the *de jure* and internationally recognized president, and at his invitation, a regional force composed of Senegalese, Nigerian, Ghanaian, Malian and Togolese troops—ECOMIG—entered Gambia.[13] ECOMIG initially consisted of some 7000 troops and was mandated to: (*a*) ensure the safety of President Barrow, political leaders and the entire population; (*b*) uphold the results of the presidential election; and (*c*) ensure that the president-elect was sworn in.[14] Under military coercion, but following a political agreement, Jammeh conceded and there was a peaceful transition of power.[15] On 9 February, President Barrow extended ECOMIG's mandate for three months.[16] The new mandate came into effect on 21 February and in addition to ensuring security, ECOMIG was asked to facilitate the establishment of trust between the new authorities and the Gambian defence and security forces. The force was subsequently downsized to 500 personnel, although in practice its numbers had already been significantly reduced.[17] The security situation remained fragile, however, and on 4 June the ECOWAS Authority of Heads of State and Government extended ECOMIG's mandate for a year and added the task of supporting the training and reorientation of the Gambian armed forces. The ECOWAS Authority requested additional troops to carry out this role.[18]

The Sahel and Maghreb regions

The Sahel and Maghreb regions are hot spots where a variety of international organizations have various peace operations deployed. The UN Multidimensional Integrated Stabilization Mission in Mali (MINUSMA) continued to be afflicted by a lack of key capabilities for operating in complex security environments. As a consequence, the asymmetric threats from frequent hostile attacks persisted. An extraordinary force generation conference on 22–23 May led to a variety of pledges to fill the capability gaps. The UN Security Council called for the rapid deployment of UNOCI's Quick Reaction Force, and the aviation unit that supports it, to Mali. It also asked the Secretary-General to consider long-term rotation schemes for critical capabilities and innovative partnerships between equipment-, troop- and police-contributing countries as new options for enhancing MINUSMA's

---

[13] Cocks, T. and Farge, E., 'West African military halt Gambia operation, issue Jammeh deadline', Reuters, 19 Jan. 2017.

[14] Jobe, A., 'ECOMIG forces explain mandate in Gambia', The Point, 31 Jan. 2017; and Williams, P. D., 'A new African model of coercion? Assessing the ECOWAS mission in the Gambia', IPI Global Observatory, 16 Mar. 2017.

[15] Office of the Spokesman for the UN Secretary-General, Note to Correspondents, Joint Declaration on the Political Situation in The Gambia, 21 Jan. 2017; and United Nations, Security Council, Statement by the President of the Security Council, S/PRST/2017/10, 24 July 2017.

[16] President Barrow extends ECOMIG mandate by 3 months, The Point, 9 Feb. 2017.

[17] De Cherisey, E., 'ECOMIG gets new mandate as some troops withdraw', Janes 360, 28 Feb. 2017.

[18] Economic Community of West African States, Final Communique of the 51st Ordinary Session of the ECOWAS Authority of Heads of States and Government, 4 June 2017.

capabilities. At MINUSMA's annual mandate renewal in June, the Security Council maintained its tasks and authorized strength of 15 209 uniformed personnel (13 289 military and 1920 police).[19] After the deployment of the Group of Five for the Sahel (G5 Sahel) Joint Force (Force Conjointe des Etats du G5 Sahel, FC-G5S), the idea of deploying a Force Intervention Brigade within MINUSMA dropped off the agenda (see section III). By the end of 2017, however, MINUSMA had still only attained 88.3 per cent of its authorized strength (11 698 military and 1725 police).

On 15 May 2017, the Council of the European Union (EU) approved a Concept of Operations for the regionalization of the EU Common Security and Defence Policy (CSDP) missions in the Sahel: EUCAP Sahel Niger, EUCAP Sahel Mali and the EU Training Mission (EUTM) Mali. The strategic objectives of regionalization are to support cross-border cooperation in the Sahel, support regional cooperation structures and enhance the national capacities of the G5 Sahel countries. A Regional Coordination Cell (RCC) was set up for this purpose within EUCAP Sahel Mali.[20]

Despite the fact that the Libyan Political Agreement (LPA), signed at Skhirat, Morocco on 17 December 2015, established a Government of National Accord (GNA), Libya remained effectively partitioned in 2017. Therefore, following a strategic assessment review, the Security Council tasked the UN Support Mission in Libya (UNSMIL) with supporting an inclusive political process within the framework of the peace agreement, in addition to its existing mandate.[21] During the year, UNSMIL and the UN Country Team continued to gradually increase their operations inside Libya and maintained a temporary rotational presence. The deployment of a guard unit to protect the UNSMIL premises in Tripoli had been completed by the end of the year.[22] In response to reports that migrants were being sold into slavery in Libya, the Security Council welcomed the work of UNSMIL on coordinating and supporting the provision of humanitarian assistance to migrants and refugees.[23]

In spite of earlier indications to the contrary, only 25 civilian staff of the UN Mission for the Referendum in Western Sahara (MINURSO) were allowed to return after the expulsion of the civilian component in 2016. Moreover,

[19] United Nations, Security Council, Report of the Secretary-General on the situation in Mali, S/2017/478, 6 June 2017; and UN Security Council Resolution 2364, 29 June 2017.

[20] Council Decision 2017/1102/CFSP of 20 June 2017 amending Decision 2014/219/CFSP on the European Union CSDP Mission in Mali (EUCAP Sahel Mali), *Official Journal of the European Union*, L158/44, 21 June 2017.

[21] 'Restoring UN Leadership of Libya's Peace Process', Statement, International Crisis Group, 18 Sep. 2017; and UN Security Council Resolution 2376, 14 Sep. 2017 On the conflict in Libya see also chapter 2, section V, in this volume.

[22] United Nations, Security Council, Report of the Secretary-General on the United Nations Support Mission in Libya, S/2018/140, 12 Feb. 2018.

[23] United Nations, Security Council, Statement by the President of the Security Council, S/PRST/2017/24, 7 Dec. 2017.

tensions continued between the Moroccan armed forces and the Popular Front for the Liberation of Saguia el Hamra and Río de Oro (Frente Popular de Liberación de Saguía el Hamra y Río de Oro, POLISARIO) in the Gueguerat buffer strip, even after the withdrawal of Moroccan forces. The combination of these issues raised questions in the Security Council about MINURSO's future mission structure and how to measure its performance. MINURSO was allowed to increase the proportion of medical personnel within its currently authorized troop ceiling.[24]

The Democratic Republic of the Congo

The Comprehensive and Inclusive Political Agreement signed in Kinshasa on 31 December 2016 determined that current President Laurent Kabila would remain Head of State until his successor was elected before the end of December 2017.[25] However, the political space in the Democratic Republic of the Congo (DRC) shrank and reports increased of serious violations of international humanitarian law and human rights. At the same time, inter-communal and militia-related violence spread from regions such as the Kivu provinces (including Beni) and Ituri to the Kasaï provinces and Tanganyika.[26] In order to support the electoral process in this deteriorating environment, the Secretary-General requested an increase in the authorized ceiling for the police component of the UN Organization Stabilization Mission in the Democratic Republic of the Congo (MONUSCO) from 1050 to 1370 personnel. He expected that although the military component was struggling to implement its mandate, reconfiguration efforts would not require additional military personnel.[27]

At the time of MONUSCO's annual mandate renewal, the 17 000 troops the mission had deployed for the past two years was already far fewer than its authorized troop ceiling of 19 815. Nonetheless, the United States and the United Kingdom called for further troop reductions, even though the other Security Council members opposed this. The USA even threatened to veto a mandate renewal in the absence of a significant personnel reduction. The UN Secretariat considered that a further reduction of 500 troops would not affect MONUSCO's ability to implement its mandate 'too adversely'. It also

[24] 'Western Sahara: Morocco to pull out of UN buffer zone', BBC News, 27 Feb. 2017; United Nations, Security Council, Report of the Secretary-General on the situation concerning Western Sahara, S/2017/307, 10 Apr. 2017; and UN Security Council Resolution 2351, 28 Apr. 2017.
[25] The electoral calendar published in December set the combined presidential, legislative and provincial elections for 23 Dec. 2018.
[26] UN Security Council Resolution 2348, 31 Mar. 2017; and United Nations, Security Council, Report of the Secretary-General on the United Nations Organization Stabilization Mission in the Democratic Republic of the Congo, S/2017/824, 2 Oct. 2017. On the conflict in the DRC see also chapter 2, section VI, in this volume.
[27] United Nations, Security Council, Report of the Secretary-General on the United Nations Organization Stabilization Mission in the Democratic Republic of the Congo, S/2017/206, 10 Mar. 2017.

suggested that the required increase in police personnel could be obtained through inter-mission cooperation.[28] Subsequently, the Security Council reduced MONUSCO's authorized troop levels from 19 815 to 16 215 military personnel, and from 760 to 660 military observers and staff officers. It did not increase the size of the police component of 391 police personnel and 1050 personnel in formed police units (FPUs), but asked the Secretary-General to explore options for inter-mission cooperation.[29]

MONUSCO's mandate remained largely the same, except that its civilian and political stabilization efforts were now framed in the context of the 31 December 2016 agreement. In addition, the Council urged MONUSCO to continually incorporate lessons learned into reforming the mission to enable it to better implement its mandate, in particular to protect civilians. In this context the Council specifically mentioned MONUSCO's chain of command, its effectiveness, the safety and security of its personnel, and its ability to manage complex situations. The Council also highlighted that undeclared national caveats, lack of effective command and control, failure to obey orders, inadequate equipment, and the failure to respond to attacks against civilians could affect the mission negatively. Finally, the Security Council requested the Secretary-General to undertake a strategic review to examine the continued relevance of the mission's tasks, priorities and related resources, and formulate an exit strategy and options for reducing the force after the implementation of the 31 December agreement.[30]

As tensions over the transition of power started to destabilize the country as a whole, analysts argued that MONUSCO's strategic review should result in a more mobile mission, less concentrated on eastern DRC.[31] The strategic review concluded that: 'Given the vastness of the country, the widening array of threats faced by the population and the limited resources' MONUSCO must shift 'from protection through presence to protection through projection'. It argued that MONUSCO's ultimate goal is to prevent the collapse of the DRC, and that only the implementation of the 31 December agreement and the containment of armed groups would allow MONUSCO to shift its focus away from protection and towards a drawdown. It stated that it is 'imperative that Member States provide MONUSCO with the resources required to implement its mandate' and that they 'should exercise caution in

[28] 'Vote on Draft Resolution Renewing MONUSCO Mandate', What's in Blue, 31 Mar. 2017; and Lynch, C. and McCormick, T., 'Nikki Haley threatened to withhold backing for UN's Congo mission, then blinked', Foreign Policy, 30 Mar. 2017.

[29] UN Security Council Resolution 2348, 31 Mar. 2017.

[30] UN Security Council Resolution 2348, 31 Mar. 2017.

[31] Guéhenno, J., 'Open Letter to the UN Secretary-General on Peacekeeping in DRC', International Crisis Group, 27 July 2017.

making further cuts to the Mission's budget that may compromise its ability to deliver on its core priorities'.[32]

A little over two months later, on 7 December, MONUSCO was hit hard when a company operating base at Semuliki, North Kivu, was attacked, reportedly by the Allied Democratic Forces (ADF). Fifteen Tanzanian peace-keepers, part of the Force Intervention Brigade (FIB), and five members of the DRC's armed forces were killed. At least 53 others were injured.[33] The event shocked the entire UN system and representatives of member states in New York. The Under-Secretary-General for Peacekeeping Operations, Jean-Pierre Lacroix, explained that the FIB had been fighting the ADF, and that he saw this as a response to MONUSCO's increasingly robust posture.[34] Some analysts questioned whether the force reduction earlier in 2017 had left MONUSCO vulnerable.[35] The attack was the start of a further increase in insecurity in the region, indicating that MONUSCO's restructuring and the closure of bases in the absence of the required air assets had at least reduced its ability to protect civilians. The troop reduction had taken place in an increasingly insecure environment and ahead of original plans. It was also implemented before the strategic review was able to provide insights on whether and where troops could be cut. As a consequence, the mission appeared to be unprepared for protection through projection.[36]

Burundi

The security situation in Burundi remained relatively calm. However, the number of refugees and internally displaced persons increased, the human rights situation remained alarming and the political impasse persisted. The Security Council did not mention the deployment of the UN police compo-nent in its presidential statement on the country, but did support efforts to implement the resolution mandating it.[37] The UN and the Government of Burundi were not able to reach agreement on the modalities of the deploy-ment of the UN police component, as the latter objected to it. Further, some

---

[32] United Nations, Security Council, 'Special report of the Secretary-General on the strategic review of the United Nations Organization Stabilization Mission in the Democratic Republic of the Congo', S/2017/826, 29 Sep. 2017.

[33] United Nations, Security Council, Press statement on attack against United Nations Organ-ization Stabilization Mission in Democratic Republic of Congo, Press Release SC/13114-PKO/699, 8 Dec. 2017.

[34] Mahamba, F, 'Rebels kill 15 peacekeepers in Congo in worst attack on UN in recent history', Reuters, 8 Dec. 2017.

[35] Vogel, C., 'UN peacekeepers were killed in Congo: Here's what we know', *Washington Post*, 8 Dec. 2017.

[36] Spink, L., *Protection With Less Presence: How the Peacekeeping Operation in The Democratic Republic of Congo is Attempting to Deliver Protection with Fewer Resources* (Center for Civilians in Conflict, 10 Jan. 2018).

[37] United Nations, Security Council, Statement by the President of the Security Council, S/PRST/2017/13, 2 Aug. 2017; and Van der Lijn, J. and Smit, T., 'Regional trends and developments', *SIPRI Yearbook 2017*, pp. 188–89.

members of the Security Council argued that the component's one-year mandate had expired one year after the resolution, whereas others argued that its mandate would only start once the component had been established on the ground.[38]

The Security Council was also concerned about the continuing delays in the deployment of AU human rights observers and military experts. By December 2017, only 37 human rights observers and 8 military observers had been deployed, far below the 200 observers the Burundian Government had agreed and fewer than the 2016 number. Both the Security Council and the AU called for the rapid signing of a memorandum of understanding to make the AU mission fully operational.[39]

Lesotho

Tensions in Lesotho were played out in a rivalry between two senior military figures, Brigadier Maaparankoe Mahao and Lieutenant General Tladi Kamoli, and their respective political allies, Tom Thabane and Pakalitha Mosisili. In 2014, South African Deputy President Cyril Ramaphosa brokered an agreement that included the removal of Kamoli and Mahao from their positions.[40] The subsequent May 2015 assassination of Mahao triggered the involvement of the Southern African Development Community (SADC). SADC set up an independent Commission of Inquiry and an Oversight Committee to serve as an early warning mechanism for potential instability in the country, and which would intervene when needed. In addition, SADC urged Lesotho to reform its constitution and security sector.[41] In November 2016, Kamoli resigned from his position as commander of the Lesotho Defence Force (LDF).[42] After two years in exile, Thabane won the 3 June 2017 elections, succeeding Mosisili as prime minister.[43]

At their August 2017 Summit in Pretoria, the Heads of State and Government of SADC gave the Government of Lesotho until November 2017 to formulate a road map for implementing all further SADC decisions.[44] This included legal action against Kamoli and two other officers who, according to the SADC Commission of Inquiry, were implicated in the assassination of Mahao. Two weeks later, the new Commander of the LDF was assassinated

[38] 'Burundi presidential statement', What's in Blue, 1 Aug. 2017.

[39] United Nations (note 37).

[40] ENCA, 'SADC agree to commission of inquiry into recent turmoil in Lesotho', African News Agency, 4 July 2017.

[41] Southern African Development Community (SADC), Communiqué, Extraordinary Summit of the Double Troika, Pretoria, Republic of South Africa, 3 July 2015.

[42] Agence France-Presse, 'Lesotho army chief accused of 2014 coup attempt resigns', News24, 9 Nov. 2016.

[43] Akwei, I., 'Lesotho: Incumbent Mosisili loses election to former Prime Minister Thabane', Africa News, 6 June 2017.

[44] SADC, Communiqué of the 37th Summit of SADC Heads of State and Government, Department of International Relations and Cooperation, Pretoria, South Africa, 19–20 Aug. 2017.

because he was unwilling to prevent the prosecution of those implicated in the assassination of Mahao.[45]

These events in turn led SADC to send a Ministerial Fact Finding Mission to Lesotho to assess the situation. The mission found that the security situation was volatile and the political stability of the country was at risk. A Double Troika Summit of SADC Heads of State and Government noted the need to assist Lesotho with restoring law, order and peace, and to enable the implementation of SADC decisions—particularly those on security sector reform (SSR) and constitutional reform, and on the establishment of a Commission of Inquiry. To this end, the summit approved the deployment of a Contingent Force consisting of military, security, intelligence and civilian experts to support the Government of Lesotho. In the meantime, it expanded the number of personnel on the Oversight Committee to 34 military, security, intelligence and civilian experts.[46]

The Contingent Force, named the SADC Preventive Mission in the Kingdom of Lesotho (SAPMIL), was launched on 2 December with the consent of the Government of Lesotho. Like the Oversight Committee before it, it consists of military (217), intelligence (15), police (24) and civilian (13) personnel. Its mandate was for an initial six months to be renewed depending on the progress made.[47] On 28 January the AU Peace and Security Council welcomed the mission and appealed to all AU member states and the UN to provide SAPMIL with technical and financial support.[48]

The Central African Republic

The UN Multidimensional Integrated Stabilization Mission in the Central African Republic (MINUSCA) came under increasing attack from anti-Balaka groups, predominantly Christian and animist militia that fought the predominantly Muslim Seleka rebel movement after it took power in 2013. These hostile acts culminated in an attack on 8 May near Bangasso that killed four peacekeepers.[49] Throughout the year, MINUSCA aimed to deal with the situation by protecting civilians and combating armed groups with operations BEKPA, MARAZE and DAMAKONGO. In coordination with the EU Training Mission in the Central African Republic (EUTM-RCA), it also supported the authorities in the Central African Republic (CAR) with

[45] Fabricius, P. and Van Schie, K., 'Lesotho: Political tensions run high following army shootings', Daily Maverick, 6 Sep. 2017.

[46] SADC, Final Communiqué of the Double Troika Summit of SADC Heads of State and Government, Department of International Relations and Cooperation, Pretoria, South Africa, 15 Sep. 2017.

[47] Reliefweb, 'SADC officially launches the SADC Preventive Mission in the Kingdom of Lesotho on December 2, 2017', Press release, SADC, 2 Dec. 2017.

[48] African Union, Peace and Security Council, 'Communiqué', 748th meeting, PSC/PR/COMM(DCCXLVIII), 24 Jan. 2018.

[49] Guilbert, K., 'Four UN peacekeepers killed, eight wounded, in Central African Republic', Reuters, 9 May 2017. On the conflict in CAR see also chapter 2, section VI, in this volume.

the development of a redeployment plan for CAR's armed forces, in order to extend state authority and security throughout the country.[50]

However, the spread of armed confrontations and violence left MINUSCA thinly spread and overstretched. Unable to respond to the security challenges, MINUSCA allowed space for armed groups to proliferate. In order to respond to the situation, the Secretary-General requested additional troops and capabilities. Although these would not allow MINUSCA to protect all civilians in the country, they would give the force more flexibility in geographical priority areas and reinforce its pre-emptive and reactive postures in high-risk areas.[51]

In response to the deteriorating security situation, the 19 June agreement signed in Rome under the auspices of the Sant-Egidio community, and the joint road map agreed by the AU and neighbouring countries in Libreville, the Security Council adjusted MINUSCA's mandate slightly compared to 2016. The mission still protects civilians and facilitates the creation of a secure environment for the delivery of humanitarian assistance. However, good offices and support to the peace process, including transitional justice, were made priority tasks, while the promotion and protection of human rights became a secondary task. In addition, the Council increased MINUSCA's authorized troop levels by 900 military personnel to 11 650, including 480 military observers and military staff, to strengthen the mission's flexibility and mobility.[52]

There were fewer reports of sexual exploitation and abuse (SEA) by members of MINUSCA in 2017. Given the very high number of reports in previous years, this was a notable, positive development. The Security Council attributed this success to the UN Secretary-General's renewed commitment to the UN's zero-tolerance policy on SEA.[53]

South Sudan and Sudan

South Sudan and Sudan remained troubled mission areas in a situation exacerbated by difficult relationships with the host governments.

The situation in South Sudan deteriorated further as the conflicting parties were unable to reach a ceasefire agreement, the coherence of the parties weakened and new rebel movements appeared. The Ceasefire and Transitional Security Arrangements Monitoring Mechanism (CTSAMM) reported regular violations of the 2015 peace agreement across South Sudan,

[50] UN Security Council Resolution 2387, 15 Nov. 2017.

[51] United Nations, Security Council, 'Report of the Secretary-General on the Central African Republic', S/2017/865, 18 Oct. 2017.

[52] United Nations, Security Council, Statement by the President of the Security Council, S/PRST/2017/9, 13 July 2017; and UN Security Council Resolution 2387, 15 Nov. 2017.

[53] UN Security Council Resolution 2387, 15 Nov. 2017.

perpetrated by both government and opposition forces.[54] The UN Mission in South Sudan (UNMISS) continued to protect over 200 000 civilians at its camps.[55] The image of UNMISS and its ability to protect civilians outside its camps improved during 2017, due to its more robust force posture.[56] However, humanitarian workers and UNMISS peacekeepers were frequently obstructed in their efforts, increasing the suffering in famine-affected regions.[57] The Security Council continued to call for the immediate removal of all obstacles to the work of UNMISS.[58]

The Security Council also, once again, demanded the removal of all obstructions of CTSAMM personnel, who continued to experience restrictions on their freedom of movement, and of the deployment of the UNMISS Regional Protection Force (RPF).[59] The Council did not follow through on its threat of an arms embargo if the Transitional Government of National Unity (TGoNU) continued to obstruct the deployment of the RPF. By May 2017, however, the first elements of the force were trickling in.[60] The security situation in Juba has significantly improved since August 2016, when the RPF was mandated, but the deployment of the RPF in Juba would allow UNMISS to reallocate resources outside Juba.[61] In spite of diplomatic efforts by the Intergovernmental Authority on Development (IGAD), little substantial progress was made.[62] In August, the TGoNU even grounded UN aircraft over a row about whether the RPF was mandated to control Juba airport.[63] At the end of the year, only 742 of the 4000 mandated RPF staff had been deployed.[64] By then, UNMISS had still only attained 76.1 per cent of its total authorized strength of 17 000 troops and 2101 police (12 969 troops and

---

[54] Ceasefire and Transitional Security Arrangements Monitoring Mechanism (CTSAMM), CTSAMM Violation Reports. On the conflict in South Sudan see also chapter 2, section VI, in this volume.

[55] United Nations, Security Council, 'Report of the Secretary-General on South Sudan (covering the period from 2 September to 14 November 2017)', S/2017/1011, 1 Dec. 2017.

[56] United Nations, Security Council, 'Letter dated 17 April 2017 from the Secretary-General addressed to the President of the Security Council', S/2017/328, 17 Apr. 2017; and Patinkin, J., 'UN moves to protect South Sudan civilians after years of criticism', Reuters, 28 Aug. 2017.

[57] United Nations, Security Council, Statement by the President of the Security Council, S/PRST/2017/25, 14 Dec. 2017; and 'UN denied access to South Sudan town alleged to be massacre site', Reuters, 7 Apr. 2017.

[58] United Nations, Security Council, Statement by the President of the Security Council, S/PRST/2017/4, 23 Mar. 2017.

[59] United Nations (note 58).

[60] Nichols, M., 'Eight months after approval, new UN troops trickle into South Sudan', Reuters, 18 May 2017.

[61] United Nations, Security Council, 8056th meeting, Reports of the Secretary-General on Sudan and South Sudan (Provisional), S/PV.8056, 26 Sep. 2017.

[62] Intergovernmental Authority on Development, Communiqué of the 31st Extra-ordinary Summit of IGAD Assembly of Heads of State and Government on South Sudan, 12 June 2017, Addis Abba.

[63] Maasho, A., 'South Sudan grounds UN planes in airport row', Reuters, 21 Aug. 2017.

[64] United Nations, Security Council, 'Report of the Secretary-General on South Sudan (covering the period from 2 September to 14 November 2017)', S/2017/1011, 1 Dec. 2017.

1559 police). The UNMISS mid-December annual mandate renewal was given a technical rollover of three months to allow for the completion of its strategic review.[65]

Significant progress was lacking on achieving the benchmarks for the Joint Border Verification and Monitoring Mechanism (JBVMM) and lifting the impediments imposed on it. In the Security Council, the USA in particular wanted to suspend support for the JBVMM by the UN Interim Security Force for Abyei (UNISFA), while Ethiopia particularly wanted it to continue.[66] In the end, the Security Council warned at the first biannual mandate renewal for UNISFA that this would be the final renewal of support unless both parties could 'demonstrate through their actions clear commitment and steadfast guarantees for implementation'. In order to continue, the Council demanded the resumption of border demarcation discussions, regular meetings of the Joint Political and Security Mechanism, and full freedom of movement for the JBVMM. The Council also reduced the authorized troop ceiling by 535 to 4791.[67]

Half a year later, in November, the Council recognized some improvements, but a lack of 'significant progress'.[68] The Secretary-General agreed with the Council that the parties bear the primary responsibility for making the process a success. At the same time, he urged the Council to 'give due consideration to the imperative to preserve the achievements of relative stability' in Abyei, as he argued UNISFA was containing 'the real risk of relapse into international armed conflict'.[69] The Council eventually opted to renew UNISFA's mandate for the usual half-year term, but warned that next time the mission may no longer support the JBVMM and may instead focus only on Abyei, if the parties fail to fulfil the criteria. A reduction in the authorized troop ceiling by 556 to 4235 would then follow.[70]

In Darfur, the number of military confrontations decreased and the Government of Sudan, on the one hand, and two of the major opposition groups, the Sudan Liberation Army Minni Minnawi (SLA/MM) and the Justice and Equality Movement (JEM) Gibril, on the other, announced unilateral cessations of hostilities. Nonetheless, inter-communal violence continued. Moreover, in spite of improvements, government restrictions on the UN/AU Mission in Darfur (UNAMID), such as limits on freedom of

---

[65] UN Security Council Resolution 2392, 14 Dec. 2017.

[66] 'Council consultations and possible vote on draft resolution on UN Interim Security Force for Abyei', What's in Blue, 12 May 2017.

[67] UN Security Council Resolution 2352, 15 May 2017.

[68] UN Security Council Resolution 2386, 15 Nov. 2017.

[69] United Nations, Security Council, Report of the Secretary-General on the situation in Abyei, S/2017/870, 17 Oct. 2017.

[70] UN Security Council Resolution 2386, 15 Nov. 2017.

movement and visa restrictions, continued to affect its ability to implement its mandate.[71]

The Security Council endorsed a two-pronged strategy for the mission. This focuses on military protection and emergency relief in the Jebel Mara region while emphasizing stabilization and supporting the police and the rule of law institutions, and mediating inter-communal conflict in regions where there has not been any recent fighting. This added new peacebuilding tasks to UNAMID's mandate and it was reconfigured to optimize the mission for its new tasks. For the first six-month period, phase one, UNAMID's authorized troop ceiling was reduced by 4450 military personnel to 11 395, and by 255 police personnel to 2888, including individual police officers (IPOs) and FPUs. In phase two, starting on 31 January 2018, if a number of criteria are met, the force will then be reduced by a further 2660 military and 388 police personnel, to 8735 and 2500 respectively, by 30 June 2018. The Security Council underlined that this reduction should not affect the mission's ability to quickly respond to threats. A civilian staffing review would look at the size of UNAMID's civilian components.[72]

The downsizing of UNAMID was met with harsh criticism from analysts, advocacy groups such as Human Rights Watch and The Enough Project, and representatives of local groups. They talked of 'flagrant mistakes' and 'false narratives about Darfur's war ending', and argued that it would make several key areas insecure for the provision of humanitarian assistance and the local population.[73]

Somalia

In mid-January 2017, the AU Peace and Security Council requested the UN Security Council to authorize 4500 additional troops for the AU Mission in Somalia (AMISOM), for a non-renewable period of six months. The aim of this surge was to implement the 2016 concept of operations, and in particular to expand offensive operations and facilitate the exit strategy.[74]

On 8 February, Somalia witnessed the conclusion of its electoral process with the election of President Mohamed Abdullahi Mohamed 'Farmajo'. AMISOM played a critical role in securing these elections. At the same time, the situation in the country remained difficult and there were frequent attacks by the Islamist group Harakat al-Shabab al-Mujahideen (Mujahedin

[71] UN Security Council Resolution 2363, 29 June 2017; and UN Office for the Coordination of Humanitarian Affairs, Sudan: Darfur Humanitarian Overview, 1 Oct. 2017.
[72] UN Security Council Resolution 2363, 29 June 2017; and UN Office for the Coordination of Humanitarian Affairs, Sudan (note 71).
[73] 'UN decides to downsize peacekeeping mission in Darfur', *Dabanga*, 30 June 2017.
[74] African Union, Peace and Security Council, 'Communiqué', 649th meeting, PSC/PR/COMM(DCXLIX), 16 Jan. 2017.

Youth Movement, or al-Shabab).[75] AMISOM was also hit hard at times.[76] On the international diplomatic front, at the London Somalia Conference in May, progress was made to secure additional support for Somalia and agreements were made on the coordination of mentoring, training, equipment and remuneration for the police and military forces, such as the 10 900-strong Somali National Army.[77]

Nonetheless, AMISOM troop contributors claimed that they faced financial challenges after the EU reallocated 20 per cent of the funds for allowances into other forms of support to AMISOM, such as training and indirect costs. In addition, as the Government of Burundi is under sanctions, the EU did not reimburse the AU to cover the Burundi Government's costs. After Burundi threatened to withdraw its forces, the AU and the Burundian Government came to an agreement to funnel the remuneration for Burundian forces through a commercial bank.[78]

An AU/UN joint review of AMISOM looked into the future needs of the mission. AMISOM's increased authorized force levels after 2012 had been envisaged as enhancing the mission's capacity as part of its exit strategy. The joint review ignored the call for a surge by the African Peace and Security Council and instead recommended the start of a gradual and phased reduction of troop numbers and a reorganization of AMISOM to allow it to play a greater support role to the Somali security forces, as they progressively take the lead.[79] The Security Council subsequently adjusted AMISOM's strategic objectives in line with these recommendations.

In addition to reducing the threat from al-Shabab, the handover of security responsibilities to the Somali security forces was prioritized, and providing security to enable the political process, stabilization efforts, reconciliation and peacebuilding was replaced with providing assistance to the Somali security forces to the same end. The Security Council subsequently reduced the authorized troop level by 500 to 21 626 by the end of 2017—a figure that includes 1040 police officers in five FPUs. This reduction was scheduled to include a further 1000 troops by the end of October 2018. The civilian component of the mission was still not operational and the human rights component in particular required additional staffing. At the same time, the AU intended to develop a new concept of operations, which was intended to

---

[75] United Nations, Security Council, Statement by the President of the Security Council, S/PRST/2017/3, 10 Feb. 2017. On the conflict in Somalia see also chapter 2, section VI, in this volume.

[76] Burke, J., 'Witnesses say dozens killed in al-Shabaab attack on Kenyan troops', *The Guardian*, 27 Jan. 2017; and Omar, F., 'African Union troops ambushed in Somalia, official says 24 dead', Reuters, 30 July 2017.

[77] UN Security Council Resolution 2372, 30 Aug. 2017.

[78] Williams, P. D., 'Paying for AMISOM: Are politics and bureaucracy undermining the AU's largest peace operation?', 11 Jan. 2017, IPI Global Observatory; and Karuri, K., 'Burundi, AU resolve AMISOM pay dispute', Africa News, 16 Feb. 2017.

[79] UN Security Council Resolution 2372, 30 Aug. 2017.

strengthen the command and control structures of the mission, among other things.[80] However, analysts wondered whether, in an environment in which al-Shabab is gaining ground, a simple exit strategy is actually feasible.[81]

The Americas

There were five multilateral peace operations in the Americas in 2017, which was two more than in 2016. Two operations terminated during 2017, both of which were immediately succeeded by follow-on missions. As in the previous year, therefore, there were never more than three peace operations deployed in the region at the same time. The number of personnel deployed in multilateral peace operations in the Americas decreased by 71 per cent, from 5464 to 1606, primarily as a result of the termination of the UN Stabilization Mission in Haiti (MINUSTAH) in October 2017. The only peace operation in the Americas that did not experience any significant change in either mandate or composition in 2017 was the Organization of American States Mission to Support the Peace Process in Colombia (MAPP/OEA), which has been active in the country since 2004.

Haiti

Jovenel Moise was sworn in as Haiti's new president on 7 February 2017, ending the electoral process and, according to the UN Security Council, restoring the 'constitutional order'. The Security Council decided to terminate MINUSTAH's mandate on 15 October and that its military component should draw down in the six remaining months. MINUSTAH, which commenced operations in 2004, assisted the Haitian National Police (HNP) and the country as a whole through the 2010 earthquake, but was also connected to the 2010 cholera outbreak that affected nearly 800 000 people and caused over 9000 deaths. In spite of substantial progress, the HNP required continued international assistance to expand its territorial reach and build its technical capacity and community-based programmes.[82]

The Security Council mandated MINUJUSTH as a follow-on mission, to be established following the termination of MINUSTAH, for an initial six-month period commencing on 15 October 2017. Its mandate was to continue to provide assistance to the government and to consolidate MINUSTAH's gains by: (*a*) strengthening the government's rule of law institutions; (*b*) further supporting and developing the HNP; and (*c*) monitoring, reporting on and providing analyses of the human rights situation. It was authorized to

---

[80] UN Security Council Resolution 2372, 30 Aug. 2017.
[81] Williams, P., 'Somalia's African Union mission has a new exit strategy: But can troops actually leave?', *Washington Post*, 30 Nov. 2017.
[82] Guyler Delva, J. and Brice, M., 'Businessman Jovenel Moise takes office as President of Haiti', Reuters, 8 Feb. 2017; and UN Security Council Resolution 2350, 13 Apr. 2017.

deploy seven FPUs or 980 personnel—a reduction of four units compared to MINUSTAH. The Security Council intends to further decrease this number if the capacity of the HNP increases as projected over a two-year period. The FPUs were mandated to safeguard the security gains and provide operational assistance to the HNP. MINUJUSTH's 295 IPOs, a reduction from 1001 in MINUSTAH, will assist the development of the HNP, while its 38 corrections officers, reduced from 50, are to strengthen the administration of prisons. MINUJUSTH's quick impact projects and community violence reduction efforts will be transitioned eventually to development actors. After a benchmarking process that is projected to last two years, it is intended that assistance to Haiti will be provided by a non-peacekeeping UN presence.[83]

On the closure of MINUSTAH, the General Assembly decided to transfer $40.5 million in unspent funds to the UN Haiti Cholera Response Multi-Partner Trust Fund. The USA decided not to participate as it had already spent $100 million on the cholera epidemic.[84]

Colombia

The situation in Colombia improved further in 2017 and levels of violence were at their lowest for over 40 years. As part of the implementation of the peace agreement, the Revolutionary Armed Forces of Colombia-People's Army (Fuerzas Armadas Revolucionarias de Colombia-Ejército del Pueblo, FARC-EP) laid down its weapons and demobilized. This process was completed and verified by the UN Mission in Colombia (UNMC) on 27 June.[85] After the closure of the UNMC on 25 September, the Secretary-General drew a number of conclusions in a report on the mission, most notably that: (*a*) the strong and united support of the Security Council and the political will of the parties were essential to the mission's success; (*b*) its two-stage mandating process, involving an initial mandate followed by a more detailed one when all the information was available, proved to be an efficient process; and (*c*) even though it was not integrated with the mission, cooperation with the UN Country Team was invaluable.[86]

[83] UN Security Council Resolution 2350, 13 Apr. 2017.

[84] United Nations, General Assembly, Strengthening of the coordination of humanitarian and disaster relief assistance of the United Nations, including special economic assistance: Special economic assistance to individual countries or regions, The new United Nations approach to cholera in Haiti, A/71/L.78, 10 July 2017; and UN approves use of unspent funds on Haiti's cholera epidemic, VOA News, 13 July 2017.

[85] United Nations, Security Council, Statement by the President of the Security Council, S/PRST/2017/6, 11 May 2017; and UN Security Council Resolution 2366, 10 July 2017. On the conflict in Colombia see also chapter 2, section II, in this volume.

[86] United Nations, Security Council, Report of the Secretary-General on the United Nations Verification Mission in Colombia, S/2017/801, 26 Sep. 2017.

Implementation of further aspects of the peace agreement, such as those on reconciliation, is still to follow. In order to verify these efforts, on 26 September the Security Council established the UN Verification Mission in Colombia (UNVMC) as a follow-up to the UNMC, for an initial period of 12 months. Its tasks are to include verification of the economic and social reincorporation of the FARC-EP, implementation of the personal and collective security guarantees, and protection measures for communities and organizations.[87] The UNVMC was mandated to have approximately 120 international unarmed observers and an appropriate civilian component deployed at the mission's headquarters in Bogota, in nine regional offices and in 26 local teams. In its geographical deployment, the mission aims to cover the priority areas of reintegration and security guarantees, and to co-locate and closely coordinate with the UN Country Team.[88]

The Government of Colombia and the National Liberation Army (Ejército de Liberación Nacional, ELN) signed a temporary ceasefire on 4 September. Both parties asked the UN to become part of the monitoring and verification mechanism. Within two weeks of its establishment, the Security Council added verification of this ceasefire, as well as preventing and responding to incidents to the UNVMC's mandate. To this end, the Security Council authorized a maximum of 70 additional international observers.[89]

Asia and Oceania

There were six multilateral peace operations in Asia and Oceania in 2017, one fewer than in 2016. The number of personnel deployed in this region increased by 11 per cent during 2017, from 13 975 to 15 467. This was primarily the result of an increase in the number of troops in the North Atlantic Treaty Organization (NATO)-led Resolute Support Mission (RSM) in Afghanistan. The other peace operations in the region were two ad hoc operations— the Neutral Nations Supervisory Commission (NNSC) on the Korean Peninsula and the International Monitoring Team on the Philippine Island of Mindanao—and two UN missions—the UN Military Observer Group in India and Pakistan (UNMOGIP) in the State of Jammu and Kashmir, and the UN Assistance Mission in Afghanistan (UNAMA). The Regional Assistance Mission to the Solomon Islands (RAMSI), which was led by Australia and New Zealand under the political authority of the Pacific Islands Forum, terminated in mid-2017.

---

[87] United Nations, Security Council, Statement by the President of the Security Council, S/PRST/2017/6, 11 May 2017; and UN Security Council Resolution 2366, 10 July 2017.

[88] United Nations, Security Council, Report of the Secretary-General on the United Nations Verification Mission in Colombia, S/2017/745, 30 Aug. 2017; and UN Security Council Resolution 2377, 14 Sep. 2017.

[89] UN Security Council Resolution 2381, 6 Oct. 2017.

The RSM was one of two peace operations active in Afghanistan in 2017—the other being UNAMA following the termination of the European Police Mission in Afghanistan at the end of 2016—and was by far the largest mission in the region. The RSM was initially meant to stay in Afghanistan for a period of two years, to continue to train, advise and assist the Afghan National Security Forces (ANSF) following the termination of ISAF and the formal end of NATO-led combat operations at the end of 2014. However, NATO leaders decided to extend the RSM beyond this two-year period at their Summit in Warsaw in 2016, and announced their intention to increase the number of troops in the RSM from 13 000 to 16 000 in November 2017. This followed the decision by the Trump administration to replace the USA's existing timeline-based policy for departure from Afghanistan with a conditions-based strategy, and to deploy an additional 4000 US personnel to Afghanistan to reinforce the RSM and the regional US counterterrorism operation, Freedom's Sentinel.[90]

Europe

There were 18 multilateral peace operations in Europe in 2017—the same number as in the previous year. The number of personnel in peace operations in Europe decreased by 2.7 per cent during 2017, from 8832 to 8597. With the exception of the UN Peacekeeping Force in Cyprus (UNFICYP), all the peace operations in Europe were deployed in the states of the former Yugoslavia or states that had been part of the Soviet Union.

There were three peace operations in Ukraine in 2017, all of which were deployed in response to the armed conflict that broke out there in 2014. These were the OSCE Special Monitoring Mission (SMM), the Observer Mission at the Russian Checkpoints of Gukovo and Donetsk, and the EU Advisory Mission (EUAM). On 5 September, Russia proposed the launch of a UN Support Mission to Protect the OSCE SMM in south-eastern Ukraine along the de facto line of contact.[91] From a Ukrainian perspective this would have 'frozen' the conflict. A second Russian proposal reportedly included deploying such an operation throughout the SMM mission area. This proposal gained more interest from Ukraine and among Western countries. In response, Ukraine drafted its own proposal to deploy a broader peace operation that, among a variety tasks, would help to return the Donbas region to

---

[90] On the conflict in Afghanistan see also chapter 2, section III, in this volume.
[91] United Nations, Security Council, 'Letter dated 5 September 2017 from the Permanent Representative of the Russian Federation to the United Nations addressed to the Secretary-General and the President of the Security Council', S/2017/754, 5 Sep. 2017. On the conflict in Ukraine see also chapter 2, section IV, in this volume.

Ukrainian control and to secure the Russian border. This proposal was not tabled after the USA discouraged it in favour of continued diplomacy.[92]

There were 10 peace operations in the Western Balkans. Four of these were located in Kosovo, three in Bosnia and Herzegovina, and one each in Albania, Macedonia and Serbia. The NATO-led Kosovo Force (KFOR) and the EU Rule of Law Mission (EULEX) in Kosovo were the largest of these missions. All the others were relatively small. The remaining peace operations were located in Georgia, Moldova and Nagorno-Karabakh.

The Middle East

There were nine multilateral peace operations in the Middle East in 2017, one more than in the previous year. The number of personnel deployed in missions in this region also remained fairly constant during the year. At the end of 2017 there were 14 001 personnel deployed in peace operations in the Middle East, compared with 13 928 at the end of 2016.

On 19 June 2017, the Council of the EU announced that it had received a request from the Iraqi authorities to deploy an EU Security Sector Reform Advise and Assist Team. The EU Advisory Mission in support of Security Sector Reform in Iraq (EUAM Iraq) was established on 16 October to: (a) provide advice and expertise at the strategic level to contribute to the implementation of the Iraqi National Security Strategy; (b) analyse, assess and identify opportunities for further EU support for SSR in Iraq; and (c) assist with the coordination of EU and member states' support in the field of SSR in Iraq. More concretely, it will assist efforts to implement the National Counter-Terrorism Strategy and with the drafting of a national strategy against organized crime, and map ongoing activities to identify lessons and gaps. It deployed to Baghdad on 17 November.[93]

Despite continued fighting in the area of separation between Israel and Syria, the UN Disengagement Observer Force (UNDOF) slowly returned to previously vacated positions, starting with Camp Faouar on the eastern border of the buffer zone (the bravo side). However, it continued to struggle to achieve the capacity and resources required to implement its mandate in a safe way.[94]

---

[92] International Crisis Group (ICG), *Can Peacekeepers Break the Deadlock in Ukraine?* Report no. 246 (ICG Europe: Brussels, 15 Dec. 2017).

[93] Council Decision 2017/1869/CFSP of 16 October 2017 on the European Union Advisory Mission in support of Security Sector Reform in Iraq (EUAM Iraq), *Official Journal of the European Union*, L266/18, 17 Oct. 2017; and European External Action Service, Common Security and Defence Policy, EU Advisory Mission in support of Security Sector Reform in Iraq (EUAM Iraq), Nov. 2017. On the conflict in Iraq see also chapter 2, section V, in this volume.

[94] UN Security Council Resolution 2361, 29 June 2017; and UN Security Council Resolution 2394, 21 Dec. 2017.

Incidents in the area of operations of the UN Interim Force in Lebanon (UNIFIL) demonstrated the continuing fragility of the situation there.[95] Nonetheless, it was perhaps in the Security Council that the most notable developments and heated debates took place. The Trump administration and Israel called for a more forceful attitude from UNIFIL and sought a strengthened mandate to proactively confront Hezbollah, which the USA alleged was illegally stockpiling weapons. Other members of the Security Council—particularly those that were contributing troops to the mission, such as France and Italy—strongly disagreed, as they argued that this might destabilize southern Lebanon.[96] The final text of UNIFIL's renewed mandate contained tougher language against Hezbollah than before and requested the Secretary-General 'to look at ways to enhance UNIFIL's efforts . . . including ways to increase UNIFIL's visible presence, including through patrols and inspections, within its existing mandate and capabilities'. UNIFIL's mandate, however, was not changed.[97]

Finally, the Multinational Force and Observers (MFO) continued to monitor the implementation of the 1979 peace treaty between Egypt and Israel. The personnel strength of the MFO decreased further in 2017, from 1383 to 1300. This reduction resulted from a reconfiguration of the force in 2016 and 2017, in which it reduced its presence in northern Sinai and increased its reliance on remote sensors rather than ground-based monitoring.[98]

[95] United Nations, Security Council, Report of the Secretary-General on the implementation of Security Council Resolution 1701 (2006), S/2017/591, 11 July 2017.

[96] 'Vote on a Resolution Renewing UNIFIL', What's in Blue, 30 Aug. 2017.

[97] UN Security Council Resolution 2373, 30 Aug. 2017.

[98] Schenker, D., 'The MFO 2.0', The Washington Institute, 16 May 2016.

III. Multilateral non-peace operations

JAÏR VAN DER LIJN

An increasing number of military and civilian personnel are being deployed in operations that fall within the grey zone of just outside the SIPRI definition of multilateral peace operations. These kinds of multilateral non-peace operations are mandated or welcomed by the United Nations Security Council but fall outside the SIPRI definition, for example, because they do not serve as instruments to facilitate the implementation of peace agreements, support peace processes, or assist conflict prevention or peacebuilding efforts. Other multilateral non-peace operations may fall outside the SIPRI definition of multilateral peace operations because their units operate on their own territory.[1]

In 2017, two operations drew extra attention in the UN Security Council: the Group of Five for the Sahel (G5 Sahel) Joint Force (Force Conjointe des Etats du G5 Sahel, FC-G5S) and the Multinational Joint Task Force (MNJTF) against Boko Haram. In addition to these two, other operations that have undertaken considerable efforts are: the 4000-troop French Operation Barkhane, which also implements Security Council-mandated tasks; the European Union Military Operation in the Southern Central Mediterranean (EUNAVFOR MED, or Operation Sophia), which deployed multiple European navy vessels and nearly 1000 personnel in 2017 and is mandated to implement the Libyan arms embargo by means of maritime interdiction; and the 1031-strong Regional Task Force (RTF) of the African Union (AU) Regional Coordination Initiative against the Lord's Resistance Army. Following the withdrawal of US Special Forces in May and the Ugandan People's Defence Forces (UPDF) in August, however, the RTF has been left toothless, despite its mandate renewal of one year by the AU Peace and Security Council in May.[2]

The Group of Five for the Sahel Joint Force

On 6 February 2017, the G5 Sahel set up FC-G5S to fight terrorism and organized crime on the territory of its member states—Burkina Faso, Chad, Mali, Mauritania and Niger.[3] On 13 April, the AU Peace and Security Council

---

[1] For a discussion of the SIPRI definition of multilateral peace operations and the missions that fall in the grey zone outside this definition see Smit, T., 'Global trends in peace operations', *SIPRI Yearbook 2017*, pp. 165–75. The increased deployment of multilateral non-peace operations, particularly when they involve military operations, will demand increased attention in future editions of the SIPRI Yearbook.

[2] African Union, Peace and Security Council, Communiqué 685th meeting, PSC/PR/COMM(D-CLXXXV), 12 May 2017.

[3] G5 Sahel, Permanent Secretariat, Resolution 00-01/2017, Relative a la creation d'une force conjointe du G5 Sahel [Resolution on the creation of a joint G5 Sahel force], 6 Feb. 2017. On the conflict in

endorsed the strategic concept and authorized a 5000-strong mission. The mission was to have military, police and civilian components, and the latter two were to deal in particular with human rights and the protection of civilians. The FC-G5S mandate is to: (a) combat terrorism, drug trafficking and human trafficking, with the aim of creating a more secure environment in the Sahel region by eradicating 'terrorist armed groups' and organized criminal groups; (b) contribute to the restoration of state authority and the return of displaced persons and refugees; (c) facilitate humanitarian assistance; and (d) assist development efforts.[4] Once it is fully operational, the FC-G5S will consist of 5000 personnel, including 500 police.

The Secretary-General recommended that the Security Council approve the deployment of the FC-G5S and authorize him to look into financial and other modalities for support.[5] The FC-G5S was of particular importance to France, as part of its strategy to reduce the pressure on its overstretched armed forces deployed in operations such as Barkhane. France was therefore willing to push hard against the United States, which was resistant to any potential UN financial or other support as it sought to reduce the UN peacekeeping budget (but perhaps could not be seen to be vetoing a counterterrorism force). The USA argued that: (a) the force did not need a UN mandate because it would be operating on the territory of its own member states; (b) its mandate was too broad and unclear, as the force would be eradicating 'undefined criminal networks'; (c) it lacked sufficient accountability and oversight; (d) coordination with other operations in the region needed to be further operationalized; and (e) the lack of an exit strategy meant that it would be prone to mission creep.[6] Eventually, the Security Council welcomed—rather than authorized as France had wanted but the USA had opposed—the deployment of the FC-G5S, encouraged bilateral and non-UN funding and agreed to review the mission after four months.[7] The Security Council also requested MINUSMA to coordinate with the FC-G5S, through information and intelligence sharing among other things.[8]

The FC-G5S reached its initial operational capacity by 17 October and undertook its first operation, Hawbi, in the central boundary zone. It is scheduled to be fully operational by March 2018.[9] The FC-G5S managed to

the Sahel region see also chapter 2, section VI, in this volume.

[4] African Union, Peace and Security Council, Communiqué, 679th meeting, PSC/PR/COMM (DCLXXIX), 13 Apr. 2017.

[5] United Nations, Security Council, Report of the Secretary-General on the situation in Mali, S/2017/478, 6 June 2017.

[6] Lynch, C., 'Trump weighs vetoing France's African anti-terrorism plan', *Foreign Policy*, 13 June 2017; and Nichols, M., 'US wary of French push for UN to back Sahel force: Diplomats', Reuters, 6 June 2017.

[7] UN Security Council Resolution 2359, 21 June 2017.

[8] UN Security Council Resolution 2364, 29 June 2017.

[9] UN Security Council Resolution 2391, 8 Dec. 2017.

collect over half of its estimated budget of €500 million from donors such as the European Union (€50 million), Saudi Arabia (€100 million), the United Arab Emirates (€30 million) and the USA ($60 million).[10] In addition, the Security Council decided after four months that the FC-G5S was contributing to the stability of Mali and, as such, to the fulfilment of MINUSMA's mandate. It therefore requested MINUSMA to provide operational and logistical support to the FC-G5S on Malian territory until it becomes self-reliant. This will include the provision of medical and casualty evacuation (MEDEVAC and CASEVAC), access to water, rations and fuel, and use of engineers to assist with the preparation of operational bases in Mali. Moreover, given that military operations like FC-G5S run the risk of having adverse effects if they do not fully respect human rights, the support guarantees a compliance framework based on the Human Rights Due Diligence Policy (HRDDP) on UN support to non-UN security forces.[11]

The Multinational Joint Task Force against Boko Haram

Like the FC-G5S, the 10 772-strong MNJTF involves countries deploying operations on their own territory. The Lake Chad Basin Commission (LCBC) member states (Cameroon, Chad, Niger and Nigeria) and Benin are working together to combat Boko Haram. The MNJTF developed its concept of operations and received support from the AU Peace and Security Council in 2014. In the context of the UN, in March 2015 the Security Council considered a draft resolution on providing assistance, including financial support, to the MNJTF under Chapter VII of the UN Charter. After the election of President Mohammadu Buhari in Nigeria, however, the country changed its position, no longer sought a Chapter VII mandate and instead chose to fund most of the operation itself.[12] Subsequently, the Security Council commended the efforts of the MNJTF and asked it to mitigate the security, development and humanitarian consequences of the fighting.[13] At the same time, the Security Council has encouraged other actors to share intelligence with the MNJTF.[14]

In 2017 the Security Council addressed the MNJTF in a separate resolution for the first time. It stressed the need for operations to be conducted in accordance with international law, and again emphasized the need for a

[10] France Diplomatie, 'G5 Sahel joint force and alliance for the Sahel' [n.d.].

[11] United Nations, Security Council, 'Report of the Secretary-General on the Joint Force of the Group of Five for the Sahel', S/2017/869, 16 Oct. 2017; and UN Security Council Resolution 2391, 8 Dec. 2017.

[12] African Union, Peace and Security Council, 484th meeting at the level of Heads of State and Government, Communiqué, PSC/AHG/COMM.2(CDLXXXIV), 29 Jan. 2015; and UN Office for West Africa, Security Council Report, 'July 2015 monthly forecast', 1 July 2015. On the conflict in the Lake Chad region see also chapter 2, section VI, in this volume.

[13] United Nations, Security Council, Statement by the President of the Security Council, S/PRST/2015/14, 28 July 2015.

[14] United Nations, Security Council, Statement by the President of the Security Council, S/PRST/2016/7, 13 May 2016.

holistic approach that goes beyond military operations to include civilian efforts such as improving governance, inclusivity and economic development.[15]

The year seemed to be a relatively successful one for the MNJTF. It was able to make important territorial gains, liberate a number of hostages and increase the number of defectors. The countries in the region also paid increasing attention to the root causes of the conflict, by means of development efforts such as the 'Buhari Plan' in Nigeria. In January 2017, however, the Nigerian Air Force accidentally bombed a refugee camp in Rann. The Security Council called for an investigation into the incident, for the deployment of civilian personnel, including human rights and gender advisers, and for donors to fulfil their pledges.[16] After losing territory, Boko Haram dispersed and instead intensified its suicide attacks. Thus, in spite of the progress made, Boko Haram remains a threat capable of causing large-scale humanitarian suffering.[17]

[15] UN Security Council Resolution 2349, 31 Mar. 2017.
[16] UN Security Council Resolution 2349, 31 Mar. 2017.
[17] United Nations, Security Council, 'Report of the Secretary-General on the situation in the Lake Chad Basin region', S/2017/764, 7 Sep. 2017.

IV. Table of multilateral peace operations, 2017

TIMO SMIT

Table 3.2 provides data on the 63 multilateral peace operations that were conducted during 2017, including operations that were launched or terminated during the year.

The table lists operations that were conducted under the authority of the United Nations, operations conducted by regional organizations and alliances, and operations conducted by ad hoc (non-standing) coalitions of states, as well as unilateral operations that were sanctioned by the UN or authorized by a UN Security Council resolution. UN operations are divided into three subgroups: (a) observer and multidimensional peace operations run by the Department of Peacekeeping Operations; (b) special political and peacebuilding missions; and (c) the joint African Union/UN Hybrid Operation in Darfur (UNAMID).

The table draws on the SIPRI Multilateral Peace Operations Database, which provides information on all UN and non-UN peace operations conducted since 2000, such as location, dates of deployment and operation, mandate, participating countries, number of personnel, budgets and fatalities.

Table 3.2. Multilateral peace operations, 2017

Unless otherwise stated, all figures are as of 31 Dec. 2017 or the date of closure. Operations that closed in 2017 are shown in italic type and are not included in the aggregate figures.

Operation	Start	Location	Mil.	Pol.	Civ.
United Nations Peacekeeping Operations			**68 957**	**8 277**	**3 947**
UNTSO	1948	Middle East	152	–	77
UNMOGIP	1951	India/Pakistan	44	–	22
UNFICYP	1964	Cyprus	888	68	32
UNDOF	1974	Syria (Golan)	990	–	45
UNIFIL	1978	Lebanon	10 492	–	245
MINURSO	1991	Western Sahara	227	2	74
MONUSCO	1999	DRC	15 856	1 351	747
UNMIK	1999	Kosovo	8	10	95
UNMIL	2003	Liberia	428	306	186
MINUSTAH	*2004*	*Haiti*	*299*	*1 497*	*136*
UNOCI	*2004*	*Côte d'Ivoire*	*–*	*–*	*25*
UNISFA	2011	Abyei	4 522	37	140
UNMISS	2011	South Sudan	12 969	1 599	861
MINUSMA	2013	Mali	11 698	1 725	663
MINUSCA	2014	CAR	10 683	2 020	649
MINUJUSTH	2017	Haiti	–	1 199	111
United Nations Special Political Mission			**1 142**	**75**	**1 070**
UNAMA	2002	Afghanistan	4	2	303
UNAMI	2003	Iraq	245	–	313
UNIOGBIS	2010	Guinea-Bissau	1	11	59
UNSMIL	2011	Libya	232	3	148
UNSOM	2013	Somalia	539	14	143
UNMC	*2016*	*Colombia*	*167*	*–*	*98*
UNVMC	2017	Colombia	121	45	104
United Nations/African Union (UN/AU)			**11 449**	**2 731**	**706**
UNAMID	2007	Sudan (Darfur)	11 449	2 731	706
African Union (AU)			**20 530**	**466**	**108**
AMISOM	2007	Somalia	20 522	466	51
MISAHEL	2013	Mali	–	–	11
MISAC	2014	CAR	–	–	9
AU Observer Mission in Burundi	2015	Burundi	8	–	37
Economic Community of West African States (ECOWAS)			**707**	**270**	**–**
ECOMIB	2012	Guinea-Bissau	332	145	–
ECOMIG	2017	Gambia	375	125	–
European Union (EU)			**1 361**	**326**	**773**
EUFOR ALTHEA	2004	Bosnia and Herzegovina	536	–	21
EUBAM Rafah	2005	Palestinian territories (Rafah Crossing Point)	–	1	7
EUPOL COPPS	2005	Palestinian territories	–	12	36

Operation	Start	Location	Mil.	Pol.	Civ.
EULEX Kosovo	2008	Kosovo	–	194	225
EUMM Georgia	2008	Georgia	–	–	206
EUTM Somalia	2010	Somalia	152	–	10
EUCAP Sahel Niger	2012	Niger	–	30	67
EUTM Mali	2013	Mali	510	–	31
EUAM Ukraine	2014	Ukraine	–	42	92
EUCAP Sahel Mali	2015	Mali	–	38	63
EUTM RCA	2016	CAR	163	–	1
EUAM Iraq	2017	Iraq	–	9	14
North Atlantic Treaty Organization (NATO)			**19 077**	**–**	**–**
KFOR	1999	Kosovo	4 031	–	–
RSM	2015	Afghanistan	15 046	–	–
Organization of American States (OAS)			**–**	**–**	**26**
MAPP/OEA	2004	Colombia	–	–	26
Organization for Security and Co-operation in Europe (OSCE)			**–**	**–**	**1 000**
OSCE Mission to Skopje	1992	Macedonia	–	–	37
OSCE Mission to Moldova	1993	Moldova	–	–	9
OSCE PRCIO	1995	Azerbaijan (Nagorno-Karabakh)	–	–	6
OSCE Mission to Bosnia and Herzegovina	1995	Bosnia and Herzegovina	–	–	29
OSCE Presence in Albania	1997	Albania	–	–	16
OMIK	1999	Kosovo	–	–	76
OSCE Mission to Serbia	2001	Serbia	–	–	20
OSCE SMM	2014	Ukraine	–	–	785
OSCE Observer Mission at the Russian Checkpoints Gukovo and Donetsk	2014	Russia (Gukovo and Donetsk checkpoints)	–	–	22
Pacific Islands Forum (PIF)			**–**	**..**	**..**
RAMSI	2003	*Solomon Islands*	–	..	..
Southern African Development Community (SADC)			**222**	**24**	**12**
SAPMIL	2017	Lesotho	222	24	12
Ad hoc coalitions of states			**2 358**	**3**	**294**
NNSC	1953	South Korea	10	–	–
MFO	1982	Egypt (Sinai)	1 187	–	113
JCC	1992	Moldova (Transnistria)	1 136	–	–
OHR	1995	Bosnia and Herzegovina	–	–	13
TIPH	1997	Palestinian territories (Hebron)	–	–	63
IMT	2004	Philippines (Mindanao)	25	3	8
CTSAMM	2015	South Sudan	–	–	97

– = not applicable; .. = information not available; AMISOM = AU Mission in Somalia; CAR = Central African Republic; Civ.= International civilian personnel; CTSAMM = Ceasefire and Transitional Security Arrangements Monitoring Mechanism; DRC = Democratic

Republic of the Congo; ECOMIB = ECOWAS Mission in Guinea-Bissau; ECOMIG = ECOWAS Mission in the Gambia; EUAM Iraq = EU Advisory Mission in Support of Security Sector Reform in Iraq; EUAM Ukraine = EU Advisory Mission for Civilian Security Sector Reform Ukraine; EUBAM Rafah = EU Border Assistance Mission for the Rafah Crossing Point; EUCAP Sahel Mali = EU Common Security and Defence Policy (CSDP) Mission in Mali; EUCAP Sahel Niger = EU CSDP Mission in Niger; EUFOR ALTHEA = EU Military Operation in Bosnia and Herzegovina; EULEX Kosovo = EU Rule of Law Mission in Kosovo; EUMM Georgia = EU Monitoring Mission in Georgia; EUPOL COPPS = EU Police Mission for the Palestinian Territories; EUTM Mali = EU Training Mission Mali; EUTM RCA = EU Training Mission in the CAR; EUTM Somalia = EU Training Mission Somalia; IMT = International Monitoring Team; JCC = Joint Control Commission Peacekeeping Force; KFOR = Kosovo Force; MAPP/OEA = OAS Mission to Support the Peace Process in Colombia; MFO = Multinational Force and Observers; MINUJUSTH = UN Mission for Justice Support in Haiti; MINURSO = UN Mission for the Referendum in Western Sahara; Mil. = military personnel (troops and military observers); MINUSCA = UN Multidimensional Integrated Stabilization Mission in the Central African Republic; MINUSMA = UN Multidimensional Integrated Stabilization Mission in Mali; MINUSTAH = UN Stabilization Mission in Haiti; MISAC = AU Mission for the Central African Republic and Central Africa; MISAHEL = AU Mission for Mali and the Sahel; MONUSCO = UN Organization Stabilization Mission in the Democratic Republic of the Congo; NNSC = Neutral Nations Supervisory Commission; OHR = Office of the High Representative; OMIK = OSCE Mission in Kosovo; OSCE SMM = OSCE Special Monitoring Mission in Ukraine; Pol. = police; PRCIO = Personal Representative of the Chairman-in-Office on the Conflict Dealt with by the OSCE Minsk Conference; RAMSI = Regional Assistance Mission to Solomon Islands; RSM = Resolute Support Mission; SAPMIL = SADC Preventive Mission in the Kingdom of Lesotho; TIPH = Temporary International Presence in Hebron; UNAMA = UN Assistance Mission in Afghanistan; UNAMI = UN Assistance Mission in Iraq; UNAMID = AU/UN Hybrid Operation in Darfur; UNDOF = UN Disengagement Observer Force; UNFICYP = UN Peacekeeping Force in Cyprus; UNIFIL = UN Interim Force in Lebanon; UNIOGBIS = UN Integrated Peace-building Office in Guinea-Bissau; UNISFA = UN Interim Security Force for Abyei; UNMIK = UN Interim Administration Mission in Kosovo; UNMIL = UN Mission in Liberia; UNMISS = UN Mission in South Sudan; UNMOGIP = UN Military Observer Group in India and Pakistan; UNOCI = UN Operation in Côte d'Ivoire; UNSMIL = UN Support Mission in Libya; UNSOM = UN Assistance Mission in Somalia; UNTSO = UN Truce Supervision Organization; UNVMC = UN Verification Mission in Colombia.

Source: SIPRI Multilateral Peace Operations Database. Data on multilateral peace operations is obtained from the following categories of open source: (*a*) official information provided by the secretariat of the organization concerned; (*b*) information provided by the operations themselves, either in official publications or in written responses to annual SIPRI question-naires; and (*c*) information from national governments contributing to the operation under consideration. In some instances, SIPRI researchers may gather additional information on an operation from the conducting organizations or governments of participating states by means of telephone interviews and email correspondence. These primary sources are supplemented by a wide selection of publicly available secondary sources consisting of specialist journals, research reports, news agencies and international, regional and local newspapers.

Part II. Military spending and armaments, 2017

Chapter 4. Military expenditure

Chapter 5. International arms transfers and developments in arms production

Chapter 6. World nuclear forces

4. Military expenditure

Overview

World military expenditure is estimated to have reached $1739 billion in 2017, the highest level since the end of the cold war. This represents 2.2 per cent of global gross domestic product (GDP) or $230 per person (see section I and table 4.1 in this chapter). Total global expenditure in 2017 was marginally higher compared with 2016, up by 1.1 per cent in real terms.

The global military spending trend in 2017 was heavily influenced by the spending patterns in the three subregions with the highest military expenditure: North America, East Asia and Western Europe. Spending in North America fell for the seventh consecutive year, down by 0.2 per cent compared with 2016. By contrast, military expenditure in East Asia continued to rise, for the 23rd year in succession, and was up by 4.1 per cent compared with 2016. In Western Europe, spending increased for the third consecutive year, up by 1.7 per cent from 2016. There were mixed spending trends in the rest of the world: military spending decreased in Africa, Central America and the Caribbean, and Eastern Europe, while spending increased in Central Europe, the Middle East (based on the countries for which data is available) and South America.

At $610 billion, military spending by the United States accounted for more than a third of the global total in 2017, and it remained the world's largest spender. Its spending was 2.7 times greater than the next highest spender, China. US military spending in 2017 accounted for 3.1 per cent of its GDP, unchanged from the level in 2016. While US military expenditure in 2017 was 22 per cent below the peak reached in 2010, the trend of falling US spending has tapered off. In late 2017 the US Senate approved a new military budget for 2018 of $700 billion, a substantial increase over the 2017 budget. The higher budget is to support increases in military personnel and the modernization of conventional and nuclear weapons.

China, the world's second largest spender, allocated an estimated $228 billion to its military in 2017, an increase of 5.6 per cent compared with 2016. This increase was the lowest since 2010 but remains in line with GDP growth plus inflation, and China's military burden thus stayed at 1.9 per cent of GDP. Saudi Arabia became the third largest spender in 2017 following a 9.2 per cent increase in military expenditure to $69.4 billion. By contrast, Russia's military spending fell by 20 per cent to $66.3 billion, making it the fourth largest spender in 2017. India, where spending rose by 5.5 per cent in 2017 to $63.9 billion, was the fifth largest spender.

SIPRI Yearbook 2018: Armaments, Disarmament and International Security
www.sipriyearbook.org

For countries whose economies are dependent on the export of oil, the size of government oil revenues plays an important role in decisions on spending. The fall in the price of oil in 2014 (and the low prices since then) has severely reduced oil revenues in these countries, leading to a need for alternative sources of finance (e.g. borrowing or debt) to fund spending, including military expenditure (see section II). Studying a set of 15 oil export-dependent countries— Algeria, Angola, Azerbaijan, Ecuador, Iran, Iraq, Kazakhstan, Kuwait, Mexico, Nigeria, Norway, Russia, Saudi Arabia, South Sudan and Venezuela—allows an assessment of the trend in the price of oil compared with the trend in military spending and debt as a share of GDP.

In the 15 countries considered, when oil revenue fell, alternative forms of finance were required and found. Debt, either local or external, has become the common first option in many of the 15 countries regardless of whether they have diversified economies, are developed or developing, or are in conflict or conflict-free. Of these 15 countries, military expenditure between 2014 and 2017 decreased by an average of 16 per cent, but the price of oil dropped by over 45 per cent and the average increase in total debt as a share of GDP was around 154 per cent (see table 4.5). The differences between revenue and expenditure in these countries have mostly been funded through debt, as shown by the specific country examples of Angola and Saudi Arabia.

SIPRI made major steps in 2017 to improve transparency in military expenditure by mapping off-budget funding in Peru and Venezuela (see section III). Off-budget spending that is not part of the state budget and is non-transparent is usually earned from natural resource exports and may be used, often outside the knowledge of the parliament or the finance ministry, to pay for arms purchases and other activities. Off-budget funds offer lucrative opportunities for self-enrichment to public officials and businesses involved in the decision-making processes. In the case of Venezuela and Peru, off-budget funding amounted to billions of dollars of spending, often without accountability or oversight (see figure 4.6 and table 4.6).

Military expenditure transparency at the international level remains a concern, specifically in the context of the United Nations Report on Military Expenditures. By 31 July 2017 at least 42 states had submitted a report to the UN on their military spending in 2016. No submission had been received from any state in Africa or the Middle East nor from four of the five largest military spenders in the world: the USA, China, Saudi Arabia and India. Continued low participation in, and the lack of comprehensiveness of, the UN reporting mechanism puts into question its future viability.

NAN TIAN

I. Global developments in military expenditure

NAN TIAN, AUDE FLEURANT, ALEXANDRA KUIMOVA,
PIETER D. WEZEMAN AND SIEMON T. WEZEMAN

Global military expenditure is estimated to have been $1739 billion in 2017, the highest level since the end of the cold war. This represents an increase of 1.1 per cent in real terms on 2016 and a 9.8 per cent increase since 2008 (see table 4.1 and figure 4.1).[1] The world military burden—global military expenditure as a share of global gross domestic product (GDP)—remained at 2.2 per cent in 2017, while military spending per capita increased to $230 per person.

The trend in global military expenditure in 2017 can be characterized by significant changes in three regions: Asia and Oceania, Europe, and the Middle East. Spending in Asia and Oceania rose by 3.6 per cent in 2017 to $477 billion, resulting almost entirely from the continued increase in China's military expenditure. In Europe, military expenditure declined by 2.2 per cent to $342 billion, mainly caused by the considerable drop in military spending by Russia (–20 per cent). Central Europe, however, had the highest percentage increase in military spending of all subregions (12 per cent), due to the perceived threat of Russia (see figure 4.2). There were particularly large relative increases in military expenditure in Latvia, Lithuania and Romania. For the third consecutive year, SIPRI cannot provide an estimate of total spending in the Middle East due to missing data from several key countries.[2] However, the combined total military expenditure of those countries in the Middle East for which data is available increased by 6.2 per cent to $151 billion in 2017. This growth in spending was principally related to an upturn in Saudi Arabia's military spending following a decrease in 2016 (see section II) and the large relative increases in spending in Iran and Iraq.

Military expenditure in the rest of the world remained largely unchanged in 2017. Spending in Africa was marginally down, by 0.5 per cent to $42.6 billion, primarily due to the first spending decrease in North Africa since 2006. Spending remained unchanged in the Americas, at $695 billion, with an increase in South America and decreases in North America and in Central America and the Caribbean.

---

[1] All figures for spending in 2017 are quoted in 2017 current US dollars. Except where otherwise stated, figures for increases or decreases in military spending are expressed in constant (2016) US dollars, often described as changes in 'real terms' or adjusted for inflation. The large differences in 2017 military expenditure when expressed in current 2017 US dollars compared with constant 2016 US dollars are caused by the overall depreciation of the US dollar against the currencies of the rest of the world. All SIPRI's military expenditure data is freely available in the SIPRI Military Expenditure Database on the SIPRI website. The sources and methods used to produce the data discussed in this chapter are also presented on the SIPRI website.

[2] No data is available for Qatar, Syria, the United Arab Emirates and Yemen.

Table 4.1. Military expenditure by region, 2008–17

Figures for 2008–17 are in US$ b. at constant (2016) prices and exchange rates. Figures for 2017 in the right-most column, marked *, are in current US$ b. Figures do not always add up to totals because of the conventions of rounding.

	2008	2009	2010	2011	2012	2013	2014	2015	2016	2017	2017*
World total	1 543	1 652	1 684	1 689	1 677	1 652	1 649	1 676	1 674	1 693	1 739
Geographical regions											
Africa	30.4	31.6	(33.2)	(36.0)	(36.8)	40.3	41.5	(39.3)	(38.9)	(38.7)	(42.6)
North Africa	9.3	(10.4)	(11.4)	(14.3)	15.4	17.7	18.7	(19.1)	(19.5)	(19.1)	(21.1)
Sub-Saharan Africa	21.1	21.2	(21.8)	(21.7)	(21.4)	(22.6)	(22.8)	20.2	19.4	19.6	21.6
Americas	759	818	841	832	789	734	694	682	675	676	695
Central America and the Caribbean	5.3	5.8	6.3	6.5	7.1	7.5	8.2	8.5	7.9	7.3	7.6
North America	710	766	785	776	732	674	634	621	618	617	630
South America	43.9	46.3	49.5	48.9	50.2	52.3	52.6	51.8	49.4	51.5	57.0
Asia and Oceania	295	332	340	354	368	387	409	431	453	469	477
Central and South Asia	52.8	60.6	61.5	62.7	63.1	63.2	66.6	68.3	74.0	77.8	82.7
East Asia	192	218	224	236	250	265	282	297	309	322	323
Oceania	21.6	23.2	23.5	23.1	22.3	22.1	23.9	26.2	28.6	28.4	29.9
South East Asia	29.1	30.5	30.9	31.9	33.1	36.5	36.2	39.8	40.5	40.5	41.1
Europe	323	329	322	316	318	312	314	324	335	327	342
Central Europe	19.2	18.6	17.9	17.5	17.2	17.0	18.0	20.4	20.7	23.1	24.1
Eastern Europe	46.2	47.5	48.2	51.8	59.6	62.4	67.1	72.3	75.5	61.5	72.9
Western Europe	257	263	256	247	241	232	229	231	239	243	245
Middle East	135	141	148	152	165	180	191	..	..	..	..
Military burden (i.e. world military spending as a % of world gross domestic product, both measured in current US$)											
World	2.4	2.6	2.5	2.4	2.4	2.3	2.1	2.3	2.2	2.2	
Africa	1.9	2.0	1.8	1.7	1.8	2.0	2.2	1.9	1.9	1.8	
Americas	1.5	1.6	1.6	1.5	1.5	1.5	1.4	1.4	1.3	1.3	
Asia and Oceania	1.7	1.9	1.7	1.7	1.7	1.7	1.8	1.9	1.9	1.7	

Europe	1.8	1.8	1.6	1.6	1.6	1.5	1.5	1.6	1.6	1.6
Middle East	4.0	4.7	4.4	4.6	5.0	5.0	5.1	5.8	5.5	5.2
World military spending per capita (current US$)	220	226	236	248	246	243	240	228	224	230

( ) = total based on country data accounting for less than 90% of the regional total; . . = estimate not provided due to unusually high levels of uncertainty and missing data.

Note: The totals for the world and regions are estimates, based on data from the SIPRI Military Expenditure Database. When military expenditure data for a country is missing for a few years, estimates are made, most often on the assumption that the rate of change in that country's military expenditure is the same as that for the region to which it belongs. When no estimates can be made, countries are excluded from the totals. The countries excluded from all totals here are Cuba, Eritrea, North Korea, Somalia, Syria, Turkmenistan and Uzbekistan. Totals for regions cover the same groups of countries for all years. Further detail on sources and methods can be found on the SIPRI website.

Sources: SIPRI Military Expenditure Database, May 2018; International Monetary Fund, World Economic Outlook Database, Oct. 2017; International Monetary Fund, International Financial Statistics Database, Sep. 2017; and United Nations Department of Economic and Social Affairs, Population Division, July 2017.

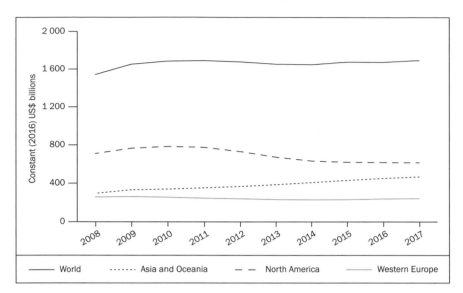

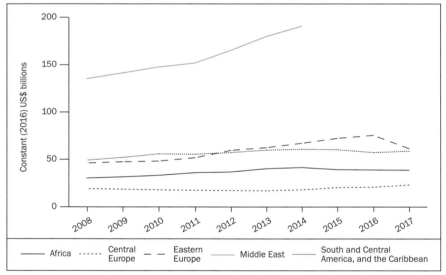

Figure 4.1. Military expenditure in major spending regions compared with other regions, 2008–17

Trends in military expenditure, 2008–17

While total global military spending continued its general upward trend in 2017, the spending trend for 2008–17 was relatively turbulent: annual increases in 2008–11, decreases in 2012–14 and then fluctuation in spending in 2015–16 (i.e. an increase and then a decrease). Various drivers have had major influences on the trends in 2008–17. The increases between 2008 and 2011 can be traced to the United States' 'global war on terrorism' and the

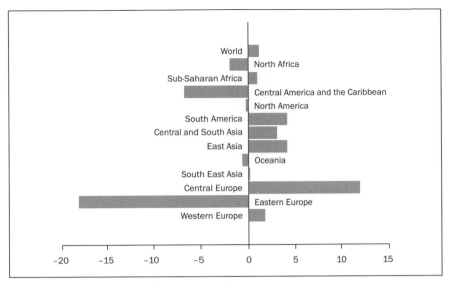

Figure 4.2. Changes in military expenditure by subregion, 2016–17

Note: No estimate of change in military expenditure in the Middle East is given since data for 2015–17 is highly uncertain. However, an estimate for the Middle East is included in the estimated world total. Totals for regions cover the same groups of countries for all years. Further detail on sources and methods can be found on the SIPRI website.

economic boom in the first half of the 2000s. The subsequent decreases until 2014 were due in part to the withdrawal of US troops from Afghanistan and Iraq, the USA's caps on government spending, and the post-2009 austerity measures adopted in many countries.[3] While spending in Asia and Oceania continues to push global military expenditure upwards, the overall effect of fluctuations in military expenditure in Europe and the Middle East since 2014—due to a fall in the price of oil and security concerns—has slowed the global rate of growth.

Between 2008 and 2017 the largest increases in military expenditure at the subregional level were in North Africa (105 per cent) and in three subregions of Asia and Oceania: East Asia (68 per cent), Central and South Asia (47 per cent) and South East Asia (39 per cent; see table 4.2). The growth in North Africa was the result of higher spending in all four countries, particularly Algeria. In East Asia, China's military spending continued to expand in line with its economic growth and its ambitions to increase global influence.[4] The higher spending in Central and South Asia can be attributed to India's procurement programmes and that in South East Asia to the tensions around the South China Sea.

[3] Fleurant, A., 'US military expenditure', *SIPRI Yearbook 2015*, pp. 353–59.
[4] Denyer, S., 'China's slowing economy leads to smallest increase in military spending in years', *Washington Post*, 4 Mar. 2016.

Table 4.2. Key military expenditure statistics by region, 2017

Spending figures are in US dollars, at current prices and exchange rates. Changes are in real terms, based on constant (2016) US dollars.

Region/ subregion	Military spending, 2017 (US$ b.)	Change (%) 2016–17	Change (%) 2008–17	Major changes, 2017 (%)[a] Increases		Major changes, 2017 (%)[a] Decreases	
World	**1 739**	*1.1*	*9.8*				
Africa[b]	(42.6)	*–0.5*	*28*	Gabon	42	South Sudan	–56
North Africa	(21.1)	*–1.9*	*105*	Benin	41	Chad	–33
Sub-Saharan Africa[b]	21.6	*0.9*	*–6.8*	Sudan	35	Mozambique	–21
				Mali	26	Côte d'Ivoire	–19
Americas	695	*0.0*	*–11*	Venezuela	20	Peru	–23
Central America and Caribbean[c]	7.6	*–6.6*	*39*	Bolivia	16	Guatemala	–9.7
North America	630	*–0.2*	*–13*	Argentina	15	Mexico	–8.1
South America	57.0	*4.1*	*17*	Uruguay	13	Trinidad and Tobago	–7.5
Asia and Oceania[d]	477	*3.6*	*59*	Philippines	21	Myanmar	–28
Central and South Asia[e]	82.7	*3.0*	*47*	Cambodia	21	Malaysia	–16
East Asia[f]	323	*4.1*	*68*	Nepal	12	Brunei Darussalam	–14
Oceania	29.9	*–0.6*	*32*	Bangladesh	7.2	Kazakhstan	–7.6
South East Asia	41.1	*0.1*	*39*				
Europe	342	*–2.2*	*1.4*	Romania	50	Russia	–20
Central Europe	24.1	*12*	*20*	Cyprus	22	Belarus	–5.6
Eastern Europe	72.9	*–18*	*33*	Lithuania	21	Georgia	–5.4
Western Europe	245	*1.7*	*–5.7*	Latvia	21	Moldova	–4.4
Middle East[g]	..	..	..	Iraq	17	Oman	–21
				Iran	15	Egypt	–11
				Turkey	9.7	Lebanon	–9.1

( ) = uncertain estimate; .. = not available.

[a] The list shows the countries with the largest increases or decreases for each region as a whole, rather than by subregion. Countries with a military expenditure in 2017 of less than $100 million (or $50 million in Africa) are excluded.
[b] Figures exclude Eritrea and Somalia.
[c] Figures exclude Cuba.
[d] Figures exclude North Korea, Turkmenistan and Uzbekistan.
[e] Figures exclude Turkmenistan and Uzbekistan.
[f] Figures exclude North Korea.
[g] No SIPRI estimate for the Middle East is available for 2015–17. A rough estimate for the Middle East (excluding Syria) is included in the world total.

Source: SIPRI Military Expenditure Database, May 2018.

By contrast, there were falls in military spending in North America (13 per cent), sub-Saharan Africa (6.8 per cent) and Western Europe (5.7 per cent). The decline in North America (which consists of Canada and the USA) was due to cuts in the US military budget. The decrease in sub-Saharan Africa was caused by the decline in Angola's and Sudan's military spending. In Western Europe, spending reductions in Italy, Spain and the United Kingdom, a relatively minor increase in Germany, and stagnancy in French military spending resulted in an overall subregional decrease between 2008 and 2017.

The largest military spenders in 2017

The 15 countries with the highest military spending in 2017 were the same set of countries as in 2016 (see table 4.3). However, there were some changes in ranking between the two years.[5] The USA (with 35 per cent of world military expenditure) and China (with 13 per cent) are by far the two largest spenders in the world. The countries ranked from third to fifth—Saudi Arabia, Russia and India—are starting to increase the spending gap with the rest of the top 15 countries: while these three countries all allocated over $60 billion to their militaries in 2017, all but one of the countries outside the top five spent less than $50 billion (the exception being France which spent $57.8 billion). Saudi Arabia regained the position of third largest spender from Russia following a 9.2 per cent increase in Saudi Arabian military spending and a 20 per cent drop in Russian spending. India moved from sixth place to fifth in the rankings.

Brazil moved up two places from 13th to 11th after its first annual increase in military spending since 2014. Italy and Australia each moved down one place in the ranking. Italy's military spending remained constant in 2017, while Australia had its first annual decline since 2013.

In analysing the trends of the top 15 military spenders over the past 10 years, several different patterns emerge. China, Turkey, India, Russia, Saudi Arabia and Australia made large increases (of more than 30 per cent) during 2008–17. There were more moderate increases (of 10–30 per cent) in the Republic of Korea (South Korea), Brazil and Canada, and minor increases (of less than 10 per cent) in Germany, France and Japan. Military spending fell in Italy, the UK and, most notably, the USA. US military expenditure decreased by 14 per cent (equivalent to $95 billion) between 2008 and 2017.

Five of the top 15 countries allocated less of their GDP to military spending in 2017 than 2008: the USA, India, the UK, Germany and Italy. Saudi Arabia, Russia, Australia and Canada spent a larger proportion of their GDP on their military, while the proportions were unchanged in China, France, Japan, South Korea, Brazil and Turkey. Of the top 15 spenders, Saudi Arabia

---

[5] The United Arab Emirates should be among the 15 largest spenders in 2017, probably ranking in the range 11–15, but a lack of data since 2014 means that no reasonable estimate of its military spending can be made and it has thus been omitted from the top 15 rankings.

Table 4.3. The 15 countries with the highest military expenditure in 2017

Spending figures and GDP are in US dollars, at current prices and exchange rates. Changes are in real terms, based on constant (2016) US dollars. Figures may not add up to stated totals due to the conventions of rounding.

Rank			Military spending, 2017 ($ b.)	Change, 2008–17 (%)	Share of GDP (%)[b]		Share of world military spending, 2017 (%)
2017	2016[a]	Country			2017	2008	
1	1	USA	610	−14	3.1	4.2	35
2	2	China	[228]	110	[1.9]	[1.9]	[13]
3	4	Saudi Arabia	[69.4]	34	[10]	7.4	[4.0]
4	3	Russia	66.3	36	4.3	3.3	3.8
5	6	India	63.9	45	2.5	2.6	3.7
Subtotal top 5			**1 038**	..	..	..	**60**
6	5	France	57.8	5.1	2.3	2.3	3.3
7	7	UK	47.2	−15	1.8	2.3	2.7
8	8	Japan	45.4	4.4	0.9	0.9	2.6
9	9	Germany	44.3	8.8	1.2	1.3	2.5
10	10	South Korea	39.2	29	2.6	2.6	2.3
Subtotal top 10			**1 271**	..	..	..	**73**
11	13	Brazil	29.3	21	1.4	1.4	1.7
12	11	Italy	29.2	−17	1.5	1.7	1.7
13	12	Australia	27.5	33	2.0	1.8	1.6
14	14	Canada	20.6	13	1.3	1.2	1.2
15	15	Turkey	18.2	46	2.2	2.2	1.0
Subtotal top 15			**1 396**	..	..	..	**80**
World			**1 739**	**9.8**	**2.2**	**2.4**	**100**

[] = estimated figure; GDP = gross domestic product.

[a] Rankings for 2016 are based on updated military expenditure figures for 2017 in the current edition of the SIPRI Military Expenditure Database. They may therefore differ from the rankings for 2016 given in *SIPRI Yearbook 2017* and in other SIPRI publications in 2017.

[b] The figures for military expenditure as a share of GDP are based on estimates of 2017 GDP from the International Monetary Fund World Economic Outlook and International Financial Statistics databases.

Sources: SIPRI Military Expenditure Database, May 2018; International Monetary Fund, World Economic Outlook Database, Oct. 2017; and International Monetary Fund, International Financial Statistics Database, Sep. 2017.

remained the country with the highest military burden, at 10 per cent of GDP, while Japan had the lowest, at 0.9 per cent of GDP.

The United States

At $610 billion, US military expenditure in 2017 was slightly lower, by 0.5 per cent, than in 2016. The country remains by far the largest spender in the world, spending 2.7 times more than the second largest military spender, China (see below). However, US military expenditure in 2017 was 22 per cent below the peak reached in 2010, which can be attributed to the US military 'surge' in Afghanistan and Iraq.[6]

Total US military expenditure covers outlays (actual expenditure) from (a) 'the base budget', that is, spending on the regular activities of the Department of Defense; (b) Department of Energy spending on the US nuclear arsenal; (c) military spending in other government departments; (d) spending on Overseas Contingency Operations, which funds military operations around the world; and (e) spending by the Department of State on foreign military aid.[7]

The failure to agree on a plan to reduce the USA's budget deficit following the impact on government revenues of the global financial crisis that began in around 2008 led to the adoption of the 2011 Budget Control Act (BCA).[8] The BCA limits US Government spending until 2021 in order to reduce the country's growing deficit.[9] Since the enactment of the BCA, negotiations on the budget, including the military budget, have been increasingly difficult and have illustrated the considerable polarization in US politics, both within the chambers of the US Congress and between the Congress and the president.[10] The election of the Republican candidate, Donald J. Trump, as US President in 2016 has not substantially changed this dynamic.[11]

In 2017 continuing discord led to an almost five-month delay in adopting the budget for the 2018 fiscal year (FY), which covers the period 1 October 2017 to 30 September 2018. During the delay, the Congress adopted short-term 'continuing' resolutions to keep government institutions open.[12]

On 19 October 2017 the Senate approved the Republican-backed military budget for FY 2018, which in turn was passed by the House of Representatives and signed by the president on 8 February 2018.[13] As Trump promised during his presidential campaign, the approved military budget for 2018 represents a significant increase (to $700 billion) over the military

---

[6] White House, Office of the Press Secretary, 'Remarks by the President in address to the nation on the way forward in Afghanistan and Pakistan', 1 Dec. 2009.

[7] Total US military aid spending in 2017 was $7 billion, or about 1.1% of total US military spending. US Department of State, *Congressional Budget Justification: Department of State, Foreign Operations, and Related Programs, Fiscal Year 2018* (US Department of State: Washington, DC, 23 May 2017).

[8] Budget Control Act of 2011, US Public Law no. 112-25, signed into law 2 Aug. 2011.

[9] The BCA mandates $1 trillion in savings between 2012 and 2021. On the BCA and its background see Sköns, E. and Perlo-Freeman, S., 'The United States' military spending and the 2011 budget crisis', *SIPRI Yearbook 2012*, pp. 162–66.

[10] Pew Research Center, 'The partisan divide on political values grows even wider', 5 Oct. 2017.

[11] Foran, C., 'America's political divide intensified during Trump's first year as president', *The Atlantic*, 5 Oct. 2017.

[12] As a general rule, continuing resolutions extend the level of resources allocated to government departments and agencies based on the previous year's budget allocations.

[13] Gambino, L., 'Senate passes Trump's budget, a first step towards contentious tax reform', *The Guardian*, 20 Oct. 2017.

Table 4.4. Components of SIPRI's estimates of China's military expenditure, 2013–17

Unless otherwise stated, figures are in yuan b. at current prices. Figures may not add up to stated totals because of the conventions of rounding.

	2013	2014	2015	2016	2017
National defence budget (central and local)	741	829	908	977	1 046
People's Armed Police	139	157	164	178	196
Additional military RDT&E spending	[116]	[120]	[122]	[132]	[140]
Payments to demobilized soldiers	68	70	76	86	92
Additional military construction spending	[45]	[49]	[52]	[56]	[60]
Arms imports	[3.7]	[8.6]	[9.3]	[8.4]	[11]
Commercial earnings of the PLA	[1.0]	[1.0]	[1.0]	[1.0]	[1.0]
Total	**1 115**	**1 233**	**1 333**	**1 437**	**1 544**
Total in US$ b. (current prices)	**180**	**201**	**214**	**216**	**228**

[ ] = estimated figure, PLA = People's Liberation Army; RDT&E = research, development, testing and evaluation.

Sources: SIPRI Military Expenditure Database, May 2018; and Chinese Ministry of Finance, various documents.

expenditure of $610 billion in 2017.[14] The higher military budget is intended to support increases in the number of military personnel as well as a comprehensive weapon modernization programme for both conventional and nuclear weapons. These projects follow from the new National Security Strategy that identifies China and Russia as rivals of the USA that 'challenge [US] power, influence and interests'.[15]

A consequence of the evolution of the US military budget in recent years is the general confusion surrounding the processes at work and a lack of clarity on the current and near future level of US military spending. Disputes between the Congress and the administration and between the political parties, as well as the use of continuing resolutions, have made the already complex US Government budget process even more difficult to follow by the public in the context of significant polarization of political life.

China

China, the world's second largest spender, allocated an estimated $228 billion to its military in 2017, an increase of 5.6 per cent since 2016. The rise in Chinese military expenditure continues to be in line with the government's

---

[14] McCarthy, T., 'Does the US really need a huge boost in military spending?', *The Guardian*, 9 Feb. 2018.

[15] White House, *National Security Strategy of the United States of America* (White House: Washington, DC, Dec. 2017), p. 2; and Gordon, M. R., 'Trump plans shift to US security strategy', *Wall Street Journal*, 18 Dec. 2017.

practice in previous years of following GDP growth plus inflation. The military burden thus remained at 1.9 per cent of GDP in 2017. If China continues to follow this approach, increases in military spending will slow down as the country's economy matures and growth stabilizes and slows down. The spending increase in 2017 was the lowest since 2010, and the rate of growth has not been this low since 1995.

China publishes a national defence budget each year, but this does not include additional important elements of total military expenditure—these lie in other parts of the state budget (see table 4.4). Data for several of these additional elements is available from official sources for at least some years (e.g. for the People's Armed Police and payments to demobilized soldiers), but data for others (e.g. additional spending on military research, development, testing and evaluation, additional spending on military construction, and spending on arms imports) is unavailable, incomplete or unreliable. As a result, the estimate of total Chinese military expenditure involves a significant degree of uncertainty.[16]

A notable element of China's military spending that is not currently included in the SIPRI estimate is 'retirement settlement' (退役安置, tuìyì ānzhì)—payments to military personnel who leave service. However, in 2015 China announced that it planned a reorganization of the People's Liberation Army, leading to a reduction of 300 000 military personnel by 2017.[17] This led to a sharp jump in the retirement settlement line of the national budget, which increased by 26 per cent from 47.4 billion yuan ($7.7 billion) in 2014 to 59.6 billion yuan ($9.6 billion) in 2015 and maintained a similar level in 2016 (with figures for 2017 yet to be released). As new information on this item of spending becomes available, SIPRI will review its methodology and, if appropriate, amend its estimate of China's military expenditure in a consistent manner.

Regional trends

Africa

Military expenditure in Africa remained roughly unchanged in real terms in 2017, marginally down by 0.5 per cent to an estimated $42.6 billion.[18] This fall continued the downward trend from the post-cold war peak reached in

[16] On SIPRI's methodology for estimating China's military spending see Perlo-Freeman. S., 'China's military expenditure', *SIPRI Yearbook 2016*, pp. 516–19.

[17] Perliz, J., 'China to raise military spending, but less than in recent years', *New York Times*, 4 Mar. 2017; and China Armed Forces, 'Experts' comments on defense and military reform', Xinhua, 27 Jan. 2016.

[18] This total excludes Eritrea and Somalia, for which it was impossible to make a reliable series of estimates for inclusion in the regional total.

2014 (see table 4.1). Despite three consecutive years of decreases, military expenditure in Africa was still 28 per cent higher in 2017 than in 2008.

Military spending in North Africa decreased for the first time since 2006, falling by 1.9 per cent to an estimated $21.1 billion in 2017. Nonetheless, spending in 2017 was 105 per cent higher than in 2008. Algeria accounts for around half of North African military expenditure and around a quarter of African military expenditure. Algeria's military spending decreased by 5.2 per cent to $10.1 billion in 2017. This was the first time since 2003 that its spending had fallen, and only the second time since 1995. The drop in spending in 2017 can be mainly attributed to the low price of oil and the continued fall in the Algerian Government's revenues from hydrocarbon extraction, which have kept the budget deficit high, depleted Algeria's national savings (down from 43 per cent of GDP in 2009 to just 4.6 per cent in 2016) and international reserves, substantially increased domestic borrowings, and prompted decreases in public spending (e.g. 5.8 per cent in 2016, with more cuts expected in 2017).[19]

Military expenditure in sub-Saharan Africa in 2017 was $21.6 billion, up 0.9 per cent from 2016 but 6.8 per cent lower than in 2008. The surge in Sudan's military expenditure in 2017 drove the upward trend, but this was partly counteracted by decreases in spending in three of the four largest spenders in the subregion: Angola, Nigeria and South Africa. Principal of those was the continued drop in Angola's military expenditure, which fell by 16 per cent to $3.1 billion in 2017. With austere government spending measures remaining in force, military spending was 61 per cent lower than at its peak in 2014.[20] While Angola was once the largest military spender in sub-Saharan Africa (with 26 per cent of the subregional total in 2014), it was in second place by 2016 and fell to third in 2017 (with 14 per cent of the subregional total), behind Sudan and South Africa (see section II).

There were also substantial cuts in military spending in 2017 in South Sudan (–56 per cent), Chad (–33 per cent), Mozambique (–21 per cent) and Côte d'Ivoire (–19 per cent). The decrease in Côte d'Ivoire's military spending, the first since 2013, was the result of the sharp drop in world prices for cocoa, the country's main export, which led to budget cuts in 2017 of around $413 million, including $117 million in military spending.[21] Chad's military expenditure has fluctuated dramatically from year to year: the 33 per cent decrease in 2017 followed a 42 per cent increase in 2016 and a 37 per cent

[19] International Monetary Fund (IMF), *Algeria: Staff Report for the 2017 Article IV Consultation*, IMF Country Report no. 17/141 (IMF: Washington, DC, 11 May 2017).

[20] International Monetary Fund (IMF), *Angola: Staff Report for the 2016 Article IV Consultation*, IMF Country Report no. 17/39 (IMF: Washington, DC, 23 Dec. 2016).

[21] 'Ivory Coast to cut budget spending by 10 pct on low cocoa prices—president', Reuters, 20 Apr. 2017; and Monnier, O., 'Ivory coast cuts budget as cocoa decline slashes export earnings', Bloomberg Markets, 12 May 2017.

decrease in 2015. The fall in 2017 can be attributed to a combination of the withdrawal of troops from fighting Boko Haram in Niger, low oil revenues and a deepening economic crisis.[22] In South Sudan, despite the renewed fighting between the national army (the Sudan People's Liberation Army, SPLA) and the Sudan People's Liberation Movement-in-Opposition (SPLM-IO), the worsening economic conditions (i.e. a fall in oil revenue, surging food prices, currency depreciation and hyperinflation) led to further reductions in military spending in 2017.[23]

The intensification in fighting between the Sudanese Government and rebels in Darfur from mid-2017 contributed to a considerable rise in Sudan's military spending, up 35 per cent to $4.4 billion in 2017.[24] The lull in armed activity in 2015 coincided with the lowest level of Sudanese military spending since the beginning of the armed conflict in Darfur, in 2003. But the government's subsequent commitment to military responses in Darfur drove up Sudanese military expenditure in 2016 and 2017 to become the highest in sub-Saharan Africa.[25]

Gabon had the highest relative increase in military expenditure in 2017 of any country in Africa. While Gabon's overall government budget decreased by 17 per cent, military spending increased by 42 per cent in 2017 to $299 million. Gabon became the third largest spender in West Africa, behind Nigeria and Côte d'Ivoire.

Nigeria's military expenditure fell for the sixth consecutive year in 2017, by 4.2 per cent to $1.6 billion, despite continued military operations against Boko Haram. Military spending by South Africa, the second largest spender in sub-Saharan Africa, has stabilized at around $3.6 billion, with a marginal decrease of 1.9 per cent in 2017.

The Americas

At $695 billion, military expenditure in the Americas in 2017 was unchanged from 2016 but was 11 per cent lower than in 2008. Spending by the two countries in North America (Canada and the USA) accounted for 91 per cent of the total for the Americas. North America's total of $630 billion was 0.2 per cent

---

[22] International Monetary Fund (IMF), *Chad: Third and Fourth Reviews under the Extended Credit Facility Arrangement, and Requests for Waivers of Nonobservance of Performance Criteria, Augmentation of Access, Extension of the Current Arrangement, and Rephasing of Disbursements*, IMF Country Report no. 16/364 (IMF: Washington, DC, 28 Oct. 2016); and Balima, B. and Farge, E., 'Chad withdraws troops from fight against Boko Haram in Niger', Reuters, 12 Oct. 2017.

[23] Pinaud, M., 'South Sudan—November 2017 update', 27 Dec. 2017, Armed Conflict Location and Event Data Project (ACLED), 27 Dec. 2017; Soi, C., 'There are no clear winners in South Sudan's war', Al Jazeera, 20 Apr. 2017; and International Monetary Fund (IMF), *Republic of South Sudan: Staff Report for the 2016 Article IV Consultation*, IMF Country Report no. 17/73 (IMF: Washington, DC, 28 Feb. 2017).

[24] Nuba Reports, 'A new conflict in Darfur, more displaced', 1 June 2017.

[25] United Nations, Security Council, Final report of the panel of experts on the Sudan established pursuant to Resolution 1591 (2005), 22 Dec. 2016, S/2017/22, 9 Jan. 2017.

lower than 2016 and 13 per cent lower than 2008. South American military spending grew by 4.1 per cent in 2017 to $57.0 billion, the first annual increase since 2014, bringing the overall increase since 2008 to 17 per cent. Between 2016 and 2017 military spending in Central America and the Caribbean fell by 6.6 per cent to $7.6 billion, but this was still 39 per cent higher than total spending in 2008. The combined military expenditure in South America and Central America and the Caribbean amounted to $64.6 billion in 2017, up by 2.7 per cent compared with 2016 and by 19 per cent compared with 2008.

The 4.1 per cent rise in military spending in South America can mainly be attributed to the increases by Argentina (by 15 per cent to $5.7 billion) and Brazil (by 6.3 per cent to $29.3 billion). Changes in Argentinian military expenditure for the latest year (in this case between 2016 and 2017) must be viewed with caution due to the regular and substantial differences between budgeted and actual spending. In each year since 1991, actual military expenditure has been on average only 94 per cent of budgeted expenditure for that year. The planned 2017 military budget of $5.7 billion could thus result in actual military expenditure of around $5.3 billion once spending is reported in 2018, representing a much lower annual increase of 6–7 per cent.

The increase in Brazil's military expenditure comes as a surprise given the country's current economic and political turmoil. The loosening of the government's budget deficit targets (up to 2020) and the release of additional funds ($4.1 billion) seem to have benefited all major sectors (education, healthcare and military spending), with the proportion of spending on these areas as a share of total government expenditure increasing in 2017 compared with 2016.[26] Military expenditure, at $29.3 billion, is the third largest area of government expenditure, behind healthcare and education.

Changes in military expenditure in Central America and the Caribbean are influenced mainly by Mexico, which accounts for 76 per cent of the subregion's spending. After many years of unofficial involvement by the military in combating Mexico's drug cartels, the 2017 Internal Security Law has now formalized that role. However, the weight of economic pressures (e.g. a high budget deficit and government debt) continues to limit government expenditure.[27] At $5.8 billion, Mexico's military spending in 2017 was 8.1 per cent lower than in 2016, down for the second consecutive year.

---

[26] Ayres, M. and Cascione, S., 'Brazil softens budget deficit goals through 2020', Reuters, 16 Aug. 2017; and Cascione, S., 'Update 1: Brazil frees up $4 billion in 2017 gov't spending', Reuters, 22 Sep. 2017.

[27] Agren, D., 'Amid criticism, Mexico is on track to strengthen military's role in fighting crime', *Washington Post*, 10 Dec. 2017; Webber, J., 'Mexico steps up austerity plans in 2017 budget', *Financial Times*, 9 Sep. 2016; and Ley de Seguridad Interior [Internal security law], *Diario Oficial de la Federación*, vol. 771, no. 18 (21 Dec. 2017).

Asia and Oceania

Military spending in Asia and Oceania amounted to $477 billion in 2017, an increase of 3.6 per cent compared with 2016. This was the lowest annual increase since the 2.4 per cent rise in 2010.

Military spending in the region grew by 59 per cent between 2008 and 2017.[28] The largest relative increases in military spending between 2008 and 2017 were made by Cambodia (332 per cent), Bangladesh (123 per cent), Indonesia (122 per cent) and China (110 per cent). There were other significant increases (higher than 40 per cent, but less than 100 per cent) in Viet Nam, the Philippines, Kyrgyzstan, Myanmar, Pakistan, Nepal and India. Military spending decreased in only five countries in Asia and Oceania over the 10-year period: Timor-Leste, Afghanistan, Fiji, Malaysia and Brunei Darussalam. Military spending in Asia and Oceania has risen from 17 per cent of global spending in 2008 to 27 per cent in 2017, primarily due to the significant increase in China's spending over the period. Moreover, five of the top 15 global spenders in 2017 are in Asia and Oceania: China (rank 2), India (rank 5), Japan (rank 8), South Korea (rank 10) and Australia (rank 13).

Many Asian states are continuing their long-term plans for modernization of their military capabilities. Existing interstate tensions in many Asian countries remain the main driving force behind the growth in military expenditure in the region.[29] The ongoing tensions include those between (*a*) the Democratic People's Republic of Korea (DPRK, or North Korea), South Korea and Japan on the Korean Peninsula; (*b*) China and Japan in the East China Sea; (*c*) China and several South East Asian countries over claims in the South China Sea; (*d*) India and Pakistan; and (*e*) India and China.

China's military spending, at an estimated $228 billion, accounted for 48 per cent of the regional total and was 3.6 times that of the second largest spender in Asia and Oceania, India. China's spending as a share of world spending rose from 5.8 per cent in 2008 to 13 per cent in 2017.

India's total military spending in 2017 was $63.9 billion, an increase of 5.5 per cent compared with 2016 and of 45 per cent compared with 2008. The Indian Government plans to modernize and enhance the operational capability of its armed forces and develop indigenous arms-production capabilities.[30] Both steps seem to be, at least partially, motivated by tensions with China and Pakistan.

---

[28] No data is available for North Korea, Turkmenistan and Uzbekistan for 2008–17 and they are not included in the totals for Asia and Oceania. The incomplete data for Tajikistan, which indicates an increase, is included in the total. Data for Laos is too incomplete to determine any clear trend.

[29] Tellis, A. J., Marble, A. and Tanner, T. (eds), *Strategic Asia 2010–11: Asia's Rising Power and America's Continued Purpose* (National Bureau of Asian Research: Seattle, WA, 2010); and Tweed, D., 'China tensions fuel acceleration in military spending in Asia', Bloomberg, 22 Feb. 2016.

[30] Jaitley, A., Indian Minister of Finance, 'Budget 2018–2019', Speech to the Lok Sabha, 1 Feb. 2018; and Magnus, G., 'Belt and road initiative stokes India–China confrontation', *Nikkei Asian*

Military spending by Japan was $45.4 billion in 2017, almost unchanged from 2016 (up by 0.2 per cent) and 4.4 per cent higher than in 2008. While perceived threats from China and North Korea remain key to Japan's security strategy, it is also focusing on improving the efficiency of, and streamlining, its armed forces.[31]

Europe

At a total of $342 billion in 2017, military spending in Europe accounted for 20 per cent of global military expenditure. It was 2.2 per cent lower than in 2016 and was only marginally (1.4 per cent) higher than in 2008. Between 2016 and 2017 military spending increased in Central Europe by 12 per cent to $24.1 billion and in Western Europe by 1.7 per cent to $245 billion, while it fell by 18 per cent in Eastern Europe to $72.9 billion. Over the 10-year period 2008–17, military spending in Central Europe and Eastern Europe rose by 20 and 33 per cent, respectively, while spending fell by 5.7 per cent in Western Europe.

Four of the 15 largest military spenders in the world in 2017 are in Western Europe: France (rank 6), the UK (rank 7), Germany (rank 9) and Italy (rank 12), all of which are members of the North Atlantic Treaty Organization (NATO). Together, they accounted for 10 per cent of global military expenditure in 2017, down from 15 per cent in 2008. This overall decrease in the share of global military spending represents a remarkable rank reversal between these largest West European spenders and China over the period 2008–17. In 2008 the combined spending of these four countries accounted for 2.6 times that of China, but by 2017 they spent only 78 per cent of China's total.

France's spending fell by 1.9 per cent to $57.8 billion in 2017, the first annual decrease since austerity measures ended in 2013. This was not unexpected following the new French Government's pledge to trim the 2017 military budget as a way to reduce the country's budget deficit.[32]

By contrast, Germany raised its military expenditure by 3.5 per cent in 2017 after a 4.2 per cent increase in 2016. At $44.3 billion, spending in 2017 was at its highest level since 1999. This followed the publication in 2016 of a government white paper on the military. In it the government concluded that the many crisis areas in the world and the increasing expectations of the role Germany should play in global security required the strengthening of

Review, 27 Feb. 2018.

[31] Japanese Ministry of Defense (MOD), *Defense Programs and Budget of Japan: Overview of FY2017 Budget Request* (MOD: Tokyo, Aug. 2016).

[32] Rubin, A. J., 'France's top general resigns in dispute over military spending', *New York Times*, 19 July 2017.

its armed forces and substantial increases in military spending.[33] It declared a long-term aim of reaching the NATO target of spending on the military—at least 2 per cent of GDP—but did not set an explicit timeline.[34] Based on Germany's GDP in 2017, reaching the NATO target would bring its military spending to about $70 billion, the highest in Europe. The stated objective of implementing such a large change prompted debate between the parties of the governing coalition during 2017 about the rate of further growth in military expenditure.[35]

British military spending rose by 0.5 per cent to $47.2 billion in 2017. This real-terms growth rate matches the government's announcement made in May 2017 that the military budget would increase by at least 0.5 per cent above the rate of inflation, a rate matched in previous years.[36] The British Ministry of Defence (MOD) estimates that the UK's military burden is around 2.2 per cent of GDP—above the NATO target of at least 2 per cent.[37] However, SIPRI estimates that it was 1.8 per cent in 2017. It is possible that this discrepancy can be attributed to differences in the definition of military spending. SIPRI's definition does not include non-monetary costs such as depreciation or amortization, which amounted to around $12 billion in 2017. By adding this figure to the SIPRI total, the UK's military burden would reach 2.2 per cent of GDP and thus match the figure quoted by the MOD.

The combined military spending of countries in Central Europe rose by 12 per cent in 2017 to $24.1 billion. All but two countries—Bosnia and Herzegovina and Serbia—increased their military expenditure in 2017, many citing the perceived threat to the subregion from Russia.[38] While Poland was by far the largest spender in Central Europe in 2017, accounting for 42 per cent of the subregional total, Romania made the largest relative increase: its military expenditure rose by 50 per cent compared with 2016 as it started to implement its military procurement, modernization and expansion plan for the period 2017–26. The plan is expected to cost a total of $11.6 billion and has already raised Romania's military burden to the NATO target of 2 per cent of GDP—the first time the country has reached that target since it became

---

[33] German Government, *Weissbuch 2016 Zur Sicherheitspolitik und zur Zukunft der Bundeswehr* [White paper 2016 on security policy and the future of the Bundeswehr] (German Ministry of Defence: Berlin, July 2016).

[34] For further detail on the NATO target see e.g. North Atlantic Council, 'Wales summit declaration', Press Release (2014) 120, 5 Sep. 2014.

[35] Werkhäuser, N., 'Mehr Geld fürs Militär?' [More money for the military?], Deutsche Welle, 8 Aug. 2017.

[36] Merrick, R., 'Theresa May pledges to increase defence spending after military chiefs warn UK losing the ability to fight wars', *The Independent*, 10 May 2017.

[37] See e.g. British Ministry of Defence, 'UK defence in numbers', Sep. 2017.

[38] Pezard, S. et al., *European Relations with Russia: Threat Perceptions, Responses and Strategies in the Wake of the Ukrainian Crisis*, Research Report no. 1579 (RAND Corporation: Santa Monica, CA, 2017).

a member of NATO in 2004.[39] Other notable increases in spending in the subregion were those of Latvia and Lithuania, both with annual increases of 21 per cent.

Military spending in Eastern Europe was $72.9 billion in 2017, a fall of 18 per cent compared with 2016. This decline in spending breaks the upward trend that began in 1998: between 1998 and 2016 military spending in Eastern Europe increased every year in real terms, and by 2016 it was almost 400 per cent higher than in 1998.

The decline in military spending in Eastern European was due almost entirely to the fall in Russian military expenditure, which in 2017 accounted for 91 per cent of the subregional total. From 2009 Russia's military spending had funded an accelerated programme for acquisition of new equipment and for modernization of arms factories.[40] This programme was intended to last until at least 2020 or 2025. However, the Russian economy has suffered a number of setbacks since 2014, including a significant drop in oil export revenues, and government spending has been falling since then. The military budget remained unaffected until 2017, when it fell for the first time since 1998. In 2017 Russian military spending was $66.3 billion, a real-terms drop of 20 per cent compared with 2016. It should be noted, however, that the Russian Government made a one-off debt repayment of roughly $11.8 billion (793 billion roubles) to Russian arms producers in 2016, which raised annual spending above the usual level. Russia plans to maintain a lower level of spending in 2018–20, which means that the 2011–20 budgets for force modernization will be significantly lower than originally planned, probably around 40 per cent lower.[41] The decrease in spending in 2017 brought Russia's military burden down to 4.3 per cent of GDP, from 5.5 per cent in 2016.

Ukraine's military expenditure in 2017 was $3.6 billion. While spending increased by 10 per cent in nominal terms, high inflation meant that military expenditure fell in real terms by 2.0 per cent. This is similar to the change in 2016 and very different from the strong real-terms growth in 2014–15, reflecting the stagnation in the scope of the conflict in eastern Ukraine since 2016.[42] Concerns, however, remain about a re-escalation of the conflict, as skirmishes between government soldiers and rebels continued into 2018.

---

[39] 'Romania commits to keep annual defence spending at 2 pct of GDP until 2026', Reuters, 1 Aug. 2017; and Wezeman, S. T. and Kuimova, A., 'Romania and Black Sea security', SIPRI Background Paper, forthcoming 2018.

[40] On Russia's state armament programme (gosudarstvennaya programma vooruzheniya, GPV) see e.g. Perlo-Freeman, S., 'Russian military expenditure, reform and restructuring', SIPRI Yearbook 2013, pp. 142–45.

[41] Cooper, J., 'Military spending in Russia's draft federal budget, 2018–20', Unpublished research note, 2 Oct. 2017.

[42] On the conflict in Ukraine see chapter 2, section IV, in this volume. See also Wezeman, S. T. and Kuimova, A., 'Ukraine and Black Sea security', SIPRI Background Paper, forthcoming 2018.

Improved economic conditions in Ukraine since 2016 have reduced its military spending as a share of GDP from a high of 4.0 per cent in 2015 to 3.4 per cent in 2017.[43]

The Middle East

Seven of the 10 countries with the highest military burden in the world in 2017 are in the Middle East.[44] However, SIPRI has not estimated total military spending in the Middle East in 2017 because of a lack of accurate data for several countries. These include Qatar and the United Arab Emirates (UAE)—which are assessed to be major military spenders based on their known large weapons acquisitions and their military spending levels in previous years—and Syria and Yemen.

The combined total military expenditure for those countries for which data is available shows a continuous increase between 2009 and 2015, resulting in a total increase between those years of 41 per cent. However, with the fall in oil prices, spending by these countries decreased by 16 per cent between 2015 and 2016. Their spending increased again in 2017, by 6.2 per cent, but their total was still 11 per cent lower than in 2015.

Saudi Arabia and the UAE are estimated to be the two largest military spenders in the region. Long-standing threat perceptions of and rivalry with Iran, along with the related military intervention in Yemen since 2015, are important drivers for their military expenditure. Major tensions between Qatar on the one side and Saudi Arabia and the UAE on the other that surfaced in 2017 have added further pressures to invest in military assets in these countries. Saudi Arabia is by far the largest military spender in the region and was the third largest in the world in 2017. Its military spending increased by 74 per cent between 2008 and 2015 to a peak of $90.3 billion. It then fell by 29 per cent in 2016, but increased again by 9.2 per cent in 2017 to $69.4 billion (see section II). The last available estimate for military spending by the UAE is for 2014 ($24.4 billion), when it was the second largest military spender in the region. Considering its military operations in Libya, Syria and Yemen, major arms procurement in recent years and developments in its overall government spending, it is reasonable to assume that the UAE's military spending remains at a similar level to 2014.

By 2014 Iran's military expenditure had declined steadily (by 31 per cent) from its peak in 2006. However, since 2014 the Iranian economy has benefited from the gradual lifting of European Union and United Nations

---

[43] World Bank, 'Ukraine economy update', 4 Apr. 2017.
[44] The 7 countries are Oman (12% of GDP), Saudi Arabia (10% of GDP), Kuwait (5.8% of GDP), Jordan (4.8% of GDP), Israel (4.7% of GDP), Lebanon (4.5% of GDP) and Bahrain (4.1% of GDP).

sanctions, which in turn facilitated a 37 per cent increase in military spending between 2014 and 2017 to $14.5 billion in 2017.[45]

Following a peak in Israel's spending in 2014–15, which coincided with its military operations in Gaza in 2014, Israel's military expenditure dropped by 13 per cent between 2015 and 2016. While military spending increased by 4.9 per cent to $16.5 billion in 2017 (excluding about $3.1 billion in military aid from the USA), this total is well below the levels of spending in 2014 and 2015.

Egyptian military expenditure in 2017 was 11 per cent lower than in 2016 and 16 per cent lower than in 2015. Considering Egypt's military operations in the Sinai, its security concerns regarding Libya, its contributions to the military intervention in Yemen and the major arms procurement programmes that it initiated in 2015, this development is notable. However, the available data may be inaccurate, possibly due to off-budget spending. Another explanation could be increased foreign military aid: while the USA has given military aid of typically $1.3 billion annually to Egypt since 1978, some of Egypt's recent arms imports from France were reportedly financed by additional military aid from Saudi Arabia.[46]

Between 2008 and 2017 Turkish military expenditure increased by 46 per cent to reach $18.2 billion, making it the 15th largest spender globally.[47] Over this decade, spending grew in real terms every year except for 2010. While the original 2017 military budget was lower than the 2016 budget, actual spending grew during the year by almost 10 per cent as military operations along the Syrian and Iraqi border increased. In 2017 Turkey spent 2.2 per cent of its GDP on the military, up from 2.1 per cent in 2016. Turkey exceeded the NATO target of 2 per cent of GDP in 8 of the 10 years between 2008 and 2017.

[45] On the lifting of sanctions see chapter 7, section V, and chapter 10, section II, in this volume.

[46] Sharp, J. M., *Egypt: Background and US Relations*, Congressional Research Service (CRS) Report for Congress RL33003 (US Congress, CRS: Washington, DC, 8 Feb. 2018), pp. 15–18; and Jova, P., 'Un des Mistral vendus à l'Egypte a pris la mer' [One of the Mistrals sold to Egypt went to sea], *Le Figaro*, 6 May 2016. SIPRI includes military aid in the military spending of the donor country, not the recipient.

[47] On Turkish military expenditure and military policy see Wezeman, S. T. and Kuimova, A., 'Turkey and Black Sea security', SIPRI Background Paper, forthcoming 2018.

II. Debt, oil price and military expenditure

NAN TIAN AND DIEGO LOPES DA SILVA

For countries whose economies are dependent on the export of oil, the size of government oil revenues plays an important role in decisions on spending. The fall in the price of oil in 2014 (and the low oil price since then) has severely reduced oil revenues in these countries. This has led them to increasingly rely on alternative sources of finance (e.g. borrowing or debt) to fund spending, including military expenditure. However, substantial increases in debt to unsustainable levels can potentially hinder economic development.

Following the oil price crash, oil export-dependent economies were exposed to sustained revenue losses, with macroeconomic consequences such as inflation, currency depreciation and severe budgetary pressures. In the process, the trade balance of countries such as Angola, Iran, Kuwait, Mexico and Saudi Arabia started to worsen because of lower exports and unchanged imports. This effect led to substantial cutbacks in government and military expenditure in many oil export-dependent countries, while debt has since soared.

This section expands the discussion in *SIPRI Yearbook 2017* on oil price shocks and military expenditure to include the role of debt.[1] It starts by providing an overview of the theoretical relationship between debt, military expenditure and the price of oil in oil export-dependent countries. This is followed by empirical analysis, which is supported by two brief country case studies, and some key conclusions.

The impact of military expenditure on debt in oil export-dependent countries during oil price shocks

The contribution that military expenditure makes to the build-up of a country's debt is an important point to consider given the potential adverse economic effects of debt. A reasonable level of borrowing can be beneficial to economic growth since it allows for capital mobility, investment and an increase in the marginal product of capital (i.e. the additional output resulting from the use of an additional unit of physical capital). Greater investment and higher rates of return will boost economic growth, allowing timely repayment of debt with overall benefits to the economy. However, excessive debt can have detrimental economic consequences since it leads to lower rates of return (because creditors have the first claim on any income) and

---

[1] Tian, N., 'Oil price shocks and military expenditure', *SIPRI Yearbook 2017*, pp. 343–49.

discourages investment, and hence economic growth. This phenomenon is known as 'debt overhang'.[2]

A fall in oil prices can have a significant effect on oil export-dependent economies. While the price of oil is volatile and varies on a daily basis, expenditure decisions are made annually with limited room for short-term adjustments. As revenue from oil drops and expenditure does not change, a gap between income and expenditure develops, which is often funded through debt (internal and external). The rise in debt following the loss of oil revenue is undesirable and governments may choose to limit it by cutting government expenditure in subsequent years (as happened in e.g. Algeria, Mexico, Russia and Saudi Arabia). However, because the loss in oil revenue is often much greater than the cuts in government spending, debt as a share of gross domestic product (GDP) will continue to increase in many countries.

These phenomena have been witnessed in all oil export-dependent countries following the sharp fall in the price of oil in late 2014. For these countries, cuts in government expenditure only occurred in the 2016 budget.

Military expenditure, a part of government expenditure, contributes to debt accumulation in two main ways. First, just like any other budget item, if revenue is insufficient to pay for military expenditure, a budget deficit will ensue. Second, arms imports must be paid for through foreign exchange, which may create a need to borrow externally.[3] One study has estimated that the external debt of developing countries would have been 20–30 per cent lower between 1970 and 1979 if arms imports were absent.[4] Even in a developed country such as Greece, military expenditure has been shown to have partially contributed to the growth of debt, in particular foreign debt through borrowing to finance arms imports.[5]

For oil export-dependent countries, a sustained low oil price creates a prolonged problem of unsustainably high levels of debt as a share of GDP. Thus, a substitution effect may occur where governments choose to prioritize certain sectors over others. In the case of military expenditure, the choice is commonly based on a country's security situation. As empirical evidence

[2] Reinhart, C. M. and Rogoff, K. S., 'Growth in a time of debt', National Bureau of Economic Research (NBER) Working Paper no. 15639, Jan. 2010; Krugman, P., 'Financing and forgiving a debt overhang', Journal of Development Economics, vol. 29, no. 3 (Nov. 1988), pp. 253–68; and Sachs, J. D., 'The debt overhang of developing countries', eds G. A. Calvo et al., Debt Stabilization and Development: Essays in Memory of Carlos Diaz Alejandro (Basil Blackwell: Oxford, 1989).

[3] Dunne, J. P., Perlo-Freeman, S. and Soydan, A., 'Military expenditure and debt in small industrialised economies: a panel analysis', Defence and Peace Economics, vol. 15, no. 2 (2004), pp. 125–32; and Dunne, J. P., Perlo-Freeman, S. and Soydan, A., 'Military expenditure and debt in South America', Defence and Peace Economics, vol. 15, no. 2 (2004), pp. 173–87.

[4] Brzoska, M., 'The military related external debt of third world countries', Journal of Peace Research, vol. 20, no. 3 (Sep. 1983), pp. 271–77.

[5] Kollias, C., Manolas, G. and Paleologouc, S., 'Military expenditure and government debt in Greece: some preliminary empirical findings', Defence and Peace Economics, vol. 15, no. 3 (2004), pp. 189–97.

shows, countries will fall into one of two categories. The first category includes countries that are involved in armed conflict or have other security concerns. These states often cannot cut military expenditure as it may threaten state survival. Since military spending in these cases must either remain constant or increase, debt as a share of GDP will probably rise if no substantial cuts are made in other areas. The second category includes countries that are not involved in armed conflict or have no pressing security concerns. For such countries, lower revenues lead to cuts in military spending. Nonetheless, the cuts in expenditure (both overall spending and military spending) remain relatively minor in comparison to the losses in oil revenue and thus debt continues to rise.

Military expenditure and debt in oil export-dependent countries, 2014–17

Studying a set of 15 oil export-dependent countries—Algeria, Angola, Azerbaijan, Ecuador, Iran, Iraq, Kazakhstan, Kuwait, Mexico, Nigeria, Norway, Russia, Saudi Arabia, South Sudan and Venezuela—allows an assessment of the trend of military spending and debt as a share of GDP for the years 2014–17. These 15 countries were chosen on the basis of data availability for military spending, healthcare and education budgets, and in order to include states with high (Angola, Iraq, Kuwait and Saudi Arabia), moderate (Algeria, Azerbaijan, Ecuador, Iran, Kazakhstan, Nigeria, South Sudan and Venezuela) and low (Mexico, Norway and Russia) dependence on revenue from oil exports.[6]

Only five of the 15 countries increased their military expenditure between 2014 and 2017 (see table 4.5). Four of those—Algeria, Iran, Iraq and Kuwait—are in regions of armed conflict or tension, while the fifth—Norway—has a diversified economy that is less reliant on oil revenues. Norway also perceives Russia as a growing threat. The average increase in total government debt of these five countries between 2014 and 2017 was 136 per cent, ranging from 17 per cent for Norway to 262 per cent for Kuwait. These countries potentially prioritized national or regional security over the consequences of high debt levels.

Debt as a share of GDP increased between 2014 and 2017 in all 10 countries that decreased their military spending. At the extreme, Saudi Arabia's debt grew by 989 per cent, partly because although military spending fell overall between 2014 and 2016, it started to rise again in 2017. Many of the remaining nine countries that cut military spending have less pronounced security concerns (except South Sudan, where there is an active intrastate conflict), but their debts as a share of GDP rose since the fall in their oil

---

[6] For further detail on this selection see also Tian (note 1).

Table 4.5. Military expenditure and debt in selected oil export-dependent countries, 2014–17

Military spending figures are in constant (2016) US dollars.

Country[a]	Military expenditure (US$ m.)			Debt as a share of GDP (%)		
	2014	2017	Change, 2014–17 (%)	2014	2017	Change, 2014–17 (%)
Algeria	9 545	9 684	1.5	7.7	18	131
Angola	6 110	2 372	–61	41	65	60
Azerbaijan	1 829	1 479	–19	14	46	222
Ecuador	2 947	2 413	–18	22	39	78
Iran	10 281	14 086	37	12	32	173
Iraq	6 956	7 284	4.7	32	64	99
Kazakhstan	1 475	1 184	–20	49	56	16
Kuwait	5 853	6 693	14	7.5	27	262
Mexico	6 514	5 533	–15	49	53	8
Nigeria	1 830	1 651	–10	12	21	71
Norway	5 821	6 330	8.7	28	33	17
Russia	59 929	55 327	–7.7	16	17	11
Saudi Arabia	85 435	69 521	–19	1.6	17	989
South Sudan[b]	569	59.5	–90	35	40	15
Venezuela[c]	535	261	–51	..	..	..

.. = not available; GDP = gross domestic product.

[a] Country selection is based on 2 factors: (*a*) the availability of data on the budget for military spending, education and healthcare; and (*b*) the heterogeneous nature of oil dependence to capture high, moderate and low oil dependence based on oil rents as a share of GDP.

[b] For South Sudan, as data for debt as a share of GDP in 2017 was unavailable, the data for 2016 was used instead.

[c] Data on Venezuelan Government debt is unavailable for the years 2014–17; however, reports have suggested substantial increases in debt amid severe economic problems.

Sources: SIPRI Military Expenditure Database, May 2018; International Monetary Fund, World Economic Outlook Database, Oct. 2017; and International Monetary Fund, *Republic of South Sudan: Staff Report for the 2016 Article IV Consultation*, IMF Country Report no. 17/73 (IMF: Washington, DC, 28 Feb. 2017).

revenues was larger than their expenditure cuts. However, at 60 per cent, the average increase in their debt was much lower than that of the five states that increased their military spending.[7]

As the price of oil peaked in 2014, debt levels in the majority of oil-exporting countries reached record lows. After 2014, there were large increases in debt across regions and income groups. The data suggests that, irrespective of the degree of oil dependence or whether military expenditure went up or down, there was a clear inverse relationship between debt and oil price.

[7] This average excludes Venezuela, for which no data on debt is available.

While the need to fund recurrent expenditure on the military no doubt contributed to debt accumulation, further impact can be attributed to payment for arms imports. Many of the countries with the largest increases in debt as a share of GDP also had substantial arms imports over the five-year period 2013–17 (e.g. Algeria, Kuwait and Saudi Arabia).[8] The decision to maintain or, in some cases, increase military spending can also be related to the country's security situation. Some of the countries that increased military spending—such as Algeria, Iran, Iraq, Kuwait and Saudi Arabia—are either situated in regions with interstate or intrastate armed conflicts or engaged in those conflicts.

Saudi Arabia

The case of Saudi Arabia is of particular interest because it is an oil export-dependent country with an undiversified economy and it is actively involved in armed conflict. Despite the oil price crash in 2014, Saudi Arabia's military intervention in Yemen, its involvement in the conflict in Syria and its threat perception of Iran pushed its military expenditure to a record high in 2015 (see figure 4.3).[9] A decrease in spending followed in 2016, as a result of the government's austerity measures, but expenditure started to rise again in 2017 because of unresolved conflicts in the region and new tensions with Qatar.[10]

As the price of crude oil dropped by 45 per cent between 2014 and 2017, Saudi Arabia's debt as a share of GDP increased by 989 per cent.[11] The immediate rise in Saudi Arabia's deficit to $367 billion in 2015 was a direct consequence of the fall in oil revenue and the government's inability to finance its spending.[12] The government subsequently implemented a set of relatively successful financial reforms (e.g. it cut spending, introduced new taxes and encouraged economic diversification). This reduced the deficit to $98 billion in 2016 and $79 billion in 2017.[13] A rise in the price of oil in 2017 also helped to ameliorate Saudi Arabia's finances.

The acute rise in indebtedness and the subsequent decline in the government deficit since 2015 suggests that Saudi Arabia looked for alternative sources of funding for its military spending—both from internal and external borrowing and from depletion of foreign exchange reserves. Although the growth in Saudi Arabia's debt cannot be solely caused by its military

---

[8] See also chapter 5, section I, in this volume.

[9] International Crisis Group, 'Yemen at war', Crisis Group Middle East Briefing no. 45, 27 Mar. 2015. See also chapter 2, section V, in this volume.

[10] Soloman, E., 'Middle East tensions rise as Iran and Saudi Arabia jostle for power', *Financial Times*, 9 Nov. 2017.

[11] Unless otherwise stated, all spending figures are quoted in current US dollars.

[12] 'Saudi Arabia cuts 2016 budget deficit, to boost 2017 spending', Reuters, 22 Dec. 2016.

[13] Bordoff, J., 'The Saudi Arabian reform slowdown and the oil price dilemma', *Financial Times*, 11 Sep. 2017.

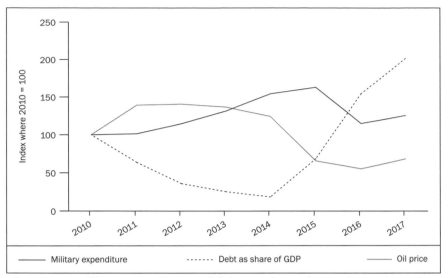

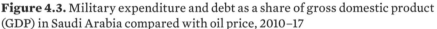

Figure 4.3. Military expenditure and debt as a share of gross domestic product (GDP) in Saudi Arabia compared with oil price, 2010–17

Note: The three lines in the graph represent indexes, with the values for 2010 set at 100 and the values for the other years showing relative difference from 2010. The time frame 2010–17 provides an indication of the trend before and after 2014.

Sources: SIPRI Military Expenditure Database, May 2018; International Monetary Fund, World Economic Outlook Database, Oct. 2017; and International Energy Agency, 'Monthly oil price statistics', various years.

expenditure, the strong positive correlation between military spending and the price of oil and the subsequent negative relationship with indebtedness suggest that Saudi Arabia used debt to fund part of its military expenditure. A separate study revealed a similar pattern in six other oil-rich Middle Eastern countries over the period 1988–2002, finding a causal relationship between military expenditure and external debt.[14]

The Saudi Arabian case indicates that armed conflict can potentially exacerbate the relationship between a low oil price and debt accumulation due to the choice to sustain high levels of military spending. The data on the 15 sample countries seems to support this argument (see table 4.5), as the growth in debt tends to be lower in countries where major armed conflict is absent: Ecuador, Kazakhstan, Norway and, as discussed below, Angola.

[14] Smyth, R. and Narayan, R. K., 'A panel data analysis of the military expenditure–external debt nexus: evidence from six Middle Eastern countries', *Journal of Peace Economics*, vol. 46, no. 2 (Mar. 2009), pp. 235–50.

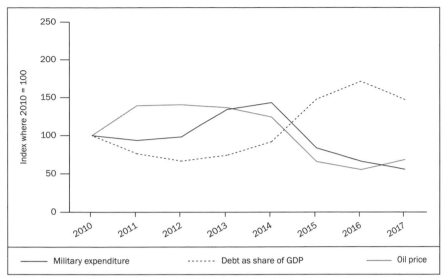

Figure 4.4. Military expenditure and debt as a share of gross domestic product (GDP) in Angola compared with oil price, 2010–17

Note: The three lines in the graph represent indexes, with the values for 2010 set at 100 and the values for the other years showing relative difference from 2010. The time frame 2010–17 provides an indication of the trend before and after 2014.

Sources: SIPRI Military Expenditure Database, May 2018; International Monetary Fund, World Economic Outlook Database, Oct. 2017; and International Energy Agency, 'Monthly oil price statistics', various years.

Angola

Angola is the second largest oil producer in Africa and has not been involved in any major armed conflict since the end of its civil war in 2002. The petroleum sector represents a third of its GDP and more than 95 per cent of its exports.[15] The Angolan economy was thus heavily affected by the oil price crash in 2014. To cope with inadequate revenues, the government has been trying to stimulate other sectors of the economy and reduce public spending.[16] Between 2014 and 2017 total government spending decreased by 48 per cent, while military expenditure shrank by 61 per cent. Unlike Saudi Arabia, where armed conflict demanded that the military budget be maintained, Angola had more leeway in reducing military spending to aid the economy's recovery. However, even reductions in military and other expenditures could not prevent an increase in Angola's total debt as a share of GDP between 2014 and 2017 (see figure 4.4).

[15] World Bank, 'The World Bank in Angola', 22 Jan. 2017.
[16] Muzima, J. and Gallardo, G., 'Angola 2017', African Economic Outlook, 2017.

Conclusions

The role of the price of oil as a significant driver of military and non-military spending by the governments of oil export-dependent countries cannot be overstated. When oil revenues fell, alternative forms of finance were required and found. Debt, either local or external, has become the common first option for many countries regardless of whether they have diversified economies, are developed or developing, or are involved in armed conflict or conflict-free.

The difficulty of quickly changing government budgets and the ability to easily find alternative sources of finance can explain why the low oil price levels in 2014 initially instigated only minor changes in military expenditure (in 2014 and 2015). It was only after rising debt levels led to a need to cut debt as a share of GDP that many oil export-dependent countries implemented austerity measures to cut expenditure, both non-military and military. However, the decrease in military spending did not always match the decrease in the oil price or oil revenue. In the 15 countries considered here, military expenditure between 2014 and 2017 fell by an average of 16 per cent, but the price of oil dropped by over 45 per cent, and the average increase in total debt as a share of GDP was around 154 per cent (see table 4.5).[17] The difference between revenue (mostly oil revenue) and expenditure in these oil export-dependent countries was mostly funded through debt.

There has been a significant build-up of debt in many oil export-dependent countries following the oil price crash in 2014. Its consequences, while not yet fully assessed, could potentially be detrimental to the economic development of these countries. The above evidence suggests that military expenditure has played an active role in the debt build-up, and indebtedness from both recurrent military spending and arms imports will probably have a cumulative effect on overall debt through interest repayments. With research suggesting that a 1 per cent increase in military expenditure results in an increase of 1.1–1.6 per cent in external debt in the long run, reducing military spending will be particularly effective because such a reduction will generate a greater than proportional reduction in external debt with potential proportional decreases in overall debt.[18]

---

[17] This average excludes Venezuela, for which no data on debt is available.

[18] Brzoska, M., 'The financing factor in military trade', *Defence and Peace Economics*, vol. 5, no. 1 (1994), pp. 67–80; and Smyth and Narayan (note 14).

III. Transparency in military expenditure

NAN TIAN, DIEGO LOPES DA SILVA AND PIETER D. WEZEMAN

Many governments choose to not completely disclose spending on military-related matters.[1] Despite calls for improvements in levels of good governance and transparency in the military sector, a large part of actual military expenditure remains unknown. Levels of transparency vary greatly between countries.[2] Some, such as Japan, New Zealand and Norway, provide substantial amounts of information on spending to the public. Others, such as Eritrea, Qatar, Uzbekistan and Viet Nam, provide no information at all to the public. The behaviour of most states lies somewhere between these extremes, providing information on military spending that lacks overall detail or context. In many cases information such as sources of funding (e.g. extra and off-budget financing), actual expenditure categories (e.g. disaggregated spending information) or purpose of spending (e.g. linked to defence policies) is missing.

One of the main difficulties in furthering transparency in military expenditure is the use of off-budget mechanisms. Using off-budget spending means that some resources are allocated to the military without being subject to the usual deliberation and debate that applies to the general budget. Several countries in Africa and South America, for instance, rely on funds from natural resource extraction and export to finance their militaries. Often, these funds are not reported. Improvements in transparency in military expenditure are key to building confidence among countries and for avoiding mismanagement of resources, reducing corruption and creating an environment for accountability and good governance.

This section looks at the current reporting situation, summarizing the problems of governmental transparency at the international and national levels. It first discusses the decline in participation in the United Nations Report on Military Expenditures. This is followed by an analysis of the transparency problems at the national level caused by off-budget military expenditure. Using two examples—Peru and Venezuela—it highlights the potential consequences of a lack of transparency in military spending.

Reporting to the United Nations

In 1981 the UN General Assembly agreed to establish an annual report in which all UN member states could voluntarily provide data on their mili-

---

[1] See e.g. Transparency International, 'Government defence anti-corruption index', [n.d.].
[2] Gorbanova, M. and Wawro, L., *The Transparency of National Defence Budgets: An Initial Review* (Transparency International UK: London, Oct. 2011).

tary expenditure. The report, now known as the UN Report on Military Expenditures, aims at promoting confidence building among states in the political–military sphere. Participation in the report declined to a low level in the period 2012–16.

In 2016 only 49 of the 193 UN member states submitted information on their military spending in 2015.[3] By 31 July 2017 at least 42 states had submitted a report on their expenditure in 2016.[4] No submission had been received from any state in Africa or the Middle East or from four of the five largest military spenders in the world: the United States, China, Saudi Arabia and India.

The functioning of the UN Report on Military Expenditures was the subject of discussions by a UN group of governmental experts (GGE) in 2016–17, which followed up on a previous GGE in 2011. The GGE agreed on the utility of the report and made some minor proposals to amend the reporting system.[5] It suggested a number of possible causes of the low rate of participation, including reporting fatigue among government officials involved in such instruments for building international confidence; a lack of confidence in the information submitted to the report; a lack of perceived benefit to reporting, in particular when the government information is already made available elsewhere in the public domain; and lingering concerns about the sensitivity of the data. However, it concluded that the causes of the low level of participation in the reporting mechanism should be established with greater confidence through an empirical study, and for that purpose the GGE produced a simple questionnaire to be completed by UN member states.[6]

The outcome of the GGE and the low participation in the instrument in 2017, including the fact that 9 of the 14 countries represented in the GGE are not listed among those that reported in 2017, do not bode well for the future of the UN Report on Military Expenditures.

Off-budget mechanisms in military expenditure

The core components of military budgets are often included in public government budgets as specific lines for 'defence', 'defence and security' or defence ministry spending. In addition, budget lines for other ministries

---

[3] Kelly, N., Lopes, D. and Tian, N., 'Transparency in military expenditure data', *SIPRI Yearbook 2017*, p. 357.

[4] United Nations, General Assembly, 'Objective information on military matters, including transparency of military expenditures', Report of the Secretary-General, A/72/328, 14 Aug. 2017. This report lists 41 submissions. At least 1 additional report was submitted in 2017: that from Russia, which is included in the online UN database. The report from Russia was submitted earlier than some submissions included in the published UN report, which raises questions about the comprehensiveness of the UN report.

[5] United Nations, General Assembly, 'Group of governmental experts to review the operation and further development of the United Nations Report on Military Expenditures', A/72/293, 4 Aug. 2017.

[6] United Nations, A/72/293 (note 5), pp. 11–12.

or functions may include spending for military purposes. These expenditure lines are often identifiable. For example, spending on fissile material for nuclear weapons is itemized in the US budget under the Department of Energy, and in Ukraine and South Korea military pensions are listed under a specific pension fund. Military spending may also include items that are less clearly identified in the budget, such as research and development spending and arms imports in China.

Even more problematic is the use by many countries of off-budget funding: spending that is outside the state budget and often non-transparent. It often includes funds earned from the export of natural resources. Off-budget funds can be used to pay for arms purchases, to receive payments from the private sector in return for security services, or to operate business activities by the military without going through the parliament or the finance ministry. When not administered according to rigorous and transparent procedures, off-budget funds offer lucrative opportunities for self-enrichment to public officials and businesses involved in the decision-making processes.

It is difficult to assess how common this type of hidden spending is or its size. However, it is suspected to be quite widely spread and it can be substantial enough to drastically change the understanding of the size and trend of a country's military spending, as shown by the examples of Peru and Venezuela.

Peru

Peru's off-budget expenditure mechanism was created by a 2004 law that established the Fund for the Armed Forces and National Police (Fondo para las Fuerzas Armadas y Policía Nacional) and funded it with revenue from natural gas fields.[7] Since 2004 it has been used to fund the acquisition, modernization, technological innovation, repair and maintenance of military equipment. In line with the usual practice for off-budget spending, the fund is managed and regulated outside of the control of the Congress, by a committee consisting of the prime minister and the ministers of foreign affairs, defence, economy and finance, and the interior.[8] It is completely outside the official national budget, and spending decisions are often unrelated to the broader economic realities of the country. Instead, they are based on the availability of natural resources, the rate of extraction, the demand for or sale of the natural resource, and the price of the commodity.

---

[7] Ley que crea el Fondo para las Fuerzas Armadas y Policía Nacional [Law creating the Fund for the Armed Forces and National Police], Peruvian Law no. 28455, signed into law 23 Dec. 2004, *El Peruano*, 31 Dec. 2014.

[8] Decreto Supremo no. 011-2005-DE Aprueban el Reglamento de la Ley No. 28455—Ley que crea el Fondo para las Fuerzas Armadas y Policía Nacional [Supreme decree no. 011-2005-DE approving the regulation of Law no. 28455—Law creating the Fund for the Armed Forces and National Police], 29 Apr. 2005, *El Peruano*, 2 May 2005.

Table 4.6. Off-budget military expenditure in Peru, 2005–17

Figures are in US$ m. at current prices and exchange rates. Figures may not add up to stated totals due to the conventions of rounding.

	Selected years					
	2005	2008	2011	2014	2017	Total, 2005–17
Lot 56	–	54.4	700	423	196	3 436
Gas	–	–	312	110	54.6	1 228
Liquified natural gas	–	54.4	388	313	141	2 208
Lot 88	191	354	574	645	387	5 380
Gas	14.9	59.2	114	185	218	1 473
Gas PLT (Pampa Melchorita Plant)	–	–	–	3.6	6.8	19.0
Liquified natural gas	177	295	461	456	162	3 888
30% of Lot 56		16.3	210	127	58.8	1 031
20% of Lot 88 (2005); 40% of Lot 88 (2006 onwards)	38.3	142	230	258	155	2 152
Total for the Fund for the Armed Forces and National Police	**38.3**	**158**	**440**	**385**	**213**	**3 183**
75% for the Peruvian armed forces	28.7	118	330	288	160	2 387
Initial payment	18.8	–	–	–	–	18.8
Total off-budget funding	**47.5**	**118**	**330**	**288**	**160**	**2 406**
Original SIPRI estimate of military expenditure	1 149	1 385	2 025	2 929	1 926	
Total military expenditure (revised SIPRI estimate)	**1 197**	**1 504**	**2 355**	**3 218**	**2 086**	

– = nil.

Sources: SIPRI Military Expenditure Database, May 2018; and Perupetro, 'Reporte de regalías histórico' [Historical reports of royalties collected], various years.

There are three sources of funding for the fund: (*a*) an initial one-off payment of $25 million from the national treasury in 2005 ($18.8 million of which went to the armed forces); (*b*) 20 per cent of the royalties from Lot 88 of the Camisea gas-extraction project in 2005 and 40 per cent from 2006 onwards; and (*c*) 30 per cent of the royalties from Lot 56 of the Camisea project.[9] Lot 88 is made up of revenues from gas and liquefied natural gas (LNG), and (since 2014) revenues from the LNG plant in Pampa Melchorita. Lot 56 is made up of revenues from gas and LNG.

The revenues from the fund are divided equally between the Peruvian Army, Navy, Air Force and National Police.[10] Thus, 75 per cent of this off-budget fund is allocated to military expenditure. Allocations have ranged from a low of $28.7 million in 2005 (excluding the one-off payment of $25 million) to a high of $346 million in 2013.[11] Between 2005 and 2017 a

[9] Ley que crea el Fondo para las Fuerzas Armadas y Policía Nacional (note 7), Article 2.
[10] Ley que crea el Fondo para las Fuerzas Armadas y Policía Nacional (note 7), Article 3.
[11] Unless otherwise stated, all spending figures are quoted in current US dollars.

total of $2.4 billion was diverted from natural resource revenues to the military (see table 4.6).[12] On average, since 2005, the off-budget funding for the Peruvian armed forces accounted for 7.7 per cent of Peru's total military expenditure, ranging from a low of 3.3 per cent following the 2014 oil price crash to a high of 14 per cent in 2011.

The SIPRI Military Expenditure Database has been revised to take this additional spending into account. However, the exact uses for this money—whether for procurement or modernization plans—remain unknown. Other questions remain regarding accountability, parliamentary oversight and possible corruption. Such questions emphasize the need for greater transparency in military expenditure.

Venezuela

Venezuela also has an off-budget funding mechanism for its military: the National Development Fund (Fondo de Desarrollo Nacional, FONDEN), created in 2005.[13] FONDEN's main objectives are to manage investments in development-related areas, such as education, health and infrastructure, and to finance public debt. It was intended to foster economic growth and sustainable development in Venezuela. The fund's resources are mainly provided by the Central Bank of Venezuela (Banco Central de Venezuela) and the state-owned oil company, Petróleos de Venezuela SA (PDVSA; see figure 4.5).[14] No information is available on the sources of funding for FONDEN after 2012.

Over the years, FONDEN has been used to finance a wide array of projects, and its scope and budget have been greatly expanded. From its inception until 2015, a total of $176 billion was used to finance 791 projects.[15] FONDEN's funds are equivalent to a small country's spending: according to one study, FONDEN's allocations in 2010 were seven times bigger than Nicaragua's

---

[12] Perupetro, 'Reporte de regalías histórico' [Historical reports of royalties collected], various years.

[13] Decree no. 3854, *Gaceta Oficial de la República Bolivariana de Venezuela*, no. 38.261, 30 Aug. 2005.

[14] In 2011 Venezuela's National Assembly implemented a new law establishing a special mechanism to collect funding, under certain conditions, based on revenues from exports of liquid hydrocarbons: Contribución Especial por Precios Extraordinarios y Precios Exorbitantes en el Mercado Internacional de Hidrocarburos [Special contribution for the extraordinary and exorbitant prices in the international hydrocarbons market] (CEPEPEMIH). Decreto no. 8163 con Rango y Valor y Fuerza de Ley que Crea una Contribución Especial por Precios Extraordinarios y Precios Exorbitantes en el Mercado Internacional de Hidrocarburos [Decree no. 8163 bringing into force the law creating a special contribution for the extraordinary and exorbitant prices in the international hydrocarbons market], *Gaceta Oficial de la República Bolivariana de Venezuela (Extraordinaria)*, no. 6.022, 18 Apr. 2011.

[15] Venezuelan Ministry of Popular Power for Planning and Finance (MPPPF), *Memoria y Cuenta 2015* [Report and accounts 2015] (MPPPF: Caracas, 2016). No information is available on projects funded by FONDEN in 2016 and 2017.

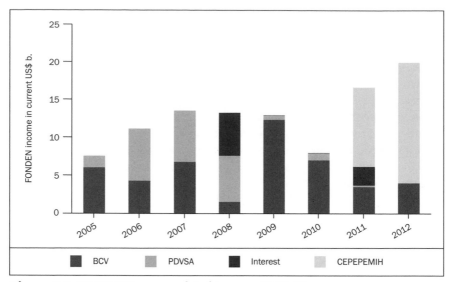

Figure 4.5. FONDEN's accumulated income, 2005–12

BCV = Banco Central de Venezuela [Central Bank of Venezuela]; CEPEPEMIH = Contribución Especial por Precios Extraordinarios y Precios Exorbitantes en el Mercado Internacional de Hidrocarburos [Special contribution for the extraordinary and exorbitant prices in the international hydrocarbons market]; FONDEN = Fondo de Desarrollo Nacional [National Development Fund]; PDVSA = Petróleos de Venezuela SA.

Source: Venezuelan Ministry of Popular Power for Planning and Finance (MPPPF), *Memoria y Cuenta 2012* [Report and accounts 2012] (MPPPF: Caracas, 2013).

state budget.[16] However, Venezuela's National Assembly has no oversight of FONDEN's investments, despite the fund's large size.

It is known that the military has received large contributions from FONDEN as off-budget allocations.[17] But FONDEN's lack of transparency means that the size of these contributions remains a matter of dispute, with estimates varying widely among analysts. Some argue that the military budget has increased sharply while social investment has remained relatively unaltered.[18] Others assert that the military budget, which includes off-budget financing, corresponds to only a small fraction of the Venezuelan state budget.[19]

[16] Transparencia Venezuela, 'Informe nuestro presupuesto' [Report of our budget], no. 11 (15 Dec. 2010), p. 8.

[17] Bromley, M. and Solmirano, C., *Transparency in Military Spending and Arms Acquisitions in Latin America and the Caribbean*, SIPRI Policy Paper no. 31 (SIPRI: Stockholm, Jan. 2012), p. 15.

[18] Corrales, J. and Penfold, M., *Dragon in the Tropics: Hugo Chávez and the Political Economy of Revolution in Venezuela* (Brookings Institution Press: Washington, DC, Feb. 2011).

[19] Gott, R., *Hugo Chávez and the Bolivarian Revolution*, new edn (Verso: New York, 2011); and Jones, B., *Hugo! The Hugo Chávez Story from Mud Hut to Perpetual Revolution* (Steerforth: Hanover, 2007).

In 2010 the accounts committee of the National Assembly demanded that the Ministry of Planning and Finance provide further clarifications on the use of FONDEN's resources. A few months later, the planning minister, Jorge Giordani, presented a document with details of all funds allocated from FONDEN in 2010.[20] This was the first credible information from an official source to back up earlier claims and assessments on Venezuela's off-budget spending. It provided insight into the types of arms purchase that were funded by off-budget oil revenues, listing all existing and new arms procurements that had been partially or fully paid for by the end of 2010.

Based on the ministry's report, SIPRI started the process of revising its Venezuelan military expenditure figures to include FONDEN's off-budget allocations.[21] Specifically, SIPRI analysed the annual report and accounts of the Ministry of Planning and Finance and the Ministry of Economy and Finance, which provide detailed figures for nearly all the projects funded by FONDEN.[22]

The information found in these reports and accounts provided further detail on Venezuela's military expenditure. For example, between 2005 and 2013 FONDEN assigned around $6.2 billion to the military to finance 39 projects. On average, off-budget allocations from FONDEN increased Venezuela's annual military spending by 26 per cent in 2005–15. These contributions have varied as oil prices have fluctuated (see figure 4.6). For example, in 2009 and 2014 the price of oil fell significantly and FONDEN's contributions were greatly reduced in those years.

The 2010 report to the National Assembly suggests that FONDEN's off-budget funds are mainly used to purchase weapon systems. For example, FONDEN assigned about $2.2 billion for the purchase of 24 Su-30 combat aircraft from Russia between 2006 and 2008. However, Russian sources suggest that the cost of the aircraft was in the region of $1.5 billion, highlighting possible misuse of funds or corruption.[23] In addition, FONDEN resources are used to cover some operational and personnel costs as well as acquisitions of small arms.

The available figures also reveal the relative priority given to funding the military in comparison with other sectors. Between 2005 and 2013, among

[20] Venezuelan Ministry of Popular Power for Planning and Finance, 'Proyectos y Recursos 2010 del Fonden y Fondo Chino' [2010 projects and resources of FONDEN and the China Fund], Apr. 2011.

[21] Tian, N. and Lopes da Silva, D., 'Improving South American military expenditure data', SIPRI Commentary, 4 Sep. 2017.

[22] Venezuelan Ministry of Popular Power for Planning and Finance (MPPPF), Memoria y Cuenta [Report and accounts], 2011–15 (MPPPF: Caracas, 2012–16). These reports provide data for spending in 2011–15. At the time of writing, there are no reports for 2016 and 2017. Data for 2005–2009 was taken from Colgan, J., 'Venezuela and military expenditure data', Journal of Peace Research, vol. 48, no. 4 (July 2011), pp. 547–56. Figures for 2010 were taken from Venezuelan Ministry of Popular Power for Planning and Finance (note 20).

[23] Makienko, K., 'The Venezuela contracts', Moscow Defense Brief, vol. 1, no. 7 (2007).

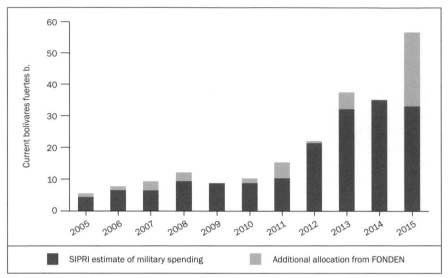

Figure 4.6. Off-budget allocations from FONDEN as a share of Venezuelan military spending, 2005–15

FONDEN = Fondo de Desarrollo Nacional [National Development Fund].

Note: Figures are in current bolívares fuertes b. rather than US dollars because of severe currency depreciation and uncertainty in the bolívar fuerte–dollar exchange rate since 2014.

Sources: Venezuelan Ministry of Popular Power for Planning and Finance (MPPPF), *Memoria y Cuenta* [Report and accounts], 2011–15 (MPPPF: Caracas, 2012–16); Colgan, J., 'Venezuela and military expenditure data', *Journal of Peace Research*, vol. 48, no. 4 (July 2011), pp. 547–56; and Venezuelan Ministry of Popular Power for Planning and Finance, 'Proyectos y Recursos 2010 del Fonden y Fondo Chino' [2010 projects and resources of FONDEN and the China Fund], Apr. 2011.

the 31 areas that received FONDEN resources, the $6.9 billion (21.3 billion bolívares fuertes) given to the military ranked it as the sixth largest recipient. Healthcare, by comparison, ranked as the 12th largest recipient, having received $1.4 billion (4.3 billion bolívares fuertes) to finance eight projects. FONDEN's allocations for education were even lower, with $1.2 billion (3.7 billion bolívares fuertes) to finance four projects.[24]

Although accounting for FONDEN's off-budget allocations is an important step towards more accurate and reliable data, Venezuela's military spending remains underestimated. Alongside FONDEN, the Venezuelan armed forces also receive funds from the China–Venezuela Joint Fund (Fondo Conjunto Chino–Venezolano) and from the Large Volume and Long-Term Fund (Fondo Gran Volumen y Largo Plazo). Future efforts should focus on collecting data on these other sources.

---

[24] Figures for allocations for healthcare and education in bolívares fuertes are based on an average exchange rate to make them consistent with SIPRI's calculation of the military allocation in that currency.

The revision of SIPRI's figures for Venezuela's military spending is particularly timely. The country now faces an acute economic crisis. Its gross domestic product (GDP) in 2017 was 34 per cent below the level in 2013, while GDP per capita fell by 37 per cent.[25] This bleak economic outlook is coupled with increasing political instability. Disclosing FONDEN's allocations to the military sector may help to elucidate whether the Venezuelan Government is managing its scarce resources according to its people's best interest.

The consequences of off-budget mechanisms in military expenditure

The non-transparent management of off-budget funds has harmful effects on democracy. The lack of accountability for and oversight of these finances can create an institutional environment prone to corruption. Questions over the management of such funds have been repeatedly raised.[26] The secrecy of arms purchases funded through Venezuela's FONDEN and, to a lesser extent, Peru's Camisea gas-extraction project, weakens democratic control since it prevents a more thorough assessment of the strategic necessity for such procurements.

The higher military spending of Peru and Venezuela, revealed by this analysis, only reinforces the importance of SIPRI's current effort to review the military spending figures of all South American countries to include off-budget allocations. It is suspected that off-budget funding is common (and not isolated to South America) and, as the above two cases show, can have a major impact on the level of military spending. Capturing off-budget mechanisms strengthens transparency within the military sector, which builds national accountability, improves trust and confidence among states and helps to discourage military corruption.

[25] International Monetary Fund, World Economic Outlook Database, Oct. 2017.
[26] Transparencia Venezuela, 'Nuestro presupuesto: seguimiento al Presupuesto Nacional en el 2012' [Our budget: tracing the National Budget in 2012], no. 25 (June 2012).

5. International arms transfers and developments in arms production

Overview

The volume of international transfers of major weapons rose by 10 per cent between 2008–12 and 2013–17, to reach its highest level since the end of the cold war (see section I in this chapter). The increase marks a continuation of the steady upward trend that began in the early 2000s.

The five largest arms suppliers in 2013–17 were the United States, Russia, France, Germany and China, and they accounted for 74 per cent of the total global volume of exports of major weapons. Since 1950 the USA and Russia (or the Soviet Union before 1992) have consistently been by far the largest suppliers and, together with West European suppliers, have historically dominated the top 10 list of suppliers.

The top five arms importers were India, Saudi Arabia, Egypt, the United Arab Emirates and China, which together accounted for 35 per cent of total arms imports. Asia and Oceania was the main recipient region, accounting for 42 per cent of the total global volume of imports of major weapons in 2013–17, followed by the Middle East, which accounted for 32 per cent. The flow of arms to the Middle East grew by 103 per cent between 2008–12 and 2013–17. The flow of arms to Asia and Oceania also rose, by 1.8 per cent. By contrast, the flow of arms to Europe decreased notably, by 22 per cent, as did those to the Americas, by 29 per cent, and Africa, by 22 per cent.

While SIPRI data on arms transfers does not represent their financial value, many arms-exporting countries publish figures on the financial value of their arms exports (see section III). Based on such data, SIPRI estimates the total value of the global arms trade in 2016 to have been at least $88.4 billion. As has been the case for the past few years, there were few positive developments in official public transparency in arms transfers in 2017 (see section II). The number of states reporting their arms exports and imports to the United Nations Register of Conventional Arms (UNROCA) dropped to an all-time low and no major changes occurred with respect to the various national and regional reporting mechanisms. However, most of the growing number of states that have ratified the 2013 Arms Trade Treaty have fulfilled their obligation of reporting arms exports and imports.

The SIPRI Top 100 arms-producing and military services companies ranks the largest companies in the arms industry (outside China) by their sales, both domestic and for export. The total sales of the SIPRI Top 100 for 2016 (the *latest year for which data is available) totalled almost $375 billion, a 1.9 per cent increase compared with 2015 (see section IV). This was the first year of increase since the peak of 2010. The rise is mainly attributable to the overall increase in the arms sales of US-based companies, which dominate the SIPRI Top 100. Taken together, the arms sales of West European arms producers were stable in 2016. The combined arms sales of Russian companies continued to grow in 2016, while there were mixed trends in arms sales for the arms producers in countries with emerging arms industries and other countries with established arms industries. Major drivers of the growth in arms sales of the Top 100 include international tensions and armed conflict on the demand side and the implementation of military industrialization strategies at the national level on the supply side. Other key causes of changes in Top 100 arms sales from year to year are company mergers, acquisitions and divestments.*

SIEMON T. WEZEMAN AND AUDE FLEURANT

I. Developments in arms transfers, 2017[1]

SIEMON T. WEZEMAN, AUDE FLEURANT, ALEXANDRA KUIMOVA,
NAN TIAN AND PIETER D. WEZEMAN

The volume of international transfers of major arms in the five-year period 2013–17 was 10 per cent higher than in 2008–12.[2] This is a continuation of the steady upward trend that began in the early 2000s (see figure 5.1).

The highest volume of transfers in any five-year period covered by SIPRI data occurred in 1980–84. The volume of transfers declined after 1980–84, until in 2000–2004 it was only 56 per cent of the peak. The total for the latest five-year period, 2013–17, was 51 per cent higher than 2000–2004 and the highest total since 1989–93 (the five-year period most directly affected by the end of the cold war). However, the total volume for 2013–17 was still 33 per cent lower than the total for 1980–84.

Major supplier developments

SIPRI has identified 67 countries as exporters of major weapons in 2013–17. The five largest suppliers of arms during that period were the United States, Russia, France, Germany and China. Together, they were responsible for 74 per cent of the total volume of exports of major arms in 2013–17 (see table 5.1). The same five countries made up the top five in 2008–12, when they also accounted for 74 per cent of the total volume of exports. However, since the total volume of transfers increased between 2008–12 and 2013–17, the top five in 2013–17 exported 11 per cent more arms than in 2008–12. The rise was due to increased exports by the USA, France and China. The USA and Russia were by far the largest exporters in 2013–17, together accounting for 56 per cent of global exports—up from 52 per cent in 2008–12.

On the whole, countries outside North America and Europe play a small role in the global export of arms, accounting for only 12 per cent of the total volume of exports of major weapons in 2013–17. Of the top 25 arms-exporting

---

[1] Except where indicated, the information on arms deliveries and contracts referred to in this chapter is taken from the SIPRI Arms Transfers Database, Mar. 2018. The database contains data on transfers of major weapons between 1950 and 2017. SIPRI data on arms transfers refers to actual deliveries of major weapons, including sales, production under licence, aid, gifts and leases. SIPRI uses a trend-indicator value (TIV) to compare the data on deliveries of different types of weapon and to identify general trends. TIVs give an indication only of the volume of international arms transfers—based on an assessment of the arms' capabilities—and not of their financial values. For a definition of 'major weapons' and a description of the TIV and its calculation see box 5.1. The figures in this chapter may differ from those in previous editions of the SIPRI Yearbook because the Arms Transfers Database is updated annually.

[2] Since year-on-year deliveries can fluctuate, SIPRI compares consecutive multi-year periods—normally 5-year periods—to provide a more stable measure for trends in transfers of major weapons. A 5-year moving average is used to measure trends in transfers over long periods.

Table 5.1. The 50 largest suppliers of major weapons, 2013–17

The table lists countries that exported major weapons in the 5-year period 2013–17. Ranking is according to 2013–17 total exports. Figures are SIPRI trend-indicator values (TIVs). Percentages above 10 per cent have been rounded to the nearest whole number, those below 10 per cent to 1 decimal place. Figures may not add up to stated totals because of the conventions of rounding.

Rank 2013–17	Rank 2008–12[a]	Supplier	Volume of exports (TIV, millions) 2017	Volume of exports (TIV, millions) 2013–17	Share (%), 2013–17	Change (%), compared with 2008–12
1	1	United States	12 394	50 062	34	25
2	2	Russia	6 148	31 722	22	−7.1
3	4	France	2 162	9 706	6.7	27
4	3	Germany	1 653	8 469	5.8	−14
5	5	China	1 131	8 312	5.7	38
6	6	United Kingdom	1 214	6 952	4.8	37
7	7	Spain	814	4 262	2.9	12
8	10	Israel	1 263	4 248	2.9	55
9	9	Italy	660	3 590	2.5	13
10	11	Netherlands	1 167	3 101	2.1	14
11	8	Ukraine	240	2 481	1.7	−26
12	15	South Korea	587	1 784	1.2	65
13	13	Switzerland	186	1 322	0.9	−11
14	12	Sweden	83	1 256	0.9	−53
15	21	Turkey	244	1 164	0.8	145
16	14	Canada	87	1 095	0.8	−18
17	16	Norway	134	862	0.6	14
18	20	Belarus	23	653	0.4	12
19	22	Australia	97	469	0.3	15
20	36	Czech Republic	110	448	0.3	467
21	17	South Africa	74	356	0.2	−51
22	38	United Arab Emirates	72	319	0.2	320
23	24	Finland	58	313	0.2	−5.7
24	23	Brazil	45	279	0.2	−20
25	29	Portugal	56	253	0.2	74
26	28	Jordan	77	242	0.2	36
27	53	Indonesia	102	196	0.1	2 078
28	42	India	56	189	0.1	278
29	26	Poland	3	184	0.1	−12
30	46	Bulgaria	–	166	0.1	337
31	31	Romania	–	108	0.1	−2.7
32	18	Uzbekistan	–	102	0.1	−84
33	30	Singapore	–	98	0.1	−32
34	19	Belgium	12	97	0.1	−84
35	27	Austria	22	91	0.1	−49
36	34	Denmark	12	89	0.1	−4.3
37	25	Iran	10	88	0.1	−63
38	35	Serbia	2	81	0.1	−12
39	52	Slovakia	22	51	0	292

Rank			Volume of exports (TIV, millions)		Share (%),	Change (%), compared
2013–17	2008–12[a]	Supplier	2017	2013–17	2013–17	with 2008–12
40	..	Hungary	–	41	0	..
41	..	Ireland	–	39	0	–63
42	..	Greece	30	30	0	..
43	..	Egypt	–	30	0	..
44	33	Chile	0	20	0	–80
45	39	New Zealand	4	17	0	–77
46	..	Georgia	7	14	0	..
47	50	Kyrgyzstan	5	14	0	0
48	47	Brunei Darussalam	–	12	0	–50
49	..	Sudan	–	11	0	..
50	61	Colombia	10	10	0	..
	..	17 others	30	112	0.1	..
		Total	31 106	145 623	..	10

.. = not available or not applicable; – = no deliveries.

Note: The SIPRI data on arms transfers relates to actual deliveries of major weapons. To permit comparison between the data on deliveries of different weapons and to identify general trends, SIPRI uses a TIV. This value is only an indicator of the volume of arms transfers and not of the financial values of such transfers. Thus, it is not comparable to economic statistics. The method for calculating the TIV is described in box 5.1.

[a] The rank order for suppliers in 2008–12 differs from that published in *SIPRI Yearbook 2013* because of subsequent revision of figures for these years.

Source: SIPRI Arms Transfers Database, Mar. 2018.

countries in 2013–17, 17 are in North America and Europe, 3 are in Asia and Oceania, 3 are in the Middle East, 1 is in Africa and 1 is in South America (see table 5.1).[3] This concentration of suppliers in the Euro-Atlantic region has been a feature of the entire period covered by the SIPRI Arms Transfers Database (i.e. 1950–2017). Many of the countries listed in the top 25 for 2013–17 also appeared there in previous periods.

The United States

The USA was the largest exporter of major weapons in 2013–17, a position it has occupied since the end of the cold war. Its arms exports in 2017 were the highest for a single year since 1998, although the contracts for most of these deliveries were signed several years ago.

The USA accounted for 34 per cent of the global volume of deliveries in 2013–17, compared with 30 per cent in 2008–12. Its arms exports increased by 25 per cent between 2008–12 and 2013–17, further widening the gap between the USA and all other arms exporters. In 2013–17 US arms exports

[3] For further detail on SIPRI's regional coverage see the 'regional coverage' page on the SIPRI website.

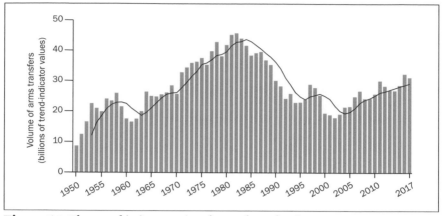

Figure 5.1. The trend in international transfers of major weapons, 1950–2017

Note: The bar graph shows annual totals and the line graph shows a 5-year moving average (plotted at the last year of each 5-year period). See box 5.1 for an explanation of the SIPRI trend-indicator value.

Source: SIPRI Arms Transfers Database, Mar. 2018.

were 58 per cent higher than those of Russia—the second largest arms exporter for that period. In 2008–12 the USA's arms exports were only 17 per cent higher than Russia's.

States in the Middle East accounted for 49 per cent of US arms exports in 2013–17, followed by states in Asia and Oceania (33 per cent), Europe (11 per cent), the Americas (4.8 per cent) and Africa (2.2 per cent; see table 5.2).

The USA delivered major weapons to at least 98 states in 2013–17, a significantly higher number of export destinations than any other supplier. It is also likely that the USA delivered a small number of light armoured vehicles to rebel forces in Syria in 2017. Of the world's 50 largest arms importers in 2013–17, only 7 did not receive or place orders for major arms from the USA during that period. By far the main recipient of US arms in 2013–17 was Saudi Arabia, accounting for 18 per cent of US arms exports. US arms exports to Saudi Arabia increased by 448 per cent between 2008–12 and 2013–17. The flow of US weapons to that country is likely to remain high for at least five more years due to large outstanding orders, including for 154 F-15SA combat aircraft (deliveries of which began in 2016). US arms supplies to Saudi Arabia led to calls in the US Congress in 2016 and 2017 for restrictions on arms supplies to Saudi Arabia, in response to Saudi Arabian military operations in Yemen (launched in 2015), which have caused many civilian casualties and were considered to be indiscriminate.[4] However, a small majority in the US Congress supported the US Government's decisions to allow continued

---

[4] On the conflict in Yemen see chapter 2, section V, in this volume.

deliveries under existing orders and to agree new orders that may surpass those signed in recent years.[5]

US arms exports to long-standing allies sometimes fluctuate based on the demand these countries have for arms. For example, US exports to Greece (a member of the North Atlantic Treaty Organization, NATO) fell by 79 per cent between 2008–12 and 2013–17 due to cuts in Greece's arms procurement after 2009, as part of austerity measures to deal with a severe economic crisis. In other cases, arms transfers are used as a tool within US foreign policy to forge new strategic partnerships. As part of its efforts to offset China's growing influence in Asia, for example, the USA has been strengthening its ties with India: its arms deliveries to India rose by 557 per cent between 2008–12 and 2013–17. The USA has also started to increase its security cooperation with Viet Nam in recent years. In 2017 it delivered one large patrol ship to Viet Nam as aid—the first US transfer of major arms to that country.

The USA exports a wide variety of weapon types. Aircraft, and in particular combat aircraft, account for a large proportion of these exports: 56 per cent in 2013–17, with the USA delivering 200 combat aircraft. These deliveries included a total of 50 F-35 combat aircraft, of which 12 were delivered to the United Kingdom, 10 to Norway, 9 each to Israel and Italy, 6 to Japan and 2 each to Australia and the Netherlands. The USA also delivered 30 F-15SG combat aircraft to Saudi Arabia and 16 to Singapore. By contrast, the volume of US exports of military ships is relatively modest. In 2013–17, for example, Germany, Spain and the Netherlands all exported a larger volume of military ships than the USA.

Russia

Russia's exports of major weapons decreased by 7.1 per cent between 2008–12 and 2013–17, while its share of total global exports fell from 26 to 22 per cent. The decrease was largely due to reductions in deliveries to some of its main recipients. Deliveries to Algeria and China, for example, continued throughout 2013–17 but were at lower levels than in 2008–12. Weapons remain on order from Russia for both countries. In addition, while Russia made significant deliveries to Venezuela in 2013, it made no arms exports to that country in the years 2015–17 as Venezuela's economy slipped deeper into crisis.[6]

Russia has fewer arms export destinations than the USA. During 2013–17 Russia delivered weapons to 47 states and to rebel forces in Ukraine. The bulk of Russian arms exports, 68 per cent, went to just four states: India accounted for 35 per cent, China for 12 per cent, and Viet Nam and Algeria

---

[5] Svet, O., 'Why Congress supports Saudi arms sales', *National Interest*, 26 Sep. 2016; Depetris, D., 'Congress must act on huge Saudi arms sales', *Breaking Defense*, 6 June 2017; and Cooper, H., 'Senate narrowly backs Trump weapons sale to Saudi Arabia', *New York Times*, 13 June 2017.

[6] On military spending, debt and transparency in Venezuela see chapter 4, sections II and III, in this volume.

Table 5.2. The 10 largest suppliers of major weapons and their destinations, by region, 2013–17

Figures are the percentage shares of the supplier's total volume of exports delivered to each recipient region. The shares may not add up to 100 because of the conventions of rounding. Percentages above 10 per cent have been rounded to the nearest whole number. For further detail on SIPRI's regional coverage see the 'regional coverage' page on the SIPRI website.

Recipient region	Supplier									
	USA	Russia	France	Germany	China	UK	Spain	Israel	Italy	Netherlands
Africa	2.2	13	7.5	8.4	21	1.2	1.4	1.1	12	1.9
North Africa	1.8	10	6.1	8.3	10	1.0	–	–	10	1.2
Sub-Saharan Africa	0.4	2.8	1.3	0.2	11	0.2	1.4	1.1	1.8	0.6
Americas	4.8	4.2	9.1	13	4.9	4.5	7.2	10	9.7	33
South America	1.4	3.8	4.6	4.6	4.7	0.8	2.9	3.7	6.7	4.9
Asia and Oceania	33	66	31	24	72	25	49	62	18	20
Central Asia	0.1	3.3	1.0	0.6	2.8	–	3.4	<0.05	1.2	1.5
East Asia	12	12	9.2	14	–	5.1	–	3.5	0.1	–
Oceania	7.0	–	4.3	0.6	–	0.3	34	0.2	4.5	–
South Asia	7.7	38	9.1	1.6	54	8.6	0.5	49	5.5	0.9
South East Asia	5.5	12	7.4	7.2	15	11	11	9.2	6.4	18
Europe	11	6.2	10	29	0.2	4.8	1.7	24	17	13
European Union	9.4	<0.05	10	28	0.2	4.7	1.7	11	15	13
Middle East	49	11	42	26	2.0	64	40	1.9	43	32
Other	<0.05	–	–	–	–	–	–	1.4	0.2	–

– = nil; <0.05 = between 0 and 0.05.

Source: SIPRI Arms Transfers Database, Mar. 2018.

for 10 per cent each. The other 44 recipients all accounted for less than 5 per cent. At the regional level, Asia and Oceania accounted for 66 per cent of Russian arms exports in 2013–17, Africa for 13 per cent, the Middle East for 11 per cent, Europe for 6.2 per cent and the Americas for 4.2 per cent.

West and Central European countries

Six West European countries—France, Germany, the UK, Spain, Italy and the Netherlands—were among the top 10 suppliers of major weapons in 2013–17. Together, they accounted for 25 per cent of the total volume of global arms transfers in that period. In addition to these six states, the top 25 arms exporters in 2013–17 included six other West and Central European states (see table 5.1). Ten of these 12 states are members of the European Union (EU). The combined total exports of all 28 EU member states was 6.7 per cent higher in 2013–17 than in 2008–12. However, the increase in the total volume of transfers meant that the EU member states' share of the global total fell from 29 per cent in 2008–12 to 27 per cent in 2013–17.

France. France was the third largest supplier of major weapons in 2013–17 and accounted for 6.7 per cent of the total volume. Its arms exports rose by 27 per cent between 2008–12 and 2013–17. It delivered arms to 81 countries in 2013–17. At the regional level, 42 per cent of its exports went to the Middle East, 31 per cent to Asia and Oceania, 10 per cent to Europe, 9.1 per cent to the Americas and 7.5 per cent to Africa. Egypt (25 per cent) was by far the largest recipient of French arms in 2013–17. This was due to the French Government's aggressive arms sales efforts, by which it made combat aircraft and warships that were in production for its own forces available for export and swift delivery to Egypt instead.[7] Other major deals were also signed in 2013–17, including for 36 combat aircraft each for India and Qatar, and 12 submarines for Australia.

Germany. Germany was the fourth largest supplier of major weapons in 2013–17. Its exports decreased by 14 per cent between 2008–12 and 2013–17, and its share of the global total fell from 7.4 per cent to 5.8 per cent. In 2013–17 Germany supplied major arms to 60 states. The main recipients were other European states, accounting for 29 per cent of Germany's total, while 24 per cent went to states in Asia and Oceania, 13 per cent to the Americas and 8.4 per cent to Africa. Arms exports to the Middle East accounted for 26 per cent of German arms exports in 2013–17, despite significant political debate in Germany about supplying weapons to states in the region. Initially, this related to concerns about the use of weapons in repression.[8] However,

---

[7] Eshel, T., 'Paris, Cairo close to agreement on Rafale, FREMM deal worth 5–6 billion euros', *Defense Update*, 16 Jan. 2015; and Hoyle, C., 'Rafale exports take off with Egyptian delivery', *Flight Global*, 20 July 2015.

[8] Wezeman, S. T. et al., 'Developments in arms transfers, 2014', *SIPRI Yearbook 2015*, pp. 413–14.

from 2015 the debate also included concerns about the use of weapons supplied by Germany in the conflict in Yemen, which resulted in early 2018 in increased restrictions on German arms exports to Saudi Arabia and other states involved in the conflict.[9]

The United Kingdom. Between 2008–12 and 2013–17 British arms exports increased by 37 per cent. Deliveries to Saudi Arabia, in particular of combat aircraft and their armaments, accounted for 49 per cent of these exports. British arms sales to Saudi Arabia were also subject to criticism. For example, in 2017 civil society groups applied to the High Court of England and Wales for a judicial review aimed at establishing whether the UK's arms exports to Saudi Arabia were lawful under its arms export regulations. The court dismissed the application and concluded that the British Government's decision to continue to license arms exports to Saudi Arabia 'was not irrational or unlawful'.[10] The British Government did not change its arms export policy towards Saudi Arabia and warned that criticism of Saudi Arabia's use of weapons in Yemen was endangering expected large British arms deals with Saudi Arabia.[11]

China

China's exports of major arms increased by 38 per cent between 2008–12 and 2013–17, while its share of global arms exports rose from 4.6 to 5.7 per cent. In 2013–17 Asia and Oceania accounted for 72 per cent of Chinese arms exports, Africa for 21 per cent, the Americas for 4.9 per cent and the Middle East for 2 per cent (a notably smaller share than any of the other top five arms exporters). China delivered major arms to 48 countries in 2013–17. Pakistan was the main recipient (35 per cent), as it has been for all five-year periods since 1991. Large increases in arms supplies to Bangladesh and Algeria accounted for much of the growth in total Chinese arms exports in 2013–17.

Other suppliers outside Europe and North America

Countries outside Europe and North America generally play a small role in international exports of major arms. Eight of the top 25 arms-exporting countries in 2013–17 were outside Europe or North America: China, Israel, the Republic of Korea (South Korea), Turkey, Australia, South Africa, the

---

[9] German Government, 'Regierungspressekonferenz vom 22. Januar 2018' [Government press conference of 22 January 2018], 22 Jan. 2018.

[10] The Queen (on the application of Campaign Against The Arms Trade) v the Secretary of State for International Trade and interveners, Case no. CO/1306/2016, High Court of England and Wales, Press summary, 10 July 2017. See also 'UK arms sales to Saudi Arabia are lawful, High Court rules', *Daily Telegraph*, 10 July 2017.

[11] Bond, D. and Hollinger, P., 'Criticism of Saudi Arabia "not helpful" for UK weapons sales', *Financial Times*, 25 Oct. 2017.

United Arab Emirates (UAE) and Brazil (in order of export volume). Of these countries, only China and Israel were placed in the top 10.

There were large increases in arms exports by Israel (55 per cent), South Korea (65 per cent) and Turkey (145 per cent) between 2008–12 and 2013–17. Israel has been among the top 15 arms exporters for decades. Israel's exports, which went to at least 42 countries in 2013–17, included missiles, radars and other sensors, and unmanned aerial vehicles. South Korea and Turkey have adopted a policy of investing heavily in their respective arms industries based on growing local demand and with the aim of becoming major exporters of weapons of all categories. In 2013–17 South Korea delivered major arms to European states for the first time: artillery to Poland and a support ship to the UK. Turkey notably increased its arms exports (mainly armoured vehicles) to other states in the Middle East in 2013–17.

Major recipient developments

In 2013–17 Asia and Oceania was the main recipient region of major weapons, accounting for 42 per cent of global imports, followed by the Middle East with 32 per cent. Deliveries to both regions increased between 2008–12 and 2013–17. Europe (11 per cent), Africa (7.2 per cent) and the Americas (7.1 per cent) accounted for much smaller shares of imports, and all three regions had lower imports in 2013–17 than in 2008–12.

In 2013–17 the top five arms importers—India, Saudi Arabia, Egypt, the UAE and China—accounted for 35 per cent of total arms imports (see tables 5.3 and 5.4). Of these, India and China were among the top five importers in both 2008–12 and 2013–17.

Africa

Between 2008–12 and 2013–17 arms imports by African states decreased by 22 per cent. The three largest importers in Africa in 2013–17 were Algeria (52 per cent of African arms imports), Morocco (12 per cent) and Nigeria (5.1 per cent). The main arms suppliers to Africa were Russia, China and the USA.

In 2013–17 Russian arms exports to Africa fell by 32 per cent compared with 2008–12. Despite the decrease, Russia remained the largest supplier to Africa, accounting for 39 per cent of total imports to the region. Algeria received 78 per cent of Russia's arms exports to Africa in 2013–17.

China's arms exports to Africa rose by 55 per cent between 2008–12 and 2013–17, and its share of total African arms imports increased from 8.4 per cent to 17 per cent. A total of 22 sub-Saharan African countries procured major arms from China in 2013–17, and China accounted for 27 per cent of sub-Saharan African arms imports, compared with 16 per cent

Table 5.3. The 50 largest recipients of major weapons, 2013–17

The table lists countries and non-state actors that imported major weapons in the 5-year period 2013–17. Ranking is according to 2013–17 total imports. Figures are SIPRI trend-indicator values (TIVs). Percentages above 10 per cent have been rounded to the nearest whole number, those below 10 per cent to 1 decimal place. Figures may not add up to stated totals because of the conventions of rounding.

Rank			Volume of imports (TIV, millions)		Share (%),	Change (%), compared
2013–17	2008–12[a]	Recipient	2017	2013–17	2013–17	with 2008–12
1	1	India	3 358	18 049	12	24
2	9	Saudi Arabia	4 111	14 805	10	225
3	21	Egypt	2 355	6 573	4.5	215
4	10	United Arab Emirates	848	6 370	4.4	51
5	2	China	1 117	5 786	4.0	–19
6	8	Australia	1 806	5 558	3.8	7.5
7	5	Algeria	905	5 414	3.7	0.8
8	17	Iraq	712	4 928	3.4	118
9	3	Pakistan	710	4 147	2.8	–36
10	26	Indonesia	1 196	4 014	2.8	193
11	19	Viet Nam	690	3 990	2.7	81
12	11	Turkey	410	3 539	2.4	–14
13	4	South Korea	918	3 239	2.2	–50
14	7	United States	547	2 930	2.0	–44
15	41	Taiwan	493	2 846	2.0	261
16	59	Oman	783	2 546	1.7	655
17	36	Israel	528	2 474	1.7	125
18	16	United Kingdom	899	2 260	1.6	–1.5
19	57	Bangladesh	320	2 239	1.5	542
20	40	Qatar	670	2 212	1.5	166
21	6	Singapore	428	2 149	1.5	–60
22	37	Italy	794	2 043	1.4	111
23	32	Azerbaijan	279	1 907	1.3	55
24	18	Japan	500	1 805	1.2	–19
25	13	Venezuela	–	1 533	1.1	–40
26	28	Canada	295	1 470	1.0	14
27	65	Kuwait	113	1 435	1.0	488
28	15	Greece	56	1 402	1.0	–44
29	44	Thailand	310	1 309	0.9	93
30	12	Morocco	351	1 288	0.9	–52
31	63	Kazakhstan	209	1 133	0.8	308
32	55	Finland	100	1 110	0.8	208
33	39	Jordan	386	1 104	0.8	26
34	22	Afghanistan	250	1 064	0.7	–48
35	43	Mexico	218	1 041	0.7	53
36	29	Myanmar	167	1 024	0.7	–20
37	30	Brazil	103	882	0.6	–31
38	31	Poland	197	872	0.6	–30
39	50	Turkmenistan	75	820	0.6	96

Rank			Volume of imports (TIV, millions)		Share (%), 2013–17	Change (%), compared with 2008–12
2013–17	2008–12[a]	Recipient	2017	2013–17		
40	20	Norway	361	749	0.5	−65
41	91	Philippines	271	744	0.5	691
42	14	Malaysia	187	700	0.5	−72
43	71	Peru	64	668	0.5	312
44	79	Russia	34	663	0.5	360
45	38	Colombia	102	651	0.4	−33
46	27	Spain	72	604	0.4	−54
47	33	Netherlands	35	556	0.4	−52
48	52	Nigeria	26	536	0.4	42
49	74	Belarus	145	491	0.3	221
50	45	Sudan	54	462	0.3	−31
..	..	153 others	1 556	9 488	6.7	..
		Total	**31 106**	**145 623**	..	**10**

.. = not available or not applicable; – = no deliveries.

Note: The SIPRI data on arms transfers relates to actual deliveries of major weapons. To permit comparison between the data on deliveries of different weapons and to identify general trends, SIPRI uses a TIV. This value is only an indicator of the volume of arms transfers and not of the financial values of such transfers. Thus, it is not comparable to economic statistics. The method for calculating the TIV is described in box 5.1.

[a] The rank order for suppliers in 2008–12 differs from that published in *SIPRI Yearbook 2013* because of subsequent revision of figures for these years.

Source: SIPRI Arms Transfers Database, Mar. 2018.

in 2008–12. In North Africa, China became an important supplier to Algeria in 2013–17, with deliveries including three frigates and artillery.

The USA accounted for 11 per cent of arms exports to Africa in 2013–17. Most of its exports went to Morocco (63 per cent of US exports to Africa). Other US transfers to Africa were typically small batches of weapons, often supplied as aid, including eight helicopters for Kenya and five for Uganda.

States in sub-Saharan Africa received 32 per cent of total African imports in 2013–17. The top five arms importers in sub-Saharan Africa were Nigeria, Sudan, Angola, Cameroon and Ethiopia. Together, they accounted for 56 per cent of arms imports in the subregion. Nigeria's arms imports grew by 42 per cent between 2008–12 and 2013–17. Major arms play an important role in the military operations by sub-Saharan African states. However, due to a lack of resources, sub-Saharan African states typically procure small numbers of older or less-advanced types of major weapons. Kenya, for example, which has a high level of internal political violence and has been fighting al-Shabab on its own territory and in Somalia since 2011, acquired 13 transport helicopters, 2 second-hand combat helicopters, 65 light armoured

Table 5.4. The 10 largest recipients of major weapons and their suppliers, 2013–17

Figures are the percentage shares of the recipient's total volume of imports received from each supplier. Only suppliers with a share of 1 per cent or more of total imports of any of the 10 largest recipients are included in the table. Smaller suppliers are grouped together under 'Others'. Figures may not add up to 100 because of the conventions of rounding. Percentages above 10 per cent have been rounded to the nearest whole number.

Supplier	Recipient									
	India	Saudi Arabia	Egypt	UAE	China	Australia	Algeria	Iraq	Pakistan	Indonesia
Australia	–	–	–	–	2.9	..	–	–	–	3.3
Belarus	–	–	–	–	–	–	–	0.8	–	–
Brazil	0.1	–	–	–	–	–	–	–	0.6	2.2
Bulgaria	–	0.1	<0.05	–	–	–	–	2.3	–	–
Canada	0.7	1.4	0.6	0.7	–	0.3	–	–	0.4	0.5
China	–	0.2	0.2	0.5	..	–	15	0.3	70	5.6
Czech Republic	–	–	–	–	–	–	–	4.0	–	0.1
France	4.5	3.6	37	13	14	6.9	0.5	–	0.4	6.8
Germany	0.7	1.8	6.3	2.1	0.7	0.7	13	0.6	0.1	7.3
Israel	11	–	–	–	–	–	–	–	–	–
Italy	0.2	1.5	0.3	6.6	–	2.9	6.5	3.4	3.5	0.4
Jordan	–	–	–	–	–	–	–	–	3.3	–
Netherlands	0.2	0.5	0.6	2.6	–	–	0.7	–	–	11
Russia	62	–	21	1.4	65	–	59	22	5.7	10
South Africa	0.2	0.1	<0.05	1.3	–	–	0.4	<0.05	–	–
South Korea	–	–	0.9	–	–	–	–	8.7	–	12
Spain	–	2.4	3.8	4.6	–	26	–	0.6	0.2	2.7
Sweden	–	1.1	–	3.4	–	0.4	1.9	–	0.5	0.2
Switzerland	0.4	1.8	–	–	3.9	0.9	–	–	0.9	3.4
Turkey	–	1.3	–	4.4	–	–	–	–	1.3	–
UAE	–	–	2.5	..	–	–	0.1	–	–	–
Ukraine	1.2	–	–	–	8.4	–	–	1.0	0.5	0.1
UK	3.2	23	–	1.0	2.8	0.3	1.3	–	0.3	17

USA	15	61	26	58	–	61	0.4	56	12	16
Uzbekistan	–	–	–	–	1.8	–	–	–	–	–
Others	0.1	0.6	0.3	0.4	–	0.7	0.6	0.9	0.1	1.0

. . = not available or not applicable; – = nil; <0.05 = between 0 and 0.05; UAE = United Arab Emirates.

Source: SIPRI Arms Transfers Database, Mar. 2018.

vehicles and a small number of self-propelled howitzers in 2013–17 for its armed and internal security forces.[12]

The Americas

Imports of major weapons by states in the Americas decreased by 29 per cent between 2008–12 and 2013–17. The USA was the largest importer of major weapons in the region in 2013–17.

Arms imports by South American states fell by 38 per cent between 2008–12 and 2013–17. In 2013–17 arms imports by South American states accounted for 43 per cent of transfers to the Americas. Russia accounted for 27 per cent of deliveries to South America, followed by the USA (15 per cent) and France (9.8 per cent). The overall fall in arms imports by South American states coincides with a generally low level of interstate tensions in the region in recent years and a decline in intrastate conflict.[13] Nevertheless, demand for major arms varies significantly between states.

Venezuela. In the years following the 1999 change of political leadership in Venezuela, the country's relationships with its main arms suppliers at the time, the USA and several European states, essentially came to an end. Venezuela rebuilt its armed forces with weapons from Russia and China, and it was the largest importer in South America for the 10-year period 2008–17. However, following the economic crisis in Venezuela, which began in 2014, its imports of major arms fell to nil by 2017.[14]

Brazil. Arms imports by Brazil decreased by 31 per cent between 2008–12 and 2013–17. However, between 2008 and 2017 Brazil signed contracts for major arms that will be delivered in 2018–25. These include 5 submarines from France and 36 combat aircraft from Sweden.

Asia and Oceania

Five of the 10 largest recipients of major weapons in 2013–17 were in Asia and Oceania—India, China, Australia, Pakistan and Indonesia (see tables 5.3 and 5.4). States in the region received 42 per cent of global imports in 2013–17, compared with 46 per cent in 2008–12. Arms imports by states in Asia and Oceania increased by 1.8 per cent between the two periods. Russia accounted for 34 per cent of arms exports to the region, the USA for 27 per cent and China for 9.7 per cent. The main importers in Asia and Oceania are all aiming to improve their local arms development and production capabilities to reduce their dependence on foreign suppliers. These efforts have had varying degrees of success.

---

[12] On conflicts involving Kenya see chapter 2, section VI, in this volume.
[13] See also chapter 2, section II, in this volume.
[14] See also chapter 4, section II, in this volume.

India and Pakistan have been among the largest importers of arms for the past few decades. India was the world's largest importer of major arms in 2008–12 and 2013–17. Pakistan was the third largest arms importer in 2008–12 and the ninth largest in 2013–17. India and Pakistan have been in conflict with each other since their independence in 1947. The tensions between India and Pakistan are compounded by each side's relations with China, which has been a close ally of Pakistan since the 1960s and has long-standing border disputes with India. In the past few years tensions have flared on a regular basis.[15] China's increasing assertiveness in the Indian Ocean region, backed by its growing capabilities to project military power, is an additional concern for India.[16] In response, India has been modernizing and expanding its armed forces, largely through imports.

India. India accounted for 12 per cent of global arms imports in 2013–17. Between 2008–12 and 2013–17 India's imports increased by 24 per cent. Russia is the main supplier of major weapons to India and will remain so for at least the next few years as existing contracts are fulfilled. It accounted for 62 per cent of India's arms imports in 2013–17, and the volume of Russian arms exports to India in that period was almost the same as in 2008–12. However, Russia is facing stronger competition from other arms-exporting countries as India is seeking to diversify the sources of its arms imports. Between 2008–12 and 2013–17 arms imports from the USA increased by 557 per cent, making it India's second largest arms supplier. This development is part of the growing strategic partnership between the two countries, under which the USA has begun to supply India with advanced military equipment. In 2013–17 such supplies included long-range maritime patrol aircraft, strategic transport aircraft and combat helicopters. India's arms imports from Israel also increased (by 285 per cent) between 2008–12 and 2013–17, making it the third largest arms supplier to India.

As Russia's competitors seek to make greater inroads into the Indian market, India has also adopted a new 'Make in India' policy for arms acquisitions. The new policy replaces a previous policy that aimed to encourage the development and production of India's weapons by Indian state-owned arms-producing companies and the state military research organization, if necessary with foreign assistance or by way of production under licence.[17] These Indian state-owned entities have a long history of working with Russian state-owned companies and state entities. The new 'Make in India'

[15] Anderson, G. et al., '2017 annual defence report', *Jane's Defence Weekly*, 13 Dec. 2017, p. 27; Krishnan, A., 'Another armed conflict with India not out of the question, says China expert', *India Today*, 4 July 2017; and Patranobis, S., 'China blames Indian troops for Ladakh clash, PLA conducts drill to strike "awe"', *Hindustan Times*, 22 Aug. 2017. See also chapter 2, section III, in this volume.

[16] Anderson et al. (note 15), p. 27.

[17] Indian Government, Make in India website; US International Trade Administration, 'India: Defense', 27 July 2017; and Unnithan, S., 'Unmade in India', *India Today*, 27 Feb. 2017.

policy allows the Indian private sector more opportunities to compete for Indian orders for weapons. India's private sector generally has closer ties with private companies in countries other than Russia and has typically linked up with those companies when offering weapons for Indian requirements.

There is also growing resistance in India, in both political and military circles, to placing too heavy a reliance on Russia as a supplier of major weapons. This resistance is based on a perception that Russia is not—or will not be—able to meet expectations and promises. The various problems connected to the joint development and production by India and Russia of the Fifth Generation Fighter Aircraft (FGFA) combat aircraft (a derivative of the Russian Su-57 combat aircraft) and the Multi-role Transport Aircraft (MTA) are perhaps the clearest recent examples of this trend. The Indian Air Force had already voiced its dissatisfaction with the FGFA/Su-57 (of which 100–27 are planned to be acquired) by 2017, and in early 2018 reports emerged that it had suggested alternatives, including the USA's F-35.[18] The MTA, which was to be designed mainly by Russia and produced in India by a state-owned company, was cancelled by India in 2017 after more than 15 years of discussions with Russia over the design. India has instead entered into negotiations for a Spanish transport aircraft to be produced by a private Indian company.[19] Moreover, India signed no major contracts for weapons with Russia in 2017. Several major deals, which were expected to be signed by the end of 2017, have been repeatedly delayed. However, Russian officials seem unconcerned by the lack of progress as delays during negotiations of large and complex contracts are common. They also point to changes in India's procedures for procurement and claim that Indian arms procurement is cyclical. According to Russian officials, the dip in 2016–17 is no different from the dip in 2008–10, which came between peaks in 2004–2008 and 2010–12.[20]

Pakistan. Pakistan has built up its arms industry over the years. However, it has been much less ambitious in its objectives than India. Rather than pursuing the indigenous development of advanced weapons, Pakistan's arms industry has remained focused on the production of foreign designs under licence or the assembly of weapons from foreign components. Since the 1960s these designs and components have mainly been of Chinese origin, although Pakistan does produce major weapons under licence from other countries.

---

[18] Noronha, J., 'Fifth-generation fighter aircraft for IAF: a mirage or reality?', *Indian Defence Review*, vol. 32, no. 4 (Oct.–Dec. 2017); Raghuvanshi, V., 'Indian Air Force wants out of fighter program with Russia', *Defense News*, 20 Oct. 2017; and Shukla, A., 'Capability jump: IAF looks to buy fifth-generation F-35 fighter', *Business Standard*, 15 Feb. 2018.

[19] Dominguez, G., 'Russia, India terminate MTA project, says report', *Jane's Defence Weekly*, 5 Apr. 2017, p. 14; and Menon, J. C., 'Indian Air Force: grand ambition', *European Security and Defence*, Feb. 2017, p. 39.

[20] *Kommersant*, [Those who criticize Iran today will fight for it], 7 Feb. 2018 (in Russian).

Recent examples include the licensed production of RBS-70 surface-to-air missiles from Sweden, and orders in 2017 for the licensed production of warships from the Netherlands and Turkey. Despite its continuing tensions with India and ongoing internal conflicts, Pakistan's arms imports decreased by 36 per cent between 2008–12 and 2013–17 and it accounted for 2.8 per cent of global arms imports in 2013–17. The bulk of Pakistan's arms imports in 2013–17 came from just two suppliers: China (70 per cent) and the USA (12 per cent).

The volume of China's arms exports to Pakistan in 2013–17 remained at roughly the same volume as in 2008–12. However, due to a decline in US arms exports to Pakistan in 2013–17, China's share of Pakistan's arms imports rose from 45 per cent in 2008–12 to 70 per cent in 2013–17.

In 2008–12 Pakistan received substantial military aid from the USA, including 28 combat aircraft and 5 maritime patrol aircraft. In 2013–17 it received far less US military aid, and its arms imports from the USA fell by 76 per cent. This coincided with growing criticism in the US Congress about what was considered to be a lack of effort by Pakistan to deal with terrorism. In 2016 the US Congress blocked Pakistan's planned procurement of eight combat aircraft, which was to be funded by US military aid.[21] In 2017 the US Government accused Pakistan of harbouring terrorists, and in January 2018 it decided to suspend military aid to Pakistan.[22]

Japan and South Korea. Arms imports by South Korea decreased by 50 per cent between 2008–12 and 2013–17 and those by Japan decreased by 19 per cent. However, Japan's tensions with China and South Korea's tensions with the Democratic People's Republic of Korea (DPRK, or North Korea) have been drivers behind major contracts for new weapons that started to be delivered or were ordered in 2013–17. Japan and South Korea have large arms industries, but remain partly dependent on arms imports. Both countries have turned to the USA for several types of advanced weapon. In 2013–17, for example, Japan started to receive the first batches of a total of 42 F-35 combat aircraft on order from the USA, while South Korea placed orders for 40 such aircraft. In the same period both countries ordered advanced air and missile defence systems from the USA. In 2013 and 2017 South Korea ordered long-range land-attack cruise missiles from Germany, the first of which were delivered in 2016. In 2017 Japan selected similar missiles from Norway.[23]

China. China is becoming increasingly capable of producing (and exporting) its own advanced weapons, and its arms imports decreased by 19 per cent

[21] 'US tells Pakistan it will have to fund F-16s itself', Reuters, 2 May 2016.
[22] US Department of State, 'Department press briefing', 4 Jan. 2018.
[23] Reynolds, I., 'Japan approves record defense budget as North Korea looms', Bloomberg, 22 Dec. 2017; and McCurry, J., 'Japan boosts defence budget to record levels with eye on North Korea', *The Guardian*, 22 Dec. 2017.

between 2008–12 and 2013–17. Despite this fall, it was the world's fifth larg-est arms importer in 2013–17. Imports included advanced combat aircraft and air defence systems from Russia. There are a number of possible reasons behind China's decision to procure these weapons. It is possible that the pro-curement was aimed at safeguarding against potential delays in the develop-ment of China's own equivalent weapons. It is also possible that, at the time of the decision, China perceived that its level of development of advanced weapons remained behind that of Russia. However, China may now have reached or even surpassed Russia's development level in the field of combat aircraft. In late 2017 China announced that its J-20 'fifth generation' combat aircraft was operational—years ahead of the Russian equivalent.[24] If the reports prove to be correct, advanced combat aircraft may be another type of weapon that China no longer needs to import.

South East Asia. In the past decade tensions between China and several countries over maritime claims in the South China Sea have directly or indirectly driven up demand for major weapons in South East Asia.[25] Although the volume of imports by countries in the subregion did not differ significantly between 2008–12 and 2013–17, the volume more than doubled between 1997–2006 and 2008–17. A large proportion of the imports in the 10-year period 2008–17 were naval and air systems, indicating a strong focus on maritime security.

Internal security and conflicts in several South East Asian countries are other drivers of arms imports. In some supplier countries concerns about the use of such weapons have led to restrictions, as in 2017 in the case of Myanmar. The use of force by the military of Myanmar against the Rohingya people, which intensified in August 2017, received widespread international condemnation.[26] Some countries, including all EU member states and the USA, have long-standing arms embargoes on Myanmar.[27] However, other countries supply Myanmar with arms. In 2013–17 China accounted for 68 per cent of Myanmar's arms imports, followed by Russia with 15 per cent. Major ongoing arms deals in 2017 included the delivery to Myanmar of combat aircraft from China and Russia.

Europe

Arms imports by states in Europe decreased by 22 per cent between 2008–12 and 2013–17. Europe accounted for 11 per cent of total global arms imports in 2013–17. In the wake of the global financial crisis that started around 2008,

[24] Mizokami, K., 'China's J-20 stealth fighter is operational', *Popular Mechanics*, 29 Sep. 2017; and Majumdar, D., 'Is China's J-20 stealth fighter really "operational"?', *National Interest*, 10 Feb. 2018.
[25] For further detail see Wezeman, S. T., 'Arms flows to South East Asia', SIPRI Policy Paper, forthcoming 2018.
[26] See also chapter 2, section III, in this volume.
[27] On the EU arms embargo see chapter 10, section II, in this volume.

several European states were forced to scale down orders for arms imports, which led to reductions in arms deliveries several years later. However, rising tensions between Russia and other European states in 2013–17 became a driver of increased arms procurement in that period and several significant arms import contracts were concluded. These procurement decisions are not reflected in the trend for 2013–17 as the majority of deliveries were planned to take place after 2017. In 2017, for example, Poland, Romania and Sweden each decided to acquire long-range air and missile defence systems from the USA, and Lithuania ordered medium-range air defence systems with components from Norway and the USA. There was also a notable rise in the demand in Europe for long-range ground attack missiles. In 2013–17 Finland and Poland received air-launched cruise missiles (ALCMs) from the USA with a range of about 400 kilometres. In 2017 Poland ordered further ALCMs from the USA with a range of 1000 km.

The short-term trend in arms imports in Europe is likely to be heavily influenced by deals with the USA for F-35 combat aircraft for Italy (90 aircraft), the Netherlands (37), Norway (52) and the UK (138), which were agreed around 2007. A total of 37 of these aircraft were supplied in 2013–17 and the pace of delivery is planned to increase in the coming years. Denmark has started the process of ordering 27 F-35 combat aircraft, while several other European states, including Belgium and Germany, are considering ordering the F-35.[28]

Despite the ongoing armed conflict in Ukraine, which started in 2014, arms imports by the Ukrainian Government remained small in the period 2013–17.[29] There were several reasons for this, including reluctance on the part of the USA and European arms-producing countries to supply weapons, Ukraine's high level of self-sufficiency in arms production, and a shortage of government funds.[30] Rebels in eastern Ukraine received tanks, armoured vehicles and portable anti-tank and surface-to-air missiles from Russia. However, a lack of reliable sources makes it impossible to provide accurate estimates of the volumes involved.

As in previous years, military clashes occurred between Armenia and Azerbaijan in 2017.[31] The volume of major arms imported by Armenia in 2013–17 was relatively small, and all its imports came from Russia. Azerbaijan's arms imports increased by 55 per cent between 2008–12 and 2013–17. In both periods Azerbaijan's imports were 12 to 14 times higher than those

[28] Belga, 'Aankoop F-16's: "Regering niet verplicht te kiezen tussen Eurofighter en F-35"' [Acquisition of F-16s: 'Government not obliged to choose between Eurofighter and F-35'], De Standaard, 14 Feb. 2017.

[29] See also chapter 2, section IV, in this volume.

[30] Wezeman, S. T. and Kuimova, A., 'Ukraine and Black Sea security', SIPRI Background Paper, forthcoming 2018.

[31] Sanamyan, E., 'Karabakh: more (relative) calm ahead in 2018?', Eurasianet, 12 Jan. 2018. See also chapter 2, section IV, in this volume.

of Armenia. Its main arms suppliers in 2013–17 were Russia (65 per cent) and Israel (29 per cent).

The Middle East

Most countries in the Middle East were directly involved in violent conflict in 2013–17, and arms imports by states in the region increased by 103 per cent between 2008–12 and 2013–17. During 2013–17, 31 per cent of arms transfers to the region went to Saudi Arabia, 14 per cent to Egypt and 13 per cent to the UAE. Iran, the second most populous state in the Middle East, accounted for only 1 per cent of the region's arms imports as it is subject to a United Nations arms embargo.[32] The USA supplied 52 per cent of total arms transfers to the Middle East, followed by the UK (9.4 per cent) and France (8.6 per cent).

In 2013–17 many states in the Middle East acquired weapons that extended their military reach. For example, Egypt procured ALCMs from France; Saudi Arabia procured ALCMs from the UK and the USA; Kuwait procured ALCMs from the UK; Qatar procured ALCMs from France and ballistic missiles from China; and the UAE procured ballistic missiles from the USA. Saudi Arabia and the UAE used some of their newly acquired missiles in Yemen. The Houthi rebels in Yemen received imprecise ballistic missiles from Iran, which were fired into Saudi Arabia in 2017.

Saudi Arabia. Saudi Arabia was the world's second largest arms importer in 2013–17, with arms imports increasing by 225 per cent compared with 2008–12. In 2013–17, 61 per cent of Saudi Arabia's arms imports came from the USA and 23 per cent from the UK. Deliveries during this period included 78 combat aircraft, 72 combat helicopters, 328 tanks and about 4000 other armoured vehicles. By the end of 2017 many more weapons were on order, indicating continuing high levels of arms transfers for at least five more years. The previous peak in Saudi Arabia's arms imports occurred in 1995–99, when it was also the world's second largest arms importer. However, its arms imports in 2013–17 were 48 per cent higher than those in 1995–99. Unlike in the late 1990s, Saudi Arabia now uses the weapons it has imported in large-scale combat, in particular in Yemen.

Qatar. From around 2011 Qatar started to become increasingly assertive in its foreign policy towards the Middle East and North Africa and initiated a rapid build-up of its armed forces.[33] Arms imports by Qatar rose by 166 per cent between 2008–12 and 2013–17. The USA accounted for 67 per cent and Germany for 20 per cent of Qatari arms imports in 2013–17. Qatar signed several major deals in 2013–17, including for 24 combat aircraft from France in 2015; for 2 frigates and 4 corvettes from Italy in 2016; and for 36 combat aircraft

---

[32] See chapter 10, section II, in this volume.
[33] Abdullah. J., 'Analysis: Qatar's foreign policy: the old and the new', Aljazeera, 21 Nov. 2014.

from the USA, 24 from the UK and 12 from France in 2017. The 2017 deals were concluded soon after tensions surfaced between Qatar and several Arab states, led by Saudi Arabia and the UAE.[34]

Egypt. Arms imports by Egypt grew by 215 per cent between 2008–12 and 2013–17, and it became the world's third largest importer. The USA has been Egypt's main arms supplier since the late 1970s and accounted for 45 per cent of Egypt's arms imports in 2008–12. However, in 2013–15 it halted deliveries to Egypt of certain arms, in particular combat aircraft. In 2014 Egypt signed major arms deals with France, and deliveries started in 2015. As a result, France accounted for 37 per cent of Egypt's arms imports in 2013–17 and overtook the USA to become the main arms supplier to Egypt for that period. This was despite the fact that the USA ended its restrictions in 2015 and increased its overall arms supplies to Egypt by 84 per cent between 2008–12 and 2013–17.

Israel. Israel's arms imports increased by 125 per cent between 2008–12 and 2013–17. The USA accounted for 60 per cent of these arms imports. Major deliveries in 2013–17 included 9 F-35 combat aircraft (of a total order for 50). These aircraft significantly strengthen Israel's ability to strike targets throughout the Middle East. Germany delivered two submarines to Israel in 2013–17, and these accounted for 30 per cent of Israel's arms imports in that period. In 2017 Germany agreed to supply a further three submarines to Israel.

[34] Hollinger, P., 'BAE Systems signs off £5bn Qatar deal for 24 Typhoon fighters', *Financial Times*, 10 Dec. 2017.

Box 5.1. Methodology

The SIPRI Arms Transfers Database, which is available on the SIPRI website, contains information on deliveries of major weapons to states, international organizations and non-state armed groups from 1950 to 2017. A new set of data is published annually, replacing data in earlier editions of the SIPRI Yearbook or other SIPRI publications.

SIPRI's definition of 'transfer' includes sales, manufacturing licences, aid, gifts, and most loans or leases. The item must have a military purpose: the recipient must be the armed forces or paramilitary forces or intelligence agency of another country, a non-state armed group, or an international organization.

The SIPRI Arms Transfers Database only includes 'major weapons', which are defined as (a) most aircraft (including unmanned), (b) most armoured vehicles, (c) artillery over 100 millimetres in calibre, (d) sensors (radars, sonars and many passive electronic sensors), (e) air defence missile systems and larger air defence guns, (f) guided missiles, torpedoes, bombs and shells, (g) most ships, (h) engines for combat-capable aircraft and other larger aircraft, for combat ships and larger support ships, and for armoured vehicles, (i) most gun or missile-armed turrets for armoured vehicles, (j) reconnaissance satellites, (k) air refuelling systems, and (l) naval guns, missile launch systems and anti-submarine weapons.

In cases where a sensor, engine, turret, refuelling system or naval gun or other system (items d, h, i, k and l) is fitted on a platform (vehicle, aircraft or ship), the transfer only appears as a separate entry in the database if the item comes from a different supplier from that of the platform.

SIPRI has developed a unique system to measure the volume of transfers of major weapons using a common unit, the trend-indicator value (TIV). The TIV is intended to represent the transfer of military resources. Each weapon has its own specific TIV. Second-hand and second-hand but significantly modernized weapons are given a reduced TIV. SIPRI calculates the volume of transfers by multiplying the weapon-specific TIV with the number of weapons delivered in a given year. SIPRI TIV figures do not represent sales prices for arms transfers.

II. Transparency in arms transfers

MARK BROMLEY AND SIEMON T. WEZEMAN

Official and publicly accessible data on arms transfers—both exports and imports—is important for assessing states' policies on arms exports, arms procurement and defence. Almost all states have published information on their arms exports and imports in the form of national reports on arms exports or through their participation in regional or international reporting mechanisms at some point in the past 25 years (although in many cases the information covers only one or a few years).[1] As of 31 December 2017, 36 states had published at least one national report on arms exports since 1990.[2] As in 2015 and 2016, no state produced a national report on arms exports in 2017 that had not done so previously, and there were no significant developments in either the types of data included or the level of detail provided.[3] A number of regional reporting instruments have been mandated or established (most notably in West Africa, the Americas and the European Union) since the early 1990s.[4] No significant developments relating to these instruments took place in 2017. The main international reporting mechanisms in the field of international arms transfers are the United Nations Register of Conventional Arms (UNROCA) and the 2013 Arms Trade Treaty (ATT) reporting instrument. This section analyses the current status of these two instruments.

The United Nations Register of Conventional Arms

UNROCA was established in 1991 and reporting started in 1993 (for arms transfers in 1992). It aims to build confidence between states and 'to prevent the excessive and destabilizing accumulation of arms'.[5] Each year all UN member states are 'requested' to report, on a voluntary basis, information on their exports and imports in the previous year of certain types of weapon, specifically those that are deemed to be 'the most lethal' or 'indispensable

---

[1] This section covers only public reporting instruments in the field of arms transfers. Confidential exchanges of information, such as those that occur within the Organization for Security and Co-operation in Europe and the Wassenaar Arrangement, are not addressed.

[2] SIPRI collects all published national reports on arms transfers and makes them available in its National Reports Database on the SIPRI website.

[3] Some states that do not publish a national report on their arms exports release data on the overall financial value of their arms exports. These states include India, Israel, Pakistan and Russia.

[4] The main regional reporting instruments include (a) the instrument created under the 2006 Economic Community of West African States (ECOWAS) Convention on Small Arms and Light Weapons, Their Ammunition and Other Related Materials; (b) instruments created by the Organization of American States; and (c) the European Union annual report. For further detail on these regional reporting instruments see Bromley, M. and Wezeman, S. T., 'Transparency in arms transfers', SIPRI Yearbook 2016, pp. 595–603.

[5] UN General Assembly Resolution 46/36L, 9 Dec. 1991.

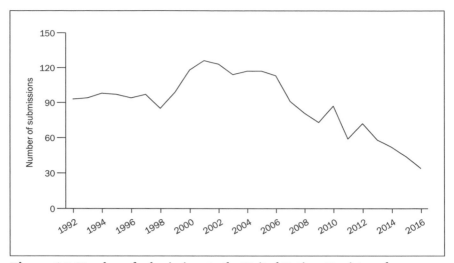

Figure 5.2. Number of submissions to the United Nations Register of Conventional Arms (UNROCA), 1992–2016

Note: Years refer to the year covered by the report, not the year of its submission.

Source: UNROCA database.

for offensive operations'.[6] Furthermore, states are 'invited' to provide additional background information on holdings of weapons and procurement from national production. Since 2003, states have also been 'invited' to provide background information on exports and imports of small arms and light weapons.

Reporting levels have decreased since the mid-2000s: over 100 states reported for each year between 2000 and 2006, compared with 44 for 2015 and 34 for 2016—the lowest level of reporting since the instrument was created (see figure 5.2). As in most years since 1993, the level of reporting for 2016 by states in Africa and the Middle East was very low: as of 31 December 2017, none of the 53 states in Africa and only 2 of the 15 states in the Middle East (i.e. 13 per cent) had submitted reports for that year. In other regions, there was an overall downward trend in reporting between 2012 and 2016 (see table 5.5).[7] One of the main reasons behind this decline is the sharp fall in the number of states submitting 'nil reports' (i.e. a report indicating that the state neither exported nor imported major weapons in the relevant period). Nil reports accounted for over 50 per cent of all submissions for 2007. For

[6] These weapons are: battle tanks, armoured combat vehicles, large-calibre artillery systems, combat aircraft, attack helicopters, warships, and missiles and missile launchers. The reports are made publicly available on the website of the United Nations Office for Disarmament Affairs (UNODA).

[7] Findings are based on information from the UNROCA website; and United Nations, General Assembly, 'United Nations Register of Conventional Arms', Report of the Secretary-General, A/72/331, 14 Aug. 2017.

Table 5.5. Reports submitted to the United Nations Register of Conventional Arms and Arms Trade Treaty, by region, 2012–16

Years refer to the year covered by the report, not the year of its submission. Figures in parentheses are the shares (%) of states (UN member states or ATT states parties) in each region that have reported.

	2012	2013	2014	2015	2016
UNROCA					
Africa	3 (6%)	1 (2%)	0 (0%)	1 (2%)	0 (0%)
Americas	11 (31%)	9 (26%)	8 (23%)	8 (23%)	3 (8.6%)
Asia	12 (41%)	5 (17%)	7 (24%)	5 (17%)	3 (10%)
Europe	43 (91%)	39 (83%)	36 (77%)	27 (57%)	28 (60%)
Middle East	1 (6.7%)	3 (20%)	0 (0%)	0 (0%)	2 (13%)
Oceania	2 (14%)	1 (7.1%)	1 (7.1%)	3 (21%)	0 (0%)
Total	**72 (37%)**	**58 (30%)**	**52 (27%)**	**44 (23%)**	**34 (18%)**
ATT					
Africa	..	..	..	4 (57%)	6 (46%)
Americas	..	..	..	8 (47%)	6 (30%)
Asia	..	..	..	1 (100%)	1 (100%)
Europe	..	..	..	32 (94%)	34 (92%)
Middle East	..	..	..	..	..
Oceania	..	..	..	3 (100%)	2 (50%)
Total	**..**	**..**	**..**	**48 (79%)**	**49 (65%)**

.. = not available or not applicable; ATT = Arms Trade Treaty; UNROCA = United Nations Register of Conventional Arms.

Sources: UNROCA database; reports on UNROCA by the UN Secretary-General to the UN General Assembly, various years; and reports by the ATT Secretariat, various years.

2014 the figure was 23 per cent, for 2015 it was 32 per cent, and for 2016 it was 6 per cent (representing only two nil reports).

Notably, certain states that are known to have exported weapons covered by UNROCA in 2015, 2016 or both years did not report for either one or both of those years. States falling into this category include China, France, Israel and Italy, all of which—according to SIPRI data—are among the world's largest arms-exporting countries (see section I).

The Arms Trade Treaty reporting instrument

Article 13 of the ATT obliges its states parties to provide annual reports on 'authorized or actual exports and imports of conventional arms', following a format similar to that of UNROCA.[8] States parties have invested significant effort in developing the reporting process: they have agreed to adopt templates for submissions and established a working group on transparency

---

[8] For a summary and other details of the ATT see annex A, section I, in this volume. On developments in the ATT in 2017 see chapter 10, section I, in this volume.

and reporting to examine reporting-related issues. During 2017 the working group developed a guidance document—which was endorsed at the third ATT Conference of States Parties in 2017—to inform states parties' practices and encourage more timely and complete submission of reports.[9] Nonetheless, reporting has been far from universal, and it declined in 2017.

By 31 December 2017, 49 of the 75 states parties (65 per cent) that were due to submit an annual report on their arms exports and imports during 2016 had done so.[10] Only 28 (37 per cent) had done so before the mandated deadline of 31 May 2017. This represents a decline on the previous year in both the proportion of states submitting annual reports and the proportion doing so before the mandated deadline. By 31 December 2017, 48 of the 61 states parties (79 per cent) that were due to submit an annual report on their arms exports and imports during 2015 had done so.[11] A total of 28 (46 per cent) had done so before the mandated deadline of 31 May 2016. An independent analysis of the reasons for non-compliance with the requirement to submit these ATT reports highlighted a number of contributing factors, including the availability of the information, a lack of capacity and coordination among government agencies, and concerns about the sensitivity of the information.[12]

To date, the impact of the ATT reporting instrument on overall levels of transparency in the international arms trade appears to be mixed. On the one hand, there are signs that becoming a state party to the ATT is encouraging states to make data available on arms transfers that they had not previously provided to UNROCA. In their ATT reports on arms transfers in 2015, for example, Austria, Costa Rica, the Dominican Republic and Liberia provided information on small arms transfers; these countries have never submitted this type of information to UNROCA.[13] On the other hand, there are also signs of states showing a growing interest in making their ATT national reports available only to other states parties. The ATT does not stipulate that the annual reports on arms exports and imports will be made public, and the

[9] Arms Trade Treaty, Working Group on Transparency and Reporting, 'Co-chairs' draft report to CSP3', ATT/CSP3.WGTR/2017/CHAIR/159/Conf.Rep, 31 July 2017, Annex D, 'Reporting authorized or actual exports and imports of conventional arms: questions and answers'.

[10] Arms Trade Treaty Secretariat, 'Reporting', 8 Mar. 2018. Greece also submitted a report despite not being required to do so.

[11] Liberia, Paraguay and Switzerland also submitted reports despite not being required to do so.

[12] Holtom, P. and Stohl, R., *Reporting in Review: Examining ATT Reporting Experiences* (Arms Trade Treaty-Baseline Assessment Project: Washington, DC, Aug. 2017), p. 15.

[13] Holtom, P. and Pavesi, I., *Trade Update 2017: Out of the Shadows* (Small Arms Survey: Geneva, Sep. 2017), p. 13.

ATT template—unlike the UNROCA template—asks states to specify if the report should be made public or distributed only to other states parties. Only one state (Slovakia) chose not to make its report on transfers in 2015 publicly available. However, three states (Liberia, Panama and Senegal) chose to keep their reports on arms exports and imports during 2016 confidential. All of these states had made their 2015 reports publicly available.

III. The financial value of states' arms exports

MARK BROMLEY AND JOHANNA TRITTENBACH

There has long been a strong interest in measuring the financial value of states' arms exports, as a means of assessing both the cost of arms transfers for importing states and the economic benefits for exporting states. The SIPRI Arms Transfers Database was not developed to measure the financial value of the international arms trade. Rather, the trend-indicator value (TIV) data produced by the database is designed to serve as an indicator of the volume of military equipment transferred (see section I). The only source of data on the financial value of states' arms exports is official data provided by governments. However, there are significant limitations on using official national data to measure the financial value of the international arms trade. In particular, the data is based on national definitions and methodologies and is thus not necessarily comparable.[1] Nevertheless, as long as these limitations are understood, the data can act as an important source of information.

Official data on the financial value of states' arms exports in the years 2007–16 is presented in table 5.6. The countries included in the table are those that provide data on the financial value of 'arms exports', 'arms export licences', 'arms export agreements' or 'arms export orders' and for which the average of the values given exceeds $10 million. The data is taken from reports by—or direct quotes from—national governments. The stated data coverage reflects the language used by the original source. National practices in this area vary, but the term 'arms exports' generally refers to the financial value of the arms actually delivered; 'arms export licences' generally refers to the financial value of the licences for arms exports issued by the national export licensing authority; and 'arms export agreements' or 'arms export orders' refers to the financial value of contracts or other agreements signed for arms exports. Conversion to constant (2016) US dollars is made using the market exchange rates of the reporting year and the US consumer price index (CPI).

According to the SIPRI Arms Transfers Database, countries that produce official data on the financial value of their arms exports account for over 90 per cent of the total volume of deliveries of major weapons. It is possible therefore to use the data in table 5.6 to attain a rough estimate of the financial value of the global arms trade. However, using the data in this way is

---

[1] There is no internationally agreed definition of what constitutes 'arms' and governments use different lists when collecting and reporting data on the financial value of their arms exports. In addition, there is no standardized methodology concerning how to collect and report such data, with some states reporting on export licences issued or used and other states using data collected from customs agencies.

problematic. First, as noted above, the data sets used are based on different definitions and methodologies and are not directly comparable. Second, several states (such as the United Kingdom) do not release data on arms exports but only on arms export licences, while other states (such as China) do not release any data on arms exports, licences, agreements or orders. Nonetheless, by adding up the data that states have made available on the financial value of their arms exports, as well as estimates for those that only provide data on arms export licences, agreements or orders, it is possible to estimate that the total value of the global arms trade in 2016 was at least $88.4 billion.[2] However, the true figure is likely to be higher.

[2] When calculating this total, figures for arms exports were used where they are available. In the case of Canada, the figure for arms exports has been doubled, as the arms export figures for Canada exclude exports to the USA, which the Canadian authorities claim account for more than half of Canada's exports of military technology. Where figures for arms exports in 2016 are not available but figures for 2015 are available, the 2015 figure has been used. Where figures for arms exports are not available in 2016 or 2015, figures for arms export agreements or orders in 2015 have been used if available. Based on an analysis of past cases in which states have released data on both arms exports and arms export agreements or orders, the full figure for arms export agreements or orders has been used, but with a one-year lag. Where figures for arms export agreements or orders are not available, figures for arms export licences in 2016 have been used if available. Based on an analysis of states that release data on both arms exports and arms export licences, half the figure for arms export licences, for the current year, has been used. This export licence-based estimate has also been used for Germany, even though it provides figures for arms exports. Germany's arms export figures only include exports of 'weapons of war', a much more limited category of goods and services than is generally covered by export licences. These figures therefore underestimate the total value of German arms exports.

Table 5.6. The financial value of states' arms exports according to national government and industry sources, 2007–16

Figures are in constant (2016) US$ m. Years are calendar years unless otherwise stated.

State	2007	2008	2009	2010	2011	2012	2013	2014	2015	2016	Explanation of data
Austria	196	343	541	544	638	611	720	722	377	707	Arms exports
	2 185	1 545	3 497	2 577	2 421	2 087	3 247	1 215	1 217	4 403	Arms export licences
Belgium	1 426	2 180	1 713	1 462	1 239	1 301	839	6 070	1 252	1 381	Arms export licences
Bosnia and Herzegovina	..	46	36	15	61	55	53	..	..	..	Arms exports
	60	95	71	41	85	62	153				Arms export licences
Bulgaria	234	245	225	376	343	294	321	543	1 574	1 122	Arms exports
	599	776	491	431	331	469	672	1 113	718	1 392	Arms export licences
Canada[a]	351	583	530	437	685	1 090	681	731	535	541	Arms exports
Croatia	..	..	..	79	52	68	118	95	44	82	Arms exports
	..	..	348	649	227	320	974	648	429	419	Arms export licences
Czech Republic	276	310	272	316	271	368	394	575	632	762	Arms exports
	756	346	606	657	513	356	449	673	833	380	Arms export licences
Denmark	311	266	392	548	352	298	1 070	197	150	224	Arms export licences
Estonia	5	10	5	<1	4	<1	1	4	4	4	Arms exports
	5	10	12	3	519	4	4	5	16	10	Arms export licences
Finland	119	152	135	86	144	78	305	300	110	146	Arms exports
	90	550	291	89	273	158	471	305	407	108	Arms export licences
France	7 158	5 129	5 736	5 400	5 409	4 491	5 308	5 174	6 805	7 721	Arms exports
	8 967	10 751	12 688	7 461	9 666	6 470	9 403	11 054	19 004	15 420	Arms export licences
Germany	2 392	2 330	2 081	3 089	1 906	1 271	1 276	2 452	1 746	2 767	Arms exports[b]
	13 817	13 609	10 939	8 005	16 012	11 922	11 408	8 768	14 396	7 638	Arms export licences[c]
Greece	52	78	353	430	335	457	..	..	..	..	Arms exports
Hungary	27	24	26	28	27	36	42	45	52	21	Arms exports
	152	194	197	201	231	363	702	581	1 441	651	Arms export licences
India[d]	96	220	77	..	..	90	121	165	325	223	Arms exports
Ireland	52	51	70	35	40	63	85	116	48	70	Arms export licences

Country	Category										
Israel	Arms exports	..	6482	7719	7925	7469	7809	..	5738	..	..
Israel	Arms export agreements	7052	8279	8035	6210	4043	6738	4479	3792	5772	6500
Italy	Arms exports	2007	2902	3427	898	1517	3792	2940	3566	3609	3157
Italy	Arms export licences	7516	9244	10402	4739	7806	5587	3519	4479	8853	16188
Korea, South	Arms export agreements	978	1153	1304	1308	2542	2460	3662	3586	..	2548
Lithuania	Arms exports	70	51	68	22	71	26	22	25	30	45
Lithuania	Arms export licences	100	77	123	34	76	27	30	21	66	102
Montenegro	Arms exports	..	28	12	9	..	4	4	12	4	..
Montenegro	Arms export licences	49	33	12	15	6	7	8	15	12	..
Netherlands	Arms exports	1385	816	881	985	1145	1104	346	337	665	626
Netherlands	Arms export licences	1136	2054	2044	1331	617	1264	1317	2778	980	1566
Norway	Arms exports	632	769	801	668	681	697	579	473	410	427
Norway	Arms export agreements	22	58	16	19	11	14	13	17	61	..
Pakistan[e]	Arms export agreements	56	27	..	37	26	29	23	57	95	..
Poland	Arms export licences	455	601	2162	666	1259	850	1174	1237	1425	1357
Portugal	Arms exports	..	116	25	29	37	42	241	211	214	660
Portugal	Arms export licences	43	124	44	31	46	70	200	343	76	270
Romania	Arms exports	97	93	110	135	140	87	182	161	163	181
Romania	Arms export licences	196	133	185	167	196	187	305	252	223	241
Russia	Arms exports	8566	9308	9509	11007	14618	15889	16175	15816	14683	15000
Russia	Arms export licences	147	366	227	281	243	207	317	360	..	..
Serbia	Arms exports	475	949	726	1105	547	618	1051	995	..	..
Serbia	Arms export licences	59	62	68	22	15	34	42	49	64	66
Slovakia	Arms exports	117	116	166	85	44	98	167	360	318	230
Slovakia	Arms export licences	5	10	8	9	13	5	4	12	12	18
Slovenia	Arms exports	8	10	19	16	18	12	12	4	35	48
South Africa	Arms exports	657	796	1031	1252	1350	1350	337	278	217	283
South Africa	Arms export licences	1478	1525	2093	1644	3606	2623	5346	4308	4178	4481
Spain	Arms exports	3108	4125	4962	3262	4258	10698	5911	4931	11990	6138
Spain	Arms export licences	..	..	..	..	..	..	..	..	..	..

State	2007	2008	2009	2010	2011	2012	2013	2014	2015	2016	Explanation of data
Sweden	1 645	2 148	1 982	2 099	2 286	1 506	1 889	1 176	896	1 283	Arms exports
	1 170	1 624	1 623	2 020	1 791	1 224	1 555	662	594	7 224	Arms export licences
Switzerland	448	743	748	677	1 049	780	512	624	470	418	Arms exports
Turkey	486	642	750	698	872	1 254	1 432	1 673	1 681	1 678	Arms exports
United Kingdom	22 353	8 929	12 637	9 913	9 231	14 523	15 784	14 190	11 912	7 961	Arms export orders[f]
	2 079	4 027	5 380	4 136	10 387	3 578	7 157	3 478	9 005	4 369	Arms export licences
Ukraine	810	892	895	1 053	1 071	1 070	1 030	..	577	770	Arms exports
United States[g]	24 571	50 418	23 993	20 035	20 870	18 347	20 948	19 696	21 524	21 665	Arms exports[h]
	19 297	30 433	32 412	23 375	27 618	65 629	24 260	31 873	45 516	27 532	Arms export agreements[i]
	28 396	38 114	40 244	37 516	46 813	35 094	21 426	63 905	74 883	49 840	Arms export licences[j]

.. = not available or not applicable.

Note: The countries included in this table are those that provide official data on the financial value of either 'arms exports', 'contracts signed for arms exports', 'arms export orders placed' or 'licences for arms exports' for at least 6 of the 10 years covered and where the average of the values given in at least 1 of the data sets exceeds $10 million. The arms export data for the different states in this table is not necessarily comparable and may be based on significantly different definitions and methodologies.

[a] Figures for Canada exclude exports to the USA.
[b] These figures only include exports of 'war weapons' as defined under German legislation.
[c] These figures include arms export licences for international collaborative projects.
[d] Figures for India for 2007–2008 and 2012–16 cover the period 1 Apr.–31 Mar. (e.g. the figure for 2016 covers the period 1 Apr. 2016–31 Mar. 2017). The figure for 2009 covers the period 1 Apr. 2009–31 Dec. 2009.
[e] Figures for Pakistan cover the period 1 Apr.–31 Mar. (e.g. the figure for 2016 covers the period 1 Apr. 2016–31 Mar. 2017).
[f] These figures cover defence equipment and additional aerospace equipment and services.
[g] Figures for the USA cover the period 1 Oct.–30 Sep. (e.g. the figure for 2016 covers the period 1 Oct. 2015–30 Sep. 2016).
[h] These figures include items sold under the government-to-government Foreign Military Sales programme and sales by US industry directly to foreign governments as direct commercial sales.
[i] These figures only include items sold under the government-to-government Foreign Military Sales programme.
[j] These figures only include sales by US industry directly to foreign governments as direct commercial sales.

Sources: Reports by—or direct quotes from—national governments. For a full list of sources and all available financial data on arms exports see the SIPRI website.

IV. Arms production and military services

AUDE FLEURANT AND NAN TIAN

Overview of developments in the arms industry, 2016

Sales of arms and military services by the SIPRI Top 100—a ranking of the world's largest arms-producing and military services companies (excluding China) according to arms sales—totalled almost $375 billion in 2016, a 1.9 per cent increase compared with 2015 (see table 5.7).[1] This is the first year-on-year real-terms rise in Top 100 arms sales since they reached a peak of $420 billion in 2010, which was followed by five consecutive years of decline. Despite the growth in 2016, the total arms sales of the Top 100 were still 13 per cent lower than those of 2010. However, they were 38 per cent higher than those of 2002, the year when SIPRI began reporting corporate arms sales.

The growth in the total arms sales of the Top 100 for 2016 was largely driven by a 4.0 per cent increase in the arms sales of companies based in the United States (see table 5.8). The USA has a decisive influence on the annual global trend in arms sales due to (a) the high number of US-based companies listed in the Top 100 (38 are ranked in 2016); and (b) the scale of the arms sales of the highest-ranked companies from the USA compared with companies from other countries (6 of the top 10 companies listed in 2016, including the top 3, are based in the USA). Arms sales by US-based companies accounted for 58 per cent of total arms sales by the Top 100 for 2016.

The annual trend in arms sales by the Top 100 is also heavily influenced by companies based in Western Europe. The combined arms sales of the 25 ranked West European companies amounted to $91.6 billion in 2016, which accounted for 24 per cent of total sales by the Top 100. Companies from eight West European countries, as well as two entities categorized as 'West European', were ranked in 2016 (see table 5.8).[2] There were overall increases

---

[1] Companies included in the SIPRI Top 100 may change from year to year, especially those situated at lower ranks. Consequently, comparisons between total revenues do not necessarily include the same companies each year.

SIPRI estimates that several Chinese arms-producing companies are large enough to be ranked in the Top 100. However, due to a lack of comparable and sufficiently accurate data, it has not been possible to include them in the rankings.

'Arms sales' refers to sales of military equipment and services to armed forces and ministries of defence worldwide; sales are only for those companies that are ranked. Unless otherwise stated, all arms sales figures in this section are presented in nominal (current) US dollars, while percentage changes and shares are in constant 2016 US dollars (i.e. real terms). For further detail see the SIPRI Arms Industry Database, Dec. 2017. See also Fleurant, A. et al., 'The SIPRI Top 100 arms-producing and military services companies, 2016', SIPRI Fact Sheet, Dec. 2017.

[2] The category 'West European' refers to companies whose ownership and control structures are located in more than 1 European country. The West European companies listed in the Top 100 for 2016 are Airbus and MBDA.

Table 5.7. Trends in arms sales of companies in the SIPRI Top 100 arms-producing companies, 2007–16

Percentages above 10 per cent have been rounded to the nearest whole number, those below 10 per cent to 1 decimal place.

	2007	2008	2009	2010	2011	2012	2013	2014	2015	2016
Arms sales in current prices and exchange rates										
Total ($ b.)	349	392	406	420	420	405	406	397	370	375
Change (%)	*11*	*12*	*3.4*	*3.6*	*0.0*	*–3.7*	*0.3*	*–2.1*	*–6.9*	*1.3*
Arms sales in constant (2016) prices and exchange rates										
Total ($ b.)	371	398	426	432	408	389	381	369	368	375
Change (%)	*4.6*	*7.1*	*7.1*	*1.3*	*–5.4*	*–4.7*	*–2.2*	*–3.0*	*–0.4*	*1.9*
Cumulative change since 2007 (%)	*0*	*7.1*	*15*	*16*	*10*	*4.9*	*2.5*	*–0.6*	*–1.0*	*0.9*

Note: Figures in this table refer to the companies in the SIPRI Top 100 for each year, which means they refer to a different set of companies each year, as ranked from a consistent set of data.

Source: SIPRI Arms Industry Database, Dec. 2017.

in the arms sales of companies based in Germany, Norway, Sweden, Switzerland and the United Kingdom. By contrast, there were overall decreases in the arms sales of the two West European entities and of companies based in France, Italy and Spain. Despite the diverging trends in Western Europe, the combined arms sales of companies based in that region remained stable in 2016, increasing by 0.2 per cent compared with 2015, mostly due to the growth in arms sales of British and German companies.

The combined arms sales of companies based in Russia rose by 3.8 per cent. This increase was mainly driven by domestic demand and by the implementation of a long-term and comprehensive modernization programme, which is intended to improve and update the capabilities of Russia's arms industry and allow it to reach higher standards in weapons performance. A total of 10 Russian companies appear in the Top 100 for 2016, 7 of which are in the top 50. No Russian company appears in the top 10, however.

SIPRI's 2016 ranking underlines the stability of the world's top arms-producing and military services companies. Several of the companies, such as Lockheed Martin, BAE Systems, Thales and Rheinmetall, listed in the first half of the ranking in 2016 have been listed in all previous years since 2002—the first year covered by the SIPRI Arms Industry Database. Major changes in rank in the upper half of the Top 100 tend to be caused primarily by mergers, acquisitions and divestments of companies that were ranked in previous years. By contrast, there is often more fluctuation from year to year in the rankings of companies in the lower half of the Top 100. This is mainly due to the fact that a year-on-year change in the total arms sales of a lower-ranked company (with smaller arms sales) will often have a comparatively larger impact on ranking than a change of the same value for a higher-ranked company (with larger arms sales). The smaller the original arms sales total, the more important a change will be relative to that total.

Three categories of arms producers: 'major', 'other established' and 'emerging'

The USA, Canada, Russia and countries in Western Europe with arms-producing or military services companies ranked in the Top 100 are categorized by SIPRI as 'major arms producers', since these countries are widely acknowledged to have comprehensive arms-production capabilities. The 'other established producers' category includes countries that rank arms producers and military services companies in the Top 100 and have mature and, in many cases, significant arms-producing capabilities, but do not intend to develop their capabilities further. The countries in this category for 2016 are Australia, Israel, Japan, Poland, Singapore and Ukraine. The 'emerging producers' category includes countries with arms producers and military services companies that rank in the Top 100 and have stated objectives to build significant indigenous arms-production capabilities and achieve some greater level of self-sufficiency in arms procurement. The countries in this category for 2016 are Brazil, India, the Republic of Korea (South Korea) and Turkey.

Undoubtedly, these classifications are imperfect but, as an analytical tool, they can provide insights into trends and developments in arms-production capabilities, both within and across categories. Trends in 2016 and longer-term trends (between 2002 and 2016) in each category are discussed in more detail in the following subsections.

Major arms producers

While the arms sales of major arms producers in the Top 100 increased by 35 per cent between 2002 and 2016, their share of total arms sales dropped by 3 percentage points (from 93 to 90 per cent) for the same period. In other words, the total arms sales of the Top 100 companies as a whole grew faster (by 39 per cent) between 2002 and 2016 than the overall arms sales of the major arms producers in the Top 100 over that period.[3] Fewer companies from major arms producers were ranked in 2016 (74 companies) than in 2002 (81 companies). In addition, the share of total Top 100 sales by the 10 largest arms producers (6 in the USA, 1 each in France, Italy and the UK and 1 West European entity) decreased from 60 per cent in 2002 to 52 per cent in 2016. This suggests that the arms industry is becoming slightly less concentrated, with the largest companies now holding a smaller proportion of the Top 100 market share.

---

[3] Note that the companies included in the SIPRI Top 100 change from year to year.

Table 5.8. Regional and national shares of arms sales for the SIPRI Top 100 arms-producing companies in the world excluding China, 2016 compared with 2015[a]

Percentages above 10 per cent have been rounded to the nearest whole number, those below 10 per cent to 1 decimal place.

Number of companies	Region/country[b]	Arms sales ($ b.) 2016	Arms sales ($ b.) 2015[c]	Changes in arms sales, 2016–15 (%) Nominal[d]	Changes in arms sales, 2016–15 (%) Real[e]	Share of total Top 100 arms sales, 2016 (%)
39	**North America**	**218**	**207**	*5.3*	*4.0*	*58*
38	United States	217	206	5.3	4.0	58
1	Canada	0.8	0.8	2.6	4.8	0.2
25	**Western Europe**	**91.6**	**95.9**	*−4.5*	*0.2*	*24*
8	United Kingdom	36.1	39.8	*−9.2*	*2.0*	*9.6*
6	France	18.6	18.7	*−0.9*	*−0.8*	*5.0*
2	West European[f]	15.8	16	*−1.5*	*−1.6*	*4.2*
2	Italy	10.1	10.8	*−6.5*	*−6.1*	*2.7*
3	Germany	6.0	5.6	*6.8*	*6.6*	*1.6*
1	Sweden	2.8	2.6	*4.9*	*5.5*	*0.7*
1	Switzerland	0.8	0.8	*0.0*	*2.8*	*0.2*
1	Norway	0.7	0.7	*5.5*	*6.1*	*0.2*
1	Spain	0.7	0.7	*−4.1*	*−3.6*	*0.2*
10	**Eastern Europe**	**26.6**	**26.3**	*1.0*	*3.8*	*7.1*
10	Russia	26.6	26.3	1.0	3.8	7.1
12	**Other established producers**	**20.9**	**20.3**	*2.8*	*−1.2*	*5.6*
5	Japan	8.2	7.9	*4.1*	*−6.4*	*2.2*
3	Israel	7.8	7.7	*1.6*	*0.9*	*2.1*
1	Singapore	1.7	1.7	*1.8*	*2.8*	*0.5*
1	Poland	1.1	1.2	*−4.2*	*0.8*	*0.3*
1	Ukraine	1.1	0.9	*22*	*25*	*0.3*
1	Australia	0.9	1.0	*−4.1*	*−4.3*	*0.3*
14	**Emerging producers**	**17.8**	**16**	*12*	*12*	*4.7*
7	South Korea	8.4	7.0	*19*	*21*	*2.2*
4	India	6.2	6.2	*−1.0*	*−1.2*	*1.6*
2	Turkey	2.3	1.9	*24*	*28*	*0.6*
1	Brazil	0.9	0.8	*15*	*11*	*0.2*
100	**Total**	**375**	**366**	*2.5*	*3.1*	*100*

Note: Arms sales figures are in US$ b., at current prices and exchange rates. Figures do not always add up to stated totals due to the conventions of rounding.

[a] Although it is known that several Chinese arms-producing enterprises are large enough to rank among the SIPRI Top 100, a lack of comparable and accurate data makes it impossible to include them.

[b] Figures for a country or region refer to the arms sales of the Top 100 companies headquartered in that country or region, including those in its foreign subsidiaries. They do not reflect the sales of arms actually produced in that country or region.

[c] Arms sales figures for 2015 refer to companies in the SIPRI Top 100 for 2015, and not to the companies in the Top 100 for 2016. Figures are given in current (2016) prices and exchange rates.

^{d} This column gives the change in sales 2016–15 in current US dollars.
^{e} This column gives the change in sales 2016–15 in constant (2016) dollars.
^{f} The 2 companies classified as 'West European' are Airbus and MBDA.
Source: SIPRI Arms Industry Database, Dec. 2017.

United States

US-based companies benefit from the largest domestic demand in the world and also capture a significant share of the international market for arms and military services (see section I). For 2016, US weapons procurement funding was just under $103 billion and research, development, testing and evaluation was $64.9 billion.[4] Moreover, the USA's enduring defence posture and foreign policy, which seek to preserve US primacy in world affairs, necessitate maintaining large, technologically advanced and comprehensive national arms-production capabilities.[5]

Since SIPRI started collecting data on the global arms industry, the yearly trend in total Top 100 arms sales has invariably been set by US-based companies, and 2016 was no exception. The combined sales of the 38 US-based companies in the Top 100 amounted to $217 billion in 2016, accounting for 58 per cent of the Top 100 total. Lockheed Martin, the world's largest arms producer, increased its arms sales by 11 per cent in 2016 to reach $40.8 billion, significantly widening the gap between it and Boeing, the second largest arms producer. Growth in Lockheed Martin's arms revenues was expected following the acquisition of helicopter manufacturer Sikorsky from United Technologies in 2015 and increased deliveries of F-35 combat aircraft.

Several key developments in the USA in 2017 are likely to shape the annual trend in the total value of arms sales for the Top 100 in 2017. In his first budget request to the US Congress following his inauguration in 2017, US President Donald J. Trump committed to continue implementation of a programme to modernize the country's military nuclear capabilities that was initiated under the previous administration. The cost of this programme is estimated by the US Congressional Budget Office (CBO) to be $1.2 trillion over a period of 30 years.[6] Notably, although the CBO estimate accounts for inflation, other estimates forecast that the total cost will be closer to $1.7 trillion.[7] As the modernization programme includes major systems, such as intercontinental ballistic missiles, nuclear-powered ballistic missile submarines

---

[4] US Department of Defense (DOD), Office of the Under Secretary of Defense (Comptroller), *National Defense Budget Estimates for FY 2018 (Revised)* (DOD: Washington, DC, Aug. 2017). On the international arms trade see section I above; and the SIPRI Arms Transfers Database.

[5] O'Hanlon, M., *The National Security Industrial Base: A Crucial Aspect of the United States, Whose Future May Be in Jeopardy*, 21st Century Defense Initiative Policy Paper (Brookings: Washington, DC, Feb. 2011).

[6] US Congressional Budget Office (CBO), *Approaches for Managing the Costs of US Nuclear Forces, 2017–2046* (CBO: Washington, DC, Oct. 2017).

[7] Reif, K., 'Trump continues Obama nuclear funding', *Arms Control Today*, July/Aug. 2017; and Reif, K., 'CBO: nuclear arsenal to cost $1.2 trillion', *Arms Control Today*, Dec. 2017.

and nuclear-capable long-range bombers, US-based arms producers stand to benefit significantly.[8] However, a cut to US Government tax revenues implemented at the end of 2017 may place additional constraints on the US military budget and undermine the USA's capacity to implement this and other (non-nuclear) military modernization programmes.[9] In addition, the spending limitations on the US Government budget imposed by the 2011 Budget Control Act, which remained in place in 2017, will continue to have an impact on the arms sales of US-based companies.[10]

Western Europe

The collective arms sales of companies based in Western Europe amounted to $91.6 billion in 2016. Overall sales in the region remained stable compared with 2016. However, while the ranking hierarchy of the largest West European arms-producing companies in the Top 100 does not change significantly from year to year, the overall arms sales totals of the companies in each West European country tend to follow different trajectories because the European market and industry remain fragmented by national borders.

With arms sales of $36.1 billion in 2016, the eight British companies ranked in the Top 100 accounted for 9.6 per cent of the Top 100 total and the largest proportion of the West European total. The combined arms sales of British companies grew by 2.0 per cent compared with 2015. BAE Systems, the UK's largest arms producer, increased its sales by 0.4 per cent, while arms sales by Rolls-Royce, the UK's second largest arms producer, rose by 4.5 per cent. GKN, an aerospace components manufacturer, recorded the highest growth in arms sales (43 per cent) among British companies between 2015 and 2016. The short-term outlook for British arms manufacturers remains uncertain following the UK's decision in 2016 to leave the European Union (EU).

The combined arms sales of the six French companies ranked in the Top 100 amounted to $18.6 billion, accounting for 5.0 per cent of the overall total for 2016. This represents a decrease in sales of 0.8 per cent compared with 2015. The slight fall was mostly due to a slowdown in deliveries of Rafale combat aircraft (produced by Dassault) compared with 2015. Dassault's arms sales decreased by 25 per cent in 2016. The arms sales of land systems producer Nexter also fell, by 19 per cent.

---

[8] On US nuclear force modernization plans see chapter 6, section I, in this volume.

[9] Goodkind, N., 'Republican tax bill could hurt US military, according to top generals', *Newsweek*, 12 Dec. 2017; and Gould, J., 'US defense industry to Congress: don't let tax cuts add to the deficit', *Defense News*, 28 Oct. 2017.

[10] Budget Control Act of 2011, US Public Law no. 112-25, signed into law 2 Aug. 2011. See also Sköns, E. and Perlo-Freeman, S., 'The United States' military spending and the 2011 budget crisis', *SIPRI Yearbook 2012*, pp. 162–66. On the spending limitations on the US budget see also chapter 4, section I, in this volume.

Following a corporate restructuring, Italy's largest arms producer, Finmeccanica, was renamed Leonardo in 2016.[11] The company's subsidiaries (such as AgustaWestland) were all consolidated into the parent company, except for the US-based Leonardo DRS. The company also sold its civilian transportation business and will now chiefly focus its activities on aerospace and military capabilities. Leonardo's arms sales were $8.5 billion in 2016—a decrease of 8.5 per cent compared with 2015. The arms sales of Italy's second largest arms producer, the naval shipyard Fincantieri, totalled $1.6 billion in 2016, representing an increase of 7.1 per cent. This was due to deliveries of littoral combat ships to the USA and of frigates and submarines to Italy.

The combined arms sales of the three German companies listed in the Top 100 for 2016 rose by 6.6 per cent to $6.0 billion. The arms sales of land systems producers Krauss-Maffei Wegmann and Rheinmetall each rose by 13 per cent due to increased German arms procurement. By contrast, ThyssenKrupp's sales fell by 6.6 per cent.

Two companies are categorized as 'West European': MBDA (France, Italy and the UK) and Airbus Group (Germany, Spain and the UK). MBDA was formerly categorized as a subsidiary of Airbus but is listed as an independent company in the Top 100 for 2016.[12] Its arms sales grew by 3.1 per cent to $3.3 billion in 2016. The arms sales of Airbus Group, which is ranked in the top 10 for 2016, totalled $12.5 billion—a decrease of 2.7 per cent compared with 2015. The fall is partly due to delays in delivering the A400 military transport aircraft.

One enduring issue for West European arms-producing countries is the sustainability of their arms-production capabilities as national resources are stretched and the costs of planned new generations of weapons are high. Attempts to generate greater trans-European cooperation and create European arms companies have been limited.[13] In 2017, following announcements of new and continuing arms modernization plans by the USA and Russia, the EU launched a programme to create better conditions for cooperation in arms production among EU member states, called Permanent Structured Cooperation (PESCO). Under the programme, the EU has, for the first time, allocated research and development funds that are specifically dedicated

---

[11] Leonardo, 'Finmeccanica: shareholders' meeting approves the change of the company's name and the 2015 financial statements', Press release, 28 Apr. 2016.

[12] Following a reassessment of MBDA, its status has been changed from 'joint venture' to 'company'. Its new status is reflected in adjustments for arms sales of the SIPRI Top 100 for previous years.

[13] An example would be the union between armoured vehicles manufacturers KMW (Germany) and Nexter (France). In 2016, sales were still made by the individual companies as the combination of the 2 companies, called KNDS, was still a holding company. Reuters, 'KMW and Nexter complete Franco-German tank deal', 5 Dec. 2015.

to the arms industry.[14] Access to funding is conditional on the submission of cross-border cooperation projects, the objective being to create larger, trans-European arms producers.

Russia

With 10 companies ranked in the Top 100 for 2016, Russia's share of total Top 100 arms sales was 7.1 per cent. The combined arms sales of Russian companies increased by 3.8 per cent in 2016, reaching a total of $26.6 billion. However, this rate of increase is lower than it was between 2014 and 2015. The central drivers of this deceleration are constraints on public finances and the effects of EU and US sanctions, which have limited Russian companies' access to some components and subsystems, causing delays in production and delivery of weapons. In 2016 Russia's gross domestic product dropped by 3.7 per cent following the fall in oil and gas prices and the implementation of sanctions.[15]

The Russian state armament programme (gosudarstvennaya programma vooruzheniya, GPV) for the period 2011–20 ended in December 2017.[16] The new GPV is intended to cover 2018–27 and includes a $283 billion (19 trillion rouble) fund for procurement and $14.9 billion (1 trillion roubles) for infrastructure construction.[17] According to reports, the GPV for 2018–27 aims to provide Russia with new generations of major weapon systems, such as hypersonic weapons, latest-generation combat aircraft (and their engines) and a modernized nuclear arsenal.[18] Precision-guided weapons and air defence systems have also been prioritized by the Russian Ministry of Defence.[19] However, doubts have been expressed regarding Russia's capacity to conduct modernization programmes, especially for new generations of weapons, within the existing budgetary constraints, assuming that sanctions remain in place and there is no significant increase in oil and gas prices.[20]

---

[14] European External Action Service, 'Permanent Structured Cooperation (PESCO): deepening defence cooperation among EU member states', Fact Sheet, 5 Mar. 2018.

[15] Luhn, A., 'Russia's GDP falls 3.7% as sanctions and low oil prices take effect', *The Guardian*, 25 Jan. 2016; and Aksenov, P., 'Ukraine crisis: why a lack of parts has hamstrung Russia's military', BBC News, 8 Aug. 2015.

[16] Mills, C., 'Russia's rearmament programme', House of Commons Library, Briefing Paper no. 877, 24 Jan. 2017.

[17] Russian Ministry of Defence, 'New 2018–2027 state armaments programme stipulates first-ever fund allocations for infrastructure construction', 10 Jan. 2018.

[18] Gorenburg, D., 'Russia's military modernization plans: 2018–2027', Ponars Eurasia, Policy Memo no. 495 (Nov. 2017).

[19] Boulègue, M., 'Russia's new state armament programme offers a glimpse at military priorities', Chatham House, Expert Comment, 27 Nov. 2017.

[20] Wezeman, S. T., 'China, Russia, and the shifting landscape of arms sales', SIPRI Commentary, 5 July 2017.

Other established producers

The general approach taken by countries in the established producers category is based on a policy of selective support of national arms-production capabilities. Each country's policy also reflects its own national preferences, funding priorities and budgetary constraints. The country in this category with the highest number of companies ranked in the Top 100 for 2016 was Japan with five, followed by Israel with three. Australia, Poland, Singapore and Ukraine each had one company ranked in the Top 100 for 2016. The combined arms sales of companies in this category fell by 1.2 per cent in 2016 to a total of $20.9 billion. However, only companies based in Japan (–6.4 per cent) and the Australian company (–4.3 per cent) recorded overall decreases in arms sales.

The other established producers category is heavily influenced by trends in Japan due to the number of Japanese companies ranked and their comparatively high volume of arms sales. The fall in Japan's arms sales in 2016 was driven by a decline in the sales of its largest arms companies: Mitsubishi Heavy Industries (–4.8 per cent), Kawasaki Heavy Industries (–16 per cent) and Mitsubishi Electric Corporation (–29 per cent). The decline is partially attributable to the appreciation of the yen against the US dollar, leading to a reduction in orders.

The arms sales of the Ukrainian company UkrOboronProm rose by 25 per cent in 2016. This was mainly due to high local demand caused by the ongoing conflict in eastern Ukraine, its absorption of the aircraft producer Antonov in 2016, and arms exports.

In the longer-term trends, the arms sales of other established producers in the Top 100 rose by 44 per cent between 2002 and 2016, slightly outpacing the overall arms sales growth (39 per cent) of the Top 100 for that period. As a result, there was a minor increase in these producers' share of total Top 100 arms sales over that period: their share rose from 5.4 per cent in 2002 to 5.6 per cent in 2016. There were two fewer companies in this category ranked in 2016 than in 2002.

Emerging producers

The country in the emerging producers category with the highest number of companies ranked in the Top 100 for 2016 was South Korea with seven companies, followed by India (four companies), Turkey (two companies) and Brazil (one company). For some of these countries, such as Turkey and South Korea, there were some successes in export markets (see section I).[21] The

---

[21] For further detail see the SIPRI Arms Transfers Database.

combined arms sales of companies in this category increased by 12 per cent in 2016 to a total of $17.8 billion.

South Korean arms producers heavily influence annual developments in the emerging producers category. Their combined arms sales totalled $8.4 billion in 2016, representing a 21 per cent increase compared with 2015 and a 430 per cent increase since 2002. South Korean arms producers held a 2.2 per cent share of total Top 100 sales in 2016, putting South Korea along-side countries in the other established producers category such as Israel and Japan. The arms sales of Brazilian and Turkish companies also increased in 2016, growing by 11 and 28 per cent, respectively. India was the only emerging producer whose Top 100 companies had lower arms sales (–1.2 per cent) in 2016.

The longer-term trends show that emerging producers' overall share of total Top 100 arm sales grew from 2.1 per cent in 2002 to 4.7 per cent in 2016. The rise in the emerging producers' share of the Top 100 arms sales appears to correlate with the previously discussed fall in the major arms producers' share during the period. There were also more companies in the Top 100 for 2016 from countries classified as emerging producers (14 companies) than in 2002 (5 companies).

Drivers of arms sales

Identifying specific drivers behind changes at category and country levels is problematic due to methodological limitations in Top 100 data. However, some general observations can be made. The first and most significant driver of arms sales is the strength of domestic demand in the country in which a company is based. This is true for all companies included in the Top 100, but is especially clear in countries in which the arms industry has been grow-ing rapidly, such as South Korea. Other central drivers are cycles of weapon modernization, tensions and conflict, which increase national demand for arms. In terms of cycles of modernization, some major arms producers are planning multiple and costly new weapon programmes, including nuclear modernization programmes, which have either started or will begin soon. This is the case, notably, for the USA, Russia and France. In general, there is a delay between a country announcing the procurement of new generations of weapons and a corresponding increase in arms sales for the companies involved, as these programmes take time to materialize, often spanning decades. However, if the planned programmes are implemented in these countries, they will have a notable effect on the Top 100 ranking in the coming years.

Regional tensions and wars may partially explain why Top 100 arms sales rose in the 2000s and peaked in 2010, with demand led by members of the North Atlantic Treaty Organization (NATO) and countries involved in the wars in Afghanistan and Iraq. This driver is also often the catalyst for a country to implement comprehensive military industrialization programmes. Indeed, procurement funding to support military industrialization is probably one of the principal factors behind the rise in emerging producers' arms sales, as military industrialization projects usually involve significant research and development and procurement resources. Other key drivers of change in arms sales from year to year are mergers, acquisitions and divestments, each of which may either increase or decrease individual company's arms sales and a country's (or region's) overall share of Top 100 arms sales.

6. World nuclear forces

Overview

At the start of 2018 nine states—the United States, Russia, the United Kingdom, France, China, India, Pakistan, Israel and the Democratic People's Republic of Korea (DPRK, or North Korea)—possessed approximately 14 465 nuclear weapons, of which 3750 were deployed with operational forces (see table 6.1). Nearly 2000 of these are kept in a state of high operational alert.

Overall, inventories of nuclear warheads continue to decline. This is mainly due to the USA and Russia, which collectively account for approximately 92 per cent of global nuclear weapons, reducing their deployed nuclear forces in line with the 2010 Treaty on Measures for the Further Reduction and Limitation of Strategic Offensive Arms (New START). Despite making reductions in their arsenals, both the USA and Russia have extensive and expensive programmes under way to replace and modernize their nuclear warheads, missile and aircraft delivery systems, and nuclear weapon production facilities (see sections I and II in this chapter).

The nuclear arsenals of the other nuclear-armed states are considerably smaller (see sections III–IX), but all are either developing or deploying new weapon systems or have announced their intention to do so. China, India, North Korea and Pakistan are thought to be expanding the size of their nuclear arsenals.

The availability of reliable information on the status of the nuclear arsenals and capabilities of the nuclear-armed states varies considerably. The USA has disclosed important information about its stockpile and nuclear capabilities, and the UK and France have also declared some information. Russia refuses to disclose the detailed breakdown of its forces counted under New START even though it shares the information with the USA, and the US Government has stopped releasing detailed information about Russian and Chinese nuclear forces. The governments of India and Pakistan make statements about some of their missile tests but provide no information about the status or size of their arsenals. Israel has a policy of not commenting on its nuclear arsenal and North Korea provides no information about its nuclear capabilities.

North Korea continues to prioritize its military nuclear programme as a central element of its national security strategy, and conducted its sixth test explosion in 2017. The test took the total number of nuclear explosions recorded worldwide since 1945 to 2058 (see section XI).

The raw material for nuclear weapons is fissile material, either highly enriched uranium (HEU) or separated plutonium. China, France, Russia, the UK and the

SIPRI Yearbook 2018: Armaments, Disarmament and International Security
www.sipriyearbook.org

Table 6.1. World nuclear forces, January 2018

All figures are approximate. The estimates presented here are based on public information and contain some uncertainties, as reflected in the notes to tables 6.1–6.10.

Country	Year of first nuclear test	Deployed warheads[a]	Stored warheads[b]	Other warheads	Total inventory
United States	1945	1 750[c]	2 050[d]	2 650[e]	6 450
Russia	1949	1 600[f]	2 750[g]	2 500[e]	6 850
United Kingdom	1952	120	95	–	215
France	1960	280	10	10	300
China	1964	–	280	–	280
India	1974	–	130–140	..	130–140
Pakistan	1998	–	140–150	..	140–150
Israel	..	–	80	..	80
North Korea	2006	–	..	(10–20)	(10–20)[h]
Total[i]		**3 750**	**5 555**	**5 160**	**14 465**

.. = not applicable or not available; – = zero; ( ) = uncertain figure.

[a] These are warheads placed on missiles or located on bases with operational forces.

[b] These are warheads in central storage that would require some preparation (e.g. transport and loading on to launchers) before they could become fully operationally available.

[c] This figure includes approximately 1600 strategic warheads (about 1300 on ballistic missiles and nearly 300 on bomber bases), as well as c. 150 non-strategic (tactical) nuclear bombs deployed in Europe for delivery by US and other North Atlantic Treaty Organization combat aircraft.

[d] This figure includes c. 50 non-strategic nuclear bombs stored in the USA.

[e] This figure is for retired warheads awaiting dismantlement.

[f] This figure includes approximately 1400 strategic warheads on ballistic missiles and about 200 deployed on heavy bomber bases.

[g] This figure includes c. 920 warheads for strategic bombers and nuclear-powered ballistic missile submarines (SSBNs) in overhaul and c. 1830 non-strategic nuclear weapons for use by short-range naval, air force and air defence forces.

[h] There is no authoritative open-source evidence to confirm that North Korea has produced or deployed operational nuclear warheads.

[i] Total figures assume the highest estimate when a range is given. Figures for North Korea are not included.

USA have produced both HEU and plutonium for use in their nuclear weapons; India and Israel have produced mainly plutonium; and Pakistan has produced mainly HEU, but is increasing its ability to produce plutonium. North Korea has produced plutonium for use in nuclear weapons but may have produced HEU as well. All states with a civilian nuclear industry are capable of producing fissile materials (see section X).

SHANNON N. KILE AND HANS M. KRISTENSEN

I. US nuclear forces

HANS M. KRISTENSEN

As of January 2018, the United States maintained a military stockpile of about 3800 nuclear warheads, a reduction of nearly 200 warheads compared with the total in early 2017.[1] The stockpile included approximately 1750 deployed nuclear warheads, consisting of about 1600 strategic and 150 non-strategic warheads. In addition, about 2050 warheads were held in reserve and around 2650 retired warheads were awaiting dismantlement, giving a total inventory of approximately 6450 nuclear warheads (see table 6.2). The reduction in warheads was due to the USA's implementation of its warhead life-extension programmes and continuing implementation of the 2010 Treaty on Measures for the Further Reduction and Limitation of Strategic Offensive Arms (New START) during 2017.[2]

Nuclear modernization

The USA has initiated a large-scale nuclear modernization programme (known as the 'program of record'), which aims to replace or upgrade (a) US land-, sea- and air-based nuclear delivery systems; (b) the command and control systems at the US Department of Defense; and (c) the nuclear warheads and their supporting infrastructure at the US Department of Energy's National Nuclear Security Administration.[3] According to an estimate published in February 2017 by the US Congressional Budget Office (CBO), modernizing and operating the US nuclear arsenal and the facilities that support it will cost around $400 billion for the period 2017–26 (a 15 per cent increase on the CBO's estimate covering the period 2015–24).[4] The nuclear modernization (and maintenance) programme will continue well beyond 2026 and, based on the CBO's estimate, will cost $1.2 trillion for the period 2017–46. Notably, although the CBO estimate accounts for inflation, other estimates forecast that the total cost will be closer to $1.7 trillion.[5] The CBO estimates that the planned modernization would increase the total costs of US nuclear forces for 2017–46 by roughly 50 per cent when compared with

---

[1] Kristensen, H. M., 'Despite rhetoric, US stockpile continues to decline', FAS Strategic Security Blog, Federation of Atomic Scientists, 22 Mar. 2018.

[2] For a summary and other details of New START see annex A, section III, in this volume. On the implementation of New START see chapter 7, section II, in this volume.

[3] Kristensen, H. M., 'US nuclear forces', *SIPRI Yearbook 2017*, pp. 413–15.

[4] US Congressional Budget Office, 'Projected costs of US nuclear forces, 2017 to 2026', Feb. 2017, p. 1.

[5] See e.g. Reif, K., 'US nuclear modernization programs', Arms Control Association, Fact Sheet, Mar. 2018.

Table 6.2. US nuclear forces, January 2018

Type	Designation	No. of launchers	Year first deployed	Range (km)[a]	Warheads x yield	No. of warheads[b]
Strategic forces						3 600
Bombers		60/107[c]				880[d]
B-52H	Stratofortress	44/87	1961	16 000	20 x ALCM 5–150 kt[e]	528
B-2A	Spirit	16/20	1994	11 000	16 x B61-7, -11, B83-1 bombs[f]	282
ICBMs		400				800[g]
LGM-30G	Minuteman III					
	Mk-12A	200	1979	13 000	1-3 x W78 335 kt	600[h]
	Mk-21 SERV	200	2006	13 000	1 x W87 300 kt	200[i]
SSBNs/SLBMs		240[j]				1 920[k]
UGM-133A	Trident II (D5/D5LE)					
	Mk-4	..	1992	>7 400	1-8 x W76-0 100 kt	216
	Mk-4A	..	2008	>7 400	1-8 x W76-1 100 kt	1 320
	Mk-5	..	1990	>7 400	1-8 x W88 455 kt	384
Non-strategic forces						200[l]
F-15E	Strike Eagle	..	1988	3 840	5 x B61-3, -4[m]	70
F-16C/D	Falcon	..	1987	3 200[n]	2 x B61-3, -4	70
F-16MLU	Falcon (NATO)	..	1985	3 200	2 x B61-3, -4	30
PA-200	Tornado (NATO)	..	1983	2 400	2 x B61-3, -4	30
Total stockpile						3 800[o]
Deployed warheads						1 750
Reserve warheads						2 050
Retired warheads awaiting dismantlement						2 650
Total inventory						6 450[p]

.. = not available or not applicable; ALCM = air-launched cruise missile; ICBM = intercontinental ballistic missile; kt = kiloton; NATO = North Atlantic Treaty Organization; SERV = security-enhanced re-entry vehicle; SLBM = submarine-launched ballistic missile; SSBN = nuclear-powered ballistic missile submarine.

Note: The figures in the USA's New START Treaty declaration do not necessarily correspond to those contained in the table because of the treaty's counting rules.

[a] Maximum unrefuelled range. All nuclear-equipped aircraft can be refuelled in the air. Actual mission range will vary according to flight profile and weapon loading.

[b] The number shows the total number of warheads assigned to nuclear-capable delivery systems. Only some of these warheads are deployed on missiles and aircraft bases.

[c] Bombers have 2 numbers: the first is the number assigned to the nuclear mission; the second is the total inventory. The US Air Force has 66 nuclear-capable bombers (20 B-2As and 46 B-52Hs) of which no more than 60 will be deployed at any given time.

[d] Of the bomber weapons, c. 300 (200 ALCMs and 100 bombs) are deployed at the bomber bases; all the rest are in central storage. The total bomb inventory is listed as higher than in *SIPRI Yearbook 2017* to compensate for a recount of the ICBM warhead estimate, but many of the gravity bombs are no longer fully active and are slated for retirement after the B61-12 is fielded in 2020.

[e] The B-52H is no longer configured to carry nuclear gravity bombs.

[f] Strategic gravity bombs are only assigned to B-2A bombers. The maximum yields of strategic bombs are: B61-7 (360 kt), B61-11 (400 kt), B83-1 (1200 kt). However, they also have lower yields. Many B83-1s have been moved to the inactive stockpile. The administration of President Barack Obama decided that the B83-1 would be retired once the B61-12 was deployed, but

the administration of President Donald J. Trump has indicated that it might retain the B83-1 for a longer period.

g Of these ICBM warheads, only 400 are deployed on the missiles. The remaining warheads are in central storage.

h Only 200 of these W78 warheads are deployed. The rest are in central storage.

i Another 340 W87s are possibly in long-term storage outside the stockpile for planned use in future so-called interoperable warheads.

j Of the 14 SSBNs, 2 are normally undergoing refuelling overhaul at any given time. They are not assigned weapons. Another 2 or more submarines may be undergoing maintenance at any given time and may not be carrying missiles. The number of deployable missiles has been reduced to 240 to meet the New START limit on deployed strategic missile launchers.

k Of these warheads, only about 900 are deployed on submarines; all the rest are in central storage. Although each D5 missile was counted under the 1991 Strategic Arms Reduction Treaty as carrying 8 warheads and was initially flight tested with 14, the US Navy has downloaded each missile to an average of 4–5 warheads. All deployed W76 warheads are of the new W76-1 type. Once production of the W76-1 is finished in 2019, all remaining W76-0s will be retired.

l Approximately 150 of the tactical bombs are deployed in Europe. The remaining bombs are in central storage in the USA. Once the B61-12 is deployed, all other B61 versions will be retired.

m The maximum yields of tactical bombs are as follows: B61-3 (170 kt) and B61-4 (50 kt). All have selective lower yields. The B61-10 was retired in 2016.

n Most sources list 2400 km unrefuelled ferry range but Lockheed Martin, which produces the F-16, lists 3200 km.

o Of these weapons, approximately 1750 are deployed on ballistic missiles, at bomber bases, and in Europe; all the rest are in central storage.

p In addition to these intact warheads, there are more than 20 000 plutonium pits stored at the Pantex Plant, Texas, and perhaps 4000 uranium secondaries stored at the Y-12 facility at Oak Ridge, Tennessee.

Sources: US Department of Defense, various budget reports, press releases and documents obtained under the Freedom of Information Act; US Department of Energy, various budget reports and plans; US Air Force, US Navy and US Department of Energy, personal communications; 'Nuclear notebook', *Bulletin of the Atomic Scientists*, various issues; and authors' estimates.

the costs of operating and sustaining only the forces that are already fielded.[6] It remains to be seen to what extent the US Congress will agree to fund these expensive projects (instead of building cheaper life-extended versions of existing designs) or whether it will decide to delay some of them.

Bombers

The US Air Force currently operates a fleet of 169 heavy bombers: 62 B-1Bs, 20 B-2As, and 87 B-52Hs. Of these, 66 (20 B-2As and 46 B-52Hs) were declared to be nuclear-capable as of 1 September 2017, although only 60 (18 B-2As and 42 B-52Hs) are thought to be assigned nuclear delivery

---

[6] US Congressional Budget Office (CBO), *Approaches for Managing the Costs of US Nuclear Forces, 2017 to 2046* (CBO: Washington, DC, Oct 2017), p. 1.

roles.[7] The bombers are being equipped with new command and control systems to improve interconnectivity with other forces and the US National Command Authority.[8]

The development of the next-generation long-range strike bomber, known as the B-21 Raider, is well under way. The B-21 is scheduled to enter service in the mid-2020s.[9]

To arm its bombers, the Air Force is developing a controversial new nuclear air-launched cruise missile, known as the LRSO (Long-Range Standoff missile), for deployment from 2030.[10] The Air Force plans to acquire 1000 missiles, of which about half will be nuclear-armed and the rest used for test launches. The weapon is intended for integration on the B-2A, the B-52H and the new B-21.[11]

Land-based ballistic missiles

As part of its implementation of New START, in 2017 the USA completed the reduction of its intercontinental ballistic missile (ICBM) force from 450 to 400 deployed Minuteman III missiles, which are deployed in silos across three missile wings. Following the reduction, each of the three ICBM bases has 133–34 deployed missiles. The 50 emptied silos are being kept in a state of readiness and can be reloaded with stored missiles if necessary.

Each Minuteman III ICBM is armed with one warhead: either a 335-kiloton W78/Mk12A or a 300-kt W87/Mk21. Missiles carrying the W78 can be uploaded with up to two more warheads for a maximum of three multiple independently targetable re-entry vehicles (MIRVs). The entire Minuteman III force completed a decade-long upgrade in 2015 to extend its life through the 2020s. Moreover, an upgrade is under way of the W87/Mk21 re-entry vehicle to a new fuze (arming, fuzing and firing unit).[12]

---

[7] US Department of State, 'New START Treaty aggregate numbers of strategic offensive arms', Fact Sheet, 12 Jan. 2018.

[8] US Air Force, Presentation to the US House of Representatives Armed Services Committee, Strategic Forces Subcommittee, Subject: FY19 Posture for Department of Defense Nuclear Forces, Statement of Rand, R. (Gen.), Commander Air Force Global Strike Command, 22 Mar. 2018.

[9] Gertler, J., *Air Force B-21 Raider Long-Range Strike Bomber*, Congressional Research Service (CRS) Report for Congress R44463 (US Congress, CRS: Washington, DC, 7 June 2017).

[10] For background and context on the LRSO see e.g. Kristensen, H. M., 'LRSO: the nuclear cruise missile mission', FAS Strategic Security Blog, Federation of American Scientists, 20 Oct. 2015; Kristensen, H. M., 'Forget LRSO: JASSM-ER can do the job', FAS Strategic Security Blog, Federation of American Scientists, 16 Dec. 2015; and Reif, K., 'Examining the flawed rationale for a new nuclear air-launched cruise missile', *Arms Control Today*, vol. 8, no. 2 (12 June 2016).

[11] US Air Force, 'USAF awards contracts for new nuclear missile to Lockheed, Raytheon', 23 Aug. 2017; Stone, M., 'US Air Force picks Raytheon, Lockheed for next-gen cruise missile', Reuters, 24 Aug. 2017; and Majumdar, D., 'B-52, B-2 and B-21 bombers are getting nuclear-tipped cruise missiles', *National Interest*, 24 Aug. 2017.

[12] Woolf, A. F., *US Strategic Nuclear Forces: Background, Developments, and Issues*, Congressional Research Service (CRS) Report for Congress RL33640 (US Congress, CRS: Washington, DC, 6 Mar. 2018), pp. 24–26.

The Air Force has begun development of a next-generation ICBM, known as the Ground Based Strategic Deterrent (GBSD), which is scheduled to begin replacing the Minuteman III in 2028. It plans to buy 642 missiles, of which 400 would be deployed, 50 stored and the rest used for test launches and as spares.[13] The expected cost of developing and producing the GBSD is increasing, and in 2017 it was projected to be around $100 billion, up from an initial projection of $62.3 billion in 2015.[14]

The Air Force conducted four test launches of the Minuteman III in 2017. The tests took place on 8 February, 26 April, 3 May and 2 August.[15] All four missiles were launched from Vandenberg Air Force Base (AFB) in California with re-entry vehicle impact some 6760 kilometres away at the Ronald Reagan Ballistic Missile Defense Test Site in the Kwajalein Atoll in the Marshall Islands. Several simulated ICBM launches were also conducted in 2017, including one at F. E. Warren AFB in Wyoming that involved six missiles.[16]

Ballistic missile submarines

In 2017 the US Navy completed the reduction of missile launch tubes (from 24 to 20) on each of its Ohio class nuclear-powered ballistic missile submarines (SSBNs). The reduction was necessary to meet the New START Treaty limit of no more than 700 deployed strategic launchers. Following the reductions, the navy's SSBN fleet can deploy up to 240 strategic missiles.[17]

All of the 14 Ohio class SSBNs, 8 of which are based in the Pacific and 6 in the Atlantic, carry Trident II (D5) submarine-launched ballistic missiles (SLBMs). Of the 14 SSBNs, 12 are normally considered to be operational and 2 are typically undergoing refuelling overhaul at any given time. Around 8 to 10 SSBNs are normally at sea, of which 4 or 5 are on alert in their designated patrol areas and ready to fire their missiles within 15 minutes of receiving the launch order.

In 2017 the navy started replacing the Trident II (D5) SLBMs with an enhanced version known as the D5LE. The D5LE is equipped with the new Mk-6 guidance system, designed to improve the D5LE's effectiveness. The D5LE will arm Ohio class submarines for the remainder of their service lives (up to 2042), and will also be deployed on British Trident submarines (see

[13] Reif, K., 'Air Force drafts plan for follow-on ICBM', *Arms Control Today*, 8 July 2015.
[14] Reif, K., 'New ICBM replacement cost revealed', *Arms Control Today*, Mar. 2017.
[15] US Air Force, Vandenberg Air Force Base, 30th Space Wing Public Affairs, 'Minuteman III launches from Vandenberg', 9 Feb. 2017; US Air Force, Global Strike Command, 'F. E. Warren tests Minuteman III missile with launch from Vandenberg', 26 Apr. 2017; US Air Force, Global Strike Command, 'Malmstrom tests Minuteman III missile with launch from Vandenberg', 3 May 2017; and US Air Force, Global Strike Command, 'F.E. Warren tests Minuteman III missile with launch from Vandenberg', 2 Aug. 2017.
[16] US Air Force, '90th MW provides unwavering nuclear deterrence', 13 Apr. 2017.
[17] Woolf (note 12).

242 MILITARY SPENDING AND ARMAMENTS, 2017

section III). The D5LE will initially also arm the new Columbia class SSBN, the first of which is scheduled to start patrols in 2031, but will eventually be replaced with a new SLBM in the early 2040s.[18]

The Trident SLBMs carry two basic warhead types: either the 455-kt W88 or the 100-kt W76. The navy has almost completed deployment of a life-extended version of the W76, known as W76-1. The W76-1 is equipped with a new fuze that improves its targeting effectiveness. Each SLBM can carry up to eight warheads but normally carries fewer. The navy does not disclose how many warheads it carries on each submarine but, in practice, each missile carries an average of four to five warheads, depending on mission requirements. The New START data indicates that the SSBN fleet carried a total of 945 warheads as of September 2017.[19]

The navy test launched four Trident II (D5) SLBMs from one SSBN in 2017. As part of Follow-on Commander Evaluation Test number 53, the missiles were launched in the Pacific from the USS Kentucky (SSBN-737) over the course of three days.[20] The event marked the final test launch of the original Trident II (D5). All future Trident II test launches will be for the D5LE.

Non-strategic nuclear weapons

The USA has one type of non-strategic weapon in its stockpile—the B61 gravity bomb. The weapon exists in two modifications: the B61-3 and B61-4. A third modification (B61-10) was retired in late 2016. There are an estimated 200 tactical B61 bombs in the US stockpile. Approximately 150 of these are deployed at six North Atlantic Treaty Organization (NATO) airbases in five European countries: Aviano and Ghedi, Italy; Büchel, Germany; Incirlik, Turkey; Kleine Brogel, Belgium; and Volkel, the Netherlands. The Belgian, Dutch and possibly Turkish air forces (using F-16 combat aircraft) and German and Italian air forces (using PA-200 Tornado combat aircraft) are assigned nuclear strike missions with the US B61 bombs. In peacetime, however, they are kept under the custodial control of US Air Force personnel.

Concerns were raised about the security of the nuclear weapons at the Incirlik base during the failed coup attempt in Turkey in July 2016, and reports emerged in late 2017 suggesting that the weapons might have been 'quietly withdrawn'.[21] These reports have not been confirmed, and Incirlik is still included in scheduled nuclear storage base upgrades for 2019.[22]

---

[18] Woolf (note 12).

[19] US Department of State (note 7).

[20] Daniels, J. M., US Navy, Strategic Systems Programs Public Affairs, 'FCET success: SSBN launches fleet ballistic missile', NNS170216-21, 16 Feb. 2017.

[21] Hammond, J., 'The future of Incirlik Air Base', Real Clear Defense, 30 Nov. 2017.

[22] For background and context see Nuclear Threat Initiative (NTI), Building a Safe, Secure, and Credible NATO Nuclear Posture (NTI: Washington, DC, Jan. 2018).

The remaining 50 B61 bombs are stored in the (continental) USA for potential use by US fighter-bombers in support of allies outside Europe, including in East Asia and the Middle East.

NATO has approved a modernization of its nuclear posture in Europe through deployment, beginning in 2022–24, of the US B61-12 guided nuclear gravity bomb.[23] The B61-12 will use the nuclear explosive package of the B61-4, which has a maximum yield of approximately 50 kt, but will be equipped with a new tail kit to increase its accuracy and standoff capability. The B61-12 will be able to destroy hardened targets that could not be destroyed by the B61-3 or B61-4. It will also enable strike planners to select lower yields for existing targets, which would reduce collateral damage.[24]

Integration flight tests have begun of the B61-12 bombs on F-15E, F-16 and Tornado combat aircraft. The B61-12 will also be integrated on the US-built F-35A combat aircraft, which is expected to be nuclear certified in 2024–26.[25] Italy and the Netherlands have received the first of their F-35A combat aircraft, some of which will later be designated for a nuclear delivery role.[26] Belgium is considering whether to buy the F-35A. Although in early 2018 the US State Department approved a possible sale of 34 F-35A aircraft, Belgium has not yet officially announced a decision to buy the F-35A.[27] Germany does not currently have a plan to replace the PA-200 Tornado in its nuclear role and is expected to extend its service life into the 2020s, despite the German Air Force's apparent preference for the F-35A.[28]

[23] US Government Accountability Office (GAO), *Nuclear Weapons: DOD and NNSA Need to Better Manage Scope of Future Refurbishments and Risks to Maintaining US Commitments to NATO*, Report to Congressional Requesters, GAO-11-387 (GAO: Washington, DC, May 2011), p. 13.

[24] For a description of the B61-12 and its implications see Kristensen, H. M., 'B61 LEP: increasing NATO nuclear capability and precision low-yield strikes', FAS Strategic Security Blog, Federation of American Scientists, 15 June 2011.

[25] Kristensen, H. M. and Norris, R. S., 'The B61 family of nuclear bombs', *Bulletin of the Atomic Scientists*, vol. 70, no. 3 (2014).

[26] Seligman, L., 'Dutch F-35s land in the Netherlands', *Defense News*, 23 May 2016; and Peruzzi, L., 'Italy receives first Cameri-assembled F-35A', Flight Global, 8 Dec. 2015.

[27] Defense Security Cooperation Agency, 'Belgium: F-35 Joint Strike Fighter Aircraft', News Release 17-80, 18 Jan. 2018.

[28] Reuters, '"F-35" für die Bundeswehr? Luftwaffe benennt Anforderungen an "Tornado": Nachfolger' ['F-35' for the Bundeswehr? Air Force calls requirements on 'Tornado' successor], *Der Spiegel*, 8 Nov. 2017.

II. Russian nuclear forces

HANS M. KRISTENSEN

As of January 2018, Russia maintained an arsenal of approximately 4350 nuclear warheads. About 2520 of these are strategic warheads, of which nearly 1600 are deployed on land- and sea-based ballistic missiles and at bomber bases. Russia also possessed approximately 1830 non-strategic (tactical) nuclear warheads, all of which are in central storage sites.[1] An estimated additional 2500 warheads were retired or awaiting dismantlement, giving a total inventory of approximately 6850 warheads (see table 6.3). The reduction in Russia's deployed strategic warheads from the estimated total of 1950 in early 2017 was due to its continuing implementation of the 2010 Treaty on Measures for the Further Reduction and Limitation of Strategic Offensive Arms (New START) during 2017.[2]

Strategic bombers

Russia's Long-range Aviation Command operates a fleet of approximately 13 Tu-160 (Blackjack), 30 Tu-95MS16 (Bear-H16) and 25 Tu-95MS6 (Bear-H6) bombers. Some of these may not be fully operational and others are undergoing various upgrades. The maximum loading on the operational bombers is more than 600 nuclear weapons, of which approximately 200 might be stored at the two strategic bomber bases. Modernization of the bombers is well under way. Nearly all of the Tu-160s and some of the Tu-95s will be upgraded to maintain a bomber force of 50–60 aircraft. The upgraded bombers are capable of carrying the new Kh-102 (AS-23B) nuclear air-launched cruise missile.[3] The Russian Government has also announced plans to resume production of the Tu-160 to produce up to 50 modified aircraft known as Tu-160M2, with serial production starting in 2023.[4] The additional bombers would probably replace many of the old Tu-95 (MS16 and MS6) aircraft and provide a bridge to the future next-generation bomber, known as PAK-DA, which is scheduled to begin fielding in the late 2020s.[5]

---

[1] For a recent overview of Russia's nuclear weapon storage facilities see Podvig, P. and Serrat, J., 'Lock them up: zero-deployed non-strategic nuclear weapons in Europe', United Nations Institute for Disarmament Research, 2017.

[2] For a summary and other details of New START see annex A, section III, in this volume. On the implementation of New START see chapter 7, section II, in this volume.

[3] Roblin, S., 'The Tu-95 Bear: the 60-year-old Russian bomber America still chases all over the world', *National Interest*, 11 June 2017.

[4] TASS, 'Russia's upgraded Tu-160M2 bomber to remain state-of-the-art for four more decades', 1 Nov. 2017.

[5] TASS, 'Russia to develop first prototype of next-generation strategic bomber by early 2020s', 13 Apr. 2017.

Land-based ballistic missiles

As of January 2018, Russia's Strategic Rocket Forces—the branch of the armed forces that controls land-based intercontinental ballistic missiles (ICBMs)—consisted of 12 missile divisions grouped into 3 armies and deploying an estimated 318 ICBMs of 7 different types and variations. These ICBMs can carry a total of 1138 warheads but SIPRI estimates that they have been downloaded to carry just under 800 warheads, nearly 50 per cent of Russia's deployed strategic warheads. In contrast to the frequent claims in recent years about a Russian nuclear 'build-up', the US Air Force's National Intelligence and Space Center (NASIC) estimates that 'the number of missiles in the Russian ICBM force will continue to decrease because of arms control agreements, aging missiles, and resource constraints'.[6]

Russia's ICBM force is in the middle of a significant modernization programme to replace all Soviet-era missiles with new types, albeit not on a one-for-one basis. The replacement programme, which started in 1997, appears to be progressing more slowly than planned. About 60 per cent of the force had been upgraded by the end of 2017. All the remaining Soviet-era ICBMs are scheduled to be withdrawn by 2024, three years later than previously announced. In addition to the procurement of new missiles, the modernization involves substantial reconstruction of silos, launch control centres, garrisons and support facilities.[7]

Russia's current ICBM modernization is focused on the multiple-warhead version of the RS-12, known as RS-24 Yars (SS-27 Mod 2). Three mobile divisions have already been completed, with two more in progress, and two more to begin upgrade by 2020. The first silo-based RS-24 regiment with 10 missiles is operational at Kozelsk and a second regiment is in the early stages of construction.[8] Russia is developing a third modification of the RS-12M, known as the RS-26 Yars-M (SS-X-28), which will be lighter than the RS-24. However, final development and deployment of the RS-26 has been delayed.[9] In addition, Russia is developing a new 'heavy' liquid-fuelled, silo-based ICBM, known as the RS-28 Sarmat (SS-X-29), as a replacement for the RS-20V (SS-18). According to Russia's Deputy Defence Minister, Yuriy Borisov, the RS-28 will carry 'new types of warheads', including

---

[6] US Air Force, National Air and Space Intelligence Center (NASIC), *Ballistic and Cruise Missile Threat* (NASIC: Wright-Patterson Air Force Base, OH, July 2017), p. 27. On the alleged Russian nuclear 'build-up' see e.g. Gertz, B., 'Russia sharply expanding nuclear arsenal, upgrading underground facilities', Washington Free Beacon, 13 Dec. 2017.

[7] Azanov, R., 'Russia's Strategic Missile Forces as its decisive defense', TASS, 19 Dec. 2017.

[8] Azanov (note 7); and Andreyev, D. and Zotov, I., [The nuclear shield is reliable], *Krasnaya Zvezda*, 14 Dec. 2017 (in Russian).

[9] Kristensen, H. M., 'Review of NASIC Report 2017: nuclear force developments', FAS Strategic Security Blog, Federation of American Scientists, 30 June 2017.

Table 6.3. Russian nuclear forces, January 2018

All estimated figures are approximate. Figures may not add up to stated totals due to the conventions of rounding.

Type/ Russian designation (NATO designation)	No. of launchers	Year first deployed	Range (km)[a]	Warhead loading	No. of warheads[b]
Strategic offensive forces					2 520[c]
Bombers	50/68[d]				616[e]
Tu-95MS6 (Bear-H6)	14/25	1981	6 500–10 500	6 x AS-15A or AS-23B ALCMs, bombs	84
Tu-95MS16 (Bear-H16)	25/30	1981	6 500–10 500	16 x AS-15A or AS-23B ALCMs, bombs	400
Tu-160 (Blackjack)	11/13	1987	10 500–13 200	12 x AS-15B or AS-23B ALCM, bombs	132
ICBMs	318				1 138[f]
RS-20V (SS-18 Satan)	46	1992	11 000–15 000	10 x 500–800 kt	460
RS-18 (SS-19 Stiletto)	20	1980	10 000	6 x 400 kt	120
RS-12M Topol (SS-25 Sickle)	72[g]	1985	10 500	1 x 800 kt	72
RS-12M2 Topol-M (SS-27 Mod 1/silo)	60	1997	10 500	1 x 800 kt	60
RS-12M1 Topol-M (SS-27 Mod 1/mobile)	18	2006	10 500	1 x (800 kt)	18
RS-24 Yars (SS-27 Mod 2/ mobile)	90	2010	10 500	4 x (100 kt)	360
RS-24 Yars (SS-27 Mod 2/silo)	12	2014	10 500	4 x (100 kt)	48
RS-26 Yars-M (SS-X-28)	..	(2018)	5 500+	MIRV (.. kt)	..
RS-28 Sarmat (SS-X-29)	..	(2020)	10 000+	MIRV (.. kt)	..
SLBMs	11/176[h]				768[h]
RSM-50 Volna (SS-N-18 M1 Stingray)	2/32	1978	6 500	3 x 50 kt	96
RSM-54 Sineva (SS-N-23 M1)	6/96	1986/2007	9 000	4 x 100 kt	384
RSM-56 Bulava (SS-N-32)	3/48	2014	>8 050	6 x (100 kt)	288
Non-strategic forces					1 830[i]
ABM, air/coastal defence	898				373
53T6 (SH-08, Gazelle)	68	1986	30	1 x 10 kt	68
S-300 (SA-10/20)	800[j]	1980/1992	..	1 x low kt	290
3M-55 Yakhont (SS-N-26)	20	(2014)	400+	1 x (.. kt)	10
SSC-1B (Sepal)	10	1973	500	1 x 350	5
Air Force weapons[k]	358				498
Tu-22M3 (Backfire-C)	100	1974	..	3 x ASM, bombs	250
Su-24M/M2 (Fencer-D)	150	1974	..	2 x bombs	150
Su-34 (Fullback)	98	2006	..	2 x bombs	98
MiG-31K (Foxhound)	10	1983	..	1 x ASM	..
Army weapons	148				148
Tochka (SS-21 Scarab)	12	1981	120	(1 x 10–100 kt)	12

Type/ Russian designation (NATO designation)	No. of launchers	Year first deployed	Range (km)[a]	Warhead loading	No. of warheads[b]
Iskander-M (SS-26 Stone)	120	2005	350[l]	(1 x 10–100 kt)	120
9M729 (SSC-8)	16	2016	(2 500)	1 x .. kt	16
Navy weapons					*810*
Submarines/surface ships/air			LACM, SLCM, ASW, SAM, depth bombs, torpedoes[m]		
Total stockpile					**4 350**
Deployed warheads					1 600[n]
Reserve warheads					2 750
Retired warheads awaiting dismantlement					**2 500**
Total inventory					**6 850**

.. = not available or not applicable; ( ) = uncertain figure; ABM = anti-ballistic missile; ALCM = air-launched cruise missile; ASM = air-to-surface missile; ASW = anti-submarine warfare; ICBM = intercontinental ballistic missile; kt = kiloton; LACM = land-attack cruise missile; MIRV = multiple independently targetable re-entry vehicle; NATO = North Atlantic Treaty Organization; SAM = surface-to-air missile; SLBM = submarine-launched ballistic missile; SLCM = sea-launched cruise missile.

Note: The table lists the total number of warheads estimated to be available for the delivery systems. Only some of these are deployed and they do not necessarily correspond to the New START Treaty data counting rules.

[a] Aircraft range is for illustrative purposes only; actual mission range will vary according to flight profile and weapon loading.

[b] The number shows the total number of available warheads, both deployed and in storage, assigned to the delivery systems.

[c] Approximately 1600 of these strategic warheads are deployed on land- and sea-based ballistic missiles and at bomber bases. The remaining warheads are in central storage.

[d] The first number is the number of bombers estimated to be counted under the New START Treaty. The second number is the total number of bombers in the inventory. Because of ongoing bomber modernization, there is considerable uncertainty about how many bombers are operational.

[e] Of the 616 weapons estimated to be assigned to long-range bombers, only 200 weapons are thought to be present at the 2 strategic bomber bases. The remaining weapons are in central storage facilities.

[f] Of the 1138 warheads available for operational ICBMs, nearly 800 are thought to be deployed on the missiles, with the remaining warheads in storage.

[g] The number is uncertain because several SS-25 garrisons are upgrading to the SS-27 Mod 2.

[h] Two of the Delta SSBNs are in overhaul at any given time and do not carry their assigned nuclear missiles and warheads. It is possible that only 1 Delta III is operational.

[i] Non-strategic nuclear warheads are not deployed with their delivery systems but are kept in a central storage facility, according to the Russian Government. Some storage facilities are near operational bases.

[j] There are at least 80 S-300 sites across Russia, each with an average of 12 launchers, each with 2–4 interceptors. Each launcher has several reloads. The SA-10 has almost been replaced by the SA-20.

[k] The numbers show total nuclear-capable aircraft but only some of them are thought to have nuclear missions. Most can carry more than 1 nuclear weapon. Other potential nuclear-capable aircraft include Su-25 Frogfoot and MiG-25 Foxbat.

l Although many unofficial sources and news media reports say the SS-26 has a range of nearly 500 km, the US Air Force, National Air and Space Intelligence Center (NASIC) lists the range as 350 km.

m Only submarines are thought to be assigned nuclear torpedoes.

n Note that the number is different from the New START Treaty number for deployed warheads because of the treaty's counting rules.

Sources: Russian Ministry of Defence, various press releases; US Department of State, START Treaty Memoranda of Understanding, 1990–July 2009; New START aggregate data releases, various years; US Air Force, National Air and Space Intelligence Center (NASIC), *Ballistic and Cruise Missile Threat* (NASIC: Wright-Patterson Air Force Base, OH, July 2017); BBC Monitoring; Russian news media; Russian Strategic Nuclear Forces website; International Institute for Strategic Studies, *The Military Balance* (Routledge: London, various issues); Cochran, T. B. et al., *Nuclear Weapons Databook*, vol. 4, *Soviet Nuclear Weapons* (Harper & Row: New York, 1989); IHS Jane's *Strategic Weapon Systems*, various issues; *Proceedings*, US Naval Institute, various issues; 'Nuclear notebook', *Bulletin of the Atomic Scientists*, various issues; and authors' estimates.

'manoeuvrable warheads'.[10] Test launches of the 200-tonne missile have begun and will be followed by serial production, before eventual deployment in upgraded RS-20V silos in a few years. Production of a rail-based ICBM seems to have been delayed or cancelled.[11]

Russia normally conducts two large-scale exercises with road-mobile ICBMs each year. The biannual exercises in 2017 involved RS-12M Topol (SS-25), RS-12M1 Topol-M (SS-27 Mod 1) and RS-24 mobile launchers from all the operational missile divisions. The launchers were deployed further from their bases and for longer periods than in previous years. Russian ICBMs also participated in broader strategic exercises along with nuclear-powered ballistic missile submarines (SSBNs) and bombers.[12] These included several test launches of strategic missiles, some of which took place around the time of the Zapad-17 exercise in western Russia and Belarus in September 2017.[13]

Ballistic missile submarines and sea-launched ballistic missiles

The Russian Navy has a fleet of 11 deployable nuclear-armed SSBNs. The fleet includes 9 Soviet-era SSBNs and 3 (of a planned total of 8) SSBNs of a new class that will gradually replace the old SSBNs over the next decade. A

[10] Gavrilov, Y., 'Sarmat will fly over pole: Russia designing unique missile', *Rossiyskaya Gazeta*, 2 June 2014. Translation from Russian, BBC Monitoring.

[11] TASS, 'Russia excludes rail-mobile ICBM system from armament, focuses on Sarmat missile', 6 Dec. 2017. For further detail on the planned rail-based ICBM see Kristensen H. M., 'Russian nuclear forces', *SIPRI Yearbook 2017*, p. 423.

[12] See e.g. TASS, 'Some 20 Topol-M, Yars mobile ICBM systems take part in massive Central Russian drills', 28 Mar. 2017; TASS, 'Eleven strategic missile regiments to hold large-scale drills across Russia', 4 Sep. 2017; and TASS, 'Topol ballistic missile test launched from range in Russia's south', 26 Sep. 2017.

[13] For further detail on the Zapad-17 exercise see Johnson, D., 'Zapad 2017 and Euro-Atlantic security', NATO Review, 14 Dec. 2017.

former SSBN has been converted to a test-launch platform for submarine-launched ballistic missiles (SLBMs) but it is not nuclear armed.

The current backbone of the Russian SSBN fleet is made up of six Project 667BDRM Delfin (designated Delta IV class by the North Atlantic Treaty Organization, NATO) submarines assigned to the Northern Fleet. Two Project 667BDR Kalmar (Delta III) SSBNs are believed to be operational with the Pacific Fleet, although reports in early 2018 suggested that it is possible that only one of these is still operational.[14] A third Project 667BDR Kalmar SSBN is held in reserve. All three will be decommissioned in the near future.

Three of the new Borei class SSBNs (Project 955/A) are operational: two with the Pacific Fleet and one with the Northern Fleet. Five more of an improved design, known as Borei-A (Project 955A), are under construction and scheduled to enter service between 2018 and 2022. Each Borei class SSBN carries 16 RSM-56 Bulava (SS-N-32) SLBMs. It is possible that Russia will buy four more Borei class SSBNs to maintain an SSBN fleet comparable in size to that of the United States.[15]

Non-strategic nuclear weapons

According to SIPRI data, as of January 2018, Russia had approximately 1830 warheads assigned for potential use by non-strategic forces. Many more Soviet-era non-strategic warheads have been retired and are awaiting dismantlement (see table 6.3).

Russia's large arsenal of non-strategic nuclear weapons chiefly serves to compensate for perceived weaknesses in its conventional forces. There has been considerable debate about the role that non-strategic nuclear weapons have in Russian nuclear strategy, including potential first use.[16] Development of new dual-capable weapons demonstrates that Russia continues to see non-strategic nuclear weapons as important in its military strategy. As targeting accuracy has improved, some weapons have been equipped with warheads with lower yields than they had during the cold war. Others are likely to be replaced with advanced conventional weapons over the next decade.

The most significant naval development is the fielding of a nuclear version of the new long-range, land-attack Kalibr sea-launched cruise missile

---

[14] The scheduled defuelling was first published by Rosatom and reported on Twitter by @7FBTK. The Rosatom notification is no longer available, but a description is available at the Russianforces. org website. Podvig, P., 'Two Project 667BDR submarines withdrawn from service', Russianforces. org, 14 Mar. 2018.

[15] Bogdanov, K., ['Great Fleet' on the horizon], Lenta, 23 Jan. 2015 (in Russian).

[16] See e.g. Scaparrotti, C. M., 'NATO's military commander concerned about Russia's tactical nuclear weapons in Europe', Atlantic Council, NATO Source, 3 May 2017; and Ven Bruusgaard, K., 'The myths of Russia's lowered nuclear threshold', War on the Rocks, 22 Sep. 2017.

(SLCM), known as the 3M-14 (SS-N-30A).[17] While the conventional version is being fielded on a wide range of ships and submarines, the nuclear version will probably be integrated on front-line nuclear-powered attack submarines to replace the S-10 Granat (SS-N-21 Sampson) SLCM. However, it is possible that the nuclear 3M-14 might also be integrated on some surface ships. It is estimated that there are about 810 warheads for non-strategic naval nuclear weapons, which include land-attack cruise missiles, anti-ship cruise missiles, anti-submarine rockets, depth charges, torpedoes, and naval aviation.

The 3M-55 Yakhont (SS-N-26) SLCM has been included in the estimate of Russia's non-strategic forces for January 2018 because NASIC designates it as 'nuclear possible' and notes that it is used to arm submarines, ships and coastal defence units (see table 6.3).[18] The 3M-55 is replacing the SS-N-9 (P-120), SS-N-12 (P-500) and SS-N-19 (P-700) anti-ship cruise missiles, which are dual-capable.[19]

The Russian Air Force has an estimated 498 weapons for use by Tu-22M3 (Backfire-C) intermediate-range bombers, Su-24M (Fencer-D) fighter-bombers and the new Su-34 (Fullback) fighter-bomber. A new air-to-surface missile (Kh-32) is in development to replace the Kh-22N (AS-4) used on the Tu-22M3. The Air Force also appears close to deploying a hypersonic air-launched ballistic missile, known as the Kh-47M2 Kinzhal.[20]

It is estimated that a total of around 373 nuclear warheads are in use by dual-capable air defence forces, the Moscow A-135 missile defence system and coastal defence units (although only a small number of warheads are assigned to the coastal defence units). All these defensive systems are being modernized.[21]

It is estimated that there are approximately 148 warheads assigned to Russian short-range ballistic missiles (SRBMs) and ground-launched cruise missiles (GLCMs). Ground-based non-strategic nuclear forces include the dual-capable Iskander-M (SS-26) SRBM, which is replacing the Tochka (SS-21) SRBM in 10 or more missile brigades. Deployment started in 2004

---

[17] There is considerable confusion about the designation of what is commonly referred to as the Kalibr missile. The Kalibr designation is actually not a missile but a family of weapons that, in addition to the 3M-14 (SSN30/A) land-attack versions, includes the 3M-54 (SS-N-27) anti-ship cruise missile and the 91R anti-submarine missile. For further detail see US Navy, Office of Naval Intelligence (ONI), *The Russian Navy: A Historic Transition* (ONI: Washington, DC, Dec. 2015), pp. 34–35; and US Air Force, National Air and Space Intelligence Center (note 6), p. 37.

[18] US Air Force, National Air and Space Intelligence Center (note 6), p 37.

[19] US Navy, Office of Naval Intelligence (note 17), p. 34.

[20] TASS, 'Russian Aerospace Forces test launch Kinzhal hypersonic missile', 11 Mar. 2018.

[21] TASS, 'Russia's missile early warning system helps ward off any threat', 29 June 2017; and Novichkov, N., 'Russian Defence Minister summarises modernisation progress in 2017', *Jane's Defence Weekly*, 4 Jan. 2018.

and, by the end of 2017, the army had received 10 Iskander-M brigades.[22] Facilities in the Kaliningrad oblast were nearing completion at the end of 2017 and were expected to receive the Iskander-M in early 2018.[23] Construction of a missile storage facility, similar to those constructed at other Iskander bases, has yet to be identified in Kaliningrad.

Army non-strategic nuclear weapons also include a new dual-capable GLCM, known as the 9M729 (SSC-8), which is a modified version of the 9M728 (SSC-7) used on the Iskander-M system.[24] According to the USA, the new cruise missile violates the 1987 Soviet–US Treaty on the Elimination of Intermediate-Range and Shorter-Range Missiles (INF Treaty).[25] Russia has rejected the accusation. Unconfirmed reports suggest that the 9M729 has been deployed in at least one garrison and it appears that further deployments are planned.[26]

---

[22] Interfax, 'Ten brigade sets of Iskander-M missile systems delivered to Russia's ground forces: commander', 22 Dec. 2017.

[23] Blank, S., 'Baltic build-up', *Jane's Intelligence Review*, vol. 29, no. 5 (May 2017), pp. 6–13.

[24] US Department of State, Bureau of Arms Control, Verification and Compliance, 'INF Treaty: at a glance', Fact Sheet, 8 Dec. 2017, p. 1.

[25] For a summary and other details of the INF Treaty see annex A, section III, in this volume. On the INF Treaty controversy see chapter 7, section II, in this volume; and Kile, S., 'Russian–US nuclear arms control and disarmament', *SIPRI Yearbook 2017*, pp. 477–78.

[26] Gordon, M., 'Russia deploys missile, violating treaty, and challenging Trump', *New York Times*, 14 Feb. 2017.

III. British nuclear forces

SHANNON N. KILE AND HANS M. KRISTENSEN

As of January 2018, the British nuclear stockpile consisted of approximately 215 warheads (see table 6.4). In its 2015 Strategic Defence and Security Review (SDSR), the British Government reaffirmed its plans to cut the size of the nuclear arsenal. The number of operationally available nuclear warheads has been reduced to no more than 120. The overall size of the nuclear stockpile, including non-deployed warheads, will decrease to no more than 180 by the mid-2020s.[1]

The British nuclear deterrent consists exclusively of a sea-based component: four Vanguard class Trident nuclear-powered ballistic missile submarines (SSBNs).[2] In a posture known as continuous at-sea deterrent, one British SSBN is on patrol at all times.[3] While the second and third SSBNs can be put to sea rapidly, the fourth would take longer because of the cycle of extensive overhaul and maintenance. In September 2017, the British Ministry of Defence (MOD) marked the 350th nuclear deterrence patrol conducted by Royal Navy submarines since 1969.[4]

The Vanguard class SSBNs can each be armed with up to 16 UGM-133 Trident II (D5) submarine-launched ballistic missiles (SLBMs). The United Kingdom does not own the missiles but leases them from a pool of 58 Trident SLBMs shared with the United States Navy. Under limits set out in the 2010 SDSR, when on patrol, the submarines are armed with no more than 8 operational missiles with a total of 40 nuclear warheads.[5] The missiles are kept on a reduced operational alert status and would require several days' notice to be able to fire.[6]

In January 2017 the Trident programme became the centre of controversy when a newspaper revealed that the British Government had not publicly disclosed the failed test launch of a Trident SLBM the previous summer, shortly before a vote in the British House of Commons on the Trident submarine successor programme.[7] US officials confirmed that a missile test fired in June 2016 at a US test range off the Florida coast had deviated from its

---

[1] British Government, *National Security Strategy and Strategic Defence and Security Review 2015: A Secure and Prosperous United Kingdom*, Cm 9161 (Stationery Office: London, Nov. 2015), para. 4.66.

[2] *HMS Vanguard* entered service in Dec. 1994, while the last in class, *HMS Vengeance*, entered service in Feb. 2001. Mills, C. and Dempsey, N., 'Replacing the UK's nuclear deterrent: progress of the Dreadnought class', Briefing Paper 8010, House of Commons Library, 19 June 2017, p. 7.

[3] British Government (note 1), para. 4.65.

[4] British Royal Navy, 'UK marks 350th UK deterrent patrol', Press release, 29 Sep. 2017.

[5] British Ministry of Defence, *Securing Britain in an Age of Uncertainty: The Strategic Defence and Security Review*, Cm 7948 (Stationery Office: London, Oct. 2010), pp. 5, 38.

[6] British Ministry of Defence, 'UK nuclear deterrent', Fact sheet, updated 24 Mar. 2016, p. 1.

[7] *Sunday Times*, 'Nuclear cover-up', 22 Jan. 2017.

programmed course and crashed into the sea.[8] The MOD declined to comment on the cause of the failure, which marked its first unsuccessful Trident missile flight test.[9] The UK had previously conducted successful flight tests in 2000, 2005, 2009 and 2012.

The Trident submarine successor programme

In 2016 the House of Commons approved by a large majority a motion supporting the government's commitment to a 'like-for-like' replacement of the current Vanguard class SSBNs with four new SSBNs.[10] While recognizing that the UK's nuclear deterrent would 'remain essential to the UK's security today as it has for over 60 years', the motion did not give final approval for the new submarine programme. In order to control costs, the government had previously announced that approval of the investment would be made in stages rather than as a single 'main gate' decision.[11]

The new class of SSBN, which has been named Dreadnought, will carry the new life-extended Trident II D5LE SLBMs but will have a missile compartment that holds 12 missile launch tubes, a reduction from the 16 carried by the Vanguard class. As a cost-saving measure, a common missile compartment is being designed in cooperation with the US Navy that will also equip the latter's new Columbia class SSBNs.[12] The replacement of the Trident II (D5) missile is not part of the Dreadnought development and acquisition programme. However, the UK is participating in the US Navy's current programme to extend the service life of the Trident II (D5) missile to the early 2060s.[13]

The Dreadnought submarines were originally expected to begin to enter into service by 2028 but are now expected to enter into service in the early 2030s. The delay was part of the extended development and acquisition programme announced in the 2015 SDSR. The service life of the Vanguard class SSBNs was commensurately extended.[14]

---

[8] Star, B. and Masters, J., 'US official confirms Trident missile failure', CNN, 23 Jan. 2017.

[9] Kuenssberg, L., 'Trident: defence secretary refuses to give test missile details', BBC News, 23 Jan. 2017; and MacAskill, E., 'How did the Trident test fail and what did Theresa May know?', *The Guardian*, 23 Jan. 2017.

[10] British Parliament, House of Commons, 'UK's nuclear deterrent', *House of Commons Hansard*, col. 559, vol. 613, 18 July 2016; and Kuenssberg, L., 'MPs vote to renew Trident weapons system', BBC News, 19 July 2016.

[11] British Government (note 1), para. 4.75.

[12] British Ministry of Defence, 'The United Kingdom's future nuclear deterrent: the Dreadnought programme', 2017 Update to Parliament, 20 Dec. 2017; Allison, G., 'A guide to the Dreadnought class nuclear submarine', UK Defence Journal, 3 Jan. 2018; and US Navy, 'United States Navy: fact file: Trident II (D5) missile', 11 May 2017.

[13] Mills, C. and Brooke-Holland, L., 'The costs of the UK strategic nuclear deterrent', Briefing Paper 08166, House of Commons Library, 8 Dec. 2017, p. 9.

[14] Mills and Dempsey (note 2).

Table 6.4. British nuclear forces, January 2018

Type	Designation	No. deployed	Year first deployed	Range (km)[a]	Warheads x yield	No. of warheads
Submarine-launched ballistic missiles[b]						
D5	Trident II	48	1994	>7 400	1–3 x 100 kt[c]	215[d]

kt = kilotons.

[a] Range is for illustrative purposes only; actual mission range will vary according to flight profile and weapon loading.

[b] The operational nuclear-powered ballistic missile submarines (SSBNs) carry a reduced loading of no more than 8 Trident II missiles and 40 nuclear warheads. One submarine is on patrol at any given time.

[c] The British warhead is called the Holbrook, a modified version of the United States' W76-1 warhead, with a lower-yield option.

[d] Of the estimated 215 warheads currently in the stockpile, 120 are operationally available. The process to reduce the stockpile to 180 warheads by the mid-2020s is under way.

Sources: British Ministry of Defence, white papers, press releases and website; British House of Commons, *Hansard*, various issues; 'Nuclear notebook', *Bulletin of the Atomic Scientists*, various issues; and authors' estimates.

The 2015 SDSR also postponed the replacement of the current British-manufactured Holbrook warhead for the Trident II missiles, at least until the late 2030s.[15] A decision on a new warhead is planned for the current parliament, and work continues on developing replacement options.[16] In the meantime, the British Atomic Weapons Establishment (AWE) has begun a programme to improve the performance and extend the life of the current Trident warhead—which is modelled on the US W76-1 warhead and incorporated into the US-produced Mk4A re-entry vehicle—in collaboration with US nuclear weapon laboratories.[17]

The MOD has estimated the cost of the Dreadnought programme to be £31 billion ($47.4 billion), including defence inflation over the life of the programme. It has set aside a further contingency of £10 billion ($15.3 billion) to cover possible increases.[18] In its 2017 update to parliament, the MOD confirmed that the programme remained within budget, and that £4.3 billion

[15] British Government (note 1), paras 4.72, 4.76.

[16] Mills and Dempsey (note 2), p. 3; and British Ministry of Defence (note 12).

[17] Nuclear Information Service, 'AWE: past, present, and possibilities for the future', June 2016, pp. 26–28.

[18] British Government (note 1), para. 4.76.

($5.5 billion) had been spent so far on the design and early manufacture phases.[19] However, there were reports during the year of significant cost overruns related to the submarine's next-generation nuclear reactor propulsion plant.[20] As the year ended, concerns were raised in parliament about the impact of the Trident successor programme on the affordability of the MOD's overall equipment plan.[21]

[19] British Ministry of Defence (note 12).

[20] Hookham, M. and Ripley, T., '"Red alert" over Trident reactor costs', *Sunday Times*, 23 July 2017.

[21] MacAskill, E., 'Trident may be removed from MoD budget, MPs told', *The Guardian*, 18 Dec. 2017; and Haynes, D., 'Defence cuts: take expensive Trident out of MoD budget, Hammond urged', *Sunday Times*, 25 Nov. 2017.

IV. French nuclear forces

SHANNON N. KILE AND HANS M. KRISTENSEN

France's nuclear arsenal contains approximately 300 warheads, a number that has remained stable in recent years. The warheads are earmarked for delivery by 48 submarine-launched ballistic missiles (SLBMs) and 54 air-launched cruise missiles, which provides France with both strategic and tactical nuclear capabilities.[1]

The main component of France's strategic nuclear deterrence force consists of four Triomphant class nuclear-powered ballistic missile submarines (SSBNs), each of which carries 16 submarine-launched ballistic missiles (SLBMs). The submarines began to enter operational service in 1997. The French Navy maintains a continuous at-sea deterrent posture, whereby one SSBN is on patrol at all times. The SSBN force is complemented by nuclear-capable land- and sea-based combat aircraft (see table 6.5).

France continues to modernize its Strategic Oceanic Force (Force Océanique Stratégique, FOST). The French Navy is modifying the Triomphant class submarines to carry the M51 SLBM, which has replaced the M45 missile.[2] As of December 2017, all four submarines had been upgraded to the M51.1 SLBM.[3] Each of the M51 missiles is capable of carrying up to six multiple independently targetable re-entry vehicle (MIRV) TN-75 warheads. The number of warheads on some of the missiles is believed to have been reduced in order to improve targeting flexibility.

The French SSBN fleet will be equipped with a longer-range version of the missile, the M51.2, by 2020. An M51.2 missile was successfully test launched under operational conditions from Le Triomphant in July 2016, after which the missile was certified and commissioned for service.[4] The French Minister of the Armed Forces, Florence Parly, confirmed in December 2017 that the M51.2 was operational.[5] The M51.2 is designed to carry the new, stealthier tête nucléaire océanique (TNO, oceanic nuclear warhead) with a

---

[1] Hollande, F., French President, 'Discours sur la dissuasion nucléaire: Déplacement auprès des forces aériennes stratégiques' [Speech on nuclear deterrence: visit to the strategic air forces], Istres, 19 Feb. 2015.

[2] French Navy, 'Modernisation de la force océanique stratégique: le SNLE Le Triomphant adapté au M51' [Modernization of the strategic naval force: the SSBN Le Triomphant adapted for M51], 13 Aug. 2015.

[3] French Ministry of the Armed Forces, 'Madame Florence Parly, Ministre des armées Visite de l'usine des Mureaux: Ariane Group' [Florence Parly, Minister of the Armed Forces, Visit to the Mureaux factory: Ariane Group], Mureaux, 14 Dec. 2017, p. 6.

[4] Groizeleau, V., 'DCNS débute la refonte du Téméraire' [DCNS begins the recasting of Le Téméraire], Mer et Marine, 8 Dec. 2016; and French Ministry of Defence, 'Le système d'armes SNLE Le Triomphant/M51 validé en conditions opérationnelles' [Le Triomphant/M51 SSBN weapon system validated under operational conditions], Press release, updated 20 Sep. 2016.

[5] French Ministry of the Armed Forces (note 3).

Table 6.5. French nuclear forces, January 2018

Type	No. deployed	Year first deployed	Range (km)[a]	Warheads x yield	No. of warheads
Land-based aircraft					
Mirage 2000N	20	1988	2 750	1 x up to 300 kt TNA	20
Rafale F3[b]	20	2010–11	2 000	1 x up to 300 kt TNA	20
Carrier-based aircraft					
Rafale MF3	10	2010–11	2 000	1 x up to 300 kt TNA	10
Submarine-launched ballistic missiles[c]					
M51.1	32	2010	>6 000	4–6 x 100 kt TN-75	160[d]
M51.2	16	2016	>6 000[e]	4–6 x 150 kt TNO	80
M51.3[f]	0	(2025)	>(6 000)	(up to 6 x 150 kt) TNO	0
Reserves					10[g]
Total					**300[h]**

.. = not available or not applicable; ( ) = uncertain figure; kt = kiloton; TNA = tête nucléaire aéroportée (airborne nuclear warhead); TNO = tête nucléaire océanique (oceanic nuclear warhead).

[a] Aircraft range is for illustrative purposes only; actual mission range will vary according to flight profile and weapon loading.

[b] The Mirage 2000N and Rafale carry the air-sol moyenne portée-améliorée (ASMP-A, improved medium-range air-to-surface) air-launched cruise missile. A mid-life upgrade of the ASMP-A is scheduled to begin in 2022.

[c] France has only produced enough submarine-launched ballistic missiles (SLBMs) to equip 3 operational nuclear-powered ballistic missile submarines (SSBNs); the 4th SSBN is out of service for overhaul and maintenance work at any given time.

[d] Although the M51 SLBM can carry up to 6 warheads, the number of warheads is believed to have been reduced on some of the missiles in order to improve targeting flexibility.

[e] The M51.2 has a 'much greater range' than the M51.1, according to the French Ministry of Defence.

[f] The M51.3 is under development and has not yet been deployed.

[g] The reserve includes 4 ASMP-A missiles.

[h] President François Hollande confirmed a cap of 300 warheads in a speech in Feb. 2015.

Sources: French Ministry of the Armed Forces, 'Madame Florence Parly, Ministre des armées Visite de l'usine des Mureaux: Ariane Group' [Florence Parly, Minister of the Armed Forces, Visit to the Mureaux factory: Ariane Group], Mureaux, 14 Dec. 2017; Hollande, F., French President, 'Discours sur la dissuasion nucléaire–Déplacement auprès des forces aériennes stratégiques' [Speech on nuclear deterrence: visit to the strategic air forces], Istres, 19 Feb. 2015; Sarkozy, N., French President, Speech on defence and national security, Porte de Versailles, 17 June 2008; Sarkozy, N., French President, 'Presentation of SSBM "Le Terrible"', Speech, Cherbourg, 21 Mar. 2008; Chirac, J., French President, Speech during visit to the Strategic Forces, Landivisiau–L'lle Longue, Brest, 19 Jan. 2006; French Ministry of Defence, various publications; French National Assembly, various defence bills; International Institute for Strategic Studies, *The Military Balance 2018* (Routledge: London, 2018); *Air Actualités*, various issues; *Aviation Week & Space Technology*, various issues; 'Nuclear notebook', *Bulletin of the Atomic Scientists*, various issues; and authors' estimates.

reported yield of up to 150 kilotons.[6] France has commenced design work on a new M51.3 SLBM with improved accuracy.[7] It is scheduled to become operational in 2025.[8] France is also beginning preliminary design work on a third-generation SSBN, designated the SNLE 3G, which will be equipped with the M51.3 SLBM. The goal is to have an operational successor to the Triomphant class submarine by 2035.[9]

The airborne component of the French nuclear forces consists of two squadrons of the land-based Mirage 2000N and Rafale F3 combat aircraft. The remaining Mirage 2000Ns will be replaced by Rafale B aircraft by 2018.[10] The French Navy also operates a single squadron of Rafale MF3 aircraft deployed aboard its aircraft carrier the *Charles de Gaulle*.

The Rafale aircraft are equipped with the extended-range air-sol moyenne portée-améliorée (ASMP-A, improved medium-range air-to-surface) cruise missile, which entered service in 2009. There are 54 ASMP-As in France's nuclear arsenal.[11] A mid-life refurbishment programme for the ASMP-A is scheduled to begin in 2022.[12] The missiles are armed with the tête nucléaire aéroportée (TNA, airborne nuclear warhead), which has a reported yield of up to 300 kt. The French Ministry of Defence has initiated research on a successor missile, designated air-sol nucléaire (air-to-surface nuclear) fourth-generation (ASN-4G), with enhanced stealth and manoeuvrability to counter potential technological improvements in air defences.[13]

The French Government's commitment to the long-term modernization of the country's air- and sea-based nuclear deterrent forces will require a substantial increase in military nuclear expenditure.[14] The draft law on military

---

[6] French Senate, 'Avis présenté au nom de la Commission des Affaires Étrangères, de la Défense et des Forces Armées (1) sur le Projet de Loi de Finances pour 2014, adopté par L'Assemblée Nationale: Défense: equipement des forces et excellence technologique des industries de défense' [Opinions submitted on behalf of the committee on foreign affairs, defence and the armed forces (1) on the draft finance law for 2014, adopted by the National Assembly: defence: equipment of the forces and technological excellence of the defence industries], no. 158, 21 Nov. 2013, pp. 51–52.

[7] Loi relative à la programmation militaire pour les années 2014 à 2019 [Law on military planning for the years 2014 to 2019], French Law no. 2013-1168 of 18 Dec. 2013.

[8] French Ministry of the Armed Forces (note 3).

[9] Hollande (note 1); and Le Drian, J. Y., French Minister of Defence, 'Discours de clôture du colloque pour les 50 ans de la dissuasion' [Conference closing speech on the 50th anniversary of deterrence], French Ministry of Defence, Paris, 20 Nov. 2014.

[10] Hollande (note 1).

[11] Hollande (note 1).

[12] French Senate (note 6), p. 52.

[13] Le Drian (note 9); and Tran, P., 'France studies nuclear missile replacement', *Defense News*, 29 Nov. 2014.

[14] Guisnel, J., 'Le casse-tête financier de la modernisation de la dissuasion nucléaire' [The financial puzzle of modernization of nuclear deterrence], *Le Point*, 12 May 2016.

planning for 2019–25 has allocated €37 billion to maintain and modernize France's nuclear forces and infrastructure.[15] This is a significant increase on the €23 billion allocated to nuclear forces and infrastructure in the military planning law for 2014–19.[16]

[15] Agence France-Presse, 'La France va consacrer 295 milliards d'euros à sa défense entre 2019 et 2025' [France will spend €295 billion on defence between 2019 and 2025], *Le Figaro*, 7 Feb. 2018.

[16] Collin, J. M., 'Dissuasion nucléaire: l'obstination française' [Nuclear deterence: French obstinance], Group for Research and Information on Peace and Security (GRIP), Report, 19 Feb. 2015.

V. Chinese nuclear forces

SHANNON N. KILE AND HANS M. KRISTENSEN

China maintains an estimated stockpile of about 280 nuclear warheads. The size of the stockpile has remained fairly stable over the past decade but is now increasing slowly. Around 234 warheads are assigned to China's land- and sea-based ballistic missiles. The remainder are assigned to non-operational forces, such as new systems in development, operational systems that may increase in number in the future and reserves. China may also have some residual nuclear air-strike capability (see table 6.6). China's nuclear warheads are believed to be 'de-mated' from their delivery vehicles—that is, stored separately and not available for immediate use.[1]

China continues to modernize its nuclear arsenal as part of a long-term programme to develop more survivable and robust forces consistent with its nuclear strategy of assured retaliation. The Chinese Government's stated goal is to 'strengthen [China's] capabilities for strategic deterrence and nuclear counterattack' by improving the 'strategic early warning, command and control, rapid reaction, and survivability and protection' capabilities of its nuclear forces.[2] In accordance with its self-declared minimum deterrence posture, China has focused on making qualitative improvements to its nuclear arsenal rather than significantly increasing its size.[3] These have included the development of new capabilities in response to the ballistic missile defences and precision-guided conventional strike systems being deployed by the United States and other countries.[4]

The Chinese Government has reorganized the country's nuclear forces as part of a larger move to restructure and modernize the military under a streamlined command system.[5] At the beginning of 2016 it established a new People's Liberation Army (PLA) Rocket Force (PLARF) as the fourth service in China's military. It has command responsibility for all three legs of China's nuclear triad and maintains custodial and operational control over the country's nuclear warheads.[6] While remaining the 'core force of strategic deterrence', the PLARF has also been put in charge of conventional

---

[1] Stokes, M. A., *China's Nuclear Warhead Storage and Handling System* (Project 2049 Institute: Arlington, VA, 12 Mar. 2010), p. 8; and Bin, L., 'China's potential to contribute to multilateral nuclear disarmament', *Arms Control Today*, vol. 41, no. 2 (Mar. 2011), pp. 17–21.

[2] Chinese State Council, *China's Military Strategy*, Defense White Paper, section 4 (Information Office of the State Council: Beijing, May 2015).

[3] Cunningham, F. and Fravel, M. T., 'Assuring assured retaliation: China's nuclear posture and US–China strategic stability', *International Security*, vol. 40, no. 2 (fall 2015), pp. 12–15.

[4] Saalman, L., 'China's calculus on hypersonic glide', SIPRI Commentary, 15 Aug. 2017.

[5] Chinese Ministry of National Defense, 'China establishes Rocket Force and Strategic Support Force', 1 Jan. 2016.

[6] Cordesman, A. and Kendall, J., *The PLA Rocket Force: Evolving Beyond the Second Artillery Corps (SAC) and Nuclear Dimension* (Center for Strategic and International Studies: Washington,

missile systems and tasked with strengthening China's medium- and long-range precision strike capabilities.[7]

Chinese officials have emphasized that the reorganization of the country's nuclear command structure does not herald changes to its nuclear policies or strategy. China remains committed to its no-first-use policy on nuclear weapons and has pledged to keep its 'nuclear capability at the minimum level required for safeguarding its national security'.[8] Nor has the Chinese Government given any indication that it will change its long-standing policy of maintaining nuclear forces at a low level of alert in peacetime. In recent years there have been internal discussions within the Chinese military about raising the alert level and moving towards a more launch-ready posture in order to ensure responsiveness.[9]

Land-based ballistic missiles

China's nuclear-capable land-based ballistic missile arsenal is undergoing gradual modernization as China replaces ageing silo-based, liquid-fuelled missiles with new mobile solid-fuelled models. China's shift towards more survivable mobile missiles has been motivated by concerns that US advances in intelligence, surveillance and reconnaissance (ISR) capabilities and in precision-guided conventional weapons pose a pre-emptive threat to fixed missile launch sites and supporting infrastructure.[10]

In its most recent annual report on Chinese military developments, the US Department of Defense (DOD) estimated that China deployed 75–100 intercontinental ballistic missiles (ICBMs) in 2017.[11] The silo-based, liquid-fuelled, two-stage Dong Feng (DF)-5A and the road-mobile, solid-fuelled, three-stage DF-31A are currently China's longest-range operational ICBMs and the only missiles in its arsenal capable of targeting all of the continental USA.

China is developing another longer-range ICBM: the road-mobile, solid-fuelled, three-stage DF-41, which has an estimated range in excess of 12 000 kilometres, making it capable of striking targets throughout the

---

DC, 13 Oct. 2016); and Tiezzi, S., 'The new military force in charge of China's nuclear weapons', The Diplomat, 5 Jan. 2016.

[7] Chinese Ministry of National Defense (note 5).

[8] Xinhau, 'China's nuclear policy, strategy consistent: spokesperson', 1 Jan. 2016.

[9] See Heginbotham, E. et al. (eds), *China's Evolving Nuclear Deterrent: Major Drivers and Issues for the United States* (RAND Corporation: Santa Monica, CA, 2017), pp. 131–33; and Kulacki, G., 'China's military calls for putting its nuclear forces on alert', Union of Concerned Scientists, Jan. 2016.

[10] O'Connor, S., 'Sharpened Fengs: China's ICBM modernisation alters threat profile', *Jane's Intelligence Review*, vol. 27, no. 12 (Dec. 2015), pp. 44–49.

[11] US Department of Defense (DOD), *Military and Security Developments Involving the People's Republic of China 2017*, Annual Report to Congress (DOD: Washington, DC, May 2017), p. 31.

Table 6.6. Chinese nuclear forces, January 2018

Type/Chinese designation (US designation)	Launchers deployed	Year first deployed	Range (km)[a]	Warheads x yield	No. of warheads[b]
Land-based ballistic missiles[c]	*131[d]*				*186*
DF-4 (CSS-3)	5	1980	5 500	1 x 3.3 Mt	10
DF-5A (CSS-4 Mod 2)	10	2015	12 000	3 x 200–300 kt	10
DF-5B (CSS-4 Mod 3)	10	..	..	MIRV	30
DF-15 (CCS-6 Mod 1)	..	1994	600	(1 x 10–50 kt)	..[e]
DF-21 (CSS-5 Mods 1/2)	<50	1991	2 100[f]	1 x 200–300 kt	80
DF-21 (CSS-5 Mod 6)	..	2016	2 100[f]	1 x 200–300 kt	..
DF-26 (CSS-..)	16	(2018)	>4 000	1 x 200–300 kt	16
DF-31 (CSS-10 Mod 1)	8	2006	>7 000	(1 x 200–300 kt)	8
DF-31A (CSS-10 Mod 2)	32	2007	>11 200	(1 x 200–300 kt)	32
DF-31AG (CSS-10 Mod ..)	..	(2018)	..	..	..
DF-41 (CSS-X-20)	..	(2018)	(12 000)	MIRV	..
Sea-based ballistic missiles[g]	48				*48[h]*
JL-2 (CSS-NX-14)	48	(2016)	>7 000	(1 x 200–300 kt)	48
Aircraft[i]	*(20)*				*(20)*
H-6 (B-6)	(20)	1965	3 100	1 x bomb/ (ALCM)	(20)
Attack (..)	..	1972–..	..	1 x bomb	..
Cruise missiles[j]	..				..
Total					**280[k]**

.. = not available or not applicable; ( ) = uncertain figure; ALCM = air-launched cruise missile; kt = kiloton; Mt = megaton; MIRV = multiple independently targetable re-entry vehicle.

[a] Aircraft range is for illustrative purposes only; actual mission range will vary according to flight profile and weapon loading.

[b] Figures are based on estimates of 1 warhead per nuclear-capable launcher, except the MIRVed DF-5B, which is estimated to have 3 warheads. The DF-4 and DF-21 have reload missiles with additional warheads. The warheads are not thought to be deployed on launchers under normal circumstances but kept in storage facilities. All estimates are approximate.

[c] China defines missile ranges as short range, <1000 km; medium range, 1000–3000 km; long range, 3000–8000 km; and intercontinental range, >8000 km.

[d] The estimate only counts nuclear launchers. Some launchers might have 1 or more reloads of missiles.

[e] The US Central Intelligence Agency concluded in 1993 that China had 'almost certainly' developed a warhead for the DF-15, although it is unclear whether the capability was ever fielded.

[f] The range of the nuclear DF-21 variants (CSS-5 Mods 1, 2, and 6) is thought to be greater than the 1750 km normally reported.

[g] The JL-1 submarine-launched ballistic missile (SLBM), which dates from the 1980s, is no longer considered to be operational.

[h] The estimate is based on the assumption that warheads have been produced for the JL-2 SLBMs on China's 4 Type 094 (Jin class) nuclear-powered ballistic missile submarines (SSBNs). The operational status of the missile is unclear.

[i] Chinese aircraft do not currently have a nuclear weapon delivery mission but it is assumed here that some residual nuclear capability exists.

[j] The US Air Force National Air and Space Intelligence Center's (NASIC) 2013 assessment on ballistic and cruise missile threats listed the DH-10 ground-launched cruise missile as

'conventional or nuclear' and the US Air Force Global Strike Command's command brief from 2013 listed the CJ-20 as nuclear. These designations were not used in the NASIC 2017 assessment on ballistic and cruise missile threats but it is possible that China is developing nuclear-capable cruise missiles.

[k] As well as the c. 254 warheads thought to be assigned to operational forces (which includes the estimate for residual air-strike capability), a further 26 or so warheads are believed to be in storage or production to arm additional DF-26s and future DF-41 missiles. The total stockpile is believed to comprise c. 280 warheads and is slowly increasing.

Sources: US Air Force, National Air and Space Intelligence Center (NASIC), Ballistic and Cruise Missile Threat, various years; US Air Force Global Strike Command, various documents; US Central Intelligence Agency, various documents; US Defense Intelligence Agency, various documents; US Department of Defense, Military and Security Developments Involving the People's Republic of China, various years; International Institute for Strategic Studies, The Military Balance 2018 (Routledge: London, 2018); Kristensen, H. M., Norris, R. S. and McKinzie, M. G., Chinese Nuclear Forces and US Nuclear War Planning (Federation of American Scientists/Natural Resources Defense Council: Washington, DC, Nov. 2006); 'Nuclear notebook', Bulletin of the Atomic Scientists, various issues; Google Earth; and authors' estimates.

continental USA.[12] It is also believed to be developing rail- and silo-based versions of the missile.[13] According to a Chinese state media report in 2017, the DF-41 could enter service in the first half of 2018.[14] The PLARF carried out a flight test of a DF-41 ICBM, apparently carrying two dummy warheads, near the South China Sea on 6 November 2017. This was the eighth test of the system since 2012.[15]

After many years of research and development, China has modified a small number of ICBMs to deliver nuclear warheads in multiple independently targetable re-entry vehicles (MIRVs). China has prioritized the deployment of MIRVs in order to improve its warhead penetration capabilities in response to advances in US and, to a lesser extent, Indian and Russian missile defences.[16] The missile identified as being MIRV-equipped is a modified version of the liquid-fuelled, silo-based DF-5A ICBM, the DF-5B.[17] In February 2017 the Chinese Ministry of National Defense acknowledged the test launch of a new variant of the missile, the DF-5C, and cited US media reports that it might carry as many as 10 warheads. However, it did not confirm the reports.[18] The deployment of MIRVs on the ageing DF-5 missiles may have

[12] Gady, F. S., 'China tests new missile capable of hitting entire United States', The Diplomat, 19 Aug. 2015.
[13] O'Halloran, J. (ed.), 'DF-41', IHS Jane's Weapons: Strategic, 2015–16 (IHS Jane's: Coulsdon, 2015), pp. 21–22.
[14] Deng, X., 'Missile Dongfeng-41 matures considerably, will serve PLA within months: analysts', Global Times, 19 Nov. 2017.
[15] Gertz, B., 'China confirms DF-41 missile test', Washington Free Beacon, 6 Dec. 2017.
[16] Lewis, J., 'China's belated embrace of MIRVs', eds M. Krepon, T. Wheeler and S. Mason, The Lure and Pitfalls of MIRVs: From the First to the Second Nuclear Age (Stimson Center: Washington, DC, May 2016), pp. 95–99.
[17] US Department of Defense (note 11).
[18] Chinese Ministry of National Defense, 'China says its trial launch of DF-5C missile normal', Press release, 6 Feb. 2017; and Gertz, B., 'China tests missile with 10 warheads', Washington Free Beacon, 31 Jan. 2017.

been an interim arrangement necessitated by delays in the development of the DF-41 mobile ICBM.[19] Chinese analysts have speculated that the DF-41 can carry 6–10 MIRVed warheads, although there is significant uncertainty about the actual capability.[20] In 2017 Chinese state media reports indicated that a new variant of the DF-31A ICBM, the DF-31AG, might be armed with MIRVed warheads.[21] However, MIRVed warheads would require a significantly modified DF-31A missile, which according to the US Air Force National Air and Space Intelligence Center (NASIC) carries only one warhead.[22] The DF-31AG might therefore be an improved launcher for the existing DF-31A.

In 2016 China began deploying the new DF-26 intermediate-range ballistic missile (IRBM), which is capable of precision conventional or nuclear strikes against ground targets, as well as conventional strikes against naval targets. It has an estimated maximum range exceeding 4000 km and can reach targets in the western Pacific Ocean, including the US territory of Guam.[23]

The PLARF currently deploys one nuclear-capable medium-range ballistic missile. The DF-21 is a two-stage, solid-fuelled mobile missile that was first deployed in 1991. A modified version, the DF-21A, was deployed beginning in 1996.[24] Reports indicate that a new version of the DF-21 was deployed in 2016.[25]

Ballistic missile submarines

China continues to pursue its long-standing strategic goal of developing and deploying a sea-based nuclear deterrent. According to the US DOD's 2017 annual report on China's military power, the PLA Navy (PLAN) has commissioned four Type 094 nuclear-powered ballistic missile submarines (SSBNs).[26] A fifth submarine with a modified hull structure, designated by some sources as the Type 094A, may be under construction.[27]

[19] Minnick, W., 'Chinese parade proves Xi in charge', *Defense News*, 6 Sep. 2015.

[20] Deng (note 14); and Gertz (note 15).

[21] Fisher, R., 'DF-31AG ICBM can carry multiple warheads, claims China's state media', *Jane's Defence Weekly*, 16 Aug. 2017, p. 9.

[22] US Air Force, National Air and Space Intelligence Center (NASIC), *Ballistic and Cruise Missile Threat* (NASIC: Wright-Patterson Air Force Base, OH, July 2017), p. 29.

[23] US Department of Defense (note 11), pp. 31, 49; and Wilson, J., 'China's expanding ability to conduct conventional missile strikes on Guam', US–China Economic and Security Review Commission, Staff Research Report, 10 May 2016, p. 8.

[24] O'Halloran, J. (ed.), 'DF-21', *IHS Jane's Weapons: Strategic, 2015–16* (IHS Jane's: Coulsdon, 2015), pp. 15–17. Two subsequent versions of the missile were designed for conventional anti-ship and anti-access/area-denial (A2/AD) missions.

[25] US Department of Defense (DOD), *Military and Security Developments Involving the People's Republic of China 2016*, Annual Report to Congress (DOD: Washington, DC, May 2016), p. 58.

[26] US Department of Defense (note 11), p. 24. The Type 094 SSBN is designated the Jin class by the United States and the North Atlantic Treaty Organization.

[27] Fisher, R., 'Images show possible new variant of China's Type 094 SSBN', *Jane's Defence Weekly*, 15 July 2016.

The Type 094 submarine can carry up to 12 three-stage, solid-fuelled JL-2 submarine-launched ballistic missiles (SLBMs). The JL-2 is a sea-based variant of the DF-31 ICBM. It has an estimated maximum range in excess of 7000 km and is believed to carry a single nuclear warhead. The PLAN is thought to have deployed the JL-2 SLBM. According to the US DOD's 2017 annual report, the four operational Type 094 SSBNs are equipped to carry up to 12 JL-2s.[28]

There has been considerable speculation about when a Type 094 SSBN carrying nuclear-armed JL-2 SLBMs will begin deterrence patrols. Although there were media reports in 2016 that China would soon commence patrols, there was no evidence in 2017 that they had begun.[29] In May 2017 the Director of the US Defense Intelligence Agency, Lieutenant General Vincent R. Stewart, stated that, when armed with a JL-2 SLBM, the PLAN's Type 094 SSBN 'will provide Beijing with its first sea-based nuclear deterrent'.[30] The annual US DOD reports on China's military power have been predicting since 2014 that commencement of submarine deterrence patrols was imminent, but the 2017 report does not refer to the issue. The routine deployment by China of nuclear weapons on its SSBNs would constitute a significant change to the country's long-held practice of keeping nuclear warheads in central storage in peacetime.

The PLAN is developing its next-generation SSBN, the Type 096. In 2017 the US DOD assessed that construction is likely to begin in the early 2020s.[31] Reports vary widely on the design parameters, but the new submarine is expected to be larger, quieter and equipped with more missile launch tubes than the Type 094. The Type 096 will reportedly be armed with a longer-range successor to the JL-2, the JL-3 SLBM.[32]

Aircraft and cruise missiles

According to the US DOD's 2017 annual report on China's military power, the PLA Air Force (PLAAF) 'does not currently have a nuclear mission'.[33] However, it is likely that some residual nuclear capability exists. In 2016 the

---

[28] US Department of Defense (note 11), p. 60.

[29] Borger, J., 'China to send nuclear-armed submarines into Pacific amid tensions with US', *The Guardian*, 26 May 2016.

[30] Stewart, V. R., Director, US Defense Intelligence Agency, Statement for the Record, 'Worldwide Threat Assessment', Armed Services Committee, US Senate, 23 May 2017, p. 10.

[31] US Department of Defense (note 11), p. 24.

[32] Dempsey, J. and Boyd, H., 'Beyond JL-2: China's development of a successor SLBM continues', Military Balance blog, International Institute for Strategic Studies, 7 Aug. 2017.

[33] US Department of Defense (note 11), p. 61. Medium-range combat aircraft were China's earliest means of delivering nuclear weapons and were used to conduct more than 12 atmospheric nuclear tests in the 1960s and 1970s. Norris, R., Burrows, A. S. and Fieldhouse, R. W., *Nuclear Weapons Databook, vol. 5: British, French, and Chinese Nuclear Weapons*, National Resources Defense Council (Westview Press: Boulder, CO, 1994), pp. 367–68.

PLAAF confirmed reports in the Chinese state media that it was building a long-range strategic bomber.[34] According to Chinese military sources, the aircraft, known as the H-20, will have stealth characteristics comparable to those of the US B-2 bomber.[35] The PLAAF was reportedly assigned a 'strategic deterrence' mission in 2012.[36] However, it has not confirmed whether the new aircraft will have a nuclear role.

The PLA currently deploys or is believed to be developing several types of ground-, sea- and air-launched cruise missiles. In its 2017 assessment of ballistic missile and cruise missile threats, NASIC did not list any Chinese cruise missile as being nuclear-capable.[37] In its previous assessment, published in 2013, NASIC had listed the ground-launched Donghai-10 (DH-10, also designated Changjian-10, CJ-10) as a 'conventional or nuclear' (dual-capable) system. In his statement in May 2017, Stewart noted that China was developing two new air-launched ballistic missiles, 'one of which may include a nuclear payload', but he did not identify the systems.[38]

---

[34] Zhao, L., 'PLA Air Force commander confirms new strategic bomber', *China Daily*, 2 Sep. 2016; and Zhao, L., 'Long-range bomber may be in China's plans', *China Daily*, 7 July 2015.

[35] Tate, A., 'Details emerge about requirement for China's new strategic bomber', *Jane's Defence Weekly*, 4 Jan. 2017, p. 4.

[36] US Department of Defense (note 25), p. 38.

[37] US Air Force, National Air and Space Intelligence Center (note 22).

[38] Stewart (note 30).

VI. Indian nuclear forces

SHANNON N. KILE AND HANS M. KRISTENSEN

India is estimated to have a growing arsenal of 130–40 nuclear weapons (see table 6.7). This figure is based on calculations of India's inventory of weapon-grade plutonium and the number of operational nuclear-capable delivery systems. India is widely believed to be gradually expanding the size of its nuclear weapon stockpile as well as its infrastructure for producing nuclear warheads.

Military fissile material production

India's nuclear weapons are believed to be plutonium-based. The plutonium was produced at the Bhabha Atomic Research Centre (BARC) in Trombay, Mumbai, by the 40-megawatt-thermal (MW(t)) heavy water CIRUS reactor, which was shut down at the end of 2010, and the 100-MW(t) Dhruva heavy water reactor. India operates a plutonium reprocessing plant for military purposes at the BARC.[1]

India plans to build six fast breeder reactors by the 2030s, which will significantly increase its capacity to produce plutonium that could be used for building weapons.[2] An unsafeguarded 500-megawatt-electric (MW(e)) prototype fast breeder reactor (PFBR) is being built at the Indira Gandhi Centre for Atomic Research (IGCAR) complex at Kalpakkam, Tamil Nadu. The PFBR is expected to be commissioned in mid-2018 following a series of technical delays.[3] The IGCAR has announced that a fast reactor fuel cycle facility will be built at Kalpakkam to reprocess spent fuel from the PFBR and future fast breeder reactors. The plant is scheduled to be commissioned by 2022.[4]

India is currently expanding its uranium enrichment capabilities. It continues to enrich uranium at the small gas centrifuge facility at the Rattehalli Rare Materials Plant (RMP) near Mysore, Karnataka, to produce highly enriched uranium (HEU) for use as naval reactor fuel. India has begun construction of a new industrial-scale centrifuge enrichment plant, the Special Material Enrichment Facility (SMEF), at a site in Karnataka. This will be a dual-use facility that produces HEU for both military and civilian purposes.[5]

[1] International Panel on Fissile Material (IPFM), 'Facilities: reprocessing plants', 12 Feb. 2018.

[2] Ramana, M. V., 'A fast reactor at any cost: the perverse pursuit of breeder reactors in India', *Bulletin of the Atomic Scientists*, 3 Nov. 2016.

[3] *Deccan Herald*, 'Plan to make 6 N-reactors operational by 2039', 5 Nov. 2017.

[4] *The Hindu*, 'HCC to construct fuel processing facility at Kalpakkam', 7 Aug. 2017; and World Nuclear News, 'India awards contract for fast reactor fuel cycle facility', 8 Aug. 2017.

[5] Albright, D. and Kelleher-Vergantini, S., *India's Stocks of Civil and Military Plutonium and Highly Enriched Uranium, End 2014* (Institute for Science and International Security: Washington, DC,

Table 6.7. Indian nuclear forces, January 2018

Type (US/Indian designation)	Launchers deployed	Year first deployed	Range (km)[a]	Warheads x yield[b]	No. of warheads[c]
Aircraft[d]	48				48
Mirage 2000H	32	1985	1 850	1 x bomb	32
Jaguar IS	16	1981	1 600	1 x bomb	16
Land-based ballistic missiles	60				60
Prithvi-II	24	2003	250	1 x 12 kt	24
Agni-I	20	2007	>700	1 x 10–40 kt	20
Agni-II	8	2011	>2 000	1 x 10–40 kt	8
Agni-III	8	2014	>3 200	1 x 10–40 kt	8
Agni-IV	0	(2018)	>3 500	1 x 10–40 kt	0
Agni-V	0	(2020)	>5 200	1 x 10–40 kt	0
Sea-based ballistic missiles	14				16
Dhanush	2	(2013)	400	1 x 12 kt	4[e]
K-15 (B05)[f]	(12)[g]	(2018)	700	1 x 12 kt	(12)
K-4	(4)[g]	..	3 500	1 x 10–40 kt	0
Cruise missiles	..	..	..	..	..
Nirbhay ALCM[h]	..	..	(>700)	..	..
Total					**130–140[i]**

.. = not available or not applicable; ( ) = uncertain figure; ALCM = air-launched cruise missile; kt = kiloton.

[a] Aircraft range is for illustrative purposes only; actual mission range will vary according to flight profile and weapon loading. Missile payloads may have to be reduced in order to achieve maximum range.

[b] The yields of India's nuclear warheads are not known. The 1998 nuclear tests demonstrated yields of up to 12 kt. Since then it is possible that boosted warheads have been introduced with a higher yield, perhaps up to 40 kt. There is no open-source evidence that India has developed 2-stage thermonuclear warheads.

[c] Aircraft and several missile types are dual-capable. Cruise missile launchers carry more than 1 missile. This estimate counts an average of 1 warhead per launcher. Warheads are not deployed on launchers but kept in separate storage facilities. All estimates are approximate.

[d] Other fighter-bombers that could potentially have a secondary nuclear role include the Su-30MKI.

[e] Each Dhanush-equipped ship is thought to have possibly 1 reload.

[f] Some sources have referred to the K-15 submarine-launched ballistic missile (SLBM) as Sagarika, which was the name of the missile development project.

[g] The K-15 and K-4 use the same 4 launch tubes on the *INS Arihant* nuclear-powered ballistic missile submarine (SSBN). Each launch tube can hold either 3 K-15s contained in a triple-missile canister or 1 of the larger K-4 SLBMs (once the K-4 becomes operational). Thus, according to the US Air Force National Air and Space Intelligence Center (NASIC), the K-15 has 12 possible launchers and the K-4 has 4.

[h] There are reports that the Nirbhay, which is in development, might have a nuclear capability, but the Indian Government has not confirmed them.

[i] In addition to the 124 warheads estimated to be assigned to fielded launchers, warheads for additional Agni-III and future Agni-IV medium-range ballistic missiles may already have been produced giving a total stockpile of 130–40 warheads.

Sources: Indian Ministry of Defence, annual reports and press releases; International Institute for Strategic Studies, *The Military Balance 2018* (Routledge: London, 2018); US Air Force, National Air and Space Intelligence Center (NASIC), *Ballistic and Cruise Missile Threat*, various years; Indian news media reports; 'Nuclear notebook', *Bulletin of the Atomic Scientists*, various issues; and authors' estimates.

India's expanding centrifuge enrichment capacity is motivated by plans to build new naval propulsion reactors. However, the HEU produced at the plants could also hypothetically be used to manufacture thermonuclear or boosted-fission nuclear weapons.[6]

Aircraft

Aircraft constitute the most mature component of India's nuclear strike capabilities. The Indian Air Force has reportedly certified the Mirage 2000H multi-role combat aircraft for delivery of nuclear gravity bombs.[7] It is widely speculated that the Air Force's Jaguar IS fighter-bomber may also have a nuclear delivery role.[8]

Land-based missiles

Under its Integrated Guided Missile Development Programme, which began in 1983, India's Defence Research and Development Organization (DRDO) has developed two families of nuclear-capable, land-based ballistic missiles: the Prithvi family (although only the Prithvi-II is thought to be nuclear-capable), consisting of three types of road-mobile, short-range missiles; and the Agni family of longer-range, solid-fuelled ballistic missiles. The latter are designed to provide a quick-reaction nuclear capability and have taken over much of the Prithvi's nuclear delivery role.

The Agni-I is a single-stage, road-mobile missile that has a range of 700 kilometres. The nuclear-capable missile was first deployed in 2007. The Agni-II is a two-stage, solid-fuelled rail-mobile ballistic missile that can deliver a 1000-kilogram payload to a range exceeding 2000 km. The missile is in service with the Indian Army under the Strategic Forces Command (SFC), which is the body responsible for exercising operational command and control over the country's nuclear weapons. The Agni-II appears to have been plagued by technical problems; according to estimates in 2017,

2 Nov. 2015).

[6] Levy, A., 'India is building a top-secret nuclear city to produce thermonuclear weapons, experts say', *Foreign Policy*, 16 Dec. 2015.

[7] Kampani, G., 'New Delhi's long nuclear journey: how secrecy and institutional roadblocks delayed India's weaponization', *International Security*, vol. 38, no. 4 (spring 2014), pp. 94, 97–98.

[8] Cohen, S. and Dasgupta, S., *Arming Without Aiming: India's Military Modernization* (Brookings Institution Press: Washington, DC, 2010), pp. 77–78; and India Defence Update, 'SEPECAT Jaguar is India's only tactical nuclear carrying and ground attack aircraft', 13 Dec. 2016.

fewer than 10 launchers have been deployed.[9] On 4 May 2017 a user trial of an Agni-II failed when the test had to be aborted shortly after the launch of the missile. Indian defence officials did not comment on the cause of the failure.[10]

The Agni-III is a two-stage, rail-mobile missile with a range exceeding 3200 km. It was inducted into service in 2011 but, according to estimates in 2017, fewer than 10 launchers have been deployed.[11] On 27 April 2017 the SFC successfully test launched an Agni-III as part of a user training exercise. The missile was randomly chosen from the production lot.[12]

India is developing two longer-range ballistic missiles, the Agni-IV and the Agni-V, which would give it the capability to strike targets throughout China for the first time. The two-stage, road-mobile Agni-IV missile, which has a range of over 3500 km, is in development and undergoing user trials. An Agni-IV was successfully test launched by the SFC on 2 January 2017— the sixth consecutive successful test of the missile.[13]

The DRDO has prioritized the development of the three-stage, road-mobile Agni-V missile with a range in excess of 5000 km. Unlike the other Agni missiles, the Agni-V is designed to be stored in and launched from a new mobile canister system, an arrangement that, among other things, increases operational readiness by reducing the time required to place the missiles on alert in a crisis.[14] On 18 January 2018 an Agni-V missile was test launched from a sealed canister mounted on a truck located at the Integrated Test Range complex on Abdul Kalam Island (formerly Wheeler Island). The missile flew on a programmed trajectory for 4900 km. This was the third consecutive launch from a canister on a road-mobile launcher and the fifth successful flight test of the Agni-V since 2012.[15] The missile will undergo several additional test flights before it is inducted into service.

India is pursuing a technology development programme for multiple independently targetable re-entry vehicles (MIRVs). However, there are conflicting statements from DRDO officials as to whether India will deploy MIRVs on the Agni-V or a future Agni-VI with an even longer range.[16] The

[9] US Air Force, National Air and Space Intelligence Center (NASIC), *Ballistic and Cruise Missile Threat* (NASIC: Wright-Patterson Air Force Base, OH, July 2017), p. 25.

[10] Pandit, R., 'Trial of Agni-II ballistic missile fails: sources', *Times of India*, 4 May 2017.

[11] US Air Force, National Air and Space Intelligence Center (note 9).

[12] *New Indian Express*, 'India successfully test fires nuclear capable Agni-III missile off Odisha coast', 27 Apr. 2017.

[13] Subramanian, T. S., 'Agni-IV test a "grand success"', *The Hindu*, 2 Jan. 2017.

[14] Aroor, S., 'New chief of India's military research complex reveals brave new mandate', *India Today*, 13 July 2013.

[15] Gurung, S. K., 'India successfully test-fires nuclear-capable Agni-5 ballistic missile', *Economic Times*, 18 Jan. 2018.

[16] Basrur, R. and Sankaran, J., 'India's slow and unstoppable move to MIRV', eds M. Krepon, T. Wheeler and S. Mason, *The Lure and Pitfalls of MIRVs: From the First to the Second Nuclear Age* (Stimson Center: Washington, DC, May 2016), pp. 149–76.

Agni-VI is in the design phase and awaiting approval but may begin testing as early as 2018.

Sea-based missiles

India continues to develop the naval component of its triad of nuclear forces in pursuit of an assured second-strike capability. It is building a fleet of up to five nuclear-powered ballistic missile submarines (SSBNs) as part of its four-decade-old Advanced Technology Vessel project.

India's first indigenously built SSBN, the *INS Arihant*, was launched in 2009 and formally commissioned in 2016.[17] According to Indian media reports in January 2018, the *Arihant* had been out of service for 10 months for repairs after its propulsion compartment suffered significant flood damage when a hatch was left open by mistake while leaving harbour.[18] A second SSBN, the *INS Arighat* (originally thought to have been named *Aridhaman*), was launched in November 2017.[19] Construction work has reportedly begun on a third and fourth submarine, with expected launch dates in 2020 and 2022, respectively.[20]

The *Arihant* is equipped with a four-tube vertical launch system and will carry up to 12 two-stage, 700-km range K-15 (also known as B05) submarine-launched ballistic missiles (SLBMs). Unconfirmed reports have claimed that the *Arighat* is equipped with eight launch tubes to carry up to 24 K-15 missiles (three per launch tube), but the United States Air Force National Air and Space Intelligence Center made no mention of additional launch tubes on a second submarine in its 2017 assessment of ballistic missile and cruise missile threats.[21] In November 2015 the SFC and the DRDO conducted an underwater ejection test of a dummy missile, reportedly from the *Arihant*, but the maiden flight test of a K-15 from the submarine had not been conducted as of the end of 2017.[22]

The DRDO is developing a two-stage, 3500-km range SLBM, known as the K-4, that will eventually replace the K-15.[23] The *Arihant* will be capable of carrying four K-4s but the *Arighat* and subsequent SSBNs will be able

[17] Dinakar, P., 'Now, India has a nuclear triad', *The Hindu*, 18 Oct. 2016.

[18] Peri, D. and Joseph, J., '*INS Arihant* left crippled after "accident" 10 months ago', *The Hindu*, 8 Jan. 2018.

[19] Gady, F. S., 'The Indian Navy's second nuclear-powered ballistic missile submarine was quietly launched in November', The Diplomat, 13 Dec. 2017.

[20] Unnithan, S., 'A peek into India's top secret and costliest defence project, nuclear submarines', *India Today*, 10 Dec. 2017.

[21] Indian Defence Update, 'India's 2nd nuclear submarine "*INS Aridhaman*" to be deadlier than *INS Arihant*', 27 Dec. 2016; and US Air Force, National Air and Space Intelligence Center (note 9).

[22] Indian Defence News, 'Confirmed: first ejection test of K-15 (B-05) SLBM from *INS Arihant* SSBN', 28 Nov. 2015.

[23] Jha, S., 'India's undersea deterrent', The Diplomat, 30 Mar. 2016; and US Air Force, National Air and Space Intelligence Center (note 9), p. 33.

to carry eight. On 17 December 2017 the test launch of a K-4 missile from an underwater pontoon in the Bay of Bengal failed. Indian officials did not release information on the cause of the failure.[24] The missile had previously been tested four times, including a test launch from the *Arihant* in 2016.[25] The DRDO is currently developing a K-5 SLBM, which is expected to have a range in excess of 5000 km, and has announced plans to develop a longer-range K-6 SLBM.[26]

The nuclear-capable Dhanush missile is a naval version of the Prithvi-II that is launched from a surface ship. It can reportedly carry a 500-kg warhead to a maximum range of 400 km and is designed to be able to hit both sea- and shore-based targets.[27] The Dhanush has been inducted into service with the Indian Navy on two Sukanya class coastal patrol ships based at the naval base near Karwar on the west coast of India.

Cruise missiles

The DRDO has been developing a long-range subsonic cruise missile since 2004. Known as the Nirbhay, it has a range exceeding 700 km and is believed to have ground-, sea- and air-launched versions. Development of the missile has been delayed by technical problems with its flight control software and navigation system. Following a second consecutive failed test flight in December 2016, sources within the DRDO indicated that the Nirbhay programme was likely to be terminated.[28] However, on 7 November 2017 the Indian Ministry of Defence announced that the DRDO had conducted a successful test flight of a Nirbhay cruise missile at the Integrated Test Range on Abdul Kalam Island that 'had achieved all the mission objectives'.[29] The Indian Government has not confirmed media reports that the Nirbhay has the capability to carry nuclear warheads.[30]

[24] Pubby, M., 'Setback for Indian missile programme: two failures in a week, submarine version stuck', *The Print*, 24 Dec. 2017.

[25] Rout, H. K., 'Maiden test of undersea K-4 missile from Arihant submarine', *New Indian Express*, 9 Apr. 2016.

[26] Unnithan (note 20); and Jha (note 23).

[27] Mallikarjun, Y., 'Dhanush missile successfully test-fired from ship', *The Hindu*, updated 3 Nov. 2016; and US Air Force, National Air and Space Intelligence Center (note 9), p. 33.

[28] Subramanian, T. S., 'Nirbhay missile test "an utter failure"', *The Hindu*, 21 Dec. 2016; and Rout, H. K., 'DRDO's cruise missile project Nirbhay on verge of closure', *New Indian Express*, 23 Dec. 2016.

[29] Indian Ministry of Defence, Press Information Bureau, 'DRDO conducts successful flight trial of "Nirbhay" sub-sonic cruise missile', 7 Nov. 2017.

[30] Pandit, R., 'India successfully tests its first nuclear-capable cruise missile', *Times of India*, 8 Nov. 2017; and Gady, F. S., 'India successfully test fires indigenous nuclear-capable cruise missile', The Diplomat, 8 Nov. 2017.

VII. Pakistani nuclear forces

SHANNON N. KILE AND HANS M. KRISTENSEN

Pakistan continues to prioritize the development and deployment of new nuclear weapons and delivery systems as part of its 'full spectrum deterrence posture' vis-à-vis India. It is estimated that Pakistan possessed 140–50 warheads as of January 2018 (see table 6.8). Pakistan's nuclear weapon arsenal is likely to expand significantly over the next decade, although estimates of the increase in warhead numbers vary considerably.[1]

Pakistan is believed to be gradually increasing its military fissile material holdings, which include both plutonium and highly enriched uranium (HEU) (see section X). Pakistan's plutonium production complex is located at Khushab in the province of Punjab. It consists of four operational heavy water nuclear reactors and a heavy water production plant.[2] Pakistan appears to be increasing its capacity to reprocess spent nuclear fuel—that is, to chemically separate plutonium from irradiated reactor fuel. A small reprocessing plant has been expanded at the New Laboratories facility of the Pakistan Institute of Science and Technology (PINSTECH) near Rawalpindi. A larger reprocessing plant has been constructed at the Chashma Nuclear Power Complex in Punjab and may already be operational.[3]

Uranium enrichment takes place at the gas centrifuge plant in the Khan Research Laboratories (KRL) complex at Kahuta in Punjab and at a smaller plant located at Gadwal, also in Punjab. A new uranium enrichment centrifuge plant may be under construction in the KRL complex at Kahuta.[4] Pakistan's capacity to produce HEU for nuclear weapons is constrained by its limited indigenous supply of natural uranium.[5]

Aircraft

The Pakistan Air Force's (PAF) Mirage III and Mirage V combat aircraft are the most likely aircraft to have been given a nuclear delivery role. The Mirage III has been used for developmental test flights of the nuclear-capable

[1] Dalton, T. and Krepon, M., *A Normal Nuclear Pakistan* (Stimson Center and Carnegie Endowment for International Peace: Washington, DC, Aug. 2015); and Kristensen, H. M. and Norris, R., 'Pakistani nuclear forces, 2016', *Bulletin of the Atomic Scientists*, vol. 72, no. 6 (Oct.–Nov. 2016), pp. 368–76.

[2] Burkhard, S., Lach, A. and Pabian, F., 'Khushab update', Institute for Science and International Security, Report, 7 Sep. 2017.

[3] Albright, D. and Kelleher-Vergantini, S., 'Pakistan's Chashma plutonium separation plant: possibly operational', Institute for Science and International Security, Imagery Brief, 20 Feb. 2015.

[4] Cartwright, C. and Dewey, K., 'Spin strategy: likely uranium facility identified in Pakistan', *Jane's Intelligence Review*, vol. 28, no. 11 (Nov. 2016), pp. 48–52.

[5] International Panel on Fissile Material (IPFM), 'Pakistan may be building a new enrichment facility', IPFM Blog, 16 Sep. 2016.

Table 6.8. Pakistani nuclear forces, January 2018

Type (US/Pakistani designation)	Launchers deployed	Year first deployed	Range (km)^a	Warheads x yield^b	No. of warheads^c
Aircraft	*36*				*36*
F-16A/B^d	24	1998	1 600	1 x bomb	24
Mirage III/V	12	1998	2 100	1 x bomb or Ra'ad ALCM	12
Land-based missiles	*102^e*				*102*
Abdali (Hatf-2)	10	(2015)	200	1 x 12 kt	10
Ghaznavi (Hatf-3)	16	2004	290	1 x 12 kt	16
Shaheen-I (Hatf-4)	16	2003	750	1 x 12 kt	16
Shaheen-IA (Hatf-4)^f	..	(2017)	900	1 x 12 kt	..
Shaheen-II (Hatf-6)	12	2014	1 500	1 x 10–40 kt	12
Shaheen-III (Hatf-6)^g	..	(2018)	2 750	1 x 10–40 kt	..
Ghauri (Hatf-5)	24	2003	1 250	1 x 10–40 kt	24
Nasr (Hatf-9)	24	(2013)	60–70	1 x 12 kt	24
Ababeel (Hatf-..)	0	..	2 200	MIRV or MRV	0^h
Cruise missiles	*12*				*12*
Babur GLCM (Hatf-7)	12	(2014)	350^i	1 x 12 kt	12
Babur-2 GLCM (Hatf-..)	..	..^{j}	700	1 x 12 kt	..
Babur-3 SLCM (Hatf-..)	0	..^{k}	450	1 x 12 kt	0
Ra'ad ALCM (Hatf-8)	..	(2017)	350	1 x 12 kt	..
Ra'ad-2 ALCM (Hatf-..)	..	(2018)	>350	1 x 12 kt	..
Total					**140–150**

.. = not available or not applicable; ( ) = uncertain figure; ALCM = air-launched cruise missile; GLCM = ground-launched cruise missile; kt = kiloton; MIRV = multiple independently targetable re-entry vehicle; MRV = multiple re-entry vehicle; SLCM = sea-launched cruise missile.

^{a} Aircraft range is for illustrative purposes only; actual mission range will vary according to flight profile and weapon loading. Missile payloads may have to be reduced in order to achieve maximum range.

^{b} The yields of Pakistan's nuclear warheads are not known. The 1998 nuclear tests demonstrated a yield of up to 12 kt. Since then it is possible that boosted warheads have been introduced with higher yields. There is no open-source evidence that Pakistan has developed 2-stage thermonuclear warheads.

^{c} Aircraft and several missile types are dual-capable. Cruise missile launchers carry more than 1 missile. This estimate counts an average of 1 warhead per launcher. Warheads are not deployed on launchers but kept in separate storage facilities.

^{d} There are unconfirmed reports that some of the 40 F-16 combat aircraft procured from the USA in the 1980s were modified by Pakistan for a nuclear delivery role.

^{e} Some launchers might have 1 or more reloads of missiles.

^{f} It is unclear whether the Shaheen-IA has the same designation as the Shaheen-I.

^{g} It is unclear whether the Shaheen-III has the same designation as the Shaheen-II.

^{h} According to the Pakistani armed forces, the missile is 'capable of delivering multiple warheads', using MIRV technology.

^{i} The Pakistani Government claims the range is 700 km, double the range reported by the US Air Force, National Air and Space Intelligence Center (NASIC).

^{j} The Babur-2, which was first test launched on 14 Dec. 2016, is an improved version of the original Babur GLCM.

^{k} The first test launch of a Babur-3 SLCM was carried out from an underwater platform on 9 Jan. 2017.

Sources: Pakistani Ministry of Defence; various documents; US Air Force, National Air and Space Intelligence Center (NASIC), *Ballistic and Cruise Missile Threat*, various years; International Institute for Strategic Studies, *The Military Balance 2018* (Routledge: London, 2018); 'Nuclear notebook', *Bulletin of the Atomic Scientists*, various issues; and authors' estimates.

Ra'ad air-launched cruise missile (ALCM), while the Mirage V is believed to have been given a strike role with nuclear gravity bombs.[6]

Pakistan is acquiring the JF-17 Thunder aircraft, a multi-role lightweight fighter jointly developed with China, to replace the ageing Mirage aircraft. There are reports that the PAF intends to integrate the dual-capable Ra'ad ALCM on to the JF-17, although whether this signifies a nuclear delivery role for the aircraft is unclear.[7]

Pakistan procured 40 F-16A/B combat aircraft from the United States in the mid-1980s. There are unconfirmed reports that some of these aircraft were modified by Pakistan for a nuclear delivery role.[8]

Land-based missiles

Pakistan is expanding its nuclear-capable ballistic missile arsenal, which consists of a series of short- and medium-range systems. It currently deploys the Ghaznavi (also designated Hatf-3) and Shaheen-I (Hatf-4) solid-fuelled, road-mobile short-range ballistic missiles (SRBMs). An extended-range version of the Shaheen-I, the Shaheen-IA, is still in development.

Pakistan deploys two types of nuclear-capable medium-range ballistic missile (MRBM): the liquid-fuelled, road-mobile Ghauri (Hatf-5) with a range of 1250 kilometres; and the two-stage, solid-fuelled, road-mobile Shaheen-II (Hatf-6) with a range of 1500 km.[9] A longer-range variant, the Shaheen-III, is currently in development and was first test launched in 2015.[10] The missile has a declared range of 2750 km, making it the longest-range system to be tested by Pakistan to date.

Pakistan's National Defence Complex is developing a new MRBM, the nuclear-capable Ababeel, based on the Shaheen-III's airframe and solid-fuel motors.[11] On 24 January 2017 Pakistan announced that the first test launch

---

[6] Kerr, P. and Nikitin, M. B., *Pakistan's Nuclear Weapons*, Congressional Research Service (CRS) Report for Congress RL3248 (US Congress, CRS: Washington, DC, 1 Aug. 2016), p. 7.

[7] Fisher, R., 'JF-17 Block II advances with new refuelling probe', *Jane's Defence Weekly*, 27 Jan. 2016; and Ansari, U., 'Despite missile integration, nuke role unlikely for Pakistan's JF-17', *Defense News*, 7 Feb. 2013.

[8] For further analysis on the role of the F-16 see Kristensen and Norris (note 1).

[9] US Air Force, National Air and Space Intelligence Center (NASIC), *Ballistic and Cruise Missile Threat* (NASIC: Wright-Patterson Air Force Base, OH, July 2017), p. 25.

[10] Pakistan Inter Services Public Relations, 'Shaheen 3 missile test', Press Release PR-61/2015-ISPR, 9 Mar. 2015.

[11] The National Defence Complex (also referred to as the National Development Complex or National Development Centre) and its supervisory organization, the National Engineering and Scientific Commission (NESCOM), are the principal bodies responsible for Pakistan's missile

of the Ababeel, aimed at 'validating various design and technical parameters of the weapon system', had been successfully carried out.[12] According to the armed forces' press service, the missile is 'capable of delivering multiple warheads, using Multiple Independent Re-entry Vehicle (MIRV) technology' and is being developed to '[ensure the] survivability of Pakistan's ballistic missiles in the growing regional Ballistic Missile Defence (BMD) environment'.[13] Pakistan's National Defence Complex is reportedly developing the technology to deploy MIRV-equipped missiles as a countermeasure to India's prospective ballistic missile defence system.[14]

Pakistan has prioritized the development of nuclear-capable short-range missiles that appear to be intended for tactical nuclear roles and missions. In pursuing its 'full-spectrum deterrence' posture, Pakistan's defence planners have given particular attention to nuclear options for responding to an Indian military doctrine that envisages carrying out rapid but limited conventional attacks on Pakistani territory using forward-deployed forces.[15]

Pakistan has deployed two land-based, single-stage ballistic missiles capable of delivering compact, low-yield nuclear warheads as well as conventional warheads: the 200-km range, road-mobile Abdali (Hatf-2); and the 60-km range, road-mobile Nasr (Hatf-9). The Nasr system was initially tested in 2011 using a single-tube launcher but has subsequently appeared with a mobile multi-tube launcher that can fire a four-missile salvo.[16] An improved 70-km range version was test launched on 5 July 2017.[17]

Sea-based cruise missiles

As part of its efforts to achieve a secure second-strike capability, Pakistan is seeking to match India's nuclear triad by developing a sea-based nuclear force. On 9 January 2017 Pakistan announced that the first test launch of a submarine-launched cruise missile (SLCM), the Babur-3, had been successfully carried out from 'an underwater, mobile platform' deployed in the Indian Ocean.[18] The missile was said to be a sea-based variant of the

development programmes. Nuclear Threat Initiative, 'National Defence Complex', updated 27 Sep. 2011.

[12] Pakistan Inter Services Public Relations, Press Release PR-34/2017-ISPR, 24 Jan. 2017.

[13] Pakistan Inter Services Public Relations (note 12).

[14] Tasleem, S., 'No Indian BMD for no Pakistani MIRVS', Stimson Center, Off Ramps Initiative, Paper, 2 Oct. 2017.

[15] Ahmed, M., 'Pakistan's tactical nuclear weapons and their impact on stability', Carnegie Endowment for International Peace, Regional Insight, 30 June 2016; and Sankaran, J., 'Pakistan's battlefield nuclear policy: a risky solution to an exaggerated threat', International Security, vol. 39, no. 3 (winter 2014/15), pp. 118–51.

[16] Ansari, U., 'Pakistan holds parade after 7-year break', Defense News, 24 Mar. 2015; and Haroon, A., 'Pakistan test fires Hatf-IX', Dispatch News Desk, 26 Sep. 2014.

[17] Pakistan Inter Services Public Relations, Press Release PR-344/2017-ISPR, 5 July 2017.

[18] Pakistan Inter Services Public Relations, Press Release PR-10/2017-ISPR, 9 Jan. 2017.

Babur-2 ground-launched cruise missile (GLCM) and to have a range of 450 km. It is most likely to be deployed on the Pakistan Navy's diesel-electric Agosta class submarines, which are currently in service.[19]

In 2012 Pakistan established a Naval Strategic Force Command as the 'custodian of the nation's second-strike capability'.[20] It is unclear whether the Pakistan Navy has developed a command and control infrastructure to manage a submarine-based nuclear force or custodial arrangements for nuclear warheads deployed on patrol.[21]

Ground- and air-launched cruise missiles

In addition to the sea-based Babur-3 SLCM, Pakistan continues to develop two types of nuclear-capable cruise missile as an integral part of its pursuit of a full-spectrum deterrence posture. The 700-km range Babur-2 is an improved version of the Babur (Hatf-7) GLCM that incorporates stealth design features. It was first test launched in 2016.[22] The Ra'ad (Hatf-8) ALCM, which Pakistan claims can carry either conventional or nuclear warheads to a range of over 350 km, has been flight tested seven times since 2007.[23] Although the initial tests were conducted using a PAF Mirage III combat aircraft, some reports indicate that the missile may have been integrated with the JF-17 aircraft.[24] In 2017 Pakistan revealed an improved version, the Ra'ad-2 ALCM, which reportedly has an extended range.[25]

[19] See e.g. Khan, F. H., 'Going tactical: Pakistan's nuclear posture and implications for stability', Institut Français des Relations Internationales (IFRI), *Proliferation Papers*, no. 53, Sep. 2015, p. 41.

[20] Iskander, R., *Murky Waters: Naval Nuclear Dynamics in the Indian Ocean* (Carnegie Endowment for International Peace: Washington, DC, Mar. 2015), p. 17.

[21] Panda, A. and Narang, V., 'Pakistan tests new sub-launched nuclear-capable cruise missile: what now?', The Diplomat, 10 Jan. 2017.

[22] Pakistan Inter Services Public Relations, Press Release PR-482/2016-ISPR, 14 Dec. 2016.

[23] Pakistan Inter Services Public Relations, Press Release PR-16/2016-ISPR, 19 Jan. 2016.

[24] Fisher (note 7).

[25] Khan, B., 'Pakistan officially unveils extended range Ra'ad 2 air-launched cruise missile', Quwa Defence News and Analysis Group, 23 Mar. 2017.

VIII. Israeli nuclear forces

SHANNON N. KILE AND HANS M. KRISTENSEN

Israel continues to maintain its long-standing policy of nuclear opacity: it neither officially confirms nor denies that it possesses nuclear weapons.[1] Like India and Pakistan, Israel has never been a party to the 1968 Treaty on the Non-Proliferation of Nuclear Weapons (Non-Proliferation Treaty, NPT).[2]

Declassified US and Israeli government documents indicate that Israel began building a stockpile of nuclear weapons in the early 1960s, using plutonium produced by the Israel Research Reactor 2 (IRR-2) at the Negev Nuclear Research Center near Dimona.[3] There is little publicly available information about the operating history and power capacity of the unsafe-guarded IRR-2. The ageing heavy water reactor remained operational in 2017 despite the existence of a number of identified structural problems.[4] It may now be operated primarily to produce tritium.[5]

It is estimated that Israel has approximately 80 nuclear weapons (see table 6.9). Of these, approximately 30 are gravity bombs for delivery by combat aircraft. Several bunkers thought to contain nuclear bombs are located at the Tel Nof airbase south of Tel Aviv. The remaining 50 weapons are for delivery by land-based ballistic missiles. Israel's arsenal includes solid-fuelled, two-stage Jericho II medium-range ballistic missiles, which are believed to be based, along with their mobile transporter-erector-launchers, in caves at an airbase near Zekharia in the Negev desert.[6] A three-stage Jericho III intermediate-range ballistic missile, with a range exceeding 4000 kilometres, was declared operational in 2011.[7] In 2013 Israel tested a Jericho III with a new motor that some sources believe may give the missile an intercontinental range—that is, a range exceeding 5500 km.[8] Its development status is unknown.

There are numerous unconfirmed reports that Israel has equipped its fleet of German-built Dolphin class diesel-electric submarines with

---

[1] On the role of this policy in Israel's national security decision making see Cohen, A., 'Israel', eds H. Born, B. Gill and H. Hänggi, SIPRI, *Governing the Bomb: Civilian Control and Democratic Account-ability of Nuclear Weapons* (Oxford University Press: Oxford, 2010).

[2] For a summary and other details of the NPT see annex A, section I, in this volume.

[3] For a history of Israel's nuclear weapon programme see Cohen, A., *The Worst-kept Secret: Israel's Bargain with the Bomb* (Columbia University Press: New York, 2010).

[4] *Times of Israel*, 'Government has no plans to close aging Dimona nuclear facility', 19 Sep. 2017.

[5] International Panel on Fissile Material (IPFM), *Global Fissile Material Report 2015: Nuclear Weapon and Fissile Material Stockpiles and Production* (IPFM: Princeton, NJ, Dec. 2015), p. 26.

[6] O'Halloran, J. (ed.), 'Jericho missiles', *IHS Jane's Weapons: Strategic, 2015–16* (IHS Jane's: Coulsdon, 2015), p. 53.

[7] O'Halloran, ed. (note 6).

[8] Ben David, A., 'Israel tests Jericho III missile', *Aviation Week & Space Technology*, 22 July 2013.

Table 6.9. Israeli nuclear forces, January 2018

Type	Range (km)[a]	Payload (kg)	Status	No. of warheads
Aircraft[b]				..
F-16A/B/C/D/I Falcon	1 600	5 400	205 aircraft in the inventory; some are believed to be equipped for nuclear weapon delivery	30
Land-based ballistic missiles[c]				..
Jericho II	1 500– 1 800	750– 1 000	c. 25 missiles; first deployed in 1990	25
Jericho III	>4 000	1 000– 1 300	First became operational in 2011–15 and is gradually replacing Jericho II	25
Cruise missiles				
..	..	..	Dolphin class diesel-electric submarines are rumoured to have been equipped with nuclear-armed SLCMs; denied by Israeli officials	..
Total				**80**[d]

.. = not available or not applicable; SLCM = sea-launched cruise missile.

[a] Aircraft range is for illustrative purposes only; actual mission range will vary. Missile payloads may have to be reduced in order to achieve maximum range.

[b] Some of Israel's 25 F-15I aircraft may also have a long-range nuclear delivery role.

[c] The Jericho III is based on the Shavit space launch vehicle, which if converted to a ballistic missile, could deliver a 775-kg payload to a distance of 4000 km.

[d] SIPRI's estimate, which is approximate, is that Israel has 80 stored warheads. There is significant uncertainty about the size of Israel's nuclear arsenal and its warhead capabilities.

Sources: Cohen, A., *The Worst-kept Secret: Israel's Bargain with the Bomb* (Columbia University Press: New York, 2010); Cohen, A. and Burr, W., 'Israel crosses the threshold', *Bulletin of the Atomic Scientists*, vol. 62, no. 3 (May/June 2006); Cohen, A., *Israel and the Bomb* (Columbia University Press: New York, 1998); Albright, D., Berkhout, F. and Walker, W., SIPRI, *Plutonium and Highly Enriched Uranium 1996: World Inventories, Capabilities and Policies* (Oxford University Press: Oxford, 1997); *IHS Jane's Strategic Weapon Systems*, various issues; International Institute for Strategic Studies, *The Military Balance 2018* (Routledge: London, 2018); Fetter, S., 'Israeli ballistic missile capabilities', *Physics and Society*, vol. 19, no. 3 (July 1990); 'Nuclear notebook', *Bulletin of the Atomic Scientists*, various issues; and authors' estimates.

nuclear-armed sea-launched cruise missiles, giving it a sea-based second-strike capability. German and Israeli officials have consistently denied these reports. Israel has purchased six Dolphin class submarines, five of which have been delivered to Israel. The sixth submarine is scheduled to be delivered by the end of 2019.[9] In October 2017 the German Government announced that it had agreed to subsidize the sale of three new submarines to Israel to replace the first three Dolphin class boats, which were delivered in the late 1990s.[10] The new submarines will enter service from 2027.

[9] Opall-Rome, B., 'Israeli Navy backs Netanyahu's submarine scheme', *Defense News*, 19 Apr. 2017.

[10] Reuters, 'Deutschland beteiligt sich finanziell an U-Booten für Israel' [Germany participates financially in submarines for Israel], *Der Spiegel*, 23 Oct. 2017.

IX. North Korea's military nuclear capabilities

SHANNON N. KILE AND HANS M. KRISTENSEN

The Democratic People's Republic of Korea (DPRK, or North Korea) maintains an active but highly opaque nuclear weapon programme. It is estimated that North Korea may have produced 10–20 nuclear weapons (see table 6.10). This is based on calculations of the amount of plutonium that North Korea may have separated from the spent fuel produced by its 5 megawatt-electric (MW(e)) graphite-moderated research reactor at the Yongbyon Nuclear Scientific Research Center (YNSRC) and assumptions about North Korean weapon design and fabrication skills. North Korea is believed to be increasing its limited holdings of weapon-usable plutonium (see section X), although assessments differ about the scale and pace of the increase.[1] In 2017 commercial satellite imagery and thermal imagery indicated that the Radiochemical Laboratory at the YNSRC might be continuing to operate intermittently to separate plutonium from the reactor's spent fuel rods.[2]

In 2016 North Korea publicly acknowledged that it was producing highly enriched uranium (HEU) for nuclear weapons.[3] There has been considerable speculation that North Korea is seeking to build warheads using HEU as the fissile material in order to overcome the constraints imposed by its limited holding of separated plutonium. However, it is not known whether it has done so. Furthermore, little is known about North Korea's stock of HEU or its uranium enrichment capacity.[4]

On 3 September 2017 North Korea conducted its sixth nuclear test explosion at the Punggye-ri underground test site in the north-east of the country.[5] Following the explosion, the North Korean Nuclear Weapons Institute announced that the event was a successful test of a hydrogen bomb that could be delivered by an intercontinental ballistic missile (ICBM).[6] Many commentators assessed, based on indirect evidence, that North Korea's

---

[1] See e.g. Yonhap News Agency, 'North Korea has 50 kg of weapons-grade plutonium: Seoul's Defense White Paper', 11 Jan. 2017; and Albright, D. and Kelleher-Vergantini, S., 'Plutonium, tritium and highly enriched uranium production at the Yongbyon nuclear site', Institute for Science and International Security, Imagery Brief, 14 June 2016.

[2] Bermudez, J. et al., 'North Korea's Yongbyon facility: probable production of additional plutonium for nuclear weapons', 38 North, US–Korea Institute, 14 July 2017.

[3] Kyodo News Agency, 'North Korea confirms restart of plutonium processing', Japan Times, 17 Aug. 2016.

[4] Albright and Kelleher-Vergantini (note 1); and Hecker, S. et al., North Korean Nuclear Facilities After the Agreed Framework, Working Paper (Freeman Spogli Institute for International Studies, Stanford University: Stanford, CA, 2016).

[5] For a technical assessment of the test and an overview of global nuclear weapon tests since 1945 see section XI of this chapter.

[6] Korean Central News Agency, 'DPRK Nuclear Weapons Institute on successful test of H-bomb for ICBM', 3 Sep. 2017.

claim that the nuclear explosive device tested was a thermonuclear weapon was plausible.[7] However, some experts noted that in the absence of the detection of leaked radioactive debris characteristic of a thermonuclear explosion, it was not possible to rule out that North Korea had tested another type of weapon design, such as a boosted composite device or even a large fission-only device.[8]

North Korea had previously conducted nuclear tests at the site in October 2006, May 2009, February 2013, and January and September 2016.[9] The estimated yields (explosive energy) of the tests have progressively increased.

Ballistic missiles

North Korea is expanding and modernizing its ballistic missile force, which consists of 10 types of indigenously produced short-, medium- and intermediate-range systems that are either deployed or under development. It is developing a road-mobile ICBM as well as a submarine-launched ballistic missile (SLBM). In 2017 North Korea conducted 20 known missile tests, compared with 24 tests in 2016. Of the seven different types of missile tested in 2017, four had not been previously tested.[10]

In a speech on 1 January 2018, the North Korean leader, Kim Jong Un, said that the country would begin to mass-produce nuclear warheads and ballistic missiles.[11] There is no publicly available evidence to confirm North Korea's claim that it has built a nuclear warhead that is sufficiently compact to be delivered by a ballistic missile. In 2017 the Defense Intelligence Agency of the United States reportedly concluded that North Korea had successfully designed and produced an operational nuclear weapon that could be delivered by a ballistic missile.[12] In the 2016 edition of its biennial Defense White Paper, South Korea's Ministry of National Defense noted that North Korea had 'reached a significant level' of technical progress towards building a miniaturized warhead, but it did not state whether it believed that North Korea had succeeded in doing so.[13] Other elements of the

---

[7] See e.g. Lewis, J., 'Welcome to the thermonuclear club, North Korea!', *Foreign Policy*, 4 Sep. 2017.

[8] Dominguez, G., 'North Korea conducts its sixth and largest nuclear test', *Jane's Defence Weekly*, 13 Sep. 2017, p. 6.

[9] On the earlier tests see Fedchenko, V. and Ferm Hellgren, R., 'Nuclear explosions, 1945–2006', *SIPRI Yearbook 2007*; Fedchenko, V., 'Nuclear explosions, 1945–2009', *SIPRI Yearbook 2010*; Fedchenko, V., 'Nuclear explosions, 1945–2013', *SIPRI Yearbook 2014*; and Fedchenko, V., 'Nuclear explosions, 1945–2016', *SIPRI Yearbook 2017*.

[10] James Martin Center for Nonproliferation Studies, North Korea Missile Test Database, 30 Nov. 2017. North Korea conducted an additional test in 2017 but the missile type is not known.

[11] Korean Central News Agency, 'Kim Jong-un makes new year address', 1 Jan. 2018.

[12] Warrick, J., Nakashima, E. and Fifield, A., 'North Korea now making missile-ready nuclear weapons, US analysts say', *Washington Post*, 8 Aug. 2017.

[13] Park, B., '2016 Defense White Paper estimates North Korea has 50kg of plutonium', *Hankyoreh*, 12 Jan. 2017.

Table 6.10. North Korean forces with potential nuclear capability, January 2018

Type[a]	Range (km)	Payload (kg)	Status	No. of warheads
Land-based ballistic missiles				..
Hwasong-7 (Nodong)	>1 200	1 000	Single-stage, liquid-fuel missile. Fewer than 100 launchers; first deployed in 1990	
Hwasong-9 (Scud-ER)	1 000	500	Scud missile variant, lengthened to carry additional fuel	
Bukkeukseong-2 (KN-15)	1 000	..	2-stage, solid-fuel missile launched from canister launcher. Land-based version of Bukkeukseong-1 SLBM; test launched twice in 2017	
Hwasong-10 (BM-25, Musudan)	>3 000	(1 000)	Single-stage, liquid-fuel missile under development; several failed test launches in 2016	
Hwasong-12 (KN-17)	3 300– 4 500	1 000	Single-stage, liquid-fuel missile under development; although half of 2017 test launches failed, North Korea declared it operational after Sep. 2017 test launch	
Hwasong-13 (KN-08)[b]	>5 500	..	3-stage, liquid-fuel missile with potential intercontinental range under development; no known test launches	
Hwasong-14 (KN-20)	6 700– 10 400	500– 1 000	2-stage, liquid-fuel missile under development; test launched twice in 2017	
Hwasong-15 (KN-22)	8 500– 13 000	1 000– 1 500	2-stage, liquid-fuel missile under development; test launched once in 2017	
Taepodong-2[c]	12 000	..	Under development; 3-stage space launch vehicle variant placed satellites in orbit in 2012 and 2016	
Submarine-launched ballistic missiles				
Bukkeukseong-1 (KN-11)	..	..	2-stage, solid-fuel SLBM under development, replacing earlier liquid-fuel version	
Total				(10–20)[d]

.. = not available or not applicable; ( ) = uncertain figure; SLBM = submarine-launched ballistic missile.

[a] The operational capability of North Korean warheads is uncertain. While there is speculation that some medium-range ballistic missiles might have operational nuclear capability, there is no authoritative open-source evidence that North Korea has developed and tested a functioning re-entry vehicle that is capable of carrying a nuclear warhead on a long-range ballistic missile and deployed warheads with operational forces. This table lists the ballistic missiles that could potentially have a nuclear delivery role, although that does not imply that each type is a mass-produced operational weapon system.

[b] A longer-range variant, the KN-14, is under development but has yet to be test launched.

[c] A 2-stage Taepodong-1 missile was unsuccessfully flight tested in 1998.

[d] SIPRI's estimate is that North Korea may have fissile material for between 20 and 30 warheads. After 6 tests, 1 of which was more than 200 kilotons, North Korea might have a small number of deliverable nuclear warheads.

Sources: US Air Force, National Air and Space Intelligence Center (NASIC), *Ballistic and Cruise Missile Threat*, various years; *IHS Jane's Strategic Weapon Systems*, various issues; International Institute for Strategic Studies, *The Military Balance 2018* (Routledge: London, 2018); 'Nuclear notebook', *Bulletin of the Atomic Scientists*, various issues; and authors' estimates.

US intelligence community and military have expressed doubt about the operational capability of, in particular, the warheads on long-range missiles. The South Korean Vice Defense Minister, Suh Choo-suk, stated in August 2017 that 'Both the United States and South Korea do not believe North Korea has yet completely gained re-entry technology in material engineering terms'.[14] Vice Chairman of the Joint Chiefs of Staff, US General Paul Selva, added in January 2018 that 'What [North Korea] has not demonstrated yet are the fusing and targeting technologies and survivable re-entry vehicle'.[15]

Medium- and intermediate-range ballistic missiles

Assuming that North Korea is able to produce a sufficiently compact warhead, some observers assess that the size, range and operational status of the Hwasong-7, also known as the Nodong, medium-range missile make it the system most likely to be given a nuclear delivery role.[16] Based on a Soviet-era Scud missile design, the Nodong is a single-stage, liquid-fuelled ballistic missile with an estimated range exceeding 1200 kilometres. The North Korean Army's Strategic Rocket Force Command carried out five test launches of Nodong missiles in 2016.[17] No tests were conducted in 2017.

North Korea has developed the single-stage, liquid-fuelled Hwasong-9, also known as the Scud-ER (extended-range) system. Based on the Hwasong-6 (Scud C variant) missile with a lengthened fuselage to carry additional fuel, the Scud-ER has an estimated range of 1000 km.[18] On 6 March 2017 four Scud-ER missiles were test fired simultaneously from the Sohae Satellite Launch complex in north-western North Korea.[19] According to some reports, a fifth Scud-ER may have failed to launch.[20] The missiles flew nearly 1000 km and landed in the Sea of Japan, approximately

[14] 'N. Korea still needs time to perfect re-entry technology: S. Korea vice def min', Reuters, 13 Aug. 2017.

[15] Ali, I., 'US general says North Korea not demonstrated all components of ICBM', Reuters, 30 Jan. 2018.

[16] See e.g. Fitzpatrick, M., 'North Korea nuclear test on hold?', Shangri-La Voices, International Institute for Strategic Studies, 27 May 2014.

[17] Three of the missile flight tests were apparently successful, but 2 of the missiles exploded (1 in July 2016 and 1 in Aug. 2016) shortly after launch. Kwon, K., Berlinger, J. and Hanna, J., 'North Korea fires 2 ballistic missiles, South Korea and US say', CNN, 3 Aug. 2016.

[18] US Air Force, National Air and Space Intelligence Center (NASIC), *Ballistic and Cruise Missile Threat* (NASIC: Wright-Patterson Air Force Base, OH, July 2017), pp. 18, 25.

[19] Bermudez, J. and Liu, J., 'North Korea's Sohae Satellite Launching Station: Scud-ER launch site visible; activity at vertical engine test stand', 38 North, US–Korea Institute, 17 Mar. 2017.

[20] Schmerler, D., 'Did North Korea test a fifth missile last week?', NK News, 16 Mar. 2017.

350 km from the Japanese island of Honshu.[21] The test raised concerns in Japan that North Korea was developing an ability to launch salvos of missiles capable of overwhelming Japan's ballistic missile defence systems, including those that have yet to be deployed.[22]

The Hwasong-10 missile, also designated the Musudan or BM-25, is a single-stage, liquid-fuelled missile with an estimated range exceeding 3000 km. The Musudan was first unveiled at a military parade in 2010. Flight testing began in 2016, with multiple failures.[23] No flight tests of the Musudan are known to have been conducted in 2017 and the status of the missile development programme is unclear.

The Hwasong-12 (also referred to by the US Department of Defense, DOD, designation KN-17) is a single-stage, intermediate-range missile that is believed to have a new liquid-propellant booster engine as well as design features that may serve as a technology test bed for a future ICBM.[24] Some analysts have speculated that the missile carries a small post-boost vehicle (PBV) that, in addition to increasing its maximum range, can be used to improve warhead accuracy.[25] The missile has an estimated range of 3300–4500 km, which would be sufficient to strike US military bases in the western Pacific Ocean, including on the island of Guam. A Hwasong-12 missile was successfully test launched for the first time on 14 May 2017.[26] Three tests conducted the previous month reportedly all failed.[27] On 28 August the North Korean Army's Strategic Rocket Force Command test launched a Hwasong-12 missile that travelled 2700 km, flying over Hokkaido in northern Japan before breaking up into three pieces during re-entry and falling into the Pacific Ocean.[28] The missile's flight path over Japan was strongly condemned by the Japanese Government.[29] A Hwasong-12 missile that was

[21] Hancocks, P. and Westcott, B., 'North Korea fires four missiles into the Sea of Japan', CNN, 7 Mar. 2017.

[22] Rich, M., 'North Korea launch could be test of new attack strategy, Japan analysts say', New York Times, 6 Mar. 2017.

[23] Savelsberg, R. and Kiessling, J., 'North Korea's Musudan missile: a performance assessment', 38 North, US–Korea Institute, 20 Dec. 2016. In 2016 North Korea conducted 8 flight tests of the Musudan system. Only 1 of the tests was judged to have been successful. In the other tests, the missiles exploded on launch or shortly thereafter.

[24] Yi, Y., 'Hwasong-12 a stepping stone in North Korea's ICBM development', Hankyoreh, 16 May 2017; and Savelsberg, R., 'A quick technical analysis of the Hwasong-12 missile', 38 North, US–Korea Institute, 19 May 2017.

[25] Elleman, M., 'North Korea's Hwasong-12 launch: a disturbing development', 38 North, US–Korea Institute, 30 Aug. 2017.

[26] Felstead, P. and Gibson, N., 'North Korea fires new missile to 2000 km altitude', Jane's Defence Weekly, 24 May 2017, p. 8.

[27] Panda, A., 'Exclusive: North Korea tested its new intermediate-range ballistic missile 3 times in April 2017', The Diplomat, 3 June 2017.

[28] Elleman (note 25); and Felstead, P. and Gibson, N., 'North Korean IRBM flies over Japan', Jane's Defence Weekly, 6 Sep. 2017, p. 5.

[29] Fifield, A., 'North Korean missile flies over Japan escalating tensions and prompting an angry response from Tokyo', Washington Post, 28 Aug. 2017; and McCurry, J., 'Trump and Abe vow to

test launched on 15 September also flew over Japan and travelled 3700 km—the longest distance by a North Korean missile to date—before landing in the Pacific Ocean.[30] Unlike previous tests, the missile was fired from a transporter-erector-launcher vehicle rather than from a concrete platform, which indicates a higher level of operational readiness.[31]

North Korea is developing the Bukkeukseong-2 missile ('Polaris-2', US DOD designation, KN-15), which is a land-based variant of the Bukkeukseong-1 SLBM. The two-stage, solid-fuelled missile has an estimated maximum range exceeding 1000 km.[32] The missile was first flight tested on 12 February 2017, followed by a second test on 21 May 2017.[33] Some analysts noted that North Korea's development of the Bukkeukseong-2 was probably part of an effort to improve the survivability of its nuclear-capable ballistic missile systems. Solid-fuelled missiles can be fired more quickly than liquid-fuelled systems and require fewer support vehicles that might give away their position to overhead surveillance.[34]

Intercontinental-range ballistic missiles

North Korea is widely believed to have prioritized building and deploying a long-range ballistic missile that can deliver a nuclear warhead to targets in the continental USA. In recent years it has pursued the serial development of several missile systems with progressively longer ranges and increasingly sophisticated delivery capabilities.

The Hwasong-13 (US DOD designation, KN-08) was first presented by North Korea as a road-mobile, three-stage missile with intercontinental range at a military parade in April 2012, although some non-governmental analysts have argued that the missiles displayed were only mock-ups.[35] Estimates of the range and payload capabilities of the missile are highly speculative. No test launch had been conducted as of the end of 2017.

North Korea has developed the Hwasong-14 (US DOD designation, KN-20), a prototype ICBM that first appeared in 2015 at a military parade in Pyongyang.[36] The two-stage missile appears to use the same high-energy

increase pressure after North Korea fires missile over Japan', *The Guardian*, 29 Aug. 2017.

[30] 'North Korea fires second missile over Japan', BBC News, 15 Sep. 2017.

[31] Graham, C., Boyle, D. and Connor, N., 'North Korea fires second missile over Japan as US tells China and Russia to take "direct action"', *Daily Telegraph*, 15 Sep. 2017; and Panda, A. 'North Korea shows increased operational confidence in the Hwasong-12 IRBM', The Diplomat, 17 Sep. 2017.

[32] US Air Force, National Air and Space Intelligence Center (note 18), p. 25.

[33] Felstead, P. and Gibson, N., 'North Korea tests Trump with ballistic missile launch', *Jane's Defence Weekly*, 22 Feb. 2017, p. 16; and BBC News, 'North Korea confirms "successful" new ballistic missile test', 21 May 2017.

[34] Panda, A., 'It wasn't an ICBM, but North Korea's first missile test of 2017 is a big deal', The Diplomat, 14 Feb. 2017.

[35] Schiller, M. and Kelley, R., 'Evolving threat: North Korea's quest for an ICBM', *Jane's Defence Weekly*, 18 Jan. 2017, p. 24.

[36] Schiller and Kelley (note 35).

liquid-propellant booster engine as the single-stage Hwasong-12.[37] The missile was test launched from mobile platforms twice in 2017, on 4 July and 28 July. In both tests the missiles were fired on elevated trajectories to avoid flying over Japan and reached maximum altitudes of 2800 km and 3700 km, respectively. The second test might not have been completely successful, as a lightweight re-entry vehicle carried by the missile apparently disintegrated before reaching the ground.[38] The Hwasong-14 is estimated to have a range of up to 10 400 km, depending on the payload and flight trajectory.[39]

North Korea is developing a new two-stage ICBM, the Hwasong-15 (US DOD designation, KN-22) that has a significantly larger second stage and more powerful booster engines than the Hwasong-14. The first flight test was conducted on 28 November 2017, when a Hwasong-15 was launched on an elevated trajectory and flew higher and for a longer duration than any previous North Korean missile. One estimate put the theoretical maximum range of the Hwasong-15 on a normal trajectory at up to 13 000 km—sufficient to reach Washington, DC, and other targets on the east coast of the USA.[40] The missile was assessed to be carrying a light payload, however, and the range would be significantly reduced if it were carrying a heavier payload such as a nuclear warhead.[41] According to a North Korean Government statement issued after the test, the Hwasong-15 is 'an intercontinental ballistic rocket tipped with super-large heavy warhead which is capable of striking the whole mainland of the US' that 'meets the goal of the completion of the rocket weaponry system'.[42]

Overall, in 2017 North Korea made progress towards building an operational ICBM across a range of technical challenges at a pace that surprised many experts.[43] Some analysts pointed out that North Korea had yet to validate the performance and reliability of an ICBM system, in particular that of the missile's re-entry vehicle.[44] However, estimates of the time required for it to do so shortened during the year. According to a July 2017 media report, the US Defense Intelligence Agency had concluded that North Korea would be able to produce a 'reliable, nuclear-capable ICBM' some time in 2018. The

[37] According to 1 non-governmental analyst, North Korea probably acquired the engine through illicit channels operating in Russia or Ukraine. Elleman, M., 'The secret to North Korea's ICBM success', IISS Voices blog, International Institute for Strategic Studies, 14 Aug. 2017.

[38] Schilling, J., 'What's next for North Korea's ICBM?', 38 North, US–Korea Institute, 1 Aug. 2017.

[39] Wright, D., 'North Korean ICBM appears able to reach major US cities', All Things Nuclear blog, Union of Concerned Scientists, 28 July 2017.

[40] Wright, D., 'Re-entry of North Korea's Hwasong-15 missile', All Things Nuclear blog, Union of Concerned Scientists, 7 Dec. 2017.

[41] Elleman, M., 'North Korea's third ICBM launch', 38 North, US–Korea Institute, 29 Nov. 2017; and Wright (note 40).

[42] Korean Central News Agency, 'DPRK Gov't statement on successful test-fire of new-type ICBM', 29 Nov. 2017.

[43] Broad, W. and Sanger, D., 'How US Intelligence agencies underestimated North Korea', New York Times, 6 Jan. 2018.

[44] Wright (note 40); and Elleman (note 41).

US intelligence community had previously assessed that North Korea would not have a credible ICBM capability until 2020 at the earliest.[45] In his statement in August 2017, Choo-suk noted that North Korea would need 'at least one or two more years' to master the re-entry vehicle technology required for a long-range missile delivery system.[46]

Submarine-launched ballistic missiles

North Korea is developing an SLBM called the Bukkeukseong-1 ('Polaris-1', US DOD designation, KN-11). The missile is now a two-stage, solid-fuelled design after initial test failures using a liquid-fuelled missile.[47] In August 2016, following a series of failed attempts, North Korea conducted the first successful underwater test launch of the Bukkeukseong-1 missile from an experimental submarine.[48] In 2017 North Korea conducted a series of successful underwater ejection tests—that is, tests designed to evaluate stabilization systems and the process of ejecting the missile from a submerged launch tube—but it did not conduct any flight tests of the missile.[49] Most observers assess that North Korea still has numerous technical challenges to overcome before it will be able to design, build and deploy an operational SLBM force. However, commercial satellite imagery of the shipyard in Sinpo from November 2017 revealed that North Korea appeared to be building a new, larger submarine capable of launching an SLBM.[50] As the year ended, concerns about North Korea's technical progress towards achieving an SLBM capability spurred the USA, Japan and South Korea to conduct military drills for tracking submarine missile launches by North Korea.[51]

[45] Nakashima, E., Fifield, A. and Warrick J., 'North Korea could cross ICBM threshold next year, US officials warn in new assessment', *Washington Post*, 25 July 2017.

[46] 'N. Korea still needs time to perfect re-entry technology: S. Korea vice def min' (note 14).

[47] Schilling, J., 'A new submarine-launched ballistic missile for North Korea', 38 North, US–Korea Institute, 25 Apr. 2016.

[48] Park, J. M. and Kim, J., 'North Korea fires submarine-launched ballistic missile towards Japan', Reuters, 24 Aug. 2016.

[49] Ryall, J., 'North Korea carries out "unprecedented" test of submarine missile system', *Daily Telegraph*, 1 Aug. 2017.

[50] Bermudez, J., 'North Korea's submarine ballistic missile program moves ahead: indications of shipbuilding and missile ejection testing', 38 North, US–Korea Institute, 16 Nov. 2017.

[51] Mullany, G., 'North Korean submarine missile threat prompts US-led military drills', *New York Times*, 11 Dec. 2017.

X. Global stocks and production of fissile materials, 2017

MORITZ KÜTT, ZIA MIAN AND PAVEL PODVIG

INTERNATIONAL PANEL ON FISSILE MATERIALS

Materials that can sustain an explosive fission chain reaction are essential for all types of nuclear explosives, from first-generation fission weapons to advanced thermonuclear weapons. The most common of these fissile materials are highly enriched uranium (HEU) and plutonium. This section gives details of military and civilian stocks as of the beginning of 2017 of HEU (see table 6.11) and separated plutonium (see table 6.12), including in weapons, and details of the current capacity to produce these materials (see tables 6.13 and 6.14, respectively). The information in the tables is based on estimates prepared for the International Panel on Fissile Materials (IPFM). The most recent annual declarations on civilian plutonium and HEU stocks to the International Atomic Energy Agency (IAEA) were released in late 2017 and give data for the end of 2016.

The production of both HEU and plutonium starts with natural uranium. Natural uranium consists almost entirely of the non-chain-reacting isotope uranium-238 (U-238) and is only about 0.7 per cent uranium-235 (U-235). The concentration of U-235, however, can be increased through enrichment—typically using gas centrifuges. Uranium that has been enriched to less than 20 per cent U-235 (typically, 3–5 per cent)—known as low-enriched uranium—is suitable for use in power reactors. Uranium that has been enriched to contain at least 20 per cent U-235—known as HEU—is generally taken to be the lowest concentration practicable for use in weapons. However, in order to minimize the mass of the nuclear explosive, weapon-grade uranium is usually enriched to over 90 per cent U-235. Plutonium is produced in nuclear reactors when U-238 is exposed to neutrons. The plutonium is subsequently chemically separated from spent fuel in a reprocessing operation. Plutonium comes in a variety of isotopic mixtures, most of which are weapon-usable. Weapon designers prefer to work with a mixture that predominantly consists of plutonium-239 (Pu-239) because of its relatively low rate of spontaneous emission of neutrons and gamma rays and the low level of heat generation from radioactive alpha decay. Weapon-grade plutonium typically contains more than 90 per cent of the isotope Pu-239. The plutonium in typical spent fuel from power reactors (reactor-grade plutonium) contains 50–60 per cent Pu-239 but is weapon-usable, even in a first-generation weapon design. All states with a civil nuclear industry have some capability to produce fissile materials that could be used for weapons.

Table 6.11. Global stocks of highly enriched uranium, 2017

State	National stockpile (tonnes)[a]	Production status	Comments
China[b]	14 ± 3	Stopped 1987–89	
France[c]	30 ± 6	Stopped 1996	Includes 4.8 tonnes declared civilian
India[d]	4 ± 1.4	Continuing	Includes HEU in naval reactor cores
Israel[e]	0.3	–	
Pakistan	3.4 ± 0.4	Continuing	
Russia[f]	679 ± 120	Stopped 1987–88	
UK[g]	21.1	Stopped 1962	Includes 1.37 tonnes declared civilian
USA[h]	574.5 (95 not available for military purposes)	Stopped 1992	Includes HEU in a naval reserve
Other states[i]	~15		
Total[j]	**~1340 (95 not available for military purposes)**		

HEU = highly enriched uranium.

[a] Most of this material is 90–93% enriched uranium-235 (U-235), which is typically considered weapon-grade. Important exceptions are noted. Blending down (i.e. reducing the concentration of U-235) of excess Russian and US weapon-grade HEU and civilian HEU declarations up to the end of 2016 has been taken into account. The estimates are in effect for the end of 2016.

[b] This revised estimate is based on a new assessment for the International Panel on Fissile Materials (IPFM) of fissile material production and stocks in China.

[c] France declared 4.8 tonnes of civilian HEU to the International Atomic Energy Agency (IAEA) as of the end of 2016; it is assumed here to be 93% enriched HEU, even though 1.54 tonnes of the material is in irradiated form. The uncertainty in the estimate applies only to the military stockpile of about 26 tonnes and does not apply to the declared civilian stock. A recent analysis offers grounds for a significantly lower estimate of the stockpile of weapon-grade HEU (as large as 10 ± 2 tonnes or as low as 6 ± 2 tonnes), based on evidence that the Pierrelatte enrichment plant may have had both a much shorter effective period of operation and a smaller weapon-grade HEU production capacity than previously assumed.

[d] It is believed that India is producing HEU (enriched to 30–45%) for use as naval reactor fuel. The estimate is for HEU enriched to 30%.

[e] Israel may have acquired about 300 kg of weapon-grade HEU from the USA in or before 1965.

[f] This estimate may understate the amount of HEU in Russia since it assumes that it ceased production of all HEU in 1988. However, Russia may have continued producing HEU for civilian and non-weapon military uses after that date. The material in discharged naval cores is not included in the current stock since the enrichment of uranium in these cores is believed to be less than 20% U-235.

[g] The UK declared a stockpile of 21.9 tonnes of HEU as of 31 Mar. 2002, the average enrichment of which was not given. Some of this has been consumed since then in naval fuel. The UK declared a stock of 1.37 tonnes of civilian HEU to the IAEA as of the end of 2016.

[h] The amount of US HEU is given in actual tonnes, not 93% enriched equivalent. In 2016 the USA declared that as of 30 Sep. 2013 its HEU inventory was 585.6 tonnes, of which 499.4 tonnes was declared to be for 'national security or non-national security programs including nuclear weapons, naval propulsion, nuclear energy, and science'. The remaining 86.2 tonnes was composed of 41.6 tonnes 'available for potential down-blend to low enriched uranium or, if not possible, disposal as low-level waste', and 44.6 tonnes in spent reactor fuel. As of the end

of Dec. 2016, another 11.1 tonnes had been down blended or shipped for blending down. The 95 tonnes declared excess includes the remaining 75.1 tonnes and 20 tonnes of HEU reserved for HEU fuel for research reactors.

[i] The 2016 IAEA Annual Report lists 181 significant quantities of HEU under comprehensive safeguards in non-nuclear weapon states as of the end of 2016. In order to reflect the uncertainty in the enrichment levels of this material, mostly in research reactor fuel, a total of 15 tonnes of HEU is assumed. About 10 tonnes of this is in Kazakhstan and has been irradiated; it was initially slightly higher than 20%-enriched fuel. It is possible that this material is no longer HEU.

[j] Totals are rounded to the nearest 5 tonnes.

Sources: International Panel on Fissile Materials (IPFM), *Global Fissile Material Report 2015: Nuclear Weapon and Fissile Material Stockpiles and Production* (IPFM: Princeton, NJ, Dec. 2015). China: Zhang, H., *China's Fissile Material Production and Stockpile* (IPFM: Princeton, NJ, Dec. 2017). France: International Atomic Energy Agency (IAEA), Communication Received from France Concerning its Policies Regarding the Management of Plutonium, INFCIRC/549/Add.5/21, 29 Sep. 2017; and Philippe, S. and Glaser, A., 'Nuclear archaeology for gaseous diffusion enrichment plants', *Science & Global Security*, vol. 22, no. 1 (2014), pp. 27–49. Israel: Myers, H., 'The real source of Israel's first fissile material', *Arms Control Today*, vol. 37, no. 8 (Oct. 2007), p. 56; and Gilinsky, V. and Mattson, R. J., 'Revisiting the NUMEC affair', *Bulletin of the Atomic Scientists*, vol. 66, no. 2 (Mar./Apr. 2010). UK: British Ministry of Defence, 'Historical accounting for UK defence highly enriched uranium', Mar. 2006; and Office for Nuclear Regulation, 'Annual figures for holdings of civil unirradiated plutonium as at 31 December 2016', 2017. USA: US Department of Energy (DOE), *Highly Enriched Uranium, Striking a Balance: A Historical Report on the United States Highly Enriched Uranium Production, Acquisition, and Utilization Activities from 1945 through September 30, 1996* (DOE: Washington, DC, 2001); Personal communication, US DOE, Office of Fissile Material Disposition, National Nuclear Security Administration; White House, Office of the Press Secretary, 'Fact sheet: transparency in the US highly enriched uranium inventory', 31 Mar. 2016; and Irons, C. W., 'Status of surplus HEU disposition in the United States', Institute of Nuclear Materials Management, 57th Annual Meeting, Atlanta, 26 July 2016. Non-nuclear weapon states: IAEA, *IAEA Annual Report 2016* (IAEA: Vienna, 2017), Annex, Table A4, p. 123.

Table 6.12. Global stocks of separated plutonium, 2017

State	Military stocks (tonnes)	Military production status	Civilian stocks (tonnes)[a]
China	2.9 ± 0.6	Stopped in 1991	0.04
France	6 ± 1.0	Stopped in 1992	65.4 (excludes 16.3 foreign owned)
Germany[b]	–	–	0.6
India[c]	0.58 ± 0.15	Continuing	6.4 ± 3.5 (includes 0.4 under safeguards)
Israel[d]	0.9 ± 0.13	Continuing	–
Japan	–	–	47.0 (includes 37.1 in France and UK)
Korea, North[e]	0.04	Continuing	–
Pakistan[f]	0.28 ± 0.09	Continuing	–
Russia[g]	128 ± 8 (40 not available for weapons)	Stopped in 2010	57.2
UK[h]	3.2	Stopped in 1995	110.3 (excludes 23.2 foreign owned)
USA[i]	87.8 (49.4 not available for weapons)	Stopped in 1988	–
Other states[j]	–	–	2.3
Totals[k]	~230 (89 not available for weapons)		~290

[a] Some countries with civilian plutonium stocks do not submit an International Atomic Energy Agency (IAEA) INFCIRC/549 declaration. Of these countries, Italy, the Netherlands, Spain and Sweden store their plutonium abroad. The data is for the end of 2016.

[b] This may be an overestimate since Germany apparently reports plutonium as being in unirradiated mixed oxide (MOX) fuel even if the fuel is being irradiated in a reactor.

[c] India's estimate for military plutonium is reduced because of new publicly available information about the performance of its Dhruva reactor. As part of the 2005 Indian–US Civil Nuclear Cooperation Initiative, India has included in the military sector much of the plutonium separated from its spent power-reactor fuel. While it is labelled civilian here since it is intended for breeder reactor fuel, this plutonium was not placed under safeguards in the 'India-specific' safeguards agreement signed by the Indian Government and the IAEA on 2 Feb. 2009. India does not submit an IAEA INFCIRC/549 declaration.

[d] Israel is believed to still be operating the Dimona plutonium production reactor but may be using it primarily for tritium production. The estimate is for the end of 2016.

[e] North Korea reportedly declared a plutonium stock of 37 kg in June 2008. It resumed plutonium production in 2009, but has probably expended some material in the nuclear tests conducted in 2009–17.

[f] As of the end of 2016, Pakistan was operating 4 plutonium production reactors at its Khushab site. This estimate assumes that in 2016 Pakistan separated plutonium from the cooled spent fuel from 2 new reactors, 1 of which began operating some time in 2013 and the other in late 2014 or early 2015.

[g] The 40 tonnes of plutonium not available for weapons comprises 25 tonnes of weapon-origin plutonium stored at the Mayak Fissile Material Storage Facility and about 15 tonnes of weapon-grade plutonium produced between 1 Jan. 1995 and 15 Apr. 2010, when the last plutonium production reactor was shut down. The post-1994 plutonium, which is currently stored at Zheleznogorsk, cannot be used for weapon purposes under the terms of the US–Russian agreement on plutonium production reactors signed in 1997. Russia made a commitment to eliminate 34 tonnes of the plutonium not available for weapons (including all 25 tonnes of plutonium stored at Mayak) as part of the US–Russian Plutonium Management

and Disposition Agreement, concluded in 2000. Russia does not include the plutonium that is not available for weapons in its INFCIRC/549 statement. Nor does it make the plutonium it reports as civilian available to IAEA safeguards.

[h] The UK declared 110.3 tonnes of civilian plutonium (not including 23.2 tonnes of foreign-owned plutonium in the UK) as of the end of 2016. This includes 4.4 tonnes of military plutonium declared excess and placed under Euratom safeguards.

[i] In 2012 the USA declared a government-owned plutonium inventory of 95.4 tonnes as of 30 Sep. 2009. In its 2016 IAEA INFCIRC/549 statement, the USA declared 49 tonnes of unirradiated plutonium (both separated and in MOX) as part of the stock that was identified as excess for military purposes. Since most of this material is stored in classified form, it is considered military stock. The USA considers a total of 61.5 tonnes of plutonium as declared excess to national security needs. This includes 49 tonnes of unirradiated plutonium, 4.5 tonnes of plutonium disposed of as waste, 0.2 tonnes lost to radioactive decay since 1994 and 7.8 tonnes of irradiated government-owned plutonium. The plutonium reported in INFCIRC/549 also includes 0.4 tonnes of plutonium brought to the USA in 2016 from Japan, Germany and Switzerland (331 kg, 30 kg, and 18 kg, respectively). Like the 49 tonnes of unirradiated excess plutonium, this material will not be used for weapons. However, it has not been placed under IAEA safeguards, so it is accounted for together with military material.

[j] This is estimated by reconciling the amounts of plutonium declared as 'held in locations in other countries' and 'belonging to foreign bodies' in the INFCIRC/549 reports.

[k] Totals are rounded to the nearest 5 tonnes.

Sources: International Panel on Fissile Materials (IPFM), *Global Fissile Material Report 2015: Nuclear Weapon and Fissile Material Stockpiles and Production* (IPFM: Princeton, NJ, Dec. 2015). Civilian stocks (except for India): declarations by countries to the International Atomic Energy Agency (IAEA) under INFCIRC/549. China: Zhang, H., *China's Fissile Material Production and Stockpile* (IPFM: Princeton, NJ, Dec. 2017). North Korea: Kessler, G., 'Message to US preceded nuclear declaration by North Korea', *Washington Post*, 2 July 2008; and Hecker, S. S., 'What we really know about North Korea's nuclear weapons', *Foreign Affairs*, 4 Dec. 2017. Russia: Agreement Concerning the Management and Disposition of Plutonium Designated as No Longer Required for Defense Purposes and Related Cooperation (Russian–US Plutonium Management and Disposition Agreement), signed 29 Aug. and 1 Sep. 2000, amended Apr. 2010, entered into force July 2011. USA: National Nuclear Security Administration (NNSA), *The United States Plutonium Balance, 1944–2009* (NNSA: Washington, DC, June 2012).

Table 6.13. Significant uranium enrichment facilities and capacity worldwide, 2017

State	Facility name or location	Type	Status	Enrichment process[a]	Capacity (thousands SWU/yr)[b]
Argentina[c]	Pilcaniyeu	Civilian	Resuming operation	GD	20
Brazil	Resende Enrichment	Civilian	Expanding capacity	GC	120
China[d]	Lanzhou	Civilian	Operational	GC	2 600
	Hanzhong (Shaanxi)	Civilian	Operational	GC	2 000
	Emeishan	Civilian	Operational	GC	1 050
	Heping	Dual-use	Operational	GD	230
France	Georges Besse II	Civilian	Operational	GC	7 500
Germany	Urenco Gronau	Civilian	Operational	GC	4 000
India	Rattehalli	Military	Operational	GC	15–30
Iran[e]	Natanz	Civilian	Limited operation	GC	3.5–5
	Qom (Fordow)	Civilian	Idle	GC	..
Japan	Rokkasho[f]	Civilian	Resuming operation	GC	75
Korea, North	Yongbyon[g]	..	Uncertain	GC	8
Netherlands	Urenco Almelo	Civilian	Operational	GC	5 400
Pakistan	Gadwal	Military	Operational	GC	..
	Kahuta	Military	Operational	GC	15–45
Russia[h]	Angarsk	Civilian	Operational	GC	4 000
	Novouralsk	Civilian	Operational	GC	13 300
	Seversk	Civilian	Operational	GC	3 800
	Zelenogorsk	Civilian	Operational	GC	7 900
UK	Capenhurst	Civilian	Operational	GC	4 700
USA[i]	Urenco Eunice	Civilian	Operational	GC	4 700

[a] The gas centrifuge (GC) is the main isotope-separation technology used to increase the percentage of uranium-235 (U-235) in uranium, but a few facilities continue to use gaseous diffusion (GD).

[b] SWU/yr = Separative work units per year: an SWU is a measure of the effort required in an enrichment facility to separate uranium of a given content of U-235 into 2 components, 1 with a higher and 1 with a lower percentage of U-235. Where a range of capacities is shown, the capacity is uncertain or the facility is expanding its capacity.

[c] In Dec. 2015 Argentina announced resumption of production at its Pilcaniyeu GD uranium enrichment plant, which was shut down in the 1990s.

[d] A new assessment of China's enrichment capacity in 2015 identified new enrichment sites and suggested a much larger total capacity than had previously been estimated. These estimates were again updated in a new report in 2017.

[e] In July 2015 Iran agreed a Joint Comprehensive Plan of Action that ended uranium enrichment at Fordow but kept centrifuges operating, and limited the enrichment capacity at Natanz to 5060 IR1 centrifuges (equivalent to 3500–5000 SWU/yr) for 10 years.

[f] The Rokkasho centrifuge plant is being refitted with new centrifuge technology and is operating at very low capacity, about 75 000 SWU/yr as of Dec. 2016.

[g] North Korea revealed its Yongbyon enrichment facility in 2010. Its operating status is unknown.

[h] Zelenogorsk is operating a cascade for highly enriched uranium production for fast reactor and research reactor fuel.

[i] Plans for new centrifuge enrichment plants at Piketon (United States Enrichment Corporation, USEC) and Eagle Rock (AREVA) have been shelved for technical and financial reasons, respectively.

Table 6.14. Significant reprocessing facilities worldwide, as of 2017

All facilities process light water reactor (LWR) fuel, except where indicated.

State	Facility name or location	Type	Status	Design capacity (tHM/yr)[a]
China[b]	Jiuquan pilot plant	Civilian	Operational	50
France	La Hague UP2	Civilian	Operational	1 000
	La Hague UP3	Civilian	Operational	1 000
India[c]	Kalpakkam (HWR fuel)	Dual-use	Operational	100
	Tarapur (HWR fuel)	Dual-use	Operational	100
	Tarapur-II (HWR fuel)	Dual-use	Operational	100
	Trombay (HWR fuel)	Military	Operational	50
Israel	Dimona (HWR fuel)	Military	Operational	40–100
Japan	JNC Tokai	Civilian	To be shut down[d]	200
	Rokkasho	Civilian	Start planned for 2021	800
Korea, North	Yongbyon	Military	Operational	100–150
Pakistan	Chashma (HWR fuel)	Military	Starting up	50–100
	Nilore (HWR fuel)	Military	Operational	20–40
Russia[e]	Mayak RT-1, Ozersk	Civilian	Operational	400
UK	BNFL B205 (Magnox fuel)	Civilian	To be shut down 2018	1 500
	BNFL Thorp, Sellafield	Civilian	To be shut down 2020	1 200
USA	H-canyon, Savannah River Site	Civilian	Operational	15

HWR = heavy water reactor.

[a] Design capacity refers to the highest amount of spent fuel the plant is designed to process and is measured in tonnes of heavy metal per year (tHM/yr), tHM being a measure of the amount of heavy metal—uranium in these cases—that is in the spent fuel. Actual throughput is often a small fraction of the design capacity. LWR spent fuel contains about 1% plutonium, and heavy water- and graphite-moderated reactor fuel about 0.4%.

[b] China is planning to build a pilot reprocessing facility at Jiuquan with a capacity of 200 tHM/yr.

[c] As part of the 2005 Indian–US Civil Nuclear Cooperation Initiative, India has decided that none of its reprocessing plants will be opened for International Atomic Energy Agency safeguards inspections.

[d] In 2014 the Japan Atomic Energy Agency announced the planned closure of the head-end of its Tokai reprocessing plant, effectively ending further plutonium separation activity. In 2016 it was still working with very small amounts of plutonium.

[e] A 250 tHM/yr Pilot Experimental Centre is under construction in Zheleznogorsk. It is supposed to begin operation in 2018.

Sources for table 6.13: Indo-Asian News Service, 'Argentina president inaugurates enriched uranium plant', *Business Standard*, 1 Dec. 2015; Zhang, H., 'China's uranium enrichment complex', *Science & Global Security*, vol. 23, no. 3 (2015), pp. 171–90; and Zhang, H., *China's Fissile Material Production and Stockpile* (International Panel on Fissile Materials: Princeton, NJ, Dec. 2017). Enrichment capacity data is based on International Atomic Energy Agency, Integrated Nuclear Fuel Cycle Information Systems (INFCIS); Urenco website; and International Panel on Fissile Materials (IPFM), *Global Fissile Material Report 2015: Nuclear Weapon and Fissile Material Stockpiles and Production* (IPFM: Princeton, NJ, Dec. 2015).

Sources for table 6.14: Data on design capacity is based on International Atomic Energy Agency, Integrated Nuclear Fuel Cycle Information Systems (INFCIS); and International Panel on Fissile Materials (IPFM), *Global Fissile Material Report 2015: Nuclear Weapon and Fissile Material Stockpiles and Production* (IPFM: Princeton, NJ, Dec. 2015).

XI. Nuclear explosions, 1945–2017

VITALY FEDCHENKO

On 3 September 2017 the Democratic People's Republic of Korea (DPRK, or North Korea) conducted its sixth nuclear test explosion, following tests conducted in January and September 2016, February 2013, May 2009 and October 2006.[1] This 2017 test brought the total number of nuclear explosions recorded since 1945 to 2058.

The September 2017 nuclear test

On 3 September 2017 at 03:30 Coordinated Universal Time (12:00 local time) North Korea conducted an underground test explosion at the Punggye-ri Nuclear Test Facility under Mount Mantap in the north-east of the country.[2] Shortly after, the Korean Central News Agency (KCNA) announced that the event was a successful test of a hydrogen bomb for an intercontinental ballistic missile (ICBM) and published a statement by the Nuclear Weapons Institute (NWI) of North Korea detailing the features of the test device.[3]

The publication after a test of discussion by the NWI of the test device's features is a new development: it occurred for the first time after the fifth test in September 2016. The NWI noted that the test carried out in September 2017 was of a bomb of 'unprecedentedly big power' and proclaimed the test a success. The NWI also stated that North Korea had conducted 'experimental measurements' to verify the performance of a new 'H-bomb' design, in terms of (a) its 'total explosion power' (yield); (b) its 'fission to fusion power' ratio; (c) the 'precision of the compression technology and the fission chain reaction start control technology of the first system of the H-bomb', meaning the performance of the high explosive implosion assembly and the neutron initiator in the primary; and (d) the 'nuclear material utility rate in the first system and the second system', or the proportion of the fissile material in the primary that underwent fission, as opposed to being scattered by the explosion, and the amount of material that underwent either fusion or fission in the secondary.[4] Some descriptions of the test device's features,

---

[1] On the earlier tests see Fedchenko, V. and Ferm Hellgren, R., 'Nuclear explosions, 1945–2006', *SIPRI Yearbook 2007*; Fedchenko, V., 'Nuclear explosions, 1945–2009', *SIPRI Yearbook 2010*; Fedchenko, V., 'Nuclear explosions, 1945–2013', *SIPRI Yearbook 2014*; and Fedchenko, V., 'Nuclear explosions, 1945–2016', *SIPRI Yearbook 2017*.

[2] Lee, M. Y. H., 'North Korea's latest nuclear test was so powerful it reshaped the mountain above it', *Washington Post*, 14 Sep. 2017.

[3] Korean Central News Agency, 'DPRK Nuclear Weapons Institute on successful test of H-bomb for ICBM', 3 Sep. 2017.

[4] The ratio of fission to fusion energy (i.e. the share of energy from fission and fusion reactions in the total yield) determines the amount of long-term contamination by radioactive isotopes. Less fission means less long-lived radioactive isotopes in the fallout, so the weapon can be treated

Table 6.15. Data on North Korea's nuclear explosion, 3 September 2017

Source[a]	Origin time (UTC)	Latitude	Longitude	Error margin[b]	Body-wave magnitude[c]
IDC[d]	03:30:06.09 ± 3.7	41.3256° N	129.0760° E	±6.7 km[e]	6.07 ± 0.1
CEME	03:29:59.0	41.3° N	129.1° E	..	6.3
NEIC	03:30:01.760	41.332° N	129.030° E	±1.4 km[f]	6.3
IES CAS	03:30:00	41.3° N	129.1° E	..	6.3
KMA	03:29:58	41.302° N	129.080° E	..	5.7
FOI	03:30	41.3° N	129.1° E	..	6.1

.. = data not available; CEME = Russian Academy of Sciences, Geophysical Survey, Central Experimental Methodical Expedition, Obninsk, Kaluga oblast, Russia; FOI = Swedish Defence Research Agency, Stockholm, Sweden; IDC = Comprehensive Nuclear-Test-Ban Treaty Organization (CTBTO), International Data Centre, Vienna, Austria; IES CAS = Institutions of Earth Science, Chinese Academy of Science, Beijing, China; km = kilometres; KMA = Korean Meteorological Administration, Seoul, South Korea; NEIC = US Geological Survey, National Earthquake Information Center, Denver, CO, United States; UTC = Coordinated Universal Time.

[a] Because of differences between estimates regarding the precise location and magnitude of the explosion, data from 6 sources—1 internationally recognized body and 5 national bodies—is provided for comparison.

[b] The error margins are as defined by the data sources.

[c] Body-wave magnitude indicates the size of the event. In order to give a reasonably correct estimate of the yield of an underground explosion, detailed information is needed (e.g. on the geological conditions in the area where the explosion took place). Body-wave magnitude is an unambiguous way of indicating the size of an explosion.

[d] The IDC was 'in a test and provisional operation mode only' so 41 of the 50 primary and 96 of the 120 auxiliary seismic monitoring stations in the CTBTO's International Monitoring System were contributing data at the time of the event.

[e] This figure is the length of the semi-major axis of the confidence ellipse. The confidence ellipse area was 109 square km, or almost 10 times smaller than the maximum area allowed to be inspected under the Comprehensive Nuclear-Test-Ban Treaty On-Site Inspection regime (1000 square km).

[f] This figure is the horizontal location error, defined as the 'length of the largest projection of the three principal errors on a horizontal plane'.

Sources: CTBTO, IDC, 'Technical briefing', 3 Sep. 2017; and CTBTO, IDC, 'Technical findings', 7 Sep. 2017; CEME, [Information message about underground nuclear explosion made in North Korea on 3 September 2017], 4 Sep. 2017 (in Russian); NEIC, 'M 6.3 nuclear explosion: 21 km ENE of Sungjibaegam, North Korea', US Geological Survey, [n.d.]; IES CAS, 'Research letters: September 3, 2017, preliminary results of seismological discrimination, depth and equivalence estimates for North Korea's nuclear tests', 4 Sep. 2017; KMA, Earthquake Volcano Monitoring Division, 'Artificial earthquake occurred in North Hamkyung Province', Press release, 3 Sep. 2017; and FOI, 'Nuclear weapons test in North Korea', Press release, 11 Sep. 2017.

such as 'the directional combination structure and multi-layer radiation explosion-proof structural design of the first system and the second system' and the 'light thermal radiation-resisting materials and neutron-resisting

as 'cleaner' by military planners. This could be important for those considering the tactical use of nuclear weapons.

materials', are harder to interpret specifically on the basis of open-source descriptions of thermonuclear weapon designs. However, these statements seem to be consistent with the 'Teller–Ulam' thermonuclear design, which is ostensibly used by all states with thermonuclear weapons.[5]

As was the case with the fifth test, the NWI statement noted that 'there were neither emission through ground surface nor leakage of radioactive materials nor did it have any adverse impact on the surrounding ecological environment'.

Verification of the September 2017 North Korean test by the international community

The international community—international organizations, individual states and many research institutions—sought to verify North Korea's claims concerning the test using a combination of available technologies, including seismology, radionuclide monitoring and satellite imagery analysis.[6]

The 1996 Comprehensive Nuclear-Test-Ban Treaty (CTBT) is a multilateral treaty that, once it enters into force, will prohibit the carrying out of any nuclear explosion.[7] The Preparatory Commission for the Comprehensive Nuclear-Test-Ban Treaty Organization (CTBTO) has been established to prepare for the entry into force of the CTBT. These preparations include the creation of an International Monitoring System (IMS) to detect nuclear explosions. While the CTBT had been ratified by 166 states as of 1 February 2018, it cannot enter into force until it has been signed and ratified by 44 states that possess certain nuclear facilities. North Korea, which is one of these 44 states, has not signed the treaty and therefore does not participate in the IMS.

Seismic data recorded at monitoring stations around the world was used to estimate the time, location and size of the 3 September 2017 explosion (see table 6.15). The seismic wave patterns recorded, the depth of the event (less than 1 kilometre) and the fact that it occurred so close to the five previous nuclear tests (a characteristic distance being a few hundred metres) all indicate that it was an explosion rather than an earthquake.[8] The characteristic feature of this test was that its yield was large enough to produce aftershocks that themselves were large enough to be detected by seismic monitoring

---

[5] Korean Central News Agency (note 3).

[6] US National Academy of Sciences, *Technical Issues Related to the Comprehensive Nuclear Test Ban Treaty* (National Academy Press: Washington, DC, 2002), pp. 39–41; and Dahlman, O. et al., *Detect and Deter: Can Countries Verify the Nuclear Test Ban?* (Springer: Dordrecht, 2011), pp. 29–76.

[7] For a summary and other details of the CTBT see annex A, section I, in this volume.

[8] Comprehensive Nuclear-Test-Ban Treaty Organization, International Data Centre, 'Technical findings', 7 Sep. 2017.

stations.[9] In addition, synthetic aperture radar (SAR) satellite imagery was used to show that the peak of Mount Mantap had 'incurred a visible amount of subsidence', and an area of about 35 hectares 'of the southwest flank of the mountain was displaced by several meters'.[10] The seismic events that followed the test explosion have reportedly led the governments of the United States and China to conclude that a collapse of an explosion cavity or tunnels had taken place.[11]

Even though there can be little doubt in cases of an explosion of this size, strictly speaking, seismic data alone is insufficient to confirm that an underground explosion is a nuclear explosion. Following North Korea's 2006 and 2013 tests, the nuclear nature of the explosion was confirmed when air sampling detected traces of radioxenon—radioactive isotopes of xenon that are released from a nuclear explosion.[12] No trace of radioxenon or other radioactive debris was reported found after the 2009 event, or after either of the events in 2016. Radioxenon detection after the 2017 test produced ambiguous results. The Government of the Republic of Korea (South Korea) announced that its Nuclear Safety and Security Commission found xenon-133 in 'ground, air and maritime' samples collected locally after the test.[13] The CTBTO also detected and investigated elevated concentrations of radioxenon, but found these 'not conclusive with regard to a possible association to the seismic event on 3 September'. It therefore determined that 'no CTBT-relevant radionuclides were detected by the IMS that could be unambiguously linked to a nuclear test in DPRK in September 2017'.[14]

Discussion of the September 2017 test results

North Korea does not announce the planned or measured yields from its test explosions. Estimates made by international researchers vary significantly. The published body-wave magnitude measurements—an unambiguous way of registering the size of a seismic event—ranged from 5.7 to 6.3.[15] As a result of this discrepancy and differences in the empirical methods used to convert

[9] Kitov, I. O. and Rozhkov, M. V., 'Discrimination of the DPRK underground explosions and their aftershocks using the P/S spectral amplitude ratio', Cornell University Library, Preprint, 5 Dec. 2017.

[10] Lee (note 2).

[11] Dill, C., 'North Korea nuclear test: "tunnel collapse" may provide clues', BBC News, 3 Sep. 2017.

[12] Fedchenko and Ferm Hellgren (note 1), p. 553; and Comprehensive Nuclear-Test-Ban Treaty Organization (CTBTO), 'CTBTO detects radioactivity consistent with 12 February announced North Korean nuclear test', Press release, 23 Apr. 2013.

[13] Yonhap News Agency, 'Traces of xenon detected in S. Korea following N. Korea's nuke test', 8 Sep. 2017.

[14] American Geophysical Union (AGU), Proceedings of the AGU Fall Meeting 2017, New Orleans, 11–15 Dec. 2017. For a detailed discussion of CTBT-relevant radionuclides and the CTBTO procedures for their detection and analysis see De Geer, L. E., 'Radionuclide signatures for post-explosion environments', ed. V. Fedchenko, SIPRI, The New Nuclear Forensics: Analysis of Nuclear Materials for Security Purposes (Oxford University Press: Oxford, 2015), pp. 128–55.

[15] For further detail on body-wave magnitude see the United States Geological Survey website.

these values into explosive yields, yield estimates ranged from 50 kilotons to 1 megaton.[16] Most researchers agree, however, that the September 2017 test was about an order of magnitude larger than the previous one in September 2016. For example, the US Government's assessment of the explosive yield is 140 kt, the Norwegian Government's figure is 120 kt and the Swedish Government and Chinese university researchers, working independently, estimate a yield in the range of 100–200 kt.[17]

Most commentators found North Korea's claim that the nuclear explosive device tested on 3 September 2017 was a thermonuclear weapon to be plausible.[18] It should be noted, however, that these findings, which may indeed be correct, are based on indirect evidence. The only direct evidence associated with the event that is described in open sources is seismic wave data. Seismic waves can provide evidence of the size of the explosion but do not give information on the nuclear, boosted or thermonuclear nature of the explosive device, or on whether the test device used uranium or plutonium. The radioactive debris—and specifically the radioactive micro-particles—associated with the explosion must be analysed to discern that kind of detail.[19]

The explosive yield of the tested device is consistent with all three of the above-mentioned types of weapon (nuclear, boosted or thermonuclear) and therefore cannot be used to discriminate between them. For example, the B61 nuclear bomb—a true thermonuclear two-stage gravity bomb currently deployed in the US arsenal—reportedly has variants with yields of between a few kilotons and 300 kt.[20] By contrast, the largest publicly known pure-fission nuclear explosive device ever tested by the USA, the Ivy King test explosion on 16 November 1952, had a yield of about 500 kt.[21] Moreover, some commentators point out that it is technically easier to achieve a 100-kt yield in an underground test with no constraints on size and weight than to design a miniature warhead with a yield of 10–20 kt.[22]

[16] See table 6.15; and Incorporated Research Institutions of Seismology, 'Special event: 2017 North Korean nuclear test', 23 Jan. 2018.

[17] Panda, A., 'US intelligence: North Korea's sixth test was a 140 kiloton "advanced nuclear" device', The Diplomat, 6 Sep. 2017; NORSAR, 'Large nuclear test in North Korea on 3 September 2017', 3 Sep. 2017; University of Science and Technology of China (USTC), 'North Korea's 3 September 2017 nuclear test location and yield: seismic results from USTC', [n.d.]; and Swedish Defence Research Agency (FOI), 'Nuclear weapons test in North Korea', Press release, 11 Sep. 2017.

[18] See e.g. Lewis, J., 'Welcome to the thermonuclear club, North Korea!', Foreign Policy, 4 Sep. 2017.

[19] De Geer (note 14), pp. 128–55.

[20] Hansen, C., Swords of Armageddon, vol. 5 (Chukelea Publications: Sunnyvale, CA, 2007), p. 473.

[21] Hansen (note 20), pp. 96–97.

[22] Kelley, R., 'North Korea's sixth nuclear test: what do we know so far?', SIPRI Expert Comment, 5 Sep. 2017.

Table 6.16. Estimated number of nuclear explosions, 1945–2017

	USA[b]		Russia/ USSR		UK[b]		France		China		India		Pakistan		North Korea		
Year[a]	a	u	a	u	a	u	a	u	a	u	a	u	a	u	a	u	Total
1945	3	–	–	–	–	–	–	–	–	–	–	–	–	–	–	–	3
1946	2[c]	–	–	–	–	–	–	–	–	–	–	–	–	–	–	–	2
1948	3	–	–	–	–	–	–	–	–	–	–	–	–	–	–	–	3
1949	–	–	1	–	–	–	–	–	–	–	–	–	–	–	–	–	1
1951	15	1	2	–	–	–	–	–	–	–	–	–	–	–	–	–	18
1952	10	–	–	–	1	–	–	–	–	–	–	–	–	–	–	–	11
1953	11	–	5	–	2	–	–	–	–	–	–	–	–	–	–	–	18
1954	6	–	10	–	–	–	–	–	–	–	–	–	–	–	–	–	16
1955	17[c]	1	6[c]	–	–	–	–	–	–	–	–	–	–	–	–	–	24
1956	18	–	9	–	6	–	–	–	–	–	–	–	–	–	–	–	33
1957	27	5	16[c]	–	7	–	–	–	–	–	–	–	–	–	–	–	55
1958	62[d]	15	34	–	5	–	–	–	–	–	–	–	–	–	–	–	116
1960	–	–	–	–	–	–	3	–	–	–	–	–	–	–	–	–	3
1961	–	10	58[c]	1	–	–	1	1	–	–	–	–	–	–	–	–	71
1962	39[c]	57	78	1	–	2	–	1	–	–	–	–	–	–	–	–	178
1963	4	43	–	–	–	–	3	–	–	–	–	–	–	–	–	–	50
1964	–	45	–	9	–	2	–	3	1	–	–	–	–	–	–	–	60
1965	–	38	–	14	–	1	–	4	1	–	–	–	–	–	–	–	58
1966	–	48	–	18	–	–	6	1	3	–	–	–	–	–	–	–	76
1967	–	42	–	17	–	–	3	–	2	–	–	–	–	–	–	–	64
1968	–	56	–	17	–	–	5	–	1	–	–	–	–	–	–	–	79
1969	–	46	–	19	–	–	–	–	1	1	–	–	–	–	–	–	67
1970	–	39	–	16	–	–	8	–	1	–	–	–	–	–	–	–	64
1971	–	24	–	23	–	–	5	–	1	–	–	–	–	–	–	–	53
1972	–	27	–	24	–	–	4	–	2	–	–	–	–	–	–	–	57
1973	–	24	–	17	–	–	6	–	1	–	–	–	–	–	–	–	48
1974	–	22	–	21	–	1	9	–	1	–	–	1	–	–	–	–	55
1975	–	22	–	19	–	–	–	2	–	1	–	–	–	–	–	–	44
1976	–	20	–	21	–	1	–	5	3	1	–	–	–	–	–	–	51
1977	–	20	–	24	–	–	–	9	1	–	–	–	–	–	–	–	54
1978	–	19	–	31	–	2	–	11	2	1	–	–	–	–	–	–	66
1979	–	15	–	31	–	1	–	10	1	–	–	–	–	–	–	–	58
1980	–	14	–	24	–	3	–	12	1	–	–	–	–	–	–	–	54
1981	–	16	–	21	–	1	–	12	–	–	–	–	–	–	–	–	50
1982	–	18	–	19	–	1	–	10	–	1	–	–	–	–	–	–	49
1983	–	18	–	25	–	1	–	9	–	2	–	–	–	–	–	–	55
1984	–	18	–	27	–	2	–	8	–	2	–	–	–	–	–	–	57
1985	–	17	–	10	–	1	–	8	–	–	–	–	–	–	–	–	36
1986	–	14	–	–	–	1	–	8	–	–	–	–	–	–	–	–	23
1987	–	14	–	23	–	1	–	8	–	1	–	–	–	–	–	–	47
1988	–	15	–	16	–	–	–	8	–	1	–	–	–	–	–	–	40
1989	–	11	–	7	–	1	–	9	–	–	–	–	–	–	–	–	28
1990	–	8	–	1	–	1	–	6	–	2	–	–	–	–	–	–	18
1991	–	7	–	–	–	1	–	6	–	–	–	–	–	–	–	–	14
1992	–	6	–	–	–	–	–	–	–	2	–	–	–	–	–	–	8

Year[a]	USA[b] a	USA[b] u	Russia/ USSR a	Russia/ USSR u	UK[b] a	UK[b] u	France a	France u	China a	China u	India a	India u	Pakistan a	Pakistan u	North Korea a	North Korea u	Total
1993	–	–	–	–	–	–	–	–	–	1	–	–	–	–	–	–	1
1994	–	–	–	–	–	–	–	–	–	2	–	–	–	–	–	–	2
1995	–	–	–	–	–	–	–	5	–	2	–	–	–	–	–	–	7
1996	–	–	–	–	–	–	–	1	–	2	–	–	–	–	–	–	3
1998	–	–	–	–	–	–	–	–	–	–	–	2[e]	–	2[e]	–	–	4
2006	–	–	–	–	–	–	–	–	–	–	–	–	–	–	–	1	1
2009	–	–	–	–	–	–	–	–	–	–	–	–	–	–	–	1	1
2013	–	–	–	–	–	–	–	–	–	–	–	–	–	–	–	1	1
2016	–	–	–	–	–	–	–	–	–	–	–	–	–	–	–	2	2
2017	–	–	–	–	–	–	–	–	–	–	–	–	–	–	–	1	1
Subtotal	217	815	219	496	21	24	50	160	23	22	–	3	–	2	–	6	
Total	1 032		715		45		210		45		3		2		6		2 058

– = no known test; a = atmospheric (or in a few cases underwater); u = underground[f]; USSR = Soviet Union.

[a] The table includes only those years in which a known explosion took place.

[b] All British tests from 1962 were conducted jointly with the USA at the US Nevada Test Site but are listed only under 'UK' in this table. Thus, the number of US tests is higher than shown. Safety tests carried out by the UK are not included in the table.

[c] One of these tests was carried out underwater.

[d] Two of these tests were carried out underwater.

[e] India's detonations on 11 and 13 May 1998 are listed as 1 test for each date. The 5 detonations by Pakistan on 28 May 1998 are also listed as 1 test.

[f] 'Underground nuclear test' is defined by the 1990 Protocol to the 1974 Soviet–US Threshold Test-Ban Treaty (TTBT) as 'either a single underground nuclear explosion conducted at a test site, or two or more underground nuclear explosions conducted at a test site within an area delineated by a circle having a diameter of two kilometres and conducted within a total period of time of 0.1 second' (section I, para. 2). 'Underground nuclear explosion' is defined by the 1976 Soviet–US Peaceful Nuclear Explosions Treaty (PNET) as 'any individual or group underground nuclear explosion for peaceful purposes' (Article II(a)). 'Group explosion' is defined as 'two or more individual explosions for which the time interval between successive individual explosions does not exceed five seconds and for which the emplacement points of all explosives can be inter-connected by straight line segments, each of which joins two emplacement points and each of which does not exceed 40 kilometres' (Article II(c)).

Sources: Bergkvist, N.-O. and Ferm, R., Nuclear Explosions 1945–1998 (Swedish Defence Research Establishment/SIPRI: Stockholm, July 2000); Swedish Defence Research Agency (FOI), various estimates, including information from the Comprehensive Nuclear-Test-Ban Treaty Organization (CTBTO) International Data Centre and from the Swedish National Data Centre provided to the author in Feb. 2007 and Oct. 2009; Reports from the Australian Seismological Centre, Australian Geological Survey Organisation, Canberra; US Department of Energy (DOE), United States Nuclear Tests: July 1945 through September 1992 (DOE: Washington, DC, 1994); Norris, R. S., Burrows, A. S. and Fieldhouse, R. W., Natural Resources Defense Council, Nuclear Weapons Databook, vol. 5, British, French and Chinese Nuclear Weapons (Westview: Boulder, CO, 1994); Direction des centres d'experimentations nucléaires (DIRCEN) and Commissariat à l'Énergie Atomique (CEA), Assessment of French Nuclear Testing (DIRCEN and CEA: Paris, 1998); Russian ministries of Atomic Energy and Defence, USSR Nuclear Weapons Tests and Peaceful Nuclear Explosions, 1949 through 1990 (Russian Federal Nuclear Centre (VNIIEF): Sarov, 1996); and Natural Resources Defense Council, 'Archive of nuclear data', various years.

The estimated number of nuclear explosions, 1945–2017

Since 1945 there have been 2058 known nuclear explosions carried out by eight states—the USA, the Soviet Union, the United Kingdom, France, China, India, Pakistan and North Korea (see table 6.16). This total includes nuclear tests conducted in nuclear weapon test programmes, explosions carried out for peaceful purposes and the nuclear bombs dropped on Hiroshima and Nagasaki in August 1945. The total also includes tests for safety purposes carried out by France, the Soviet Union and the USA, irrespective of the yield and of whether they caused a nuclear explosion.[23] It does not include subcritical experiments that did not sustain a nuclear chain reaction. Simultaneous detonations, also known as salvo explosions, were carried out by the USA (from 1963) and the Soviet Union (from 1965), mainly for economic reasons.[24] A total of 20 per cent of the Soviet tests and 6 per cent of the US tests were salvo experiments.

No verified nuclear tests have been carried out by Israel. There are assertions that the unexpected 'double flash' registered by the US Vela 6911 satellite in September 1979 was an indication of a nuclear weapon test conducted by Israel with support from South Africa. However, this assertion has never been officially confirmed by either government.[25]

A number of moratoriums on testing, both voluntary and legal, have been observed. The Soviet Union, the UK and the USA observed a moratorium from November 1958 to September 1961. The 1963 Partial Test-Ban Treaty (PTBT), which prohibits nuclear explosions in the atmosphere, in outer space and underwater, entered into force on 10 October 1963.[26] The Soviet Union observed a unilateral moratorium on testing between August 1985 and February 1987. The Soviet Union and then Russia observed a moratorium on testing from January 1991 and the USA from October 1992, until they signed the CTBT on 24 September 1996. France observed a similar moratorium from April 1992 to September 1995. The CTBT, which has not yet entered into force, would prohibit the carrying out of any nuclear explosion.[27]

---

[23] In a safety experiment, or a safety trial, more or less fully developed nuclear devices are subjected to simulated accident conditions. The nuclear weapon core is destroyed by conventional explosives with either no or a very small release of fission energy. The UK has also carried out numerous safety tests but they are not included in table 6.16.

[24] The Soviet Union conducted simultaneous tests of up to 8 devices on 23 Aug. 1975 and 24 Oct. 1990 (the last Soviet test).

[25] Weiss, L., 'Flash from the past: why an apparent Israeli nuclear test in 1979 matters today', *Bulletin of the Atomic Scientists*, 8 Sep. 2015.

[26] India, Pakistan, Russia, the UK and the USA are among the parties. For a full list see annex A, section I, in this volume.

[27] China, France, Russia, the UK and the USA are among the parties. For a full list see annex A, section I, in this volume.

Part III. Non-proliferation, arms control and disarmament, 2017

Chapter 7. Nuclear disarmament, arms control and non-proliferation

Chapter 8. Chemical and biological security threats

Chapter 9. Conventional arms control

Chapter 10. Dual-use and arms trade controls

7. Nuclear disarmament, arms control and non-proliferation

Overview

There was important new momentum behind global efforts to promote nuclear disarmament and non-proliferation in 2017. The year was marked by the negotiation and opening for signature of the new Treaty on the Prohibition of Nuclear Weapons (TPNW). The treaty is the first legally binding international agreement to comprehensively prohibit nuclear weapons, with the ultimate goal of their total elimination. The opening of negotiations on the treaty had been mandated by a United Nations General Assembly resolution at the end of 2016 that had in turn been motivated by the growing international awareness of the devastating humanitarian consequences of any use of nuclear weapons (see section I). These steps reflected the frustration of many non-nuclear weapon states that the nuclear weapon states were not taking seriously their obligation under the 1968 Non-Proliferation Treaty (NPT) to pursue nuclear disarmament. While proponents of the TPNW acknowledged that it would probably have no immediate impact on existing nuclear arsenals, they highlighted its long-term normative impact—it would serve to delegitimize and stigmatize nuclear weapons and thereby contribute to achieving the ultimate goal of nuclear disarmament. At the same time, there was a recognition during the year that the relationship between the TPNW, the NPT and related agreements would have to be defined over time in order to prevent the fragmentation of nuclear disarmament efforts.

Russia and the United States continued to implement the 2010 Treaty on Measures for the Further Reduction and Limitation of Strategic Offensive Arms (New START). However, the prospects for sustaining the progress made in Russian–US nuclear arms control since the end of the cold war appeared to be increasingly remote. New START will expire in 2021 unless both parties agree to extend it, and neither Russia nor the USA expressed interest in negotiating deeper reductions in their deployed strategic nuclear forces beyond those mandated by New START. At the same time, the USA continued to allege that Russia was violating an important cold war-era arms control treaty, the 1987 Soviet–US Treaty on the Elimination of Intermediate-Range and Shorter-Range Missiles (INF Treaty), by deploying a new ground-launched cruise missile proscribed by the treaty (see section II). These developments come against the background of the further deterioration in political relations between Russia and the USA that underscored fundamental differences in their respective goals and priorities for arms control.

SIPRI Yearbook 2018: Armaments, Disarmament and International Security
www.sipriyearbook.org

There were also developments during the year related to other multilateral treaties and initiatives on nuclear disarmament, arms control and non-proliferation (see section III). In February the Conference on Disarmament (CD), the world's sole multilateral forum for negotiating arms control and disarmament agreements, renewed efforts to break the deadlock that has left it unable to adopt a programme of work since 2009. It established a working group on 'the way ahead' to take stock of the progress on all CD agenda items and to identify common ground for a programme of work with a negotiating mandate. In May the first session of the Preparatory Committee for the 2020 NPT Review Conference was convened in Vienna. There were also events connectedwithtwoitemsof'unfinishedbusiness'onthemultilateraldisarmament and non-proliferation agenda: a fissile material cut-off treaty (FMCT) and the 1996 Comprehensive Nuclear-Test-Ban Treaty (CTBT). In July and August a high-level expert preparatory group met in Geneva to consider ways to commence negotiations on an FMCT. In September the 10th Conference on Facilitating the Entry into Force of the CTBT was held in New York.

North Korea's programmes to develop nuclear and other weapons of mass destruction, in contravention of UN Security Council resolutions, remained the source of grave international concern (see section IV). During the year, the Security Council adopted three additional resolutions imposing new or expanded sanctions on North Korea in response to its nuclear weapon and ballistic missile testing activities.

In 2017 Iran continued to implement the Joint Comprehensive Plan of Action (JCPOA) to limit its nuclear programme (see section V). The JCPOA was agreed in July 2015 between Iran and the E3/EU+3. During the year, however, political tensions between Iran and the USA threatened to undermine the JCPOA. In October US President Donald J. Trump refused to certify that the continued lifting of US sanctions was proportional to Iran's actions under the JCPOA—a decision that under US law triggered a 60-day review period for the US Congress to decide whether to reimpose the sanctions on Iran that were lifted under the agreement. Although Congress did not subsequently decide to do so, Trump's decertification decision put the USA at odds with all the other signatories of the JCPOA.

SHANNON N. KILE AND TYTTI ERÄSTÖ

I. Treaty on the Prohibition of Nuclear Weapons

SHANNON N. KILE

The landmark Treaty on the Prohibition of Nuclear Weapons (TPNW) was opened for signature on 20 September 2017 after a relatively short period of negotiation. The treaty is the first legally binding international agreement to comprehensively prohibit the development, deployment or use of nuclear weapons, with the ultimate goal of their total elimination. As such, it marks the culmination of an international movement to establish a normative and legal basis for banning nuclear weapons. As of 31 December 2017, the TPNW had been signed by 56 states and ratified by 3.[1] The treaty will enter into force 90 days after 50 states have ratified it.

The TPNW remains controversial, and international support for it remains far from universal. None of the nuclear weapon-possessing states or their allies have expressed a willingness to join the treaty. While the TPNW's practical and normative implications will only be discernible with time, it has already sparked debate about the future of nuclear weapons and the multilateral juridical framework for nuclear disarmament.

This section recounts the origins of the negotiation of the TPNW, summarizes the main issues considered during the talks and the steps leading to the treaty's adoption, and examines the principal arguments that have been made in favour of and against a nuclear weapon ban treaty. Finally, it highlights the key issues to be addressed to ensure that the treaty supplements rather than supplants existing nuclear arms control and related regulatory measures.

The origins of the nuclear weapon ban treaty negotiations

The interest in a treaty prohibiting the possession or use of nuclear weapons reflects the growing international awareness in recent years of the catastrophic humanitarian consequences of any use of nuclear weapons.[2] The humanitarian dimension was raised in the final document of the 2010 Review Conference of the 1968 Treaty on the Non-Proliferation of Nuclear Weapons (Non-Proliferation Treaty, NPT). The states parties to the NPT expressed 'deep concern at the catastrophic humanitarian consequences of any use of nuclear weapons' and reaffirmed the need 'for all States at all times to comply with applicable international law, including international

---

[1] For a summary and other details of the TPNW see annex A, section I, in this volume.

[2] Kmentt, A., 'The development of the international initiative on the humanitarian impact of nuclear weapons and its effect on the nuclear weapons debate', *International Review of the Red Cross*, vol. 97, no. 899 (Sep. 2015), pp. 681–709.

humanitarian law'.[3] This language was interpreted as a mandate to take action to highlight the humanitarian impact of nuclear weapons.

A series of international conferences on the humanitarian impact of nuclear weapons was subsequently convened, which brought together states, international organizations and civil society groups. These were held in Oslo on 4–5 March 2013, in Nayarit, Mexico, on 13–14 February 2014 and in Vienna on 8–9 December 2014.

One of the main achievements of the conferences was to call international attention to the humanitarian dimension of nuclear disarmament by providing well-documented analyses of the ways in which the use of nuclear weapons would cause profound and long-term damage to the environment, the climate, human health and well-being, and socio-economic development irrespective of national borders. The overarching conclusion from the conference presentations was that no single state or international body could address in an adequate manner the immediate humanitarian emergency caused by a nuclear weapon detonation or provide sufficient assistance to those affected.[4]

At the end of the third and final conference, Austria made a national pledge to work 'to fill the legal gap for the prohibition and elimination of nuclear weapons' and 'to cooperate . . . in efforts to stigmatise, prohibit and eliminate nuclear weapons in light of their unacceptable humanitarian consequences and associated risks'.[5] The Austrian pledge was subsequently internationalized as the Humanitarian Pledge for the Prohibition and Elimination of Nuclear Weapons, which was adopted in a resolution by the United Nations General Assembly on 7 December 2015.[6]

The open-ended working group and diverging approaches to disarmament

Concurrent with the adoption of the Humanitarian Pledge, the UN General Assembly established an open-ended working group (OEWG) to consider concrete legal measures, norms and recommendations for the advancement of multilateral nuclear disarmament negotiations that would lead to a world without nuclear weapons.[7] Three OEWG meetings were held in Geneva, in

---

[3] 2010 NPT Review Conference, Final Document, Vol. I, NPT/CONF.2010/50 (Vol. I), para. 80, 28 May 2010, p. 19; and for a summary and other details of the NPT see annex A, section I, in this volume.

[4] Williams, H., Lewis, P. and Aghlani, S., *The Humanitarian Impacts of Nuclear Weapons Initiative: The 'Big Tent' in Disarmament*, Research paper (Royal Institute of International Affairs, Chatham House: London, Mar. 2015), pp. 10–12.

[5] Austrian Federal Ministry for Europe, Integration and Foreign Affairs, 'Pledge presented at the Vienna Conference on the Humanitarian Impact of Nuclear Weapons', 9 Dec. 2014.

[6] UN General Assembly Resolution 70/48, 'Humanitarian pledge for the prohibition and elimination of nuclear weapons', adopted 7 Dec. 2015, A/RES/70/48, 11 Dec. 2015.

[7] UN General Assembly Resolution 70/33, 'Taking forward multilateral nuclear disarmament negotiations', adopted 7 Dec. 2015, A/RES/70/33, 11 Dec. 2015. An OEWG is 'open' in the sense that all UN member states can participate.

February, May and August 2016. None of the nuclear weapon-possessing states participated in the meetings.

The OEWG considered four distinct approaches to nuclear disarmament that had featured frequently in debates in the First Committee of the UN General Assembly (on disarmament and international security) and the NPT review cycle. These approaches focused on: (*a*) a comprehensive nuclear weapons convention that would involve the participation of all nuclear weapon-possessing states from the outset and would establish provisions for the prohibition and elimination of nuclear weapons, including effective means for verification and inspection; (*b*) a nuclear weapon ban treaty that would provide the basic prohibitions and obligations for all states parties and establish political objectives for the complete elimination of nuclear weapons but would not include provisions on existing nuclear arsenals and their elimination or on verification, and would not necessarily need to be universal from the outset; (*c*) a framework (or 'chapeau') agreement that would establish key prohibitions and provide for the subsequent negotiation of protocols to elaborate measures for the elimination of nuclear weapons and related objectives; and (*d*) a progressive approach, building on existing nuclear disarmament, non-proliferation and security agreements and arrangements, that would elaborate parallel legal and non-legal measures as well as confidence-building measures leading to a comprehensive nuclear weapons convention after a 'minimization point' has been reached.[8]

The OEWG discussions on the feasibility and effectiveness of the various approaches revealed a clear division among the participating states on pre-ferred approaches to taking forward multilateral nuclear disarmament. This division tended to reflect a country's status under the NPT and its member-ship of other treaty regimes and military alliances.[9]

A majority of the non-nuclear weapon states (NNWS) in the OEWG expressed support for a treaty banning nuclear weapons. At the May 2016 session, 10 NNWS jointly submitted a working paper formally proposing a 2017 conference to launch negotiations on a nuclear weapon ban treaty (approach b above).[10] The proposal was opposed by, among others, many of the NNWS members of the North Atlantic Treaty Organization (NATO),

[8] United Nations, General Assembly, Report of the open-ended working group taking forward multilateral nuclear disarmament negotiations, A/71/371, 1 Sep. 2016. The 'minimization point' refers to a situation where nuclear weapons have been greatly reduced from current numbers to a minimal number from which the next step would be the elimination of all nuclear weapons.

[9] Nielsen, J., '2016 open ended working group: Towards 2017 nuclear weapon ban negotiations?', Arms Control Wonk, 13 Sep. 2016.

[10] United Nations, General Assembly, Open-ended working group taking forward multilateral nuclear disarmament negotiations, 'Addressing nuclear disarmament: Recommendations from the perspective of nuclear-weapon-free zones', Working paper submitted by Argentina, Brazil, Costa Rica, Ecuador, Guatemala, Indonesia, Malaysia, Mexico, Philippines and Zambia, A/AC.286/WP.34/Rev.1, 11 May 2016.

which along with Australia, Japan and the Republic of Korea (South Korea) have defence arrangements with the United States that include extended nuclear deterrence. These so-called nuclear umbrella states favoured the progressive approach (*d* above), based on using effective legal and practical measures as 'building blocks' to support progress towards nuclear disarmament, without a defined timeline.[11]

Despite this and other substantive disagreements, the OEWG was able to adopt, through a series of procedural manoeuvres, a final report in its concluding session in August 2016. The report recommended that the UN General Assembly convene a conference in 2017 to begin negotiations on a legally binding instrument for the prohibition and elimination of nuclear weapons.[12]

The UN General Assembly adopts a ban resolution

The 2016 session of the UN General Assembly's First Committee approved a draft resolution on convening negotiations in 2017 on 'a legally binding instrument to prohibit nuclear weapons, leading towards their total elimination'.[13] Among the states voting against the draft resolution were France, the United Kingdom and the USA, which released a joint explanation of their votes in which they declared that the ban on nuclear weapons proposed in the resolution 'can in no way constitute an acceptable basis for negotiations'. They stated that a consensus-based, 'step-by-step approach is the only way to combine the imperatives of disarmament and of the maintenance of global security'.[14]

On 23 December 2016 the UN General Assembly adopted the draft resolution forwarded by the First Committee as Resolution 71/258 by a vote of 113 states in favour, 35 against and 13 abstentions.[15] Of the nine states that are known or believed to possess nuclear weapons, only the Democratic People's Republic of Korea (DPRK, or North Korea) voted in favour; China, India and Pakistan abstained; and France, Israel, Russia, the UK and the USA voted against.[16] Among the other states voting against the resolution were all the

---

[11] United Nations, General Assembly, Open-ended working group taking forward multilateral nuclear disarmament negotiations, 'A progressive approach to a world free of nuclear weapons: Revisiting the building blocks paradigm', Working paper submitted by Australia, Belgium, Bulgaria, Canada, Estonia, Finland, Germany, Hungary, Italy, Japan, Latvia, Lithuania, Netherlands, Poland, Portugal, Romania, Slovakia and Spain, A/AC.286/WP.9, 24 Feb. 2016.

[12] United Nations, General Assembly, Report of the open-ended working group taking forward multilateral nuclear disarmament negotiations, A/71/371, 1 Sep. 2016, para. 67.

[13] United Nations, General Assembly, First Committee, Resolution on 'Taking forward multilateral nuclear disarmament negotiations', A/C.1/71/L.41, 14 Oct. 2016, para. 8.

[14] France, United Kingdom and United States, 'Explanation of vote', delivered by France, 27 Oct. 2016.

[15] UN General Assembly Resolution 71/258, 'Taking forward multilateral nuclear disarmament negotiations', adopted 23 Dec. 2016, A/RES/71/258, 11 Jan. 2017.

[16] International Campaign to Abolish Nuclear Weapons, 'Voting on UN resolution for nuclear ban treaty', 23 Dec. 2016.

NATO member states except the Netherlands, which abstained, as well as Australia, Japan and South Korea, which have extended nuclear deterrence commitments from the USA.

The negotiation of the treaty

Opening of the negotiations

Prior to the opening of the UN Conference to Negotiate a Legally Binding Instrument to Prohibit Nuclear Weapons, a one-day organizational meeting was held in New York on 16 February 2017, attended by more than 100 states. The participating states elected Ambassador Elayne Whyte Gómez of Costa Rica as the president of the conference and adopted a provisional agenda for the first substantive session, which was scheduled for March.[17] The states also agreed that the conference's rules of procedure would be those used by the UN General Assembly, which require, among other things, a two-thirds majority for matters of substance and a simple majority for procedural matters. This meant that no single state or small group of states would be able to block the conference's decisions.[18]

The opening session of the conference took place in New York on 27–31 March 2017. More than 130 states participated, along with representatives from international organizations and civil society groups. No nuclear weapon-possessing state took part in the meeting, and of the NNWS allied with the USA only the Netherlands participated in the talks.[19] In an October 2016 memorandum, the USA had warned other NATO members that efforts to negotiate a treaty prohibiting nuclear weapons or to delegitimize nuclear deterrence were 'fundamentally at odds with NATO's basic policies on deterrence' and urged them not to participate in the negotiations on a ban treaty.[20]

The discussion in the opening session focused on the purpose and scope of the proposed treaty. There was general agreement among the states about the core prohibitions to be codified in the treaty text. These included prohibitions on the use, possession, development, acquisition, transfer and

---

[17] United Nations, 'United Nations conference to negotiate ban on nuclear weapons holds first organizational meeting, adopts agenda for 2017 substantive session', Press Release DC/3685, 16 Feb. 2017; and Ware, A., 'UN commences nuclear abolition negotiations', Abolition 2000, 24 Feb. 2017.

[18] Rauf, T., '2017: The year in which nuclear weapons could be banned?', Commentary, SIPRI, 20 Mar. 2017.

[19] The Dutch Government attended the meeting at the insistence of a majority of the parties in parliament, which in turn reflected civil society sentiment. In May 2016 the Dutch Parliament adopted a motion urging the government to work for an international ban on nuclear weapons. Van Oostward, S., 'The Netherlands should actively negotiate an international nuclear weapons ban treaty', International Campaign to Abolish Nuclear Weapons, 23 May 2016.

[20] US Mission to NATO, 'Defense impacts of potential United Nations General Assembly nuclear weapons ban treaty', Non-paper, AC/333-N(2016)0029 (INV), 17 Oct. 2016; and International Campaign to Abolish Nuclear Weapons, 'US pressured NATO states to vote no to a ban', 1 Nov. 2016.

deployment of nuclear weapons as well as on assistance with prohibited activities.

However, there were disagreements on a number of questions regarding the treaty's scope. These included differences over whether to prohibit the threat of use of nuclear weapons. Proposed language to prohibit nuclear threats 'under any circumstances' was eventually dropped, in part because of concern that many NNWS members of NATO would see it as being incompatible with their NATO obligations and would hence reject the treaty. Proposed language prohibiting the transit of nuclear weapons through the territories of signatory states—a prohibition set out in existing nuclear weapon-free-zone treaties—was similarly excluded from the draft text of the treaty. States were also divided over whether the treaty text should include language banning nuclear testing; some expressed concern that such a prohibition could come into conflict with the 1996 Comprehensive Nuclear-Test-Ban Treaty (CTBT) and therefore undermine efforts to secure its entry into force.[21]

More fundamentally, states diverged on whether the TPNW would need its own verification protocols in addition to those that exist under the NPT. There was disagreement over whether the treaty should contain provisions for the verified dismantlement and physical elimination of nuclear weapon stockpiles, or leave this for later negotiations with nuclear weapon states— possibly in connection with discussions on a process for the accession by these states to the treaty. There was also no consensus on whether the treaty should be formally linked with the verification system established by the International Atomic Energy Agency (IAEA), in particular, with the application of IAEA safeguards.[22]

There was broad agreement among the participating states that the treaty should have a relatively simple text that codified the norms of the non-use and non-possession of nuclear weapons. By leaving more detailed legal and technical measures for subsequent negotiations, the initial agreement could be concluded relatively quickly. A few states, including Iran and Egypt, expressed interest in a more comprehensive treaty with extensive prohibitions and verification provisions that would probably have taken considerably longer to negotiate.[23]

[21] Acheson, R., *Banning Nuclear Weapons: Principles and Elements for a Legally Binding Instrument* (Women's International League for Peace and Freedom: Geneva, Mar. 2017); and Meier, O., Cordes, S. and Suh, E., 'What participants in a nuclear weapons ban treaty (do not) want', *Bulletin of the Atomic Scientists*, 9 June 2017.

[22] Carlson, J., 'Nuclear weapon ban convention: Overview of first draft', Nuclear Threats Monitor, Asia-Pacific Leadership Network, 26 May 2017; and Meier, Cordes and Suh (note 21).

[23] Potter, W. C., 'Disarmament diplomacy and the nuclear ban treaty', *Survival*, vol. 59, no. 4 (Aug.–Sep. 2017), p. 96.

Completion of the negotiations

On 22 May 2017 the president of the conference circulated an initial draft of the treaty.[24] The draft text reflected debates and informal consultations during the first round of negotiations and served as the basis for the second round, which began at the UN headquarters in New York on 15 June.

There was general agreement among the participating states about the basic purpose of the treaty, as explained in the preamble, and the general obligations set out in Article 1. It would oblige all state parties to prohibit the possession, development, production, transfer and use of nuclear weapons, and to prohibit assisting any other state with any of these activities. In addition, the treaty would prohibit a state party from stationing another state's nuclear weapons on its territory.

The draft text included a prohibition on the parties from carrying out 'any nuclear weapon test explosion or any other nuclear explosion', but this was excluded from the final text. Cuba and Iran also proposed the addition of prohibitions on the financing and transit of nuclear weapons, but these too were not included in the final text.[25]

One of the most controversial issues during the second round of negotiations dealt with safeguards and related legal instruments intended to ensure that civilian nuclear material and facilities are not used for military purposes. A number of states, led by Sweden and Switzerland, wanted to require all parties to the treaty to agree to negotiate an Additional Protocol to their safeguards agreements with the IAEA.[26] However, Brazil and other states opposed making mandatory what had previously been a voluntary agreement. The final text instead required states that have yet to negotiate a comprehensive safeguards agreement with the IAEA to do so, and for all other states to maintain at a minimum their IAEA safeguards obligations in force at the time of the treaty's entry into force. This led some observers to complain that the treaty framers had missed an opportunity to promote state-of-the-art safeguards practices that would strengthen nuclear disarmament efforts.[27]

Following a series of parallel consultations led by the conference president, a final draft of the treaty was completed on 7 July 2017, which was the end date recommended in UN General Assembly Resolution 71/258. The

[24] United Nations Conference to Negotiate a Legally Binding Instrument to Prohibit Nuclear Weapons, Leading Towards Their Total Elimination, 'Draft convention on the prohibition of nuclear weapons', A/CONF.229/2017/CRP.1, 22 May 2017.

[25] Sanders-Zakre, A., 'Nuclear weapons ban treaty adopted', *Arms Control Today*, vol. 47, no. 6 (July/Aug. 2017), pp. 21–22.

[26] An Additional Protocol significantly enhances the IAEA's ability to verify the peaceful use of all nuclear material in states with comprehensive safeguards agreements. International Atomic Energy Agency, 'Additional Protocol', [n.d.].

[27] Wolfsthal, J., 'Second time is not a charm for the nuclear ban treaty', Arms Control Wonk, 29 June 2017.

participating states adopted the treaty text by a vote of 122 in favour, with 1 state (the Netherlands) voting against and 1 state (Singapore) abstaining.[28]

Opening for signature

On 20 September 2017 the Treaty on the Prohibition of Nuclear Weapons opened for signature at the UN headquarters in New York. More than 50 heads of state, heads of government and foreign ministers took part in a signing ceremony held on the margins of the annual opening of the UN General Assembly.[29]

The TPNW will enter into force 90 days after its 50th instrument of ratification has been deposited. This will not be contingent on the ratification of any particular state or group of states. During the treaty negotiations, many states had argued that the TPNW should have simple requirements for entry into force in order to avoid the long-running procedural impasse that has blocked the CTBT's entry into force (see section III).

Contending views on the treaty

The opening for signature of the TPNW highlighted long-standing disputes and divisions over a nuclear weapon ban.[30] Some states have emphasized the need to bridge the division between nuclear weapon-possessing states and non-nuclear weapon states. For example, the Netherlands, the only NATO member state to take part in the negotiations, said that, while it supported a legally binding prohibition in principle, in order to be meaningful it must be comprehensive and verifiable and must eventually gain the support of the nuclear weapon-possessing states.[31]

Arguments in favour of the nuclear weapon ban treaty

Proponents of the prohibition treaty make at least four broad arguments in support of a legal ban on nuclear weapons. These focus primarily on its normative and legal implications.

---

[28] UN News Centre, 'UN conference adopts treaty banning nuclear weapons', 7 July 2017. The Netherlands voted against the treaty on the grounds that it was incompatible with the country's NATO obligations, contained inadequate verification provisions and could undermine the NPT. Permanent Representation of the Netherlands to the United Nations in New York, 'Explanation of vote of the Netherlands on text of Nuclear Ban Treaty', 7 July 2017.

[29] International Campaign to Abolish Nuclear Weapons, 'UN nuclear weapon ban treaty opens for signature', 20 Sep. 2017.

[30] Borrie, J. et al., *A Prohibition on Nuclear Weapons: A Guide to the Issues* (United Nations Institute for Disarmament Research (UNIDIR) and International Law and Policy Institute: Geneva and Oslo, Feb. 2016).

[31] United Nations Conference to negotiate a legally binding instrument to prohibit nuclear weapons, leading towards their total elimination, Statement by the Netherlands, Agenda item 8(b), 28 Mar. 2017.

First, many proponents argue that outlawing nuclear weapons is, above all, a moral and humanitarian imperative.[32] As shown during the conferences on the humanitarian impact of nuclear weapons, the case for prohibiting nuclear weapons is clear: they are by nature inhumane and indiscriminate; and they are uniquely dangerous because they are uniquely destructive. Accordingly, the preamble to the ban treaty acknowledges 'the ethical imperatives for nuclear disarmament and the urgency of achieving and maintaining a nuclear-weapon-free world, which is a global public good of the highest order'.[33]

Second, support for a ban treaty reflects the growing frustration of many non-nuclear weapon states over the lack of progress on multilateral nuclear disarmament under the NPT.[34] The nuclear weapon states have come under increased criticism for their perceived unwillingness to take seriously the commitment under Article VI of the NPT to 'pursue negotiations in good faith on effective measures relating to cessation of the nuclear arms race at an early date and to nuclear disarmament'.[35] There has been particular disappointment that the nuclear weapon states failed to implement many of the steps toward nuclear disarmament agreed at the 2000 and 2010 NPT Review Conferences.[36] This in turn led many non-nuclear weapon states to support the convening of negotiations on a nuclear ban treaty within the UN but outside the context of the NPT.[37]

Third, proponents of a ban treaty argue that it is also a legal imperative, required to fill a gap in international law.[38] They note that biological and chemical weapons, the other two categories of non-conventional weapon, are explicitly prohibited because their use would conflict with the requirements of international humanitarian law. In contrast, although nuclear weapons would have a far more devastating humanitarian impact, there is no general and universally applicable prohibition in international law regarding their possession or use. In the view of many proponents of a nuclear weapon ban treaty, weapons that cause unacceptable harm to civilians cannot remain legal or be considered legitimate options in times of war.

---

[32] Fihn, B., 'The logic of banning nuclear weapons', *Survival*, vol. 59, no. 1 (Feb./Mar. 2017), pp. 43–50; and Sauer, T. and Pretorius, J., 'Nuclear weapons and the humanitarian approach', *Global Change, Peace and Security*, vol. 26, no. 3 (Sep. 2014), pp. 233–50.

[33] Treaty on the Prohibition of Nuclear Weapons (note 1).

[34] Nielsen, J. and Ingram, P., 'Opportunities for effective strategic dialogue: Bridging the nuclear deterrence and disarmament constituencies', British–American Security Information Council (BASIC), 1 Jan. 2017.

[35] Treaty on the Non-Proliferation of Nuclear Weapons (note 3).

[36] See 2000 NPT Review Conference, Final Document, NPT/CONF.2000/28 (Vol. I), section 15, 24 Apr. 2000, pp. 14–15; and 2010 NPT Review Conference, Final Document (note 3), pp. 19–29.

[37] Cronberg, T., 'After 72 years, nuclear weapons have been prohibited', Commentary, SIPRI, 21 July 2017.

[38] Nystuen, G. and Egeland, K., 'A "legal gap"? Nuclear weapons under international law', *Arms Control Today*, vol. 46, no. 3 (Mar. 2016).

Finally, many proponents of the TPNW maintain that the treaty will engender a normative shift in the political discourse about nuclear weapons, away from long-standing claims about the security benefits allegedly provided by nuclear deterrence, and towards the consideration of alternative political and diplomatic strategies based on humanitarian and moral imperatives.[39] The existing NPT regime is unable to unequivocally delegitimize nuclear weapons and the practice of nuclear deterrence, given that it discriminates between nuclear weapon states and non-nuclear weapon states. By prohibiting the possession of nuclear weapons and threats to use them, the TPNW reflects the opposition of the majority of countries in the world to security policies and practices that are premised on nuclear deterrence.[40]

Arguments against the nuclear weapon ban treaty

Opponents of the TPNW tend to argue that the prohibition of nuclear weapons is unnecessary, unrealistic and potentially detrimental to multilateral nuclear disarmament efforts.

First, a number of states that oppose a nuclear weapon ban treaty, such as Canada and the Netherlands, have explicitly rejected the claim that the absence of a law or legal norm prohibiting the possession of nuclear weapons constitutes a legal gap.[41] They note that, while an advisory opinion issued by the International Court of Justice in 1996 imposed strict limits on the permissible circumstances in which nuclear weapons can be used, under current customary international law the possession and use of such weapons is not illegal. In the view of these states, the NPT continues to provide the necessary and sufficient legal basis for making progress towards disarmament.

Second, many opponents of the TPNW have stressed that it is both an unrealistic nuclear disarmament measure and inadvisable, since the nuclear weapon ban could have adverse consequences for international security. The nuclear weapon states and many states under the US nuclear umbrella have complained that the ban does not take account of the international security environment, the current geopolitical situation and the role of nuclear weapons in existing security doctrines. The USA has cautioned that efforts to delegitimize nuclear weapons will undermine the long-standing strategic stability that underpins the international security structure and regional security arrangements. In particular, the treaty could—and is 'designed by ban advocates to'—'destroy the basis for US nuclear extended deterrence' on

[39] Meyer, P., 'The mirage of nuclear deterrence', *The NPT and the Prohibition Negotiation: Scope for Bridge-building* (UNIDIR: Geneva, May 2017), pp. 3–10.

[40] Mian, Z., 'After the nuclear weapons ban treaty: A new disarmament politics', *Bulletin of the Atomic Scientists*, 7 July 2017.

[41] United Nations, General Assembly, Open-ended Working Group on taking forward multilateral nuclear disarmament negotiations, 'Reflections on the "Legal Gap for the elimination and prohibition of nuclear weapons"', Submitted by Canada, A/AC.286/WP.20, 12 Apr. 2016.

which many US allies and partners depend.[42] In this context, some observers have argued that, intentionally or not, the ban treaty will create divisions between democratic allies and could weaken deterrence of non-democratic governments that will be less constrained by public opinion and the norms reflected in the treaty. This, in turn, would make actual nuclear disarmament less likely.[43]

Third, opponents have expressed concern that the TPNW could create confusion regarding the implementation of the NPT and complicate fulfilment of the NPT's nuclear disarmament obligations. Some states have pointed out that the TPNW provides for a comprehensive parallel review mechanism with a mandate that at least partially overlaps with that of the NPT. This could in turn lead to a fragmentation of disarmament efforts.[44] Concerns have also been raised that the ban treaty could distract attention from the consideration in international forums of important operational steps connected with reducing the risks and dangers posed by nuclear weapons.[45]

Finally, some observers have warned that the TPNW could exacerbate existing non-proliferation challenges. For example, the creation of an alternative treaty structure governing nuclear weapons could lead to 'forum-shopping', in which a state might hope to dilute international condemnation over its non-compliance with the strict verification requirements of the existing NPT by participating in the new, less rigorous treaty.[46] In addition, critics have noted that the inclusion of a three-month withdrawal procedure in Article 18 of the TPNW creates a risk that a state with a clandestine nuclear weapon programme could use the treaty and its protections until it decided to stage a nuclear 'breakout' with little warning.[47]

Next steps

While the adoption and opening for signature of the TPNW marked an important achievement, the treaty itself provides only a general legal and normative framework for nuclear disarmament. The TPNW must ultimately be complemented by a verifiable, enforceable nuclear disarmament regime if the current divide between the nuclear weapon 'haves' and 'have nots' is to be bridged. The process of designing a prototype disarmament regime will

---

[42] US Mission to NATO (note 20).

[43] Harries, M., 'The real problem with a nuclear ban treaty', Nuclear Policy Program, Carnegie Endowment for International Peace, 15 Mar. 2017.

[44] Permanent Representation of the Netherlands to the United Nations in New York (note 28).

[45] Sagan, S. and Valentino, B. A., 'The nuclear weapons ban treaty: Opportunities lost', Bulletin of the Atomic Scientists, 16 July 2017.

[46] Mount, A. and Nephew, R., 'A nuclear weapons ban should first do no harm to the NPT', Bulletin of the Atomic Scientists, 7 Mar. 2017.

[47] Wolfsthal (note 27).

have to address questions not considered in the treaty negotiations, such as which activities, materials and facilities useful for developing and producing nuclear weapons must be prohibited, and how to manage and monitor nuclear activities with both military and civilian applications.[48]

While the treaty provides for the accession of nuclear weapon-possessing states and allows for the designation of a 'competent international authority' to verify the irreversible disarmament of such a state, that authority is not identified in the treaty. As a result, there is a need to identify the national and international transparency and verification protocols required by disarming states, and which international body or bodies would have responsibility for enforcing such a regime.[49]

The TPNW is unlikely to have any impact for the foreseeable future on the nuclear arsenals and modernization plans of the nine nuclear weapon-possessing states.[50] None of these states participated in the treaty negotiations and none has indicated that it will join the treaty. Against this background, critics of the TPNW are likely to continue to challenge what many treaty proponents highlight as its main long-term contribution: that it will serve to delegitimize and stigmatize nuclear weapons for future generations and thereby contribute to achieving the ultimate goal of nuclear disarmament.

---

[48] Perkovich, G., 'The nuclear ban treaty: What would follow?', Nuclear Policy Program, Carnegie Endowment for International Peace, 31 May 2017.

[49] Perkovich (note 48); and Arms Control Association, 'The Treaty on the Prohibition of Nuclear Weapons at a glance', Fact sheet, July 2017.

[50] For detail about the size and composition of the nuclear warhead inventories of the 9 nuclear weapon-possessing states see chapter 6, sections I–IX, in this volume.

II. Russian–United States nuclear arms control

SHANNON N. KILE

In 2017 the prospects for advancing the Russian–US nuclear arms control and disarmament agenda continued to diminish. The role of arms control as one of the foundations of the post-cold war strategic relationship between Russia and the United States came under increasing strain as political relations between the two countries deteriorated further. The situation was complicated by the new US administration's emphasis on making future discussions about arms control and disarmament contingent on effective verification of compliance with existing agreements.

Implementation of New START

Russia and the USA continued to implement the bilateral 2010 Treaty on Measures for the Further Reduction and Limitation of Strategic Offensive Arms (New START).[1] Under the treaty the two parties agreed to limit the number of their deployed strategic nuclear warheads to 1550 each and to limit the number of their deployed strategic missile launchers and heavy bombers equipped for nuclear armaments to 700 each.[2] The biannual treaty data collected in September 2017 showed that both Russian and US holdings were under most of the final treaty limits (see table 7.1).[3]

New START contains transparency and verification measures—such as biannual data exchanges, notifications and up to 18 on-site inspections annually—that have contributed to building mutual confidence between the parties about the size and composition of their respective strategic nuclear forces.[4] The 13th session of the treaty's Bilateral Consultative Commission was held in Geneva on 29 March–11 April 2017 to discuss practical issues related to its implementation.[5]

When fully implemented by February 2018, New START will result in modest reductions in Russian and US deployed strategic nuclear forces. However, these forces constitute only a relatively small proportion of their total nuclear weapon inventories. New START does not limit the two coun-

---

[1] For a summary and other details of New START see annex A, section III, in this volume.

[2] Due to New START's counting rules, these numbers do not reflect the actual deployment of strategic warheads and launchers. This is mainly because bombers are counted as carrying only 1 weapon each, even though they can carry many more air-launched cruise missiles. See also chapter 6, sections I and II, in this volume.

[3] US Department of State, Bureau of Arms Control, Verification and Compliance, 'New START Treaty aggregate numbers of strategic offensive arms', Fact sheet, 18 Jan. 2018.

[4] For a summary of inspection activities see US Department of State, 'New START treaty inspection activities', [n.d.].

[5] US Department of State, Office of the Spokesperson, 'Thirteenth session of the bilateral consultative commission under the New START Treaty', Media note, 12 Apr. 2017.

Table 7.1. Russian and US aggregate numbers of strategic offensive arms under New START, as of 5 Feb. 2011 and 1 Sep. 2017

Category of data	Treaty limits[a]	Russia		United States	
		Feb. 2011	Sep. 2017	Feb. 2011	Sep. 2017
Deployed ICBMs, SLBMs and heavy bombers	700	521	501	882	660
Warheads on deployed ICBMs, SLBMs and heavy bombers[b]	1550	1537	1561	1800	1393
Deployed and non-deployed launchers of ICBMs, SLBMs and heavy bombers	800	865	790	1124	800

ICBM = intercontinental ballistic missile; SLBM = submarine-launched ballistic missile.

[a] To be reached by 5 Feb. 2018.

[b] Each heavy bomber, whether equipped with cruise missiles or gravity bombs, is counted as carrying only 1 warhead, even though the aircraft can carry larger weapon payloads.

Source: US Department of State, Bureau of Arms Control, Verification and Compliance, 'New START Treaty aggregate numbers of strategic offensive arms', Fact sheets, 1 June 2011 and 18 Jan. 2018.

tries' stocks of operational non-deployed strategic nuclear warheads or retired warheads awaiting dismantlement, which constitute a significant proportion of their overall warhead holdings. Nor does it limit their holdings of non-strategic (tactical) nuclear weapons, which in Russia's case is nearly a quarter of its total inventory of nuclear warheads. As of January 2018 Russia possessed an estimated total of approximately 6600 nuclear warheads, while the USA had approximately 6800 warheads.[6]

New START will expire in February 2021, 10 years after it entered into force, but the treaty stipulates that the parties may agree to extend it for a further 5 years. Against the background of growing pessimism about the future of US–Russian arms control, the year ended with no clear indication of whether the two sides would agree to an extension.[7] Many US officials have expressed an unwillingness to extend the treaty with Russia while the latter is alleged by the USA to be in violation of a seminal cold war-era agreement, still in force, that limits specified types of intermediate-range missile.[8]

[6] For details of the size and composition of Russian and US nuclear warhead inventories see chapter 6, sections I and II, in this volume.

[7] Stewart, P., 'Despite tensions, US sees value in New START treaty with Russia', Reuters, 23 Sep. 2017; and Kozin, V., 'Nuclear disarmament is unthinkable until trust is restored between Russia and the US', OrientalReview.org, 26 Oct. 2017.

[8] Brooks, L., 'After the end of bilateral nuclear arms control', Center for Strategic and International Studies, CSIS Next Generation Nuclear Network, 3 Nov. 2017.

The INF Treaty dispute

In 2017 Russian–US tensions continued to rise over US allegations that Russia was violating the 1987 Soviet–US Treaty on the Elimination of Intermediate-Range and Shorter-Range Missiles (INF Treaty).[9] Under the INF Treaty, the Soviet Union and the USA agreed not to possess, produce or flight test a ballistic missile or ground-launched cruise missile (GLCM) with a range capability of 500 to 5500 kilometres, or to possess or produce launchers for such missiles. In 2014 the USA alleged that Russia was conducting flight tests of a new GLCM with a range proscribed by the treaty. Russia rejected the US allegation as baseless and complained that the USA had failed to provide any evidence or specific facts about the alleged Russian violation.[10]

Russia countered with its own allegations of US non-compliance with the INF Treaty. These included charges that the USA was deploying a missile defence interceptor system in Europe that could also be used to launch prohibited GLCMs; using targets for missile defence tests with similar characteristics to proscribed intermediate-range missiles; and manufacturing armed unmanned aerial vehicles (UAVs, drones) that fall under the treaty's definition of GLCM.[11] The USA dismissed Russia's allegations as an attempt to draw attention away from its own violation of the treaty. According to the US State Department, since 2014 the USA had repeatedly engaged with Russian officials in multiple venues to explain why the US systems and activities of concern are in compliance with the INF Treaty.[12]

New public information about alleged Russian treaty violation

The INF Treaty dispute moved increasingly into the public domain in 2017 after a US decision to provide more information, based on intelligence sources, about the Russian missile system in question. During a hearing in the US Congress in March 2017, the vice chairman of the US Joint Chiefs of Staff, General Paul Selva, confirmed media reports that the USA believed that Russia had begun to deploy the new missile, in violation of 'the spirit and intent' of the INF Treaty.[13] Selva testified that Russia has 'deliberately deployed' the missile to military units 'in order to pose a threat to NATO [the

[9] The current parties to the INF Treaty are the USA and the 4 relevant successor states of the Soviet Union—Belarus, Kazakhstan, Russia and Ukraine. For a summary and other details of the INF Treaty see annex A, section III, in this volume.
[10] Russian Ministry of Foreign Affairs, 'Comments by the Russian Ministry of Foreign Affairs on the report of the US Department of State on Adherence to and Compliance with Arms Control, Nonproliferation, and Disarmament Agreements and Commitments', 1 Aug. 2014.
[11] Russian Ministry of Foreign Affairs (note 10).
[12] US State Department, Bureau of Arms Control, Verification and Compliance, 'Refuting Russian allegations of US noncompliance with the INF Treaty', Fact sheet, 8 Dec. 2017.
[13] US House of Representatives, Armed Services Committee, 'Transcript of hearing on military assessment of nuclear deterrence requirements', 8 Mar. 2017, p. 10; and Gordon, M. R., 'Russia deploys missile, violating treaty and challenging Trump', New York Times, 14 Feb. 2017.

North Atlantic Treaty Organization] and to facilities within the NATO area of responsibility'.

In November 2017 a senior official of the US National Security Council, Christopher Ford, publicly identified the Russian missile system under US scrutiny as the Novator 9M729, which has the NATO designation SSC-8.[14] The existence of the missile had been known for some time, but its technical characteristics and relationship to existing Russian missile systems remained the subject of speculation. It is widely believed to be a ground-based version of the Novator 3M14 Kalibr sea-launched cruise missile.[15] It is unclear, however, whether the new missile can be fitted on the same launcher used by the INF Treaty-compliant 9M728 Iskander-M missile, which would make it difficult for US satellite surveillance to distinguish between the two.[16]

The USA has not made public the evidence that it used in determining that the Novator 9M729 violates the INF Treaty. The US State Department's latest annual report on arms control compliance, released in April 2017, explains the types of information the USA has shared with Russia to support its claim of Russian non-compliance but does not reveal the substance of that information.[17] Some analysts have speculated that the missile may not have been tested to a treaty-proscribed range from a mobile ground-based launcher and that evidence of a violation was indirect, based on a US technical assessment of its range capability.[18] According to the 2017 State Department report, the USA provided Russia with information to show that: 'The violating GLCM has a range capability between 500 and 5500 kilometers'.[19]

Continued deadlock over INF Treaty compliance

On 8 December 2017, the 30th anniversary of the signing of the INF Treaty, the US State Department announced a new US strategy for resolving the INF Treaty dispute. This involved the use of economic and military measures in order 'to induce the Russian Federation to return to compliance', which included a review of the options for new US 'conventional, ground-launched, intermediate-range missile systems'. The announcement noted that the USA

---

[14] Majumdar, D., 'Novator 9M729: The Russian missile that broke INF Treaty's back?', *National Interest*, 7 Dec. 2017.

[15] Podvig, P., 'The INF Treaty culprit identified: Now what?', Russian Strategic Nuclear Forces, 5 Dec. 2017.

[16] Gibbons-Neff, T., 'This is the ground-launched cruise missile that Russia has reportedly just deployed', *Washington Post*, 15 Feb. 2017.

[17] US Department of State, *Adherence to and Compliance with Arms Control, Nonproliferation, and Disarmament Agreements and Commitments* (Department of State: Washington, DC, Apr. 2017), p. 14.

[18] Podvig (note 15). Under the INF Treaty, a ground-launched cruise missile does not have to be flight-tested to a proscribed range to be in violation of the treaty; it is sufficient if the missile has the range capability to be so.

[19] US Department of State (note 17), pp. 13–14.

was prepared to halt such research and development activities if Russia returned to 'full and verifiable compliance with its INF Treaty obligations'.[20] In the previous month, the US Congress approved funding for development work on a new US GLCM system with a range prohibited by the INF Treaty.[21]

In response to the US announcement, the Russian Deputy Foreign Minister, Sergey Ryabkov, denied that the missile system in question contravened the INF Treaty, stating that it had a much shorter range than the USA alleged.[22] A Russian Foreign Ministry statement charged that the USA continued 'to bring forward unfounded accusations of Russia's breaching the treaty'. The statement added that 'attempts to communicate with us in the language of ultimatums or to put military and political pressure on Russia through sanctions . . . are unacceptable'.[23]

On 12–14 December 2017 delegations from the five parties to the INF Treaty—Belarus, Kazakhstan, Russia, Ukraine and the USA—held a meeting in Geneva of the treaty's dispute-resolution mechanism, known as the Special Verification Commission.[24] The delegations expressed a shared view that the INF Treaty continued to play an important role in the existing system of international security, nuclear disarmament and non-proliferation, and should be preserved and strengthened. However, there were no reports of progress being made on resolving the mutual recriminations between Russia and the USA that the other party was not in compliance with the INF Treaty.

Following the meeting, the USA's allies in NATO expressed solidarity with US efforts to ensure Russian compliance with the INF Treaty. The North Atlantic Council—NATO's principal political decision-making body—said in a statement that 'Allies have identified a Russian missile system that raises serious concerns'. It urged Russia 'to address these concerns in a substantial and transparent way, and actively engage in a technical dialogue with the United States'.[25]

[20] US Department of State, 'Trump administration INF Treaty integrated strategy', Press statement, 8 Dec. 2017. Research and development work on an intermediate-range GLCM is not prohibited under the INF Treaty. However, the production and flight-testing of such a missile would violate the treaty.

[21] Reif, K., 'Hill wants development of banned missile', Arms Control Today, vol. 47, no. 10 (Dec. 2017), p. 5; and National Defense Authorization Act for Fiscal Year 2018, US Public Law no. 115-91, signed into law 12 Dec. 2017.

[22] 'Russia hits back at US charges of INF Treaty violations', Radio Free Europe/Radio Liberty, 10 Dec. 2017.

[23] Russian Ministry of Foreign Affairs, 'Comment by the Information and Press Department on the 30th anniversary of the INF Treaty', 2380-08-12-2017, 8 Dec. 2017.

[24] Russian Ministry of Foreign Affairs, 'Press release on the 31st session of the Special Verification Commission under the INF Treaty', 2442-15-12-2017, 15 Dec. 2017. The purpose of the commission is to serve as a forum to 'resolve questions relating to compliance' and to 'agree upon such measures as may be necessary to improve the viability and effectiveness of this Treaty'. INF Treaty (note 9), Article XIII.

[25] North Atlantic Council, 'Statement by the North Atlantic Council on the Intermediate-Range Nuclear Forces (INF) Treaty', Press Release (2017) 180, 15 Dec. 2017.

The future of the INF Treaty

The year ended with growing concern that the INF Treaty dispute between Russia and the USA was building up to a breakdown of the treaty at a time when neither side was showing a strong commitment to preserving it. There was particular concern that the US administration's efforts to put pressure on Russia to return to 'full and verifiable compliance' by pursuing the development of a new cruise missile delivery system that does not comply with the INF Treaty would prove counterproductive. Rather than helping to repair and preserve the INF Treaty, some experts predicted that this could accelerate the treaty's collapse and precipitate a new Russian–US missile competition.[26] Others warned that US allies in Europe may not be willing to accept the deployment of the new missile, and that, as was the case before the INF Treaty was concluded in the 1980s, plans to do so might split NATO.[27]

Moreover, the continued impasse between Russia and the USA over alleged INF Treaty violations threatened to destabilize other agreements such as New START. In doing so, it further eroded the role of arms control in Russian–US strategic relations and raised the prospect that, when New START expires in 2021, there will be no treaty regulating the nuclear balance between the two sides either in force or under negotiation for the first time since the end of the cold war.

[26] Pifer, S., 'The looming end of the INF Treaty', Order from Chaos, Brookings Institution, 8 Dec. 2017.
[27] Krepon, M., 'Responding to the INF Treaty violation', Arms Control Wonk, 5 Mar. 2017.

III. Developments in multilateral nuclear disarmament and non-proliferation

SHANNON N. KILE

Preparatory Committee for the 2020 Non-Proliferation Treaty Review Conference

The Preparatory Committee for the 2020 Review Conference of the Parties to the 1968 Treaty on the Non-proliferation of Nuclear Weapons (Non-Proliferation Treaty, NPT) held the first of three planned sessions in Vienna on 2–12 May 2017.[1] The session was chaired by Ambassador Henk Cor Van der Kwast of the Netherlands.[2]

The discussions were generally restrained and avoided the acrimonious disputes that had paralysed the 2015 NPT Review Conference.[3] The latter was widely seen as having ended in failure when the states parties were unable to achieve consensus on a final document.[4] During the 2017 meeting, the parties largely refrained from debating long-standing differences over arrangements for establishing a weapon of mass destruction-free zone in the Middle East and over the perceived lack of progress towards nuclear disarmament by the five NPT-defined nuclear weapon states.[5] These differences had been the principal sources of contention that had prevented the adoption by consensus of a final document at the 2015 Review Conference.[6]

During the 2017 Preparatory Committee discussions, there was general agreement among the states parties on many issues related to the three pillars of the NPT: nuclear disarmament, non-proliferation and nuclear energy. Many states expressed support for bringing into force the 1996 Comprehensive Nuclear-Test-Ban Treaty (CTBT); convening a panel of experts on a fissile material cut-off treaty (FMCT); promoting International Atomic

---

[1] For a summary and other details of the NPT see annex A, section I, in this volume. In order to strengthen the treaty's review process, the 1995 NPT Review and Extension Conference decided that preparatory committee meetings would be held in each of the 3 years leading up to the 5-yearly review conferences. The purpose of the preparatory committee meetings is to 'consider principles, objectives and ways to promote the full implementation of the Treaty, as well as its universality, and to make recommendations thereon to the Review Conference'. 1995 Review and Extension Conference of the Parties to the Treaty on the Non-Proliferation of Nuclear Weapons, NPT/CONF.1995/32 (Part I), New York, 11 May 1995, Decision 1, para. 4.

[2] United Nations Office for Disarmament Affairs (UNODA), '2017 Preparatory Committee for the 2020 Nuclear Non-Proliferation Treaty Review Conference', [n.d.].

[3] See Elbahtimy, H., 'More heat than light: Reflections on the 2017 NPT Prepcom', Commentary, European Leadership Network, 26 June 2017.

[4] The NPT review conferences in 1980, 1990 and 2005 also failed to reach consensus on a final document.

[5] The NPT designates a state as a nuclear weapon state if it exploded a nuclear device before 1 Jan. 1967. The 5 NPT-defined nuclear weapon states are China, France, Russia, the UK and the USA.

[6] Meier, O., *The 2015 NPT Review Conference Failure: Implications for the Nuclear Order* (German Institute for International and Security Affairs: Berlin, Oct. 2015).

Energy Agency (IAEA) safeguards, including comprehensive safeguards agreements and the IAEA Model Additional Protocol; and reaffirming the right of states parties to peaceful uses of nuclear energy under Article IV of the NPT.[7] There was also consensus support for a statement condemning the continued nuclear weapon and ballistic missile tests by the Democratic People's Republic of Korea (DPRK, or North Korea).[8]

One key issue that emerged during the discussion concerned the potential impact of the proposed treaty prohibiting the possession of nuclear weapons, which was under negotiation at the time (see section I). Specifically, questions were raised about whether a nuclear weapon ban, once in place, would distract attention from disarmament efforts under the NPT and might widen existing divisions among the states parties to the NPT. There were also questions about whether countries might choose to prioritize ways to implement the proposed ban treaty, through the development of protocols, verification mechanisms or other follow-on actions, at the expense of measures under the NPT.[9]

As the Preparatory Committee meeting drew to a close, the chairman prepared a factual summary of the meeting's deliberations that was later circulated as a working paper.[10] During the final plenary session, the states parties had the opportunity to comment on the summary. Their remarks generally reaffirmed support for the principles and goals of the NPT but also highlighted long-standing differences in views about the nature of the main challenges facing the NPT regime.[11] In the light of these unresolved differences, some observers renewed calls for consideration to be given to procedural changes in the review process, including the required adoption by consensus of a final document at the end of a review conference, so that disagreements over certain issues do not lead to the breakdown of the conference.[12]

---

[7] Preparatory Committee for the 2020 Review Conference of the Parties to the Treaty on the Non-Proliferation of Nuclear Weapons, First Session, 'Chair's factual summary (working paper)', NPT/CONF.2020/PC.I/WP.40, 25 May 2017.

[8] Preparatory Committee for the 2020 Review Conference of the Parties to the Treaty on the Non-Proliferation of Nuclear Weapons, First Session, Joint statement on 'Democratic People's Republic of Korea's nuclear challenge to the Treaty on the Non-Proliferation of Nuclear Weapons', NPT/CONF.2020/PC.I/13, 11 May 2017.

[9] Pitts-Kiefer, S. and Williams, I., '2017 NPT PrepCom: Sleepy conference masks continuing tensions', PrepCom Primer, Nuclear Threat Initiative (NTI), 15 May 2017.

[10] Preparatory Committee for the 2020 Review Conference of the Parties to the Treaty on the Non-Proliferation of Nuclear Weapons, NPT/CONF.2020/PC.I/WP.40 (note 7).

[11] Preparatory Committee for the 2020 Review Conference of the Parties to the Treaty on the Non-Proliferation of Nuclear Weapons, First Session, 'Summary record of the 16th meeting', NPT/CONF.2020/PC.I/SR.16, 28 July 2017.

[12] Cronberg, T. and van der Meer, S., 'Working toward a successful NPT 2020 Review Conference', Policy Brief, Clingendael–Netherlands Institute of International Relations, Sep. 2017.

Preparations for opening future negotiations on a fissile material cut-off treaty

The fissile material cut-off treaty is a proposed international treaty to prohibit the further production of fissile material for use in nuclear weapons or other nuclear explosive devices.[13] In 1995 the Conference on Disarmament (CD) approved a mandate for an ad hoc committee to negotiate, without preconditions, 'a non-discriminatory, multilateral and internationally and effectively verifiable treaty banning the production of fissile material for nuclear weapons or other nuclear explosive devices'.[14] However, the CD was subsequently unable to adopt a programme of work for all but two of its subsequent sessions. This was due primarily to procedural reservations from Pakistan arising from its position that fissile material stockpiles existing at the time an FMCT is agreed should be covered by the treaty. To date, no substantive negotiations have taken place, and the terms of the proposed treaty have yet to be defined.

In December 2016 the United Nations General Assembly adopted a resolution urging the CD to agree on and implement a balanced and comprehensive programme of work that includes the immediate commencement of negotiations on an FMCT on the basis of the 1995 mandate.[15] The resolution requested the UN Secretary-General to establish 'a high-level fissile material cut-off treaty (FMCT) expert preparatory group' with a membership of 25 states, which would operate by consensus to consider and make recommendations on substantial elements of a future non-discriminatory, multilateral and internationally and effectively verifiable FMCT (i.e. on the basis of the 1995 CD mandate). The group's deliberations would draw on earlier work in this field, in particular the 2015 final report of the group of governmental experts established by the UN Secretary-General on possible elements for an FMCT.[16]

After its establishment, the high-level FMCT expert preparatory group met for informal consultations at the UN headquarters in New York on 2–3 March 2017.[17] The purpose of the meeting was to engage all UN member

[13] On the FMCT see, inter alia, Nuclear Threat Initiative, 'Proposed fissile material (cut-off) treaty (FMCT)', 31 May 2017.

[14] Conference on Disarmament, 'Report of Ambassador Gerald E. Shannon of Canada on consultations on the most appropriate arrangement to negotiate a treaty banning the production of fissile material for nuclear weapons or other nuclear explosive devices', CD/1299, 24 Mar. 1995.

[15] UN General Assembly Resolution 71/259, 'Treaty banning the production of fissile material for nuclear weapons or other nuclear explosive devices', adopted 23 Dec. 2016, A/RES/71/259, 11 Jan. 2017.

[16] United Nations, General Assembly, 'Group of governmental experts to make recommendations on possible aspects that could contribute to but not negotiate a treaty banning the production of fissile material for nuclear weapons or other nuclear explosive devices', A/70/81, 7 May 2015.

[17] United Nations Office at Geneva, 'High Level Fissile Material Cut-Off Treaty (FMCT) Expert Preparatory Group', 28 July 2017. The high-level group is composed of experts from the following 25 countries, invited by the UN Secretary-General on the basis of equitable geographical rep-

states in discussions about several issues that were left unresolved in the 1995 mandate and that will be addressed in future negotiations. These concerned definition of the fissile materials to be covered; the scope of a future treaty—specifically, whether the treaty's provisions will apply to stocks of fissile material produced prior to its entry into force; verification and monitoring requirements; and associated legal and institutional arrangements.[18]

The expert group held its first formal session on 31 July–11 August 2017 in Geneva.[19] A second session will be held in 2018. The group will present a final report to the UN General Assembly in September 2018, which will elaborate options to be considered in future negotiations on an FMCT.

Comprehensive Nuclear-Test-Ban Treaty entry into force conference

As of 31 December 2017 the 1996 Comprehensive Nuclear-Test-Ban Treaty had been ratified by 166 states and signed by an additional 17 states.[20] However, the CTBT cannot enter into force until all 44 of the states listed in Annex 2 to the treaty have ratified it, and eight of these states—China, Egypt, India, Iran, Israel, North Korea, Pakistan and the United States—have yet to do so.[21] In September 2016, on the 20th anniversary of the CTBT, the UN Security Council affirmed that 'entry into force of the Treaty will contribute to the enhancement of international peace and security' and urged all of the states listed in Annex 2 to ratify the treaty 'without further delay'.[22]

On 20 September 2017 a Conference on Facilitating the Entry into Force of the Comprehensive Nuclear-Test-Ban Treaty (the so-called Article XIV conference) was held at the UN headquarters in New York.[23] This was the 10th such conference held since the CTBT was opened for signature in 1996.

The conference reaffirmed 'the vital importance and urgency of the entry into force of the CTBT' and reiterated 'that the cessation of all nuclear

resentation: Algeria, Argentina, Australia, Brazil, Canada, China, Columbia, Egypt, Estonia, France, Germany, India, Indonesia, Japan, Mexico, Morocco, the Netherlands, Poland, Russia, Senegal, South Africa, South Korea, Sweden, the UK and the USA.

[18] For detail about these issues see Kile, S. N. and Kelley, R., *Verifying a Fissile Material Cut-off Treaty: Technical and Organizational Considerations*, SIPRI Policy Paper no. 33 (SIPRI: Stockholm, Jan. 2012).

[19] United Nations Office at Geneva, 'High-Level Fissile Material Cut-off Treaty (FMCT) Expert Preparatory Group concludes its first session', 11 Aug. 2017.

[20] For a summary and other details of the CTBT see annex A, section I, in this volume.

[21] The CTBT will enter into force 180 days after it has been ratified by these 44 states, which were members of the CD with nuclear power or research reactors on their territories when the treaty was signed. As of Dec. 2017 India, North Korea and Pakistan had not signed the treaty. The other 5 of these 8 states had signed but not ratified.

[22] United Nations Security Council Resolution 2310, 23 Sep. 2016. See also Rauf, T., '"Unfinished business" on the anniversary of the Comprehensive Nuclear-Test-Ban Treaty', Commentary, SIPRI, 26 Sep. 2016.

[23] Article XIV of the CTBT provides for the convening of a biennial conference by the states that have deposited their instruments of ratification (other states may participate as observers) to 'consider measures to facilitate the early entry into force of the treaty'.

weapon test explosions and all other nuclear explosions . . . constitutes an effective measure of nuclear disarmament and non-proliferation'.[24] It discussed a number of steps and measures to promote the early entry into force and universalization of the treaty. These focused primarily on education, training and public outreach initiatives. They also involved support for the work of the Preparatory Commission for the Comprehensive Nuclear-Test-Ban Treaty Organization (CTBTO) in completing the treaty's verification regime.[25] The conference's final declaration noted that the verification regime, in addition to its treaty-defined mandate, had demonstrated its utility in 'bringing tangible scientific and civil benefits', including for tsunami warning systems and possibly other disaster alert systems.[26]

The conference's deliberations took on added urgency in the wake of North Korea's sixth nuclear test explosion, purportedly of a thermonuclear device, which was carried out on 3 September.[27] The final declaration condemned the test, and all previous North Korean nuclear tests, 'in the strongest terms'. It urged North Korea not to conduct any further nuclear test and to fully and immediately comply with all relevant UN Security Council resolutions. The declaration also expressed appreciation for the effectiveness of the CTBT verification regime in responding to North Korea's nuclear tests.[28]

[24] Conference on Facilitating the Entry into Force of the Comprehensive Nuclear-Test-Ban Treaty, 'Report of the conference', CTBT-Art.XIV/2017/6, 16 Nov. 2017, Final declaration, paras 1, 5.

[25] The CTBT verification regime consists of an International Monitoring System (IMS), which will consist of a global network of 321 monitoring stations and 16 laboratories to detect evidence of a nuclear explosion; and an International Data Centre (IDC) to process and analyse the data registered at the monitoring stations and transmit it to member states. CTBTO Preparatory Commission, 'How the International Monitoring System works'.

[26] Conference on Facilitating the Entry into Force of the Comprehensive Nuclear-Test-Ban Treaty (note 24), Final declaration, para. 8. See also Venturini, G., 'The CTBTO PrepCom at twenty: Beyond the CTBT?', *Nonproliferation Review*, vol. 23, nos. 3–4 (2017), pp. 345–56.

[27] See chapter 6, section XI, in this volume.

[28] Conference on Facilitating the Entry into Force of the Comprehensive Nuclear-Test-Ban Treaty (note 24), Final declaration, para. 6.

IV. International non-proliferation sanctions against North Korea

SHANNON N. KILE

The long-running efforts of the Democratic People's Republic of Korea (DPRK, or North Korea) to develop nuclear weapons and their ballistic missile delivery systems continue to draw strong international condemnation and demands that the country immediately halt all activities related to these programmes. In 2017 North Korea conducted a sixth nuclear test explosion and 23 test launches of ballistic missiles, including new long-range missile systems.[1] The tests prompted the United Nations Security Council, as well as individual states, to impose additional financial sanctions and sanctions on key sectors of the North Korean economy, and to tighten enforcement of the existing arms embargo.[2] At the same time, significant difficulties remained in implementing and enforcing the sanctions, which continued to be vulnerable to circumvention by an increasingly sophisticated range of smuggling activities and deceptive practices.

United Nations Security Council sanctions

By the end of December 2017 the Security Council had adopted nine resolutions imposing sanctions and other restrictive measures on North Korea in response to the country's nuclear weapon and ballistic missile tests since 2006 (see table 7.2). All nine resolutions were adopted unanimously and cited Chapter VII of the UN Charter in demanding that North Korea abandon its nuclear weapons and nuclear weapon programmes in a complete, verifiable and irreversible manner and immediately cease all related activities.[3] The Security Council monitors implementation of the sanctions through a committee established by Resolution 1718 (of 2006) and a panel of experts established by Resolution 1874 (of 2009).[4] The panel produces regular reports on the status of the sanctions and their enforcement.

In 2017 the Security Council adopted three new sanctions resolutions in response to North Korea's nuclear weapon and ballistic missile tests during the year. Resolution 2371 was adopted unanimously on 5 August following North Korea's test launches in July of two long-range ballistic missiles. The

---

[1] See chapter 6, section IX, in this volume.

[2] On the arms embargo see chapter 10, section II, in this volume.

[3] Chapter VII powers ('action with respect to threats to the peace, breaches of the peace, and acts of aggression') must be used for the establishment of Security Council-mandated sanctions regimes, although an explicit reference to the chapter is not essential. Charter of the United Nations, signed 26 June 1945, entered into force 24 Oct. 1945.

[4] For the text of the United Nations Security Council resolutions mentioned in this section see United Nations, 'Security Council resolutions'.

Table 7.2. Summary of UN Security Council sanctions resolutions in response to North Korea's nuclear and ballistic missile tests

Date	Resolution	Main provisions
14 Oct. 2006	1718	Condemned 9 Oct. 2006 nuclear test; called on states to inspect cargo shipments to and from North Korea suspected of trafficking WMD-related material; established a sanctions committee to monitor and review sanctions and report to the Security Council
12 June 2009	1874	Condemned 25 May 2009 nuclear test; expanded sanctions to ban all weapon exports from North Korea and most imports except for small arms; prohibited financial transactions, technical training or assistance for the provision, manufacture, maintenance or use of WMD and missile systems; established a 7-person panel of experts to assist the sanctions committee established by Resolution 1718
22 Jan. 2013	2087	Condemned 12 Dec. 2012 long-range rocket launch; designated new subjects of sanctions measures previously adopted by the Security Council
7 Mar. 2013	2094	Condemned 12 Feb. 2013 nuclear test; added to the prohibited list of equipment and technologies and made new entities and individuals subject to sanctions; authorized states to inspect all cargo transiting through their territories to and from North Korea
2 Mar. 2016	2270	Condemned 6 Jan. 2016 nuclear test; banned North Korea's exports of coal and iron, except for 'livelihood purposes'; banned North Korea's exports of gold, titanium and rare earth metals
30 Nov. 2016	2321	Condemned 9 Sep. 2016 nuclear test; banned North Korea's exports of non-ferrous metals (copper, nickel, silver and zinc); placed limit on North Korea's exports of coal; restricted activities of North Korean diplomats and diplomatic missions
5 Aug. 2017	2371	Condemned test launches of long-range ballistic missiles on 3 July and 28 July 2017; banned North Korea's exports of lead, iron and seafood; imposed new restrictions on North Korea's Foreign Trade Bank; prohibited new joint ventures between North Korea and foreign partners
11 Sep. 2017	2375	Condemned nuclear test of 3 Sep. 2017; limited North Korea's imports of crude oil and refined petroleum products; banned all North Korean textile exports; required termination of joint ventures with North Korean entities; prohibited new work permits for North Korean nationals to work in foreign countries
22 Dec. 2017	2397	Condemned test launch of long-range ballistic missile on 28 Nov. 2017; imposed new limit on North Korea's annual import of refined petroleum products; required the repatriation of all North Korean nationals earning income abroad within 2 years; strengthened maritime interdiction measures targeting North Korean vessels

WMD = weapon of mass destruction.

Source: United Nations, Security Council, Committee established pursuant to Resolution 1718 (2006), 'Resolutions'.

resolution banned the export by North Korea of several materials that previous sanctions resolutions had restricted the export of, such as coal, iron and iron ore, lead and lead ore, and seafood. It also imposed new sanctions against North Korean individuals and entities, including the Foreign Trade Bank (FTB), and prohibited new joint ventures between North Korea and foreign partners.[5]

On 11 September 2017 the Security Council unanimously approved Resolution 2375 in response to North Korea's sixth nuclear test explosion, thought to be a hydrogen bomb, which was conducted on 3 September.[6] The resolution contained several measures that strengthened sanctions on the North Korean economy. Specifically, it imposed an annual ceiling on imports by North Korea of refined petroleum products (gasoline, diesel, heavy fuel oil, etc.) while freezing imports of crude oil at the current level. The resolution also banned the supply to North Korea of all natural gas and natural gas condensates in order to prevent it from obtaining substitutes for refined petroleum products. It banned the export by North Korea of all textiles—targeting the country's largest economic sector which the Security Council had not previously restricted. The resolution also eliminated a major source of revenue by prohibiting UN member states from issuing new permits for North Korean nationals to work in their jurisdictions.[7] Finally, the resolution contained strengthened maritime provisions enabling countries to counter North Korean smuggling activities of prohibited exports by sea.[8]

On 28 November 2017 North Korea test launched a new type of long-range ballistic missile. In response, on 22 December the Security Council unanimously approved Resolution 2397, which further tightened sanctions against the country.[9] The resolution reduced by 75 per cent the annual cap on the supply of refined petroleum products to North Korea imposed by Resolution 2375, to a maximum of 500 000 barrels in 2018; and it capped crude oil imports in 2018 at the current level of 4 million barrels.[10] The resolution called for UN member states to repatriate all North Korean nationals earning income within their jurisdictions, with some humanitarian exceptions, within two years. Finally, the resolution strengthened maritime interdiction measures to prevent sanctions evasion, including a new requirement for countries to seize and impound ships caught smuggling illicit items such as oil and coal.

---

[5] UN Security Council Resolution 2371, 5 Aug. 2017.

[6] UN Security Council Resolution 2375, 11 Sep. 2017. See also chapter 6, section XI, in this volume.

[7] According to a US Government estimate, c. 100 000 North Koreans were working abroad and generating more than $500 million in revenue for the North Korean Government each year. US Mission to the United Nations, 'UN Security Council Resolution 2397 on North Korea', Fact sheet, 22 Dec. 2017.

[8] UN Security Council Resolution 2375 (note 6).

[9] UN Security Council Resolution 2397, 22 Dec. 2017.

[10] US Mission to the United Nations (note 7).

Divergent views on sanctions

The negotiations on the Security Council resolutions were marked by disagreements between China and Russia on one side and the United States on the other over the scope and severity of the proposed sanctions. The USA sought to impose stringent measures, calling for the 'strongest possible' sanctions against North Korea during the negotiation of Resolution 2375.[11] China and Russia consistently rejected US calls to impose stringent sanctions targeting North Korea's economy as ineffectual and potentially destabilizing. Chinese officials in particular reportedly feared that an oil embargo or similar measures risked causing social unrest inside North Korea that could spill over its border with China.[12] This concern was supported by reports during the year about the steady deterioration in living conditions for ordinary North Koreans.[13] The USA eventually dropped several proposed measures—including a total oil embargo—in order to win the support of China and Russia.[14]

China and Russia emphasized that the tightening of economic and financial sanctions on North Korea must be accompanied by serious diplomatic efforts to advance the prospects for reaching a comprehensive political settlement.[15] They continued to express support for a Chinese-proposed 'freeze-for-freeze' deal as an interim step. This would involve North Korea agreeing to cease all nuclear weapon testing and missile launches in exchange for the USA reducing its military presence on the Korean peninsula and ceasing all joint military exercises with the Republic of Korea (South Korea).[16] However, the US ambassador to the United Nations dismissed the freeze-for-freeze proposal as 'insulting' following North Korea's sixth nuclear weapon test.[17]

UN panel of experts midterm report

In September 2017 the panel of experts established by Resolution 1874 issued a mid-term report conveying to the Security Council its most recent findings and recommendations.[18] The panel reported that North Korea had

---

[11] Smith, D., 'North Korea "begging for war" says US, calling for strongest possible sanctions', *The Guardian*, 4 Sep. 2017.

[12] Rahn, W., 'Why China won't help US against North Korea', Deutsche Welle, 15 Sep. 2017;

[13] E.g. McCurry, J., '"Too many soldiers to feed": North Koreans fear more sanctions as drought threatens famine', *The Guardian*, 23 Aug. 2017.

[14] Sengupta, S., 'After US compromise, Security Council strengthens North Korea sanctions', *New York Times*, 11 Sep. 2017.

[15] Nichols, M., 'UN Security Council unanimously steps up sanctions on North Korea', Reuters, 11 Sep. 2017.

[16] Nichols (note 15). For a description of the freeze-for-freeze proposal see Russian Ministry of Foreign Affairs, 'Joint statement by the Russian and Chinese foreign ministries on the Korean Peninsula's problems', Press Statement 1317-04-07-2017, 4 July 2017.

[17] Haley, N., US Permanent Representative to the United Nations, 'Remarks at an emergency UN Security Council briefing on North Korea', US Mission to the United Nations, 4 Sep. 2017.

[18] United Nations, Security Council, 'Midterm report of the panel of experts established pursuant to Resolution 1874 (2009)', 4 Aug. 2917, S/2017/742, 5 Sep. 2017.

made significant technological progress in its nuclear and ballistic missile programmes 'in defiance of the most comprehensive and targeted sanctions regime in United Nations history'. Its investigation revealed that North Korea continued to violate the financial sanctions through the use of a range of illicit activities and deceptive practices. It also revealed that North Korea continued to violate the sanctions on various sectors of its economy through the export of almost all of the commodities prohibited in the resolutions, using indirect channels and third countries to evade sanctions. According to the panel, these developments showed that 'as the sanctions regime expands, so does the scope of evasion'.[19]

The panel's report stated that, despite an increased rate of submission of national implementation reports to the Security Council, 'the actual implementation of the sanctions lags far behind what is necessary to achieve the goal of denuclearization'.[20] It argued that this was due in part to the 'lack of appropriate domestic legal and regulatory frameworks' in some UN member states.[21] The practical consequence was that 'Lax enforcement of the sanctions regime, coupled with [North Korea's] evolving evasion techniques are undermining the goals of the resolutions that [North Korea] abandon all weapons of mass destruction and cease all related programmes and activities'.[22]

Other national and international sanctions

In 2017 several countries and the European Union (EU) imposed autonomous sanctions against North Korea. In some cases, these went beyond the measures contained in UN Security Council resolutions.

On 20 September a US executive order blocked from the US financial system any foreign business, organization or individual that facilitated trade with North Korea.[23] The new measure was reportedly designed to counteract sanction-evasion tactics and was aimed at Chinese financial institutions in particular.[24] China has opposed unilateral US sanctions that go beyond Security Council sanctions, especially those that impose de facto long-arm jurisdiction over Chinese entities and individuals.[25]

---

[19] United Nations, S/2017/742 (note 18), p. 4. See also Abrahamian, A., 'The art of sanctions: Can North Korea navigate expanded measures?', 38 North, 21 Mar. 2016. See also chapter 10, section II, in this volume.

[20] United Nations, S/2017/742 (note 18), p. 5.

[21] United Nations, S/2017/742 (note 18), para. 60.

[22] United Nations, S/2017/742 (note 18), p. 5.

[23] White House, Presidential Executive Order on imposing additional sanctions with respect to North Korea, 20 Sep. 2017.

[24] Reiss, M., 'With new North Korea sanctions in place, all eyes are on China', Lawfare, 22 Sep. 2017.

[25] Meyers, J., 'China denounces US sanctions on North Korea trade', Los Angeles Times, 20 Aug. 2017.

The USA had previously imposed unilateral sanctions against North Korea in response to cyberattacks attributed to it, human rights violations, money laundering and other activities.[26] In August 2017 the US Congress approved a controversial law, the Countering America's Adversaries Through Sanctions Act, that imposes new or expanded sanctions on North Korea as well as on Iran and Russia.[27] Among other provisions, the law tightens US restrictions on North Korea's cargo and shipping as well as its use of forced labour.[28]

On 16 October 2017 the Council of the European Union adopted new autonomous EU measures to complement and reinforce those in UN Security Council Resolution 2375. These include banning all EU investment in North Korea; banning the sale of refined petroleum products and crude oil to North Korea; reducing the amount of personal remittances that can be transferred to North Korea; and prohibiting the renewal of work permits for North Korean nationals currently employed in EU member states. The EU also added individuals and entities to the lists of those subject to an asset freeze and travel restrictions.[29]

In November and December 2017 the Japanese Government approved measures freezing assets of additional individuals and entities, including some based in China and Russia, which it had identified as assisting North Korea to circumvent UN Security Council sanctions.[30]

The impact of sanctions

The year 2017 ended with international sanctions of unprecedented scope and severity in place against North Korea but no indication that the country was prepared to abandon its nuclear weapons or halt their development. Following the adoption of UN Security Council Resolution 2397, the North Korean Government issued a statement denouncing the sanctions as 'an act of war' that had been 'rigged up by the US and its followers'.[31] The statement vowed that, despite the 'worn out "sanctions"', North Korea would 'further consolidate [its] self-defensive nuclear deterrence aimed at fundamentally eradicating the US nuclear threats, blackmail and hostile moves'.

[26] Albert, E., 'What to know about sanctions on North Korea', Backgrounder, Council on Foreign Relations, 3 Jan. 2018.

[27] Countering America's Adversaries Through Sanctions Act, US Public Law 155-44, signed into law 2 Aug. 2017; and Rampton, R. and Zengerle, P., 'Trump signs Russia sanctions bill, Moscow calls it "trade war"', Reuters, 2 Aug. 2017.

[28] Countering America's Adversaries Through Sanctions Act (note 27), sections 314–15, 321; and Korean Central News Agency (KCNA), 'US sanctions racket slammed', Naenara, 2 Aug. 2017.

[29] Council of the European Union, 'North Korea: EU adopts new sanctions', Press Release 575/17, 16 Oct. 2017.

[30] Kyodo news agency, 'Japan to ratchet up economic sanctions on North Korea', Japan Times, 7 Nov. 2017; and 'Japan expands unilateral sanctions against North Korea', BBC News, 15 Dec. 2017.

[31] Korean Central News Agency (KCNA), 'Statement by the DPRK Foreign Ministry spokesman', 24 Dec. 2017.

The statement heightened the debate among Western analysts about how effective sanctions can be in compelling North Korea to halt and eventually give up its nuclear weapon and ballistic missile programmes. Some analysts argued that the robust enforcement of increasingly stringent financial and economic sanctions would eventually compel the North Korean leadership to seek a denuclearization deal in order to preserve the current political system.[32] Others argued that sanctions alone would not force the leadership to change its strategic cost–benefit calculations about nuclear weapons.[33] In particular, the available trade data indicated that sanctions had not worked to date and were unlikely to force North Korea to abandon its nuclear weapon programme and related activities even if they were tightened further.[34] The enforcement of existing UN sanctions remained problematic, as evidenced by North Korea's reported use of cargo ships to circumvent restrictions on the export of oil to the country.[35] This in turn suggested that the international community needed to give greater attention to non-punitive diplomatic options for engaging with North Korea to address concerns about its nuclear programme.

[32] Stanton, J., Lee, S. and Klinger, B., 'Getting tough on North Korea: How to hit Pyongyang where it hurts', *Foreign Affairs*, May/June 2017.

[33] Delury, J., 'North Korea sanctions: Futile, counterproductive and dangerous', CNN, 2 Dec. 2016; and Alcaro, R. and Greco, E., 'The challenge from North Korea: Fostering regional security and nonproliferation', International Institutions and Global Governance Program, Council on Foreign Relations, 29 Nov. 2017.

[34] Frank, R., 'Engagement, not sanctions, deserve a second chance', 38 North, 13 Oct. 2017.

[35] 'North Korea: South seizes ship amid row over illegal oil transfer', BBC News, 29 Dec. 2017.

V. Implementation of the Joint Comprehensive Plan of Action in Iran

TYTTI ERÄSTÖ

After years of international concern about the purpose, extent and apparent furtiveness of its nuclear programme, Iran agreed to a Joint Comprehensive Plan of Action (JCPOA) in July 2015.[1] Iran's main commitments under the JCPOA are designed to prevent the production of highly enriched uranium and plutonium—the two 'pathways' to a nuclear weapon. Together with more intrusive inspections, these measures seek to build international confidence in Iran's intentions, to allow its nuclear programme to be 'treated in the same manner as that of any other non-nuclear weapon state party to the [1968 Non-Proliferation Treaty]'.[2] Iran's compliance with the JCPOA has been verified by the International Atomic Energy Agency (IAEA) in nine consecutive reports.

Despite its successful implementation, the future of the JCPOA began to look increasingly uncertain in 2017 largely due to political tensions between Iran and the United States. This section first reviews Iran's compliance during 2017 with the various aspects of the JCPOA. It then describes the political context, focusing on the responses by the other JCPOA participants to the controversial decision of US President Donald J. Trump in October 2017 to 'decertify' the JCPOA, based on his assessment that the continued lifting of US sanctions was not proportional to Iran's actions under the deal.

Iran's compliance with its JCPOA commitments

Under the JCPOA, Iran is required to limit its uranium enrichment activities, to cut its stockpiles of enriched uranium, and to redesign and rebuild the heavy water reactor in Arak with international support. In addition to the long-standing obligations under its comprehensive safeguards agreement (CSA) with the IAEA, Iran also agreed to provisionally apply the stricter provisions of a standard Additional Protocol to its CSA.

Iran's counterparts in the JCPOA are three member states of the European Union (EU)—France, Germany and the United Kingdom, known as the E3—and three other permanent members of the United Nations Security Council—China, Russia and the USA. The EU itself plays a facilitating role.

---

[1] Joint Comprehensive Plan of Action (JCPOA), 14 July 2015, Vienna, reproduced as Annex A of UN Security Council Resolution 2231, 20 July 2015. For background see Rauf, T., 'Resolving concerns about Iran's nuclear programme', *SIPRI Yearbook 2016*, pp. 673–88; and Rauf, T., 'Implementation of the Joint Comprehensive Plan of Action in Iran', *SIPRI Yearbook 2017*, pp. 505–10.

[2] JCPOA (note 1), Preamble.

Collectively they are known as the E3/EU+3. Their main commitment under the JCPOA is to gradually lift their nuclear-related sanctions.

In 2017 the IAEA issued four reports verifying Iran's continued compliance with its commitments.[3]

Activities related to heavy water and reprocessing

The previous design of Iran's heavy water reactor near Arak raised proliferation concerns because it would have produced spent nuclear fuel containing weapon-grade plutonium. The new design to which Iran agreed in the JCPOA minimizes the amount of plutonium produced. To address concerns over reprocessing of the spent nuclear fuel, which would involve the separation of plutonium, Iran agreed to ship abroad all the spent fuel produced by the new reactor throughout its lifetime.

Iran also agreed not to accumulate heavy water exceeding its immediate needs (estimated to be 130 tonnes before and 90 tonnes after the commissioning of the new reactor). Any heavy water produced by the Arak plant that exceeds these amounts is to be sold abroad, reportedly to Russia and the USA.[4] This practice will continue until 2030.[5]

The 2017 IAEA reports confirmed that Iran complied with all of the above commitments—including the cap on heavy water, which had been temporarily exceeded in 2016.[6] Iran had not pursued the construction of the Arak reactor based on its original design, and the natural uranium pellets, fuel pins and assemblies meant for that design remained in storage.[7] On 12 April 2017 the Atomic Energy Organization of Iran signed a contract with the China National Nuclear Corporation for the design concept of the new reactor.[8]

Activities related to enrichment and fuel

Under the JCPOA, Iran also agreed not to enrich uranium above 3.67 per cent, to keep its stockpile of enriched uranium below 300 kilogrammes and to limit its enrichment activities to a single location, in Natanz. These restrictions apply for 15 years (until 2030). In addition, Iran agreed to reduce the number of its operating centrifuges to 5060—about a quarter of pre-JCPOA

[3] IAEA, Board of Governors, 'Verification and monitoring in the Islamic Republic of Iran in light of United Nations Security Council Resolution 2231 (2015)', Report by the Director General, 24 Feb. 2017, GOV/2017/10; 2 June 2017, GOV/2017/24; 31 Aug. 2017, GOV/2017/35; and 13 Nov. 2017, GOV/2017/48.

[4] Katzman, K. and Kerr, P. K., *Iran Nuclear Agreement*, US Congressional Research Service (CRS) Report for Congress R43333 (US Congress, CRS: Washington, DC, 15 Sep. 2017), p. 12.

[5] JCPOA (note 1), Annex I.

[6] Iran's stock of heavy water was between 111 and 128.2 tonnes. IAEA, GOV/2017/10, GOV/2017/24, GOV/2017/35 and GOV/2017/48 (note 3).

[7] IAEA, GOV/2017/10, GOV/2017/24, GOV/2017/35 and GOV/2017/48 (note 3).

[8] 'China, Iran sign first contract for Arak redesign', World Nuclear News, 24 Apr. 2017.

levels—and to place all excess centrifuges in storage for 10 years (until 2025), to be removed only to replace failed or damaged ones.

The 2017 IAEA reports reconfirmed that Iran was continuing to abide by the above limitations, with an enriched uranium stockpile of 79.8–101.7 kg.[9] The IAEA monitored the substitution of 245 failed or damaged centrifuges with those held in storage.[10] In February 2017 Iran provided a revised estimate of the quantity of enriched uranium recovered from the enriched UO_2 powder plant (EUPP) in Esfahan. This material had been held in the process lines at the EUPP. The reported quantity (99.9 kg) was consistent with the IAEA's previous assessment. By June 2017 Iran had down-blended 35.7 kg of this material to the level of natural uranium.[11]

Centrifuge research and development, manufacturing and inventory

The JCPOA allows Iran to conduct limited research on new centrifuges.[12] According to the 2017 IAEA reports, Iran's research and development activities continued to be consistent with the JCPOA. In January 2017 the IAEA monitored the process of feeding natural UF_6 into an advanced IR-8 centrifuge for the first time.[13]

Transparency, Additional Protocol and other issues

In 2017 the IAEA reconfirmed that Iran continued to apply the Additional Protocol and that it was evaluating Iran's declarations under the Additional Protocol. The IAEA also noted that Iran had permitted it to use online and electronic monitoring techniques and had granted long-term visas for nuclear inspectors.[14]

The IAEA continued to verify that declared nuclear material at declared nuclear facilities in Iran had not been diverted to prohibited uses, but was not yet able to verify the absence of undeclared materials and activities, noting that evaluations in this regard remained ongoing.[15] To verify that all nuclear material in Iran is in peaceful use, the IAEA would need to reach a 'broader conclusion', based on enhanced authorities provided by the Additional Protocol. Completing this process usually takes several years.[16]

---

[9] IAEA, GOV/2017/10, GOV/2017/24, GOV/2017/35 and GOV/2017/48 (note 3).
[10] In Feb., the Agency reported that Iran had replaced 124 centrifuges in the reporting period. In June that number was 48, in Aug. it was 57 and in Nov. it was 16.
[11] IAEA, GOV/2017/24 (note 3).
[12] JCPOA (note 1), Annex I.
[13] IAEA, GOV/2017/10 (note 3).
[14] IAEA, GOV/2017/10, GOV/2017/24, GOV/2017/35 and GOV/2017/48 (note 3).
[15] IAEA, GOV/2017/10, GOV/2017/24, GOV/2017/35 and GOV/2017/48 (note 3).
[16] See e.g. Joyner, D., 'The JCPOA and the broader conclusion', Arms Control Law: Analysis and Discussion of Legal Issues Relevant to Arms Control, 8 Dec. 2015.

In 2017 the IAEA reported that verification and monitoring of Iran's other commitments were continuing.[17] These included section T ('Activities which could contribute to the design and development of a nuclear explosive device') of Annex I of the JCPOA. Although the IAEA has not questioned Iran's compliance with Section T, the issue caught the attention of JCPOA critics when the IAEA Director General, Yukiya Amano, asked the JCPOA Joint Commission—which brings the parties together to discuss implementation of the agreement—for clearer guidance on how to verify these commitments.[18]

The IAEA also verified that all the uranium ore concentrate (yellowcake) in Iran had been taken to the uranium conversion facility at Esfahan— including the 125.4 tonnes that Iran received in February 2017, reportedly from Kazakhstan.[19] Iran also began feeding depleted uranium through the process lines at the EUPP under IAEA monitoring, with the aim of increasing uranium-235 content close to the level of natural uranium.[20]

In October 2017 Iran informed the IAEA of its plans to build a light water critical reactor 'for research purposes in the near future'.[21] The plans are in line with the JCPOA, which encourages Iran to rely on light (instead of heavy) water reactors in the future.[22]

Political tensions threatening the JCPOA

The future of the JCPOA began to look increasingly uncertain after the 2016 US presidential election, during which the current president, Donald J. Trump, expressed reservations about the agreement. A US law, the 2015 Iran Nuclear Agreement Review Act (INARA), requires the US president to publicly certify every 90 days that Iran is in technical compliance with the deal and, more broadly, that 'suspension of sanctions [is] appropriate and proportionate to the specific and verifiable measures taken by Iran with respect to terminating its illicit nuclear program' as well as 'vital to the national security interests of the United States'.[23] While President Trump

---

[17] IAEA, GOV/2017/24, GOV/2017/35 and GOV/2017/48 (note 3).

[18] Murphy, F., 'IAEA chief calls for clarity on disputed section of Iran nuclear deal', Reuters, 26 Sep. 2017.

[19] IAEA, GOV/2017/10 (note 3); and 'Iran to import 950 tons of yellow cake, England getting in way', *Tehran Times*, 25 Feb. 2017.

[20] IAEA, GOV/2017/24 (note 3). Depleted uranium is a by-product of enrichment that contains less U-235 than natural uranium.

[21] IAEA, GOV/2017/48 (note 3).

[22] Iran's commitment to 'keep pace with the trend of international technological advancement in relying only on light water for its future nuclear power and research reactors' in JCPOA (note 1), Annex I, is matched by a commitment by the E3/EU+3 to 'facilitate Iran's acquisition of light-water research and power reactors, for research, development and testing, and for the supply of electricity and desalination' in JCPOA (note 1), Annex III.

[23] Iran Nuclear Agreement Review Act, US Public Law 114-17, signed into law 22 May 2015. It is unclear whether this law also applies after certification has been refused.

did reluctantly certify the deal in April and July, on 13 October 2017 he chose not to do so.[24] While a US president 'decertifying' the nuclear deal with Iran under US law is not the same as leaving the deal, it does set in motion special legislative rules that temporarily increase the powers of the US Congress to make such a decision. The other members of the E3/EU+3 reacted to the US decertification decision by restating their commitment to the agreement, but the resulting uncertainty led many Iranians to question the merits of the JCPOA.

The decertification decision and debate in the US Congress

The Trump administration has criticized the JCPOA because of the temporary nature of the limits to Iran's nuclear programme. It has also called for the IAEA to use its inspection authority more widely, by demanding access to Iran's military sites.[25] While Iran has stated that such sites are out of bounds to inspectors, the IAEA has not indicated any need for additional inspection powers. In November 2017 Amano reiterated that: 'As of today, we have had access to all the locations that we needed to visit. However, for reasons of confidentiality, we do not disclose details, including which locations were visited by our inspectors, or whether these were civilian or military . . . Whether or not a particular location is civilian or military is not relevant for the Agency'.[26]

For the most part, however, the US administration's misgivings are not related to the implementation of the JCPOA itself. While acknowledging Iran's 'technical' compliance with the nuclear deal, the USA argues that Iran's missile tests, satellite launches and activities in the region violate the spirit of the JCPOA and the letter of UN Security Council Resolution 2231, which calls on Iran 'not to undertake any activity related to ballistic missiles designed to be capable of delivering nuclear weapons'.[27] A launch by Iran of a satellite on 27 July 2017 prompted the US Congress to impose the first new US sanctions on Iran since the negotiation of the JCPOA.[28]

President Trump's decertification decision opened a two-month window for the US Congress to consider reimposing nuclear-related sanctions against

[24] White House, Office of the Press Secretary, 'Remarks by President Trump on Iran strategy', 13 Oct. 2017.

[25] 'Nuclear inspectors should have access to Iran military bases: Haley', Reuters, 25 Aug. 2017.

[26] Amano, Y., IAEA Director General, Speech on Iran, the JCPOA and the IAEA, Belfer Center for Science and International Affairs, John F. Kennedy School of Government, Cambridge, MA, 14 Nov. 2017.

[27] UN Security Council Resolution 2231 (JCPOA) (note 1), Annex B. See also e.g. Labott, E., Koran, L. and Diamond, J., 'US to extend sanctions waivers on Iran as Trump signals frustration with nuclear deal', CNN, 14 Sep. 2017; and 'Ambassador Haley on Iran's threats to quit the JCPOA', US Mission to the United Nations, 15 Aug. 2017.

[28] Harris, B., 'Congress closes in on first new Iran sanctions since nuclear deal', Al-Monitor, 25 July 2017; and Countering America's Adversaries Through Sanctions Act, US Public Law 115-44, signed into law 2 Aug. 2017.

Iran through an expedited process. The president urged Congress to address the JCPOA's 'many serious flaws' with legislation making all restrictions on Iran's nuclear activity permanent under US law and preventing Iran from developing an intercontinental ballistic missile. Trump also warned that he might unilaterally terminate US participation in the JCPOA.[29] Congress could not agree on any new legislation that would have compromised the JCPOA. A bill proposed by US senators Bob Corker and Tom Cotton would have made the deal's restrictions permanent and added limits to Iran's centrifuge programme, among other things. However, it failed to get enough support among US lawmakers and was never formally introduced.[30]

Reaction from the rest of the E3/EU+3

Throughout 2017, EU leaders actively defended the JCPOA. In January Federica Mogherini, High Representative of the EU for Foreign Affairs and Security Policy, wrote 'despite criticism that deceitfully stresses the deal's perceived shortcomings . . . it is important to state very clearly: the nuclear agreement with Iran is working' and 'the EU stands firmly by the deal'.[31] Both the E3 and the EU itself issued statements of support for the JCPOA in response to the US decertification.[32] As concrete signs of the EU's commitment to the JCPOA, shortly before President Trump's certification deadline in October the European Commission proposed that the European Investment Bank be allowed to operate in Iran and European credit agencies provided guarantees for exports to Iran.[33] While most EU leaders stressed that the JCPOA covers only Iran's nuclear activities and opposed renegotiating it, the E3 joined the USA in condemning Iran's missile tests and satellite launches.[34] President of France Emmanuel Macron also called for a new agreement to address Iran's ballistic missile programme.[35]

---

[29] White House (note 24).

[30] Corker, B. and Cotton, T., US Senate, 'Fixing the Iran deal: Background and key details', [13 Oct. 2017]; and Manson, K., 'Fate of Iran deal to land back in Trump's hands', *Financial Times*, 12 Dec. 2017.

[31] Mogherini, F., 'The Iran nuclear deal is a success, and the whole world is safer for it', *The Guardian*, 17 Jan. 2017.

[32] Joint statement from Prime Minister Theresa May, Chancellor Angela Merkel and President Emmanuel Macron following President Trump's statement on the US' Iran Strategy, 'Declaration by the Heads of State and Government of France, Germany and the United Kingdom', 13 Oct. 2017; and Council of the European Union, 'Iran nuclear deal: EU statement on the Joint Comprehensive Plan of Action', Press Release 590/17, 16 Oct. 2017.

[33] Schmid, H., Secretary General of the European External Action Service, 'European commitment to the JCPOA', Keynote speech, Zurich, 4 Oct. 2017; Kamali Dehghan, S., 'Europe's business heads aim to keep Iran nuclear deal despite US threat', *The Guardian*, 6 Oct. 2017; and Nasseri, L., 'Trump's Iran policy is a headache for EU business', Bloomberg, 17 Oct. 2017.

[34] E.g. Joint Statement (note 32). See also Erästö, T., 'Time for Europe to put Iran's missile programme in context', Commentary, SIPRI, 30 Oct. 2017.

[35] 'Emmanuel Macron's exclusive interview with CNN', CNN, 19 Sep. 2017.

The Russian Ministry of Foreign Affairs described the US decertification decision as 'counter to the spirit and the letter of the JCPOA' but hoped that it would 'have no adverse impacts on the implementation of the deal'.[36] Russia's Foreign Minister, Sergey Lavrov, also criticized the new US sanctions against Iran, arguing that they 'threaten the realization' of the JCPOA, which he described as 'one of the key factors of international and regional stability'.[37] Russia is opposed to renegotiating the JCPOA.[38]

China's Foreign Minister, Wang Yi, said in September that 'all parties should look at the positive side of the JCPOA as no agreement is perfect. Should the agreement be discarded, the international non-proliferation regime would be severely impacted and the situation in the Middle East might worsen'.[39]

Discussion in Iran

From Iran's perspective, the USA has breached articles 26, 27 and 28 of the JCPOA by creating a negative atmosphere that undermines sanctions relief.[40] Iran has raised these concerns at meetings of the Joint Commission.[41] Iran distinguishes between the above breaches and the potential reimposition of nuclear-related sanctions, which it terms a 'gross violation' of the JCPOA.[42] Iran's Supreme Leader, Ali Khamenei, has warned that Iran would 'set fire' to the deal if the USA violates the JCPOA, and the Iranian Parliament has called for reciprocity regarding US actions.[43] However, the President of Iran, Hassan Rouhani, and the Foreign Minister, Javad Zarif, have suggested that Iran might stick to the deal even if the USA does not.[44]

Public support in Iran for the JCPOA has fallen as a result of the slow pace of economic recovery and the renewed confrontation with the USA. According to an opinion poll in June 2017, while two-thirds of respondents

---

[36] 'Russia hopes US refusal to recertify Iran nuclear deal will not impact JCPOA realization', TASS, 13 Oct. 2017.

[37] Lavrov, S. V., Russian Minister of Foreign Affairs, Statement at the UN General Assembly, 21 Sep. 2017.

[38] Comments by Russian Deputy Foreign Minister Sergey Riabkov at the Moscow Nonproliferation Conference, 21 Oct. 2017.

[39] Xinhua, 'China calls for support for Iran nuclear deal', *China Daily*, 21 Sep. 2017.

[40] Comments by Iran's Deputy Foreign Minister, Abbas Araghchi, at the Moscow Nonproliferation Conference, 21 Oct. 2017, YouTube; and 'Iran Foreign Ministry submits 7th report on JCPOA to parliament', Press TV, 24 Oct. 2017.

[41] See e.g. Press release on behalf of the Joint Commission of the JCPOA (10 Jan. 2017), Brussels, 10 Jan. 2017; 'Chair's statement following the 21 July 2017 meeting of the JCPOA Joint Commission', Brussels, 21 July 2017; and 'Iran reserves right to respond to US violation of JCPOA: Araqchi', Press TV, 21 July 2017.

[42] 'Iran Foreign Ministry submits 7th report on JCPOA to parliament' (note 40).

[43] 'Iran's Khamenei threatens to "set fire" to nuclear deal if West violates', Reuters, 14 June 2017; and 'Iran Majlis committee passes motion to counter US hostilities', Press TV, 29 July 2017.

[44] See e.g. 'President in a live televised speech', Official Website of the President of the Islamic Republic of Iran, 13 Oct. 2017; and 'Iran: We will stick to nuclear deal if Europe does', Deutsche Welle, 15 Oct. 2017.

still supported the JCPOA, the majority felt that it had not led to economic improvement and that Iran should respond to a US violation by restarting parts of its nuclear programme.[45] The street protests that began in various Iranian cities in late December 2017 also reflected widespread discontent with the poor state of the economy and with living standards in the country.[46]

Calls for Iran to limit its missile programme have found little understanding among Iranians. In response to the US decertification, President Rouhani said 'Our . . . missiles are for our defence. We have always been determined to defend our country and we became more determined today'.[47] The June 2017 poll also found that 63 per cent of Iranians viewed the demand that Iran reduce its missile testing as unacceptable.[48]

Conclusions

Iran continued to live up to its commitments under the JCPOA throughout 2017. However, the future of the deal looks bleak because the USA is reconsidering the value of the continued implementation of its reciprocal commitments. Although the US Congress chose not to undermine the JCPOA following the October decertification decision, in May 2018 President Trump might decide not to waive the sanctions that were suspended as part of the JCPOA, thus unilaterally violating the deal. In that case, Iran might also withdraw from the deal. However, it might instead decide to stick to the deal's provisions if the reciprocity of the collective commitments is preserved by other means—notably by a European refusal to comply with reimposed extraterritorial US sanctions.

Even if the rest of the E3/EU+3 manage to convince President Trump to waive sanctions in May, he could keep referring the matter back to Congress every 90 days through decertification.[49] The resulting atmosphere of uncertainty would make business and financial institutions increasingly wary of entering the Iranian market, thereby undermining the benefits of the JCPOA that Iran was supposed to enjoy through sanctions relief. This could lead to a slow-motion erosion of the deal through decreasing domestic support in Iran. Given the precariousness of the situation, the JCPOA will also be more vulnerable to political shifts, notably to increasing animosity between the

[45] Gallagher, N., 'Three ways Trump's nuclear strategy misunderstands the mood in Iran', The Conversation, 14 Oct. 2017.

[46] Kottasová, I., 'The economic forces driving protests in Iran', CNN Money, 2 Jan. 2018.

[47] 'President in a live televised speech' (note 44).

[48] Gallagher (note 45).

[49] Aleem, Z., 'Trump punted the Iran deal to Congress: Congress just punted it back'. Vox, 12 Dec. 2017.

USA and Iran over the latter's missile tests, regional issues or the Iranian Government's responses to possible domestic unrest in the country.

To preserve the JCPOA, the E3/EU, Russia and China will need to work particularly hard not only to prevent outright violations of the deal, but also to address the less apparent dangers related to obstacles to sanctions relief and the escalation of tensions on issues not directly related to the JCPOA.

8. Chemical and biological security threats

Overview

The United Nations, the Organisation for the Prohibition of Chemical Weapons (OPCW) and governments continued to evaluate allegations of chemical weapon (CW) use in Iraq and Syria in 2017. Both the UN Security Council and the OPCW Executive Council remained deadlocked on the question of Syrian Government responsibility for CW use (see section I), including with regard to the use of sarin at Khan Shaykhun on 4 April. This attack prompted the United States to launch retaliatory Tomahawk cruise missile strikes against a Syrian airbase.

The mandate of the OPCW–UN Joint Investigative Mechanism (JIM) in Syria expired in November because the Security Council was unable to agree terms for an extension. While it operated, the JIM issued seven reports and concluded that the Syrian Government was responsible for four cases of CW use and that non-state actors were responsible for two cases. The work of the OPCW Declaration Assessment Team on the completeness and correctness of Syria's declarations to the Technical Secretariat and of the OPCW Fact-finding Mission (FFM) to evaluate allegations of CW use in Syria will continue in 2018. The FFM provided the information baseline on allegations of CW use to the JIM.

As the Islamic State group lost territory in both Iraq and Syria, various governments undertook further efforts to ascertain the group's CW-related intentions and capabilities. The work of international criminal investigations and prosecutions, such as the 'International, Impartial and Independent Mechanism to Assist in the Most Serious Crimes under International Law Committed in the Syrian Arab Republic since March 2011' established by the UN General Assembly at the end of 2016, could eventually facilitate the achievement of a common international understanding on responsibility for all the documented instances of confirmed CW use.

No authoritative public information was made available on the sampling and analysis of the chemical (understood to be VX) used to kill Kim Jong Nam, the half-brother of Kim Jong Un, the leader of North Korea, at Kuala Lumpur International Airport, Malaysia, in February 2017. The Malaysian authorities put on trial the two women who were recorded by surveillance cameras applying a substance to the face of the victim. The OPCW and several of its member states provided Malaysia with unspecified technical support with the investigation (see section II).

SIPRI Yearbook 2018: Armaments, Disarmament and International Security
www.sipriyearbook.org

Russia—formerly the largest possessor of chemical weapons—completed the destruction of its stockpile in 2017, as required by the 1993 Chemical Weapons Convention (CWC). The 22nd Conference of the States Parties (CSP) to the CWC convened in November 2017 (see section III). It reviewed the status of planning for the Fourth CWC Review Conference, which will be held in 2018, and elected Ambassador Fernando Arias of Spain as the next Director-General. It remains to be seen how Syria, which became a party to the CWC in 2013, will operate within the treaty regime (including in relation to forthcoming changes to the senior OPCW leadership) where relations among the parties are informed by a strongly held concept of equal rights and obligations. In particular, the parties have been unable to reach common understanding on whether Syria should be treated as uncooperative and in fundamental non-compliance with its treaty obligations, or if the country should be treated as a 'normal' party working towards clarifying concerns regarding its treaty obligations in good faith.

In December the annual meeting of states parties (MSP) to the 1972 Biological and Toxin Weapons Convention (BTWC) agreed a further intersessional process of annual meetings for the period 2018–20. The parties will continue to discuss and promote common understanding and effective action on selected topics. Some states parties wish to move the interactions among the membership towards more specific discussions about compliance. These parties have continued to focus on modifications to the content, structure and handling of the current politically binding information exchanges that are intended to serve as confidence-building measures. The 2017 outcome represents a continuation of the status quo, whereby information, views and best practices on the convention's various provisions are exchanged in annual Meetings of Experts and MSPs with the support of the Geneva-based Implementation Support Unit (ISU). The BTWC regime also continued to experience financial difficulties due to the continuing underpayment or non-payment of assessed contributions by many states parties (see section IV).

JOHN HART

I. Allegations of use of chemical weapons in Syria

JOHN HART

The United Nations, the Organisation for the Prohibition of Chemical Weapons (OPCW), various governments and civil society continued to examine allegations of chemical weapon (CW) use in Syria throughout 2017. However, the UN Security Council and the OPCW Executive Council remained deadlocked on the question of Syrian Government responsibility for CW use. This section describes the ad hoc international arrangements used to evaluate Syria's declarations under the 1993 Chemical Weapons Convention (CWC) and reviews the reports of the OPCW Fact-finding Mission (FFM).[1] It also describes developments in Syria in 2017, including the use of sarin at Khan Shaykhun on 4 April, which prompted the United States to launch retaliatory Tomahawk cruise missile strikes against a Syrian airbase. Finally, the section discusses the likely future focus of the work of the OPCW in Syria and the issue of CW-related sanctions.

The ad hoc arrangements for evaluating Syria's CWC declarations

The OPCW FFM has collected and analysed information related to the numerous instances of suspected CW use in Syria since it was established in 2014.[2] The FFM provided the information baseline that supported the work of the OPCW–UN Joint Investigative Mechanism (JIM), which was established in August 2015.[3] While it operated, the JIM issued seven reports and attributed responsibility for CW use to both the Syrian Government and non-state actors.[4] The JIM's mandate ended on 16 November 2017. The ad hoc arrangements involving the FFM on CW use allegations and the OPCW Declarations Assessment Team (DAT) continued to investigate the completeness and correctness of Syria's declarations under the CWC.

The CWC negotiators intended that the convention's provisions on investigations of alleged use of CWs and, in other suspected cases of fundamental non-compliance, challenge inspections, should be used, rather than such ad

---

[1] On the Convention on the Prohibition of the Development, Production, Stockpiling and Use of Chemical Weapons and on their Destruction (Chemical Weapons Convention, CWC) see also annex A, section I, in this volume.

[2] See Hart, J., 'Chemical disarmament in conflict areas', *SIPRI Yearbook 2015*, pp. 584–85; Hart, J., 'Investigation of alleged chemical weapon use in Syria and other locations in the Middle East', *SIPRI Yearbook 2016*, pp. 731–39; and Hart, J., 'Achieving clarity on Syrian chemical weapon declarations to the OPCW and continued chemical weapon use allegations', *SIPRI Yearbook 2017*, pp. 518–19.

[3] UN Security Council Resolution 2235, 7 Aug. 2015.

[4] United Nations, Security Council, first–seventh reports of the Organization for the Prohibition of Chemical Weapons–United Nations Joint Investigative Mechanism, S/2016/142, 12 Feb. 2016; S/2016/530, 10 June 2016; S/2016/738, 24 Aug. 2016; S/2016/888, 21 Oct. 2016; S/2017/131, 13 Feb. 2017; S/2017/552, 28 June 2017; and S/2017/904, 26 Oct. 2017.

Table 8.1. Summary of attributions by the Joint Investigative Mechanism of responsibility for chemical weapon use in Syria

Location	Date	Attribution	Chemical weapon agent
Marea	21 Aug. 2015	Non-state actor	Sulphur mustard
Umm Hawsh	16 Sep. 2016	Non-state actor	Sulphur mustard
Talmenes	21 Apr. 2014	Syrian Government	Chlorine
Qmenas	16 Mar. 2015	Syrian Government	Chlorine
Sarmin	16 Mar. 2015	Syrian Government	Chlorine
Khan Shaykhun	4 Apr. 2017	Syrian Government	Sarin (or 'sarin-like')

Source: United Nations, Security Council, 'Third report of the Organization for the Prohibition of Chemical Weapons–United Nations Joint Investigative Mechanism', S/2016/738, 24 Aug. 2016; and United Nations, Security Council, 'Seventh report of the Organisation for the Prohibition of Chemical Weapons–United Nations Joint Investigative Mechanism', S/2017/904, 26 Oct. 2017.

hoc arrangements.[5] However, they did not anticipate that a state might join the convention in a time of civil war, much less one that was part of a wider, longer-term regional armed conflict. In addition, a state's legal obligations are based on the understanding that its territory is under full governmental jurisdiction and control. Given the lack of security and clear understanding of who has controlled much of Syria's territory since 2013 when Syria joined the CWC, the OPCW declaration and verification procedures have had to be adjusted to reflect variable, on-the-ground physical security exigencies. Nor did the negotiators anticipate a geopolitical process whereby accession to the convention would be facilitated by an agreed framework concluded by two permanent members of the UN Security Council—Russia and the USA—or that the Security Council and the OPCW Executive Council would jointly supervise specially created verification mechanisms over a multi-year period, yielding results that have been partly interpreted according to broader, political interests. In particular, the UN Security Council and the OPCW Executive Council were unable to achieve consensus on the JIM's attribution of responsibility to the Syrian Government (see table 8.1).

Of the 27 chemical weapon production facilities (CWPFs) ultimately declared by Syria, the final two to remain outside of Syrian Government control—Al Dhamir 1 near Aleppo and Al Dhamir 2 near Damascus—were finally visited by the OPCW in late 2017, following a reduction in the fighting.

The DAT continued to seek further clarity on the nature and role of facilities belonging to Syria's Scientific Studies and Research Centre (SSRC). In

---

[5] Such violations are distinct from lesser violations of a more technical or administrative nature. CWC (note 1), Article IX, paras 8–25, Verification Annex, Parts X and XI. See also Hart, J., 'Political and technical aspects of challenge inspections under the Chemical Weapons Convention', Paper presented at 'EU seminar on "challenge inspections" in the framework of the CWC', Vienna, 24–25 June 2004.

2017 the OPCW Technical Secretariat conducted two rounds of inspections of SSRC facilities, triggered by the results of previous visits and analyses of samples taken during inspections conducted prior to 2017. The results indicated that Syria had not fully disclosed all the relevant chemicals in its CW programme. The identity of these chemicals has not been officially released to the public.[6]

On 30 September 2017 Syria supplemented its initial declaration to the OPCW by declaring additional laboratories and rooms at the SSRC.[7] On 2 October 2017 Syria also provided an overview of general activities at the SSRC, including Institute 3000.[8] On 10 November 2017 Syria provided 19 documents (around 450 pages) to the OPCW describing research and development activities at SSRC declared laboratories for the period 1995–2010.[9] The OPCW conducted a second round of inspections at the Barzah and Jamraya facilities of the SSRC on 14–21 November 2017.[10]

Reports by the OPCW Fact-finding Mission

In 2017 the FFM issued at least eight reports dealing with three incidents of alleged chemical weapon use and a summary report of its investigation activities throughout 2017.[11]

The first report was on an incident involving the use of sulphur mustard at Um-Housh on 16 September 2016.[12] The FFM interviewed casualties, took blood samples for analysis and examined a mortar round that had been made available by specialists from a Russian chemical, biological, radiological and nuclear technical team working with the SSRC in Barzi. The FFM found that

[6] Hart, *SIPRI Yearbook 2017* (note 2), pp. 514–15.
[7] OPCW, 'Progress in the elimination of the Syrian Chemical weapons programme', Note by the Director-General, EC-87/DG.4, 24 Nov. 2017, para. 8, p. 2.
[8] OPCW, EC-87/DG.4 (note 7), para. 8, p. 2.
[9] OPCW, EC-87/DG.4 (note 7), para. 10, p. 3.
[10] OPCW, EC-87/DG.4 (note 7), para. 11, p. 3.
[11] OPCW, Technical Secretariat, 'Report of the OPCW Fact-finding Mission in Syria regarding the incident of 16 September 2016 as reported in the note verbale of the Syrian Arab Republic number 113 dated 29 November 2016', S/1491/2017, 1 May 2017; 'Status update of the OPCW Fact-finding Mission in Syria regarding a reported incident in Khan Shaykhun, 4 April 2017', S/1497/2017, 12 May 2017; 'Report of the OPCW Fact-finding Mission in Syria regarding an alleged incident in Khan Shaykhun, Syrian Arab Republic, April 2017', S/1510/2017, 29 June 2017; 'Analysis results of the samples provided by the Government of the Syrian Arab Republic in relation to the alleged incident in Khan Shaykhun, Syrian Arab Republic, April 2017', S/1521/2017, 28 July 2017; 'Analysis results of samples relating to the alleged use of chemicals as weapons in Ltamenah, Hama Governorate, Syrian Arab Republic, March 2017', S/1544/2017, 12 Oct. 2017; 'Further clarifications why the OPCW Fact-finding Mission did not deploy to Khan Shaykhun', S/1545/2017, 17 Oct. 2017; 'Report of the OPCW Fact-finding Mission in Syria regarding an alleged incident in Ltamenah, the Syrian Arab Republic, 30 March 2017', S/1548/2017, 2 Nov. 2017; and 'Summary update of the activities carried out by the OPCW Fact-finding Mission in Syria in 2017', S/1556/2017, 14 Nov. 2017.
[12] OPCW, S/1491/2017 (note 11).

a 217-millimetre calibre projectile had contained sulphur mustard, and that two casualties had been exposed to sulphur mustard.

The FFM issued two reports—a preliminary report dated 12 May 2017 followed by a full FFM report of 29 June 2017—on the 4 April sarin incident at Khan Shaykhun.[13] The FFM concluded that at least 86 people had died from exposure to sarin or a sarin-like substance but did not attribute responsibility as this was outside its mandate. The chemical originated from a single crater caused by an aerial munition, either an air-launched rocket or an aerial bomb. The normal OPCW chain-of-custody procedure was not observed for the samples analysed. Russia has been highly critical on this point. The FFM did not deploy to Khan Shaykhun or the Shayrat Airfield, which housed the aircraft that had attacked the location.[14] FFM members did, however, attend autopsies in a neighbouring country, collect biomedical specimens and receive environmental samples from third parties. DNA analyses of biomedical samples obtained by third parties and samples collected by the FFM team enabled it to link the individuals it had interviewed and who tested positive for sarin to samples collected in Khan Shaykhun by third parties. The FFM also received samples from the Government of Syria, which were analysed by the OPCW chemical laboratory as well as two designated laboratories. These showed the presence of CWC-relevant chemicals, such as sarin, diisopropyl methylphosphonate (DIMP) and hexamine.[15] Hexamine and methylphosphonyl difluoride (DF) have been used by Syria in the synthesis of sarin as part of its prior programme declared to the OPCW in 2013.

The FFM also investigated the alleged use of a chemical weapon in Ltamenah, Hama Governorate, in March 2017. The FFM was unable to visit the incident location but it did interview casualties and medical staff in a neighbouring country and obtained environmental samples, including munition parts. A report on the analysis of these soil and metal samples confirmed the presence of sarin and a number of related degradation products, as well as products related to sarin synthesis.[16] The FFM report published on the incident in November 2017 concluded that it was 'more than likely' that sarin had been used at Ltamenah.[17] Once again it did not attribute responsibility as this was outside its mandate.

---

[13] OPCW, S/1497/2017 (note 11); and OPCW, S/1510/2017 (note 11).
[14] For a detailed explanation see OPCW, S/1545/2017 (note 11).
[15] OPCW, S/1521/2017 (note 11).
[16] OPCW, S/1544/2017 (note 11).
[17] OPCW, S/1548/2017 (note 11).

Developments in Syria in 2017

The fighting in Syria intensified early in 2017 but diminished towards the end of the year.[18] Government forces recaptured Wadi Barada and al-Waar in Homs in mid-February, while in February and March opposition forces with some coordination with the al-Nusra Front launched offensives in Daraa, Damascus and Hama.[19]

On 28 February 2017 China and Russia vetoed a UN Security Council resolution that would have sanctioned Syria for CW use based on the findings of the JIM.[20] On 27 April 2017 the three-member Senior Leadership Panel of the JIM was reconstituted by the new UN Secretary-General, António Guterres. Ambassador Edmond Mulet of Guatemala replaced Virginia Gamba of Argentina as head of the JIM. The other two new members were Stefan Mogl of Switzerland and Judy Cheng-Hopkins of Malaysia.[21]

Chemical weapon attack at Khan Shaykhun

The CW attack on Khan Shaykhun in southern Idlib on 4 April 2017 occurred in the context of fighting by government forces to retake territory recently lost in northern Hama.[22] As noted above, the incident resulted in the deaths of at least 86 people.[23] In response, the USA attacked the Shayrat Airfield in Homs Governorate with 59 Raytheon RGM-109 Tomahawk Land Attack Missiles (TLAMs) on 7 April.[24] According to the US Department of Defense (DOD), the purpose of the strike was to 'deter the [Syrian] regime from using chemical weapons' and thus 'proportionality is measured against that outcome'.[25] The USA stated that the airbase had stored chemical weapons previously and that it had a high level of confidence that the airbase was used to launch the CW attack.[26] The Syrian General Command characterized the US strike as a 'blatant act of aggression'.[27]

---

[18] Ripley, T., 'Syrian Government forces complete multiple encirclements of IS fighters', *Jane's Defence Weekly*, vol. 54, no. 35 (30 Aug. 2017), p. 4. On the conflict in Syria see chapter 2, section V, this volume.

[19] United Nations, 'Syria: As US responds militarily to chemical attack, UN urges restraint to avoid escalation', UN News Centre, 7 Apr. 2017.

[20] United Nations, 'Russia blocks Security Council action on reported use of chemical weapons in Syria's Khan Shaykhun', UN News Centre, 12 Apr. 2017.

[21] United Nations, 'Secretary-General appoints Edmond Mulet of Guatemala head of Security Council Joint Investigative Mechanism on chemical weapon use in Syria', Press release, 27 Apr. 2017.

[22] United Nations (note 19).

[23] United Nations (note 19).

[24] Ferdinando, L., 'US strike designed to deter Assad regime's use of chemical weapons', US DOD Press release, 7 Apr. 2017. For a summary of Russian air defence systems in Syria at the time see Johnson, R. F., 'Tomahawk strike in Syria stokes debate about Russian air defences', *Jane's Defence Weekly*, vol. 54, no. 16 (19 Apr. 2017), p. 4.

[25] Ferdinando (note 24).

[26] Ferdinando (note 24).

[27] United Nations (note 19).

At the UN Security Council, Iran and Russia condemned the US strike, while Australia, Germany, Italy, Japan, the Netherlands, New Zealand, Saudi Arabia, Turkey and the United Kingdom expressed 'some support' for the USA.[28] US President Donald J. Trump justified the attack as a proportionate response, arguing that it was in the 'vital national security interest of the United States to prevent and deter the spread and use of deadly chemical weapons'.[29]

According to the US DOD, although the USA was not 'tracking the airfield as an active chemical site', it did take precautions against hitting items that might result in the release of toxic chemicals or their precursors.[30] The attack resulted in the destruction of approximately 20 aircraft, as well as some surface-to-air missile systems and hangars.[31] The DOD estimated that there had been damage to aircraft, hardened aircraft shelters, petroleum and logistical storage, ammunition supply bunkers, air defence systems and radar.[32]

Saudi Arabia characterized the US strike as a 'courageous decision'.[33] On 8 April Iran's President Hassan Rouhani called for an impartial investigation into the Khan Shaykhun attack.[34] The following day he criticized the US strike as 'flagrant US aggression on Syria'.[35] On the same day the Joint Command Centre, comprising Iranian, Russian and Syrian Government forces and allied militia groups, issued a statement that the US attack on the Syrian airbase had crossed 'red lines', and that the USA would be responsible for any increase in their level of support for the Syrian Government and associated additional violence.[36]

On 11 April the White House released a summary of US Government intelligence concerning the Syrian Government's responsibility for the chemical weapon attack.[37] On 12 April Russia vetoed a proposed UN Security Council resolution drafted by France, the UK and the USA that would have condemned the 4 April attack and would have called on the Syrian Government to comply with the relevant recommendations of the OPCW FFM and

---

[28] United Nations (note 19).

[29] The White House, Office of the Press Secretary, 'Statement by President Trump on Syria', Press release, 6 Apr. 2017.

[30] Ferdinando (note 24).

[31] Ferdinando (note 24).

[32] Garamone, J., 'Trump orders missile attack in retaliation for Syrian chemical strikes', Press release, US Department of Defense, 6 Apr. 2017.

[33] 'Iran's Rouhani condemns US attack on Syria, chides Gulf Arabs', Reuters, 9 Apr. 2017.

[34] 'Iran's Rouhani condemns US attack on Syria, chides Gulf Arabs' (note 33).

[35] 'Iran's Rouhani condemns US attack on Syria, chides Gulf Arabs' (note 33).

[36] Al-Khalidi, S., 'Assad's allies say US attack crosses "red lines"', Reuters, 9 Apr. 2017.

[37] The White House, 'The Assad regime's use of chemical weapons on April 4, 2017', Press release, 11 Apr. 2017.

the JIM.[38] Ten Security Council members voted in favour, two (including Russia) voted against, while China, Ethiopia and Kazakhstan abstained.[39]

In an interview published on 13 April 2017 the Syrian President, Bashar al-Assad, stated that Syria did not possess any chemical weapons, having relinquished its CW stockpile, and that even if Syria did have CWs it would not use them. He added that Syria had never used CWs, that the children seen in news footage could have been brought in from elsewhere, that al-Qaeda members have been known to 'shave their beards and put on white helmets' [i.e. Syrian Civil Defence Forces which operate in opposition-controlled areas], and that the USA was working hand in hand with 'terrorists' and had fabricated the sarin attack story.[40] On 12 April Syria proposed that the OPCW Director-General send a new 'technical mission' to Khan Shaykhun and Shayrat airbase to investigate the matter.[41]

April meeting of the OPCW Executive Council

On 13 April the OPCW Executive Council met to review the FFM's preliminary analysis and findings on the CW attack. Some members of the Executive Council did not take a position on whether Syria was responsible for the attack, while some that made statements did not authorize the OPCW to place them on its website.

Canada accused 'Syria and its allies of deflecting attention from technical conclusions they do not like by questioning the credibility of the exercise and seeking to introduce competing processes to the mix'.[42]

Cuba, by contrast, stated that 'using the alleged use of chemical weapons by the government of Syria as a pretext is a grave violation of the Charter of the United Nations and International Law and an outrage against a sovereign State, which worsens the conflict in the country and the region and delays the achievement of a negotiated solution'.[43]

Iran stated that:

every necessary step towards the complete removal and elimination of the Syrian chemical weapons programme have been undertaken by the OPCW and this significant and noticeable progress has been made in the light of full cooperation by the Syrian Arab Republic . . . the government of Syria was verifiably disarmed from all chemical arms by the United Nations. Thus, the undeniable fact is that, among others, Al-Nusrah Front and Daesh, are the only parties in possession of chemical weapons, with internationally documented track record of having used them, in

---

[38] United Nations (note 20).

[39] United Nations (note 20).

[40] ClarityNews43, 'President Assad: Latest interview 4/13/2017', 13 Apr. 2017, YouTube; and 'Syria chemical attack "fabricated", Assad', BBC News, 13 Apr. 2017.

[41] The proposal itself does not appear to be public. Canada referred to it in its statement to the Executive Council. OPCW, Executive Council, 54th meeting, Statement of Canada, 13 Apr. 2017, p. 1.

[42] OPCW, Statement of Canada (note 41), p. 2.

[43] OPCW, Executive Council, 54th meeting, Statement of Cuba, 13 Apr. 2017, pp. 1–2.

Iraq and Syria. In this regard, the Islamic Republic of Iran calls for formation of an impartial and professional international Team of experts to investigate comprehensively both incidents on-site and clarify how and through what borders these chemical weapons entered and used in the Syrian Arab Republic.[44]

Ireland supported the referral of 'possible war crimes and crimes against humanity perpetrated in Syria to the International Criminal Court'.[45] The UK stated that, based on analysis of samples taken from Khan Shaykhun which tested positive for sarin or a 'sarin-like substance', 'it is highly likely that the Syrian Government was responsible for a sarin attack on Khan Shaykhun on 4 April'.[46]

The USA was critical of Russia's stance:

On April 7, the Press Service of the President of Russia issued an official statement asserting 'the fact of the destruction of all Syrian Chemical weapons' stockpiles has been recorded and verified by the OPCW, a specialized UN body.' . . . As Russia is no doubt aware, nothing could be further from the truth as the Director-General on several occasions has made clear that 'the Secretariat is not able to resolve all identified gaps, inconsistencies and discrepancies in Syria's declaration, and therefore cannot fully verify that Syria has submitted a declaration that can be considered accurate and complete in accordance with the Chemical Weapons Convention or Council decision EC-M-33/DEC.1, dated 27 September 2013.' Russia should immediately issue an official retraction of this blatant distortion.[47]

The Executive Council reconvened on 19 April to discuss the 4 April attack. The OPCW Director-General, Ahmet Üzümcü, reported that:

The bio-medical samples collected from three victims at autopsy were analysed at two OPCW designated labs. The results of analysis indicate that these victims were exposed to sarin or a sarin like substance. Bio-medical samples from seven individuals undergoing treatment at hospitals were also analysed in two other OPCW designated labs . . . the results of these analyses indicate exposure to Sarin or a Sarin like substance . . . while further details of laboratory analyses will follow, the analytical results are incontrovertible.[48]

'Sarin-like' may refer to detection of the methyl-phosphonate moiety (functional group) in the biomedical samples. The biomedical analytical techniques employed do not detect intact sarin. In principle the methylphosphonate moiety could derive from a sarin analogue based on a different alcohol. The term may also have been used to avoid the use of more definite language in legal and political circles.

[44] OPCW, Executive Council, 54th meeting, Statement of Iran, 13 Apr. 2017, pp. 1–3.

[45] OPCW, Executive Council, 54th meeting, Statement of Ireland, 13 Apr. 2017, p. 2.

[46] OPCW, Executive Council, 54th meeting, Statement of the United Kingdom, 13 Apr. 2017, pp. 1–3.

[47] OPCW, Executive Council, 54th meeting, Statement of the United States, 13 Apr. 2017, pp. 1–3.

[48] OPCW, 'OPCW Director-General shares incontrovertible laboratory results concluding exposure to sarin', Press release, 19 Apr. 2017.

France later issued statements and summaries of unclassified intelligence reports on the 4 April attack.[49] Russia maintained that there was no reliable evidence to indicate Syrian Government responsibility for CW use.[50]

The Executive Council rejected a draft decision tabled by Iran and Russia that would have entailed the establishment of a new technical investigative body.[51]

Towards an attribution of responsibility by the JIM

On 6 July Mulet briefed the UN Security Council on the progress made by the JIM. After the meeting, Mulet told media representatives: 'We do receive, unfortunately, direct and indirect messages all the time from many sides telling us how to do our work'. He added that nearly 20 actors had provided their views to JIM members on whether the Syrian Government was responsible for any (or none) of the CW attacks.

As of 6 July the FFM was prioritizing six or seven other investigations of alleged use. Mulet remained open to the idea of the JIM visiting the Khan Shahkhun site and the Shayrat airbase if the security situation allowed. Mulet stated that Syria had not provided the information required for the airbase visit, such as flight logs, details of movement around the base and the names of the people that the JIM would be interviewing.

Mulet observed that the JIM was working in a highly politicized environment and appealed to the members of the UN Security Council to allow it to carry out its work. He promised that any findings would be based on facts and science.[52]

JIM October report

On 6 October Russia sent a letter to the UN Secretary-General criticizing the methods of work of the FFM and the JIM.[53] Russia stated that it wished to review the report on Khan Shaykhun prior to deciding whether to extend

[49] French Ministry for Europe and Foreign Affairs, 'Chemical attack in Syria: National evaluation presented by Jean-Marc Ayrault following the Defense Council Meeting', 26 Apr. 2017.

[50] Russian Ministry of Foreign Affairs, 'Comment by the Information and Press Department on the investigation launched by France into the alleged use of chemical weapons in Khan Shaykhun', 27 Apr. 2017, Press release.

[51] OPCW, Executive Council, 'Addressing the situation around the alleged use of chemical weapons in the Khan Shaykhun area of southern Idlib in the Syrian Arab Republic', Draft decision EC-M-54/DEC/CRP.1, 13 Apr. 2017.

[52] United Nations Radio, 'Syria chemical weapons investigations proceeding "objectively, impartially"', 6 July 2017. See also United Nations, 'Edmond Mulet (OPCW–UN Joint Investigative Mechanism) on chemical weapon use in Syria—SC stakeout', 6 July 2017.

[53] United Nations, General Assembly and Security Council, Letter dated 6 October 2017 from the Permanent Representative of the Russian Federation to the United Nations addressed to the Secretary-General, S/2017/848, 10 Oct. 2017; and 'Vote on the Syria Joint Investigative Mechanism', What's in Blue, 23 Oct. 2017.

the JIM's mandate for a further 12 months. The USA maintained that the JIM's mandate should be extended prior to the report's release.[54]

According to the Director of the Russian Foreign Ministry's Non-proliferation and Arms Control Department, Mikhail Ulyanov:

the JIM staff investigated the incident in Khan Shaykhun remotely, mostly from The Hague and New York offices . . . Although they should have visited both Khan Shaykhun, where the April 4 chemical weapon incident took place, and the Shayrat air base, where according to Americans, sarin used in Khan Shaykhun had been stored . . . the situation looks like a subversion . . . . First, the UN mission refused to visit the incident scene in Khan Shaykhun. They carried out their investigations in a country neighboring Syria, referring to a lack of necessary security conditions . . . it has turned out recently that this does not correspond to reality. Two weeks ago, the UN Secretariat's Department of Safety and Security confirmed at the Security Council that in fact safe and secure access to the scene was guaranteed to UN staff by local field commanders.[55]

Syria rejected the findings of the JIM's seventh report, condemning 'the reliance of the [JIM] on the words of criminals who committed this immoral act in Khan Sheikhoun and those of suspect witnesses, as well as so-called open sources'.[56]

The JIM's mandate expired in November.[57] Consequently, the OPCW can only formally investigate the continued use of CWs in Syria via the FFM or on the basis of a request by its members to initiate an investigation of alleged use or a challenge inspection. It is possible that the OPCW could use the forensic capacity of its Rapid Response and Assistance Mission (RRAM), which was established in 2016.[58] The consideration of such factors will be informed by impending changes to the OPCW leadership, when Fernando Arias replaces Üzümcü as OPCW Director-General in July 2018.

Other developments

The work of international bodies that do not specialize in arms control and the understandings and statements of security and defence sector officials with close or direct involvement in Syria provide further insight into this case and its wider geopolitical implications. In 2017 the Independent International Commission of Inquiry on the Syrian Arab Republic, which was established by the UN Human Rights Council in 2011 to investigate human

[54] Landry, C., 'US, Russia headed for clash over UN gas attack probe', AFP News, 18 Oct. 2017.

[55] 'Probe into chemical weapon incidents in Syria looks like subversion, diplomat says', TASS, 20 Oct. 2017.

[56] Dadouch, S., 'Syria rejects report blaming it for April sarin attack: State media', Reuters, 27 Oct. 2017.

[57] On the work of the JIM see also Hart, *SIPRI Yearbook 2016* (note 2), pp. 730–31; and Hart, *SIPRI Yearbook 2017* (note 2), pp. 519–22.

[58] The RRAM was meant to strengthen the treaty regime's general response capacity and is not Syria-specific. See OPCW, Technical Secretariat, 'Establishment of a rapid response assistance team', S/1381/2016, 10 May 2016.

rights abuses, noted that 'Throughout 2016, Syrian air forces launched air strikes using chlorine bombs in eastern Aleppo city. There is no information to support the claim that the Russian military ever used any chemical weapons in the Syrian Arab Republic. While civilians exposed to chlorine may exhibit symptoms similar to those exposed to vesicants, such as sulphur mustard, chlorine gas was identified as the most likely agent in several cases.'[59]

Brigadier-General Zaher al-Sakat, who reportedly headed the chemical warfare unit of the 5th Division of the Syrian Army prior to defecting in 2013, told a British newspaper in 2017 that the Syrian Government had not declared to the OPCW 'large amounts of sarin precursor chemicals and other toxic materials'.[60]

On 19 April 2017 an unnamed senior member of the Israel Defense Forces (IDF) stated that the 4 April attack had been authorized by senior Syrian Government officials 'possibly with the full personal knowledge of President Assad himself'.[61] The officer observed 'In the past, Assad had possessed some 1200 tons of chemical warfare agents fitted to missiles, artillery shells and airborne munitions, and most of this arsenal was destroyed. What he has now are just a few remaining tons of chemical warfare agents. The attack using Sarin gas reflects frustration and distress on Assad's part.'[62]

The future of the Syria case

The future focus of the OPCW in Syria will be on (a) clarifying the completeness and correctness of Syria's declaration, with a focus on SSRC facilities through the DAT; (b) reaching closure on the allegations of CW use through the FFM; (c) verifying the destruction of two above-ground CWPFs; and (d) conducting routine annual CWC-mandated inspections of underground structures already destroyed, including CWPFs. The DAT's focus on Syria's declarations will be on (a) the role of the SSRC in Syria's CW programme; (b) clarifying the results of analyses of samples taken by the OPCW at multiple locations in Syria; and (c) clarifying the nature of 'other chemical

---

[59] United Nations, Human Rights Council, 'Report of the Independent International Commission of Inquiry on the Syrian Arab Republic', A/HRC/34/64, 2 Feb. 2017, para. 17, p. 6.

[60] Ensor, J., 'Bashar al-Assad still has "hundreds of tons" of chemicals stockpiled, former Syrian weapons research chief claims', *Daily Telegraph*, 15 Apr. 2017.

[61] Heller, O., 'IDF: "High-ranking Syrian officers ordered the chemical attack in Idlib', Israel Defense, 20 Apr. 2017. More complete information is provided in the Hebrew-language version, <http://www.israeldefense.co.il/he/node/29287>.

[62] Heller (note 61). See also Chulov, M., 'Qatari royal family members used as leverage in Syrian population swap', *The Guardian*, 14 Apr. 2017.

weapons-related activities' that occurred prior to Syria's accession to the CWC in 2013.[63]

In addition, scientific research on the victims of CWs in Iraq and Syria underwent peer review in 2017 prior to publication. The research included a cohort study of a family exposed to sulphur mustard in Syria in August 2015 and analyses of degradation products characteristic of the impurities associated with sulphur mustard produced by the Levinstein process.[64] Further information and studies were published on conventional weapons research and development projects, including improvised explosive devices (IEDs), carried out by Islamic State affiliates in Iraq and Syria. As a consequence of the use of CWs in Iraq and Syria, biomedical sampling and analysis protocols have now been standardized in the chemical weapons disarmament and arms control fields, including in annual OPCW laboratory proficiency tests. The preliminary procedures, which began to be adopted in 2016, were agreed on a provisional basis within the framework of the OPCW Scientific Advisory Board. The OPCW continued to conduct proficiency tests to designate laboratories for the analysis of biomedical samples.[65]

Finally the fact that some JIM staff are no longer employed on the Syria case and are therefore more able to speak publicly may help eventually to achieve a common understanding among governments on the responsibility for all documented instances of CW use in Syria.

Sanctions related to the use of chemical weapons in Syria

Canada, France, the UK, the USA and the European Union (EU) are among those to have publicly identified individuals and entities involved in the acquisition of toxic chemicals and their precursors for use as a method of warfare in Syria.[66]

---

[63] OPCW, Executive Council, 'Progress in the elimination of the Syrian chemical weapons programme', Note by the Director-General, EC-87/DG.2, 23 Oct. 2017, para. 8, pp. 2–3.

[64] Sezigen, S. et al. 'A Syrian family who were exposed to blister agent', poster presented by University of Health Sciences (Ankara) and Tarsus State Hospital (Mersin) at 16th Medical Chemical Defense Conference proceedings, Bundeswehr Institute of Pharmacology and Toxicology, Munich, 5–6 Apr. 2017; and OPCW, Scientific Advisory Board, 'Report of the Scientific Advisory Board at its twenty-fifth session', SAB-25/1, 31 Mar. 2017. See also Blum, M.-M., Bickelhaupt, M. and Poater, J., 'P 01 investigation of sulfur mustard, polysulfide analogues and reactive intermediates from Levinstein mustard density functional theory (DFT)', 16th Medical Chemical Defense Conference proceedings, Bundeswehr Institute of Pharmacology and Toxicology, Munich, 5–6 Apr. 2017, p. 76. The Levinstein process involves reacting disulphur dichloride and ethylene. The process typically yields mixtures of approximately 70% H/HD.

[65] See OPCW, Technical Secretariat, 'Status of the laboratories designated for the analysis of authentic biomedical samples', Note by the Director-General, S/1516/2017, 11 July 2017.

[66] E.g. for Canada, 'Special Economic Measures Act: Regulations amending the special economic measures (Syria) regulations', Canada Gazette, vol. 151, no. 9 (3 May 2017); for the EU, European Council, 'Use of chemical weapons in Syria: EU imposes sanctions against 16 additional persons', Press release, 17 July 2017; for France, French Treasury, 'Liste unique de gels' [Single list of asset

On 20 March the EU imposed sanctions against four Syrian military officials for their role in the use of CWs.[67]

In January 2017 the US Department of the Treasury published the names of the individuals and entities it was sanctioning in connection with Syria's CW-related activities, and in connection with the findings of the JIM.[68] On 24 April it imposed sanctions on 271 SSRC staff members in connection with the sarin attack on Khan Shaykhun.[69] On 12 June 2017 the US Treasury targeted an Islamic State leader, Attallah Salman 'Abd Kafi al-Jaburi, for, among other things the development of CWs. Al-Jaburi is described as 'an Iraq-based [Islamic State] senior leader in charge of factories producing [IEDs], vehicle-borne [IEDs], and explosives', and as being 'involved in the development of chemical weapons'.[70] On the same day the US Department of State designated Marwan Ibrahim Hussayn Tah al-Azawi an 'Iraqi [Islamic State] leader connected to [Islamic State's] development of chemical weapons for use in ongoing combat against Iraqi Security Forces'. It also stated that since mid-2016 al-Jaburi had been the Islamic State's 'chemical weapons and explosives manager' located in Kirkuk Province, and in mid-January 2016 the Islamic State had asked al-Jaburi to work on a chemical weapons project for use against the Peshmerga forces operating in the northern region of Iraq. The USA stated that al-Jaburi had received chemical weapon training in Syria (presumably during the civil war) and returned to Iraq in 2015.[71]

freezes], [n.d.]; and for the UK, British Treasury, 'Guidance: Financial sanctions targets, list of all asset freeze targets', 1 Mar. 2018.

[67] European Council, 'Use of chemical weapons in Syria: EU imposes sanctions against 4 high-ranking military officials', Press Release 137/17, 20 Mar. 2017.

[68] US Department of the Treasury, 'Treasury sanctions Syrian officials in connection with OPCW-UN findings of regime's use of chemical weapons on civilians', Press release, 12 Jan. 2017; and US Department of the Treasury, 'Resource Center: Non-proliferation designations; Syria designations; Zimbabwe designations removal', 12 Jan. 2017.

[69] US Department of the Treasury, 'Treasury sanctions 271 Syrian Scientific Studies and Research Center staff in response to sarin attack on Khan Sheikhoun', Press release, 24 Apr. 2017; and US Department of the Treasury, 'Syria designations', 24 Apr. 2017.

[70] US Department of the Treasury, 'Treasury targets ISIS leader involved in chemical weapons development', Press release, 12 June 2017.

[71] US Department of the Treasury (note 70).

II. Allegations of use of chemical weapons in Iraq and by North Korea

JOHN HART

Iraq

In October 2016 the Iraqi Army began a major campaign to regain control of Mosul, in northern Iraq, from the Islamic State group. On 3 March 2017 the International Committee of the Red Cross (ICRC) condemned the use of chemical weapons in Mosul.[1] The ICRC stated that seven patients had symptoms 'consistent with exposure to a toxic chemical agent' and were being treated at Rozhawa hospital, where ICRC medical staff were assisting.[2] While the ICRC did not attribute blame for the use of chemical weapons, the attacks appeared to be launched from areas held by the Islamic State.[3] On 10 March, however, Iraq's Ambassador to the United Nations, Mohamed Ali Alhakim, stated there was 'no evidence' that the Islamic State had used chemical weapons in Mosul.[4]

There have also been reports that evidence was found in January 2017 that Islamic State personnel had converted chemistry laboratories at Mosul University to produce chemical weapons.[5] After parts of Mosul were recaptured, Iraqi forces reportedly found sulphur mustard and Russian-made surface-to-surface missiles in the city.[6] Brigadier General Haider Fadhil of the Iraqi Army stated that French specialists had found that a chemical sample taken from Mosul had tested positive for sulphur mustard agent.[7] Fadhil added that a chemical weapon production facility had originally been located in the ruins of Nineveh, on the outskirts of Mosul, but was subsequently moved to a residential neighbourhood to improve operational security.[8] Iraqi officials stated that it appeared that Islamic State personnel had been attempting to fill missiles with the agent.[9] In June 2017 Brigadier General Hajar Ismail stated that there were thousands of tonnes of sulphur and chlorine around Al Mishraq that the Iraqi security forces need to protect.[10]

---

[1] ICRC, 'Iraq: ICRC strongly condemns use of chemical weapons around Mosul', Press release, 3 Mar. 2017; and Hart, J., 'Allegations of use of chemical weapons in Iraq', *SIPRI Yearbook 2017*, pp. 523–25.

[2] ICRC (note 1).

[3] '"First chemical attack" in Mosul battle injures twelve', BBC News, 3 Mar. 2017.

[4] 'Iraq says "no evidence" of chemical weapons attacks in Mosul', Reuters, 10 Mar. 2017.

[5] 'Iraqi forces discover chemical warfare agent in Mosul', Associated Press, 28 Jan. 2017.

[6] 'Iraqi forces discover chemical warfare agent in Mosul (note 5).

[7] 'Iraqi forces discover chemical warfare agent in Mosul (note 5).

[8] 'Iraqi forces discover chemical warfare agent in Mosul (note 5).

[9] 'Iraqi forces discover chemical warfare agent in Mosul (note 5).

[10] Winfield, G., 'What came next', *CBRNe World*, June 2017, p. 22.

Further analysis was conducted of the nature of the Islamic State's research and development and its weapon-production capacity, including of improvised explosive devices.[11] The Islamic State sought to standardize weapon components, including injection-moulded munition fuses, shoulder-fired rockets, mortar rounds, modular bomb parts and plastic-bodied landmines.[12] Unfired rocket-propelled grenades were found in Mosul that contained 'a crude blister agent resembling sulfur mustard'.[13] Conflict Armament Research (CAR), a London-based organization, and others have recovered documentation and visited facilities that show that the Islamic State engaged in 'a system of armaments production that combined research and development, mass production and organized distribution to amplify [the group's] endurance and power'.[14] CAR found no clear evidence that chemicals had been used by the Islamic State for anything other than explosives manufacture.[15]

Finally, PAX, a Dutch non-governmental organization, sought to further document the environmental effects of the burning of elemental sulphur at the Mishraq Sulphur Plant near Mosul. It reported that the Islamic State undertook the development of chlorine and sulphur mustard at the Al-Hekma pharmaceutical complex, north of Mosul.[16]

North Korea

Kim Jong Nam, half-brother of Kim Jong Un, the leader of the Democratic People's Republic of Korea (DPRK, or North Korea), was assassinated at Kuala Lumpur International Airport on 13 February 2017.[17] Two attackers applied a substance understood to be VX onto his face. North Korean authorities denied responsibility for the act.[18]

---

[11] Ismay, J., Gibbons-Neff, T. and Chivers, C. J., 'How ISIS produced its cruel arsenal on an industrial scale', *New York Times*, 10 Dec. 2017.

[12] Ismay, Gibbons-Neff and Chivers (note 11).

[13] Ismay, Gibbons-Neff and Chivers (note 11).

[14] Ismay, Gibbons-Neff and Chivers (note 11).

[15] Conflict Armament Research (CAR), *Weapons of the Islamic State: A Three-year Investigation in Iraq and Syria* (CAR: London, Dec. 2017).

[16] Zwijnenburg, W. and Postma, F., *Living Under a Black Sky: Conflict Pollution and Environmental Health Concerns in Iraq* (Colophon: Utrecht, Nov. 2017), pp. 16–18. The information in the report is based on media reports.

[17] Fifield, A., 'North Korean leader's half brother killed in Malaysia in possible poison attack, police say', *Washington Post*, 15 Feb. 2017. On the legal status of assassination in international human rights law see Murray, D., *Practitioners' Guide to Human Rights Law in Armed Conflict* (Oxford University Press: Oxford, 2016), section 5.171, p. 159.

[18] Korea Central News Agency (KCNA), 'US, S. Korea's absurd sophism against DPRK over its citizen's death abroad blasted', 1 Mar. 2017.

Malaysian authorities undertook decontamination work at the airport and on 26 February declared it safe.[19] The Organisation for the Prohibition of Chemical Weapons (OPCW) provided Malaysia with 'technical materials to assist with [its] internal investigation'.[20] No authoritative information has been published on the sampling and analysis work.[21]

During the trial of the alleged attackers, it was revealed that Kim Jong Nam had been carrying 12 atropine tablets at the time of the attack.[22] (atropine can be used to treat cases of organophosphate poisoning and is normally administered intravenously).

The US Treasury identified Korea Ryonbong General Corporation (Ryonbong) as specializing in acquisitions for North Korea's defence industries and providing support for its military-related sales. It concluded that the organization's procurements 'probably support North Korea's chemical weapons program'.[23]

---

[19] Sipalan, J. and Teo, A., 'Malaysia declares airport safe for travel after nerve agent attack', Reuters, 26 Feb. 2017.

[20] OPCW, 'Opening statement by the Director-General to the Executive Council at its eighty-fourth session', EC-84/DG.26, 7 Mar. 2017, para. 9, p. 2.

[21] Chai, P. R. et al., 'Toxic chemical weapons of assassination and warfare: Nerve agents VX and sarin', *Toxicology Communications*, vol. 1, no. 1 (2017), pp. 21–23.

[22] Harris, B., 'Kim's poisoned half-brother was carrying antidote, court told', *Financial Times*, 2–3 Dec. 2017, p. 6.

[23] US Department of the Treasury, 'Treasury sanctions agents linked to North Korea's weapons of mass destruction proliferation and financial networks', Press release, 31 Mar. 2017.

III. Chemical arms control and disarmament

JOHN HART

The 1993 Chemical Weapons Convention (CWC) is the principal international legal basis for the prohibition of chemical warfare.[1] No state acceded to the convention in 2017, although South Sudan indicated that it intended to do so shortly. As of December 2017, there were 192 states parties to the convention, which is implemented by the Organisation for the Prohibition of Chemical Weapons (OPCW).[2]

OPCW developments

The OPCW focused much of its attention and resources on investigating continued allegations of chemical weapon (CW) use in Iraq and Syria, and confirming the completeness and correctness of Syria's declarations (see sections I and II).

Since 1 January 2017, the 2017 edition of the Harmonized Commodity Description and Coding System (HS) nomenclature has allocated a unique international code to 33 of the most traded CWC-scheduled chemicals.[3] In conjunction with this development, a revised edition of the OPCW Handbook on Chemicals was issued.[4]

In January 2017 the OPCW Technical Secretariat hosted a tabletop exercise under the auspices of the United Nations Counter-Terrorism Implementation Task Force (UNCTITF) to test interagency cooperation in response to a chemical or biological weapon attack. The exercise utilized the Rapid Response Assistance Mission (RRAM), which was established in 2016.[5]

In 2017 the Technical Secretariat issued the results of a survey on the extent of employment of biomediated processes.[6] Of the 32 states parties that responded to the survey, at least 12 maintain a policy of declaring relevant discrete organic chemicals (DOCs) produced through chemical, biochemical

---

[1] For a summary and other details of the Convention on the Prohibition of the Development, Production, Stockpiling and Use of Chemical Weapons and on their Destruction (Chemical Weapons Convention, CWC) see annex A, section I, in this volume.

[2] The remaining non-member states are Egypt, Israel and North Korea. Israel is a signatory.

[3] OPCW, 'Opening statement by the Director-General to the Executive Council at its eighty-fourth session', EC-84/DG.26, 7 Mar. 2017, para. 49, p. 7. The HS nomenclature is established by the International Convention on the Harmonized Commodity Description and Coding System, opened for signature 14 June 1983, entered into force 1 Jan. 1988.

[4] OPCW, *Handbook on Chemicals, 2017*, rev. 1 (OPCW: The Hague, Jan. 2017).

[5] OPCW (note 3), para. 19, p. 3. On the responsibilities and capabilities of the RRAM see OPCW, Technical Secretariat, 'Establishment of a rapid response assistance team', S/1381/2016, 10 May 2016.

[6] OPCW, Technical Secretariat, 'Results of the survey on biomediated processes', S/1534/2017, 14 Sep. 2017. See also OPCW, Scientific Advisory Board, 'Report of the Scientific Advisory Board's workshop on trends in chemical production', SAB-26/WP.2, 19 Oct. 2017.

or biological processes to the OPCW.[7] China, Germany and India were among the parties with substantial chemical industries that did not participate. The survey (a) provides insight into the OPCW's routine verification procedures; (b) suggests possible implications of modifying the cost, scope and level of intrusiveness of the CWC; and (c) illustrates potential overlaps between chemical and biological arms control verification. An important component of the CWC's routine declaration and verification regime for the chemical industry is focused on chemical plants that produce 'by synthesis' certain DOCs. The parties have long considered whether the definition of such production should include biological and biologically mediated processes, mainly in order to include certain types of enzyme catalysis processes. The OPCW has adjusted DOC-selection methodologies to reduce, for example, the number of urea-production plants that receive routine inspections.[8] It is possible that similar adjustments will be made in relation to biomediated processes. This issue remains under review within the OPCW's Industry Cluster and elsewhere. The methodology for collecting and analysing such information could be further developed and harmonized.

The OPCW Scientific Advisory Board (SAB) considered the possible integration of existing verification practices with a capability for chemical forensics and evidence management, partly through the use of unmanned aerial vehicles. Such an approach would strengthen the response to chemical emergencies, including by enhancing the organization's detection, identification and monitoring capacities.[9] If used to support investigations of alleged use or to conduct challenge inspections, the Conference of the States Parties (CSP) and Executive Council would first have to evaluate and approve the underlying work instructions and standard operating procedures in order to ensure that the principles and procedures for CWC 'managed access' verification are observed. Finally, the Chemical Forensics International Technical Working Group (CFITWG) was established in April 2017 with a mandate to address gaps between theoretical science and practical capabilities in the performance of chemical forensics on weaponized chemicals. The work of the CFITWG will be further considered by a newly established SAB temporary working group on investigative science and technology starting in 2018.

---

[7] OPCW (note 6), para. 5(a), p. 3. The 32 states were Andorra, Argentina, Australia, Austria, Bangladesh, Belarus, Brazil, Burkina Faso, Canada, Chile, Costa Rica, Croatia, Cuba, the Czech Republic, France, Greece, Iran, Ireland, Italy, Japan, the Netherlands, New Zealand, Portugal, Russia, Slovakia, Slovenia, Switzerland, Thailand, Turkey, the UK, the USA and Uzbekistan.

[8] DOC and phosphorus, sulphur or fluorine (PSF) producing plant sites are of relevance to CWC verification due to the potential to reconfigure them at short notice for prohibited purposes. Urea is an organic compound with wide application, including for explosives. However, it poses a low risk to the object and purpose of the CWC.

[9] OPCW, Scientific Advisory Board, 'Report of the Scientific Advisory Board's workshop on emerging technologies', SAB-26/WP.1, 21 July 2017.

The Conference of the States Parties

The CSP met on 27 November–1 December 2017. It agreed a programme of work and a budget of €67 248 655 (*c.* $82 million) for 2018, of which €28 984 106 (*c.* $35.5 million) is related to verification costs and €37 830 816 (*c.* $46 million) to administrative and other costs.[10] The remaining balance was essentially earmarked for the Fourth CWC Review Conference. The CSP elected by consensus Ambassador Fernando Arias of Spain as the fourth Director-General of the OPCW.[11] Arias will begin work on 25 July 2018.

There was general agreement among the parties that the treaty regime has now entered its 'post-CW destruction phase'.

In its opening plenary statement, Russia stated that criticisms of the completeness and correctness of Syria's declarations at the OPCW and the conclusions of the OPCW–United Nations Joint Investigative Mechanism (JIM) holding Syria responsible for CW use were politically motivated.[12] Syria reiterated its continued willingness to work with the OPCW on questions concerning the completeness and correctness of its declarations. It also underlined its commitment to the object and purpose of the CWC and called for the establishment of a zone free of weapons of mass destruction in the Middle East.[13]

The United States stated that 'Chemical weapons use by the Syrian Arab Republic remains the most serious violation of the Chemical Weapons Convention in the Convention's twenty year history, and the greatest modern challenge to the global norm against chemical weapons use'.[14]

Essentially, only the states in the Western European and Other States Group sought to hold the Syrian Government responsible for CW use in their plenary statements.[15] China, India, Jordan and Pakistan, as well as the Africa Group and the Latin America and the Caribbean Group, refrained from taking a public position on Syrian Government responsibility for chemical weapon use. The reasons are not clear and somewhat speculative. Most governments are informally willing to accept that the Syrian Government is

[10] OPCW, 'Decision, programme and budget of the OPCW for 2018', C-22/DEC.5, 30 Nov. 2017, para. 9(c), p. 3.

[11] Dr John Gee of Australia, the organization's first Deputy Director-General, briefly served as an acting Director-General.

[12] Russia, [Statement by G. V. Kalamanov, Deputy Minister of Industry and Trade of the Russian Federation, Head of the Russian Delegation at the 22nd Session of the Conference of the States Parties to the Convention on the Prohibition of Chemical Weapons], [no number], 27 Nov. 2017, The Hague (in Russian).

[13] Syrian plenary statement [simultaneous translation to English].

[14] OPCW, Conference of the States Parties, 'United States of America: Statement by Andrea Hall, Senior Director for Weapons of Mass Destruction and Counterproliferation, National Security Council Delegation of the United States of America to the Twenty-Second Session of the Conference of the States Parties', C-22/NAT.7, 27 Nov. 2017, p. 2.

[15] In addition to West European states, the group includes Australia, Canada, New Zealand, Turkey and the USA.

responsible for some CW attacks. Some governments do not wish to become entangled in a Russian–US dispute. Many governments take the view that if others reflect their position, they need not take a public stance. The intelligence and security analytical capabilities among governments are variable. Some governments do not necessarily have the capacity (or the will) to draw their own analytical conclusions and act on them.

Drawing on the efforts of Australia and Switzerland in recent years, 39 states issued a joint paper drawing attention to the potential risks posed by chemicals that affect the central nervous system (CNS) to the object and purpose of the CWC.[16] These states called for a further clarification of positions on this matter among the member states. In support of this initiative, the USA stated that 'If our first responders are at risk when they encounter illicit fentanyl, how can our unsuspecting populations be safe when fentanyl is aerosolised and used as a law enforcement tool? Despite these dangers, countries continue to pursue these chemicals. . . . CNS-acting chemicals pose to the Chemical Weapons Convention—a threat that will increase, not decrease, over time.'[17]

Among the side events were (a) an update on the upgrading or construction of a new OPCW Central Laboratory; (b) presentations on and discussion of CNS-acting chemicals and their relation to CWC provisions, to avoid the re-emergence of chemical warfare and misuse of 'law enforcement' provisions; (c) presentations on and discussion of the potential applicability of CWC provisions to sea-dumped chemical weapons and an update on environmental assessments and munitions remediation activity; (d) an introduction to the OPCW's secure information exchange (SIX) for the digital transmission of data between the parties and the Technical Secretariat; (e) a presentation on 'science for diplomats' in the context of recent SAB activity and reports; (f) presentations by France on preventing the misuse of chemical facilities and chemical products; (g) an update on the activities of the OPCW Staff Council; (h) an exhibit by the delegation of Japan updating the status of operations to destroy abandoned chemical weapons (ACWs) in China; (i) an exhibit by the Gesellschaft zur Entsorgung von chemischen Kampstoffen und Rüstungsaltlasten mbH (GEKA mbH) on the destruction of chemicals shipped to the facility from Libya in 2016; (j) presentations on

---

[16] The states are Albania, Argentina, Australia, Austria, Belgium, Brazil, Bulgaria, Canada, Chile, Colombia, Croatia, Cyprus, the Czech Republic, Ecuador, Estonia, Finland, Germany, Greece, Ireland, Japan, Latvia, Lithuania, Luxembourg, Malta, New Zealand, Norway, the Philippines, Poland, Portugal, Romania, Senegal, Slovenia, South Korea, Spain, Switzerland, Turkey, the UK, the USA and Uruguay. OPCW, Conference of the States Parties, 'Joint paper: Aerosolisation of central nervous system-acting chemicals for law enforcement purposes', C-22/NAT.5, 28 Nov. 2017. See also OPCW (note 9); and OPCW, Scientific Advisory Board, 'Response to the Director-General's request to the Scientific Advisory Board to provide consideration on which riot control agents are subject to declaration under the Chemical Weapons Convention', SAB-25/WP.1, 27 Mar. 2017.

[17] OPCW, C-22/NAT.7 (note 14), pp. 2–3.

the long-term health effects of CW exposure, such as cohort studies of those exposed during the 1980–88 Iran–Iraq War; (k) an update on the work of the OPCW Fact-finding Mission (FFM) in Syria; and (l) a presentation on a newly published book on the history of CWs.[18]

Destruction of chemical weapons

As of December 2017 approximately 96 per cent of declared CW stockpiles had been destroyed. Eight parties have declared CW stockpiles since the convention's entry into force: Albania, India, Iraq, the Republic of Korea (South Korea), Libya, Russia, Syria and the USA. In 2017 the OPCW conducted six inspections of old chemical weapons (OCWs) in Belgium, France, Germany, Italy, Panama and the United Kingdom. China and Japan continued to cooperate on the destruction of World War II-era ACWs left behind by the latter. At the end of 2016 there were 10 CW destruction facilities (see table 8.2), which are distinct from the destruction facilities and technologies used for the destruction of ACWs and OCWs.

China

As of 31 October 2017, 62 416 ACWs had been declared and 48 851 destroyed.[19] As of October 2017 Japan had spent approximately €1.3 billion (c. $1.6 billion) on ACW-related activities in China.[20]

Japan expressed its hope that the destruction of all currently identified ACWs in China would be completed by 2022.[21] Japan intends to complete destruction operations at Haerbaling by 2022 of all ACW declared on or before 31 December 2016.[22] In 2017, 81 ACW were recovered from Hunchun on 13–27 June and 62 ACW from Shangzhi on 3–16 July (see table 8.3).[23]

---

[18] Friedrish, B. et al. (eds), *One Hundred Years of Chemical Warfare: Research, Deployment, Consequences* (Springer: Cham, 2017); 'Translating ambitions: Upgrading the OPCW Chemical Laboratory to a Centre for Chemistry and Technology', Presentation slides by private contractor, The Hague; and OPCW, Technical Secretariat, 'Request from the Director-General to states parties for voluntary contributions to a new trust fund for upgrading the OPCW Chemical Laboratory to a Centre for Chemistry and Technology', S/1561/2017, 8 Dec. 2017.

[19] Japan, '5. Achievements and PLAN', poster no. 5, Poster exhibit at 22nd CSP, The Hague, 27 Nov.–1 Dec. 2017.

[20] Japan, 'Statement by HE Mr Hiroshi Inomata, Ambassador of Japan and Permanent Representative to the OPCW at the Eighty-Sixth Session of the Executive Council of the OPCW', 10–13 Oct. 2017, The Hague, p. 3.

[21] OPCW, Executive Council, 'Japan: Statement by H.E. Ambassador Hiroshi Inomata, Permanent Representative of Japan to the OPCW at the Eighty-Sixth Session of the Executive Council', EC-86/NAT.14, 10 Oct. 2017, p. 3.

[22] Japan, '2. characteristics of ACW destruction project', poster no. 2, Poster exhibit at 22nd CSP, The Hague, 27 Nov.–1 Dec. 2017.

[23] Japan, '4. Haerbaling area', poster no. 4, Poster exhibit at 22nd CSP, The Hague, 27 Nov.–1 Dec. 2017.

Table 8.2. Chemical weapon destruction facilities in service or under construction as of 31 Dec. 2016

Facility	Location
Rabta Toxic Chemicals Destruction Facility	Libya
Gesellschaft zur Entsorgung von chemischen Kampfstoffen und Rüstungsaltlasten mbH (GEKA mbH)	Lower Saxony, Germany[a]
Kizner[b]	Udmurtia, Russia
Pueblo Chemical Agent-Destruction Pilot Plant (PCAPP)	Colorado, United States
Pueblo Chemical Agent-Destruction Pilot Plant Explosive Destruction System (PCAPP-EDS)	Colorado, United States
Blue Grass Chemical Agent-Destruction Pilot Plant (BGCAPP)	Kentucky, United States
Blue Grass Chemical Agent-Destruction Pilot Plant Static Detonation Chamber (BGCAPP-SDC)	Kentucky, United States
Prototype Detonation Test and Destruction Facility (PDTDF)	Maryland, United States
Aberdeen Proving Ground Chemical Transfer Facility (APG/CTF)	Maryland, United States
Recovered Chemical Weapons Destruction Facility (RCWDF)	United States

[a] This facility destroys old chemical weapons, as well as chemical weapons removed from Libya.

[b] Destruction operations at this facility were completed in 2017.

Source: OPCW, Technical Secretariat, 'Summary of verification activities in 2016', Note by the Director-General, S/1537/2017, 19 Sep. 2017, table 4, p. 11.

Iraq

Iraq announced that two CW bunkers at the Al Muthanna Complex in Saladin Governorate left over from the time of President Saddam Hussein had been encapsulated in concrete.[24]

Libya

A number of the CWC parties, including European Union (EU) member states, continued to allocate funds and to provide other support to remediate 350 tonnes of sulphur mustard hydrolysate at the Ruwagha Tank Farm, south-eastern Libya.[25] The EU funded an environmental scoping study of the site in 2017, which was carried out by the Hotzone Solutions Group. The

---

[24] OPCW, Conference of the States Parties, 'Opening statement by the Director-General to the Conference of the States Parties at its Twenty-Second Session', C-22/DG.20, 27 Nov. 2017, para. 17, p. 3.

[25] OPCW, Executive Council, 'Status of the implementation of the plan for the destruction of Libya's remaining Category 2 chemical weapons outside the territory of Libya', Report by the Director-General, EC-87/DG.1, 23 Oct. 2017, para. 15, p. 3.

Table 8.3. Status of abandoned chemical weapon destruction operations in China

Site	Destruction approach	Status
Guangzhou MDF	..	Site selection under way
Haerbaling TDF	CDC and SDC	Operational since 2014; 7112 ACW destroyed as of Nov. 2017
Harbin MDF	CDC	Under construction
Nanjing MDF	CDC	Operations completed in 2012; 35 861 ACW destroyed
Shijiazhuang MDF	CDC	Operations completed in Dec. 2016; 2567 ACW destroyed
Taiyuan MDF	..	Site selection under way
Wuhan MDF	CDC	Operations completed in 2015; 264 ACW destroyed

ACW = abandoned chemical weapon; CDC = cold detonation chamber/controlled detonation chamber; MDF = mobile destruction facility; SDC = static detonation chamber; TDF = temporary destruction facility.

Source: Japan, '3. Overview: Destruction operations', poster no. 3, Poster session at 22nd CSP, The Hague, 27 Nov.–1 Dec. 2017.

destruction of chemicals shipped to GEKA in Germany from Ruwagha in 2017 was completed in January 2018.[26]

Panama

During World War II the USA operated a CW testing facility on San José Island, off the Pacific coast of Panama.[27] Panama declared the possession of ACWs on its territory in 2002. However, it has since redesignated the weapons as OCWs.

In 2017 Panama declared eight OCWs, all located on the island. They comprise: six M79 1000-pound (454-kilogram) air bombs believed to have originally been filled with phosgene (CG), one M78 500-lb (227-kg) air bombs believed to have originally been filled with cyanogen chloride (CK) and one M1A1 cylinder that is rusted through and empty. Later in the year

---

[26] NDR1, '500 Tonnen Chemiewaffen in Munster Vernichtet' [500 tonnes of chemical weapons destroyed in Munster], NDR.de, 11 Jan. 2018; and German Federal Foreign Office, 'Vernichtung von restbeständen des libyschen chemiewaffenprogramms in Deutschland erfolgreich beendet' [Successful completion of the destruction in Germany of the remnants of Libya's chemical weapon programme], Press release, 5 Jan. 2018.

[27] Brophy, L. P. and Fisher, G. J. B., *The Chemical Warfare Service: Organizing for War*, United States in World War II, the Technical Services (US Army Center of Military History: Washington, DC, 1959, reprinted 1989), p. 106. See also Lindsay-Poland, J., *Emperors in the Jungle: The Hidden History of the US in Panama* (Duke University Press: Durham, NC, 2003); and Johnston, H., *A Bridge Not Attacked: Chemical Warfare Civilian Research during World War II* (World Scientific: London, 2003).

Panama destroyed the munitions *in situ* through explosive venting during the rainy season. The solids were rinsed with caustic solution and the rinsate collected in containers that meet international standards for disposal by a licensed off-site treatment, storage and disposal facility. The explosive components of the munitions were detonated using donor charges and the metal fragments were collected and checked for contamination, after which they were to be recycled.[28]

Russia

Russia completed the destruction of its CW stockpile on 27 September 2017.[29] Russia thanked those states that had assisted it in this effort. Their combined contributions over 20 years comprised approximately 10 per cent of the total destruction cost.[30]

The United States

As of 31 October 2017 the USA had completed the destruction of 91 per cent of its Category 1 CWs.[31] Construction of its final chemical weapon destruction facility, at Blue Grass, Kentucky, was almost complete and it is scheduled to commence full-scale operations in 2020.[32]

---

[28] OPCW, Executive Council, 'Panama: Concept plan for the destruction of eight old chemical weapons', EC-85/NAT.2, 16 June 2017.

[29] OPCW, 'OPCW marks completion of destruction of Russian chemical weapons stockpile', Press release, 11 Oct. 2017.

[30] These states were Belgium, Canada, the Czech Republic, Finland, France, Germany, Ireland, Italy, the Netherlands, New Zealand, Norway, Poland, Switzerland, Sweden, the UK and the USA. On Russian CW destruction assistance see Hart, J., 'Assistance for the destruction of chemical weapons in the Russian Federation: Political and technical aspects', Paper presented at the Conference on Strengthening European Action on WMD Non-Proliferation and Disarmament: How Can Community Instruments Contribute?, 7–8 Dec. 2005, Brussels.

[31] OPCW, C-22/DG.20 (note 24), para. 9, p. 2. Category 1 CWs are those weapons based on chemicals appearing in Schedule 1 of the CWC's Annex on Chemicals and their parts and components. For 'order of destruction' of Category 1 CW see CWC (note 1), Verification Annex, Part IV(A), paras 15–17.

[32] OPCW, C-22/DG.20 (note 24), para. 9, p. 2.

IV. Biological arms control

JOHN HART

The principal legal instrument against biological warfare is the 1972 Biological and Toxin Weapons Convention (BTWC).[1] Samoa acceded to the convention in 2017 and, as of December 2017, the convention had 179 states parties.

The BTWC treaty regime

The BTWC treaty regime is based on an evolving process that dates to 2002, when the reconvened Fifth Review Conference agreed an initial set of annual intersessional process meetings. The most divisive issue at both the Eighth Review Conference, in 2016, and the 2017 Meeting of States Parties (MSP) was whether an annual intersessional process should refer to a legally binding instrument (LBI) as a negotiating objective and, if so, whether the mandate for an intersessional process should include the possibility of an expert meeting to reconsider an LBI, or to recommend that the Ninth Review Conference revisit the 1995–2001 negotiations by setting up an ad hoc group to strengthen treaty compliance.[2] The final document of the Eighth Review Conference contained no reference to an LBI but the final document of the 2017 MSP document does allude to one.[3]

The treaty regime continued to operate under financial constraints due to late payment and non-payment by governments of their assessed contributions.[4] On 7 December 2017 the Implementation Support Unit (ISU) summarized the budgetary status and requirements of the treaty regime.[5] It estimated the cost of holding MSPs in 2017–20 to be $208 100.[6] It also summarized the costs of the annual BTWC meetings to date (see table 8.4).

---

[1] For a summary and other details of the Convention on the Prohibition of the Development, Production and Stockpiling of Bacteriological (Biological) and Toxin Weapons and on their Destruction (Biological and Toxin Weapons Convention, BTWC) see annex A, section I, in this volume.

[2] BTWC 2017 Meeting of States Parties, 'Intersessional programme', Submitted by Venezuela on behalf of the Group of the Non-Aligned Movement and Other States, BWC/MSP/2017/WP.21, 5 Dec. 2017, para. 9, pp. 2–3. See also Sims, N., *The Evolution of Biological Disarmament*, SIPRI Chemical & Biological Warfare Studies no. 19 (Oxford University Press: Oxford, 2001), pp. 112–91.

[3] Thus the 5th Meeting of Exports shall be devoted to the 'Consideration of the full range of approaches and options to further strengthen the Convention and its functioning through possible additional legal measures or other measures in the framework of the Convention'. BTWC 2017 Meeting of States Parties, 'Report of the Meeting of States Parties', BWC/MSP/2017/6, 19 Dec. 2017, p. 8. On the LBI see also BTWC 2017 Meeting of States Parties, BWC/MSP/2017/WP.21 (note 2), p. 2.

[4] E.g. United Nations, Secretariat, 'Status of contributions of BWC, CCW, CCM, OTW as at 30 September 2017', 30 Sep. 2017.

[5] Feakes, D., 'Potential cost implications', BTWC Implementation Support Unit, 7 Dec. 2017.

[6] Feakes (note 5), slide 3.

Table 8.4. Estimated cost of BTWC intersessional processes

Intersessional programme	Cost per year (US$)
2017–20 Meetings of States Parties	1 109 500*
2016 8th Review Conference	1 966 700
2012–15	1 943 400
2011 7th Review Conference	2 010 300
2007–10	721 700
2006 6th Review Conference	1 344 900
2003–2005	542 700
Ad Hoc Group 2001	1 357 100
Ad Hoc Group 2000	2 926 300
Ad Hoc Group 1999	2 489 739
Total	**16 412 339**

* = estimated figure; BTWC = Biological and Toxin Weapons Convention.

Source: Feakes, D., 'Potential cost implications', BTWC Implementation Support Unit, 7 Dec. 2017.

The 2017 Meeting of States Parties

The Eighth Review Conference of the BTWC, which met in 2016, deferred until 2017 the question of whether further intersessional Meetings of Experts (MXs) and annual MSPs should be held in 2018–20 and, if so, how the programme of work should be structured.[7] These were the major issues considered during the 2017 MSP, which was convened on 4–8 December under the chairmanship of Ambassador Singh Gill of India.

Numerous meetings were convened in the lead-up to the MSP, motivated partly by the perceived need to reduce the risk of bioterrorism and for better preparedness for disease outbreaks. For example, Russia demonstrated a mobile laboratory capacity at a conference on 1–2 November 2017 organized in Sochi by the Russian Ministry of Foreign Affairs.[8] Other meetings sought to increase treaty membership and to improve national implementation of the treaty's provisions. A workshop for Pacific Island states was hosted by Fiji with support from the United Nations Office for Disarmament Affairs, the ISU and the European Union (EU) on 27–28 July.[9] The EU funded a workshop in support of the BTWC extended assistance programmes on

[7] Pearson, G. and Sims, N. A., *Report from Geneva: The BTWC Eighth Review Conference: A Disappointing Outcome*, Review no. 46 (Harvard Sussex Program: Brighton, Apr. 2017).

[8] 'International Conference "Global Biosecurity Challenges: Problems and Solutions"', 1–2 Nov. 2017, Annex 1.

[9] UN Office for Disarmament Affairs, 'Fiji hosts regional workshop to promote universalization of the Biological and Toxin Weapons Convention in the Pacific', Press release, 3 Aug. 2017.

28–29 March, and the Regional Africa Parliamentary Workshop brought together African officials to discuss and review the BTWC on 27–28 March.[10]

The Inter-Academy Partnership (IAP) held a workshop on assessing the security implications of genome editing technology in Germany in October.[11] Spiez Laboratory hosted its third workshop on developing a laboratory network to support the convention in June.[12] The Robert Koch Institute hosted a bio-reference laboratory workshop in September.[13]

The BTWC depositaries—Russia, the United Kingdom and the United States—met to develop a common approach to a further intersessional process. The results were circulated at the MSP as a working paper that enjoyed wide support from the parties.[14] Governments considered the working paper to be an unusual and welcome piece of statecraft in view of the broader geopolitical tensions between the three states.

The EU maintained, in a position paper supported by nine other states parties and tabled at the MSP, that 'further concrete progress' should be made on 'all key issues', but especially national implementation and compliance, confidence-building measures (CBMs), science and technology, Article V on consultation and cooperation, Article VII on assistance, and achieving universal treaty membership.[15] The EU stated that it considered 'the primary objective' of the meeting to be 'to agree on an intersessional programme that would strengthen the [BTWC] and enhance its implementation and universalisation'.[16]

The EU suggested that the meeting focus on six areas: (a) 'national implementation and compliance, including information sharing on national legislation and implementation measures to [maintain] control over pathogenic microorganisms, biosafety and biosecurity standards, engagement with non-governmental stakeholders'; (b) 'further work on [CBMs] to provide reassurance on compliance by means of information exchanges and

[10] 'PGA Regional Africa Workshop to Promote Ratification and Implementation of the Biological and Toxin Weapons Convention (BTWC)', 27–28 Mar. 2017, Sierra Leone; and Permanent Delegation of the EU to the UN and Other International Organisations in Geneva, 'Report: Workshop in support of the Biological Weapons Convention Extended Assistance Programmes', 28–29 Mar. 2017.

[11] Inter-Academy Partnership, 'Statement by the IAP Biosecurity Working Group', Dec. 2017.

[12] Spiez Laboratory, 'UNSGM Designated Laboratories workshop report, Spiez, Switzerland, 20–22 June 2017', Sep. 2017.

[13] On the Robert Koch Institute's project on the UN Secretary-General's investigative mechanism (UNSGM) see Robert Koch Institute, 'UNSGM-Projekt', 24 June 2014.

[14] BTWC 2017 Meeting of States Parties, 'Elements of a possible intersessional process', Submitted by Russia, the UK and the USA, BWC/MSP/2017/WP.10, 30 Nov. 2017.

[15] European Union External Action Service, 'EU statement on the outcome of the 2017 Meeting of States Parties of the Biological and Toxin Weapons Convention (BTWC) Geneva', 8 Dec. 2017, p. 1.

[16] European Union External Action Service, 'Meeting of States Parties to the Biological and Toxin Weapons Convention—EU key messages: Reaching consensus on an intersessional programme', 6 Dec. 2017, p. 1. Albania, Bosnia and Herzegovina, Georgia, the Former Yugoslav Republic of Macedonia, Moldova, Montenegro, Serbia, Turkey and Ukraine associated themselves with this statement.

enhancing transparency, including increasing the relevance of CBM forms and conducting voluntary peer review initiatives'; (c) 'assistance and cooperation under Article VII taking into account the pressing capacity building needs as regards responding to outbreaks of infectious diseases'; (d) 'science and technology in order to review relevant developments in a more systematic way and assess their impact, positive and negative, on the BTWC'; (e) 'review of the Consultative Committee procedure making it possible for States Parties to resort to consultation and cooperation bilaterally and multilaterally, as set out in Article V'; and (f) 'universalisation, including the adoption of an action plan and dedicated sessions to promote universal adherence to the BTWC'.[17]

Since 2006 the EU has spent €6.3 million (c. $7.7 million) and organized 26 workshops to support achieving universal treaty membership and effective treaty implementation.[18] There was continued support among the parties for the creation of a network of designated laboratories to support the UN Secretary-General's mechanism for investigating allegations of use of chemical or biological weapons.[19] Germany and Switzerland hosted a side event devoted to this topic on 7 December.

MSP outcomes

The outcomes of the MSP were shaped by the structure and language developed on an intersessional process as outlined in the joint paper circulated by the convention's three depositary states.[20] Three annual MSPs and five sets of Meetings of Experts will be held in the period 2018–20.[21]

MX1 will meet three times, each for two days, to discuss and promote common understanding and effective action on cooperation and assistance, with a particular focus on strengthening cooperation and assistance under Article X, which encourages peaceful uses of the life sciences and associated technologies. These meetings will, among other things, review the operation of the assistance and cooperation database by the ISU.

MX2 will meet three times, each for two days, to discuss and promote common understanding and effective action on reviewing developments, including genome editing, in the fields of science and technology related to the convention. This will include consideration of 'any other science and technology developments of relevance to the Convention and also to the activities of relevant multilateral organizations' such as the World Health

---

[17] European Union External Action Service (note 16), p. 2.

[18] European Union External Action Service, 'Meeting of the States Parties to the Biological and Toxin Weapons Convention—EU key messages on universalisation', 7 Dec. 2017, p. 1.

[19] The Secretary-General's mechanism was last invoked in 2013, at the request of the Syrian Government. On the mechanism see United Nations Office for Disarmament Affairs.

[20] BTWC 2017 Meeting of States Parties, BWC/MSP/2017/WP.10 (note 14).

[21] BTWC 2017 Meeting of States Parties, BWC/MSP/2017/6 (note 3).

Organization (WHO), the World Organisation for Animal Health (OIE), the Food and Agricultural Organization of the UN (FAO), the International Plant Protection Convention (IPPC) and the Organisation for the Prohibition of Chemical Weapons (OPCW). This will require further interaction between the OPCW Scientific Advisory Board (SAB) and the BTWC framework meetings and processes.

MX3 will meet three times, each for one day, to discuss and promote common understanding and effective action on strengthening national implementation. This will include consideration of the quantity and quality of CBM submissions and 'effective measures of export control, in full conformity with all Articles of the Convention, including Article X'. Despite the Article X reference, this does not constitute a general endorsement by the parties of strategic trade controls.

MX4 will meet three times, each for two days, to discuss and promote common understanding and effective action on assistance, response and preparedness. This will entail further consideration of previous Russian proposals to examine how the concept of mobile biomedical units might contribute to the preparedness of parties to react to naturally occurring or deliberate biological threats.

MX5 will meet three times, each for one day, to discuss and promote common understanding and effective action on institutional strengthening of the convention. These meetings will consider the full range of approaches to and options for strengthening the convention, including through 'possible additional legal measures or other measures in the framework of the Convention'. This could mean possible modifications to the content, structure and legal status of CBMs or interactions with other legal regimes, either existing or proposed. For example, the parties might agree to make CBMs legally binding at the Ninth Review Conference.

The annual MSPs will discuss and promote common understanding of and effective action on the outputs of the MXs. The 2018–20 intersessional process has no decision-making authority. In 2021 the Ninth Review Conference will consider the work and outcomes of this process as a possible basis for taking legally binding or other types of decisions.

Some of the parties that wish to move the interactions among the members towards more specific compliance discussions—either to more fully and systematically demonstrate current compliance or to revisit past allegations of violations—have continued to focus on possible modifications to the content, structure and handling of the current politically binding information exchanges, which are intended to serve as CBMs, including on the basis of the Benelux practice visits to life sciences facilities conducted in 2015.[22] Some

---

[22] E.g. Revill, J., *Compliance Revisited: An Incremental Approach to Compliance in the Biological and Toxin Weapons Convention*, Occasional Paper no. 31 (Center for Nonproliferation Studies: Monterey,

parties maintain that CBMs in themselves are insufficient and that agreeing an LBI should instead be the objective. The 2017 outcome represents a continuation of the status quo whereby information, views and best practices on the convention's various provisions are exchanged in annual MXs and MSPs with the support of the Geneva-based ISU. The treaty regime continues to be process-oriented. The evolution of the treaty regime since at least the early 1980s remains relevant—even if this is unstated and somewhat overlooked.[23]

In 1961 Fred Iklé, a professor at the Massachusetts Institute of Technology (MIT) and later Director of the US Arms Control and Disarmament Agency, offered a standard framework for consideration of the handling of violations of disarmament and arms control agreements. In it he observed: 'The evidence of [a] violation must . . . be such as to impress the public as authoritative and impartial. A finding by an international organization will be influential in this regard, especially with public opinion outside the countries directly affected'.[24] Looking ahead, the parties to the BTWC could further consider the extent to which Iklé's analysis and admonition that verification frameworks should provide evidence that is accepted by all states as authoritative and impartial hold lessons for the convention.

In addition, a recently concluded three-year historical project carried out by Sussex University and University College London confirmed that chemical and biological arms control issues are inextricably linked.[25] This implies continued synergies between the implementation of the BTWC and of the 1993 Chemical Weapons Convention, such as through further consultations by the ISU and the SAB on relevant scientific and technological developments in the life sciences and chemistry. The 2018–20 intersessional process meetings will provide a platform for achieving a common understanding on longer-term treaty regime trends and their implications for multilateral disarmament and arms control more generally.

CA, Aug. 2017); Carus, W. S., 'A century of biological-weapons programs, 1915–2015: Reviewing the evidence', *Nonproliferation Review*, vol. 24, nos. 1–2 (2017), pp. 129–53; and BTWC 2015 Meeting of States Parties, 'Outline of key features and objectives', Submitted by Belgium, Luxembourg and the Netherlands, BWC/MSP/2015/MX/WP.13, 6 Aug. 2015.

[23] See e.g. Zanders, J. P., Hart, J. and Kuhlau, F., 'Biotechnology, biological defence research and the BTWC', *SIPRI Yearbook 2002*, pp. 680–83 [on biodefence projects]; Leitenberg, M. and Zilinskas, R. A., *The Soviet Biological Weapons Program: A History* (Harvard University Press: Cambridge, MA, 2012) [on legacies of former state BW programmes]; Wheelis, M., Rózsa, L. and Dando, M., *Deadly Cultures: Biological Weapons Since 1945* (Harvard University Press: Cambridge, MA, 2005); and Sims (note 2).

[24] Iklé, F. C., 'After detection—what?', *Foreign Affairs*, vol. 39, no. 2 (Jan. 1961) , p. 218.

[25] Balmer, B., McLeish, C. and Spelling, A., *Understanding Biological Disarmament: The Historical Context of the Origins of the Biological Weapons Convention (BWC)* (University College London: London, July 2017).

9. Conventional arms control

Overview

The regulation of different categories of weapons as a means of trying to improve compliance with international humanitarian law has become an important theme in conventional arms control. However, participation in humanitarian arms control agreements is far from universal and states parties to such agreements still face many implementation challenges. According to some states and civil society groups, there are also gaps in humanitarian arms control and disarmament law that need to be addressed. In 2017, negotiations to address some of these challenges continued within the framework of the 1981 Convention on Prohibitions or Restrictions on the Use of Certain Conventional Weapons which may be Deemed to be Excessively Injurious or to have Indiscriminate Effects (CCW Convention), see section I; the 1997 Convention on the Prohibition of the Use, Stockpiling, Production, and Transfer of Anti-Personnel Mines and on their Destruction (APM Convention), see section II; and the 2008 Convention on Cluster Munitions (CCM), which is discussed in section III.

Afghanistan and Lebanon joined the CCW in 2017, taking the total number of states parties to 125. The CCW Convention has also been a vehicle for discussions on how to regulate new or emerging technologies. The focus in 2017 was on lethal autonomous weapon systems (LAWS). For the first time, these discussions took place in the format of a Group of Governmental Experts (GGE), which focused on the technological, military and ethical/legal dimensions of emerging technologies in the area of LAWS. While no substantive decisions were made, it was recommended that the GGE would convene again in 2018 for 10 days, with a focus on the characterization of systems under consideration and the implications of human-machine interaction.

In the first 11 months of 2017 at least 15 399 civilians were reported killed by explosive weapons, representing an increase of 42 per cent on the same period in 2016. The growing international concern over the use of incendiary weapons and explosive weapons in populated areas, including the use of improvised explosive devices (IEDs) by non-state armed groups, failed to generate new concrete outcomes during discussions within the CCW. The lack of consensus was compounded by the fact that several expert meetings were cancelled due to a lack of funding. States parties agreed to discuss some of the issues further in 2018.

Sri Lanka and Palestine became the 163rd and 164th states parties to the APM Convention in 2017, which celebrated its 20th anniversary in September. Global casualties from APMs in 2016 were at their highest level since 1999, largely as a result of the armed conflicts in Afghanistan, Libya, Ukraine and Yemen. Algeria and Mozambique declared themselves free of landmines in 2017, but 57 states and four other areas remained contaminated by mines. Discussions on mines other than anti-personnel mines (MOTAPM) also took place at the CCW in 2017.

Benin and Madagascar ratified the CCM in 2017 taking the total number of states parties to 102. There was continued use of cluster munitions in Syria and Yemen in 2017.

IAN DAVIS

I. The Convention on Certain Conventional Weapons

IAN DAVIS AND MAAIKE VERBRUGGEN

Humanitarian arms control

Many arms control and disarmament regimes are underpinned by humanitarian norms and principles.[1] Much of the focus on conventional technologies in the recent past (1990–2010) was on cluster munitions and landmines, as well as efforts to restrict the proliferation of small arms. These efforts included steps to improve standards in the production, trade and use of weaponry as well as bans on an entire class of weaponry. The 1981 Convention on Prohibitions or Restrictions on the Use of Certain Conventional Weapons which may be Deemed to be Excessively Injurious or to have Indiscriminate Effects (CCW Convention) takes both approaches. The 1997 Convention on the Prohibition of the Use, Stockpiling, Production and Transfer of Anti-Personnel Mines and on their Destruction (APM Convention) and the 2008 Convention on Cluster Munitions (CCM)—which are discussed in sections II and III, respectively—both ban an entire class of weapon, albeit relatively narrow ones. This section reviews the negotiations that took place within the CCW Convention. It also examines ongoing efforts to expand the scope of the CCW Convention, especially the discussions on lethal autonomous weapon systems (LAWS), the use of explosive weapons in populated areas (EWIPA) and incendiary weapons, which have been the main focus of negotiations on conventional technologies in recent years.

Scope of the convention

The CCW Convention and its five protocols ban or restrict the use of specific types of weapon that are considered to cause unnecessary or unjustifiable suffering to combatants or to affect civilians indiscriminately.[2] It is a so-called umbrella treaty, under which specific agreements can be concluded in the form of protocols. As of the end of December 2017 there were 125 states parties to the original convention and its protocols. Afghanistan and Leba-

---

[1] The body of international humanitarian disarmament law was further expanded in 2017 with the adoption on 7 July of the Treaty on the Prohibition of Nuclear Weapons. See the discussion in chapter 7, section I, in this volume. On the broader application of humanitarian norms and principles to arms control see Anthony, I., 'International humanitarian law: ICRC guidance and its application in urban warfare', SIPRI Yearbook 2017, pp. 545–53. For a critical, and historically informed, reading of the humanitarian arms control agenda see Cooper, N., 'Humanitarian arms control and processes of securitization: Moving weapons along the security continuum', Contemporary Security Policy, vol. 32, no. 1 (2011), pp. 134–58; and Docherty, B., 'Ending civilian suffering: The purpose, provisions, and promise of humanitarian disarmament law', Austrian Review of International and European Law, vol. 15 (2010), pp. 7–44.

[2] For a summary of the CCW Convention see annex A, section I, in this volume.

non joined the CCW in 2017. However, not all the states parties have ratified all the amended or additional protocols.

The CCW Convention is also important for addressing the challenges posed by the development or use of new weapons and their systems with respect to international humanitarian law (IHL). The convention originally contained three protocols: prohibiting the use of weapons that employ fragments not detectable in the human body by X-ray (Protocol I); regulating the use of landmines, booby traps and similar devices (Protocol II); and limiting the use of incendiary weapons (Protocol III). In subsequent years states added two protocols: Protocol IV prohibiting the use and transfer of blinding laser weapons was added in 1996; and Protocol V on explosive remnants of war in 2003. In addition, amendments have expanded and strengthened the convention. Its scope was expanded in 2001, for instance, to situations of intra-state armed conflict.

These developments demonstrated that the CCW Convention could— despite often having to tread a careful path between humanitarian and strategic military needs—be a dynamic instrument for responding to advances in weapons technology and developments in the nature and conduct of armed conflict. In recent years, however, it has become increasingly difficult to reconcile humanitarian demands with strategic military needs—in part, because of differing interpretations of 'strategic military needs' and the exploitation of the convention's consensus-based methods of working—with the result that many of the discussions within the convention have become deadlocked. Nonetheless, all CCW states parties meet regularly either at an annual meeting of the high contracting parties (states parties) or at a review conference (every fifth year), in which they also consider the work done by the Group of Governmental Experts (GGE) established in 2001 and convened in various formats since then.

At the Fifth Review Conference in 2016, states were divided between those that supported either new measures or reviews of some of the existing protocols to address the humanitarian harm arising from the use of EWIPA, incendiary weapons and new technologies, and those that argued that existing law is sufficient but that compliance needs to be improved. The net result was that the 2016 Review Conference failed to make any progress in addressing these issues.[3]

In the run-up to the Meeting of the High Contracting Parties to the Convention in Geneva on 22–24 November 2017, a number of CCW meetings took place in the city in November 2017: (a) the Group of Governmental Experts on LAWS, on 13–17 November 2017; (b) the Eleventh Conference of the High Contracting Parties on Protocol V, on 20 November 2017; and

---

[3] See the discussion on the 2016 CCW Review Conference in Davis, I. et al., 'Humanitarian arms control regimes: Key developments in 2016', *SIPRI Yearbook 2017*, pp. 554–61.

(c) the Nineteenth Annual Conference of the High Contracting Parties on Amended Protocol II, on 21 November 2017. However, the GGE meetings on LAWS planned for April and August, as well as Experts Meetings to prepare for the Protocol V and Amended Protocol II conferences, did not take place for financial reasons. Proposals to address the poor financial situation of the convention were circulated by the 2017 Chair, Ambassador Matthew Rowland of the United Kingdom, in July.[4] The underfunding of the convention was due to a combination of outstanding debts by certain member states that had not paid their assessed contributions and the implementation of a complex UN financial management system that requires all money relating to a particular meeting to be paid in advance of the meeting itself.

Group of Governmental Experts on Lethal Autonomous Weapons Systems

The CCW was again the centre of diplomatic discussion on the risks posed by LAWS.[5] Despite several years of ongoing expert discussions, LAWS still lack a generally agreed definition, but they are commonly described by civil society as weapons that are capable of selecting and attacking targets, including human targets, without the direct involvement of a human operator.[6]

LAWS have been taken up for international intergovernmental discussion under the framework of the CCW since 2014, and between 2014–16 they were discussed in the context of informal Meetings of Experts. During the Fifth Review Conference of the CCW in December 2016 it was decided that the issue of LAWS would be taken up within a GGE, as recommended by the Meeting of Experts. The Fifth Review Conference also adopted its recommendations on the subjects to discuss. These were first and foremost the identification of characteristics of LAWS and the elaboration of a working definition of LAWS, as well as the application of the relevant principles and rules of international law, in particular IHL. It was also recommended that the GGE examine (a) compliance with international human rights law when applicable; (b) legal and political responsibility and accountability; (c) ethical and moral questions; (d) the effects on regional and global security and stability; (e) the effects on the threshold for armed conflicts; (f) the risk of an arms race; (g) proliferation risks, including to and by non-state actors; (h) and related risks posed by cyber operations.[7] It was decided that the GGE

---

[4] Letter of the Chairperson, Ambassador Matthew Rowland of the United Kingdom, dated 6 July 2017, containing the Non-paper on the financial issue.

[5] See *SIPRI Yearbook 2014* and *SIPRI Yearbook 2017* for earlier accounts of the discussion on the regulation of LAWS: Anthony, I. and Holland, C., 'The governance of autonomous weapons', *SIPRI Yearbook 2014*; and Davis et al. (note 3).

[6] For a detailed overview of what LAWS are and how they function see Boulanin, V. and Verbruggen, M., *Mapping the Development of Autonomy in Weapon Systems* (SIPRI: Stockholm, 2017).

[7] Davis et al. (note 3), p. 560.

would meet for 10 days in 2017, with a first session on 24–28 April 2017 or 21–25 August 2017, and a second session on 13–17 November 2017. However, due to the above-mentioned budgetary difficulties, only the second session took place. The GGE was chaired by India's Ambassador to the Conference of Disarmament, Amandeep Singh Gill.[8]

There are no agreed definitions of LAWS and many previous diplomatic discussions on the issue have floundered in attempting to reach a working definition. To avoid this deadlock Chair Singh Gill steered the GGE away from discussions on defining LAWS, and instead aimed to develop a better shared understanding of the underlying issues.[9] The main body of the programme of work was made up of three panels on the technological, military, and legal and ethical dimensions of emerging technologies in the area of LAWS. It also featured panels on the cross-cutting dimensions of emerging technologies in the area of LAWS, an interactive discussion on the Chair's food-for-thought paper and a discussion on the way ahead.[10]

Both the expert presentations and the general debates showed a wide range of views in all three subject areas. The first panel focused on the technical dimensions and assessed issues such as the existence of Artificial General Intelligence (or superintelligence), the speed of development of artificial intelligence (AI) and the challenges in developing reliable and safe AI. While the analyses of and predictions on these technological developments varied, the panellists all agreed that a ban on LAWS would be unlikely to interfere with peaceful uses of AI.[11]

The second panel centred on the military dimensions and reviewed the impact of autonomy in warfare, such as where it would be most likely to be deployed and have the greatest impact, and how it would fit in with existing command and control systems. It was widely agreed by experts and states alike that a form of human control must be maintained over the weapon systems, especially over the selection and engagement of targets. However, there was no consensus on exactly what meaningful human control entails, and some states maintain that there are other risks associated with LAWS that would not be adequately addressed by only ensuring meaningful human control.

The third panel dealt with the legal and ethical dimensions, but agreement was only reached on the most basic of issues. First, while most states agreed that Article 36 reviews can serve as an excellent tool for ensuring compliance

---

[8] United Nations, 'Final Document of the Fifth Review Conference', CCW/CONF.V/10, 23 Dec. 2016.
[9] Singh Gill, A., Chairperson of the Group of Governmental Experts on LAWS, United Nations, Food-for-thought Paper, CCW/GGE.1/2017/WP.1, 4 Sep. 2017.
[10] Singh Gill, A., Chairperson of the Group of Governmental Experts on LAWS, United Nations, 'Provisional Programme of Work', CCW/GGE.1/2017/2/Rev.1, 8 Nov. 2017.
[11] Reaching Critical Will, 'CCW Report', vol. 5, no. 2 (14 Nov. 2017), p. 5.

with IHL, there was no consensus that they are sufficient on their own to deal with the challenges that LAWS raise.[12] Second, while all states agreed on the applicability of IHL to LAWS, opinions varied on whether international human rights law applies to LAWS, for instance the rights to life, a fair trial, peaceful assembly and human dignity.[13]

In his summary of the debates, Chair Singh Gill referred to the need to improve the shared understanding of LAWS. Many states proposed adopting a working definition, but once again this approach was not successful. Chair Singh Gill stated that this was the result of disagreement over scope. Significant items of contention were whether the definition should include already deployed systems, and apply only to offensive or also to defensive systems, and whether to distinguish between fully and semi-autonomous systems. While some states consider that fully autonomous weapon systems do not yet exist, others highlighted precursor technologies or the deployment of increasingly autonomous technologies to show how difficult it is to make this distinction. Certain states also considered working definitions premature at this stage of the debate. Aside from the issue of working definitions, Chair Singh Gill noted that it was regrettable that 18 months had passed without a formal discussion on LAWS. A majority of states have expressed their interest in transitioning to a new phase and starting to develop concrete political and legal responses, but consensus is required to do so, which has not yet been achieved. The states therefore affirmed their intention to undertake more frequent discussion of the subject in 2018.[14]

A number of different solutions were proposed to move the discussions forward. The civil society coalition Campaign to Stop Killer Robots, which has put the issue on the agenda of the CCW, advocates a prohibition on the use and development of LAWS. Brazil, Iraq and Uganda are the latest states to express support for a ban and 22 states now favour this approach.[15] The two other most discussed options in 2017 were a new legally binding instrument to regulate LAWS, as proposed by the Non-Aligned Movement; and a political declaration on LAWS, as suggested by France and Germany. In addition, the possibility of a moratorium on the development and use of LAWS

[12] Article 36 reviews are legal reviews to test whether new weapons, means or methods of warfare comply with a country's obligations under international law. For more information on Article 36 reviews see Boulanin V., and Verbruggen, M., *Article 36 Reviews: Dealing with the Challenges Posed by Emerging Technologies* (SIPRI: Stockholm, 2017).

[13] Reaching Critical Will, 'CCW Report', vol. 5, no. 3, 15 Nov. 2017.

[14] United Nations, Group of Governmental Experts of the High Contracting Parties to the Convention on Prohibitions or Restrictions on the Use of Certain Conventional Weapons Which May Be Deemed to Be Excessively Injurious or to Have Indiscriminate Effects, Report of the 2017 Group of Governmental Experts on Lethal Autonomous Weapons Systems (LAWS), CCW/GGE.1/2017/CRP.1, Geneva, 20 Nov. 2017, Annex II: Chair's Summary of the discussion.

[15] The other 19 states are Algeria, Argentina, Bolivia, Chile, Costa Rica, Cuba, Ecuador, Egypt, Ghana, Guatemala, Holy See, Mexico, Nicaragua, Pakistan, Panama, Peru, Palestine, Venezuela and Zimbabwe. See Campaign to Stop Killer robots, 'Country views on killer robots', 16 Nov. 2016.

was discussed. However, a small number of states, most notably the United States and Russia, considered it too early to move the discussion forward and focus on tangible outcomes.[16] The GGE concluded by recommending that the group meet for 10 days in 2018 to resume discussions. The Final Report of the GGE suggested that there would be merit in focusing discussions on the characterization of the systems under consideration to promote a common understanding and further assess human-machine interaction.[17]

There were some noteworthy developments in the discussion on LAWS outside of the CCW. In Australia, Belgium and Canada, scientists signed a call to ban LAWS and presented it to their national governments.[18] In addition, 116 experts from industry called for renewed efforts on the discussions on LAWS in August 2017, when it became clear that the first session at the CCW would not take place.[19]

Protocol V and Amended Protocol II meetings

Protocol V Meeting: Explosive remnants of war

The Eleventh Annual Conference of the High Contracting Parties to Protocol V was presided over by Ambassador Andre Pung of Estonia. The Protocol recognizes the serious post-conflict humanitarian problems caused by explosive remnants of war (ERW)—landmines, unexploded ordnance and abandoned explosive ordnance—and addresses remedial measures to minimize their occurrence, effects and risks. The conference focused on the practical implementation of Article 4 of the CCW, on the recording, retaining and transmission of information, which can have a significant impact on the clearance of ERW and ultimately the protection of civilians.[20] A proposal for a new national reporting assistance mechanism to improve the rate and quality of reporting was discussed and adopted.[21] Finally, the conference

---

[16] Reaching Critical Will (note 13).

[17] United Nations, Report of the 2017 Group of Governmental Experts on Lethal Autonomous Weapons Systems (LAWS) (note 14).

[18] Members of the Australian AI research community, Letter to Australian Prime Minister Malcolm Turnbull, Re: An international ban on the weaponization of artificial intelligence, 2 Nov. 2017; Members of the Belgian artificial intelligence (AI) and robotics research community, 'Autonomous weapon systems: An open letter from Belgian scientists', 6 Dec. 2017; and Members of the Canadian AI research community, Letter to Canadian Prime Minister Justin Trudeau, Re: An international ban on the weaponization of artificial intelligence, 2 Nov. 2017.

[19] 'An open letter to the Convention on Certain Conventional Weapons', The Future of Life Institute, 21 Aug. 2017.

[20] UNODA, Joint Letter by the Presidents-designate of the Conferences of the High Contracting Parties to Amended Protocol II and to Protocol V, 2 Nov. 2017.

[21] Proposal on the Provision of Expert Assistance for National Reporting under Protocol V on Explosive Remnants for War (ERW), CCW/P.V/CONF/2017/2, 26 Sep. 2017; and Eleventh Conference of the High Contracting Parties to Protocol V on Explosive Remnants of War to the Convention on Prohibitions or Restrictions on the Use of Certain Conventional Weapons Which May Be

agreed to focus work under Protocol V in 2018 on the clearance of explosive remnants of war and to continue efforts on national reporting.

Amended Protocol II Meeting: Landmines and improvised explosive devices

The Nineteenth Annual Conference of the High Contracting Parties to Amended Protocol II was presided over by Beatriz Londono Soto, Ambassador of Colombia. The conference reviewed the status and operation of the protocol and considered matters arising from the national reports by states parties. These reports contained information on a range of protocol-related matters, such as: (*a*) dissemination of information on the protocol to armed forces and civilian populations; (*b*) mine clearance and rehabilitation programmes; (*c*) the steps taken to meet the technical requirements of the protocol; (*d*) legislation related to the protocol; (*e*) and measures taken on international technical information exchange, international cooperation on mine clearance and technical cooperation and assistance, as well as the development of technologies to protect civilians against the indiscriminate effects of mines.[22]

The meeting also considered the issue of improvised explosive devices (IEDs), with a focus on information exchange on national measures and best practices with regard to the general features of IEDs and new types of IED; methods of humanitarian clearance of IEDs; and methods to protect civilians from IEDs.[23] The latter issue has become increasingly salient in recent years. More than 109 000 deaths or injuries linked to IEDs were recorded from 2011 until 2016, of which over 81 per cent were civilian. This represents around 57 per cent of all civilian casualties from explosive weapons during this period.[24] Non-state armed groups use IEDs in a variety of forms, such as remote detonation, with timer devices or in suicide attacks, and sometimes use commercial unmanned aerial vehicles to deliver IEDs.[25]

While there is clear scope for action in the CCW on IEDs, given that it is both a humanitarian and a military strategic concern, the key difficulties are more practical: What would a CCW protocol on IEDs look like? How can states control materials that can be used in IEDs that are invariably dual-use and so diffuse in society? The Conference reached no concrete conclusions on this issue, although states parties agreed to discuss IEDs further in 2018,

Deemed to Be Excessively Injurious or to Have Indiscriminate Effects, 'Final Report', CCW/P.V/CONF/2017/5, 4 Dec. 2017.

[22] UNODA (note 20); and Nineteenth Annual Conference of the High Contracting Parties to Amended Protocol II to the Convention on Prohibitions or Restrictions on the Use of Certain Conventional Weapons Which May Be Deemed to Be Excessively Injurious or to Have Indiscriminate Effects, 'Final Document', Advance version, 1 Dec. 2017.

[23] UNODA (note 20). See also the discussion on IEDs in Davis et al. (note 3), p. 554.

[24] Action on Armed Violence, *Improvised Explosive Device (IED) Monitor 2017*, Oct. 2017.

[25] Davies, R., 'Drones and the IED threat', *Action on Armed Violence*, 26 July 2017.

and to continue to review the operation and status of the protocol more generally.

Other efforts to address the IED threat in 2017 were the adoption of UN Security Council Resolution 2370 of 2 August 2017, which calls for more stringent national measures to prevent the supply of weapons and explosive precursors to terrorists, and a UN General Assembly First Committee Resolution on the issue in October.[26]

Meeting of the High Contracting Parties

The 2017 CCW Meeting of the High Contracting Parties was held in Geneva on 22–24 November 2017, chaired by Ambassador Matthew Rowland of the UK. The meeting reviewed progress towards the universalization of, and compliance with, the convention. It tasked the GGE on LAWS to meet for 10 days in 2018 under the continuing chair of India (as discussed above); and agreed to place on the agenda of its next meeting 'Emerging issues in the context of the objectives and purposes of the Convention', with an open invitation to states parties to submit working papers on the issues they intend to raise. The meeting also agreed a number of measures to improve the financial situation of the convention.[27] The three substantive issues discussed were incendiary weapons, EWIPA and mines other than anti-personnel mines (MOTAPM).

Incendiary weapons

Protocol III to the CCW Convention prohibits certain uses of incendiary weapons but its restrictions have failed to stop the civilian harm from their use in recent years in Syria, Ukraine, Yemen and elsewhere. The protocol has two major loopholes: weaker regulation of ground-launched incendiary weapons in comparison with air-dropped models; and inadequate wording on multipurpose munitions, such as white phosphorus, which can be used for several purposes on the battlefield—as an obscurant or smoke screen, for signalling and marking, and as an incendiary weapon.

In 2017, according to Human Rights Watch (HRW) and other reports, the Syrian Government and Russian forces used incendiary weapons in populated areas in Syria.[28] More specifically, HRW documented 22 attacks with incendiary weapons in Syria in 2017, which represented about a quarter of

[26] UN Security Council Resolution 2370, 2 Aug. 2017; and UN General Assembly, First Committee, Countering the threat posed by improvised explosive devices, A/C.1/72/L.15/Rev.1, 24 Oct. 2017.
[27] Meeting of the High Contracting Parties to the Convention on Prohibitions or Restrictions on the Use of Certain Conventional Weapons Which May Be Deemed to Be Excessively Injurious or to Have Indiscriminate Effects, Geneva, 22–24 Nov. 2017, Final Report, Advance version, 29 Nov. 2017.
[28] Human Rights Watch and Harvard Law School International Human Rights Clinic, *An Overdue Review: Addressing Incendiary Weapons in the Contemporary Context, Memorandum to Delegates at the Meeting of States Parties to the Convention on Conventional Weapons*, Nov. 2017, pp. 14–19.

the total number it had documented over the past five years of armed conflict in Syria. For example, an online video from 16 March showed the use of incendiary weapons in the town of Om al-Krameel, close to Aleppo.[29]

Syria is not a state party to Protocol III and is therefore not bound by its restrictions, and has been using Russian-made or Soviet-era incendiary weapons since 2012. Russia, however, has ratified the protocol and is prohibited from using air-dropped incendiary weapons in areas with concentrations of civilians. Despite evidence to the contrary, Russia has denied using incendiary or other forbidden weapons or ammunition in Syria.[30]

In addition, the US-led coalition used white phosphorus munitions while fighting the Islamic State group in Raqqah, Syria, and Mosul, Iraq, in 2017.[31] After incidents documented in March and June 2017, a spokesman for the US-led coalition stated that 'white phosphorous rounds are used for screening, obscuring and marking in a way that fully considers the possible incidental effects on civilians and civilian structures'.[32] With regard to the incident in Mosul, Iraqi Security Forces stated that they used the munitions to create a smokescreen, and the US-led coalition issued a statement explaining it 'used smoke and precision munitions to suppress the enemy and provide cover for fleeing civilians'.[33]

Several states, along with the International Committee of the Red Cross (ICRC), the UN Secretary-General and many non-governmental organizations (NGOs), have condemned recent incendiary weapon attacks and called for Protocol III to be revisited and strengthened.[34] While little progress was made at the Fifth Review Conference in 2016, it was anticipated that, given that the protocol was appearing as a separate item on the agenda of a meeting of states parties for the first time since the CCW was adopted in 1980, this would be an opportunity for a robust discussion on the harm caused by incendiary weapons and the adequacy of the protocol. However, outcomes were limited to states parties collectively condemning the use of incendiary weapons, reaffirming the importance of the protocol and calling for its universalization and full implementation. There was no commitment to a future strengthening of the protocol, although the states parties did decide to retain the issue as a separate agenda item for the 2018 meeting.[35]

---

[29] Broomfield, M., 'New footage shows Russia using "white phosphorous" in Syria, activists claim', *The Independent*, 16 Mar. 2017.

[30] See e.g. Broomfield (note 29); and Human Rights Watch, 'Syria/Russia: Incendiary weapons burn in Aleppo, Idlib', 16 Aug. 2016.

[31] Barnard, A., 'US-led forces said to have used white phosphorus in Syria', *New York Times*, 10 June 2017.

[32] Barnard (note 31); Gibbons-Neff, T., 'US-led forces appear to be using white phosphorous in populated areas in Iraq and Syria', *Washington Post*, 9 June 2017; and Human Rights Watch, 'Iraq/Syria: Danger from US White Phosphorus', 14 June 2017.

[33] Human Rights Watch (note 32).

[34] See the discussion on incendiary weapons in Davis et al. (note 3), pp. 556–57.

[35] Meeting of the High Contracting Parties, Final Report (note 27).

Explosive weapons in populated areas

According to the ICRC, 'Armed conflicts are increasingly fought in population centres, but often with weapon systems that were originally designed for use in open battlefields. When used in populated areas, explosive weapons that have wide-area effects are very likely to have indiscriminate effects. They are a major cause of harm to civilians and of disruption of services essential for their survival'.[36] In particular, the use of explosive weapons with a large destructive radius, an inaccurate delivery system, or the capacity to deliver multiple munitions over a wide area is likely to have an enormous humanitarian impact in urban areas. This is due to both the direct blast and the fragmentation effects, but also to the related destruction of civilian housing and essential civilian infrastructure, which may result in subsequent civilian death, injury and displacement that outweighs the immediate civilian casualties caused by an attack.[37] Where explosive weapons are used in populated areas, it is not unusual for over 90 per cent of the casualties to be civilian.[38]

In the first 11 months of 2017 at least 15 399 civilians were reported killed by explosive weapons—an increase of 42 per cent on the same period in 2016, when the total was 10 877. The majority of civilian deaths (8932) were caused by air-launched weapons. This was an increase of 82 per cent from 4902 in 2016 and an increase of 1169 per cent compared to 2011, when 704 civilian deaths were caused by airstrikes.[39] The use of IEDs by non-state armed groups killed 3874 civilians in the first 11 months of 2017, a similar number to those killed in 2016. The worst single explosive weapon incident of 2017 globally saw at least 512 people killed by a truck bomb in Mogadishu, Somalia, in October 2017.[40]

Conflicts in Afghanistan, Iraq, Syria, Ukraine, Yemen and elsewhere have provided clear evidence of this persistent pattern of destruction. In Yemen, for example, the indiscriminate and disproportionate use of explosive weapons by all parties, including airstrikes by a Saudi-led coalition, has caused many civilian casualties. At least 10 000 people have been killed since the start of the war in March 2015.[41] Even when precision-guided munitions

---

[36] ICRC, 'Explosive weapons in populated areas', Fact sheet, 14 June 2016. See also 'Areas of harm: Understanding explosive weapons with wide area effects', PAX and Article 36, Oct. 2016.

[37] On the impact of the destruction of civilian infrastructure see e.g. ICRC, 'Diary: ICRC president on the ground in Yemen', 25 July 2017.

[38] ICRC (note 36); and International Network on Explosive Weapons (INEW) website.

[39] 'First 11 months of 2017 sees 42% increase in civilian deaths from explosive weapons compared to 2016', Action on Armed Violence, 8 Jan. 2018; and McVeigh, K., '"Crazy numbers": Civilian deaths from airstrikes almost double in a year', *The Guardian*, 8 Jan. 2018.

[40] 'Death toll from Somalia truck bomb in October now at 512: Probe committee', Reuters, 30 Nov. 2017. On the conflict in Somalia see chapter 2, section VI, in this volume.

[41] Wintour, P., 'Saudi-led airstrikes kill 68 civilians in one day of Yemen's "absurd" war', *The Guardian*, 28 Dec. 2017. On the conflict in Yemen see chapter 2, section V, in this volume.

(PGMs) are used in populated areas the civilian casualties can be unacceptably high.

In the fight against the Islamic State in Iraq and Syria, for example, the US-led coalition has conducted more than 27 500 airstrikes since August 2014. The coalition claims to have a meticulous target-selection process and often uses PGMs to minimize civilian casualties. However, an independent assessment of coalition airstrikes carried out in Iraq over an 18-month period found that one in five of the airstrikes resulted in civilian deaths—a rate more than 31 times that acknowledged by the coalition.[42] Four problems have been identified that may have contributed to this lack of precision: (a) a decrease in the strategic military incentives that come with protecting civilians; (b) new shifts in targeting tactics, techniques and procedures; (c) a 'guilt by association' approach to targeting—whereby people killed in close proximity to the intended target are counted as non-civilians; (d) and a reduction in the military's investigative resources for monitoring civilian casualties.[43]

Since current IHL does not draw clear boundaries on the use of EWIPA, some states and NGOs see the need for a specific treaty-based restriction that would provide clear and universal guidance on the application of IHL to the use of EWIPA. Discussions aimed at developing a political instrument to address this humanitarian problem are being led by Austria with the support of the leading civil society coalition on this issue, the International Network on Explosive Weapons. Some states, led by Germany, have sought to bring the use of EWIPA within the framework of the CCW Convention. The 2016 Review Conference agreed that the 2017 meeting should explore the 'challenges presented by the use of conventional weapons in armed conflicts and their impact on civilians, particularly in areas where there are concentrations of civilians'.[44]

In his first report to the UN Security Council on the protection of civilians in armed conflict in May 2017, UN Secretary-General António Guterres underlined the destructive impacts for civilians when explosive weapons with wide-area effect are used in populated areas during conflict, and called on states to engage constructively in the process being led by Austria.[45] His predecessor, Ban Ki-moon, as well as the ICRC, had consistently called on states to refrain from using EWIPA. Both Austria and Germany submitted working papers on EWIPA to the November CCW meeting.[46] However,

---

[42] Khan, A. and Gopal, A., 'The Uncounted', *New York Times Magazine*, 16 Nov. 2017.

[43] Garlasco, M., 'How to fix the US Military's broken targeting system', Just Security, 12 Dec. 2017.

[44] See the discussion on EWIPA in Davis et al. (note 3), pp. 557–58.

[45] United Nations, Security Council, Report of the Secretary-General on the protection of civilians in armed conflict, S/2017/414, 10 May 2017.

[46] Convention on Certain Conventional Weapons, Meeting of High Contracting Parties, Emerging issues of relevance to the Convention, Submitted by Austria, CCW/MSP/2017/WP.1, 19 Oct.

at the meeting the issue was relegated to 'other matters' after objections from Turkey, one of the five countries Austria cited as having the highest number of civilian deaths and injuries linked to explosive weapons (alongside Afghanistan, Iran, Syria and Yemen).[47] The lack of consensus on how to address the problem of EWIPA meant that no concrete proposals emerged from the meeting and there was no mention of the issue in the final report document.

Representatives of 19 African countries, the United Nations Office for the Coordination of Humanitarian Affairs, the ICRC and civil society organizations met in Maputo, Mozambique, on 27–28 November 2017 for a regional conference on the protection of civilians from the use of EWIPA.[48]

Mines other than anti-personnel mines

Discussions on MOTAPM are focused on anti-vehicle mines, which include anti-tank mines. It is a topic that has been discussed several times within the CCW for over a decade, but without any agreed consensus among states parties on how to move the debate forward. The UN Office of Disarmament Affairs, the UN Mine Action Service and the Geneva International Centre for Humanitarian Demining held an informal meeting on MOTAPM on 29 August 2017.[49] At the November meeting of the CCW, however, progress was again stymied, although in the final report the chairperson-elect was tasked with holding an informal open consultation on how best to address the continuing differences of view on MOTAPM and reporting back to the 2018 meeting.[50]

2017; and Use of Explosive Weapons in Populated Areas (EWIPA), Submission by Germany, CCW/MSP/2017/WP.2, 25 Oct. 2017.

[47] See the Tweet by the Austrian Ambassador, Thomas Hajnoczi. @ThomasHajnoczi, Twitter, 22 Nov. 2017.

[48] Communique from Maputo regional conference on the protection of civilians from the use of explosive weapons in populated areas, 28 Nov. 2017.

[49] The presentations are available at UN Office at Geneva, 'MOTAPM: Latest news!'.

[50] Meeting of the High Contracting Parties, Final report (note 27).

II. The Anti-Personnel Mines Convention

IAN DAVIS

The 1997 Convention on the Prohibition of the Use, Stockpiling, Production, and Transfer of Anti-Personnel Mines and on their Destruction (APM Convention) prohibits, among other things, the use, development, production and transfer of anti-personnel mines (APMs)—mines that detonate due to human contact, also known as 'victim-activated', and thereby encompassing improvised explosive devices (IEDs) that act as anti-personnel mines, also known as 'improvised mines'.

Key developments in 2017

In 2017 two states, Sri Lanka and Palestine, joined the convention, bringing the total to 164 states parties by the end of the year, including all members of the European Union, every state in sub-Saharan Africa and every state in the Americas except for Cuba and the United States. Only 33 states remained outside the treaty.[1] Sri Lanka's accession was significant since the country has used APMs in the past and is currently undertaking an extensive mine clearance effort.[2] Similarly, Palestine's accession to the convention is important, given that some 20 square kilometres of its territory is contaminated by landmines, anti-vehicle mines and other explosive remnants of war (ERW).[3]

September 2017 marked the 20th anniversary of the signing of the convention and the establishment of both the United Nations Mine Action Service (UNMAS) and the Inter-Agency Coordination Group on Mine Action, which brings together working-level representatives of UN organizations involved in mine action to develop or revise policies and strategies, set priorities among UN players and share information.[4] Mine action involves the clearance of landmines and other ERW, including explosive munitions left behind after conflicts end, in order to release land back to the community. Mine clearance encompasses a range of activities to achieve clearance of mine- and ERW-affected areas such as technical and non-technical surveys, and mapping and marking to identify mined and demined areas.

New use of APMs by states is now extremely rare. Only Myanmar and Syria—both states outside the treaty—recorded use in the period October

---

[1] For a summary of the APM Convention see annex A, section I, in this volume.
[2] Human Rights Watch, 'Sri Lanka joins global landmine treaty', 14 Dec. 2017.
[3] ICBL, 'Palestine accedes to the mine ban treaty', News release, 3 Jan. 2018.
[4] UN Mine Action Service; and United Nations, General Assembly, Assistance in mine action, Report of the Secretary-General, A/72/226.

2016 to October 2017.[5] In Myanmar, for example, the security forces have been deploying APMs for the past 20 years and in 2017 were alleged to have built fences and placed landmines along the border to deter the Rohingya people fleeing government attacks from crossing into Bangladesh.[6] In September, the President of the APM Convention called on the Myanmar Government to clarify the situation and consider allowing an independent fact-finding mission into the country.[7]

The use of APMs, including victim-activated improvised mines, by non-state armed groups in conflicts is a growing problem. Such improvised mines and APMs were used by non-state armed groups in at least nine countries from October 2016 to October 2017: Afghanistan, India, Iraq, Myanmar, Nigeria, Pakistan, Syria (including extensive use of improvised mines by the retreating Islamic State group), Ukraine and Yemen.[8] There were no new uses of APMs by non-state armed groups in Colombia for the first time since monitoring began in 1999.

According to *Landmine Monitor 2017*, global casualties from APMs are at an 18-year high. The armed conflicts in Afghanistan, Libya, Ukraine and Yemen contributed to a second successive year of exceptionally high casualties caused by mines and other ERW in 2016. In 2016, the last year for which data is available, *Landmine Monitor* recorded 8605 mine/ERW casualties, of which at least 2089 were fatal, marking the highest recorded total since 1999 (when 9228 casualties were recorded) and the highest number of annual casualties caused by improvised mines ever.[9]

After hitting a 10-year low in 2015, international support for mine action in 2016 increased by over $85 million: 32 donors contributed $479.5 million to 40 states and 3 other areas. The top five mine action donors—the United States, the EU, Japan, Germany and Norway—contributed 70 per cent of all international funding in 2016.[10] In 2017 there were three further pledging conferences, building on the three held in 2016, to support mine action: a second international pledging conference for the implementation of the convention held in Geneva on 28 February 2017, and two individual conferences in support of Iraq (in July) and Colombia (in September).[11] In April 2017 the United Kingdom announced a £100 million ($124 million) aid package to

---

[5] ICBL–CMC, *Landmine Monitor 2017* (ICBL–CMC: Geneva, Dec. 2017), pp. 1, 8–18. The report focuses on calendar year 2016, with information included up to November 2017 when possible.

[6] Das, K. N., 'Bangladesh protests over Myanmar's suspected landmine use near border', Reuters, 5 Sep. 2017; and ICBL-CMC (note 5), pp. 9–10. On the conflict in Myanmar see also chapter 2, section III, in this volume.

[7] 'Landmine treaty president calls for fact-finding mission in Myanmar', APM Convention, Press release, 22 Sep. 2017.

[8] ICBL–CMC (note 5), pp. 1, 8–18.

[9] ICBL–CMC (note 5), pp. 2, 51–62.

[10] ICBL–CMC (note 5), pp. 3, 81–91.

[11] 'Second Pledging Conference for the Anti-Personnel Mine ban convention', APM website; and ICBL-CMC (note 5), pp. 82–83. Three pledging conferences were held in 2016, including the first

support landmine clearance projects in Afghanistan, Cambodia, Somalia and South Sudan over the next three years.[12]

In 2014, states parties set a shared goal of completing landmine clearance by 2025. In 2016, about 170 km² of land was cleared of landmines—an area similar to 2015—and more than 232 000 landmines were destroyed—a significant increase compared to 2015.[13] In 2017 Algeria and Mozambique declared themselves free of landmines.[14] Among the 57 states and four other sovereignty-disputed areas that are known to have mine contamination, 33 are states parties to the APM Convention. Only four of those appear to be on track to meet the 10-year deadline for clearance of known landmine contamination: Chile, the Democratic Republic of the Congo, Mauritania and Peru.[15] Among the states parties that must still fulfil their mine clearance obligation are some of the most mine-affected in the world: Afghanistan, Angola, Bosnia and Herzegovina, Cambodia, Colombia, Iraq, Serbia, Thailand and Zimbabwe.

Ukraine is in violation of the APM Convention having missed its 1 June 2016 deadline for mine clearance without having requested a deadline extension. It is also in violation for having missed its stockpile destruction deadline.[16] Collectively, states parties have destroyed more than 53 million stockpiled APMs, including the more than 2.2 million destroyed in 2016. The total global stockpile remaining today is estimated to be less than 50 million. Russia (26.5 million), Pakistan (6 million), India (4–5 million), China (5 million) and the USA (3 million) are estimated to be the largest stockpilers.[17] After missing its original deadline, Belarus completed the destruction of its stockpiles in 2017, including more than 3 million Soviet-era PFM-1 mines. These are extremely hazardous and their destruction poses serious technical difficulties.[18]

International Pledging Conference for the Implementation of the APM Convention in March. See Davis et al. (note 3), p. 564.

[12] UK Department for International Development (DFID), 'UK triples support for action against landmines on 20th anniversary of Princess Diana's iconic Angola visit', DFID Press release, 4 Apr. 2017.

[13] ICBL-CMC (note 5), pp. 2–3, 31–48.

[14] 'After decades of work, Algeria one of the most mine-affected countries in the world, is now free from this scourge', APM Convention website, 10 Feb. 2017.

[15] ICBL-CMC (note 5), pp. 2–3, 31–48.

[16] See the discussion on Ukraine and landmines in Davis et al. (note 3), pp. 565–66.

[17] ICBL-CMC (note 5), pp. 3–4, 18–19.

[18] 'Belarus destroys over three million hazardous landmines fulfilling its Ottawa Convention obligations: Over 50 million landmines have now been destroyed', APM Convention website, 7 Apr. 2017.

The 16th Meeting of States Parties to the APM Convention

Annual meetings of treaty member states are held at different locations around the world. The 16th Meeting of States Parties (MSP) to the APM Convention took place in Vienna on 18–21 December 2017 and was chaired by the Austrian Ambassador Thomas Hajnoczi.[19]

The conference expressed concern over the growing use of improvised landmines, called for sustained assistance to victims of these weapons and agreed that more sustained and targeted efforts in mine clearance were needed to meet the 2025 mine-free ambition. The conference also expressed concern that Ukraine is now in a state of non-compliance and called on the country to submit a request for extension of its mine clearance deadline as soon as possible.[20]

Five states parties—Angola, Ecuador, Iraq, Thailand and Zimbabwe— requested and were granted extensions on their mine clearance deadlines.[21] Iraq, which joined the convention in 2007, requested and was granted an extension to 2028 due to new contamination from IEDs from the conflict with the Islamic State. Since 2008, Iraq has allocated almost $250 million to its mine action activities, demined over 551 million square metres of land and destroyed 124 072 APMs.[22] The other four states were all granted deadline extensions that fell within the global 2025 mine-free target.

On 21 December, the last day of the conference, Palestine indicated that it would accede to the convention, which it did on 29 December. Ambassador Suraya Dalil of Afghanistan was elected chair of the convention's 17th MSP, which is scheduled to take place on 26–30 November 2018.[23]

---

[19] For details of proceedings, documents and statements by states parties see 'Sixteenth Meeting of the States Parties', APM website.

[20] 'Landmine Treaty at 20: Gains made in mine clearance, stockpile destruction and universalization', APM Convention press release, 22 Dec. 2017.

[21] Analysis of the request submitted by Angola for an extension of the deadline for completing the destruction of anti-personnel mines in accordance with Article 5 of the Convention, APLC/MSP.16/2017/WP.2, 1 Dec. 2017; Analysis of the request submitted by Ecuador for an extension of the deadline for completing the destruction of anti-personnel mines in accordance with Article 5 of the Convention, APLC/MSP.16/2017/WP.4, 20 Oct. 2017; Analysis of the request submitted by Iraq for an extension of the deadline for completing the destruction of anti-personnel mines in accordance with Article 5 of the Convention, APLC/MSP.16/2017/WP.6, 24 Oct. 2017; Analysis of the request submitted by Thailand for an extension of the deadline for completing the destruction of anti-personnel mines in accordance with Article 5 of the Convention, APLC/MSP.16/2017/WP.10, 23 Oct. 2017; and Analysis of the request submitted by Zimbabwe for an extension of the deadline for completing the destruction of anti-personnel mines in accordance with Article 5 of the Convention, APLC/MSP.16/2017/WP.14, 23 Oct. 2017.

[22] APM Convention press release (note 20). On the challenges facing mine action in the Middle East more generally see 'Death fields: Challenges facing mine action in the Middle East', Future for Advanced Research and Studies, 31 Oct. 2017.

[23] APM Convention press release (note 20).

Conclusions

The International Campaign to Ban Landmines–Cluster Munition Coalition (ICBL–CMC) concluded in its 2017 report that implementation of, and compliance with, the APM Convention has generally been 'excellent'. Core obligations have largely been respected and ambiguities, when they have arisen, have been dealt with in a satisfactory manner.[24] Similarly, the President of the APM Convention described progress since 1997 as 'outstanding', while noting with concern the recent increases in mine victims, largely due to the use of improvised anti-personnel mines by non-state actors.[25] However, the APM Convention also continues to be undercut by the refusal of some of the most powerful states, such as China, Iran, Israel, North Korea, Russia, Saudi Arabia and the USA, to sign it.[26]

Compliance concerns remain regarding a small number of issues: Ukraine's violation of Article 5 due to missing its 1 June 2016 clearance deadline (noted above); investigations still pending in relation to Yemen's acknowledged use of APMs in 2011; missed deadlines by Greece and Ukraine to complete their stockpile destruction; the 71 states parties that retain APMs for training and research purposes, of which 37 retain more than 1000 mines (Bangladesh, Finland and Turkey each retain more than 12 000 mines); and poor annual reporting by states parties—only 48 per cent have submitted annual reports for 2016, a slight increase on the previous year (45 per cent).[27]

[24] ICBL-CMC (note 5), pp. 4, 93–95.
[25] 'President's Final Declaration–Towards a mine-free world', AP Mine Ban Convention, Dec. 2017.
[26] 'Why do land mines still kill so many?', *New York Times*, 6 Jan. 2018.
[27] ICBL-CMC (note 5), pp. 4, 93–95.

III. The Convention on Cluster Munitions

IAN DAVIS

The 2008 Convention on Cluster Munitions (CCM) addresses the humanitarian consequences of and unacceptable harm to civilians caused by cluster munitions. The CCM establishes an unconditional prohibition and a framework for action. It also requires the destruction of stockpiles within eight years, the clearance of areas contaminated by cluster munition remnants within 10 years and the provision of assistance for victims of the weapon. As of 31 December 2017, the convention had 102 states parties and 17 signatory states.[1]

Key developments in 2017

In October 2017, 134 states, including 30 non-signatories to the convention, voted to adopt the third UN General Assembly resolution supporting the Convention on Cluster Munitions.[2] The resolution provides states outside the CCM with an important opportunity to indicate their support for the humanitarian rationale of the treaty and the objective of its universalization. Russia and Zimbabwe were the only states to vote against the resolution (as they were in respect of the 2016 resolution), while 36 states abstained.[3]

Most of the states still outside the convention abide de facto by the ban on the use and production of cluster munitions. However, despite international condemnation, there was continued use of cluster munitions in two countries in 2017: in Syria, where they have been used since mid-2012, and in Yemen, where they have been used since 2015.[4] According to *Cluster Munition Monitor 2017*, more than 600 cluster munition attacks occurred in Syria in the five-year period to July 2017, and there have been at least 238 separate attacks since August 2016, mostly carried out by the armed forces of the Syrian Government.[5] Other attacks have been attributed to Russia, which began joint operations with Syria in September 2015. However, in a position paper attached to a December 2016 letter to Human Rights Watch, the Russian Foreign Minister, Sergey Lavrov, claimed that the use of cluster

---

[1] In 2017 Benin and Madagascar ratified the CCM. South Sudan announced that it would also accede, but had not submitted its instrument of accession by the end of the year. For a summary of the Convention on Cluster Munitions see annex A, section I, in this volume.

[2] United Nations General Assembly, Implementation of the Convention on Cluster Munitions, A/C.1/72/L.41, 12 Oct. 2017.

[3] Cluster Munitions Coalition, 'United Nations votes on cluster munitions resolution', 9 Nov. 2017.

[4] On the conflict in Syria see chapter 2, section V, in this volume.

[5] *Cluster Munition Monitor 2017* focuses on calendar year 2016, with information included to July 2017 where possible. International Campaign to Ban Landmines–Cluster Munition Coalition (ICBL–CMC), *Cluster Munition Monitor 2017* (ICBL–CMC: Geneva, Aug. 2017), pp. 15–18.

munitions in Syria was in accordance with IHL, without explicitly denying or admitting to their use.[6]

In Yemen, a coalition of states led by Saudi Arabia has been involved in military operations against the Houthi—a predominantly Shia-led religious-political movement that emerged from Sa'dah, northern Yemen in the 1990s—and their allies since March 2015. At least 23 cluster munition attacks have been documented in Yemen since the start of the conflict, but fewer attacks since the second half of 2016.[7] On 15 June 2017 the European Parliament adopted a third resolution condemning Saudi-led coalition airstrikes in Yemen, including its use of cluster munitions.[8] Similar resolutions were agreed in February 2016 and July 2015. In addition, there were unverified allegations of cluster munitions use by Libyan National Army (LNA) forces in Libya and by the Islamic State in Iraq in 2016 or the first half of 2017.[9]

Under the CCM, 28 of the 41 states parties that have possessed stockpiles of cluster munitions have completed the destruction of nearly 1.4 million stockpiled cluster munitions containing 175 million submunitions. This represents the destruction of 97 per cent of all cluster munitions and 98 per cent of all submunitions declared as stockpiled under the treaty. No state party completed the destruction of its cluster munition stocks in the second half of 2016 or the first half of 2017, but Spain and Switzerland are expected to do so in 2018.[10] *Cluster Munition Monitor* is unable to provide a global estimate of the quantity of cluster munitions currently stockpiled by non-signatories to the CCM as too few have disclosed information on the types and quantities they possess.

The United States, a non-signatory to the convention, views cluster munitions as a military necessity but in 2008 introduced a policy to reduce the failure rate of the weapon to 1 per cent or less by 2019—a standard considered important given the hazard to civilians of unexploded submunitions in conflict zones. In November 2017, however, the US Department of Defense (DOD) said that it would be unable to fulfil the 2008 pledge. Under the new policy, the US military can continue to use cluster munitions that do not meet the 1 per cent or less unexploded submunitions standard in extreme situations to meet immediate warfighting demands. Furthermore, while the

[6] Lavrov, S., 'Russia's Position on the Use of Cluster Munitions in Syria', Position Paper annexed to letter to HRW from Sergey Lavrov, Russian Minister of Foreign Affairs, 9 Dec. 2016 (in Russian, with unofficial translation).

[7] ICBL–CMC (note 5), pp. 18–22; Amnesty International, 'Yemen: Saudi Arabia-led coalition uses banned Brazilian cluster munitions on residential areas', 9 Mar. 2017; and HRW, 'Yemen: Cluster munitions wound children', 17 Mar. 2017.

[8] European Parliament, Resolution on the humanitarian situation in Yemen, P8_TA(2017)0273, Strasbourg, 15 June 2017.

[9] ICBL–CMC (note 5), pp. 22–23; and Bulos, N., 'Islamic State fires cluster bombs at Iraqi government forces', *Los Angeles Times*, 21 Feb. 2017.

[10] ICBL–CMC (note 5), pp. 26–34.

US DOD will continue to replace cluster munitions that exceed the 1 per cent rate, the new policy does not set a deadline for achieving this. Instead, the US military 'will retain cluster munitions currently in active inventories until the capabilities they provide are replaced with enhanced and more reliable munitions'.[11]

As of July 2017, 82 states parties had submitted an initial transparency report as required by the convention, while 18 states parties had failed to do so—including five that were originally due in 2011. As of 30 June 2017, 50 states parties had submitted their annual updated transparency report covering activities in 2016, and 27 states parties were yet to do so.[12]

Conflict and insecurity made the clearance of cluster munitions more challenging in several countries, but at least 88 square kilometres of contaminated land was cleared in 2016, resulting in the destruction of 140 000 submunitions—both increases compared with 2015.[13] Between 2010 and 2016, more than 535 000 submunitions were destroyed and at least 425 km² of land was cleared worldwide. At least 26 states and three other areas remain contaminated by cluster munitions.[14] An accurate estimate of the total size of the contaminated area is not possible because the extent of contamination and the progress of clearance are difficult to discern in many states, especially non-signatory states.

Mozambique reported the completion of its clearance of cluster munitions in December 2016, bringing the total number of states parties that have done so under the convention to eight.[15] Only one (Croatia) of 13 states parties with declared contaminated areas and ongoing clearance programmes is judged to be on track to meet its mandated 10-year clearance deadline.[16]

Following an earlier workshop in Africa in August 2016, three regional workshops aimed at encouraging the universalization and implementation of the convention took place in 2017: in Bangkok on 16–17 March, in Kampala on 29–30 May and in Rakitje, Croatia, on 12–13 June.[17]

[11] Burns, R., 'US putting off planned ban of its use of cluster bombs', Associated Press, 30 Nov. 2017; and Feickert, A. and Kerr, P. K., *Cluster Munitions: Background and Issues for Congress*, RS22907 (Congressional Research Service: Washington, DC, 13 Dec. 2017).

[12] ICBL–CMC (note 5), pp. 36–37.

[13] ICBL–CMC (note 5), pp. 53–54.

[14] The states parties with cluster munition remnants are: Afghanistan, Bosnia and Herzegovina, Chad, Chile, Croatia, Germany, Iraq, Laos, Lebanon, Montenegro, Somalia and the United Kingdom; signatory: Angola; non-signatories: Azerbaijan, Cambodia, Georgia, Iran, Libya, Serbia, South Sudan, Sudan, Syria, Tajikistan, Ukraine, Viet Nam and Yemen; other areas: Kosovo, Nagorno-Karabakh and Western Sahara. ICBL–CMC (note 5), pp. 53–63.

[15] The others are: Albania, the Republic of the Congo, Grenada, Guinea-Bissau, Mauritania, Norway and Zambia. ICBL–CMC (note 5), p. 63.

[16] The other 12 are: Afghanistan, Bosnia and Herzegovina, Chad, Chile, Colombia, Germany, Laos, Iraq, Lebanon, Montenegro, Somalia and the UK. ICBL–CMC (note 5), pp. 63–69.

[17] CCM, Seminar Final Report, 'Cooperating to implement the CCM: The Country Coalition Concept', 16–17 Mar. 2017, Bangkok; CCM, 'Final Report on Convention on Cluster Munitions Ratification Seminar', Kampala, 29–30 May 2017; and CCM, 'The Workshop on Enhancing Implementa-

Seventh Meeting of States Parties to the CCM

The Seventh Meeting of States Parties to the CCM took place in Geneva on 4–6 September 2017 under the presidency of Germany. Earlier in the year Germany held bilateral meetings with at least 14 states that have produced and/or stockpiled cluster munitions, including Brazil, Saudi Arabia, Syria and Ukraine.[18] The meeting of the states parties was the second formal meeting since the adoption of the 2015 Dubrovnik Action Plan, a five-year action plan that provides a roadmap for states to implement and universalize the convention.[19] In the final report of the meeting, states parties 'expressed their strong concern regarding recent incidents and evidence of use of cluster munitions in different parts of the world and condemned any use by any actor'.[20] In addition, having noted that less than half of states parties had made a financial contribution to the 2016 CCM Implementation Support Unit (ISU) budget—which was fully covered only because a few states parties made significant contributions in excess of their assessed contributions—the meeting adopted a political declaration as an annex to the final report that identified a number of specific measures to improve the CCM's financial procedures.[21]

tion of Articles 3 and 4 of the CCM in South-East Europe: The Country Coalition Concept', Croatia, 12–13 June 2017.

[18] Minutes of the CCM Coordination Committee Meeting, Geneva, 23 Mar. 2017.

[19] The Dubrovnik Action Plan was adopted at the First Review Conference of the CCM in Dubrovnik, Croatia, on 11 Sep. 2015. For the text of the plan see CCM, 'Dubrovnik Action Plan', [n.d.]. For an update on progress see CCM, 'Convention on Cluster Munitions, 7MSP Progress Report: Monitoring progress in implementing the Dubrovnik Action Plan, Submitted by the President of the Seventh Meeting of States Parties, CCM/MSP/2017/9, 10 July 2017.

[20] CCM, Final Report, CCM/MSP/2017/12, 25 Sep. 2017. See also the coverage of the meeting by the Cluster Munition Coalition, 'The Seventh Meeting of States Parties'.

[21] CCM, Final Report (note 20).

10. Dual-use and arms trade controls

Overview

Global, multilateral and regional efforts continued in 2017 to strengthen controls on the trade in conventional arms and in dual-use items connected with conventional, biological, chemical and nuclear weapons and their delivery systems. Membership of the different international and multilateral instruments that are aimed at establishing and promoting agreed standards for dual-use and arms trade controls continued to expand. At the same time, ensuring effective implementation of these instruments—and reaching agreement about what 'effective implementation' means—continued to be a challenge. This could be seen in disagreements between non-governmental organizations (NGOs) and states about how to measure and ensure effective implementation of the 2013 Arms Trade Treaty (ATT) and the many reported violations of United Nations (UN) arms embargoes. The difficulties associated with ensuring that dual-use and arms trade controls keep pace with advances in technology and evolving trade patterns were also evident. This was visible in the discussions in the export control regime meetings about updating their control lists and guidance documents and efforts to regulate intangible transfers of technology (ITT).

The third conference of ATT states parties took place in Geneva in September 2017 (see section I). While the conference took a number of key decisions, the tensions between states parties and the community of NGOs that supported the creation of the ATT were again on display. Moreover, while the number of states parties to the treaty continued to increase, levels of compliance with reporting and funding obligations continued to fall short in several areas. Efforts to increase the number of states parties have focused on Asia in recent years and this trend seems likely to continue, given the appointment of Ambassador Nobushige Takamizawa of Japan as president of the fourth conference of states parties. However, while Asia faces a number of the security challenges that the ATT is intended to address, its current political dynamics also place significant obstacles in the way of further increases in the number of parties.

Thirty-five multilateral arms embargoes were in force in 2017: 13 imposed by the UN, 21 by the European Union (EU) and 1 by the League of Arab States (see section II). Of the EU's 21 embargoes, 9 implemented UN arms embargoes directly, 3 were similar to UN embargoes but differed in geographical scope or the types of weapon covered, and 9 had no UN counterpart. Most of these embargoes only covered conventional arms. However, the UN and EU embargoes on Iran and North Korea and the EU embargo on Russia also covered exports of dual-use items. One new multilateral arms embargo was imposed in 2017: an EU embargo on Venezuela. As in previous years, investigations by the UN revealed problems in the implementation of its embargoes, with numerous reported cases of violations. However, the scope and significance of these violations varied considerably, with some involving large shipments of arms in contravention of the embargo and others involving a failure by a supplier or recipient state to notify a sanctions committee about a transfer.

Each of the four multilateral export control regimes—the Australia Group (on chemical and biological weapons), the Missile Technology Control Regime (MTCR), the Nuclear Suppliers Group (NSG) and the Wassenaar Arrangement on Export Controls for Conventional Arms and Dual-use Goods and Technologies (Wassenaar Arrangement, WA)—updated its respective trade control lists and guidelines. As in previous years, a key challenge that all the regimes faced was ensuring that control lists were able to keep pace with the often rapid advances in goods, software and technology (see section III). In recent years all of the regimes have faced difficulties with admitting new members, owing to the requirement that all existing members must approve an application. However, in 2017 India was admitted to the Wassenaar Arrangement and in early 2018 it was admitted to the Australia Group. This follows its admission to the MTCR in 2016. India's application to join the NSG continues to be strongly opposed by a group of countries led by China. There were few changes in the EU's export controls during 2017. The main developments involved discussions concerning the ongoing review of the EU Dual-use Regulation.

The main export control regimes, the EU's controls on the trade in arms and dual-use items, and UN and EU arms embargoes all include requirements to exert and enforce controls on ITT. ITT are generally divided between those that involve transfers of technical data and software and transfers of knowledge and technical assistance. ITT are seen as being particularly difficult to detect, making enforcement hard for national authorities. In addition, controls on ITT also generate significant compliance costs for companies and research institutes (see section IV). The problems in this area are only going to become more acute in the years to come, as new trading patterns and technologies increase the volume and range of ITT that are potentially subject to export controls. During 2017 there were discussions—particularly within the context of the review of the EU Dual-use Regulation but also in the export control regimes—about how controls on ITT should be best structured and applied. Key challenges in this area include if and how export controls should apply to cloud computing and academic publishing, as well as the challenges presented by additive manufacturing—also known as 3D printing—as both an enabler of ITT and a multiplier of associated proliferation risks.

MARK BROMLEY

I. The Arms Trade Treaty

MARK BROMLEY AND KOLJA BROCKMANN

The 2013 Arms Trade Treaty (ATT) is the first legally binding international agreement to establish standards regulating the trade in conventional arms and preventing illicit arms transfers.[1] Since its entry into force in December 2014, much of the focus of states parties and interested sections of civil society has been on the bureaucratic modalities of establishing a working secretariat and other aspects of treaty architecture. By the end of 2016, the ATT Secretariat had been established and the parties had agreed templates for the initial report on steps taken to implement the treaty and the annual report on arms imports and exports. During 2017 attention increasingly shifted to treaty universalization and the issue of how to measure and ensure effective implementation by states parties. Both issues are likely to prove challenging.

As of 31 December 2017, 94 states were party to the ATT. An additional 41 states had signed but not yet ratified the treaty. In 2017 three states became party to the ATT—Honduras, Kazakhstan and Palestine—down from 12 in 2016. Representation is particularly low in the Middle East and Asia, while leading arms exporting countries such as China, Russia and the United States are yet to become party to the treaty and seem unlikely to do so in the near future. Meanwhile, discussions about treaty implementation have the potential to generate schisms—particularly between states parties and the community of non-governmental organizations (NGOs) that championed the treaty—about how this should be assessed and ensured.

The third conference of states parties (CSP3) was held in Geneva on 11–15 September 2017, with Ambassador Klaus Korhonen of Finland as president. It was attended by 79 of the 92 states parties—roughly the same proportion as for CSP2—along with 23 states signatories, 4 observer states, and 24 regional and international organizations, NGOs and industry associations.[2] Discussions were broadly divided into six areas: treaty implementation; transparency and reporting; the work of the ATT Secretariat; preparations for CSP4; treaty universalization; and international assistance.[3] This section summarizes the key aspects of discussions in these areas, while

---

[1] For a summary and other details of the Arms Trade Treaty see annex A, section I, in this volume. The 2001 UN Firearms Protocol is also legally binding but only covers controls on the trade in firearms. United Nations, General Assembly, Resolution 55/255, Protocol against the Illicit Manufacturing of and Trafficking in Firearms, their Parts and Components and Ammunition, supplementing the UN Convention against Transnational Organized Crime (UN Firearms Protocol), adopted 31 May 2001, entered into force 3 July 2005.

[2] Arms Trade Treaty, 3rd Conference of States Parties, 'Final report', ATT/CSP3/2017/SEC/184/Conf.FinRep.Rev1, 15 Sep. 2017.

[3] Arms Trade Treaty, 3rd Conference of States Parties, 'CSP3 provisional annotated programme of work', ATT/CSP3/2017/SEC/152/Conf.AnnPoW, 13 July 2017.

making broader points about the future prospects of the ATT. For treaty universalization and international assistance, this includes a more detailed focus on Asia, where ATT participation has been particularly low.

Treaty implementation

As was the case at CSP2, there was a clear division at CSP3 between the states parties and most of the NGOs present about which issues should be included in the discussion about the implementation of the ATT. In particular, many of the NGOs wished to engage in a debate about whether certain arms exports of states parties—and particularly arms transfers to Saudi Arabia for use in the conflict in Yemen—were in line with treaty requirements.[4] However, the majority of states present were keen to avoid what they saw as potentially sensitive and contentious discussions of particular cases and focus instead on how national legislative and regulatory instruments should be adjusted in order to allow for effective treaty implementation. States parties agreed to turn the existing ad hoc working group on effective treaty implementation into a standing working group and endorsed the group's draft list of priority areas of discussion in the run-up to CSP4.[5] The list includes national control systems, export assessment procedures, transit and trans-shipment controls, diversion, and record-keeping.[6] The list of topics appears to leave little room for discussions about particular arms exports and further underlines the limited interest in this topic among the majority of states parties.

Nonetheless, there were small indications that future CSPs might become forums where controversial arms transfers could be discussed and normative standards developed and applied. In particular, at CSP3 a group of states from the Americas called on all ATT states parties—in the light of their obligations under articles 6 and 7 of the treaty and the conduct of the Government of Venezuela during the ongoing crisis in the country—to abstain from all arms transfers to Venezuela.[7] Venezuela has not signed or acceded to the treaty. The European Union (EU) subsequently imposed an arms embargo on Venezuela (see section II), but it is unclear if this decision was influenced by events at CSP3. States have made similar calls for restraint

---

[4] Isbister, R., 'Much ado about nothing? Reflections on the third ATT conference of states parties', Saferworld, 20 Sep. 2017.

[5] Arms Trade Treaty, 3rd Conference of States Parties (note 2).

[6] Arms Trade Treaty, Ad Hoc Working Group on Effective Treaty Implementation, 'Co-chairs' draft report to CSP3', ATT/CSP3.WGETI/2017/CHAIR/158/Conf.Rep, 31 July 2017.

[7] These states were Argentina, Brazil, Canada, Chile, Colombia, Costa Rica, Guatemala, Honduras, Mexico, Panama, Paraguay and Peru. At the time statement was issued Brazil, Canada, Chile and Colombia had signed but not ratified the ATT. Arms Trade Treaty, 3rd Conference of States Parties, 'Intervención de los países que suscribieron la Declaración de Lima en ocasión de la Tercera Conferencia de los Estados Partes del Tratado sobre el Comercio de Armas [Statement of the countries that signed the Declaration of Lima at the Third Conference of States Parties to the Arms Trade Treaty]', 11 Sep. 2017.

in arms exports to particular destinations in meetings of the United Nations Security Council.[8] The declaration on Venezuela demonstrates that the ATT has created a new forum for states that are not members of the UN Security Council to make such calls, as well as a new set of normative standards to reference. However, it is unclear whether the ATT can continue to serve this function if the goal of universalization is achieved since it may be hard for states parties to 'name and shame' another state party to the ATT in an ATT forum.

The sessions dealing with treaty implementation also included a discussion of the relationship between the ATT and the Sustainable Development Goals (SDGs), in particularly Goal 16.4, which commits states to reducing illicit flows of arms. The inclusion of the SDGs on the agenda of CSP3 followed a pattern set by the 2016 biennial meeting of states on the UN Programme of Action (UNPOA) on small arms and light weapons. The outcome document of that meeting highlights that effective implementation of the UNPOA can help to achieve the SDGs and that measuring UNPOA implementation can act as a proxy for measuring the achievement of the SDGs.[9] The final report of CSP3 highlights the links between implementation of the ATT and achievement of the SDGs and commits the three intersessional working groups (on effective treaty implementation, on transparency and reporting, and on treaty universalization) to further explore synergies between the ATT and the SDGs.[10] One key implication of making this link—drawn by a number of states and NGOs—is that it can help to convince states to sign and ratify the ATT.[11] However, many of the states that are key targets of treaty universalization outreach efforts—particularly those in Asia—appear to be mainly concerned with the short-term national security implications of treaty accession and may not be swayed by arguments about the more long-term benefits for sustainable development.

Transparency and reporting, the ATT Secretariat and the fourth conference of states parties

One key hope for the ATT was that its requirements on reporting would increase the levels of transparency of both arms transfer controls and arms transfers. Each state party is obliged to provide the ATT Secretariat with an initial report detailing the 'measures undertaken in order to implement this

---

[8] E.g. in 2017 the USA called in the UN Security Council for states to halt arms exports to Myanmar. Haley, N., 'Remarks at a UN Security Council briefing on the situation in Burma', US Permanent Representative to the United Nations, New York, 28 Sep. 2017.

[9] See Davis, I. et al., 'Humanitarian arms control regimes: Key developments in 2016', *SIPRI Yearbook 2017*, pp. 566–69.

[10] Arms Trade Treaty, 3rd Conference of States Parties (note 2).

[11] See Spano, L. and Alpers, P., *Reinvigorating the Narrative: The Broader Benefits of the Arms Trade Treaty* (Centre for Armed Violence Reduction: Sydney, Sep. 2017).

Table 10.1. Arms Trade Treaty ratifications, accessions and signatories by region, as of 31 December 2017

Region	No. of states	No. of parties	No. of signatories	No. of non-signatories
Africa	53	22	17	14
Americas	35	23	6	6
Asia	29	3	7	19
Europe	48[a]	41	2	5
Middle East	16[b]	1	5	10
Oceania	14	4	4	6
Total	195	94	41	60

Note: The treaty was open for signature until it entered into force in Dec. 2014. A state may no longer sign it. An existing state signatory may accept, approve or ratify the treaty to become a state party. A non-signatory state must directly accede to the treaty in order to become a state party.

[a] This figure includes the Holy See.
[b] This figure includes Palestine.

Source: United Nations, Treaty Collection.

Treaty'.[12] States parties must also provide the Secretariat with an annual report 'for the preceding calendar year concerning authorized or actual exports and imports of conventional arms'.[13] However, although reporting levels have been high, they have been far from universal. As of 3 March 2018, 62 of the 91 state parties (68 per cent) that were due to submit an initial report on their implementation of the ATT had done so.[14] Moreover, as of the same date, only 49 of the 75 states parties (65 per cent) that were due to submit an annual report on their arms imports and exports during 2016 by May 2017 had done so.[15]

Another area in which states parties are failing to fully meet their obligations is that of financial contributions. All states parties to the ATT are required to make an annual assessed financial contribution to cover the costs of organizing the CSPs and the work of the ATT Secretariat. However, a significant number of states are failing to pay their bills. As of 5 February 2018, only 58 of the 86 assessed states parties (67 per cent) and 14 of the 30 assessed states signatories (47 per cent) had paid their contributions for 2017, totalling 86 per cent of the annual budget. Taken with the shortfall in contributions to the 2015–16 budget, the ATT had accumulated a deficit of

[12] Arms Trade Treaty (note 1), Article 13(1).

[13] Arms Trade Treaty (ATT), opened for signature 3 June 2013, entered into force 24 Dec. 2014, Article 13(3). The ATT does not explicitly state that either of these reports will be made public, noting only that they 'shall be made available, and distributed to States Parties by the Secretariat'.

[14] Arms Trade Treaty Secretariat, 'Reporting', 3 Mar. 2018.

[15] Arms Trade Treaty Secretariat (note 14). Greece also submitted a report despite not being required to do so. For a more detailed description of the content of states reports on arms imports and exports see chapter 5, section 2, in this volume.

$270 760.[16] The final report of CSP3 noted that states parties expressed 'deep concern' about the unpaid contributions as well as the possible impact 'of a potential shortage of funds for the organization of any future meetings'.[17]

Other key decisions were made at CSP3 regarding the format and functioning of CSP4 and the plan of work for the interim period. Ambassador Nobushige Takamizawa of Japan was appointed as president of CSP4, which is scheduled to take place in Tokyo on 20–24 August 2018.[18] Following decisions made at CSP3, the working groups on effective treaty implementation, on transparency and reporting, and on treaty universalization are now all standing bodies with ambitious programmes of work in the run-up to CSP4. However, discussions about the future activities of the working groups also generated one of the few areas of genuine disagreement among states parties at CSP3. In particular, states struggled to agree rules that would govern the circumstances in which working group meetings could be closed to observers—such as NGOs—or states signatories.[19] In the end, the final report of CSP3 notes that the rules for when meetings would be closed 'will be considered during the informal preparatory process for [CSP4] with a view to resolving this at [CSP4]'.[20]

Treaty universalization and international assistance: A focus on Asia

There is a geographic imbalance in states' levels of engagement with the ATT process and this seems likely to persist for the foreseeable future. In particular, rates of signature, accession and ratification remain far higher in Europe, Africa and the Americas than in Asia and the Middle East (see table 10.1). Universalization remains one of the key challenges for the ATT and was a key focus of discussions at CSP3. As well as agreeing to turn the existing ad hoc working group on treaty universalization into a standing working group, states parties explored a range of potential initiatives aimed at increasing the number of parties to the Treaty.[21]

Since the entry into force of the ATT, the low rate of participation among states in Asia has been a particular cause for concern. With the exception of the Middle East, Asia has the lowest level of both signatories and states parties. Of the 29 states in Asia, only three were party to the ATT as of 31 December 2017: Japan, Kazakhstan and South Korea.[22] A further seven

---

[16] Arms Trade Treaty Secretariat, 'Status of Contributions to ATT Budgets as at 05 February 2018'.

[17] Arms Trade Treaty, 3rd Conference of States Parties (note 2).

[18] Arms Trade Treaty, 3rd Conference of States Parties (note 2).

[19] Isbister (note 4).

[20] Arms Trade Treaty, 3rd Conference of States Parties (note 2).

[21] Arms Trade Treaty, 3rd Conference of States Parties (note 2).

[22] Kazakhstan acceded to the ATT in Dec. 2017 and the treaty will thus only enter into force for it in Mar. 2018.

Asian states—Bangladesh, Cambodia, Malaysia, Mongolia, the Philippines, Singapore and Thailand—signed the treaty but had yet to ratify it by the end of 2017. In their official statements at CSP3, Malaysia, the Philippines and Singapore all indicated that they are likely to ratify the treaty soon, but challenges in a variety of areas remain in all three states.[23]

The low level of acceptance of the ATT in Asia is widely recognized and has been a focus of diplomatic attention and effort in recent years. In March 2017, Ambassador Korhonen, president of CSP3, visited China, Indonesia and Thailand in order to promote the universalization of the ATT in Asia.[24] In the run-up to CSP4, increased attention is likely to be paid to Asia, especially with Japan assuming the presidency of this session.

In addition, a range of legal, technical and material assistance projects as well as capacity building and training efforts have been carried out in Asia. These include substantial outreach projects such as the EU Partner-to-Partner (EUP2P) outreach project, a new round of which was approved in 2017, and the regional and national workshops implemented by the UN Regional Centre for Peace and Disarmament in Asia and the Pacific (UNRCPD) and others.[25] However, of the 17 projects that the ATT Secretariat approved for funding by its voluntary trust fund (VTF) in 2017, only 1 is being implemented by an Asian state—the Philippines.[26] In contrast to Africa, Latin America and the Caribbean, significant work has also been carried out in Asia on dual-use export controls outreach and assistance, among others by the EU and the USA. Future capacity building work for the ATT could potentially build more on such existing capabilities in related areas and create synergies between the respective capacity-building projects.

Proponents of the ATT argue that Asia faces a range of significant security-related challenges of the type that the treaty is intended to alleviate. In particular, amid a range of continued and re-emerging tensions, many states in Asia—and particularly South East Asia—are increasing their arms imports and strengthening their national defence capabilities.[27] For example, Indonesia, the Philippines and Viet Nam have all significantly increased their arms imports in recent years, while Malaysia and Singapore are engaged in

[23] Arms Trade Treaty, 3rd Conference of States Parties, 'Statements'.

[24] Arms Trade Treaty Secretariat, 'Universalization trip China and ASEAN—March 2017'.

[25] For an overview of these activities see the activities database of the Mapping ATT-relevant Cooperation and Assistance Activities Project.

[26] Arms Trade Treaty Secretariat, '1st Voluntary Trust Fund cycle (2017): Overview of projects approved for ATT VTF funding', 8 Nov. 2017. The VTF was established in 2016 to support projects carried out to assist ATT states parties and states signatories as well as 'other States having shown clear and unambiguous political commitment to accede to the ATT'. It is funded by donations from states parties and other entities and is administered by the ATT Secretariat. Arms Trade Treaty, 2nd Conference of States Parties, 'Terms of reference for the ATT Voluntary Trust Fund', ATT/CSP2/2016/WP.3/Rev.1, 24 Aug. 2016.

[27] Stohl, R. and Holtom, P., 'Assessing ATT implementation in the Asia-Pacific Region', Arms Trade Treaty Baseline Assessment Project, 2017, p. 1.

wide-ranging expansions of their military forces.[28] In such a context, robust and systematic reporting on arms imports, as is required under the ATT, could act as a means of reducing regional tensions. In addition, improved controls on arms transfers and better mechanisms for sharing information on routes of diversion, both of which are mandated under the ATT, could be of significant benefit for the many parts of Asia where arms trafficking is a major concern.

A number of states in Asia have stated that they are wary of the legally binding nature of the ATT and are unwilling to ratify it until they have ensured that their national legislation meets all treaty requirements.[29] However, in many cases, the impediments to ATT accession appear to have less to do with the technical challenges of implementation and more to do with broader political concerns. In particular, many states in the region already have the necessary legal and regulatory instruments in place that meet the standards laid down in the ATT.[30] For some of these states, the level of interest in ratifying the ATT may be diminished by a fear that it would reduce their trade with key arms suppliers to the region—particularly China, Russia and the USA, which are unlikely to become parties to the ATT in the near future. In addition, concerns that increased transparency will reveal national capabilities and weaknesses further adds to states' reluctance to join the ATT. Questions of domestic politics and regional security will continue to affect the political will of Asian states to sign and ratify the ATT.[31]

The limited penetration of the ATT in Asia is also both a reflection and a consequence of the region's low prior engagement with security cooperation, arms control and confidence-building measures. In other parts of the world, regional organizations such as the Economic Community of West African States (ECOWAS), the EU, the Organization of American States (OAS), and the Organization for Security and Co-operation in Europe (OSCE) have established common standards on arms export controls and mechanisms for sharing information on arms exports or imports.[32] These mechanisms represent a willingness to engage in multilateral discussions about sensitive security issues and have also created a familiarity with and mutual confidence in such measures. This is reflected in the correlation between mem-

---

[28] Wezeman P. D. et al., 'Trends in international arms transfers, 2017', SIPRI Fact Sheet, Mar. 2017; and Heiduk, F., *An Arms Race in Southeast Asia? Changing Arms Dynamics, Regional Security and the Role of European Arms Exports*, SWP Research Paper RP10 (Stiftung Wissenschaft und Politik: Berlin, Aug. 2017), pp. 9–20.

[29] Persi Paoli, G. and Kytomaki, E., *Towards a Universal Arms Trade Treaty: Understanding Barriers and Challenges in South-East Asia* (RAND Corporation: Santa Monica, CA, 2016), pp. 29–31.

[30] Stohl and Holtom (note 27), p. 1.

[31] Weiss, M., 'The Arms Trade Treaty in the Asia-Pacific: Small steps toward improving a difficult relationship', *The Diplomat*, 22 Dec. 2017.

[32] See Holtom, P. and Bromley, M., *Implementing an Arms Trade Treaty: Lessons on Reporting and Monitoring from Existing Mechanisms*, SIPRI Policy Paper no. 28 (SIPRI: Stockholm, July 2011).

bership of these organizations on the one hand and strong support for and high levels of signatures and ratifications of the ATT on the other.[33] Nothing of equivalent ambition has been established by the Association of Southeast Asian Nations (ASEAN) or the other regional and subregional groupings in Asia.[34] This absence likewise reflects a more limited interest among Asian states in the creation of such mechanisms and feeds a general wariness about the implications of new instruments, such as the ATT.[35]

[33] Control Arms, *ATT Monitor Report 2017* (Control Arms Secretariat: New York, 11 Sep. 2017), pp. 9–11.

[34] Some limited mechanisms related to controls on small arms and light weapons have been established by e.g. the Asia-Pacific Economic Cooperation (APEC), the Conference on Interaction and Confidence-building Measures in Asia (CICA) and the Shanghai Cooperation Organisation (SCO). However, the extent to which they are being applied is unclear. See Heiduk (note 28), p. 28.

[35] Weiss (note 31).

II. Multilateral embargoes on arms and dual-use items

MARK BROMLEY AND PIETER D. WEZEMAN

Thirty-five multilateral arms embargoes were in force in 2017: 13 imposed by the United Nations (UN), 21 by the European Union (EU) and 1 by the League of Arab States (see table 10.2).[1] Nine of the EU embargoes implemented UN arms embargoes directly, three were similar to UN embargoes but differed in geographical scope or the types of weapon covered, and nine had no UN counterpart.[2] The single Arab League arms embargo, on Syria, had no UN counterpart. One new multilateral arms embargo was imposed in 2017, by the EU on Venezuela.

Most of these embargoes only covered conventional arms and military goods and services. However, three embargoes also covered certain exports of dual-use items: goods, software and technologies that can be used for both civilian purposes and in connection with conventional, biological, chemical or nuclear weapons or their delivery systems. These were the UN and EU embargoes on Iran and on the Democratic People's Republic of Korea (DPRK, or North Korea) and the EU embargo on Russia.[3]

During 2017 the various UN investigations on the implementation of UN arms embargoes highlighted violations of varying scope and significance. Unlike UN arms embargoes, there are no systematic mechanisms in place for monitoring compliance with EU and Arab League arms embargoes.

This section reviews in turn proposals to impose new UN arms embargoes on South Sudan and Syria, the implementation of certain existing UN embargoes, and developments in EU embargoes.

Threats to impose new United Nations arms embargoes

During 2017 only one draft resolution proposing a UN arms embargo, on Syria, was tabled in the UN Security Council. Calls for an arms embargo on

---

[1] In addition, 1 voluntary multilateral embargo was in force in which the Conference on Security and Co-operation in Europe (CSCE, now renamed the Organization for Security and Co-operation in Europe) requests that all participating states impose an embargo on arms deliveries to Armenian and Azerbaijani forces engaged in combat in the Nagorno-Karabakh area. Conference on Security and Co-operation in Europe, Committee of Senior Officials, Statement, annex 1 to Journal no. 2 of the Seventh Meeting of the Committee, Prague, 27–28 Feb. 1992.

[2] The 3 that differed from equivalent UN embargoes were those on Iran and North Korea, which covered more weapon types than the UN embargo, and on Sudan, which covered the whole country, whereas the UN embargo applied only to the Darfur region. The 9 with no UN counterpart were those on Belarus, China, Egypt, Myanmar, Russia, South Sudan, Syria, Venezuela and Zimbabwe. The 9 that implement UN embargoes are indicated in table 10.2.

[3] The UN and EU embargoes on Iran and North Korea apply to dual-use items on the control lists of the Nuclear Suppliers Group and the Missile Technology Control Regime. The EU embargo on Russia applies to transfers to military end-users of all items on the EU's dual-use list.

the belligerents in South Sudan had been repeated regularly since the war in the country started in 2013.[4] In March 2017 France, the United Kingdom and the United States once again stated their support in the UN Security Council for the imposition of an arms embargo, but no resolution calling for this measure was formally submitted.[5]

Syria

In February 2017 France and the UK proposed a draft resolution at the UN Security Council that included a ban on the transfer to Syria of: (*a*) chlorine; (*b*) the chemicals listed in schedules to the 1993 Chemical Weapons Convention (CWC) and a supplementary list; and (*c*) arms and related materiel used to deliver chemicals as weapons, mentioning in particular helicopters.[6] This was the first time since 2011 that a resolution calling for an arms embargo on Syria had been tabled at the UN Security Council.

The resolution was a response to an October 2016 report by the Organization for the Prohibition of Chemical Weapons–United Nations Joint Investigative Mechanism (JIM), which concluded that Syrian Government forces had used helicopters to drop bombs containing chlorine gas.[7] The resolution was drafted in December 2016, but its formal submission was reportedly delayed while states determined the policy of the incoming US administration.[8]

Nine of the 15 members of the Security Council voted in favour of the resolution, but it was vetoed by China and Russia. China argued that investigations into the use of chemical weapons in Syria were not yet complete and that the resolution was not helpful in sustaining peace talks.[9] Russia's main argument in support of its veto was that it considered the conclusions of the JIM unconvincing. It argued that they were based on questionable information and that the JIM report was biased since the JIM was staffed largely by representatives of states that pursue regime change in Syria. It also argued

---

[4] For a full analysis of developments prior to 2017 see Bromley, M., Kelly, N. and Wezeman, P. D., 'Multilateral embargoes on arms and dual-use goods', *SIPRI Yearbook 2017*, pp. 589–90.

[5] United Nations, 'No military solution in South Sudan, Security Council presidential statement stresses, urging immediate end to violence against aid workers', UN Meeting Coverage SC/12761, 23 Mar. 2017.

[6] United Nations, Security Council, Draft resolution, S/2017/172, 28 Feb. 2017. For a summary and other details of the Convention on the Prohibition of the Development, Production, Stockpiling and Use of Chemical Weapons and on their Destruction (Chemical Weapons Convention, CWC) see annex A, section I, in this volume.

[7] United Nations, Security Council, 'Fourth report of the Organization for the Prohibition of Chemical Weapons–United Nations Joint Investigative Mechanism', S/2016/888, 21 Oct. 2016. On the JIM investigation in Syria see also chapter 8, section I, in this volume; on the conflict in Syria see also chapter 2, section V, in this volume.

[8] What's in Blue, 'Syria: Draft resolution imposing sanctions regarding the use and production of chemical weapons', Security Council Report, 25 Feb. 2017.

[9] United Nations, Security Council, 7893rd meeting, S/PV.7893, 28 Feb. 2017, pp. 6–8, 9–10.

that the real purpose of the proposed sanctions was not to control chemical weapons, but to undermine the Syrian Government.

Implementation of United Nations arms embargoes

As in previous years, there were numerous reported cases of alleged violations of UN arms embargoes in 2017. The scope and significance of these violations varied considerably, with some involving large shipments of arms in contravention of the embargo and others involving a failure by a supplier or recipient state to notify a sanctions committee about a transfer. This section illustrates this variety along with other problems related to the implementation of UN arms embargoes by looking in more detail at the cases of Iran, Yemen, North Korea, Libya and Somalia.

Iran and Yemen

The UN arms embargo on Iran was substantially modified in January 2016, following the adoption of the Joint Comprehensive Plan of Action (JCPOA) and UN Security Council 2231 in July 2015.[10] The modification permitted transfers of arms and dual-use items to and from Iran, provided that they have been approved in advance by the UN Security Council.[11] Only one request to export arms to Iran was submitted between January 2016 and December 2017, by an unnamed state. However, the UN Security Council failed to reach the consensus necessary to approve the request.[12] Between January 2016 and December 2017 four states submitted 24 requests to approve transfers to Iran of items on the Nuclear Suppliers Group (NSG) control list.[13]

Between January 2016 and December 2017 no request was submitted to the UN Security Council to approve an arms export from Iran.[14] Nonetheless, there have been numerous allegations that Iran has exported arms to Syria, Iraq and Yemen (see below).[15] Iran's compliance with the mechanism for approving exports of arms and dual-use items to and from Iran is not

---

[10] Joint Comprehensive Plan of Action (JCPOA), Vienna, 14 July 2015, reproduced as Annex A of UN Security Council Resolution 2231, 20 July 2015. For a full analysis of the JCPOA and the schedule for lifting the UN arms embargo on Iran see Anthony, I., Bromley, M. and Wezeman P. D., 'The role and impact of international sanctions on Iran', *SIPRI Yearbook 2016*, pp. 87–114; and Rauf, T., 'Resolving concerns about Iran's nuclear programme', *SIPRI Yearbook 2016*, pp. 673–88. On the implementation of the JCPOA in 2017 see chapter 7, section V, in this volume.

[11] UN Security Council Resolution 2231 (note 10).

[12] United Nations, Security Council, 'Third six-month report of the facilitator on the implementation of Security Council Resolution 2231 (2015)', S/2017/537, 27 June 2017, para. 32.

[13] United Nations, Security Council, 'Fourth six-month report of the facilitator on the implementation of Security Council Resolution 2231 (2015)', S/2017/1058, 15 Dec. 2017, para. 31.

[14] United Nations, S/2017/1058 (note 13), para. 38.

[15] Qaidaari, A., 'Is Iran becoming a major regional arms producer?', Iran Business News, 24 Mar. 2016; and Schmitt, E., 'Iran is smuggling increasingly potent weapons into Yemen, US admiral says', *New York Times*, 18 Sep. 2017.

listed among its commitments under the JCPOA. However, the alleged Iranian arms transfers would be a violation of UN Security Council Resolution 2231 and, in the case of the transfers to Yemen, Resolution 2216.[16]

The UN arms embargo on Yemen prohibits arms transfers to non-state actors in Yemen. Allegations and investigations regarding the violation of the embargo have focused on reports about arms supplies from Iran to the Houthi forces, which controlled large parts of the north of Yemen. In 2017 the UN panel of experts on Yemen and the UN Secretariat continued investigations into small arms and light weapons produced in Iran that were seized in international waters in 2015 and 2016 and were assumed to be destined for end-users in Yemen.[17] In addition, the UN Secretariat investigated claims by Saudi Arabia that Iran had supplied unmanned aerial vehicles (UAVs, drones) and components for explosive boats to the Houthi forces and examined items that Saudi Arabia said it had recovered in Yemen.[18]

In 2017 the Houthi forces continued the use of ballistic missiles against Saudi Arabia, including against Riyadh, which is 800 kilometres from Yemen.[19] In January 2018 the UN panel of experts on Yemen concluded that it had identified missile remnants, related military equipment and military UAVs of Iranian origin that arrived in Yemen after the imposition of the arms embargo on Yemen. The panel concluded that Iran had breached the arms embargo as it had failed to take the necessary measures to prevent the direct or indirect supply, sale, or transfer of ballistic missiles, storage tanks for propellants for missiles and UAVs to the Houthi–Saleh alliance.[20]

North Korea

The UN arms embargo on North Korea prohibits the transfer of arms and certain dual-use items to and from the country. The embargo forms part of a wide array of sanctions that the UN Security Council has imposed in response to North Korea's nuclear weapon and ballistic missile programmes.[21] In recent years, the mechanisms for monitoring compliance with the sanctions regime have been significantly expanded.

In August and September 2017 the UN sanctions were further expanded in response to North Korea's ballistic missile tests in July 2017 and its sixth

---

[16] UN Security Council Resolution 2216, 14 Apr. 2015.

[17] United Nations, Security Council, 'Fourth report of the Secretary-General on the implementation of Security Council Resolution 2231 (2015)', S/2017/1030, 8 Dec. 2017, para. 33. On the conflict in Yemen see chapter 2, section V, in this volume.

[18] United Nations, S/2017/1030 (note 17), paras 34–35.

[19] United Nations, Security Council, 'Final report of the panel of experts on Yemen', S/2018/68, 26 Jan. 2018, p. 25.

[20] United Nations, S/2018/68 (note 19), p. 2.

[21] On North Korea's nuclear weapon and ballistic missile programmes see chapter 6, section IX, in this volume; on the sanctions regime against these programmes see chapter 7, section IV, in this volume.

nuclear test, on 3 September 2017.[22] The second of these expansions also included a widening of the sanction's associated monitoring mechanisms. In particular, the Security Council called on states to inspect a vessel on the high seas, with the consent of the flag state, 'if they have information that provides reasonable grounds to believe' that it contains cargo prohibited by Council resolutions.[23] The resolution also directs the associated sanctions committee to consider adding any vessel that refuses a request for inspection to the list of sanctioned entities.[24]

Despite being subject to one of the most wide-ranging and intrusive UN sanctions regimes, North Korea continued to make rapid advances in both its nuclear weapon and missile programmes during 2017.[25] The UN panel of experts on North Korea also documented wide-ranging and extensive violations of UN sanctions by the country. As the panel's August 2017 report notes, 'as the sanctions regime expands, so does the scope of evasion'.[26] However, events in 2017 demonstrated the difficulty of determining exactly where North Korea is acquiring the technology needed to advance its weapons programmes and—in particular—the extent to which it is dependent on acquisitions from abroad or is able to rely on indigenous technological developments.

In August 2017 the International Institute for Strategic Studies (IISS), a London-based think tank, claimed that North Korea's rapid progress in developing ballistic missiles had been made possible by the recent acquisition of R-250 engines.[27] The precise source for the engines was a matter of dispute. The report indicated that they may have been obtained from Yuzhnoye State Design Office in Ukraine, although other possible sources in Ukraine and Russia were also indicated. Yuzhnoye denied that it was the source of the engines and highlighted the conviction of two North Koreans who had been caught trying to steal information from it in 2011 as evidence of the controls it has in place.[28]

Other reports emphasized that, while North Korea is reliant on acquisitions from abroad for key aspects of its nuclear weapon and ballistic missile programmes, it is also showing an increasing ability to master certain com-

---

[22] UN Security Council Resolution 2371, 5 Aug. 2017; and UN Security Council Resolution 2375, 11 Sep. 2017.
[23] UN Security Council Resolution 2375 (note 22), para. 7.
[24] UN Security Council Resolution 2375 (note 22), para. 8.
[25] For more information see chapter 6, section IX and XI, in this volume.
[26] United Nations, Security Council, 'Midterm report of the panel of experts established pursuant to Resolution 1874 (2009)', S/2017/742, 5 Sep. 2017, p. 4.
[27] Elleman, M., 'The secret to North Korea's ICBM success', International Institute for Strategic Studies (IISS), IISS Voices, 14 Aug. 2017; and Broad, W. J. and Sanger, D. E., 'North Korea's missile success is linked to Ukrainian plant, investigators say', New York Times, 14 Aug. 2017.
[28] Broad and Sanger (note 27).

plex production techniques domestically.[29] These findings would suggest that, while the UN-imposed controls on transfers of arms and dual-use items—even if it were rigidly enforced—might slow the advance of North Korea's nuclear weapon and ballistic missile programmes, they are unlikely to completely halt progress.

The UN panel of experts also continued its investigations into past cases where North Korea violated UN restrictions on its arms exports by supplying arms, military technology and military services to six countries, all in Africa; Angola, the Democratic Republic of the Congo, Eritrea, Mozambique, Namibia and Uganda. In all cases, the panel reported that the recipient country had not fully responded to its inquiries about the alleged violations.[30] The panel also investigated reports from 2017 that North Korean companies were involved in ballistic missile activities in Syria and maintenance of air defence systems in Syria and Tanzania.[31] The panel reported that two states had intercepted shipments from North Korea to Syria and that it was investigating reports from another state that the intended recipient of these transfers was connected to Syria's chemical weapon programme.[32]

During 2017 new information was reported about the intended destination of 30 000 rocket-propelled grenades found on a North Korean vessel that was intercepted near the coast of Egypt in August 2016. The UN panel of experts described this as the 'largest seizure of ammunition in the history of sanctions against [North Korea]'.[33] Although the Egyptian authorities played a key role in seizing the weapons and subsequently destroyed them, several sources indicated that their intended recipient was the Egyptian military.[34] The case highlights the extent to which North Korea remains integrated into global arms supply networks.

Libya

The UN arms embargo on Libya permits transfers of arms to the internationally recognized Government of National Accord (GNA), provided that they have been approved in advance by the relevant UN sanctions committee.[35] During 2017 the UN panel of experts on Libya highlighted numerous cases in which the various armed groups in Libya received supplies of

[29] Salisbury, D., 'Why didn't sanctions stop North Korea's missile program?', *Defense News*, 15 Aug. 2017.

[30] United Nations, S/2017/742 (note 26), paras 22–27, 29.

[31] United Nations, S/2017/742 (note 26), paras 28, 30.

[32] United Nations, S/2017/742 (note 26), para. 28.

[33] United Nations, Security Council, 'Report of the panel of experts established pursuant to Resolution 1874 (2009)', 30 Jan. 2017, S/2017/150, 27 Feb. 2017, p. 4.

[34] Warrick, J., 'A North Korean ship was seized off Egypt with a huge cache of weapons destined for a surprising buyer', *Washington Post*, 1 Oct. 2017.

[35] United Nations, Security Council, 'Final report of the panel of experts established pursuant to Resolution 1973 (2011)', S/2015/128, 23 Feb. 2015. On the conflict in Libya see chapter 2, section V, in this volume.

military equipment and other related items from foreign governments that had not been given prior approval. Among the more significant transfers in 2017 were additional suppliers by the UAE of pick-up trucks and armoured vehicles to the Libyan National Army, which is under the control of General Khalifa Haftar.[36]

Determining what constitutes a transfer of arms to the GNA remains difficult given the range of forces that are nominally under its control. In May 2016 the Prime Minister of the GNA, Fayez Sarraj, established the Libyan Presidential Guard. The Libyan National Army views this new force as a rival.[37] In June 2017 General Najmi al-Naqou, commander of the Libyan Presidential Guard, stated that the UN Security Council had been formally requested to exclude his forces from all restrictions on arms imports.[38] However, no modification to the coverage of the arms embargo was made in 2017. As the UN panel of experts on Libya noted in 2017, 'The political process that the exceptions to the arms embargo were designed to support has not developed in the manner anticipated, as the relationship between armed groups and political entities remains transactional and transitional'.[39]

Somalia

In 2017 the UN monitoring group on Somalia concluded that weapons continued to reach armed groups in the country. In particular they highlighted evidence suggesting that the rate of arrival of weapons in Puntland alone was approximately one shipment a month, predominantly from Yemen.[40]

The UN arms embargo on Somalia requires the Government of Somalia to report to the relevant Security Council sanctions committee in advance on all of its arms acquisitions from abroad, to provide information on the structure of its armed forces and to take steps to secure its arms stockpiles. During 2017 the Government of Somalia repeated its past calls for the restrictions on its arms acquisitions to be fully lifted. However, the monitoring group argued against this, noting that over the past two years a number of weapon supplies to government bodies had been only partially notified or not notified at all.[41]

---

[36] United Nations, Security Council, 'Final report of the panel of experts on Libya established pursuant to Resolution 1973 (2011)', S/2017/466, 1 June 2017, para. 166.

[37] El Amrani, I., 'New risks in Libya as Khalifa Haftar dismisses UN-backed accord', 21 Dec. 2017.

[38] Xinhua, 'Interview: Libyan general requests UNSC to exclude Libyan Presidential Guard from arms embargo', 19 June 2017.

[39] United Nations, S/2017/466 (note 36), para. 107.

[40] United Nations, Security Council, Report on Somalia of the monitoring group on Somalia and Eritrea, S/2017/924, 2 Nov. 2017, p. 6. On the conflict in Somalia see chapter 2, section VI, in this volume.

[41] United Nations, S/2017/924 (note 40), pp. 6–7.

Despite modest improvements, there remain flaws in the weapon and ammunition management by the Government of Somalia, particularly with respect to distribution and tracking.[42]

European Union arms embargoes

Venezuela

On 13 November 2017 the Council of the EU imposed sanctions on Venezuela, including an embargo on the supply of arms and on material that might be used for internal repression.[43] The immediate reason for the sanctions was the Council's assessment that there had been numerous irregularities in the Venezuelan gubernatorial elections of October 2017 and that a large part of the opposition did not recognize the results. In addition the Council argued that the setting-up of an 'all-powerful' Constituent Assembly had further eroded the democratic and independent institutions in Venezuela and that 'Reports . . . of violations of human rights and fundamental freedoms are an additional reason for alarm'.[44]

The arms embargo covers all transfers of goods and technology listed in the EU Common List of Military Equipment, unless the contracts for such transfers were signed before 13 November 2017. In addition the embargo bans transfers of 'equipment which might be used for internal repression', such as riot control vehicles, certain types of explosive and body armour.[45] As is the case with EU sanctions on Iran and Syria, the sanctions on Venezuela also place restrictions on the transfer of a range of equipment, technology or software that can be used for monitoring internet or telephone communications. However, the restrictions on Venezuela are more narrowly defined than those on Iran and Syria. Exports to Iran and Syria must be blocked if the items will be used 'for monitoring or interception . . . of internet or telephone communications'.[46] In contrast, exports to Venezuela must be blocked if they will be used 'for internal repression'.[47] The sanctions do not provide a definition of what is meant by 'internal repression' in this context.

[42] Gaffey, C., 'Why Somalia wants a 25-year arms embargo lifted', *Newsweek*, 12 May 2017.

[43] Council Decision (CFSP) 2017/2074 of 13 November 2017 concerning restrictive measures in view of the situation in Venezuela, *Official Journal of the European Union*, L 295, 14 Nov. 2017.

[44] Council of the European Union, 'Venezuela: EU adopts conclusions and targeted sanctions', Press Release 643/17, 13 Nov. 2017.

[45] Council Regulation (EU) 2017/2063 of 13 November 2017 concerning restrictive measures in view of the situation in Venezuela, *Official Journal of the European Union*, L 295, 14 Nov. 2017.

[46] Council Regulation (EU) 359/2011 of 12 April 2011 concerning restrictive measures directed against certain persons, entities and bodies in view of the situation in Iran, *Official Journal of the European Union*, L 100, 14 Apr. 2011, Article 1b; and Council Regulation (EU) 36/2012 of 18 January 2012 concerning restrictive measures in view of the situation in Syria and repealing Regulation (EU) 442/2011, *Official Journal of the European Union*, L 16, 19 Jan. 2012, Article 4.

[47] Council Regulation (EU) 2017/2063 (note 45), Article 6.

Egypt

In 2013 the EU member states reached a political agreement that they would suspend exports to Egypt of equipment that might be used for internal repression, re-evaluate export licences for military equipment and review their security assistance to Egypt. These measures remained in place in 2017.[48]

The measures seem to have had little impact on the overall flow of weapons to Egypt or the military or security aspects of EU–Egyptian relations. Since 2013 several EU member states have exported significant quantities of arms to Egypt.[49] Neither the measures nor the arms exports to Egypt were mentioned in a European Commission report on EU–Egypt relations or in a joint EU–Egypt statement of July 2017.[50] However, both documents mentioned the possibility for security- and counterterrorism-related cooperation between the EU and Egypt.

Myanmar

The EU has maintained an arms embargo on Myanmar since 1991. It was part of a broader set of sanctions intended to exert pressure for democratization and in response to human rights abuses. In 2013 political reforms in Myanmar led to the EU lifting all sanctions other than the arms embargo.

In response to the violence by the Myanmar military against Rohingya people, in October 2017 the Council of the EU called on all sides to bring an immediate end to the violence and called on the Myanmar military to end its operations.[51] In this context the EU confirmed the relevance of the current EU embargo on supplies to Myanmar of arms and on equipment that can be used for internal repression.[52]

Saudi Arabia

In February 2016 the European Parliament concluded that there was strong evidence that Saudi military operations in Yemen that began in 2015 involved violations of international humanitarian law. It therefore adopted a non-binding resolution that asked the High Representative of the EU for

---

[48] European External Action Service, Communication with authors, 3 Oct. 2017. On the conflict in Egypt see chapter 2, section V, in this volume.

[49] See e.g. SIPRI Arms Transfers Database.

[50] European Commission, High Representative of the Union for Foreign Affairs and Security Policy, 'Report on EU–Egypt relations in the framework of the revised ENP', Joint staff working paper, SWD(2017) 271 final, 13 July 2017; and Council of the EU, 'Joint statement by Federica Mogherini, High Representative of the Union for Foreign Affairs and Security Policy and Sameh Shoukry, Minister of Foreign Affairs of Egypt following the 7th session of the EU–Egypt Association Council', Statements and Remarks 496/17, 25 July 2017.

[51] On the conflict in Myanmar see chapter 2, section III, in this volume.

[52] Council of the European Union, 'Council conclusions on Myanmar/Burma', 13099/17, 16 Oct. 2016.

Table 10.2. Multilateral arms embargoes in force during 2017

Target[a]	Date embargo first imposed	Key developments during 2017
United Nations arms embargoes		
Central African Republic (NGF)	5 Dec. 2013	Extended until 31 Jan. 2018
Democratic Republic of the Congo (NGF)	28 July 2003	Extended until 1 July 2018
Eritrea	23 Dec. 2009	
Iran	23 Dec. 2006	
Iraq (NGF)	6 Aug. 1990	
ISIL (Da'esh), al-Qaeda and associated individuals and entities	16 Jan. 2002	
Korea, North	15 July 2006	
Lebanon (NGF)	11 Aug. 2006	
Libya (NGF)	26 Feb. 2011	
Somalia (NGF)	23 Jan. 1992	Extended until 15 Nov. 2018
Sudan (Darfur)	30 July 2004	
Yemen (NGF)	14 Apr. 2015	Extended until 26 Mar. 2018
Taliban	16 Jan. 2002	
European Union arms embargoes		
Al-Qaeda, the Taliban and associated individuals and entities*	17 Dec. 1996	
Belarus	20 June 2011	Extended until 28 Feb. 2018
China[b]	27 June 1989	
Central African Republic (NGF)*	23 Dec. 2013	
Democratic Republic of the Congo (NGF)*	7 Apr. 1993	
Egypt[b]	21 Aug. 2013	
Eritrea*	1 Mar. 2010	
Iran	27 Feb. 2007	
Iraq (NGF)*	4 Aug. 1990	
Korea, North	20 Nov. 2006	
Lebanon (NGF)*	15 Sep. 2006	
Libya (NGF)*	28 Feb. 2011	
Myanmar	29 July 1991[c]	Extended until 30 Apr. 2018
Russia	31 July 2014	Extended until 31 Jan. 2018
Somalia (NGF)*	10 Dec. 2002	
South Sudan	18 July 2011	
Sudan	15 Mar. 1994	
Syria	9 May 2011	
Venezuela	13 Nov. 2017	
Yemen (NGF)*	8 June 2015	
Zimbabwe	18 Feb. 2002	Extended until 20 Feb. 2018
League of Arab States arms embargoes		
Syria	3 Dec. 2011	

* = European Union embargo directly implementing a UN embargo; ISIL = Islamic State in Iraq and the Levant; NGF = Embargo applies to non-governmental forces (and may allow transfers of arms to the target state provided that certain conditions have been met).

[a] The target may have changed since the first imposition of the embargo. The target stated here is as of the end of 2017.

[b] The EU embargoes on China and Egypt are political commitments whereas the rest are legally binding.

[c] The EU and its member states first imposed an arms embargo on Myanmar in 1990.

Sources: United Nations, Security Council, 'Sanctions'; and European Commission, 'Restrictive measures (sanctions) in force', 4 Aug. 2017. The SIPRI Arms Embargo Archive, provides a detailed overview of most multilateral arms embargoes that have been in force since 1950 along with the principle instruments establishing or amending the embargoes.

Foreign Affairs and Security Policy to 'launch an initiative aimed at imposing an EU arms embargo against Saudi Arabia'.[53] In September and November 2017 the parliament adopted resolutions that reiterated the call for an EU arms embargo on Saudi Arabia.[54]

No ensuing action had been taken by the Council of the EU by the end of 2017, and Saudi Arabia continued to be an important arms export market for several EU member states.[55]

[53] European Parliament, Resolution of 25 Feb. 2016 on the humanitarian situation in Yemen, 2016/2515(RSP). On the conflict in Yemen see chapter 2, section V, in this chapter; on Saudi Arabia's role in the region see chapter 1, section II, in this volume.

[54] European Parliament, Resolution of 13 Sep. 2017 on arms export: Implementation of Common Position 2008/944/CFSP, 2017/2029(INI); and European Parliament, Resolution of 30 Nov. 2017 on the situation in Yemen, 2017/2849(RSP).

[55] See chapter 5, section I, in this volume.

III. The export control regimes

SIBYLLE BAUER, KOLJA BROCKMANN, MARK BROMLEY AND
GIOVANNA MALETTA

There are four multilateral export control regimes—the Australia Group
(AG), the Missile Technology Control Regime (MTCR), the Nuclear Suppliers Group (NSG) and the Wassenaar Arrangement on Export Controls
for Conventional Arms and Dual-use Goods and Technologies (Wassenaar
Arrangement, WA)—that coordinate trade controls on goods and technologies that have uses in connection with chemical, biological, nuclear and
conventional weapons (see table 10.3).[1] These politically binding agreements
operate by consensus and are implemented and enforced through national
and regional laws.[2] The regimes also have an important norm-setting function as an ever-increasing number of non-members apply the regimes' control lists and standards.

Government representatives from policy, licensing, enforcement, technical and intelligence backgrounds meet annually in different groupings
within the regimes and report to the respective plenary meeting, which
decides on changes to control lists and issues guidance and good practice
documents. The regime chair rotates among participating states on an
annual basis, except for the AG, which has been chaired by Australia since
its establishment. The chairs of the various sub-bodies usually serve for a
number of years and are agreed by consensus. The WA is the only regime
with a standing permanent secretariat with a head and support staff.

Although export control remains the regimes' focus, brokering, transit
and trans-shipment are also increasingly being brought within the scope of
controls and made the subject of expert group and plenary discussions. Given
that many exports are now transmitted rather than transported, this is also
true of intangible transfers of technology and emerging technologies such
as additive manufacturing (AM, or so-called 3D printing; see section IV).
The dominant cross-regime theme in 2017 was adjusting to technological
developments, including the potential exploitation of cyberspace. Engagement with non-participating states and membership expansion remains an
ongoing topic for all regimes. However, the difficulty of reaching political
consensus on admitting new applicants, combined with concerns about the
viability of a large membership and about sharing potentially sensitive infor-

---

[1] For brief descriptions and lists of the participating states in each of these regimes see annex B,
section III, in this volume.
[2] Although not all member states of the European Union (EU) participate in all the regimes,
they are legally bound by them through the EU Dual-use Regulation. Council Regulation (EC)
no. 428/2009 of 5 May 2009 setting up a Community regime for the control of exports, transfer,
brokering and transit of dual-use items, *Official Journal of the European Union*, L 134, 29 May 2009.

Table 10.3. The four multilateral export control regimes

Regime (Year established)	Scope	No. of participants (as of 31 Dec. 2017)	2017 plenary chair	2017 plenary
Australia Group (1985)	Equipment, materials, technology and software that could contribute to chemical and biological weapons activities	42[a]	Australia	26–30 June, Paris
Missile Technology Control Regime (1987)	Unmanned aerial vehicles capable of delivering weapons of mass destruction	35	Iceland and Ireland	16–20 Oct., Dublin
Nuclear Suppliers Group (1974)	Nuclear and nuclear-related materials, software and technology	48[b]	Switzerland	22–23 June, Bern
Wassenaar Arrangement (1995)	Conventional arms and dual-use items and technologies	42	France	6–7 Dec., Vienna

[a] In addition, India became the 43rd participant in the Australia Group in Jan. 2018.

[b] In addition, the European Commission and the Chair of the Zangger Committee are permanent observers of the Nuclear Suppliers Group.

Sources: Australia Group; Missile Technology Control Regime; Nuclear Supplier Group; and Wassenaar Arrangement on Export Controls for Conventional Arms and Dual-use Goods and Technologies.

mation, has limited membership to a group of 35–48 countries, depending on the regime.

Nevertheless, there were major developments in regime membership in 2017, particularly concerning India. After agreeing a civil nuclear deal with the United States in 2005, India had sought to join the NSG. This later developed into a more ambitious plan to join all four regimes. After joining the MTCR in 2016, India's efforts to join the WA and the AG succeeded in December 2017 and January 2018, respectively. However, its attempt to join the NSG remained unsuccessful. India's admission to the WA and the AG was welcomed domestically as a major diplomatic success that could support its efforts to join the NSG.[3] Admission to these regimes might have been

[3] 'Boost for NSG membership, India joins Australia Group', *Economic Times*, 19 Jan. 2018; and Kumar, A., 'Big diplomatic win as India joins Australia Group for controlling chemical & biological weapons', News18.com, 19 Jan. 2018.

facilitated both by the fact that China is not a member of these groups and by the resolution of a long-standing diplomatic dispute with Italy.[4]

In addition to the above four regimes, the European Union (EU) has established a common legal basis for controls on the export, brokering, transit and trans-shipment of dual-use items, software and technology and, to a certain degree, also military items. It is the only regional organization to have taken these steps. The EU is making major changes to its dual-use trade controls, and a 'recast' of the EU Dual-use Regulation is under way.[5] The process started in 2011 and is unlikely to be completed before the end of 2018.[6]

The Australia Group

The AG seeks to 'minimise the risk of assisting chemical and biological weapon (CBW) proliferation' through 'harmonising participating countries' national export licensing measures'.[7] Since its establishment in response to the use of chemical weapons in the 1980–88 Iran–Iraq War, its coverage has been expanded to cover biological weapons and the materials, equipment and technology that can be used in connection with them. While the lists annexed to the 1993 Chemical Weapons Convention (CWC) cover only chemicals, the AG's control lists cover also production equipment and technology.[8] Since 2004 the AG has explicitly referred to trans-shipping countries in addition to exporting countries in its official documents.[9]

The 2017 AG plenary, as in 2016, reflected on the implications of the alleged and actual use of chemical weapons in Iraq and Syria.[10] In particular, the 42 participants took note of the report of a fact-finding mission sent by the Organisation for the Prohibition of Chemical Weapons (OPCW) to Syria, which was released while the plenary meeting took place, and the related statement issued by the OPCW Director-General, which confirmed the use of sarin in an incident on 4 April 2017 at Khan Shaykhun, Syria.[11] Specific concern was also reiterated about chemical and biological weapon-related

---

[4] Panda, A., 'Wassenaar Arrangement admits India as its 42nd member', *The Diplomat*, 8 Dec. 2017. On the diplomatic dispute with Italy see Bauer, S. and Maletta, G., 'The export control regimes', *SIPRI Yearbook 2017*, pp. 603–606.

[5] Council Regulation (EC) no. 428/2009 of 5 May 2009 (note 2).

[6] Bauer, S. and Bromley, M., 'Developments in EU dual-use and arms trade control', *SIPRI Yearbook 2017*, pp. 612–15.

[7] Australia Group, 'The Australia Group: An introduction'; and Australia Group, 'Objectives of the Group'.

[8] For a summary and other details of the Convention on the Prohibition of the Development, Production, Stockpiling and Use of Chemical Weapons and on their Destruction (Chemical Weapons Convention, CWC) see annex A, section I, in this volume.

[9] Australia Group, '2004 Australia Group Plenary', June 2004.

[10] On allegations of chemical weapon use in Iraq and Syria see chapter 8, sections I and II, in this volume.

[11] OPCW, Technical Secretariat, 'Report of the OPCW fact-finding mission in Syria regarding an alleged incident in Khan Shaykhun, Syrian Arab Republic April 2017', Note by the Technical Secre-

activities in the Democratic People's Republic of Korea (DPRK, or North Korea). This followed the killing of Kim Jong Nam, the half-brother of the North Korean leader Kim Jong Un, apparently using the organophosphorus nerve agent VX in Malaysia on 13 February 2017.[12] These concerns were repeated in a separate statement issued by the AG on 30 June to celebrate the 20th anniversary of the entry into force of the CWC.[13]

As part of the AG's engagement with non-participating states, in particular in Latin America and the Caribbean, the 2016 plenary decided to hold the 2017 intersessional implementation meeting, including a meeting of experts on new and evolving technologies and an AG dialogue with Latin American countries, in Buenos Aires on 14–16 February.[14] The meeting also hosted a session open to industry and pharmaceutical companies representatives, in order to 'encourage inclusive dialogue with the private sector'.[15] The meeting was appraised as 'highly productive' and the 2017 plenary agreed 'to consider more regular Australia Group Dialogues as the model for regionally-based outreach'.[16] The 2018 AG intersessional meeting will be held in London and it will include a dialogue with Africa for the first time.[17]

More generally, the plenary agreed to strengthen outreach to relevant international forums and to 'continue an active program of international outreach and engagement in 2017–18'.[18] In addition, the AG made outreach visits to India, Malaysia, Myanmar and Serbia in 2017.[19]

To strengthen measures to counter the proliferation of chemical and biological weapons, the plenary agreed on 'increasing awareness of emerging technologies, the potential exploitation of the cyber sphere, and scientific developments', as well as on enhancing efforts to prevent biological and chemical terrorism. Focus continues to be placed on engagement with industry and academia.[20]

The annual revision of the list of chemical and biological items by technical experts resulted in the addition, among other things, of N,N-Diisopropylaminoethanethiol hydrochloride, a potential VX precursor and potential VX degradation product.

---

tariat, S/1510/2017, 29 June 2017; and Australia Group, 'Statement by the Chair of the 2017 Australia Group Plenary', 30 June 2017.

[12] Australia Group (note 11). See also chapter 8, section II, in this volume.

[13] Australia Group, 'Statement by Australia Group participants on the 20th anniversary of the entry into force of the Chemical Weapons Convention', 30 June 2017.

[14] Argentinian Ministry of Foreign Affairs and Worship, 'Intersessional meeting of the Australia Group', Press Release No. 036/17, 14 Feb. 2017; and Australia Group (note 11).

[15] Argentinian Ministry of Foreign Affairs and Worship (note 14).

[16] Australia Group (note 11).

[17] Lambert, J., 'Preventing chemical and biological weapons proliferation: The Australia Group', Presentation, 25th Asian Export Control Seminar, Tokyo, 27 Feb.–1 Mar. 2018.

[18] Australia Group (note 11).

[19] Representative of an AG participating state, Correspondence with author, 19 Nov. 2017.

[20] Australia Group (note 11).

Although 'strong support' was shown during the plenary for admitting India to the AG, the plenary concluded with no new state joining. However, consensus was reached intersessionally, and on 19 January 2018 India formally became the 43rd participant in the group.[21]

The Missile Technology Control Regime

The MTCR, which celebrated its 30th anniversary in 2017, was created in 1987 to prevent the proliferation of unmanned delivery systems for nuclear weapons by controlling the export of related goods and technologies.[22] In those 30 years, its membership grew from 7 to 35 states and its scope extended from missiles only to include all types of unmanned aerial vehicle (UAV, drone) capable of delivering nuclear, biological or chemical weapons. At its 31st plenary meeting, held in Dublin in October 2017, Ireland and Iceland jointly assumed the rotating chair for 2017–18.[23] It is the second time that this model has been used to enable smaller states to jointly assume the chairing role.[24]

During the plenary week in Dublin, the delegations of the 35 partner states discussed and exchanged information on existing and potential missile proliferation developments since the previous plenary, in Busan, Republic of Korea (South Korea), in October 2016.[25] The North Korean nuclear weapon and missile programmes was discussed 'in response to the drastic escalation of ballistic missile launches and significant missile technology development' in the past year.[26] The member states expressed their continued commitment 'to exercise extreme vigilance when controlling transfers' that could contribute to the North Korean missile programme, explicitly recalling their commitment to the related United Nations Security Council resolutions.[27]

The US delegation reportedly proposed moving UAVs with maximum speeds below 650 kilometres/hour from category I (which includes items for whose export there is a 'strong presumption of denial') to category II, which would loosen restrictions on UAV exports by the MTCR partner states.[28] The USA perceives itself at a disadvantage, compared to the main competitors on the military UAV market, China and Israel, which are not members of the

---

[21] Australia Group, 'India joins the Australia Group', Press release, 19 Jan. 2018.
[22] For further detail see the Missile Technology Control Regime (MTCR) website.
[23] Missile Technology Control Regime, 'Public statement from the plenary meeting of the Missile Technology Control Regime', Dublin, 20 Oct. 2017.
[24] The Netherlands and Luxemburg co-chaired the MTCR in 2015–16.
[25] Missile Technology Control Regime (note 23).
[26] Missile Technology Control Regime (note 23). See also chapter 7, section IV, in this volume.
[27] Missile Technology Control Regime (note 23).
[28] Insinna, V. and Mehta, A., 'Here's how the Trump administration could make it easier to sell military drones', *Defense News*, 19 Dec. 2017.

MTCR.[29] Introducing speed as a parameter to differentiate military UAVs from other category I systems would, however, represent a major change to the MTCR control list and it is unclear if the USA will be able to garner enough support for a unanimous decision to this effect.

In the plenary's opening speech, the Irish Foreign Minister, Simon Coveney, called on Iran to show its commitment to the Joint Comprehensive Plan of Action (JCPOA)—which it concluded in July 2015 with China, France, Germany, Russia, the United Kingdom, the USA and the EU to curtail its nuclear programme—'by ceasing all activities related to ballistic missiles which are not in keeping with the spirit of the agreement' and called on the US Congress to maintain its commitment to the agreement.[30] As in 2016, the public statement at the end of the plenary also mentioned the JCPOA. It confirmed the continued commitment of the partner states to the implementation of the missile-related provisions in UN Security Council Resolution 2231, which endorses the JCPOA.[31] This came only one week after the US President elected not to certify that the continued lifting of sanctions was proportional to Iran's actions under the JCPOA on 13 October and after repeated claims by members of the US administration that Iran's missile testing activities were in violation of Resolution 2231 and of the 'spirit' of the JCPOA.[32] As in previous years, the MTCR partner states reiterated concerns regarding 'ongoing missile programmes in the Middle East, Northeast Asia, and South Asia'.[33]

The plenary discussed membership issues but did not decide on any pending applications.[34] The outgoing MTCR chair, South Korea, conducted several outreach missions in 2017, including missions to Pakistan (January), Singapore (February), Kazakhstan (March), Myanmar (May) and Kuwait (July). In 2017 Kazakhstan joined Estonia and Latvia as the third state to unilaterally declare adherence to the guidelines and control lists of the MTCR.[35] This approach to universalization was only formalized by the 2014 plenary in Oslo: a state that wishes to unilaterally adhere is now asked to formally notify France, which acts as the MTCR point of contact.[36]

France hosted the annual reinforced point of contact meeting—the MTCR's intersessional policy-level meeting—in Paris in April 2017. At the meeting

---

[29] Ewers, E. C. et al., *Drone Proliferation: Policy Choices for the Trump Administration*, Papers for the President (Center for a New American Security: Washington, DC, June 2017).

[30] Coveney, S., Irish Minister for Foreign Affairs and Trade, Speech at the 31st meeting of Missile Technology Control Regime, Dublin, 18 Oct. 2017; and Joint Comprehensive Plan of Action (JCPOA), Vienna, 14 July 2015, reproduced as Annex A of UN Security Council Resolution 2231, 20 July 2015. On implementation of the JCPOA in 2017 see chapter 7, section V, in this volume.

[31] Missile Technology Control Regime (note 23).

[32] See chapter 7, section V, in this volume.

[33] Missile Technology Control Regime (note 23).

[34] Missile Technology Control Regime (note 23).

[35] Missile Technology Control Regime, 'MTCR partners'.

[36] Missile Technology Control Regime, 'Adherence policy'.

states exchanged experiences on curbing illicit procurement efforts and missile programmes of concern, especially those by states that are currently subject to UN sanctions.[37] This included discussions of the North Korean nuclear weapon and missile programmes and related UN sanctions.[38]

The annual expert meetings, held prior to the plenary, discussed proliferation trends, procurement activities, brokering, transit and trans-shipment issues, catch-all controls, and key technology trends, including 'serious risks and challenges posed by intangible technology transfers'.[39] In addition, the chair of the Hague Code of Conduct against Ballistic Missile Proliferation (HCOC) addressed the plenary.

The Hague Code of Conduct against Ballistic Missile Proliferation

The MTCR is complemented by the Hague Code of Conduct, which celebrated its 15th anniversary in 2017. The HCOC was established within the MTCR in 2002 and subsequently developed into a separate initiative for confidence building and as an instrument for transparency in ballistic missile proliferation.

The 16th annual meeting on the HCOC took place in Vienna on 6–7 June 2017, with delegations from 64 of the 138 subscribing states attending.[40] Poland assumed the chair of the HCOC for 2017–18, taking over from Kazakhstan. The new chair declared its objectives to be 'the full and comprehensive implementation of the Code in all its aspects and strengthening outreach activities for advancing the process of HCoC universalization'.[41] The countries subscribing to the HCOC lauded the subscription by India in 2016 as an important step towards universalization, especially because of its ballistic missile and space programmes. They called on more countries to join the initiative as no new countries signed on in 2017 and states with major missile programmes, such as China, Iran, North Korea and Pakistan, remain outside of the initiative.

The Nuclear Suppliers Group

The NSG aims to prevent the proliferation of nuclear weapons by controlling transfers of nuclear and nuclear-related material, equipment, software and technology.

---

[37] Missile Technology Control Regime, 'Joint statement agreed by consensus during the Reinforced Points of Contact 2017 to celebrate the 30th anniversary of the MTCR', Paris, 13 Apr. 2017.

[38] On North Korea's missile programme see chapter 6, section IX, and chapter 7, section IV, in this volume.

[39] Missile Technology Control Regime (note 23).

[40] Hague Code of Conduct, '16th regular meeting of the subscribing states to the Hague Code of Conduct against Ballistic Missile Proliferation', Press release by HCOC subscribing states, [n.d.].

[41] Hague Code of Conduct (note 40).

In 2017 Switzerland took over as chair of the NSG and will hand over to Latvia in 2018–19.[42] The chairs of the NSG consultative group and the information exchange meeting (previously held by US officials) were handed over to Mexico and Switzerland, respectively. The technical experts group will continue to be chaired by Sweden.[43]

The 2017 plenary statement highlighted proliferation concerns about North Korea and restated the NSG's support for the UN Security Council resolutions, including Resolution 2356 of 2 June 2017, strongly condemning North Korea's nuclear tests.[44]

The NSG plenary restated its interest in being briefed by the coordinator of the working group on the procurement channel under the JCPOA.[45] The agreement established a procurement working group to review proposals by states that want to provide nuclear-relevant dual-use items to Iran. It makes a recommendation to the UN Security Council, which can refuse or approve any proposed transfer.[46]

The plenary continued its discussions on enhanced outreach and 'took note of a report on outreach to non-NSG participants' while considering options for enhancing these activities.[47] It also approved revised guidance for its outreach efforts.

India and Pakistan

The current NSG rules require that participating states are party to the 1968 Non-Proliferation Treaty (NPT). Despite this, two states that are not NPT parties—India and Pakistan—have applied to join the NSG. India applied in May 2016, but this was strongly opposed by a group of countries led by China during the 2016 plenary a few weeks later.[48] However, the 'Technical, Legal and Political Aspects' of participation by non-NPT states were discussed, and the NSG demonstrated a new willingness to seek an agreement on participation criteria for non-NPT states. In particular, the chair of the 2016 plenary mandated Ambassador Rafael Mariano Grossi of Argentina (who had chaired the 2015 plenary) to consult with participants on a possible solution. The outcome of these consultations was a draft document outlining a set of criteria to be met by non-NPT applicants.[49] The document, further discussed

---

[42] Nuclear Suppliers Group, 'Public statement: Plenary meeting of the Nuclear Suppliers Group Bern, 22–23 June 2017', 23 June 2017.

[43] Nuclear Suppliers Group, 'Organisation'; and Nuclear Suppliers Group (note 42).

[44] Nuclear Suppliers Group (note 42), and UN Security Council Resolution 2356, 2 June 2017. See also chapter 7, section IV, in this volume.

[45] Nuclear Suppliers Group (note 42); and Joint Comprehensive Plan of Action (note 30).

[46] Delegation of the European Union to the International Organisations in Vienna, 'JCPOA procurement channel', 24 Aug. 2016.

[47] Nuclear Suppliers Group (note 42).

[48] Bauer and Maletta (note 4), pp. 607–609.

[49] Bauer and Maletta (note 4), pp. 607–608.

at the end of 2016, disappointed Pakistan, which termed it 'clearly discriminatory' since it would permit India's application but not that of Pakistan.[50]

The 2017 NSG plenary resumed its discussions on engagement with states that do not participate in the NSG and the plenary statement explicitly referred to a discussion on the NSG's relationship with India.[51] Notwithstanding the support expressed by the Swiss chair for India's participation in the NSG, the 2017 plenary did not register any development on the issue.[52] It again discussed the 'Technical, Legal and Political Aspects' of participation by non-NPT states and took note of the intention of the chair to organize an informal meeting on the issue. This informal meeting was held on 16 November in Vienna and gave new momentum to the discussions.[53] However, different opinions persisted on what participation criteria should include.

China's position on participation by non-NPT states in the NSG remained unchanged, as stressed by a Chinese Foreign Ministry spokesperson in May and June 2017, ahead of the plenary.[54] China remains in favour of a 'two-step approach': the NSG would first elaborate a 'non-discriminatory resolution' that would be applied to all non-NPT states and only then it would discuss applications submitted by these countries.[55] This position is based on the assumption that the NPT represents a 'political and legal foundation for the international non-proliferation regime'.[56]

The USA—which supports India's application, but not Pakistan's—maintained its position that consensus is achievable 'if pursued'.[57] Ahead of the plenary in June, India gained public support from Russia and invited other countries to follow Russia's example.[58] Remarkably, in October during an official visit to India, the Italian Prime Minister, Paolo Gentiloni, also expressed support for India's 'intensified engagement' with the WA, the AG

[50] Davenport, K., 'Export group mulls membership terms', *Arms Control Today*, vol. 47, no. 1 (Jan./Feb. 2017); and Pakistani Ministry of Foreign Affairs, 'Record of the press briefing by spokesperson on 29 December 2016', 29 Dec. 2016.

[51] Nuclear Suppliers Group (note 42).

[52] Chandrasekhar, A., 'Swiss want inclusive membership of Nuclear Suppliers Group', swissinfo.ch, 8 June 2017.

[53] Kimball, D. G., 'NSG renews membership debate', *Arms Control Today*, 1 Dec. 2017.

[54] Press Trust of India, 'On India's NSG bid, China remains roadblock, says no change in stand', New Delhi Television (NDTV), 22 May 2017; and Chinese Ministry of Foreign Affairs, 'Foreign Ministry spokesperson Hua Chunying's regular press conference on June 6, 2017', 6 June 2017.

[55] Chaudhury, D. R., 'India to keep outreach to NSG members low key', *Economic Times*, 17 June 2017; and Chinese Ministry of Foreign Affairs (note 54).

[56] Chinese Ministry of Foreign Affairs, 'Foreign Ministry spokesperson Hua Chunying's regular press conference on May 23, 2016', 23 May 2016; and Chinese Ministry of Foreign Affairs, 'Foreign Ministry spokesperson Hong Lei's remarks on issues related to enlargement of NSG', 12 June 2016.

[57] Kimball (note 53).

[58] Press Trust of India, 'Russia extends support for India's NSG membership, permanent seat in UNSC', *Hindustan Times*, 1 June 2017; and 'India asks countries friendly with China to convince it on NSG issue', *Hindustan Times*, 6 June 2017.

and the NSG, arguing that it 'strengthens global non-proliferation efforts'.[59] Prior to India joining the MTCR in 2016, Italy had been one of the strongest opponents, although this was on the grounds of an unrelated bilateral issue.[60] India did not formalize any additional civil nuclear cooperation agreement with an NSG member during 2017. However, it reportedly resumed talks with the EU on such an agreement in October.[61] In addition, the 2016 India–Japan Agreement for Cooperation in the Peaceful Uses of Nuclear Energy came into force in July 2017.[62]

Following India's admission to the WA in December 2017 and the AG in January 2018, a spokesperson of the Indian Ministry of External Affairs stated that the country remains focused on its efforts to gain support from other countries for its NSG application and that there is now hope that the country's 'credentials' for joining the NSG had been established.[63] However, China's perspective on NSG membership seemed not be affected by India's inclusion in the WA as 'different multilateral mechanisms have different roles and different criteria for accepting new members' according to a Chinese Foreign Ministry spokesman.[64]

Meanwhile, controversy continued over China's supply of nuclear technology to Pakistan, which is neither an NPT member nor under full-scope safeguards by the International Atomic Energy Agency (IAEA).[65] In July 2017 the two countries agreed to cooperate in the field of uranium exploitation and mining and Pakistan placed further orders for China to build nuclear power plants.[66] The civil nuclear cooperation between China and Pakistan long precedes recent discussions over possible NSG admission criteria for non-NPT states and it has been traditionally defended by China as being in accordance with the NSG principles and under IAEA supervision.

---

[59] India–Italy joint statement during the visit of Prime Minister of Italy to India, Indian Ministry of External Affairs, 30 Oct. 2017.

[60] Bauer and Maletta (note 4), pp. 603–604.

[61] Bagchil, I., 'India, European Union restart talks on civil nuclear agreement', *Times of India*, 19 Oct. 2017.

[62] Umeda, S., 'Japan/India: Diet approves civil nuclear cooperation agreement', US Library of Congress, Global Legal Monitor, 14 June 2017.

[63] 'India enters Australia Group, inches closer to joining Nuclear Suppliers Group', *The Wire* (New Delhi), 19 Jan. 2018.

[64] Press Trust of India, 'China downplays India's entry into Wassenaar Arrangement', *Economic Times*, 13 Dec. 2017.

[65] On this issue see also *SIPRI Yearbook 2011*, pp. 432–34; *SIPRI Yearbook 2012*, pp. 384–85; *SIPRI Yearbook 2013*, pp. 453–55; *SIPRI Yearbook 2014*, pp. 466–69; *SIPRI Yearbook 2015*, pp. 635–36; *SIPRI Yearbook 2015*, pp. 764–65; and *SIPRI Yearbook 2017*, pp. 607–609.

[66] 'China, Pakistan agree to uranium cooperation', World Nuclear News, 31 July 2017; and 'Pakistan places orders with China to build nuclear power plants', *The Nation*, 4 July 2017.

The Wassenaar Arrangement

The WA promotes 'transparency and greater responsibility' regarding transfers of conventional arms and related dual-use items. More specifically, it seeks to prevent 'destabilising accumulations' of such items and their acquisition by terrorists.[67]

The usual working groups met during 2017 to prepare for the annual plenary. The plenary itself was held on 6–7 December 2017 in Vienna, where it is usually held, with France holding the rotating chair.[68]

A key outcome of the 2017 plenary was the admission of India as the 42nd WA participating state, the first new admission since Mexico in 2011. This marked a key success in India's long-running campaign to gain admission to all of the export control regimes, and followed its admission to the MTCR in 2016.[69] Earlier in 2017 India had updated its national control lists for military goods and dual-use items in order to align them with the WA list, thereby clearing another hurdle to admission.[70]

The 2017 plenary made a wide range of amendments to different parts of the WA control lists. These included clarifications of the controls on 'ground stations for spacecraft, submarine diesel engines, technology related to intrusion software, software for testing gas turbine engines, analogue-to-digital converters, non-volatile memories and information security' as well as a relaxing of controls on 'mechanical high-speed cameras and digital computers'.[71] The wide range of items covered reflects the breadth in the coverage of the WA control lists for conventional arms and, in particular, dual-use items, the pace at which the capabilities of these items covered are evolving, and the speed with which high-performance items are becoming more widely available.

Controls on intrusion software have been a key focus of discussion and attention since they were first introduced in 2013. The controls were initially adopted in order to control systems that are used by law enforcement agencies and intelligence agencies to remotely monitor and, in certain cases, control computers and mobile phones without detection (see also section IV). However, companies and researchers quickly began to express concerns that the language used in the control lists also includes systems and processes

---

[67] Wassenaar Arrangement, 'Introduction'.

[68] Wassenaar Arrangement, Statement issued by the Plenary Chair on 2017 outcomes of the Wassenaar Arrangement on Export Controls for Conventional Arms and Dual-Use Goods and Technologies, Vienna, 7 Dec. 2017.

[69] 'India set to become member of export control regime Wassenaar Arrangement', *The Hindu*, 8 Dec. 2017.

[70] 'Updated SCOMET list as per 31/01/2018', Directorate General for Foreign Trade, Ministry of Commerce and Industry of India; and Notani, S., 'India's DGFT overhauls SCOMET', WorldECR, no. 60, June 2017.

[71] Wassenaar Arrangement (note 68).

that are essential to information technology (IT) security, particularly systems used for penetration testing and vulnerability disclosure processes.[72] In the USA, the strength of opposition from the IT sector led the government to delay national implementation of the controls, despite this being one of the obligations associated with being a WA participating state.[73] In 2016 and 2017 the USA proposed amendments to the WA controls on intrusion software.[74] In 2016 opposition from other participating states meant that only minor changes were agreed.[75] However, in 2017 more detailed explanatory notes were added to the WA controls to specify that they apply neither to software that was designed to provide software updates nor to vulnerability disclosure and cyber incident response software.[76] Vulnerability disclosure experts have broadly welcomed the new language, stating that it meets many of the concerns that they had raised.[77]

As in previous years, a key topic of discussion at the WA was 'advances in technology and market trends'.[78] The plenary chair noted that 'further work is needed to address new challenges'. Another key priority that was highlighted was 'outreach activities to non-member countries and to encouraging voluntary adherence to the WA's standards'.[79]

During the 2017 plenary, participating states also discussed several proposals for new best practices guidelines and identified other existing guidelines to be update as appropriate in 2018.[80] The WA best practices guidelines cover a broad range of topics in the field of export control implementation and are a key part of the WA's work on improving control standards among both WA participating states and non-participating states. A procedure for regularly reviewing and updating guidance documents—some of which

[72] Bratus, S. et al., 'Why Wassenaar Arrangement's definitions of intrusion software and controlled items put security research and defense at risk, and how to fix it', 9 Oct. 2014. 'Penetration testing' tools are used to test the security of a network by simulating attacks against it in order to locate vulnerabilities. 'Vulnerability disclosure' is the means through which software vulnerabilities are identified and reported.

[73] Wassenaar Arrangement, 'Initial elements', *Public Documents*, vol. I, *Founding Documents*, WA-DOC (17) PUB 001 (Wassenaar Arrangement Secretariat: [Vienna], Feb. 2017, section III(1).

[74] Galperin, E. and Cardozo, N., 'Victory! State Department will try to fix Wassenaar Arrangement', Electronic Frontier Foundation, 29 Feb. 2016.

[75] Thomson, I., 'Wassenaar weapons pact talks collapse leaving software exploit exports in limbo', The Register, 21 Dec. 2016.

[76] Wassenaar Arrangement, 'List of dual-use goods and technologies and munitions list', WA-LIST (17) 1, 7 Dec. 2017.

[77] Moussouris, K., 'Serious progress made on the Wassenaar Arrangement for global cybersecurity', The Hill, 17 Dec. 2017.

[78] Wassenaar Arrangement (note 68).

[79] Wassenaar Arrangement (note 68).

[80] Wassenaar Arrangement (note 68).

have not been updated for several years—was agreed as part of the WA's 2016 self-assessment exercise.[81]

Finally, WA participating states made improvements to the system for sharing information electronically on approvals and denials of export licences, and 'discussed how to strengthen national export control implementation in areas such as arms trade risk assessment, effective end-use and end-user assurances, re-export and controls on intangible transfers of technology, as well as catch-all provisions'.[82]

[81] Wassenaar Arrangement, Statement issued by the Plenary Chair on 2016 outcomes of the Wassenaar Arrangement on Export Controls for Conventional Arms and Dual-Use Goods and Technologies, Vienna, 8 Dec. 2016.
[82] Wassenaar Arrangement (note 68).

IV. Controls on intangible transfers of technology and additive manufacturing

MARK BROMLEY, KOLJA BROCKMANN AND GIOVANNA MALETTA

Controls on transfers of conventional arms and dual-use items apply not just to tangible transfers—that is movements of physical goods—but also intangible transfers of certain types of technology and software. These transfers, generally referred to as intangible transfers of technology (ITT), include the electronic or oral transfers of software, technical data, knowledge and technical assistance. Many of the physical items that are the subject of arms and dual-use export controls are far less useful to possess if the owner does not also have access to related software, technical data, knowledge or technical assistance. Controlling ITT is thus widely viewed as an essential component of a state's export control system. As a result, the main export control regimes, the controls of the European Union (EU), and United Nations and EU arms embargoes all include requirements to impose and enforce controls on different types of ITT. However, controls on ITT pose a particular set of problems, both for regulators when seeking to detect illicit transfers and for companies and research institutes when seeking to comply with regulations.

The difficulty of enforcement and compliance is only likely to grow. In particular, developments in areas such as cloud computing are increasing the volume of software and technical data that can be transferred electronically and raising difficult questions about if and when export controls should apply. Meanwhile, the greater ease with which individuals can travel internationally is making it harder to track and control in-person transfers of knowledge and technical assistance. Moreover, additive manufacturing (AM)—also known as 3D printing—has the potential to increase the range and complexity of controlled goods that can be produced based mostly on transferred software and technical data. AM also has the potential to change the skills and engineering expertise required compared to traditional manufacturing processes and to decrease the reliance on transfers of controlled goods. However, it is unlikely that the spread of AM will lead to a general deskilling of the production of arms and dual-use items.

During 2017 controls on ITT continued to be a major focus of discussion in the export control regimes and in the ongoing review of the EU Dual-use Regulation.[1] Within the export control regimes, states continued to try to establish common standards for the implementation of controls on ITT and examined if and how controls on AM machines and related software,

---

[1] Council Regulation (EC) no. 428/2009 of 5 May 2009 setting up a Community regime for the control of exports, transfer, brokering and transit of dual-use items, *Official Journal of the European Union*, L 134, 29 May 2009.

technology and materials could be extended (see section III). In the EU, discussions focused on how to facilitate ITT that posed a reduced proliferation risk—such as transfers between different branches of the same company—and on establishing a clear and harmonized approach to how controls should apply to cloud computing. This section describes the main challenges associated with controls on ITT, the implications for non-proliferation efforts of developments in AM, and recent discussions about these issues within the export control regimes and the EU.

Intangible transfers of technology

Controls on ITT are required—using more or less uniform wording—by all four export control regimes: the Australia Group, the Missile Technology Control Regime (MTCR), the Nuclear Suppliers Group (NSG) and the Wassenaar Arrangement on Export Controls for Conventional Arms and Dual-use Goods and Technologies (Wassenaar Arrangement, WA).[2] For example, the WA controls technology and software that is required or designed for the development, production or use of a controlled item. In turn, it defines technology as consisting of both technical data (e.g. blueprints, plans, diagrams and models) and knowledge and technical assistance (e.g. instruction, skills, training, working knowledge and consulting services).[3] Each regime also specifies that certain types of technology and software are not controlled, particularly those 'in the public domain'.[4] Certain types of technology and software can be transferred using tangible means. For example, technical data can be included in published technical manuals and training materials or software can be loaded on to a CD-ROM or pre-installed on a computer and the physical items moved from one country to another. However, many transfers of technology and software take place through intangible means.

Intangible transfers of technical data and software

An intangible transfer of technical data and software, such as blueprints, schematics, diagrams or software, can take place via email, server upload or download, cloud computing or other Internet-based sharing platform. In addition to being subject to control because it is required or designed for the development, production or use of a controlled item, some types of technical

---

[2] Wassenaar Arrangement, 'List of dual-use goods and technologies and munitions list', WA-LIST (16) 1 Corr. 1, 17 Feb. 2017; Missile Technology Control Regime, 'Equipment, software and technology annex', 19 Oct. 2017; Nuclear Suppliers Group, 'Guidelines for nuclear transfers', annexed to IAEA document INFCIRC/254/Rev.13/Part 1, 8 Nov. 2016; Nuclear Suppliers Group, 'Guidelines for transfers of nuclear-related dual-use equipment, materials, software, and related technology', annexed to IAEA document INFCIRC/254/Rev. 10/Part 2, 8 Nov. 2016; and Australia Group, 'Australia Group common control lists', [n.d.].

[3] Wassenaar Arrangement (note 2), pp. 3, 227.

[4] E.g. Missile Technology Control Regime (note 2), p. 7.

data and software can also be subject to specific controls in their own right without reference to another controlled item. For example, systems that employ a certain standard of cryptography are controlled under category 5 of the Wassenaar Arrangement dual-use list.[5] These controls cover a vast array of tangible goods that employ a certain level of cryptography in their associated systems and that are produced in a diverse range of sectors, such as telecommunications, transport and energy.[6] However, they also include goods that can be transferred electronically—particularly different forms of computer software—that are used in banking, information technology (IT) security and other areas.

The application of export controls to cryptography has long been one of the most contentious and hotly contested areas of trade controls, particularly in the United States and the EU. In the 1970s and 1980s the application by the USA of export controls to cryptography led to the so-called crypto-wars. At the time, many in the information and communications technology (ICT) sector argued that the extension of export controls to cryptography harmed commercial competitiveness, was a violation of free speech and posed a threat to IT security.[7] In response, the USA progressively eased controls on exports of cryptography through the use of exemptions and 'open licences' that allow for multiple shipments under the same authorization.[8] However, many of these exemptions and open licences do not exist in the EU.

Controls on transfers of software have recently expanded to cover the trade in so-called cyber-surveillance systems. Cyber-surveillance technologies enable the monitoring and exploitation of data or content that is stored, processed or transferred via ICT, such as computers, mobile phones and telecommunications networks.[9] From 2012 onwards the WA and subsequently the EU expanded their dual-use export controls to cover a wider array of cyber-surveillance technologies. Many of the items covered—particularly mobile telecommunications interception equipment and internet protocol (IP) network surveillance systems—are tangible goods. However, intrusion software, which is used to remotely monitor computers and mobile phones and which became subject to control by the WA in 2013 (see section III), is

---

[5] Controls on such systems have been part of the Wassenaar Arrangement dual-use list since the 1990s. See Saper, N., 'International cryptography regulation and the global information economy', *Northwestern Journal of Technology and Intellectual Property*, vol. 11, no. 7 (fall 2013).

[6] European Commission, 'Impact assessment: Report on the EU export control policy review accompanying the document Proposal for a regulation of the European Parliament and of the Council setting up a Union regime for the control of exports, transfer, brokering, technical assistance and transit of dual-use items', Commission staff working document, Brussels, SWD(2016) 315 final, p. 34.

[7] Grimmett, J. J., *Encryption Export Controls*, Congressional Research Service (CRS) Report for Congress RL30273 (Library of Congress, CRS: Washington, DC, 11 Jan. 2001).

[8] Grimmett (note 7).

[9] See Bromley, M., Steenhoek, K. J., Halink, S. and Wijkstra, E., 'ICT surveillance systems: Trade policy and the application of human security concerns', *Strategic Trade Review*, vol. 2, no. 2 (spring 2016).

transferred electronically.[10] Moreover, many cyber-surveillance systems require almost constant software updates in order to remain undetected and to function effectively.[11]

The application of export controls to intangible transfers of technical data and software has long been difficult for regulators and companies. However, the difficulties have become increasingly acute as a result of the ever larger volumes of data that are routinely transmitted electronically during marketing, production and sales processes. A company working in one of the sectors that is subject to arms and dual-use export controls may transfer controlled technical data or software numerous times a day as it moves data around its different branches and between itself and other companies in a particular supply chain.[12] When the items involved are subject to arms or dual-use export controls, every stage in this process becomes potentially subject to licensing procedures.

The challenges are likely to become more acute—for both regulators and companies—with the expanding use of cloud computing for the streamlined storage and retrieval of data. Cloud computing, which emerged in the early 2000s, can be broadly defined as 'using shared rather than private local computing resources to store software or technology and handle applications', and those shared resources can be geographically distant from the user.[13] As the use of cloud computing increases the volume of transferred technical data, it creates compliance-related challenges for both regulators and companies. One particular problem is that, depending on the model used, data may end up being physically stored in multiple locations, some of which may be subject to export control restrictions. Another problem is determining who exactly is subject to export controls, particularly when—as is increasingly common—companies outsource the provision of cloud services to a third party.

The development of more streamlined and harmonized controls on transfers of technical data has emerged as a key focus of the ongoing review of the EU Dual-use Regulation.[14] A proposal published by the European Commission in September 2016 attempts to bring greater clarity to the application of ITT controls by specifying that controls should only apply when the technology is made available to 'legal and natural persons and partnerships'

[10] Bauer, S. and Mićić, I., 'Export controls regimes', *SIPRI Yearbook 2014*, pp. 471–72.

[11] Page, K., 'Six things we know from the latest FinFisher documents', Privacy International, 15 Aug. 2014.

[12] Bromley, M. and Bauer, S., *The Dual-Use Export Control Policy Review: Balancing Security, Trade and Academic Freedom in a Changing World*, Non-proliferation Papers no. 48, EU Non-proliferation Consortium, Mar. 2016.

[13] Tauwhare, R., 'Cloud computing and export controls', Tech UK, Feb. 2016.

[14] Council Regulation (EC) no. 428/2009 (note 1), Article 2.2(iii). On the review see Bauer, S. and Bromley, M., 'Developments in EU dual-use and arms trade controls', *SIPRI Yearbook 2017* pp. 622–26.

outside the EU, rather than simply 'a destination' outside the EU, as is currently the case.[15] It also proposes a new EU general export authorization for 'Intra-company transmission of software and technology'.[16] The intention of the new language is, in part, to 'facilitate the use of cloud services'.[17] However, Digital Europe, an industrial organization representing European digital technology companies, has argued that the language needs to be further clarified, particularly by 'deleting the element of "making available" ... software and technology in electronic form'.[18] The concern appears to be that, even under the Commission's proposed language, it is the company providing cloud services that would be responsible for who downloads information, rather than just the user of the cloud services.

The review of the EU Dual-use Regulation has also created an opportunity to revisit debates about the application of export controls to cryptography. The Foreign Affairs Committee of the European Parliament emphasized in its opinion on the Commission's proposal that 'not every technology requires controls' and argued that 'exports of technologies that actually enhance human rights protection, such as encryption, should be facilitated'.[19] However, for the time being EU member states appear to be broadly in favour of retaining the existing controls on cryptography. One of the appeals of the existing controls appears to be that they enable governments to have oversight of—and the potential to control—technologies and systems that are not directly subject to export control but which are nonetheless of potential interest from a national security or human rights perspective. For example, before they were added to the Wassenaar Arrangement control list, exports of intrusion software and other cyber-surveillance systems were subject to export controls on the basis of the level of cryptography that they employ.[20]

Intangible transfers of knowledge and technical assistance

Transfers of knowledge and technical assistance can occur through a range of intangible means, including via academic courses in sensitive disciplines,

[15] European Commission, 'Proposal for a regulation of the European Parliament and of the Council setting up a Union regime for the control of exports, transfer, brokering, technical assistance and transit of dual-use items (recast)', COM(2016) 616 final, 28 Sep. 2016, p. 19.

[16] European Commission (note 15), p. 8.

[17] European Commission (note 15), p. 7.

[18] Digital Europe, 'European Commission proposed recast of the European export control regime: Making the rules fit for the digital world', Feb. 2017.

[19] European Parliament, Committee on Foreign Affairs, 'Opinion of the Committee on Foreign Affairs for the Committee on International Trade on the proposal for a regulation of the European Parliament and of the Council setting up a Union regime for the control of exports, transfer, brokering, technical assistance and transit of dual-use items (recast) (COM(2016)0616—C8-0393/2016—2016/0295(COD))', 2016/0295(COD), 31 May 2017, p. 3.

[20] 'British Government admits it has already started controlling exports of Gamma International's FinSpy', Privacy International, 9 Sep. 2012.

skills training and consulting services.[21] Activities aimed at the promotion of peaceful application of dual-use technologies (e.g. capacity building, national implementation assistance, training to respond to an attack or an incident involving hazardous materials) could also involve this type of in-person transfers of knowledge that might be used to develop, produce or make use of one of the items included in the control lists of the export control regimes.[22]

The language commonly used in most UN Security Council resolutions imposing arms embargoes also requires controls on technical assistance, mostly related to military activities or the provision, maintenance or use of arms and related materiel.[23] In the case of the Democratic People's Republic of Korea (DPRK, or North Korea), the UN Security Council specifically called on all UN member states 'to exercise vigilance and prevent specialized teaching or training of [North Korean] nationals within their territories or by their nationals, of disciplines which could contribute to [North Korea's] proliferation sensitive nuclear activities and the development of nuclear weapon delivery systems'.[24]

In the EU Dual-use Regulation, the definition of 'export' includes 'the oral transmission of technology when the technology is described over the telephone' to legal and natural persons and partnerships outside the EU.[25] Since the regulation forms part of the EU's common commercial policy, it cannot be used to regulate the cross-border movement of people. As a result, certain forms of 'in person' technical assistance are regulated separately by Council Joint Action 2000/401/CFSP.[26] However, the Joint Action only imposes controls on technical assistance provided outside the EU which is related to WMD, their related delivery mechanisms or military end-uses and provided in countries subject to EU, Organization for Security and Co-operation in Europe (OSCE) or UN arms embargoes.[27] Consequently, technical assistance and knowledge associated with other controlled dual-use items is left outside the scope of EU controls. This may change as the Commission's draft

---

[21] Rebolledo, V. G., *Intangible Transfers of Technology and Visa Screening in the European Union*, Non-proliferation Papers no. 13, EU Non-proliferation Consortium, Mar. 2012, p. 5.

[22] Hunger I. and Meier, O., 'Between Control and Cooperation: Dual-Use, Technology Transfers and the Non-Proliferation of Weapons of Mass Destruction', *Friedensforschung DSF*, no. 37, Deutschen Stiftung Friedensforschung (DSF), 2014, p. 11.

[23] E.g. UN Security Council Resolution 2216, 14 Apr. 2015, para. 14; and UN Security Council Resolution 2127, 5 Dec. 2013, para. 54.

[24] UN Security Council Resolution 1874, 12 June 2009, para. 28. See also UN Security Council Resolution 2270, 2 Mar. 2016, para. 17. The Security Council used the same language in Resolution 1737 on Iran, which was terminated on the implementation day of the Joint Comprehensive Plan of Action. UN Security Council Resolution 1737, 27 Dec. 2006, para. 17.

[25] Council Regulation (EC) no. 428/2009 (note 1), Article 2.2(iii).

[26] Council Joint Action of 22 June 2000 concerning the control of technical assistance related to certain military end-uses (2000/401/CFSP), *Official Journal of the European Union*, L 159, 30 June 2000.

[27] Council Joint Action (note 26).

revision of the EU Dual-use Regulation of September 2016 provides a legal definition of technical assistance and clarifies applicable controls.[28]

Another challenge in this field relates to transfers of knowledge or technical assistance that may occur through the arrival of a foreign citizen attending, for example, a university course or participating in an industry training programme. In the USA, this situation is covered by controls on 'deemed exports', which cover transfers of controlled technology to a foreign national.[29] In the EU this is covered by neither the Dual-use Regulation nor Joint Action 2000/401/CFSP on technical assistance, and so these legal instruments need to be complemented by other policies, such as visa policies.[30] Visa-screening mechanisms to grant short-term visas for the Schengen area (which largely overlaps with the EU) do not take into account concerns over the proliferation of weapons of mass destruction as they mainly address 'the risks of illegal immigration, terrorism and crime'.[31] Moreover, since 'long-term visas are an exclusive national competence in all EU member states, irrespective of their adherence to Schengen', controls may vary from one EU member state to the other, especially for schemes to vet foreign students.[32] For example, the United Kingdom uses the Academic Technology Approval Scheme (ATAS) to screen applications by postgraduate researchers from abroad for studies in potentially proliferation-sensitive fields.[33]

The application of controls on transfers of knowledge and technical assistance has always been difficult for regulators, companies and researchers. In particular, the provision of knowledge and technical assistance may involve the movement of people across borders carrying with them specific sensitive information in their minds. This makes it a cross-cutting issue where effective controls cannot simply be addressed by export controls, but may need to be complemented by other tools such as visa policies. For companies and research institutes, complying with controls can involve keeping track of individuals with knowledge of controlled technology and their nationalities, which can prove particularly hard.

[28] The legal basis of this possible extension in the scope of the regulation is the provision of the 2007 Lisbon Treaty, which makes 'the supply of technical assistance services involving a cross-border movement' an EU competence. European Commission (note 15), p. 13; and Treaty of Lisbon amending the Treaty on European Union and the Treaty establishing the European Community, signed 13 Dec. 2007, entered into force 1 Dec. 2009, *Official Journal of the European Union*, C 306, 17 Dec. 2007.

[29] US Department of Commerce, Bureau of Industry and Security, 'Guidance on reexports/transfers (in-country) of US-origin items or non-US-made items subject to the Export Administration Regulations (EAR)', 30 Oct. 2015.

[30] Rebolledo (note 21), p. 8.

[31] Rebolledo (note 21), p. 11.

[32] Rebolledo (note 21), p. 11.

[33] British Foreign and Commonwealth Office, 'Guidance: Academic Technology Approval Scheme (ATAS)', 3 Mar. 2017.

Additive manufacturing

AM describes certain types of manufacturing process that can form an object of practically any shape by depositing and bonding together successive layers of material. AM machines are capable of producing a variety of export-controlled items—ranging from basic small arms to key components of rocket engines—using such materials as polymers, metals or alloys.[34] Simple AM machines using polymers are often referred to as '3D printers' because of their similarity to common inkjet printers; but this term is insufficient to describe more advanced machines, particularly industrial-grade metal AM machines. AM technology has the potential to produce components required for nuclear weapons, uranium enrichment facilities, missiles and other conventional weapons. However, most of these sensitive applications are still in an experimental phase and the technology has not yet matured enough to realistically present a scenario in which an individual could simply push a button and be presented with a finished high-performance product.[35] Depending on the technology in question, additional finishing processes are often required in order to achieve key performance characteristics, such as the ability to withstand high mechanical stress. The need to specially engineer the designs for AM-produced objects may pose further hurdles for someone wishing to use these technologies to manufacture controlled items. Nonetheless, concerns have been raised about the impact of this technology on export controls and other non-proliferation efforts and the possible future impact of the technology in this area is a topic of active discussion.[36]

AM machines rely on digital build files to provide the information required to automatically produce an object of a certain shape and with certain performance characteristics. These build files can easily be transferred or made available using digital transfers, cloud computing or other types of file-sharing application. AM technology both uses intangible transfers and—by increasing the automation of manufacturing process that can be used in an attempt to bypass export controls and engage in proliferation-relevant activities—helps to reduce the knowledge barriers to producing controlled items.[37] These features of AM increase the benefit that an actor seeking to circumvent existing export controls can gain from exploiting the challenges

[34] Walther, G., 'Printing insecurity? The security implications of 3D-printing of weapons', *Science and Engineering Ethics*, vol. 21, no. 6 (Dec. 2015), pp. 1435–45; and Aerojet Rocketdyne, 'Aerojet Rocketdyne successfully tests engine made entirely with additive manufacturing', 23 June 2014.

[35] Kelley, R., *Is Three-dimensional (3D) Printing a Nuclear Proliferation Tool?*, Non-proliferation Papers no. 54, EU Non-proliferation Consortium, Feb. 2017.

[36] See Kroenig, M. and Volpe, T., '3-D printing the bomb? The nuclear nonproliferation challenge', *Washington Quarterly*, vol. 38, no. 3 (fall 2015), pp. 7–19; and Nelson, A., 'The truth about 3-D printing and nuclear proliferation', War on the Rocks, 14 Dec. 2015.

[37] Christopher, G., '3D printing: A challenge to nuclear export controls', *Strategic Trade Review*, vol. 1, no. 1 (autumn 2015), p. 18.

with controlling ITT.[38] Advances in AM thus illustrate the necessity of implementing effective controls on ITT.

AM has the potential to decentralize the production of export controlled goods. As the technology matures, the rate at which digital transfers replace transfers of goods in a product's supply chain is likely to increase.[39] By reducing the need to move controlled goods across borders, this trend will reduce the opportunities to subject a controlled item to checks and verification measures. These types of control may therefore become less effective as the opportunities to impose physical controls are reduced to transfers of AM machines and the feedstock that they use, such as special metal powders. National licensing authorities and the multilateral export control regimes have therefore considered how to apply or possibly expand existing export controls on goods and technology to address AM. For example, the 2016 MTCR plenary acknowledged that AM poses 'a major challenge to international export control efforts'.[40] In response, export controls could potentially be enhanced and expanded in three areas: (a) controls on the transfer of build files and other required technical data; (b) controls on the export of AM machines and their software; and (c) controls on the materials used in the AM process.

Controls on technology already cover transfers of build files if the item that the file describes is covered by export controls. However, the implementation of these controls varies between states, particularly in terms of the scope and complexity of information in the build files that triggers licensing requirements. No export control regime has yet produced guidance on how such controls should be enforced.

Similarly, no export control regime covers AM machines, with the exception of one specific type of production equipment in the Wassenaar Arrangement control list. However, some of the elements of AM machines, such as certain high-powered lasers, are covered by controls. Across the regimes a number of proposals have been made to include AM machines with certain dimensions and performance characteristics in the control lists, but they have all been rejected.[41] Introducing new controls may seem straightforward, and the introduction of controls on subtractive computer numerical controlled (CNC) machine tools has routinely been referred to as an example, but this example also demonstrates some of the challenges. These include

[38] Brockmann, K. and Bauer, S., '3D printing and missile technology controls', SIPRI Background Paper, Nov. 2017.

[39] Palmer, M., 'Ship a design, not a product! Is 3D printing a threat to export controls?', WorldECR, no. 43 (Sep. 2015), pp. 30–31.

[40] Missile Technology Control Regime, 'Public statement from the plenary meeting of the Missile Technology Control Regime (MTCR)', Busan, 21 Oct. 2016.

[41] Finck, R., French Secretariat-General for National Defence and Security, '3D printing', Presentation at the 20th Anniversary Practical Export Control Workshop of the Wassenaar Arrangement, 27–28 June 2016.

the potential problems of imposing controls on machines that are mainly used in the civilian field and the drawbacks of the various regimes' control lists using different metrics to define the machines subject to control.[42]

Moreover, no export control regime specifically controls materials designed for use as AM feedstock. The Wassenaar Arrangement dual-use control list covers a range of metals and alloys, some of them in powder form, but these are defined according to the specific chemical and physical properties required for other production processes and therefore only partly overlap with materials specially designed for use in AM. As AM feedstock is inherently dual-use, it will be difficult to impose new controls without affecting legitimate civilian uses. However, one possible way of expanding controls on AM feedstock is to limit new controls to powders with narrowly defined characteristics for use in high-performance metal printing.

Conclusions

The issue of how to formulate and implement effective controls on ITT is currently the subject of significant debate and discussion within the export control regimes and in the context of the review of the EU Dual-use Regulation. The fact that many of the companies and research institutes that rely on or use ITT are often operating on the cutting edge of their respective fields increases the proliferation-related risks but also strengthens the economic arguments against imposing burdensome regulations. The difficult nature of this balancing act is underscored by the extent to which effective implementation of controls on ITT relies on internal compliance and effective self-regulation by the companies and institutes involved. In particular, ITT occur in ways that leave no physical evidence. This makes it hard to prevent unauthorized transfers from taking place and to generate the evidence needed to demonstrate that controls have been violated.

In many cases, this is not necessarily a problem, since the non-proliferation concerns of regulators and the commercial confidentiality interests of companies often closely align. For example, when supplying technology to a foreign customer, many companies will have a commercial interest in ensuring that it reaches its intended destination and is not re-exported without permission. These goals would be shared by the company's national export licensing authority. The issues become more difficult when the interests of the licensing authority and the company or research institute in question do not align. For example, companies have limited commercial interest in maintaining detailed records of the cross-border movement of technology if it is passing between locations that are under its ownership and control.

---

[42] Brockmann and Bauer (note 38).

However, export licensing authorities may require the company or research institute to keep records of these movements.

More challenging is the fact that ITT bring within the scope of export controls some sectors and actors that have limited experience of these controls or where traditional methods of work are most at odds with established practices in this area. Tensions with the ICT sector with regards to cryptography indicate that export controls are unlikely—on their own—to be able to solve the proliferation-related problems that states want to address. Moreover, developments in AM and other emerging technologies look set to transform traditional models of trade and production in ways that may pose additional challenges to state-based export control frameworks. Expanding the dialogue between the export control regimes about approaches to ITT and AM would help them to develop more coordinated controls.[43]

---

[43] Brockmann and Bauer (note 38).

Annexes

Annex A. Arms control and disarmament agreements

Annex B. International security cooperation bodies

Annex C. Chronology 2017

Annex A. Arms control and disarmament agreements

This annex lists multi- and bilateral treaties, conventions, protocols and agreements relating to arms control and disarmament. Unless otherwise stated, the status of agreements and of their parties and signatories is as of 1 January 2018.

Notes

1. The agreements are divided into universal treaties (i.e. multilateral treaties open to all states; section I), regional treaties (i.e. multilateral treaties open to states of a particular region; section II) and bilateral treaties (section III). Within each section, the agreements are listed in the order of the date on which they were adopted, signed or opened for signature (multilateral agreements) or signed (bilateral agreements). The date on which they entered into force and the depositary for multilateral treaties are also given.

2. The main source of information is the lists of signatories and parties provided by the depositaries of the treaties. In lists of parties and signatories, states whose name appears in italics ratified, acceded or succeeded to, or signed the agreement during 2017.

3. States and organizations listed as parties have ratified, acceded to or succeeded to the agreements. Former non-self-governing territories, upon attaining statehood, sometimes make general statements of continuity to all agreements concluded by the former governing power. This annex lists as parties only those new states that have made an uncontested declaration on continuity or have notified the depositary of their succession. The Russian Federation continues the international obligations of the Soviet Union. Serbia continues the international obligations of the State Union of Serbia and Montenegro.

4. Unless stated otherwise, the multilateral agreements listed in this annex are open to all states or to all states in the respective zone or region for signature, ratification, accession or succession. Not all the signatories and parties are United Nations members. Taiwan, while not recognized as a sovereign state by many countries, is listed as a party to the agreements that it has ratified.

5. Where possible, the location (in a printed publication or online) of an accurate copy of the treaty text is given. This may be provided by a treaty depositary, an agency or secretariat connected with the treaty, or in the *United Nations Treaty Series* (available online at <http://treaties.un.org/>).

I. Universal treaties

Protocol for the Prohibition of the Use in War of Asphyxiating, Poisonous or Other Gases, and of Bacteriological Methods of Warfare (1925 Geneva Protocol)

Signed at Geneva on 17 June 1925; entered into force on 8 February 1928; depositary French Government

The protocol prohibits the use in war of asphyxiating, poisonous or other gases and of bacteriological methods of warfare. The protocol remains a fundamental basis of the international prohibition against chemical and biological warfare, and its principles, objectives and obligations are explicitly supported by the 1972 Biological and Toxin Weapons Convention and the 1993 Chemical Weapons Convention.

Parties (141): Afghanistan, Albania, Algeria, Angola, Antigua and Barbuda, Argentina, Australia, Austria, Bahrain, Bangladesh, Barbados, Belgium, Benin, Bhutan, Bolivia, Brazil, Bulgaria, Burkina Faso, Cabo Verde, Cambodia, Cameroon, Canada, Central African Republic, Chile, China, Colombia, Costa Rica, Côte d'Ivoire, Croatia, Cuba, Cyprus, Czech Republic, Denmark, Dominican Republic, Ecuador, Egypt, El Salvador, Equatorial Guinea, Estonia, Ethiopia, Fiji, Finland, France, Gambia, Germany, Ghana, Greece, Grenada, Guatemala, Guinea-Bissau, Holy See, Hungary, Iceland, India, Indonesia, Iran, Iraq, Ireland, Israel, Italy, Jamaica, Japan, Jordan, Kenya, Korea (North), Korea (South), Kuwait, Laos, Latvia, Lebanon, Lesotho, Liberia, Libya, Liechtenstein, Lithuania, Luxembourg, Macedonia (Former Yugoslav Republic of), Madagascar, Malawi, Malaysia, Maldives, Malta, Mauritius, Mexico, Moldova, Monaco, Mongolia, Morocco, Nepal, Netherlands, New Zealand, Nicaragua, Niger, Nigeria, Norway, Pakistan, Panama, Papua New Guinea, Paraguay, Peru, Philippines, Poland, Portugal, Qatar, Romania, Russia, Rwanda, Saint Kitts and Nevis, Saint Lucia, Saint Vincent and the Grenadines, Saudi Arabia, Senegal, Serbia, Sierra Leone, Slovakia, Slovenia, Solomon Islands, South Africa, Spain, Sri Lanka, Sudan, Swaziland, Sweden, Switzerland, Syria, Taiwan, Tanzania, Thailand, Togo, Tonga, Trinidad and Tobago, Tunisia, Turkey, Uganda, UK, Ukraine, Uruguay, USA, Venezuela, Viet Nam, Yemen

Notes: In addition to the 141 parties as of 1 Jan. 2018, Armenia acceded to the protocol in early 2018 and Palestine had applied to accede.

On joining the protocol, some states entered reservations which upheld their right to employ chemical or biological weapons against non-parties to the protocol, against coalitions which included non-parties or in response to the use of these weapons by a violating party. Many of these states have withdrawn these reservations, particularly after the conclusion of the 1972 Biological and Toxin Weapons Convention and the 1993 Chemical Weapons Convention since the reservations are incompatible with their obligation under the conventions.

In addition to these, 'explicit', reservations, a number of states that made a declaration of succession to the protocol on gaining independence inherited 'implicit' reservations from their respective predecessor states. For example, these implicit reservations apply to the states that gained independence from France and the UK before the latter states withdrew or amended their reservations. States that acceded (rather than succeeded) to the protocol did not inherit reservations in this way.

Protocol text: League of Nations, Treaty Series, vol. 94 (1929), pp. 65–74, <https://treaties.un.org/doc/Publication/UNTS/LON/Volume 94/v94.pdf>

Convention on the Prevention and Punishment of the Crime of Genocide (Genocide Convention)

Opened for signature at Paris on 9 December 1948; entered into force on 12 January 1951; depositary UN Secretary-General

Under the convention any commission of acts intended to destroy, in whole or in part, a national, ethnic, racial or religious group as such is declared to be a crime punishable under international law.

Parties (149): Afghanistan, Albania*, Algeria*, Andorra, Antigua and Barbuda, Argentina*, Armenia, Australia, Austria, Azerbaijan, Bahamas, Bahrain*, Bangladesh*, Barbados, Belarus*, Belgium, Belize, *Benin*, Bolivia, Bosnia and Herzegovina, Brazil, Bulgaria*, Burkina Faso, Burundi, Cabo Verde, Cambodia, Canada, Chile, China*, Colombia, Comoros, Congo (Democratic Republic of the), Costa Rica, Côte d'Ivoire, Croatia, Cuba, Cyprus, Czech Republic, Denmark, Ecuador, Egypt, El Salvador, Estonia, Ethiopia, Fiji, Finland, France, Gabon, Gambia, Georgia, Germany, Ghana, Greece, Guatemala, Guinea, Guinea-Bissau, Haiti, Honduras, Hungary*, Iceland, India*, Iran, Iraq, Ireland, Israel, Italy, Jamaica, Jordan, Kazakhstan, Korea (North), Korea (South), Kuwait, Kyrgyzstan, Laos, Latvia, Lebanon, Lesotho, Liberia, Libya, Liechtenstein, Lithuania, Luxembourg, Macedonia (Former Yugoslav Republic of), *Malawi*, Malaysia*, Maldives, Mali, Malta, Mexico, Moldova, Monaco, Mongolia*, Montenegro*, Morocco*, Mozambique, Myanmar*, Namibia, Nepal, Netherlands, New Zealand, Nicaragua, Nigeria, Norway, Pakistan, Palestine, Panama, Papua New Guinea, Paraguay, Peru, Philippines*, Poland*, Portugal*, Romania*, Russia*, Rwanda, Saint Vincent and the Grenadines, San Marino, Saudi Arabia, Senegal, Serbia*, Seychelles, Singapore*, Slovakia, Slovenia, South Africa, Spain*, Sri Lanka, Sudan, Sweden, Switzerland, Syria, Tajikistan, Tanzania, Togo, Tonga, Trinidad and Tobago, Tunisia, Turkey, Uganda, UK, Ukraine*, United Arab Emirates*, Uruguay, USA*, Uzbekistan, Venezuela*, Viet Nam*, Yemen*, Zimbabwe

* With reservation and/or declaration.

Signed but not ratified (1): Dominican Republic

Convention text: United Nations Treaty Collection, <https://treaties.un.org/doc/Treaties/1951/01/19510112 08-12 PM/Ch_IV_1p.pdf>

Geneva Convention (IV) Relative to the Protection of Civilian Persons in Time of War

Opened for signature at Geneva on 12 August 1949; entered into force on 21 October 1950; depositary Swiss Federal Council

The Geneva Convention (IV) establishes rules for the protection of civilians in areas covered by war and in occupied territories. Three other conventions were formulated at the same time, at a diplomatic conference held from 21 April to 12 August 1949: Convention (I) for the Amelioration of the Condition of the Wounded and Sick in Armed Forces in the Field; Convention (II) for the Amelioration of the Condition of the Wounded, Sick and Shipwrecked Members of Armed Forces at Sea; and Convention (III) Relative to the Treatment of Prisoners of War.

Parties (196): Afghanistan, Albania*, Algeria, Andorra, Angola*, Antigua and Barbuda, Argentina, Armenia, Australia*, Austria, Azerbaijan, Bahamas, Bahrain, Bangladesh*, Barbados*, Belarus, Belgium, Belize, Benin, Bhutan, Bolivia, Bosnia and Herzegovina,

Botswana, Brazil, Brunei Darussalam, Bulgaria, Burkina Faso, Burundi, Cabo Verde, Cambodia, Cameroon, Canada, Central African Republic, Chad, Chile, China*, Colombia, Comoros, Congo (Democratic Republic of the), Congo (Republic of the), Cook Islands, Costa Rica, Côte d'Ivoire, Croatia, Cuba, Cyprus, Czech Republic*, Denmark, Djibouti, Dominica, Dominican Republic, Ecuador, Egypt, El Salvador, Equatorial Guinea, Estonia, Eritrea, Ethiopia, Fiji, Finland, France, Gabon, Gambia, Georgia, Germany*, Ghana, Greece, Grenada, Guatemala, Guinea, Guinea-Bissau*, Guyana, Haiti, Holy See, Honduras, Hungary, Iceland, India, Indonesia, Iran*, Iraq, Ireland, Israel*, Italy, Jamaica, Japan, Jordan, Kazakhstan, Kenya, Kiribati, Korea (North)*, Korea (South)*, Kuwait*, Kyrgyzstan, Laos, Latvia, Lebanon, Lesotho, Liberia, Libya, Liechtenstein, Lithuania, Luxembourg, Macedonia (Former Yugoslav Republic of)*, Madagascar, Malawi, Malaysia, Maldives, Mali, Malta, Marshall Islands, Mauritania, Mauritius, Mexico, Micronesia, Moldova, Monaco, Mongolia, Montenegro, Morocco, Mozambique, Myanmar, Namibia, Nauru, Nepal, Netherlands, New Zealand*, Nicaragua, Niger, Nigeria, Norway, Oman, Pakistan*, Palau, Palestine, Panama, Papua New Guinea, Paraguay, Peru, Philippines, Poland, Portugal*, Qatar, Romania, Russia*, Rwanda, Saint Kitts and Nevis, Saint Lucia, Saint Vincent and the Grenadines, Samoa, San Marino, Sao Tome and Principe, Saudi Arabia, Senegal, Serbia, Seychelles, Sierra Leone, Singapore, Slovakia, Slovenia, Solomon Islands, Somalia, South Africa, South Sudan, Spain, Sri Lanka, Sudan, Suriname*, Swaziland, Sweden, Switzerland, Syria, Tajikistan, Tanzania, Thailand, Timor-Leste, Togo, Tonga, Trinidad and Tobago, Tunisia, Turkey, Turkmenistan, Tuvalu, Uganda, UK*, Ukraine*, United Arab Emirates, Uruguay*, USA*, Uzbekistan, Vanuatu, Venezuela, Viet Nam*, Yemen*, Zambia, Zimbabwe

* With reservation and/or declaration.

Convention text: Swiss Federal Department of Foreign Affairs, <https://www.fdfa.admin.ch/dam/eda/fr/documents/aussenpolitik/voelkerrecht/geneve/070116-conv4_e.pdf>

Protocol I Additional to the 1949 Geneva Conventions, and Relating to the Protection of Victims of International Armed Conflicts

Protocol II Additional to the 1949 Geneva Conventions, and Relating to the Protection of Victims of Non-International Armed Conflicts

Opened for signature at Bern on 12 December 1977; entered into force on 7 December 1978; depositary Swiss Federal Council

The protocols confirm that the right of parties that are engaged in international or non-international armed conflicts to choose methods or means of warfare is not unlimited and that the use of weapons or means of warfare that cause superfluous injury or unnecessary suffering is prohibited.

Parties to Protocol I (174) and Protocol II (168): Afghanistan, Albania, Algeria*, Angola[1]*, Antigua and Barbuda, Argentina*, Armenia, Australia*, Austria*, Bahamas, Bahrain, Bangladesh, Barbados, Belarus*, Belgium*, Belize, Benin, Bolivia*, Bosnia and Herzegovina*, Botswana, Brazil*, Brunei Darussalam, Bulgaria*, Burkina Faso*, Burundi, Cabo Verde*, Cambodia, Cameroon, Canada*, Central African Republic, Chad, Chile*, China*, Colombia*, Comoros, Congo (Democratic Republic of the)*, Congo (Republic of the), Cook Islands*, Costa Rica*, Côte d'Ivoire, Croatia*, Cuba, Cyprus*, Czech Republic*, Denmark*, Djibouti, Dominica, Dominican Republic, Ecuador, Egypt*, El Salvador, Equatorial Guinea, Estonia*, Ethiopia, Fiji, Finland*, France*, Gabon, Gambia, Georgia, Germany*, Ghana, Greece*, Grenada, Guatemala, Guinea*, Guinea-Bissau, Guyana, Haiti, Holy See*, Honduras, Hungary*, Iceland*,

Iraq[1], Ireland*, Italy*, Jamaica, Japan*, Jordan, Kazakhstan, Kenya, Korea (North)[1], Korea (South)*, Kuwait*, Kyrgyzstan, Laos*, Latvia, Lebanon, Lesotho*, Liberia, Libya, Liechtenstein*, Lithuania*, Luxembourg*, Macedonia (Former Yugoslav Republic of)*, Madagascar*, Malawi*, Maldives, Mali*, Malta*, Mauritania, Mauritius*, Mexico[1], Micronesia, Moldova, Monaco*, Mongolia*, Montenegro*, Morocco, Mozambique, Namibia*, Nauru, Netherlands*, New Zealand*, Nicaragua, Niger, Nigeria, Norway*, Oman*, Palau, Palestine, Panama*, Paraguay*, Peru, Philippines*, Poland*, Portugal*, Qatar*, Romania*, Russia*, Rwanda*, Saint Kitts and Nevis*, Saint Lucia, Saint Vincent and the Grenadines*, Samoa, San Marino, Sao Tome and Principe, Saudi Arabia*, Senegal, Serbia*, Seychelles*, Sierra Leone, Slovakia*, Slovenia*, Solomon Islands, South Africa, South Sudan, Spain*, Sudan, Suriname, Swaziland, Sweden*, Switzerland*, Syria*[1], Tajikistan*, Tanzania, Timor-Leste, Togo*, Tonga*, Trinidad and Tobago*, Tunisia, Turkmenistan, Uganda, UK*, Ukraine*, United Arab Emirates*, Uruguay*, Uzbekistan, Vanuatu, Venezuela, Viet Nam[1], Yemen, Zambia, Zimbabwe

* With reservation and/or declaration.
[1] Party only to Protocol I.

Protocol I text: Swiss Federal Department of Foreign Affairs, <https://www.fdfa.admin.ch/dam/eda/fr/documents/aussenpolitik/voelkerrecht/geneve/77prot1_en.pdf>

Protocol II text: Swiss Federal Department of Foreign Affairs, <https://www.fdfa.admin.ch/dam/eda/fr/documents/aussenpolitik/voelkerrecht/geneve/77prot2_en.pdf>

Antarctic Treaty

Signed by the 12 original parties at Washington, DC, on 1 December 1959; entered into force on 23 June 1961; depositary US Government

The treaty declares the Antarctic an area to be used exclusively for peaceful purposes. It prohibits any measure of a military nature in the Antarctic, such as the establishment of military bases and fortifications, and the carrying out of military manoeuvres or the testing of any type of weapon. The treaty bans any nuclear explosion as well as the disposal of radioactive waste material in Antarctica. The treaty provides a right of on-site inspection of all stations and installations in Antarctica to ensure compliance with its provisions.

States demonstrating their interest in Antarctica by conducting substantial scientific research activity there, such as the establishment of a scientific station or the dispatch of a scientific expedition, are entitled to become consultative members. In accordance with Article IX, consultative members meet at regular intervals to exchange information and hold consultations on matters pertaining to Antarctica, as well as to recommend to the governments measures in furtherance of the principles and objectives of the treaty.

Parties (53): Argentina*, Australia*, Austria, Belarus, Belgium*, Brazil*, Bulgaria*, Canada, Chile*, China*, Colombia, Cuba, Czech Republic*, Denmark, Ecuador*, Estonia, Finland*, France*, Germany*, Greece, Guatemala, Hungary, Iceland, India*, Italy*, Japan*, Kazakhstan, Korea (North), Korea (South)*, Malaysia, Monaco, Mongolia, Netherlands*, New Zealand*, Norway*, Pakistan, Papua New Guinea, Peru*, Poland*, Portugal, Romania, Russia*, Slovakia, South Africa*, Spain*, Sweden*, Switzerland, Turkey, UK*, Ukraine*, Uruguay*, USA*, Venezuela

* Consultative member under Article IX of the treaty.

Treaty text: Secretariat of the Antarctic Treaty, <http://www.ats.aq/documents/ats/treaty_original.pdf>

The Protocol on Environmental Protection (**1991 Madrid Protocol**) opened for signature on 4 October 1991 and entered into force on 14 January 1998. It designated Antarctica as a natural reserve, devoted to peace and science.

Protocol text:Secretariatof theAntarcticTreaty,<http://www.ats.aq/documents/recatt/Att006_e.pdf>

Treaty Banning Nuclear Weapon Tests in the Atmosphere, in Outer Space and Under Water (Partial Test-Ban Treaty, PTBT)

Signed by three original parties at Moscow on 5 August 1963 and opened for signature by other states at London, Moscow and Washington, DC, on 8 August 1963; entered into force on 10 October 1963; depositaries British, Russian and US governments

The treaty prohibits the carrying out of any nuclear weapon test explosion or any other nuclear explosion (*a*) in the atmosphere, beyond its limits, including outer space, or under water, including territorial waters or high seas; and (*b*) in any other environment if such explosion causes radioactive debris to be present outside the territorial limits of the state under whose jurisdiction or control the explosion is conducted.

Parties (126): Afghanistan, Antigua and Barbuda, Argentina, Armenia, Australia, Austria, Bahamas, Bangladesh, Belarus, Belgium, Benin, Bhutan, Bolivia, Bosnia and Herzegovina, Botswana, Brazil, Bulgaria, Cabo Verde, Canada, Central African Republic, Chad, Chile, Colombia, Congo (Democratic Republic of the), Costa Rica, Côte d'Ivoire, Croatia, Cyprus, Czech Republic, Denmark, Dominican Republic, Ecuador, Egypt, El Salvador, Equatorial Guinea, Fiji, Finland, Gabon, Gambia, Germany, Ghana, Greece, Guatemala, Guinea-Bissau, Honduras, Hungary, Iceland, India, Indonesia, Iran, Iraq, Ireland, Israel, Italy, Jamaica, Japan, Jordan, Kenya, Korea (South), Kuwait, Laos, Lebanon, Liberia, Libya, Luxembourg, Madagascar, Malawi, Malaysia, Malta, Mauritania, Mauritius, Mexico, Mongolia, Montenegro, Morocco, Myanmar, Nepal, Netherlands, New Zealand, Nicaragua, Niger, Nigeria, Norway, Pakistan, Panama, Papua New Guinea, Peru, Philippines, Poland, Romania, Russia, Rwanda, Samoa, San Marino, Senegal, Serbia, Seychelles, Sierra Leone, Singapore, Slovakia, Slovenia, South Africa, Spain, Sri Lanka, Sudan, Suriname, Swaziland, Sweden, Switzerland, Syria, Taiwan, Tanzania, Thailand, Togo, Tonga, Trinidad and Tobago, Tunisia, Turkey, Uganda, UK, Ukraine, Uruguay, USA, Venezuela, Yemen, Zambia

Signed but not ratified (10): Algeria, Burkina Faso, Burundi, Cameroon, Ethiopia, Haiti, Mali, Paraguay, Portugal, Somalia

Treaty text: Russian Ministry of Foreign Affairs, <http://mddoc.mid.ru/api/ia/download/?uuid=561590f5-ed1a-4e2a-a04e-f715bccb16ad>

Treaty on Principles Governing the Activities of States in the Exploration and Use of Outer Space, Including the Moon and Other Celestial Bodies (Outer Space Treaty)

Opened for signature at London, Moscow and Washington, DC, on 27 January 1967; entered into force on 10 October 1967; depositaries British, Russian and US governments

The treaty prohibits the placing into orbit around the earth of any object carrying nuclear weapons or any other kind of weapon of mass destruction, the installation of such weapons on celestial bodies, or the stationing of them in outer space in any other manner. The establishment of military bases, installations and fortifications, the testing of any type of weapon and the conducting of military manoeuvres on celestial bodies are also forbidden.

Parties (108): Afghanistan, Algeria, Antigua and Barbuda, Argentina, Australia, Austria, Azerbaijan, Bahamas, Bangladesh, Barbados, Belarus, Belgium, Benin, Brazil, Bulgaria, Burkina Faso, Canada, Chile, China, Cuba, Cyprus, Czech Republic, Denmark, Dominican Republic, Ecuador, Egypt, El Salvador, Equatorial Guinea, Estonia, Fiji, Finland, France, Germany, Greece, Guinea-Bissau, Hungary, Iceland, India, Indonesia, Iraq, Ireland, Israel, Italy, Jamaica, Japan, Kazakhstan, Kenya, Korea (North), Korea (South), Kuwait, Laos, Lebanon, Libya, Lithuania, Luxembourg, Madagascar, Mali, *Malta*, Mauritius, Mexico, Mongolia, Morocco, Myanmar, Nepal, Netherlands, New Zealand, *Nicaragua*, Niger, Nigeria, Norway, Pakistan, Papua New Guinea, Paraguay, Peru, Poland, Portugal, Qatar, Romania, Russia, Saint Vincent and the Grenadines, San Marino, Saudi Arabia, Seychelles, Sierra Leone, Singapore, Slovakia, South Africa, Spain, Sri Lanka, Sweden, Switzerland, Syria, Taiwan, Thailand, Togo, Tonga, Tunisia, Turkey, Uganda, UK, Ukraine, United Arab Emirates, Uruguay, USA, Venezuela, Viet Nam, Yemen, Zambia

Signed but not ratified (25): Bolivia, Botswana, Burundi, Cameroon, Central African Republic, Colombia, Congo (Democratic Republic of the), Ethiopia, Gambia, Ghana, Guyana, Haiti, Holy See, Honduras, Iran, Jordan, Lesotho, Malaysia, Montenegro, Panama, Philippines, Rwanda, Serbia, Somalia, Trinidad and Tobago

Treaty text: British Foreign and Commonwealth Office, Treaty Series no. 10 (1968), <https://assets.publishing.service.gov.uk/government/uploads/system/uploads/attachment_data/file/270006/Treaty_Principles_Activities_Outer_Space.pdf>

Treaty on the Non-Proliferation of Nuclear Weapons (Non-Proliferation Treaty, NPT)

Opened for signature at London, Moscow and Washington, DC, on 1 July 1968; entered into force on 5 March 1970; depositaries British, Russian and US governments

The treaty defines a nuclear weapon state to be a state that manufactured and exploded a nuclear weapon or other nuclear explosive device prior to 1 January 1967. According to this definition, there are five nuclear weapon states: China, France, Russia, the UK and the USA. All other states are defined as non-nuclear weapon states.

The treaty prohibits the nuclear weapon states from transferring nuclear weapons or other nuclear explosive devices or control over them to any recipient and prohibits them from assisting, encouraging or inducing any non-nuclear weapon state to manufacture or otherwise acquire such a weapon or device. It also prohibits non-nuclear weapon states parties from receiving nuclear weapons or other nuclear explosive devices from any source, from manufacturing them, or from acquiring them in any other way.

The parties undertake to facilitate the exchange of equipment, materials and scientific and technological information for the peaceful uses of nuclear energy and to ensure that potential benefits from peaceful applications of nuclear explosions will be made available to non-nuclear weapon states party to the treaty. They also undertake to pursue negotiations in good faith on effective measures relating to cessation of the nuclear arms race at an early date and to nuclear disarmament, and on a treaty on general and complete disarmament.

Non-nuclear weapon states parties undertake to conclude safeguard agreements with the International Atomic Energy Agency (IAEA) with a view to preventing diversion of nuclear energy from peaceful uses to nuclear weapons or other nuclear explosive devices. A Model Protocol Additional to the Safeguards Agreements, strengthening the measures, was approved in 1997; additional safeguards protocols are signed by states individually with the IAEA.

A review and extension conference, convened in 1995 in accordance with the treaty, decided that the treaty should remain in force indefinitely.

Parties (192): Afghanistan*, Albania*, Algeria*, Andorra*, Angola*, Antigua and Barbuda*, Argentina*, Armenia*, Australia*, Austria*, Azerbaijan*, Bahamas*, Bahrain*, Bangladesh*, Barbados*, Belarus*, Belgium*, Belize*, Benin*, Bhutan*, Bolivia*, Bosnia and Herzegovina*, Botswana*, Brazil*, Brunei Darussalam*, Bulgaria*, Burkina Faso*, Burundi*, Cabo Verde, Cambodia*, Cameroon*, Canada*, Central African Republic*, Chad*, Chile*, China*[†], Colombia*, Comoros*, Congo (Democratic Republic of the)*, Congo (Republic of the)*, Costa Rica*, Côte d'Ivoire*, Croatia*, Cuba*, Cyprus*, Czech Republic*, Denmark*, Djibouti*, Dominica*, Dominican Republic*, Ecuador*, Egypt*, El Salvador*, Equatorial Guinea, Eritrea, Estonia*, Ethiopia*, Fiji*, Finland*, France*[†], Gabon*, Gambia*, Georgia*, Germany*, Ghana*, Greece*, Grenada*, Guatemala*, Guinea, Guinea-Bissau, Guyana*, Haiti*, Holy See*, Honduras*, Hungary*, Iceland*, Indonesia*, Iran*, Iraq*, Ireland*, Italy*, Jamaica*, Japan*, Jordan*, Kazakhstan*, Kenya*, Kiribati*, Korea (South)*, Korea (North)[a], Kuwait*, Kyrgyzstan*, Laos*, Latvia*, Lebanon*, Lesotho*, Liberia, Libya*, Liechtenstein*, Lithuania*, Luxembourg*, Macedonia (Former Yugoslav Republic of)*, Madagascar*, Malawi*, Malaysia*, Maldives*, Mali*, Malta*, Marshall Islands*, Mauritania*, Mauritius*, Mexico*, Micronesia, Moldova*, Monaco*, Mongolia*, Montenegro*, Morocco*, Mozambique*, Myanmar*, Namibia*, Nauru*, Nepal*, Netherlands*, New Zealand*, Nicaragua*, Niger*, Nigeria*, Norway*, Oman*, Palau*, Palestine, Panama*, Papua New Guinea*, Paraguay*, Peru*, Philippines*, Poland*, Portugal*, Qatar*, Romania*, Russia*[†], Rwanda*, Saint Kitts and Nevis*, Saint Lucia*, Saint Vincent and the Grenadines*, Samoa*, San Marino*, Sao Tome and Principe, Saudi Arabia*, Senegal*, Serbia*, Seychelles*, Sierra Leone*, Singapore*, Slovakia*, Slovenia*, Solomon Islands*, Somalia, South Africa*, Spain*, Sri Lanka*, Sudan*, Suriname*, Swaziland*, Sweden*, Switzerland*, Syria*, Taiwan*, Tajikistan*, Tanzania*, Thailand*, Timor-Leste, Togo*, Tonga*, Trinidad and Tobago*, Tunisia*, Turkey*, Turkmenistan*, Tuvalu*, Uganda*, UK*[†], Ukraine*, United Arab Emirates*, Uruguay*, USA*[†], Uzbekistan*, Vanuatu*, Venezuela*, Viet Nam*, Yemen*, Zambia*, Zimbabwe*

* Party with safeguards agreements in force with the IAEA, as required by the treaty, or concluded by a nuclear weapon state on a voluntary basis.

[†] Nuclear weapon state as defined by the treaty.

[a] North Korea announced its withdrawal from the NPT on 10 Jan. 2003. A safeguards agreement was in force at that time. The current status of North Korea is disputed by the other parties.

Treaty text: International Atomic Energy Agency, INFCIRC/140, 22 Apr. 1970, <http://www. iaea.org/sites/default/files/publications/documents/infcircs/1970/infcirc140.pdf>

Additional safeguards protocols in force (133): Afghanistan, Albania, Andorra, Angola, Antigua and Barbuda, Armenia, Australia, Austria, Azerbaijan, Bahrain, Bangladesh, Belgium, Bosnia and Herzegovina, Botswana, Bulgaria, Burkina Faso, Burundi, Cambodia, Cameroon, Canada, Central African Republic, Chad, Chile, China, Colombia, Comoros, Congo (Democratic Republic of the), Congo (Republic of), Costa Rica, Côte d'Ivoire, Croatia, Cuba, Cyprus, Czech Republic, Denmark[1], Djibouti, Dominican Republic, Ecuador, El Salvador, Estonia, Euratom, Fiji, Finland, France, Gabon, Gambia, Georgia, Germany, Ghana, Greece, Guatemala, Haiti, Holy See, *Honduras*, Hungary, Iceland, India, Indonesia, Iraq, Ireland, Italy, Jamaica, Japan, Jordan, Kazakhstan, Kenya, Korea (South), Kuwait, Kyrgyzstan, Latvia, Lesotho, Libya, Liechtenstein, Lithuania, Luxembourg, Macedonia (Former Yugoslav Republic of), Madagascar, Malawi, Mali, Malta, Marshall Islands, Mauritania, Mauritius, Mexico, Moldova, Monaco, Mongolia, Montenegro, Morocco, Mozambique, Namibia, Netherlands, New Zealand, Nicaragua, Niger, Nigeria, Norway, Palau, Panama, Paraguay, Peru, Philippines, Poland, Portugal, Romania, Russia, Rwanda, Saint Kitts and Nevis, *Senegal*, Seychelles, Singapore, Slovakia, Slovenia, South Africa, Spain, Swaziland, Sweden, Switzerland, Tajikistan, Tanzania, *Thailand*, Togo, Turkey, Turkmenistan, Uganda, UK, Ukraine, United Arab Emirates, Uruguay, USA, Uzbekistan, Vanuatu, Viet Nam

[1] An additional protocol for the Danish territory of Greenland entered into force on 22 Mar. 2013.

Notes: Iran notified the IAEA that as of 16 Jan. 2016 it would provisionally apply the Additional Protocol that it signed in 2003 but has not yet ratified. Taiwan has agreed to apply the measures contained in the Model Additional Protocol.

Model Additional Safeguards Protocol text: International Atomic Energy Agency, INFCIRC/540 (corrected), Sep. 1997, <https://www.iaea.org/sites/default/files/infcirc540c.pdf>

Treaty on the Prohibition of the Emplacement of Nuclear Weapons and other Weapons of Mass Destruction on the Seabed and the Ocean Floor and in the Subsoil thereof (Seabed Treaty)

Opened for signature at London, Moscow and Washington, DC, on 11 February 1971; entered into force on 18 May 1972; depositaries British, Russian and US governments

The treaty prohibits implanting or emplacing on the seabed and the ocean floor and in the subsoil thereof beyond the outer limit of a 12-nautical mile (22-kilometre) seabed zone any nuclear weapons or any other types of weapon of mass destruction as well as structures, launching installations or any other facilities specifically designed for storing, testing or using such weapons.

Parties (95): Afghanistan, Algeria, Antigua and Barbuda, Argentina, Australia, Austria, Bahamas, Belarus, Belgium, Benin, Bosnia and Herzegovina, Botswana, Brazil*, Bulgaria, Canada*, Cabo Verde, Central African Republic, China, Congo (Republic of the), Côte d'Ivoire, Cuba, Cyprus, Czech Republic, Denmark, Dominican Republic, Ethiopia, Finland, Germany, Ghana, Greece, Guatemala, Guinea-Bissau, Hungary, Iceland, India*, Iran, Iraq, Ireland, Italy*, Jamaica, Japan, Jordan, Korea (South), Laos, Latvia, Lesotho, Libya, Liechtenstein, Luxembourg, Malaysia, Malta, Mauritius, Mexico*, Mongolia, Montenegro, Morocco, Nepal, Netherlands, New Zealand, Nicaragua, Niger, Norway, Panama, Philippines, Poland, Portugal, Qatar, Romania, Russia, Rwanda, Saint Kitts and Nevis, Saint Vincent and the Grenadines, Sao Tome and Principe, Saudi Arabia, Serbia*, Seychelles, Singapore, Slovakia, Slovenia, Solomon Islands, South Africa, Spain, Swaziland, Sweden, Switzerland, Taiwan,

Togo, Tunisia, Turkey*, UK, Ukraine, USA, Viet Nam*, Yemen, Zambia

* With reservation and/or declaration.

Signed but not ratified (21): Bolivia, Burundi, Cambodia, Cameroon, Colombia, Costa Rica, Equatorial Guinea, Gambia, Guinea, Honduras, Lebanon, Liberia, Madagascar, Mali, Myanmar, Paraguay, Senegal, Sierra Leone, Sudan, Tanzania, Uruguay

Treaty text: British Foreign and Commonwealth Office, Treaty Series no. 13 (1973), <https://assets.publishing.service.gov.uk/government/uploads/system/uploads/attachment_data/file/269694/Treaty_Prohib_Nuclear_Sea-Bed.pdf>

Convention on the Prohibition of the Development, Production and Stockpiling of Bacteriological (Biological) and Toxin Weapons and on their Destruction (Biological and Toxin Weapons Convention, BTWC)

Opened for signature at London, Moscow and Washington, DC, on 10 April 1972; entered into force on 26 March 1975; depositaries British, Russian and US governments

The convention prohibits the development, production, stockpiling or acquisition by other means or retention of microbial or other biological agents or toxins (whatever their origin or method of production) of types and in quantities that have no justification of prophylactic, protective or other peaceful purposes. It also prohibits weapons, equipment or means of delivery designed to use such agents or toxins for hostile purposes or in armed conflict. The destruction of the agents, toxins, weapons, equipment and means of delivery in the possession of the parties, or their diversion to peaceful purposes, should be effected not later than nine months after the entry into force of the convention for each country.

The parties hold annual political and technical meetings to strengthen implementation of the convention. A three-person Implementation Support Unit (ISU), based in Geneva, supports the parties in implementing the treaty, including facilitating the collection and distribution of annual confidence-building measures and supporting their efforts to achieve universal membership.

Parties (180): Afghanistan, Albania, Algeria, Andorra, Angola, Antigua and Barbuda, Argentina, Armenia, Australia, Austria*, Azerbaijan, Bahamas, Bahrain*, Bangladesh, Barbados, Belarus, Belgium, Belize, Benin, Bhutan, Bolivia, Bosnia and Herzegovina, Botswana, Brazil, Brunei Darussalam, Bulgaria, Burkina Faso, Burundi, Cabo Verde, Cambodia, Cameroon, Canada, Chile, China*, Colombia, Congo (Democratic Republic of the), Congo (Republic of the), Cook Islands, Costa Rica, Côte d'Ivoire, Croatia, Cuba, Cyprus, Czech Republic*, Denmark, Dominica, Dominican Republic, Ecuador, El Salvador, Equatorial Guinea, Estonia, Ethiopia, Fiji, Finland, France, Gabon, Gambia, Georgia, Germany, Ghana, Greece, Grenada, Guatemala, Guinea, Guinea-Bissau, Guyana, Holy See, Honduras, Hungary, Iceland, India*, Indonesia, Iran, Iraq, Ireland*, Italy, Jamaica, Japan, Jordan, Kazakhstan, Kenya, Korea (North), Korea (South)*, Kuwait*, Kyrgyzstan, Laos, Latvia, Lebanon, Lesotho, Liberia, Libya, Liechtenstein, Lithuania, Luxembourg, Macedonia (Former Yugoslav Republic of), Madagascar, Malawi, Malaysia*, Maldives, Mali, Malta, Marshall Islands, Mauritania, Mauritius, Mexico*, Moldova, Monaco, Mongolia, Montenegro, Morocco, Mozambique, Myanmar, Nauru, Nepal, Netherlands, New Zealand, Nicaragua, Niger, Nigeria, Norway, Oman, Pakistan, Palau, Panama, Papua New Guinea, Paraguay, Peru, Philippines, Poland, Portugal, Qatar, Romania, Russia, Rwanda, Saint Kitts and Nevis, Saint Lucia, Saint Vincent and the Grenadines, *Samoa*, San Marino, Sao Tome and Principe, Saudi Arabia, Senegal, Serbia, Seychelles, Sierra Leone,

Singapore, Slovakia*, Slovenia, Solomon Islands, South Africa, Spain, Sri Lanka, Sudan, Suriname, Swaziland, Sweden, Switzerland*, Taiwan, Tajikistan, Thailand, Timor-Leste, Togo, Tonga, Trinidad and Tobago, Tunisia, Turkey, Turkmenistan, Uganda, UK*, Ukraine, United Arab Emirates, Uruguay, USA, Uzbekistan, Vanuatu, Venezuela, Viet Nam, Yemen, Zambia, Zimbabwe

* With reservation and/or declaration.

Signed but not ratified (6): Central African Republic, Egypt, Haiti, Somalia, Syria, Tanzania

Note: In addition to the 180 parties as of 1 Jan. 2018, Palestine acceded to the convention on 9 Jan. 2018.

Treaty text: British Foreign and Commonwealth Office, Treaty Series no. 11 (1976), <https:// assets.publishing.service.gov.uk/government/uploads/system/uploads/attachment_data/ file/269698/Convention_Prohibition_Stock_Bacterio.pdf>

Convention on the Prohibition of Military or Any Other Hostile Use of Environmental Modification Techniques (Enmod Convention)

Opened for signature at Geneva on 18 May 1977; entered into force on 5 October 1978; depositary UN Secretary-General

The convention prohibits military or any other hostile use of environmental modification techniques that have widespread, long-lasting or severe effects as the means of destruction, damage or injury to states parties. The term 'environmental modification techniques' refers to any technique for changing—through the deliberate manipulation of natural processes—the dynamics, composition or structure of the earth, including its biota, lithosphere, hydrosphere and atmosphere, or of outer space. Understandings reached during the negotiations, but not written into the convention, define the terms 'widespread', 'long-lasting' and 'severe'.

Parties (78): Afghanistan, Algeria, Antigua and Barbuda, Argentina, Armenia, Australia, Austria, Bangladesh, Belarus, Belgium, Benin, Brazil, Bulgaria, Cabo Verde, Cameroon, Canada, Chile, China*, Costa Rica, Cuba, Cyprus, Czech Republic, Denmark, Dominica, Egypt, Estonia, Finland, Germany, Ghana, Greece, Guatemala, Honduras, Hungary, India, Ireland, Italy, Japan, Kazakhstan, Korea (North), Korea (South)*, Kuwait, Kyrgyzstan, Lithuania, Laos, Malawi, Mauritius, Mongolia, Netherlands*, New Zealand, Nicaragua, Niger, Norway, Pakistan, *Palestine*, Panama, Papua New Guinea, Poland, Romania, Russia, Saint Lucia, Saint Vincent and the Grenadines, Sao Tome and Principe, Slovakia, Slovenia, Solomon Islands, Spain, Sri Lanka, Sweden, Switzerland, Tajikistan, Tunisia, UK, Ukraine, Uruguay, USA, Uzbekistan, Viet Nam, Yemen

* With declaration.

Signed but not ratified (16): Bolivia, Congo (Democratic Republic of the), Ethiopia, Holy See, Iceland, Iran, Iraq, Lebanon, Liberia, Luxembourg, Morocco, Portugal, Sierra Leone, Syria, Turkey, Uganda

Convention text: United Nations Treaty Collection, <https://treaties.un.org/doc/ Treaties/1978/10/19781005 00-39 AM/Ch_XXVI_01p.pdf>

Convention on the Physical Protection of Nuclear Material and Nuclear Facilities

Original convention opened for signature at New York and Vienna on 3 March 1980; entered into force on 8 February 1987; amendments adopted on 8 July 2005; amended convention entered into force for its ratifying states on 8 May 2016; depositary IAEA Director General

The original convention—named the **Convention on the Physical Protection of Nuclear Material**—obligates its parties to protect nuclear material for peaceful purposes while in international transport.

The convention as amended and renamed also obligates its parties to protect nuclear facilities and material used for peaceful purposes while in storage.

Parties to the original convention (155): Afghanistan, Albania, Algeria*, Andorra*, Antigua and Barbuda, Argentina*, Armenia, Australia, Austria*, Azerbaijan*, Bahamas*, Bahrain*, Bangladesh, Belarus*, Belgium*, Bolivia, Bosnia and Herzegovina, Botswana, Brazil, Bulgaria, Burkina Faso, Cabo Verde, Cambodia, Cameroon, Canada, Central African Republic, Chile, China*, Colombia, Comoros, Congo (Democratic Republic of the), Costa Rica, Côte d'Ivoire, Croatia, Cuba*, Cyprus*, Czech Republic, Denmark*, Djibouti, Dominica, Dominican Republic, Ecuador, El Salvador*, Equatorial Guinea, Estonia, Euratom*, Fiji, Finland*, France*, Gabon, Georgia, Germany*, Ghana, Greece*, Grenada, Guatemala*, Guinea, Guinea-Bissau, Guyana, Honduras, Hungary, Iceland, India*, Indonesia*, Iraq, Ireland*, Israel*, Italy*, Jamaica, Japan, Jordan*, Kazakhstan, Kenya, Korea (South)*, Kuwait*, Kyrgyzstan, Laos*, Latvia, Lebanon, Lesotho, Libya, Liechtenstein, Lithuania, Luxembourg*, Macedonia (Former Yugoslav Republic of), Madagascar, Malawi, Mali, Malta, Marshall Islands, Mauritania, Mexico, Moldova, Monaco, Mongolia, Montenegro, Morocco, Mozambique*, *Myanmar**, Namibia, Nauru, Netherlands*, New Zealand*, Nicaragua, Niger, Nigeria, Niue, Norway*, Oman*, Pakistan*, Palau, Panama, Paraguay, Peru*, Philippines, Poland, Portugal*, Qatar*, Romania*, Russia*, Rwanda, Saint Kitts and Nevis, Saint Lucia*, San Marino, Saudi Arabia*, Senegal, Serbia, Seychelles, Singapore*, Slovakia, Slovenia, South Africa*, Spain*, Sudan, Swaziland, Sweden*, Switzerland*, Tajikistan, Tanzania, Togo, Tonga, Trinidad and Tobago, Tunisia, Turkey*, Turkmenistan, Uganda, UK*, Ukraine, United Arab Emirates, Uruguay, USA, Uzbekistan, Viet Nam*, Yemen, Zambia

* With reservation and/or declaration.

Note: In addition to the 155 parties as of 1 Jan. 2018, Palestine acceded to the convention on 11 Jan. 2018.

Signed but not ratified (1): Haiti

Convention text: International Atomic Energy Agency, INFCIRC/274, Nov. 1979, <https://www.iaea.org/sites/default/files/infcirc274.pdf>

Parties to the amended convention (115): Albania, Algeria, Antigua and Barbuda, Argentina, Armenia*, Australia, Austria, Azerbaijan*, Bahrain, *Bangladesh*, Belgium*, *Bolivia*, Bosnia and Herzegovina, Botswana, Bulgaria, Burkina Faso, Cameroon, Canada*, Chile, China, Colombia, *Costa Rica*, Côte d'Ivoire, Croatia, Cuba, Cyprus, Czech Republic, Denmark*, Djibouti, Dominican Republic, *Ecuador*, El Salvador, Estonia, Euratom*, Fiji, Finland, France, Gabon, Georgia, Germany, Ghana, Greece, Hungary, Iceland, India, Indonesia, Ireland, Israel*, Italy, Jamaica, Japan, Jordan, Kazakhstan, Kenya, Korea (South), Kuwait, Kyrgyzstan, Latvia, Lesotho, Libya, Liechtenstein, Lithuania, Luxembourg, Macedonia (Former Yugoslav Republic of), *Madagascar*, Mali, Malta, Marshall Islands, Mauritania, Mexico, Moldova, *Monaco*, Montenegro, Morocco, Myanmar*, *Namibia*, Nauru, Netherlands*, New Zealand*, Nicaragua, Niger, Nigeria, Norway, Pakistan*, Paraguay, Peru, Poland, Portugal, Qatar, Romania, Russia, Saint Lucia, San Marino, Saudi Arabia, *Senegal*, Serbia, Seychelles,

Singapore*, Slovakia, Slovenia, Spain, Swaziland, Sweden, Switzerland, Tajikistan, Tunisia, Turkey*, Turkmenistan, UK*, Ukraine, United Arab Emirates, Uruguay, USA*, Uzbekistan, Viet Nam

* With reservation and/or declaration.

Note: In addition to the 115 parties as of 1 Jan. 2018, Palestine accepted the amended convention on 11 Jan. 2018.

Amendment text and consolidated text of amended convention: International Atomic Energy Agency, INFCIRC/274/Rev.1/Mod.1, 9 May 2016, <https://www.iaea.org/sites/default/files/infcirc274r1m1.pdf>

Convention on Prohibitions or Restrictions on the Use of Certain Conventional Weapons which may be Deemed to be Excessively Injurious or to have Indiscriminate Effects (CCW Convention, or 'Inhumane Weapons' Convention)

Opened for signature with protocols I, II and III at New York on 10 April 1981; entered into force on 2 December 1983; depositary UN Secretary-General

The convention is an 'umbrella treaty', under which specific agreements can be concluded in the form of protocols. In order to become a party to the convention a state must ratify at least two of the protocols.

The amendment to Article I of the original convention was opened for signature at Geneva on 21 November 2001. It expands the scope of application to non-international armed conflicts. The amended convention entered into force on 18 May 2004.

Protocol I prohibits the use of weapons intended to injure using fragments that are not detectable in the human body by X-rays.

Protocol II prohibits or restricts the use of mines, booby-traps and other devices. Amended Protocol II, which entered into force on 3 December 1998, reinforces the constraints regarding anti-personnel mines.

Protocol III restricts the use of incendiary weapons.

Protocol IV, which entered into force on 30 July 1998, prohibits the employment of laser weapons specifically designed to cause permanent blindness to unenhanced vision.

Protocol V, which entered into force on 12 November 2006, recognizes the need for measures of a generic nature to minimize the risks and effects of explosive remnants of war.

Parties to the original convention and protocols (125): Afghanistan[2,] Algeria[2], Albania, Antigua and Barbuda[1], Argentina*, Australia, Austria, Bahrain[5], Bangladesh, Belarus, Belgium, Benin[2], Bolivia, Bosnia and Herzegovina, Brazil, Bulgaria, Burkina Faso, Burundi[4], Cabo Verde, Cambodia, Cameroon, Canada*, Chile[2], China*, Colombia, Costa Rica, Côte d'Ivoire[4], Croatia, Cuba, Cyprus*, Czech Republic, Denmark, Djibouti, Dominican Republic, Ecuador, El Salvador, Estonia[2], Finland, France*, Gabon[2], Georgia, Germany, Greece, Grenada[2], Guatemala, Guinea-Bissau, Holy See*, Honduras, Hungary, Iceland, India, Iraq, Ireland, Israel*[1], Italy*, Jamaica[2], Japan, Jordan[2], Kazakhstan[2], Korea (South)[3], Kuwait[2], Laos, Latvia, Lebanon[2], Lesotho, Liberia, Liechtenstein, Lithuania[2], Luxembourg, Macedonia (Former Yugoslav Republic of), Madagascar, Maldives[2], Mali, Malta, Mauritius, Mexico, Moldova, Monaco[3], Mongolia, Montenegro, Morocco[4], Nauru, Netherlands*, New Zealand, Nicaragua[2], Niger, Norway, Pakistan, Palestine[2], Panama, Paraguay, Peru[2], Philippines,

Poland, Portugal, Qatar[2], Romania*, Russia, Saint Vincent and the Grenadines[1], Saudi Arabia[2], Senegal[5], Serbia, Seychelles, Sierra Leone[2], Slovakia, Slovenia, South Africa, Spain, Sri Lanka, Sweden, Switzerland, Tajikistan, Togo, Tunisia, Turkey*[3], Turkmenistan[1], Uganda, UK*, Ukraine, United Arab Emirates[2], Uruguay, USA*, Uzbekistan, Venezuela, Zambia

* With reservation and/or declaration.
[1] Party only to 1981 protocols I and II.
[2] Party only to 1981 protocols I and III.
[3] Party only to 1981 Protocol I.
[4] Party only to 1981 Protocol II.
[5] Party only to 1981 Protocol III.

Signed but not ratified the original convention and protocols (4): Egypt, Nigeria, Sudan, Viet Nam

Parties to the amended convention and original protocols (86): Afghanistan, Algeria, Albania, Argentina, Australia, Austria, Bangladesh, Belarus, Belgium, *Benin*, Bosnia and Herzegovina, Brazil, Bulgaria, Burkina Faso, Canada, Chile, China, Colombia, Costa Rica, Croatia, Cuba, Czech Republic, Denmark, Dominican Republic, Ecuador, El Salvador, Estonia, Finland, France, Georgia, Germany, Greece, Grenada, Guatemala, Guinea-Bissau, Holy See*, Hungary, Iceland, India, Iraq, Ireland, Italy, Jamaica, Japan, Korea (South), Kuwait, Latvia, *Lebanon*, Lesotho, Liberia, Liechtenstein, Lithuania, Luxembourg, Macedonia (Former Yugoslav Republic of), Malta, Mexico*, Moldova, Montenegro, Netherlands, New Zealand, Nicaragua, Niger, Norway, Panama, Paraguay, Peru, Poland, Portugal, Romania, Russia, Serbia, Sierra Leone, Slovakia, Slovenia, South Africa, Spain, Sri Lanka, Sweden, Switzerland, Tunisia, Turkey, UK, Ukraine, Uruguay, USA, Zambia

* With reservation and/or declaration.

Parties to Amended Protocol II (104): Afghanistan, Albania, Argentina, Australia, Austria*, Bangladesh, Belarus*, Belgium*, Bolivia, Bosnia and Herzegovina, Brazil, Bulgaria, Burkina Faso, Cabo Verde, Cambodia, Cameroon, Canada, Chile, China*, Colombia, Costa Rica, Croatia, Cyprus, Czech Republic, Denmark*, Dominican Republic, Ecuador, El Salvador, Estonia, Finland*, France*, Gabon, Georgia, Germany*, Greece*, Grenada, Guatemala, Guinea-Bissau, Holy See, Honduras, Hungary*, Iceland, India, Iraq, Ireland*, Israel*, Italy*, Jamaica, Japan, Jordan, Korea (South)*, Kuwait, Latvia, *Lebanon*, Liberia, Liechtenstein*, Lithuania, Luxembourg, Macedonia (Former Yugoslav Republic of), Madagascar, Maldives, Mali, Malta, Moldova, Monaco, Montenegro, Morocco, Nauru, Netherlands*, New Zealand, Nicaragua, Niger, Norway, Pakistan*, Panama, Paraguay, Peru, Philippines, Poland, Portugal, Romania, Russia*, Saint Vincent and the Grenadines, Senegal, Serbia, Seychelles, Sierra Leone, Slovakia, Slovenia, South Africa*, Spain, Sri Lanka, Sweden, Switzerland, Tajikistan, Tunisia, Turkey, Turkmenistan, UK*, Ukraine*, Uruguay, USA*, Venezuela, Zambia

* With reservation and/or declaration

Parties to Protocol IV (108): Afghanistan, Algeria, Albania, Antigua and Barbuda, Argentina, Australia*, Austria*, Bahrain, Bangladesh, Belarus, Belgium*, Bolivia, Bosnia and Herzegovina, Brazil, Bulgaria, Burkina Faso, Cabo Verde, Cambodia, Cameroon, Canada*, Chile, China, Colombia, Costa Rica, Croatia, Cuba, Cyprus, Czech Republic, Denmark, Dominican Republic, Ecuador, El Salvador, Estonia, Finland, France, Gabon, Georgia, Germany*, Greece*, Grenada, Guatemala, Guinea-Bissau, Holy See, Honduras, Hungary, Iceland, India, Iraq, Ireland*, Israel*, Italy*, Jamaica, Japan, Kazakhstan, Kuwait, Latvia, Lesotho, Liberia, Liechtenstein*, Lithuania, Luxembourg, Macedonia (Former Yugoslav Republic of), Madagascar, Maldives, Mali, Malta, Mauritius, Mexico, Moldova, Mongolia, Montenegro, Morocco, Nauru, Netherlands*, New Zealand, Nicaragua, Niger, Norway, Pakistan, Panama, Paraguay, Peru, Philippines, Poland*, Portugal, Qatar, Romania, Russia, Saint Vincent and the Grenadines, Saudi Arabia, Serbia, Seychelles, Sierra Leone, Slovakia, Slovenia, South Africa*, Spain, Sri Lanka, Sweden*, Switzerland*, Tajikistan, Tunisia, Turkey,

UK*, Ukraine, Uruguay, USA*, Uzbekistan

* With reservation and/or declaration.

Parties to Protocol V (94): Afghanistan, Albania, Argentina*, Australia, Austria, Bahrain, Bangladesh, Belarus, Belgium, Bosnia and Herzegovina, Brazil, Bulgaria, Burkina Faso, Burundi, Cameroon, Canada, Chile, China*, Costa Rica, Côte d'Ivoire, Croatia, Cuba, Cyprus, Czech Republic, Denmark, Dominican Republic, Ecuador, El Salvador, Estonia, Finland, France, Gabon, Georgia, Germany, Greece, Grenada, Guatemala, Guinea-Bissau, Holy See*, Honduras, Hungary, Iceland, India, Iraq, Ireland, Italy, Jamaica, Korea (South), Kuwait, Laos, Latvia, Lesotho, Liberia, Liechtenstein, Lithuania, Luxembourg, Macedonia (Former Yugoslav Republic of), Madagascar, Mali, Malta, Moldova, Montenegro, Netherlands, New Zealand*, Nicaragua, Norway, Pakistan, *Palestine*, Panama, Paraguay, Peru, Poland, Portugal, Qatar, Romania, Russia, Saint Vincent and the Grenadines, Saudi Arabia, Senegal, Sierra Leone, Slovakia, Slovenia, South Africa, Spain, Sweden, Switzerland, Tajikistan, Tunisia, Turkmenistan, Ukraine, United Arab Emirates, Uruguay, USA*, Zambia

* With reservation and/or declaration.

Original convention and protocol text: United Nations Treaty Collection, <http://treaties. un.org/doc/Treaties/1983/12/19831202 01-19 AM/XXVI-2-revised.pdf>

Convention amendment text: United Nations Treaty Collection, <https://treaties.un.org/doc/ Treaties/2001/12/20011221 01-23 AM/Ch_XXVI_02_cp.pdf>

Amended Protocol II text: United Nations Treaty Collection, <https://treaties.un.org/doc/ Treaties/1996/05/19960503 01-38 AM/Ch_XXVI_02_bp.pdf>

Protocol IV text: United Nations Treaty Collection, <https://treaties.un.org/doc/ Treaties/1995/10/19951013 01-30 AM/Ch_XXVI_02_ap.pdf>

Protocol V text: United Nations Treaty Collection, <https://treaties.un.org/doc/ Treaties/2003/11/20031128 01-19 AM/Ch_XXVI_02_dp.pdf>

Convention on the Prohibition of the Development, Production, Stockpiling and Use of Chemical Weapons and on their Destruction (Chemical Weapons Convention, CWC)

Opened for signature at Paris on 13 January 1993; entered into force on 29 April 1997; depositary UN Secretary-General

The convention prohibits the development, production, acquisition, transfer, stockpiling and use of chemical weapons. The CWC regime consists of four 'pillars': disarmament, non-proliferation, assistance and protection against chemical weapons, and international cooperation on the peaceful uses of chemistry.

Each party undertook to destroy its chemical weapon stockpiles by 29 April 2012. Of the seven parties that had declared stocks of chemical weapons by that date, three had destroyed them (Albania, India and South Korea), Russia completed the destruction of its stockpile in 2017, while three (Iraq, Libya and the USA) continue to destroy their stocks. The stockpile of chemical weapons that Syria declared when it acceded to the CWC in 2013 was destroyed in 2016. Old and abandoned chemical weapons will continue to be destroyed as they are uncovered from, for example, former battlefields.

Parties (192): Afghanistan, Albania, Algeria, Andorra, Angola, Antigua and Barbuda, Argentina, Armenia, Australia, Austria, Azerbaijan, Bahamas, Bahrain, Bangladesh, Barbados, Belarus, Belgium, Belize, Benin, Bhutan, Bolivia, Bosnia and Herzegovina, Botswana, Brazil, Brunei

Darussalam, Bulgaria, Burkina Faso, Burundi, Cabo Verde, Cambodia, Cameroon, Canada, Central African Republic, Chad, Chile, China, Colombia, Comoros, Congo (Democratic Republic of the), Congo (Republic of the), Cook Islands, Costa Rica, Côte d'Ivoire, Croatia, Cuba, Cyprus, Czech Republic, Denmark, Djibouti, Dominica, Dominican Republic, Ecuador, El Salvador, Equatorial Guinea, Eritrea, Estonia, Ethiopia, Fiji, Finland, France, Gabon, Gambia, Georgia, Germany, Ghana, Greece, Grenada, Guatemala, Guinea, Guinea-Bissau, Guyana, Haiti, Holy See, Honduras, Hungary, Iceland, India, Indonesia, Iran, Iraq, Ireland, Italy, Jamaica, Japan, Jordan, Kazakhstan, Kenya, Kiribati, Korea (South), Kuwait, Kyrgyzstan, Laos, Latvia, Lebanon, Lesotho, Liberia, Libya, Liechtenstein, Lithuania, Luxembourg, Macedonia (Former Yugoslav Republic of), Madagascar, Malawi, Malaysia, Maldives, Mali, Malta, Marshall Islands, Mauritania, Mauritius, Mexico, Micronesia, Moldova, Monaco, Mongolia, Montenegro, Morocco, Mozambique, Myanmar, Namibia, Nauru, Nepal, Netherlands, New Zealand, Nicaragua, Niger, Nigeria, Niue, Norway, Oman, Pakistan, Palau, Panama, Papua New Guinea, Paraguay, Peru, Philippines, Poland, Portugal, Qatar, Romania, Russia, Rwanda, Saint Kitts and Nevis, Saint Lucia, Saint Vincent and the Grenadines, Samoa, San Marino, Sao Tome and Principe, Saudi Arabia, Senegal, Serbia, Seychelles, Sierra Leone, Singapore, Slovakia, Slovenia, Solomon Islands, Somalia, South Africa, Spain, Sri Lanka, Sudan, Suriname, Swaziland, Sweden, Switzerland, Syria, Tajikistan, Tanzania, Thailand, Timor-Leste, Togo, Tonga, Trinidad and Tobago, Tunisia, Turkey, Turkmenistan, Tuvalu, Uganda, UK, Ukraine, United Arab Emirates, Uruguay, USA, Uzbekistan, Vanuatu, Venezuela, Viet Nam, Yemen, Zambia, Zimbabwe

Signed but not ratified (1): Israel

Note: In addition to the 192 parties as of 1 Jan. 2018, Palestine deposited its instrument of accession to the convention on 29 Dec. 2017. However, it withdrew that instrument on 8 Jan. 2018, before the convention had entered into force for it.

Convention text: United Nations Treaty Collection, <https://treaties.un.org/doc/Treaties/1997/04/19970429 07-52 PM/CTC-XXVI_03_ocred.pdf>

Comprehensive Nuclear-Test-Ban Treaty (CTBT)

Opened for signature at New York on 24 September 1996; not in force; depositary UN Secretary-General

The treaty would prohibit the carrying out of any nuclear weapon test explosion or any other nuclear explosion and urges each party to prevent any such nuclear explosion at any place under its jurisdiction or control and refrain from causing, encouraging or in any way participating in the carrying out of any nuclear weapon test explosion or any other nuclear explosion.

The treaty will enter into force 180 days after the date that all of the 44 states listed in an annex to the treaty have deposited their instruments of ratification. All 44 states possess nuclear power reactors and/or nuclear research reactors.

States whose ratification is required for entry into force (44): Algeria, Argentina, Australia, Austria, Bangladesh, Belgium, Brazil, Bulgaria, Canada, Chile, China*, Colombia, Congo (Democratic Republic of the), Egypt*, Finland, France, Germany, Hungary, India*, Indonesia, Iran*, Israel*, Italy, Japan, Korea (North)*, Korea (South), Mexico, Netherlands, Norway, Pakistan*, Peru, Poland, Romania, Russia, Slovakia, South Africa, Spain, Sweden, Switzerland, Turkey, UK, Ukraine, USA*, Viet Nam

* Has not ratified the treaty.

Ratifications deposited (166): Afghanistan, Albania, Algeria, Andorra, Angola, Antigua and Barbuda, Argentina, Armenia, Australia, Austria, Azerbaijan, Bahamas, Bahrain, Bangladesh,

Barbados, Belarus, Belgium, Belize, Benin, Bolivia, Bosnia and Herzegovina, Botswana, Brazil, Brunei Darussalam, Bulgaria, Burkina Faso, Burundi, Cabo Verde, Cambodia, Cameroon, Canada, Central African Republic, Chad, Chile, Colombia, Congo (Democratic Republic of the), Cook Islands, Costa Rica, Côte d'Ivoire, Congo (Republic of the), Croatia, Cyprus, Czech Republic, Denmark, Djibouti, Dominican Republic, Ecuador, El Salvador, Eritrea, Estonia, Ethiopia, Fiji, Finland, France, Gabon, Georgia, Germany, Ghana, Greece, Grenada, Guatemala, Guinea, Guinea-Bissau, Guyana, Haiti, Holy See, Honduras, Hungary, Iceland, Indonesia, Iraq, Ireland, Italy, Jamaica, Japan, Jordan, Kazakhstan, Kenya, Kiribati, Korea (South), Kuwait, Kyrgyzstan, Laos, Latvia, Lebanon, Lesotho, Liberia, Libya, Liechtenstein, Lithuania, Luxembourg, Macedonia (Former Yugoslav Republic of), Madagascar, Malawi, Malaysia, Maldives, Mali, Malta, Marshall Islands, Mauritania, Mexico, Micronesia, Moldova, Monaco, Mongolia, Montenegro, Morocco, Mozambique, Myanmar, Namibia, Nauru, Netherlands, New Zealand, Nicaragua, Niger, Nigeria, Niue, Norway, Oman, Palau, Panama, Paraguay, Peru, Philippines, Poland, Portugal, Qatar, Romania, Russia, Rwanda, Saint Kitts and Nevis, Saint Lucia, Saint Vincent and the Grenadines, Samoa, San Marino, Senegal, Serbia, Seychelles, Sierra Leone, Singapore, Slovakia, Slovenia, South Africa, Spain, Sudan, Suriname, Sweden, Swaziland, Switzerland, Tajikistan, Tanzania, Togo, Trinidad and Tobago, Tunisia, Turkey, Turkmenistan, Uganda, UK, Ukraine, United Arab Emirates, Uruguay, Uzbekistan, Vanuatu, Venezuela, Viet Nam, Zambia

Signed but not ratified (17): China, Comoros, Egypt, Equatorial Guinea, Gambia, Iran, Israel, Nepal, Papua New Guinea, Sao Tome and Principe, Solomon Islands, Sri Lanka, Thailand, Timor-Leste, USA, Yemen, Zimbabwe

Treaty text: United Nations Treaty Collection, <https://treaties.un.org/doc/Treaties/1997/09/19970910 07-37 AM/Ch_XXVI_04p.pdf>

Convention on the Prohibition of the Use, Stockpiling, Production and Transfer of Anti-Personnel Mines and on their Destruction (APM Convention)

Opened for signature at Ottawa on 3–4 December 1997 and at New York on 5 December 1997; entered into force on 1 March 1999; depositary UN Secretary-General

The convention prohibits anti-personnel mines (APMs), which are defined as mines designed to be exploded by the presence, proximity or contact of a person and which will incapacitate, injure or kill one or more persons.

Each party undertakes to destroy all of its stockpiled APMs as soon as possible but not later that four years after the entry into force of the convention for that state party. Each party also undertakes to destroy all APMs in mined areas under its jurisdiction or control not later than 10 years after the entry into force of the convention for that state party.

Parties (164): Afghanistan, Albania, Algeria, Andorra, Angola, Antigua and Barbuda, Argentina*, Australia*, Austria*, Bahamas, Bangladesh, Barbados, Belarus, Belgium, Belize, Benin, Bhutan, Bolivia, Bosnia and Herzegovina, Botswana, Brazil, Brunei Darussalam, Bulgaria, Burkina Faso, Burundi, Cabo Verde, Cambodia, Cameroon, Canada*, Central African Republic, Chad, Chile*, Colombia, Comoros, Congo (Democratic Republic of the), Congo (Republic of the), Cook Islands, Costa Rica, Côte d'Ivoire, Croatia, Cyprus, Czech Republic*, Denmark, Djibouti, Dominica, Dominican Republic, Ecuador, El Salvador, Equatorial Guinea, Eritrea, Estonia, Ethiopia, Fiji, Finland, France, Gabon, Gambia, Germany, Ghana, Greece*, Grenada, Guatemala, Guinea, Guinea-Bissau, Guyana, Haiti, Holy See, Honduras, Hungary,

Iceland, Indonesia, Iraq, Ireland, Italy, Jamaica, Japan, Jordan, Kenya, Kiribati, Kuwait, Latvia, Lesotho, Liberia, Liechtenstein, Lithuania*, Luxembourg, Macedonia (Former Yugoslav Republic of), Madagascar, Malawi, Malaysia, Maldives, Mali, Malta, Mauritania, Mauritius*, Mexico, Moldova, Monaco, Montenegro*, Mozambique, Namibia, Nauru, Netherlands, New Zealand, Nicaragua, Niger, Nigeria, Niue, Norway, Oman, Palau, *Palestine*, Panama, Papua New Guinea, Paraguay, Peru, Philippines, Poland, Portugal, Qatar, Romania, Rwanda, Saint Kitts and Nevis, Saint Lucia, Saint Vincent and the Grenadines, Samoa, San Marino, Sao Tome and Principe, Senegal, Serbia*, Seychelles, Sierra Leone, Slovakia, Slovenia, Solomon Islands, Somalia, South Africa*, South Sudan, Spain, *Sri Lanka*, Sudan, Suriname, Swaziland, Sweden*, Switzerland*, Tajikistan, Tanzania, Thailand, Timor-Leste, Togo, Trinidad and Tobago, Tunisia, Turkey, Turkmenistan, Tuvalu, Uganda, UK*, Ukraine, Uruguay, Vanuatu, Venezuela, Yemen, Zambia, Zimbabwe

* With reservation and/or declaration.

Signed but not ratified (1): Marshall Islands

Convention text: United Nations Treaty Collection, <https://treaties.un.org/doc/Treaties/1997/09/19970918 07-53 AM/Ch_XXVI_05p.pdf>

Convention on Cluster Munitions

Opened for signature at Oslo on 3 December 2008; entered into force on 1 August 2010; depositary UN Secretary-General

The convention's objectives are to prohibit the use, production, transfer and stockpiling of cluster munitions that cause unacceptable harm to civilians, and to establish a framework for cooperation and assistance that ensures adequate provision of care and rehabilitation for victims, clearance of contaminated areas, risk reduction education and destruction of stockpiles. The convention does not apply to mines.

Parties (102): Afghanistan, Albania, Andorra, Antigua and Barbuda, Australia, Austria, Belgium*, Belize, *Benin*, Bolivia, Bosnia and Herzegovina, Botswana, Bulgaria, Burkina Faso, Burundi, Cabo Verde, Cameroon, Canada, Chad, Chile, Colombia, Comoros, Cook Islands, Congo (Republic of the), Costa Rica, Côte d'Ivoire, Croatia, Cuba, Czech Republic, Denmark, Dominican Republic, Ecuador, El Salvador*, Fiji, France, Germany, Ghana, Grenada, Guatemala, Guinea, Guinea-Bissau, Guyana, Holy See*, Honduras, Hungary, Iceland, Iraq, Ireland, Italy, Japan, Laos, Lebanon, Lesotho, Liechtenstein, Lithuania, Luxembourg, Macedonia (Former Yugoslav Republic of), *Madagascar*, Malawi, Mali, Malta, Mauritania, Mauritius, Mexico, Moldova, Monaco, Montenegro, Mozambique, Nauru, Netherlands, New Zealand, Nicaragua, Niger, Norway, Palestine, Palau, Panama, Paraguay, Peru, Portugal, Rwanda, Samoa, Saint Kitts and Nevis, Saint Vincent and the Grenadines, San Marino, Senegal, Seychelles, Sierra Leone, Slovakia, Slovenia, Somalia, South Africa, Spain, Swaziland, Sweden, Switzerland, Togo, Trinidad and Tobago, Tunisia, UK, Uruguay, Zambia

* With reservation and/or declaration.

Signed but not ratified (17): Angola, Central African Republic, Congo (Democratic Republic of the), Cyprus, Djibouti, Gambia, Haiti, Indonesia, Jamaica, Kenya, Liberia, Namibia, Nigeria, Philippines, Sao Tome and Principe, Tanzania, Uganda

Note: In addition to the 102 parties as of 1 Jan. 2018, Sri Lanka acceded to the convention on 1 Mar. 2018.

Convention text: United Nations Treaty Collection, <https://treaties.un.org/doc/Publication/CTC/26-6.pdf>

Arms Trade Treaty (ATT)

Opened for signature at New York on 3 June 2013; entered into force on 24 December 2014; depositary UN Secretary-General

The object of the treaty is to establish the highest possible common international standards for regulating the international trade in conventional arms; and to prevent and eradicate the illicit trade in conventional arms and prevent their diversion. Among other things, the treaty prohibits a state party from authorizing a transfer of arms if they are to be used in the commission of genocide, crimes against humanity or war crimes. The treaty also requires the exporting state to assess the potential for any arms proposed for export to undermine peace and security or be used to commit serious violations of international humanitarian law or international human rights law. Each party is to submit an annual report concerning authorized or actual exports and imports of conventional arms.

Parties (92): Albania, Antigua and Barbuda, Argentina, Australia, Austria, Bahamas, Barbados, Belgium, Belize, Benin, Bosnia and Herzegovina, Bulgaria, Burkina Faso, Cabo Verde, Central African Republic, Chad, Costa Rica, Côte d'Ivoire, Croatia, Cyprus, Czech Republic, Denmark, Dominica, Dominican Republic, El Salvador, Estonia, Finland, France, Georgia, Germany, Ghana, Greece, Grenada, Guatemala, Guinea, Guyana, *Honduras*, Hungary, Iceland, Ireland, Italy, Jamaica, Japan, Korea (South), Latvia, Lesotho, Liberia, Liechtenstein, Lithuania, Luxembourg, Macedonia (Former Yugoslav Republic of), Madagascar, Mali, Malta, Mauritania, Mauritius, Mexico, Moldova, Monaco, Montenegro, Netherlands, New Zealand, Niger, Nigeria, Norway, Panama, Paraguay, Peru, Poland, Portugal, Romania, Saint Kitts and Nevis, Saint Lucia, Saint Vincent and the Grenadines, Samoa, San Marino, Senegal, Serbia, Seychelles, Sierra Leone, Slovakia, Slovenia, South Africa, Spain, Sweden, Switzerland, Togo, Trinidad and Tobago, Tuvalu, UK, Uruguay, Zambia

Note: In addition to the 92 parties as of 1 Jan. 2018, Kazakhstan and Palestine deposited their instruments of accession in 2017 but will not become states parties until Mar. 2018.

Signed but not ratified (41): Andorra, Angola, Bahrain, Bangladesh, Brazil, Burundi, Cambodia, Cameroon, Chile, Colombia, Comoros, Congo (Republic of the), Djibouti, Gabon, Guinea-Bissau, Haiti, Israel, Kiribati, Lebanon, Libya, Malawi, Malaysia, Mongolia, Mozambique, Namibia, Nauru, Palau, Philippines, Rwanda, Sao Tome and Principe, Singapore, Suriname, Swaziland, Tanzania, Thailand, Turkey, Ukraine, United Arab Emirates, USA, Vanuatu, Zimbabwe

Treaty text: United Nations Treaty Collection, <https://treaties.un.org/doc/Treaties/2013/04/20130410 12-01 PM/Ch_XXVI_08.pdf>

Treaty on the Prohibition of Nuclear Weapons (TPNW)

Opened for signature at New York on 20 September 2017; not in force; depositary UN Secretary-General

In its preamble, the treaty cites the catastrophic humanitarian and environmental consequences of the use of nuclear weapons and invokes the principles of international humanitarian law and the rules of international law applicable in armed conflict. The treaty prohibits states parties from developing, testing, producing, manufacturing, acquiring, possessing, or stockpiling nuclear weapons or other nuclear explosive devices. States parties are prohibited from using or threatening to use nuclear weapons and other nuclear explosive devices. Finally, states parties cannot allow the stationing, installation, or deployment of nuclear weapons and other nuclear explosive devices in their territory.

The treaty outlines procedures for eliminating the nuclear weapons of any state party that owned, possessed or controlled them after 7 July 2017, to be supervised by a 'competent international authority or authorities' to be designated by the states parties. Each party is required to maintain its existing safeguards agreements with the International Atomic Energy Agency (IAEA) and must, at a minimum, conclude and bring into force a comprehensive safeguards agreement (INFCIRC/153) with the agency. The treaty also contains provisions on assisting the victims of the testing or use of nuclear weapons and taking necessary and appropriate measures towards the environmental remediation of contaminated areas.

The treaty will enter into force 90 days after the deposit of the 50th instrument of ratification. Membership of the treaty does not prejudice the parties' other, compatible international obligations (such as the NPT and the CTBT). The treaty is of unlimited duration. States parties have the right to withdraw from the treaty 12 months after giving formal notification of their intention to do so.

Ratifications deposited (3): Guyana, Holy See, Thailand

Signed but not ratified (53): Algeria, Austria, Bangladesh, Brazil, Cabo Verde, Central African Republic, Chile, Comoros, Congo (Democratic Republic of the), Congo (Republic of the), Costa Rica, Côte d'Ivoire, Cuba, Ecuador, El Salvador, Fiji, Gambia, Ghana, Guatemala, Honduras, Indonesia, Ireland, Jamaica, Kiribati, Laos, Libya, Liechtenstein, Madagascar, Malawi, Malaysia, Mexico, Namibia, Nepal, New Zealand, Nicaragua, Nigeria, Palau, Palestine, Panama, Paraguay, Peru, Philippines, Samoa, San Marino, Sao Tome and Principe, South Africa, St Vincent and the Grenadines, Togo, Tuvalu, Uruguay, Vanuatu, Venezuela, Viet Nam

Note: In addition to the 3 states that had ratified the treaty as of 1 Jan. 2018, Mexico ratified it on 16 Jan. 2018, Cuba on 30 Jan., Palestine on 22 Mar. and Venezuela on 27 Mar. In addition to the 53 states that had signed but not ratified the treaty as of 1 Jan. 2018, Kazakhstan signed it on 2 Mar.

Treaty text: United Nations Treaty Collection, <https://treaties.un.org/doc/Treaties/2017/07/20170707 03-42 PM/Ch_XXVI_9.pdf>

II. Regional treaties

Treaty for the Prohibition of Nuclear Weapons in Latin America and the Caribbean (Treaty of Tlatelolco)

Original treaty opened for signature at Mexico City on 14 February 1967; entered into force on 22 April 1968; treaty amended in 1990, 1991 and 1992; depositary Mexican Government

The treaty prohibits the testing, use, manufacture, production or acquisition by any means, as well as the receipt, storage, installation, deployment and any form of possession of any nuclear weapons by any country of Latin America and the Caribbean and in the surrounding seas.

The parties should conclude agreements individually with the IAEA for the application of safeguards to their nuclear activities. The IAEA has the exclusive power to carry out special inspections.

The treaty is open for signature by all the independent states of Latin America and the Caribbean.

Under *Additional Protocol I* states with territories within the zone—France, the Netherlands, the UK and the USA—undertake to apply the statute of military denuclearization to these territories.

Under *Additional Protocol II* the recognized nuclear weapon states—China, France, Russia, the UK and the USA—undertake to respect the military denuclearization of Latin America and the Caribbean and not to contribute to acts involving a violation of the treaty, nor to use or threaten to use nuclear weapons against the parties to the treaty.

Parties to the original treaty (33): Antigua and Barbuda[1], Argentina[1], Bahamas, Barbados[1], Belize[2], Bolivia, Brazil[1], Chile[1], Colombia[1], Costa Rica[1], Cuba, Dominica, Dominican Republic[3], Ecuador[1], El Salvador[1], Grenada[1], Guatemala[1], Guyana[3], Haiti, Honduras[1], Jamaica[1], Mexico[1], Nicaragua[3], Panama[1], Paraguay[1], Peru[1], Saint Kitts and Nevis[1], Saint Lucia[1], Saint Vincent and the Grenadines[4], Suriname[1], Trinidad and Tobago[1], Uruguay[1], Venezuela[1]

[1] Has ratified the amendments of 1990, 1991 and 1992.
[2] Has ratified the amendments of 1990 and 1992 only.
[3] Has ratified the amendment of 1992 only.
[4] Has ratified the amendments of 1991 and 1992 only.

Parties to Additional Protocol I (4): France*, Netherlands*, UK*, USA*

Parties to Additional Protocol II (5): China*, France*, Russia*, UK*, USA*

* With reservation and/or declaration.

Original treaty text: United Nations Treaty Series, vol. 634 (1968), <https://treaties.un.org/doc/Publication/UNTS/Volume 634/v634.pdf>

Amended treaty text: Agency for the Prohibition of Nuclear Weapons in Latin America and the Caribbean, S/Inf. 652 Rev. 3, 29 Jan. 2002, <http://www.opanal.org/wp-content/uploads/2015/08/Treaty_Tlatelolco.pdf>

South Pacific Nuclear Free Zone Treaty (Treaty of Rarotonga)

Opened for signature at Rarotonga on 6 August 1985; entered into force on 11 December 1986; depositary Secretary General of the Pacific Islands Forum Secretariat

The South Pacific Nuclear Free Zone is defined as the area between the zone of application of the Treaty of Tlatelolco in the east and the west coast of Australia and the western border of Papua New Guinea and between the zone of application of the Antarctic Treaty in the south and, approximately, the equator in the north.

The treaty prohibits the manufacture or acquisition of any nuclear explosive device, as well as possession or control over such device by the parties anywhere inside or outside the zone. The parties also undertake not to supply nuclear material or equipment, unless subject to IAEA safeguards, and to prevent in their territories the stationing or testing of any nuclear explosive device and undertake not to dump, and to prevent the dumping of, radioactive waste and other radioactive matter at sea anywhere within the zone. Each party remains free to allow visits, as well as transit, by foreign ships and aircraft.

The treaty is open for signature by the members of the Pacific Islands Forum.

Under *Protocol 1* France, the UK and the USA undertake to apply the treaty prohibitions relating to the manufacture, stationing and testing of nuclear explosive devices in the territories situated within the zone for which they are internationally responsible.

Under *Protocol 2* China, France, Russia, the UK and the USA undertake not to use or threaten to use a nuclear explosive device against the parties to the treaty or against any territory within the zone for which a party to Protocol 1 is internationally responsible.

Under *Protocol 3* China, France, Russia, the UK and the USA undertake not to test any nuclear explosive device anywhere within the zone.

Parties (13): Australia, Cook Islands, Fiji, Kiribati, Nauru, New Zealand, Niue, Papua New Guinea, Samoa, Solomon Islands, Tonga, Tuvalu, Vanuatu

Parties to Protocol 1 (2): France*, UK*; *signed but not ratified (1)*: USA

Parties to Protocol 2 (4): China, France*, Russia, UK*; *signed but not ratified (1)*: USA

Parties to Protocol 3 (4): China*, France*, Russia*, UK*; *signed but not ratified (1)*: USA

* With reservation and/or declaration.

Treaty text: Pacific Islands Forum Secretariat, <http://www.forumsec.org/wp-content/uploads/2018/02/South-Pacific-Nuclear-Zone-Treaty-Raratonga-Treaty-1.pdf>

Treaty on Conventional Armed Forces in Europe (CFE Treaty)

Original treaty signed by the 16 member states of the North Atlantic Treaty Organization (NATO) and the 6 member states of the Warsaw Treaty Organization (WTO) at Paris on 19 November 1990; entered into force on 9 November 1992; depositary Dutch Government

The treaty sets ceilings on five categories of treaty-limited equipment (TLE)—battle tanks, armoured combat vehicles, artillery of at least 100-mm calibre, combat aircraft and attack helicopters—in an area stretching from the Atlantic Ocean to the Ural Mountains (the Atlantic-to-the-Urals, ATTU).

The treaty was negotiated by the member states of the WTO and NATO within the framework of the Conference on Security and Co-operation in Europe (from 1995 the Organization for Security and Co-operation in Europe, OSCE).

The **1992 Tashkent Agreement**, adopted by the former Soviet republics with territories within the ATTU area of application (with the exception of Estonia, Latvia and Lithuania) and the **1992 Oslo Document** (Final Document of the Extraordinary Conference of the States Parties to the CFE Treaty) introduced modifications to the treaty required because of the emergence of new states after the break-up of the USSR.

Parties (30): Armenia, Azerbaijan, Belarus, Belgium[2], Bulgaria[2], Canada[2], Czech Republic[2], Denmark[2], France, Georgia, Germany[2], Greece, Hungary[2], Iceland[2], Italy[2], Kazakhstan, Luxembourg[2], Moldova[2], Netherlands[2], Norway, Poland, Portugal[2], Romania, Russia[1], Slovakia[2], Spain, Turkey[2], UK[2], Ukraine, USA[2]

[1] On 14 July 2007 Russia declared its intention to suspend its participation in the CFE Treaty

and associated documents and agreements, which took effect on 12 Dec. 2007. In Mar. 2015 Russia announced that it had decided to completely halt its participation in the treaty.

[2] In Nov.–Dec. 2011 these countries notified the depositary that they will cease to perform their obligations under the treaty with regard to Russia.

The first review conference of the CFE Treaty adopted the **1996 Flank Document**, which reorganized the flank areas geographically and numerically, allowing Russia and Ukraine to deploy TLE in a less constraining manner.

Original (1990) treaty text: Dutch Ministry of Foreign Affairs, <https://treatydatabase. overheid.nl/en/Verdrag/Details/004285/004285_Gewaarmerkt_0.pdf>

Consolidated (1993) treaty text: Dutch Ministry of Foreign Affairs, <http://wetten.overheid.nl/ BWBV0002009/>

Flank Document text: Organization for Security and Co-operation in Europe, <http://www. osce.org/library/14099?download=true>, annex A

Concluding Act of the Negotiation on Personnel Strength of Conventional Armed Forces in Europe (CFE-1A Agreement)

Signed by the parties to the CFE Treaty at Helsinki on 10 July 1992; entered into force simultaneously with the CFE Treaty; depositary Dutch Government

This politically binding agreement sets ceilings on the number of personnel of the conventional land-based armed forces of the parties within the ATTU area.

Agreement text: Organization for Security and Co-operation in Europe, <http:// www.osce.org/library/14093?download=true>

Agreement on Adaptation of the Treaty on Conventional Armed Forces in Europe

Signed by the parties to the CFE Treaty at Istanbul on 19 November 1999; not in force; depositary Dutch Government

With the dissolution of the WTO and the accession of some former members to NATO, this agreement would have replaced the CFE Treaty's bloc-to-bloc military balance with a regional balance, established individual state limits on TLE holdings, and provided for a new structure of limitations and new military flexibility mechanisms, flank sub-limits and enhanced transparency. It would have opened the CFE regime to all other European states. It would have entered into force when ratified by all of the signatories.

The **1999 Final Act of the Conference of the CFE States Parties**, with annexes, contains politically binding arrangements with regard to Georgia, Moldova and Central Europe and to withdrawals of armed forces from foreign territories (known as the Istanbul commitments). Many signatories of the Agreement on Adaptation made their ratification contingent on the implementation of these political commitments.

Ratifications deposited (3): Belarus, Kazakhstan, Russia*[1]

* With reservation and/or declaration.

[1] On 14 July 2007 Russia declared its intention to suspend its participation in the CFE Treaty and associated documents and agreements, which took effect on 12 Dec. 2007. In Mar. 2015 Russia announced that it had decided to completely halt its participation in the treaty.

Note: Ukraine ratified the Agreement on Adaptation on 21 Sep. 2000 but did not deposited its instrument with the depositary.

Agreement text: Dutch Ministry of Foreign Affairs, <https://treatydatabase.overheid.nl/en/Verdrag/Details/009241/009241_Gewaarmerkt_0.pdf>

Treaty text as amended by 1999 agreement: SIPRI Yearbook 2000, pp. 627–42

Final Act text: Organization for Security and Co-operation in Europe, <http://www.osce.org/library/14114>

Treaty on Open Skies

Opened for signature at Helsinki on 24 March 1992; entered into force on 1 January 2002; depositaries Canadian and Hungarian governments

The treaty obligates the parties to submit their territories to short-notice unarmed surveillance flights. The area of application stretches from Vancouver, Canada, eastward to Vladivostok, Russia.

The treaty was negotiated between the member states of the WTO and NATO. Since 1 July 2002 any state can apply to accede to the treaty.

Parties (34): Belarus, Belgium, Bosnia and Herzegovina, Bulgaria, Canada, Croatia, Czech Republic, Denmark, Estonia, Finland, France, Georgia, Germany, Greece, Hungary, Iceland, Italy, Latvia, Lithuania, Luxembourg, Netherlands, Norway, Poland, Portugal, Romania, Russia, Slovakia, Slovenia, Spain, Sweden, Turkey, UK, Ukraine, USA

Signed but not ratified (1): Kyrgyzstan

Treaty text: Canada Treaty Information, <http://www.treaty-accord.gc.ca/text-texte.aspx?id=102747>

Treaty on the Southeast Asia Nuclear Weapon-Free Zone (Treaty of Bangkok)

Signed by the 10 member states of the Association of Southeast Asian Nations (ASEAN) at Bangkok on 15 December 1995; entered into force on 27 March 1997; depositary Thai Government

The South East Asia Nuclear Weapon-Free Zone includes the territories, the continental shelves and the exclusive economic zones of the states parties. The treaty prohibits the development, manufacture, acquisition or testing of nuclear weapons inside or outside the zone as well as the stationing and transport of nuclear weapons in or through the zone. Each state party may decide for itself whether to allow visits and transit by foreign ships and aircraft. The parties undertake not to dump at sea or discharge into the atmosphere anywhere within the zone any radioactive material or waste or dispose of radioactive material on land. The parties should conclude an agreement with the IAEA for the application of full-scope safeguards to their peaceful nuclear activities.

The treaty is open for accession by all states of South East Asia.

Under a *Protocol* to the treaty, China, France, Russia, the UK and the USA are to undertake not to use or threaten to use nuclear weapons against any state party to the treaty. They should further undertake not to use nuclear weapons within the zone. The protocol will enter into force for each state party on the date of its deposit of the instrument of ratification.

Parties (10): Brunei Darussalam, Cambodia, Indonesia, Laos, Malaysia, Myanmar, Philippines, Singapore, Thailand, Viet Nam

Protocol: no signatures, no parties

Treaty text: ASEAN Secretariat, <http://asean.org/?static_post=treaty-on-the-southeast-asia-nuclear-weapon-free-zone>

Protocol text: ASEAN Secretariat, <http://asean.org/?static_post=protocol-to-the-treaty-on-the-southeeast-asia-nuclear-weapon-free-zone>

African Nuclear-Weapon-Free Zone Treaty (Treaty of Pelindaba)

Opened for signature at Cairo on 11 April 1996; entered into force on 15 July 2009; depositary Secretary-General of the African Union

The African Nuclear Weapon-Free Zone includes the territory of the continent of Africa, island states members of the African Union (AU) and all islands considered by the AU to be part of Africa.

The treaty prohibits the research, development, manufacture and acquisition of nuclear explosive devices and the testing or stationing of any nuclear explosive device in the zone. Each party remains free to allow visits and transit by foreign ships and aircraft. The treaty also prohibits any attack against nuclear installations. The parties undertake not to dump or permit the dumping of radioactive waste and other radioactive matter anywhere within the zone. Each party should individually conclude an agreement with the IAEA for the application of comprehensive safeguards to their peaceful nuclear activities.

The treaty is open for accession by all the states of Africa.

Under *Protocol I* China, France, Russia, the UK and the USA undertake not to use or threaten to use a nuclear explosive device against the parties to the treaty.

Under *Protocol II* China, France, Russia, the UK and the USA undertake not to test nuclear explosive devices within the zone.

Under *Protocol III* France and Spain are to undertake to observe certain provisions of the treaty with respect to the territories within the zone for which they are internationally responsible.

Parties (41): Algeria, Angola, Benin, Botswana, Burkina Faso, Burundi, Cameroon, Chad, Comoros, Congo (Republic of the), Côte d'Ivoire, Equatorial Guinea, Ethiopia, Gabon, Gambia, Ghana, Guinea, Guinea-Bissau, Kenya, Lesotho, Libya, Madagascar, Malawi, Mali, Mauritania, Mauritius, Mozambique, Namibia, Niger, Nigeria, Rwanda, Sahrawi Arab Democratic Republic (Western Sahara), Seychelles, Senegal, South Africa, Swaziland, Tanzania, Togo, Tunisia, Zambia, Zimbabwe

Signed but not ratified (13): Cabo Verde, Central African Republic, Congo (Democratic Republic of the), Djibouti, Egypt, Eritrea, Liberia, Morocco, Sao Tome and Principe, Sierra Leone, Somalia, Sudan, Uganda

Parties to Protocol I (4): China, France*, Russia*, UK*; *signed but not ratified (1)*: USA*

Parties to Protocol II (4): China, France*, Russia*, UK*; *signed but not ratified (1)*: USA*

Parties to Protocol III (1): France*

* With reservation and/or declaration.

Treaty text: African Union, <http://au.int/sites/default/files/treaties/7777-treaty-0018_-_ the_african_nuclear-weapon-free_zone_treaty_the_treaty_of_pelindaba_e.pdf>

Agreement on Sub-Regional Arms Control (Florence Agreement)

Adopted by the 5 original parties at Florence and entered into force on 14 June 1996

The agreement was negotiated under the auspices of the OSCE in accordance with the mandate in Article IV of Annex 1-B of the 1995 General Framework Agreement for Peace in Bosnia and Herzegovina (Dayton Agreement). It sets numerical ceilings on armaments of the former warring parties. Five categories of heavy conventional weapons are included: battle tanks, armoured combat vehicles, heavy artillery (75 mm and above), combat aircraft and attack helicopters. The limits were reached by 31 October 1997; by that date 6580 weapon items, or 46 per cent of pre-June 1996 holdings, had been destroyed. By 1 January 2010 a further 2650 items had been destroyed voluntarily.

The implementation of the agreement is monitored and assisted by the OSCE's Personal Representative of the Chairman-in-Office and the Contact Group (France, Germany, Italy, Russia, the UK and the USA) and supported by other OSCE states. Under a two-phase action plan agreed in November 2009, responsibility for the implementation of the agreement was transferred to the parties on 5 December 2014, following the signing of a new set of amendments to the agreement.

Parties (4): Bosnia and Herzegovina, Croatia, Montenegro, Serbia

Agreement text: Croatian Ministry of Defence, <https://web.archive.org/web/20120303180926/ http://arhiva.morh.hr/hvs/SPORAZUMI/tekstovi/SSKN-engleski.pdf>

Inter-American Convention Against the Illicit Manufacturing of and Trafficking in Firearms, Ammunition, Explosives, and Other Related Materials (CIFTA)

Opened for signature by the member states of the Organization of American States (OAS) at Washington, DC, on 14 November 1997; entered into force on 1 July 1998; depositary General Secretariat of the OAS

The purpose of the convention is to prevent, combat and eradicate the illicit manufacturing of and the trafficking in firearms, ammunition, explosives and other related materials; and to promote and facilitate cooperation and the exchange of information and experience among the parties.

Parties (31): Antigua and Barbuda, Argentina*, Bahamas, Barbados, Belize, Bolivia, Brazil, Chile, Colombia, Costa Rica, Dominica, Dominican Republic, Ecuador, El Salvador, Grenada, Guatemala, Guyana, Haiti, Honduras, Mexico, Nicaragua, Panama, Paraguay, Peru, Saint Kitts and Nevis, Saint Lucia, Saint Vincent and the Grenadines, Suriname, Trinidad and Tobago, Uruguay, Venezuela

* With reservation.

Signed but not ratified (3): Canada, Jamaica, USA

Convention text: OAS, <http://www.oas.org/en/sla/dil/inter_american_treaties_A-63_illicit_ manufacturing_trafficking_firearms_ammunition_explosives.asp>

Inter-American Convention on Transparency in Conventional Weapons Acquisitions

Opened for signature by the member states of the OAS at Guatemala City on 7 June 1999; entered into force on 21 November 2002; depositary General Secretariat of the OAS

The objective of the convention is to contribute more fully to regional openness and transparency in the acquisition of conventional weapons by exchanging information regarding such acquisitions, for the purpose of promoting confidence among states in the Americas.

Parties (17): Argentina, Barbados, Brazil, Canada, Chile, Costa Rica, Dominican Republic, Ecuador, El Salvador, Guatemala, Mexico, Nicaragua, Panama, Paraguay, Peru, Uruguay, Venezuela

Signed but not ratified (6): Bolivia, Colombia, Dominica, Haiti, Honduras, USA

Convention text: OAS, <http://www.oas.org/en/sla/dil/inter_american_treaties_A-64_ transparency_conventional_weapons_adquisitions.asp>

Protocol on the Control of Firearms, Ammunition and other related Materials in the Southern African Development Community (SADC) Region

Opened for signature by the members states of SADC at Blantyre on 14 August 2001; entered into force on 8 November 2004; depositary SADC Executive Secretary

The objectives of the protocol include the prevention, combating and eradication of the illicit manufacturing of firearms, ammunition and other related materials, and the prevention of their excessive and destabilizing accumulation, trafficking, possession and use in the region.

Parties (11): Botswana, Lesotho, Malawi, Mauritius, Mozambique, Namibia, South Africa, Swaziland, Tanzania, Zambia, Zimbabwe

Signed but not ratified (2*): Congo (Democratic Republic of the), Seychelles**

* Three member states of SADC—Angola, the Comoros and Madagascar—have neither signed nor ratified the protocol.
** Seychelles signed the protocol in 2001 but did not ratify it before withdrawing from SADC in 2004. It rejoined in 2008.

Protocol text: SADC, <http://www.sadc.int/files/8613/5292/8361/Protocol_on_the_Control_of_Firearms_Ammunition2001.pdf>

Nairobi Protocol for the Prevention, Control and Reduction of Small Arms and Light Weapons in the Great Lakes Region and the Horn of Africa

Signed by the 10 member states of the Nairobi Secretariat on Small Arms and Light Weapons and the Seychelles at Nairobi on 21 April 2004; entered into force on 5 May 2006; depositary Regional Centre on Small Arms in the Great Lakes Region, the Horn of Africa and Bordering States (RECSA)

The objectives of the protocol include the prevention, combating and eradication of the illicit manufacture of, trafficking in, possession and use of small arms and light weapons (SALW) in the subregion. Its implementation is overseen by RECSA.

Parties (9): Burundi, Congo (Democratic Republic of the), Djibouti, Eritrea, Ethiopia, Kenya, Rwanda, Sudan, Uganda

Signed but not ratified (6): Central African Republic, Congo (Republic of the), Seychelles, Somalia, South Sudan, Tanzania

Protocol text: RECSA, <https://web.archive.org/web/20140721014017/http://www.recsasec.org/publications/Nairobi_Protocal.pdf>

ECOWAS Convention on Small Arms and Light Weapons, their Ammunition and Other Related Materials

Adopted by the 15 member states of the Economic Community of West African States (ECOWAS) at Abuja, on 14 June 2006; entered into force on 29 September 2009; depositary President of the ECOWAS Commission

The convention obligates the parties to prevent and combat the excessive and destabilizing accumulation of SALW in the ECOWAS member states.

Parties (14): Benin, Burkina Faso, Cabo Verde, Côte d'Ivoire, Ghana, Guinea, Guinea-Bissau, Liberia, Mali, Niger, Nigeria, Senegal, Sierra Leone, Togo

Signed but not ratified (1): Gambia

Convention text: ECOWAS Executive Secretariat, <http://documentation.ecowas.int/download/en/publications/Convention on Small Arms.pdf>

Treaty on a Nuclear-Weapon-Free Zone in Central Asia (Treaty of Semipalatinsk)

Signed by the 5 Central Asian states at Semipalatinsk on 8 September 2006; entered into force on 21 March 2009; depositary Kyrgyz Government

The Central Asian Nuclear Weapon-Free Zone is defined as the territories of Kazakhstan, Kyrgyzstan, Tajikistan, Turkmenistan, Uzbekistan. The treaty obligates the parties not to conduct research on, develop, manufacture, stockpile or otherwise acquire, possess or have control over nuclear weapons or any other nuclear explosive device by any means anywhere.

Under a *Protocol* China, France, Russia, the UK and the USA undertake not to use or threaten to use a nuclear explosive device against the parties to the treaty.

Parties (5): Kazakhstan, Kyrgyzstan, Tajikistan, Turkmenistan, Uzbekistan

Parties to the protocol (4): China, France*, Russia, UK*; *signed but not ratified (1)*: USA

* With reservations and/or declaration.

Treaty and protocol text: United Nations Treaty Collection, <https://treaties.un.org/doc/ Publication/UNTS/No Volume/51633/Part/I-51633-080000028023b006.pdf>

Central African Convention for the Control of Small Arms and Light Weapons, Their Ammunition and All Parts and Components That Can Be Used for Their Manufacture, Repair and Assembly (Kinshasa Convention)

Opened for signature by the 10 member states of the Communauté économique d'États de l'Afrique Centrale (CEEAC, Economic Community of Central African States) and Rwanda at Brazzaville on 19 November 2010; entered into force on 8 March 2017; depositary UN Secretary-General

The objectives of the convention are to prevent, combat and eradicate illicit trade and trafficking in SALW in Central Africa (defined to be the territory of the members of CEEAC and Rwanda); to strengthen the control in the region of the manufacture, trade, transfer and use of SALW; to combat armed violence and ease the human suffering in the region caused by SALW; and to foster cooperation and confidence among the states parties.

Parties (7): Angola, Cameroon, Central African Republic, Chad, Congo (Republic of the), Gabon, *Sao Tome and Principe*

Signed but not ratified (4): Burundi, Congo (Democratic Republic of the), Equatorial Guinea, Rwanda

Treaty text: United Nations Treaty Collection, <https://treaties.un.org/doc/Treaties/2010/04/ 20100430 01-12 PM/Ch_xxvi-7.pdf>

Vienna Document 2011 on Confidence- and Security-Building Measures

Adopted by the participating states of the Organization for Security and Co-operation in Europe at Vienna on 30 November 2011; entered into force on 1 December 2011

The Vienna Document 2011 builds on the 1986 Stockholm Document on Confidence- and Security-Building Measures (CSBMs) and Disarmament in Europe and previous Vienna Documents (1990, 1992, 1994 and 1999). The Vienna Document 1990 provided for annual exchange of military information, military budget exchange, risk reduction procedures, a communication network and an annual CSBM implementation assessment. The Vienna Document 1992 and the Vienna Document 1994 extended the area of application and introduced new mechanisms and parameters for military activities, defence planning and military contacts. The Vienna Document 1999 introduced regional measures aimed at increasing transparency and confidence in a bilateral, multilateral and regional context and some improvements, in particular regarding the constraining measures.

The Vienna Document 2011 incorporated revisions on such matters as the timing of verification activities and demonstrations of new types of weapon and equipment system. It also established a procedure for updating the Vienna Document every five years, but the reissue due in 2016 did not occur.

Document text: Organization for Security and Co-operation in Europe, <http://www.osce.org/fsc/86597?download=true>

III. Bilateral treaties

Treaty on the Limitation of Anti-Ballistic Missile Systems (ABM Treaty)

Signed by the USA and the USSR at Moscow on 26 May 1972; entered into force on 3 October 1972; not in force from 13 June 2002

The parties—Russia and the USA—undertook not to build nationwide defences against ballistic missile attack and to limit the development and deployment of permitted strategic missile defences. The treaty prohibited the parties from giving air defence missiles, radars or launchers the technical ability to counter strategic ballistic missiles and from testing them in a strategic ABM mode. The **1974 Protocol** to the ABM Treaty introduced further numerical restrictions on permitted ballistic missile defences.

In 1997 Belarus, Kazakhstan, Russia, Ukraine and the USA signed a memorandum of understanding that would have made Belarus, Kazakhstan and Ukraine parties to the treaty along with Russia as successor states of the USSR and a set of agreed statements that would specify the demarcation line between strategic missile defences (which are not permitted under the treaty) and non-strategic or theatre missile defences (which are permitted under the treaty). The set of 1997 agreements was ratified by Russia in April 2000, but because the USA did not ratify them they did not enter into force.

On 13 December 2001 the USA announced its withdrawal from the treaty, which came into effect on 13 June 2002.

Treaty text: *United Nations Treaty Series*, vol. 944 (1974), <https://treaties.un.org/doc/Publication/UNTS/Volume 944/v944.pdf>

Protocol text: *US Department of State*, <https://www.state.gov/t/avc/trty/101888.htm#protocolabm>

Treaty on the Limitation of Underground Nuclear Weapon Tests (Threshold Test-Ban Treaty, TTBT)

Signed by the USA and the USSR at Moscow on 3 July 1974; entered into force on 11 December 1990

The parties—Russia and the USA—undertake not to carry out any underground nuclear weapon test having a yield exceeding 150 kilotons. The 1974 verification protocol was replaced in 1990 with a new protocol.

Treaty and protocol texts: *United Nations Treaty Series*, vol. 1714 (1993), <https://treaties. un.org/doc/Publication/UNTS/Volume 1714/v1714.pdf>

Treaty on Underground Nuclear Explosions for Peaceful Purposes (Peaceful Nuclear Explosions Treaty, PNET)

Signed by the USA and the USSR at Moscow and Washington, DC, on 28 May 1976; entered into force on 11 December 1990

The parties—Russia and the USA—undertake not to carry out any individual underground nuclear explosion for peaceful purposes having a yield exceeding 150 kilotons or any group explosion having an aggregate yield exceeding 150 kilotons; and not to carry out any group explosion having an aggregate yield exceeding 1500 kilotons unless the individual explosions in the group could be identified and measured by agreed verification procedures. The 1976 verification protocol was replaced in 1990 with a new protocol.

Treaty and protocol texts: *United Nations Treaty Series*, vol. 1714 (1993), <https://treaties. un.org/doc/Publication/UNTS/Volume 1714/v1714.pdf>

Treaty on the Elimination of Intermediate-Range and Shorter-Range Missiles (INF Treaty)

Signed by the USA and the USSR at Washington, DC, on 8 December 1987; entered into force on 1 June 1988

The treaty obligated the original parties—the USA and the USSR—to destroy all ground-launched ballistic and cruise missiles with a range of 500–5500 kilometres (intermediate-range, 1000–5500 km; and shorter-range, 500–1000 km) and their launchers by 1 June 1991. A total of 2692 missiles were eliminated by May 1991. For 10 years after 1 June 1991 on-site inspections were conducted to verify compliance. The use of surveillance satellites for data collection continued after the end of on-site inspections on 31 May 2001.

In 1994 treaty membership was expanded to include Belarus, Kazakhstan and Ukraine.

Treaty text: *United Nations Treaty Series*, vol. 1657 (1991), <https://treaties.un.org/doc/ Publication/UNTS/Volume 1657/v1657.pdf>

Treaty on the Reduction and Limitation of Strategic Offensive Arms (START I)

Signed by the USA and the USSR at Moscow on 31 July 1991; entered into force on 5 December 1994; expired on 5 December 2009

The treaty obligated the original parties—the USA and the USSR—to make phased reductions in their offensive strategic nuclear forces over a seven-year period. It set numerical limits on deployed strategic nuclear delivery vehicles (SNDVs)—intercontinental ballistic missiles (ICBMs), submarine-launched ballistic missiles (SLBMs) and heavy bombers—and the nuclear warheads they carry.

In the Protocol to Facilitate the Implementation of START (**1992 Lisbon Protocol**), which entered into force on 5 December 1994, Belarus, Kazakhstan and Ukraine also assumed the obligations of the former USSR under the treaty.

Treaty and protocol texts: US Department of State, <http://www.state.gov/t/avc/trty/146007.htm>

Treaty on Further Reduction and Limitation of Strategic Offensive Arms (START II)

Signed by Russia and the USA at Moscow on 3 January 1993; not in force

The treaty would have obligated the parties to eliminate their ICBMs with multiple independently targeted re-entry vehicles (MIRVs) and reduce the number of their deployed strategic nuclear warheads to no more than 3000–3500 each (of which no more than 1750 were to be deployed on SLBMs) by 1 January 2003. On 26 September 1997 the two parties signed a *Protocol* to the treaty providing for the extension until the end of 2007 of the period of implementation of the treaty.

The two signatories ratified the treaty but never exchanged the instruments of ratification. The treaty thus never entered into force. On 14 June 2002, as a response to the taking effect on 13 June of the USA's withdrawal from the ABM Treaty, Russia declared that it would no longer be bound by START II.

Treaty and protocol texts: US Department of State, <http://www.state.gov/t/avc/trty/102887.htm>

Treaty on Strategic Offensive Reductions (SORT, Moscow Treaty)

Signed by Russia and the USA at Moscow on 24 May 2002; entered into force on 1 June 2003; not in force from 5 February 2011

The treaty obligated the parties to reduce the number of their operationally deployed strategic nuclear warheads so that the aggregate numbers did not exceed 1700–2200 for each party by 31 December 2012. The treaty was superseded by New START on 5 February 2011.

Treaty text: *United Nations Treaty Series*, vol. 2350 (2005), <https://treaties.un.org/doc/Publication/UNTS/Volume 2350/v2350.pdf>

Treaty on Measures for the Further Reduction and Limitation of Strategic Offensive Arms (New START, Prague Treaty)

Signed by Russia and the USA at Prague on 8 April 2010; entered into force on 5 February 2011

The treaty obligates the parties—Russia and the USA—to each reduce their number of (*a*) deployed ICBMs, SLBMs and heavy bombers to 700; (*b*) warheads on deployed ICBMs and SLBMs and warheads counted for deployed heavy bombers to 1550; and (*c*) deployed and non-deployed ICBM launchers, SLBM launchers and heavy bombers to 800. The reductions must be achieved by 5 February 2018; a bilateral consultative commission resolves questions about compliance and other implementation issues. A protocol to the treaty contains verifications mechanisms.

The treaty follows on from START I and supersedes SORT. It will remain in force for 10 years unless superseded earlier by a subsequent agreement. If both parties agree, it can be extended for 5 years, but no more.

Treaty and protocol texts: US Department of State, <http://www.state.gov/t/avc/newstart/c44126.htm>

Annex B. International security cooperation bodies

This annex describes the main international organizations, intergovernmental bodies, treaty-implementing bodies and transfer control regimes whose aims include the promotion of security, stability, peace or arms control and lists their members or participants as of 1 January 2018. The bodies are divided into three categories: those with a global focus or membership (section I), those with a regional focus or membership (section II) and those that aim to control strategic trade (section III).

The member states of the United Nations and organs within the UN system are listed first, followed by all other bodies in alphabetical order. Not all members or participants of these bodies are UN member states. States that joined or first participated in the body during 2017 are shown in italics. The address of an Internet site with information about each organization is provided where available. On the arms control and disarmament agreements mentioned here, see annex A.

I. Bodies with a global focus or membership

United Nations (UN)

The UN, the world intergovernmental organization, was founded in 1945 through the adoption of its Charter. Its headquarters are in New York, USA. The six principal UN organs are the General Assembly, the Security Council, the Economic and Social Council (ECOSOC), the Trusteeship Council (which suspended operation in 1994), the International Court of Justice (ICJ) and the secretariat.

The General Assembly has six main committees. The First Committee (Disarmament and International Security Committee) deals with disarmament and related international security questions. The Fourth Committee (Special Political and Decolonization Committee) deals with a variety of subjects including decolonization, Palestinian refugees and human rights, peacekeeping, mine action, outer space, public information, atomic radiation and the University for Peace.

The UN Office for Disarmament Affairs (UNODA), a department of the UN secretariat, promotes disarmament of nuclear, biological, chemical and conventional weapons. The UN also has a large number of specialized agencies and other autonomous bodies.

UN member states (193) and year of membership

Afghanistan, 1946
Albania, 1955
Algeria, 1962
Andorra, 1993
Angola, 1976
Antigua and Barbuda, 1981
Argentina, 1945
Armenia, 1992
Australia, 1945
Austria, 1955
Azerbaijan, 1992
Bahamas, 1973
Bahrain, 1971
Bangladesh, 1974
Barbados, 1966
Belarus, 1945
Belgium, 1945
Belize, 1981
Benin, 1960
Bhutan, 1971
Bolivia, 1945
Bosnia and Herzegovina, 1992
Botswana, 1966
Brazil, 1945
Brunei Darussalam, 1984
Bulgaria, 1955
Burkina Faso, 1960
Burundi, 1962
Cabo Verde, 1975
Cambodia, 1955
Cameroon, 1960
Canada, 1945
Central African Republic,
   1960
Chad, 1960
Chile, 1945
China, 1945
Colombia, 1945
Comoros, 1975
Congo, Democratic Republic
   of the, 1960
Congo, Republic of the, 1960
Costa Rica, 1945
Côte d'Ivoire, 1960
Croatia, 1992
Cuba, 1945
Cyprus, 1960
Czech Republic, 1993
Denmark, 1945
Djibouti, 1977
Dominica, 1978
Dominican Republic, 1945

Ecuador, 1945
Egypt, 1945
El Salvador, 1945
Equatorial Guinea, 1968
Eritrea, 1993
Estonia, 1991
Ethiopia, 1945
Fiji, 1970
Finland, 1955
France, 1945
Gabon, 1960
Gambia, 1965
Georgia, 1992
Germany, 1973
Ghana, 1957
Greece, 1945
Grenada, 1974
Guatemala, 1945
Guinea, 1958
Guinea-Bissau, 1974
Guyana, 1966
Haiti, 1945
Honduras, 1945
Hungary, 1955
Iceland, 1946
India, 1945
Indonesia, 1950
Iran, 1945
Iraq, 1945
Ireland, 1955
Israel, 1949
Italy, 1955
Jamaica, 1962
Japan, 1956
Jordan, 1955
Kazakhstan, 1992
Kenya, 1963
Kiribati, 1999
Korea, Democratic People's
   Republic of (North Korea),
   1991
Korea, Republic of (South
   Korea), 1991
Kuwait, 1963
Kyrgyzstan, 1992
Laos, 1955
Latvia, 1991
Lebanon, 1945
Lesotho, 1966
Liberia, 1945
Libya, 1955
Liechtenstein, 1990

Lithuania, 1991
Luxembourg, 1945
Macedonia, Former Yugoslav
   Republic of, 1993
Madagascar, 1960
Malawi, 1964
Malaysia, 1957
Maldives, 1965
Mali, 1960
Malta, 1964
Marshall Islands, 1991
Mauritania, 1961
Mauritius, 1968
Mexico, 1945
Micronesia, 1991
Moldova, 1992
Monaco, 1993
Mongolia, 1961
Montenegro, 2006
Morocco, 1956
Mozambique, 1975
Myanmar, 1948
Namibia, 1990
Nauru, 1999
Nepal, 1955
Netherlands, 1945
New Zealand, 1945
Nicaragua, 1945
Niger, 1960
Nigeria, 1960
Norway, 1945
Oman, 1971
Pakistan, 1947
Palau, 1994
Panama, 1945
Papua New Guinea, 1975
Paraguay, 1945
Peru, 1945
Philippines, 1945
Poland, 1945
Portugal, 1955
Qatar, 1971
Romania, 1955
Russia, 1945
Rwanda, 1962
Saint Kitts and Nevis, 1983
Saint Lucia, 1979
Saint Vincent and the
   Grenadines, 1980
Samoa, 1976
San Marino, 1992
Sao Tome and Principe, 1975

Saudi Arabia, 1945
Senegal, 1960
Serbia, 2000
Seychelles, 1976
Sierra Leone, 1961
Singapore, 1965
Slovakia, 1993
Slovenia, 1992
Solomon Islands, 1978
Somalia, 1960
South Africa, 1945
South Sudan, 2011
Spain, 1955
Sri Lanka, 1955
Sudan, 1956

Suriname, 1975
Swaziland, 1968
Sweden, 1946
Switzerland, 2002
Syria, 1945
Tajikistan, 1992
Tanzania, 1961
Thailand, 1946
Timor-Leste, 2002
Togo, 1960
Tonga, 1999
Trinidad and Tobago, 1962
Tunisia, 1956
Turkey, 1945
Turkmenistan, 1992

Tuvalu, 2000
Uganda, 1962
UK, 1945
Ukraine, 1945
United Arab Emirates, 1971
Uruguay, 1945
USA, 1945
Uzbekistan, 1992
Vanuatu, 1981
Venezuela, 1945
Viet Nam, 1977
Yemen, 1947
Zambia, 1964
Zimbabwe, 1980

Non-member observer states (2): Holy See, Palestine

Website: <http://www.un.org/>

UN Security Council

The Security Council has responsibility for the maintenance of international peace and security. All UN members states must comply with its decisions. It has 5 permanent members, which can each exercise a veto on the Council's decisions, and 10 non-permanent members elected by the UN General Assembly for two-year terms.

Permanent members (the P5): China, France, Russia, UK, USA

Non-permanent members (10): Bolivia*, *Côte d'Ivoire***, Ethiopia*, *Equatorial Guinea****, Kazakhstan*, *Kuwait****, Netherlands*****, *Peru****, *Poland****, Sweden*

> *Note*: The 2017–18 term was the first time in over 5 decades that 2 members agreed to split a term: Italy was a member in 2017 and the Netherlands in 2018.

> * Member in 2017–18.
> ** Member in 2018–19.
> *** Member in 2018.

Website: <http://www.un.org/en/sc/>

Conference on Disarmament (CD)

The CD is intended to be the single multilateral arms control and disarmament negotiating forum of the international community. It has been enlarged and renamed several times since 1960. It is not a UN body but reports to the UN General Assembly. It is based in Geneva, Switzerland.

Members (65): Algeria, Argentina, Australia, Austria, Bangladesh, Belarus, Belgium, Brazil, Bulgaria, Cameroon, Canada, Chile, China, Colombia, Congo (Democratic Republic of the), Cuba, Ecuador, Egypt, Ethiopia, Finland, France, Germany, Hungary, India, Indonesia, Iran, Iraq, Ireland, Israel, Italy, Japan, Kazakhstan, Kenya, Korea (North), Korea (South), Malaysia, Mexico, Mongolia, Morocco, Myanmar, Netherlands, New Zealand, Nigeria, Norway, Pakistan, Peru, Poland, Romania, Russia, Senegal, Slovakia, South Africa, Spain, Sri Lanka, Sweden, Switzerland,

Syria, Tunisia, Turkey, UK, Ukraine, USA, Venezuela, Viet Nam, Zimbabwe

Website: <http://www.unog.ch/cd>

International Atomic Energy Agency (IAEA)

The IAEA is an intergovernmental organization within the UN system. It is mandated by its Statute, which entered into force in 1957, to promote the peaceful uses of atomic energy and ensure that nuclear activities are not used to further any military purpose. Under the 1968 Non-Proliferation Treaty and the nuclear weapon-free zone treaties, non-nuclear weapon states must accept IAEA nuclear safeguards to demonstrate the fulfilment of their obligation not to manufacture nuclear weapons. Its headquarters are in Vienna, Austria.

Members (169): Afghanistan, Albania, Algeria, Angola, Antigua and Barbuda, Argentina, Armenia, Australia, Austria, Azerbaijan, Bahamas, Bahrain, Bangladesh, Barbados, Belarus, Belgium, Belize, Benin, Bolivia, Bosnia and Herzegovina, Botswana, Brazil, Brunei Darussalam, Bulgaria, Burkina Faso, Burundi, Cambodia, Cameroon, Canada, Central African Republic, Chad, Chile, China, Colombia, Congo (Democratic Republic of the), Congo (Republic of the), Costa Rica, Côte d'Ivoire, Croatia, Cuba, Cyprus, Czech Republic, Denmark, Djibouti, Dominica, Dominican Republic, Ecuador, Egypt, El Salvador, Eritrea, Estonia, Ethiopia, Fiji, Finland, France, Gabon, Georgia, Germany, Ghana, Greece, Guatemala, Guyana, Haiti, Holy See, Honduras, Hungary, Iceland, India, Indonesia, Iran, Iraq, Ireland, Israel, Italy, Jamaica, Japan, Jordan, Kazakhstan, Kenya, Korea (South), Kuwait, Kyrgyzstan, Laos, Latvia, Lebanon, Lesotho, Liberia, Libya, Liechtenstein, Lithuania, Luxembourg, Macedonia (Former Yugoslav Republic of), Madagascar, Malawi, Malaysia, Mali, Malta, Marshall Islands, Mauritania, Mauritius, Mexico, Moldova, Monaco, Mongolia, Montenegro, Morocco, Mozambique, Myanmar, Namibia, Nepal, Netherlands, New Zealand, Nicaragua, Niger, Nigeria, Norway, Oman, Pakistan, Palau, Panama, Papua New Guinea, Paraguay, Peru, Philippines, Poland, Portugal, Qatar, Rwanda, Romania, Russia, *Saint Vincent and the Grenadines*, San Marino, Saudi Arabia, Senegal, Serbia, Seychelles, Sierra Leone, Singapore, Slovakia, Slovenia, South Africa, Spain, Sri Lanka, Sudan, Swaziland, Sweden, Switzerland, Syria, Tajikistan, Tanzania, Thailand, Togo, Trinidad and Tobago, Tunisia, Turkey, Turkmenistan, Uganda, UK, Ukraine, United Arab Emirates, Uruguay, USA, Uzbekistan, Vanuatu, Venezuela, Viet Nam, Yemen, Zambia, Zimbabwe

Notes: North Korea was a member of the IAEA until June 1994. In addition to the above-named states, Cabo Verde, Comoros, Gambia, Grenada, Saint Lucia and Tonga have had their membership approved by the IAEA General Conference; it will take effect once the state deposits the necessary legal instruments with the IAEA.

Website: <http://www.iaea.org/>

International Court of Justice (ICJ)

The ICJ was established in 1945 by the UN Charter and is the principal judicial organ of the UN. The court's role is to settle legal disputes submitted to it by states and to give advisory opinions on legal questions referred to it by authorized UN organs and specialized agencies. The Court is composed of 15 judges, who are elected for terms of office of nine years by the UN General Assembly and the Security Council. Its seat is at The Hague, the Netherlands.

Website: <http://www.icj-cij.org/>

Bilateral Consultative Commission (BCC)

The BCC is a forum established under the 2010 Russian–US Treaty on Measures for the Further Reduction and Limitation of Strategic Offensive Arms (New START, Prague Treaty) to discuss issues related to the treaty's implementation. It replaced the joint compliance and inspection commission (JCIC) of the 1991 START treaty. The BCC is required to meet at least twice each year in Geneva, Switzerland, unless the parties agree otherwise. Its work is confidential.

Website: US Department of Defense, Under Secretary of Defense for Acquisition and Sustainment, <https://www.acq.osd.mil/tc/nst/NSTtoc.htm>

Commonwealth of Nations

Established in its current form in 1949, the Commonwealth is an organization of developed and developing countries whose aim is to advance democracy, human rights, and sustainable economic and social development within its member states and beyond. It adopted a charter reaffirming its core values and principles in 2012. Its secretariat is in London, UK.

Members (52): Antigua and Barbuda, Australia, Bahamas, Bangladesh, Barbados, Belize, Botswana, Brunei Darussalam, Cameroon, Canada, Cyprus, Dominica, Fiji, Ghana, Grenada, Guyana, India, Jamaica, Kenya, Kiribati, Lesotho, Malawi, Malaysia, Malta, Mauritius, Mozambique, Namibia, Nauru, New Zealand, Nigeria, Pakistan, Papua New Guinea, Rwanda, Saint Kitts and Nevis, Saint Lucia, Saint Vincent and the Grenadines, Samoa, Seychelles, Sierra Leone, Singapore, Solomon Islands, South Africa, Sri Lanka, Swaziland, Tanzania, Tonga, Trinidad and Tobago, Tuvalu, Uganda, UK, Vanuatu, Zambia

   Note: In addition to the 52 members as of 1 Jan. 2018, the Gambia rejoined the Commonwealth on 8 Feb. 2018.

Website: <http://www.thecommonwealth.org/>

Comprehensive Nuclear-Test-Ban Treaty Organization (CTBTO)

The CTBTO will become operational when the 1996 Comprehensive Nuclear-Test-Ban Treaty (CTBT) has entered into force. It will resolve questions of compliance with the treaty and act as a forum for consultation and cooperation among the states parties. A Preparatory Commission was established to prepare for the work of the CTBTO, in particular by establishing the International Monitoring System, consisting of seismic, hydro-acoustic, infrasound and radionuclide stations from which data is transmitted to the CTBTO International Data Centre. Its headquarters are in Vienna, Austria.

Signatories to the CTBT (183): See annex A

Website: <http://www.ctbto.org/>

Financial Action Task Force (FATF)

The FATF is an intergovernmental policymaking body whose purpose is to establish international standards and develop and promote policies, at both national and international levels. It was established in 1989 by the Group of Seven (G7), initially to examine and develop measures to combat money laundering; its mandate was expanded in 2001 to incorporate efforts to combat terrorist financing and again in 2008 to include the financing of weapon of mass destruction (WMD) proliferation efforts. Its secretariat is in Paris, France.

Members (37): Argentina, Australia, Austria, Belgium, Brazil, Canada, China, Denmark, European Commission, Finland, France, Germany, Greece, Gulf Cooperation Council, Hong Kong (China), Iceland, India, Ireland, Italy, Japan, Korea (South), Luxembourg, Malaysia, Mexico, Netherlands, New Zealand, Norway, Portugal, Russia, Singapore, South Africa, Spain, Sweden, Switzerland, Turkey, UK, USA

Website: <http://www.fatf-gafi.org/>

Global Initiative to Combat Nuclear Terrorism (GICNT)

The GICNT was established in 2006 as a voluntary international partnership of states and international organizations that are committed to strengthening global capacity to prevent, detect and respond to nuclear terrorism. The GICNT works towards this goal by conducting multilateral activities that strengthen the plans, policies, procedures and interoperability of its partner.

Partners (88): Afghanistan, Albania, Algeria, Argentina, Armenia, Australia, Austria, Azerbaijan, Bahrain, Belarus, Belgium, Bosnia and Herzegovina, Bulgaria, Cabo Verde, Cambodia, Canada, Chile, China, Côte d'Ivoire, Croatia, Cyprus, Czech Republic, Denmark, Estonia, Finland, France, Georgia, Germany, Greece, Hungary, Iceland, India, Iraq, Ireland, Israel, Italy, Japan, Jordan, Kazakhstan, Korea (South), Kyrgyzstan, Latvia, Libya, Lithuania, Luxembourg, Macedonia (Former Yugoslav Republic of), Madagascar, Malaysia, Malta, Mauritius, Mexico, Montenegro, Morocco, Nepal, Netherlands, New Zealand, Nigeria, Norway, Pakistan, Palau, Panama, Paraguay, Philippines, Poland, Portugal, Romania, Russia, Saudi Arabia, Serbia, Seychelles, Singapore, Slovakia, Slovenia, Spain, Sri Lanka, Sweden, Switzerland, Tajikistan, Thailand, Turkey, Turkmenistan, UK, Ukraine, United Arab Emirates, USA, Uzbekistan, Viet Nam, Zambia

Official observers (5): International Atomic Energy Agency, European Union, International Criminal Police Organization (Interpol), UN Office on Drugs and Crime, UN Interregional Crime and Justice Research Institute

Website: <http://www.gicnt.org/>

Group of Seven (G7)

The G7 is a group of leading industrialized countries that have met informally, at the level of head of state or government, since the 1970s. The presidents of the European Council and the European Commission represent the European Union at summits.

Between 1997 and 2013 the G7 members and Russia met together as the Group of Eight (G8). Following Russia's annexation of Crimea, the G7 states decided in March 2014 to meet without Russia until further notice.

Members (7): Canada*, France, Germany, Italy**, Japan, UK, USA

* Summit host in 2018.
** Summit host in 2017.

Website: <https://g7.gc.ca/en/>

Global Partnership against the Spread of Weapons and Materials of Mass Destruction

The Global Partnership was launched in 2002 by the G8 to address non-proliferation, disarmament, counterterrorism and nuclear safety issues. The members meet twice each year, hosted by the state holding the G7 presidency, with the main goal of launching specific projects to tackle the abuse of weapons and materials of mass destruction and reduce chemical, biological, radioactive and nuclear risks. The Global Partnership was extended for an unspecified period in May 2011.

Members (32): Australia, Belgium, Canada, Chile, Czech Republic, Denmark, European Union, Finland, France, Georgia, Germany, Hungary, Ireland, Italy, Japan, Jordan, Kazakhstan, Korea (South), Mexico, Netherlands, New Zealand, Norway, Philippines, Poland, Portugal, Russia, Spain, Sweden, Switzerland, UK, Ukraine, USA

Note: Russia has not been formally expelled from the Global Partnership despite being excluded from the G8, but it is not invited to participate.

Website: <http://www.gpwmd.com/>

International Criminal Court (ICC)

The ICC is an independent, permanent international criminal court dealing with questions of genocide, crimes against humanity, war crimes and the crime of aggression. Its seat is at The Hague, the Netherlands.

The court's statute was adopted at Rome in 1998 and entered into force on 1 July 2002. Amendments to the Rome Statute adopted in 2010 define the crime of aggression and extend the circumstances in which use of chemical weapons is considered a war crime. Amendments adopted in 2017 extend the definition of war crime to include the use of microbial, biological or toxin weapons, weapons that injure by fragments undetectable by X-rays, and laser weapons. These amendments only apply to the states that have ratified them.

Parties to the Rome Statute (123): Afghanistan, Albania, Andorra, Antigua and Barbuda, Argentina, Australia, Austria, Bangladesh, Barbados, Belgium, Belize, Benin, Bolivia, Bosnia and Herzegovina, Botswana, Brazil, Bulgaria, Burkina Faso, Cabo Verde, Cambodia, Canada, Central African Republic, Chad, Chile, Colombia, Comoros, Congo (Democratic Republic of the), Congo (Republic of the), Cook Islands, Costa Rica, Côte d'Ivoire, Croatia, Cyprus, Czech Republic, Denmark, Djibouti, Dominica, Dominican Republic, Ecuador, El Salvador, Estonia, Fiji, Finland, France, Gabon, Gambia, Georgia, Germany, Ghana, Greece, Grenada, Guatemala, Guinea, Guyana, Honduras, Hungary, Iceland, Ireland, Italy, Japan, Jordan, Kenya, Korea (South), Latvia, Lesotho, Liberia, Liechtenstein, Lithuania, Luxembourg, Macedonia (Former Yugoslav Republic of), Madagascar, Malawi, Maldives, Mali, Malta, Marshall Islands, Mauritius, Mexico, Moldova, Mongolia, Montenegro, Namibia, Nauru,

Netherlands, New Zealand, Niger, Nigeria, Norway, Palestine, Panama, Paraguay, Peru, Philippines, Poland, Portugal, Romania, Saint Kitts and Nevis, Saint Lucia, Saint Vincent and the Grenadines, Samoa, San Marino, Senegal, Serbia, Seychelles, Sierra Leone, Slovakia, Slovenia, South Africa, Spain, Suriname, Sweden, Switzerland, Tajikistan, Tanzania, Timor-Leste, Trinidad and Tobago, Tunisia, Uganda, UK, Uruguay, Vanuatu, Venezuela, Zambia

Non-parties that have accepted ICC jurisdiction (1): Ukraine

Notes: Burundi withdrew from the ICC on 27 Oct. 2017. Gambia and South Africa, which had declared in 2016 that they would withdraw, rescinded those declarations in 2017. On 17 Mar. 2018 the Philippines gave 12 months notice that it would withdraw from the ICC.

Website: <http://www.icc-cpi.int/>

Non-Aligned Movement (NAM)

NAM was established in 1961 as a forum for consultations and coordination of positions in the UN on political, economic and arms control issues among non-aligned states.

Members (120): Afghanistan, Algeria, Angola, Antigua and Barbuda, Azerbaijan*, Bahamas, Bahrain, Bangladesh, Barbados, Belarus, Belize, Benin, Bhutan, Bolivia, Botswana, Brunei Darussalam, Burkina Faso, Burundi, Cabo Verde, Cambodia, Cameroon, Central African Republic, Chad, Chile, Colombia, Comoros, Congo (Democratic Republic of the), Congo (Republic of the), Côte d'Ivoire, Cuba, Djibouti, Dominica, Dominican Republic, Ecuador, Egypt, Equatorial Guinea, Eritrea, Ethiopia, Fiji, Gabon, Gambia, Ghana, Grenada, Guatemala, Guinea, Guinea-Bissau, Guyana, Haiti, Honduras, India, Indonesia, Iran, Iraq, Jamaica, Jordan, Kenya, Korea (North), Kuwait, Laos, Lebanon, Lesotho, Liberia, Libya, Madagascar, Malawi, Malaysia, Maldives, Mali, Mauritania, Mauritius, Mongolia, Morocco, Mozambique, Myanmar, Namibia, Nepal, Nicaragua, Niger, Nigeria, Oman, Pakistan, Palestine Liberation Organization, Panama, Papua New Guinea, Peru, Philippines, Qatar, Rwanda, Saint Kitts and Nevis, Saint Lucia, Saint Vincent and the Grenadines, Sao Tome and Principe, Saudi Arabia, Senegal, Seychelles, Sierra Leone, Singapore, Somalia, South Africa, Sri Lanka, Sudan, Suriname, Swaziland, Syria, Tanzania, Thailand, Timor-Leste, Togo, Trinidad and Tobago, Tunisia, Turkmenistan, Uganda, United Arab Emirates, Uzbekistan, Vanuatu, Venezuela**, Viet Nam, Yemen, Zambia, Zimbabwe

* Summit host in 2019
** Summit host in 2016

Website: <http://www.nambaku.org/>

Organisation for Economic Co-operation and Development (OECD)

Established in 1961, the OECD's objectives are to promote economic and social welfare by coordinating policies among the member states. Its headquarters are in Paris, France.

Members (35): Australia, Austria, Belgium, Canada, Chile, Czech Republic, Denmark, Estonia, Finland, France, Germany, Greece, Hungary, Iceland, Ireland, Israel, Italy, Japan, Korea (South), Latvia, Luxembourg, Mexico, Netherlands, New Zealand, Norway, Poland, Portugal, Slovakia, Slovenia, Spain, Sweden, Switzerland, Turkey, UK, USA

Website: <http://www.oecd.org/>

Organisation for the Prohibition of Chemical Weapons (OPCW)

The OPCW implements the 1993 Chemical Weapons Convention (CWC). Based in The Hague, the organization, among other things, oversees the destruction of chemical weapon stockpiles and associated infrastructure, implements a verification regime to ensure that such weapons do not re-emerge, provides assistance and protection to states parties threatened by such weapons, and facilitates and engages in international cooperation to strengthen treaty compliance and to promote the peaceful uses of chemistry.

Parties to the Chemical Weapons Convention (192): See annex A

Website: <http://www.opcw.org/>

Organisation of Islamic Cooperation (OIC)

The OIC (formerly the Organization of the Islamic Conference) was established in 1969 by Islamic states to promote cooperation among the members and to support peace, security and the struggle of the people of Palestine and all Muslim people. Its secretariat is in Jeddah, Saudi Arabia.

Members (57): Afghanistan, Albania, Algeria, Azerbaijan, Bahrain, Bangladesh, Benin, Brunei Darussalam, Burkina Faso, Cameroon, Chad, Comoros, Côte d'Ivoire, Djibouti, Egypt, Gabon, Gambia, Guinea, Guinea-Bissau, Guyana, Indonesia, Iran, Iraq, Jordan, Kazakhstan, Kuwait, Kyrgyzstan, Lebanon, Libya, Malaysia, Maldives, Mali, Mauritania, Morocco, Mozambique, Niger, Nigeria, Oman, Pakistan, Palestine, Qatar, Saudi Arabia, Senegal, Sierra Leone, Somalia, Sudan, Suriname, Syria, Tajikistan, Togo, Tunisia, Turkey, Turkmenistan, Uganda, United Arab Emirates, Uzbekistan, Yemen

Website: <http://www.oic-oci.org/>

Special Verification Commission (SVC)

The SVC was established by the 1987 Soviet–US Treaty on the Elimination of Intermediate-Range and Shorter-Range Missiles (INF Treaty) as a forum to resolve compliance questions and measures necessary to improve the viability and effectiveness of the treaty. The SVC, which had not met since 2000, met in November 2016 and again in December 2017.

Parties to the INF Treaty (5): See annex A

II. Bodies with a regional focus or membership

African Union (AU)

The AU was formally established in 2001 and launched in 2002. It replaced the Organization for African Unity (OAU), which was established in 1963. Membership is open to all African states. The AU promotes unity, security and conflict resolution, democracy, human rights, and political, social and economic integration in Africa. Its main organs include the Assembly (the supreme body), the Commission (the secretariat), the Pan-African Parliament and the Peace and Security Council. The AU's headquarters are in Addis Ababa, Ethiopia.

Members (55): Algeria, Angola, Benin, Botswana, Burkina Faso, Burundi, Cabo Verde, Cameroon, Central African Republic, Chad, Comoros, Congo (Democratic Republic of the), Congo (Republic of the), Côte d'Ivoire, Djibouti, Egypt, Equatorial Guinea, Eritrea, Ethiopia, Gabon, Gambia, Ghana, Guinea, Guinea-Bissau, Kenya, Lesotho, Liberia, Libya, Madagascar, Malawi, Mali, Mauritania, Mauritius, *Morocco**, Mozambique, Namibia, Niger, Nigeria, Rwanda, Sahrawi Arab Democratic Republic (Western Sahara), Sao Tome and Principe, Senegal, Seychelles, Sierra Leone, Somalia, South Africa, South Sudan, Sudan, Swaziland, Tanzania, Togo, Tunisia, Uganda, Zambia, Zimbabwe

   * Morocco was admitted to the AU in Jan. 2017 having left the OAU in 1984.

Website: <http://www.au.int/>

Peace and Security Council (PSC)

The 15-member PSC is the AU's standing decision-making organ for the prevention, management and resolution of conflicts. It is the main pillar of the African Peace and Security Architecture (APSA).

Members for a 3-year term 1 Apr. 2016–31 Mar. 2019 (5): Congo (Republic of the), Egypt, Kenya, Nigeria, Zambia

Members for a 2-year term 1 Apr. 2016–31 Mar. 2018 (10): Algeria, Botswana, Burundi, Chad, Niger, Rwanda, Sierra Leone, South Africa, Togo, Uganda

Members for a 2-year term 1 Apr. 2018–31 Mar. 2020 (10): Angola, Djibouti, Equatorial Guinea, Gabon, Liberia, Morocco, Rwanda, Sierra Leone, Togo, Zimbabwe

Asia–Pacific Economic Cooperation (APEC)

APEC was established in 1989 to enhance open trade and economic prosperity in the Asia–Pacific region. Security and political issues, including combating terrorism, non-proliferation of WMD and effective transfer control systems, have been increasingly discussed in this forum since the mid-1990s. Its seat is in Singapore.

Member economies (21): Australia, Brunei Darussalam, Canada, Chile, China, Hong Kong, Indonesia, Japan, Korea (South), Malaysia, Mexico, New Zealand, Papua New Guinea, Peru, Philippines, Russia, Singapore, Taiwan, Thailand, USA, Viet Nam

Website: <http://www.apec.org/>

Association of Southeast Asian Nations (ASEAN)

ASEAN was established in 1967 to promote economic, social and cultural development as well as regional peace and security in South East Asia. Its secretariat is in Jakarta, Indonesia.

Members (10): Brunei Darussalam, Cambodia, Indonesia, Laos, Malaysia, Myanmar, Philippines, Singapore, Thailand, Viet Nam

Website: <http://www.asean.org/>

ASEAN Regional Forum (ARF)

The ARF was established in 1994 to foster constructive dialogue and consultation on political and security issues and to contribute to confidence-building and preventive diplomacy in the Asia-Pacific region.

Participants (27): The ASEAN member states and Australia, Bangladesh, Canada, China, European Union, India, Japan, Korea (North), Korea (South), Mongolia, New Zealand, Pakistan, Papua New Guinea, Russia, Sri Lanka, Timor-Leste, USA

Website: <http://aseanregionalforum.asean.org/>

ASEAN Plus Three (APT)

The APT cooperation began in 1997, in the wake of the Asian financial crisis, and was institutionalized in 1999. It aims to foster economic, political and security cooperation and financial stability among its participants.

Participants (13): The ASEAN member states and China, Japan, Korea (South)

Website: <http://www.asean.org/asean/external-relations/asean-3>

East Asia Summit (EAS)

The East Asia Summit started in 2005 as a regional forum for dialogue on strategic, political and economic issues with the aim of promoting peace, stability and economic prosperity in East Asia. The annual meetings are held in connection with the ASEAN summits.

Participants (18): The ASEAN member states and Australia, China, India, Japan, Korea (South), New Zealand, Russia, USA

Website: <http://www.asean.org/asean/external-relations/east-asia-summit-eas/>

Collective Security Treaty Organization (CSTO)

The CSTO was formally established in 2002–2003 by six signatories of the 1992 Collective Security Treaty. It aims to promote cooperation among its members. An objective is to provide a more efficient response to strategic problems such as terrorism and narcotics trafficking. Its seat is in Moscow, Russia.

Members (6): Armenia, Belarus, Kazakhstan, Kyrgyzstan, Russia, Tajikistan

Website: <http://www.odkb-csto.org/>

Commonwealth of Independent States (CIS)

The CIS was established in 1991 as a framework for multilateral cooperation among former Soviet republics. Its headquarters are in Minsk, Belarus.

Members (11): Armenia, Azerbaijan, Belarus, Kazakhstan, Kyrgyzstan, Moldova, Russia, Tajikistan, Turkmenistan*, Ukraine*, Uzbekistan

  * Turkmenistan has not ratified the 1993 CIS charter but since 26 Aug. 2005 it has participated in CIS activities as an associate member. Ukraine has not ratified the charter and has been an

unofficial associate member since 1993.

Website: <http://www.cis.minsk.by/>

Communauté économique d'États de l'Afrique Centrale (CEEAC, Economic Community of Central African States, ECCAS)

CEEAC was established in 1983 to promote political dialogue, create a customs union and establish common policies in Central Africa. It also coordinates activities under the 2010 Central African Convention for the Control of Small Arms and Light Weapons, Their Ammunition and All Parts and Components That Can Be Used for Their Manufacture, Repair and Assembly (Kinshasa Convention). Its secretariat is in Libreville, Gabon.

The Council for Peace and Security in Central Africa (Conseil de paix et de sécurité de l'Afrique Centrale, COPAX) is a mechanism for promoting joint political and military strategies for conflict prevention, management and resolution in Central Africa.

Members (11): Angola, Burundi, Cameroon, Central African Republic, Chad, Congo (Democratic Republic of the), Congo (Republic of the), Equatorial Guinea, Gabon, Rwanda, Sao Tome and Principe

Website: <http://www.ceeac-eccas.org/>

Conference on Interaction and Confidence-building Measures in Asia (CICA)

Initiated in 1992, CICA was formally established in 1999 as a forum to enhance security cooperation and confidence-building measures among the member states. It also promotes economic, social and cultural cooperation. Its secretariat is in Astana, Kazakhstan.

Members (26): Afghanistan, Azerbaijan, Bahrain, Bangladesh, Cambodia, China, Egypt, India, Iran, Iraq, Israel, Jordan, Kazakhstan, Korea (South), Kyrgyzstan, Mongolia, Pakistan, Palestine, Qatar, Russia, Tajikistan, Thailand, Turkey, United Arab Emirates, Uzbekistan, Viet Nam

Website: <http://www.s-cica.org/>

Council of Europe (COE)

Established in 1949, the Council is open to membership of all European states that accept the principle of the rule of law and guarantee their citizens' human rights and fundamental freedoms. Its seat is in Strasbourg, France. Among its organs are the European Court of Human Rights and the Council of Europe Development Bank.

Members (47): Albania, Andorra, Armenia, Austria, Azerbaijan, Belgium, Bosnia and Herzegovina, Bulgaria, Croatia, Cyprus, Czech Republic, Denmark, Estonia, Finland, France, Georgia, Germany, Greece, Hungary, Iceland, Ireland, Italy, Latvia, Liechtenstein, Lithuania, Luxembourg, Macedonia (Former Yugoslav Republic of), Malta, Moldova, Monaco, Montenegro, Netherlands, Norway, Poland, Portugal, Romania, Russia, San Marino, Serbia, Slovakia, Slovenia, Spain, Sweden, Switzerland, Turkey, UK, Ukraine

Website: <http://www.coe.int/>

Council of the Baltic Sea States (CBSS)

The CBSS was established in 1992 as a regional intergovernmental organization for cooperation among the states of the Baltic Sea region. Its secretariat is in Stockholm, Sweden.

Members (12): Denmark, Estonia, European Union, Finland, Germany, Iceland, Latvia, Lithuania, Norway, Poland, Russia, Sweden

Website: <http://www.cbss.org/>

Economic Community of West African States (ECOWAS)

ECOWAS was established in 1975 to promote trade and cooperation and contribute to development in West Africa. In 1981 it adopted the Protocol on Mutual Assistance in Defence Matters. Its executive secretariat is in Abuja, Nigeria.

Members (15): Benin, Burkina Faso, Cabo Verde, Côte d'Ivoire, Gambia, Ghana, Guinea, Guinea-Bissau, Liberia, Mali, Niger, Nigeria, Senegal, Sierra Leone, Togo

Website: <http://www.ecowas.int/>

European Union (EU)

The EU is an organization of European states that cooperate in a wide field, including a single market with free movement of people, goods, services and capital, a common currency for some members, and a Common Foreign and Security Policy (CFSP). Its main bodies are the European Council, the Council of the European Union (also known as the Council of Ministers), the European Commission (the secretariat), the European Parliament and the European Court of Justice. The CFSP and the Common Security and Defence Policy (CSDP) are coordinated by the High Representative of the Union for Foreign Affairs and Security Policy, assisted by the European External Action Service (EEAS). The principle seat of the EU is in Brussels, Belgium.

Members (28): Austria, Belgium, Bulgaria, Croatia, Cyprus, Czech Republic, Denmark, Estonia, Finland, France, Germany, Greece, Hungary, Ireland, Italy, Latvia, Lithuania, Luxembourg, Malta, Netherlands, Poland, Portugal, Romania, Slovakia, Slovenia, Spain, Sweden, UK*

* On 29 Mar. 2017 the UK notified the European Council of its intention to leave the EU on 29 Mar. 2019 by triggering Article 50 of the Treaty on European Union.

Website: <http://europa.eu/>

European Atomic Energy Community (Euratom, or EAEC)

Euratom was created by the 1957 Treaty Establishing the European Atomic Energy Community (Euratom Treaty) to promote the development of nuclear energy for peaceful purposes and to administer (in cooperation with the IAEA) the multinational regional safeguards system covering the EU member states. The Euratom Supply Agency, located in Luxembourg, has the task of ensuring a regular and equitable supply of ores, source materials and special fissile materials to EU member states.

Members (28): The EU member states

Website: <http://ec.europa.eu/euratom/>

European Defence Agency (EDA)

The EDA is an agency of the EU, under the direction of the Council. It was established in 2004 to help develop European defence capabilities, to promote European armaments cooperation and to work for a strong European defence technological and industrial base. The EDA's decision-making body is the Steering Board, composed of the defence ministers of the participating member states and the EU's High Representative for Foreign Affairs and Security Policy (as head of the agency). The EDA is located in Brussels, Belgium.

Participating member states (27): Austria, Belgium, Bulgaria, Croatia, Cyprus, Czech Republic, Estonia, Finland, France, Germany, Greece, Hungary, Ireland, Italy, Latvia, Lithuania, Luxembourg, Malta, Netherlands, Poland, Portugal, Romania, Slovakia, Slovenia, Spain, Sweden, UK

Website: <http://eda.europa.eu/>

Gulf Cooperation Council (GCC)

Formally called the Cooperation Council for the Arab States of the Gulf, the GCC was created in 1981 to promote regional integration in such areas as economy, finance, trade, administration and legislation and to foster scientific and technical progress. The members also cooperate in areas of foreign policy and military and security matters. The Supreme Council is the highest GCC authority. Its headquarters are in Riyadh, Saudi Arabia.

Members (6): Bahrain, Kuwait, Oman, Qatar, Saudi Arabia, United Arab Emirates

Website: <http://www.gcc-sg.org/>

Intergovernmental Authority on Development (IGAD)

IGAD was established in 1996 to expand regional cooperation and promote peace and stability in the Horn of Africa. It superseded the Intergovernmental Authority on Drought and Development (IGADD), which was established in 1986. Its secretariat is in Djibouti.

Members (8): Djibouti, Eritrea, Ethiopia, Kenya, Somalia, South Sudan, Sudan, Uganda

Website: <http://www.igad.int/>

International Conference on the Great Lakes Region (ICGLR)

The ICGLR, which was initiated in 2004, works to promote peace and security, political and social stability, and growth and development in the Great Lakes region. In 2006 the member states adopted the Pact on Security, Stability and Development in the Great Lakes Region, which entered into force in 2008. Its executive secretariat is in Bujumbura, Burundi.

Members (12): Angola, Burundi, Central African Republic, Congo (Republic of the), Congo (Democratic Republic of the), Kenya, Rwanda, South Sudan, Sudan, Tanzania, Uganda, Zambia

Website: <http://www.icglr.org/>

League of Arab States

The Arab League was established in 1945 to form closer union among Arab states and foster political and economic cooperation. An agreement for collective defence and economic cooperation among the members was signed in 1950. In 2015 the Arab League agreed to create a joint Arab military force for regional peacekeeping. Its general secretariat is in Cairo, Egypt.

Members (22): Algeria, Bahrain, Comoros, Djibouti, Egypt, Iraq, Jordan, Kuwait, Lebanon, Libya, Mauritania, Morocco, Oman, Palestine, Qatar, Saudi Arabia, Somalia, Sudan, Syria*, Tunisia, United Arab Emirates, Yemen

* Syria was suspended from the organization on 16 Nov. 2011.

Website: <http://www.lasportal.org/>

North Atlantic Treaty Organization (NATO)

NATO was established in 1949 by the North Atlantic Treaty (Washington Treaty) as a Western military alliance. Article 5 of the treaty defines the members' commitment to respond to an armed attack against any party to the treaty. Its headquarters are in Brussels, Belgium.

Members (29): Albania, Belgium, Bulgaria, Canada, Croatia, Czech Republic, Denmark, Estonia, France, Germany, Greece, Hungary, Iceland, Italy, Latvia, Lithuania, Luxembourg, *Montenegro*, Netherlands, Norway, Poland, Portugal, Romania, Slovakia, Slovenia, Spain, Turkey, UK, USA

Website: <http://www.nato.int/>

Euro-Atlantic Partnership Council (EAPC)

The EAPC brings together NATO and its Partnership for Peace (PFP) partners for dialogue and consultation. It is the overall political framework for the bilateral PFP programme.

Members (50): The NATO member states and Armenia, Austria, Azerbaijan, Belarus, Bosnia and Herzegovina, Finland, Georgia, Ireland, Kazakhstan, Kyrgyzstan, Macedonia (Former Yugoslav Republic of), Malta, Moldova, Russia, Serbia, Sweden, Switzerland, Tajikistan, Turkmenistan, Ukraine, Uzbekistan

Website: <http://www.nato.int/cps/en/natolive/topics_49276.htm>

Istanbul Cooperation Initiative (ICI)

The ICI was established in 2004 to contribute to long-term global and regional security by offering practical bilateral security cooperation with NATO to countries of the broader Middle East region.

Participants (33): The NATO member states and Bahrain, Qatar, Kuwait, United Arab Emirates

Website: <http://www.nato.int/cps/en/natolive/topics_52956.htm>

Mediterranean Dialogue

NATO's Mediterranean Dialogue was established in 1994 as a forum for political dialogue and practical cooperation between NATO and countries of the Mediterranean. It reflects NATO's view that security in Europe is closely linked to security and stability in the Mediterranean.

Participants (36): The NATO member states and Algeria, Egypt, Israel, Jordan, Mauritania, Morocco, Tunisia

Website: <http://www.nato.int/cps/en/natolive/topics_52927.htm>

NATO–Georgia Commission (NGC)

The NGC was established in September 2008 to serve as a forum for political consultations and practical cooperation to help Georgia achieve its goal of joining NATO.

Participants (30): The NATO member states and Georgia

Website: <http://www.nato.int/cps/en/natohq/topics_50091.htm>

NATO–Russia Council (NRC)

The NRC was established in 2002 as a mechanism for consultation, consensus building, cooperation, and joint decisions and action on security issues. It focuses on areas of mutual interest identified in the 1997 NATO–Russia Founding Act on Mutual Relations, Cooperation and Security and new areas, such as terrorism, crisis management and non-proliferation.

Participants (30): The NATO member states and Russia

Note: In Apr. 2014, following Russian military intervention in Ukraine, NATO suspended all practical cooperation with Russia, including in the NRC, although meetings continue at the ambassadorial level or above.

Website: <https://www.nato.int/nrc-website/>

NATO–Ukraine Commission (NUC)

The NUC was established in 1997 for consultations on political and security issues, conflict prevention and resolution, non-proliferation, transfers of arms and technology, and other subjects of common concern.

Participants (30): The NATO member states and Ukraine

Website: <http://www.nato.int/cps/en/natolive/topics_50319.htm>

Organisation Conjointe de Coopération en matière d'Armement (OCCAR, Organisation for Joint Armament Cooperation)

OCCAR was established in 1996, with legal status since 2001, to provide more effective and efficient arrangements for the management of specific collaborative armament programmes. Its headquarters are in Bonn, Germany.

Members (6): Belgium, France, Germany, Italy, Spain, UK

Participants (7): Finland, Lithuania, Luxembourg, Netherlands, Poland, Sweden, Turkey

Website: <http://www.occar.int/>

Organismo para la Proscripción de las Armas Nucleares en la América Latina y el Caribe (OPANAL, Agency for the Prohibition of Nuclear Weapons in Latin America and the Caribbean)

OPANAL was established by the 1967 Treaty of Tlatelolco to resolve, together with the IAEA, questions of compliance with the treaty. Its seat is in Mexico City, Mexico.

Parties to the Treaty of Tlatelolco (33): See annex A

Website: <http://www.opanal.org/>

Organization for Democracy and Economic Development–GUAM

GUAM is a group of four states, established to promote stability and strengthen security, whose history goes back to 1997. The organization was established in 2006. The members cooperate to promote social and economic development and trade in eight working groups. Its secretariat is in Kyiv, Ukraine.

Members (4): Azerbaijan, Georgia, Moldova, Ukraine

Website: <http://guam-organization.org/>

Organization for Security and Co-operation in Europe (OSCE)

The Conference on Security and Co-operation in Europe (CSCE), which had been initiated in 1973, was renamed the OSCE in 1995. It is intended to be the primary instrument of comprehensive and cooperative security for early warning, conflict prevention, crisis management and post-conflict rehabilitation in its area. Its headquarters are in Vienna, Austria, and its other institutions are based elsewhere in Europe.

The OSCE Troika consists of representatives of the states holding the chairmanship in the current year, the previous year and the succeeding year. The Forum for Security Cooperation (FSC) deals with arms control and confidence- and security-building measures.

Participants (57): Albania, Andorra, Armenia, Austria*, Azerbaijan, Belarus, Belgium, Bosnia and Herzegovina, Bulgaria, Canada, Croatia, Cyprus, Czech Republic, Denmark, Estonia, Finland, France, Georgia, Germany, Greece, Holy See, Hungary, Iceland, Ireland, Italy**, Kazakhstan, Kyrgyzstan, Latvia, Liechtenstein, Lithuania, Luxembourg, Macedonia (Former Yugoslav Republic of), Malta, Moldova, Monaco, Mongolia, Montenegro, Netherlands, Norway, Poland, Portugal, Romania, Russia, San Marino, Serbia, Slovakia***, Slovenia, Spain, Sweden, Switzerland, Tajikistan, Turkey, Turkmenistan, UK, Ukraine, USA, Uzbekistan

    * Chairmanship in 2017.
    ** Chairmanship in 2018.
    *** Chairmanship in 2019.

Website: <http://www.osce.org/>

Joint Consultative Group (JCG)

The JCG is an OSCE-related body established by the 1990 Treaty on Conventional Armed Forces in Europe (CFE Treaty) to promote the objectives and implementation of the treaty by reconciling ambiguities of interpretation and implementation. Its seat is in Vienna, Austria.

Parties to the CFE Treaty (30): See annex A

    Note: In 2007 Russia suspended its participation in the CFE Treaty, and in Mar. 2015 it announced that it was completely halting its participation in the treaty.

Website: <http://www.osce.org/jcg/>

Minsk Group

The Minsk Group supports the Minsk Process, an ongoing forum for negotiations on a peaceful settlement of the conflict in Nagorno-Karabakh.

Members (13): Armenia, Azerbaijan, Belarus, Finland, France*, Germany, Italy, Russia*, Sweden, Turkey, USA*, OSCE Troika (Austria, Italy and Slovakia)

    * The representatives of these 3 states co-chair the group.

Website: <http://www.osce.org/mg/>

Open Skies Consultative Commission (OSCC)

The OSCC was established by the 1992 Treaty on Open Skies to resolve questions of compliance with the treaty.

Parties to the Open Skies Treaty (34): See annex A

Website: <http://www.osce.org/oscc/>

Organization of American States (OAS)

The OAS, which adopted its charter in 1948, has the objective of strengthening peace and security in the western hemisphere. Its activities are based on the four pillars of democracy, human rights, security and development. Its general secretariat is in Washington, DC, USA.

Members (35): Antigua and Barbuda, Argentina, Bahamas, Barbados, Belize, Bolivia, Brazil, Canada, Chile, Colombia, Costa Rica, Cuba*, Dominica, Dominican Republic, Ecuador, El Salvador, Grenada, Guatemala, Guyana, Haiti, Honduras, Jamaica, Mexico, Nicaragua, Panama, Paraguay, Peru, Saint Kitts and Nevis, Saint Lucia, Saint Vincent and the Grenadines, Suriname, Trinidad and Tobago, Uruguay, USA, Venezuela

  * By a resolution of 3 June 2009, the 1962 resolution that excluded Cuba from the OAS ceased to have effect; according to the 2009 resolution, Cuba's participation in the organization 'will be the result of a process of dialogue'. Cuba has declined to participate in OAS activities.

Website: <http://www.oas.org/>

Organization of the Black Sea Economic Cooperation (BSEC)

The BSEC initiative was established in 1992 and became a full regional economic organization when its charter entered into force in 1999. Its aims are to ensure peace, stability and prosperity and to promote and develop economic cooperation and progress in the Black Sea region. Its permanent secretariat is in Istanbul, Turkey.

Members (12): Albania, Armenia, Azerbaijan, Bulgaria, Georgia, Greece, Moldova, Romania, Russia, Serbia, Turkey, Ukraine

Website: <http://www.bsec-organization.org/>

Pacific Islands Forum

The forum, which was founded in 1971 as the South Pacific Forum, aims to enhance cooperation in sustainable development, economic growth, governance and security. It also monitors implementation of the 1985 Treaty of Rarotonga, which established the South Pacific Nuclear-Free Zone. Its secretariat is in Suva, Fiji.

Members (18): Australia, Cook Islands, Fiji, French Polynesia, Kiribati, Marshall Islands, Micronesia, Nauru, New Caledonia, New Zealand, Niue, Palau, Papua New Guinea, Samoa, Solomon Islands, Tonga, Tuvalu, Vanuatu

Website: <http://www.forumsec.org/>

Regional Centre on Small Arms in the Great Lakes Region, the Horn of Africa and Bordering States (RECSA)

The Nairobi Secretariat on Small Arms and Light Weapons was established to coordinate implementation of the 2000 Nairobi Declaration on the Problem of Illicit Small Arms and Light Weapons in the Great Lakes Region and the Horn of Africa. It was transformed into RECSA in 2005 to oversee the implementation of the 2004 Nairobi Protocol for the Prevention, Control and Reduction of Small Arms and Light Weapons. It is based in Nairobi, Kenya.

Members (15): Burundi, Djibouti, Central African Republic, Congo (Democratic Republic of the), Congo (Republic of the), Eritrea, Ethiopia, Kenya, Rwanda, Seychelles, Somalia, South

Sudan, Sudan, Tanzania, Uganda

Website: <http://www.recsasec.org/>

Regional Cooperation Council

The RCC was launched in 2008 as the successor of the Stability Pact for South Eastern Europe that was initiated by the EU at the 1999 Conference on South Eastern Europe. It promotes mutual cooperation and European and Euro-Atlantic integration of states in South Eastern Europe in order to inspire development in the region for the benefit of its people. It focuses on six areas: economic and social development, energy and infrastructure, justice and home affairs, security cooperation, building human capital, and parliamentary cooperation. Its secretariat is in Sarajevo, Bosnia and Herzegovina, and it has a liaison office in Brussels, Belgium.

Participants (46): Albania, Austria, Bosnia and Herzegovina, Bulgaria, Canada, Council of Europe, Council of Europe Development Bank, Croatia, Czech Republic, Denmark, European Bank for Reconstruction and Development, European Investment Bank, European Union, Germany, Finland, France, Greece, Hungary, International Organization for Migration, Ireland, Italy, Kosovo, Latvia, Macedonia (Former Yugoslav Republic of), Moldova, Montenegro, North Atlantic Treaty Organization, Norway, Organisation for Economic Co-operation and Development, Organization for Security and Cooperation in Europe, Poland, Romania, Serbia, Slovakia, Slovenia, South East European Cooperative Initiative, Spain, Sweden, Switzerland, Turkey, UK, United Nations, UN Economic Commission for Europe, UN Development Programme, USA, World Bank

Website: <http://www.rcc.int/>

Shanghai Cooperation Organisation (SCO)

The SCO's predecessor group, the Shanghai Five, was founded in 1996; it was renamed the SCO in 2001 and opened for membership of all states that support its aims. The member states cooperate on confidence-building measures and regional security and in the economic sphere. Its secretariat is in Beijing, China. The SCO Regional Anti-Terrorist Structure (RATS) is based in Tashkent, Uzbekistan.

Members (8): China, India, Kazakhstan, Kyrgyzstan, Pakistan, Russia, Tajikistan, Uzbekistan

Website: <http://www.sectsco.org/>

Sistema de la Integración Centroamericana (SICA, Central American Integration System)

SICA was founded in 1991 with the signing of the Tegucigalpa Protocol. One of the organization's purposes is to set up a new model of regional security based on the reasonable balance of forces; the strengthening of civilian authority; the overcoming of extreme poverty; the promotion of sustainable development; the protection of the environment; and the eradication of violence, corruption, terrorism, and drug and arms trafficking. The SICA headquarters are located in San Salvador, El Salvador.

Members (8): Belize, Costa Rica, Dominican Republic, El Salvador, Guatemala, Honduras, Nicaragua, Panama

Website: <http://www.sica.int/>

Six-Party Talks

The Six-Party Talks began in 2003 as a Chinese diplomatic initiative aimed at resolving the controversy over how to address North Korea's nuclear weapons programme. No negotiations have been held since 2009, when North Korea announced that it was withdrawing from the talks.

Participants (6): China, Japan, Korea (North), Korea (South), Russia, USA

Southern African Development Community (SADC)

SADC was established in 1992 to promote regional economic development and the fundamental principles of sovereignty, peace and security, human rights and democracy. It superseded the Southern African Development Coordination Conference (SADCC), established in 1980. The SADC Organ on Politics, Defence and Security Cooperation (OPDS) is intended to promote peace and security in the region. Its secretariat is in Gaborone, Botswana.

Members (16): Angola, Botswana, Comoros, Congo (Democratic Republic of the), Lesotho, Madagascar, Malawi, Mauritius, Mozambique, Namibia, Seychelles, South Africa, Swaziland, Tanzania, Zambia, Zimbabwe

Website: <http://www.sadc.int/>

Unión de Naciones Suramericanas (UNASUR, Union of South American Nations)

UNASUR is an intergovernmental organization with the aim of strengthening regional integration, political dialogue, economic development and coordination in defence matters among its member states. Its 2008 Constitutive Treaty entered into force on 11 March 2011 and it will gradually replace the Andean Community and the Mercado Común del Sur (MERCOSUR, Southern Common Market). Its headquarters are in Quito, Ecuador.

The Consejo de Defensa Suramericano (CDS, South American Defence Council) was approved by the UNASUR member states in December 2008 and had its first meeting in March 2009. The objectives of the CDS are to consolidate South America as a zone of peace and to create a regional identity and strengthen regional cooperation in defence issues.

Members (12): Argentina*, Bolivia, Brazil*, Chile*, Colombia*, Ecuador, Guyana, Paraguay*, Peru*, Suriname, Uruguay, Venezuela

* On 20 Apr. 2018 these 6 states suspended their membership of UNASUR for 1 year.

Website: <http://www.unasursg.org/>

III. Strategic trade control regimes

Australia Group (AG)

The AG is an informal group of states and the European Commission formed in 1985. The AG meets annually to exchange views and best practices on strategic trade controls in order to ensure that dual-purpose material, technology and equipment are not used to support chemical and biological warfare activity or programmes.

Participants (42): Argentina, Australia, Austria, Belgium, Bulgaria, Canada, Croatia, Cyprus, Czech Republic, Denmark, Estonia, European Commission, Finland, France, Germany, Greece, Hungary, Iceland, Ireland, Italy, Japan, Korea (South), Latvia, Lithuania, Luxembourg, Malta, Mexico, Netherlands, New Zealand, Norway, Poland, Portugal, Romania, Slovakia, Slovenia, Spain, Sweden, Switzerland, Turkey, UK, Ukraine, USA

Note: In addition to the 42 participants as of 1 Jan. 2018, India joined the AG on 18 Jan. 2018.

Website: <http://www.australiagroup.net/>

Hague Code of Conduct against Ballistic Missile Proliferation (HCOC)

The principle of the 2002 HCOC is the need to curb the proliferation of ballistic missile systems capable of delivering WMD. Subscribing states must exercise restraint in the development, testing and deployment of such missiles. The Ministry for Foreign Affairs of Austria acts as the HCOC secretariat.

Subscribing states (138): Afghanistan, Albania, Andorra, Antigua and Barbuda, Argentina, Armenia, Australia, Austria, Azerbaijan, Belarus, Belgium, Benin, Bosnia and Herzegovina, Bulgaria, Burkina Faso, Burundi, Cabo Verde, Cambodia, Cameroon, Canada, Central African Republic, Chad, Chile, Colombia, Comoros, Congo (Republic of the), Cook Islands, Costa Rica, Croatia, Cyprus, Czech Republic, Denmark, Dominica, Dominican Republic, Ecuador, El Salvador, Eritrea, Estonia, Ethiopia, Fiji, Finland, France, Gabon, Gambia, Georgia, Germany, Ghana, Greece, Guatemala, Guinea, Guinea-Bissau, Guyana, Haiti, Holy See, Honduras, Hungary, Iceland, India, Iraq, Ireland, Italy, Japan, Jordan, Kazakhstan, Kenya, Kiribati, Korea (South), Latvia, Liberia, Libya, Liechtenstein, Lithuania, Luxembourg, Macedonia (Former Yugoslav Republic of), Madagascar, Malawi, Maldives, Mali, Malta, Marshall Islands, Mauritania, Micronesia, Moldova, Monaco, Mongolia, Montenegro, Morocco, Mozambique, Netherlands, New Zealand, Nicaragua, Niger, Nigeria, Norway, Palau, Panama, Papua New Guinea, Paraguay, Peru, Philippines, Poland, Portugal, Romania, Russia, Rwanda, Saint Kitts and Nevis, Samoa, San Marino, Senegal, Serbia, Seychelles, Sierra Leone, Singapore, Slovakia, Slovenia, South Africa, Spain, Sudan, Suriname, Sweden, Switzerland, Tajikistan, Tanzania, Timor-Leste, Tonga, Tunisia, Turkey, Turkmenistan, Tuvalu, Uganda, UK, Ukraine, Uruguay, USA, Uzbekistan, Vanuatu, Venezuela, Zambia

Note: In addition to the 138 subscribing states as of 1 Jan. 2018, Lesotho subscribed to the HCOC in Jan. 2018.

Website: <http://www.hcoc.at/>

Missile Technology Control Regime (MTCR)

The MTCR is an informal group of countries that since 1987 has sought to coordinate national export licensing efforts aimed at preventing the proliferation of missile systems capable of delivering WMD. The countries apply the Guidelines for Sensitive Missile-Relevant Transfers. The MTCR has no secretariat. A point of contact based in the Ministry for Foreign Affairs of France distributes the regime's working papers and hosts regular policy and information-exchange meetings.

Partners (35): Argentina, Australia, Austria, Belgium, Brazil, Bulgaria, Canada, Czech Republic, Denmark, Finland, France, Germany, Greece, Hungary, Iceland, India, Ireland, Italy, Japan, Korea (South), Luxembourg, Netherlands, New Zealand, Norway, Poland, Portugal, Russia, South Africa, Spain, Sweden, Switzerland, Turkey, UK, Ukraine, USA

Website: <http://www.mtcr.info/>

Nuclear Suppliers Group (NSG)

The NSG, formerly also known as the London Club, was established in 1975. It coordinates national transfer controls on nuclear materials according to its Guidelines for Nuclear Transfers (London Guidelines, first agreed in 1978), which contain a 'trigger list' of materials that should trigger IAEA safeguards when they are to be exported for peaceful purposes to any non-nuclear weapon state, and the Guidelines for Transfers of Nuclear-Related Dual-Use Equipment, Materials, Software and Related Technology (Warsaw Guidelines). The NSG Guidelines are implemented by each participating state in accordance with its national laws and practices. The NSG has no secretariat. The Permanent Mission of Japan to the IAEA in Vienna acts as a point of contact and carries out practical support functions.

Participants (48): Argentina, Australia, Austria, Belarus, Belgium, Brazil, Bulgaria, Canada, China, Croatia, Cyprus, Czech Republic, Denmark, Estonia, Finland, France, Germany, Greece, Hungary, Iceland, Ireland, Italy, Japan, Kazakhstan, Korea (South), Latvia, Lithuania, Luxembourg, Malta, Mexico, Netherlands, New Zealand, Norway, Poland, Portugal, Romania, Russia, Serbia, Slovakia, Slovenia, South Africa, Spain, Sweden, Switzerland, Turkey, UK, Ukraine, USA

Website: <http://www.nuclearsuppliersgroup.org/>

Proliferation Security Initiative (PSI)

Based on a US initiative announced in 2003, the PSI is a multilateral forum focusing on law enforcement cooperation for the interdiction and seizure of illegal WMD, missile technologies and related materials when in transit on land, in the air or at sea. The PSI Statement of Interdiction Principles was issued in 2003. The PSI has no secretariat, but its activities are coordinated by a 21-member Operational Experts Group.

Participants (105): Afghanistan, Albania, Andorra, Angola, Antigua and Barbuda, Argentina*, Armenia, Australia*†, Austria, Azerbaijan, Bahamas, Bahrain, Belarus, Belgium, Belize, Bosnia and Herzegovina, Brunei Darussalam, Bulgaria, Cambodia, Canada*, Chile, Colombia, Croatia†, Cyprus, Czech Republic†, Denmark*, Djibouti†, Dominica, Dominican Republic, El Salvador, Estonia, Fiji, Finland, France*†, Georgia, Germany*†, Greece*, Holy See, Honduras, Hungary, Iceland, Iraq, Ireland, Israel, Italy*†, Japan*†, Jordan, Kazakhstan, Korea (South)*†, Kyrgyzstan, Kuwait, Latvia, Liberia, Libya, Liechtenstein, Lithuania†, Luxembourg, Macedonia (Former Yugoslav Republic of), Malaysia, Malta, Marshall Islands,

Moldova, Mongolia, Montenegro, Morocco, Netherlands*†, New Zealand*†, Norway*†, Oman, Panama, Papua New Guinea, Paraguay, Philippines, Poland*†, Portugal*†, Qatar†, Romania, Russia*, Saint Lucia, Saint Vincent and the Grenadines, Samoa, San Marino, Saudi Arabia, Serbia, Singapore*†, Slovakia, Slovenia†, Spain*†, Sri Lanka, Sweden, Switzerland, Tajikistan, Thailand, Trinidad and Tobago, Tunisia, Turkey*†, Turkmenistan, UK*†, Ukraine†, United Arab Emirates†, USA*†, Uzbekistan, Vanuatu, Viet Nam, Yemen

   * Member of the Operational Experts Group.
   † PSI exercise host, 2003–17.

Website: US Department of State, <http://www.state.gov/t/isn/c10390.htm>

Wassenaar Arrangement on Export Controls for Conventional Arms and Dual-Use Goods and Technologies (Wassenaar Arrangement, WA)

The Wassenaar Arrangement was formally established in 1996. It aims to prevent the acquisition of armaments and sensitive dual-use goods and technologies for military uses by states whose behaviour is cause for concern to the member states. The WA secretariat is in Vienna, Austria.

Participants (42): Argentina, Australia, Austria, Belgium, Bulgaria, Canada, Croatia, Czech Republic, Denmark, Estonia, Finland, France, Germany, Greece, Hungary, India, Ireland, Italy, Japan, Korea (South), Latvia, Lithuania, Luxembourg, Malta, Mexico, Netherlands, New Zealand, Norway, Poland, Portugal, Romania, Russia, Slovakia, Slovenia, South Africa, Spain, Sweden, Switzerland, Turkey, UK, Ukraine, USA

Website: <http://www.wassenaar.org/>

Zangger Committee

Established in 1971–74, the Nuclear Exporters Committee, called the Zangger Committee, is a group of nuclear supplier countries that meets informally twice a year to coordinate transfer controls on nuclear materials according to its regularly updated trigger list of items which, when exported, must be subject to IAEA safeguards. It complements the work of the Nuclear Suppliers Group.

Members (39): Argentina, Australia, Austria, Belarus, Belgium, Bulgaria, Canada, China, Croatia, Czech Republic, Denmark, Finland, France, Germany, Greece, Hungary, Ireland, Italy, Japan, Kazakhstan, Korea (South), Luxembourg, Netherlands, New Zealand, Norway, Poland, Portugal, Romania, Russia, Slovakia, Slovenia, South Africa, Spain, Sweden, Switzerland, Turkey, UK, Ukraine, USA

Website: <http://www.zanggercommittee.org/>

Annex C. Chronology 2017

IAN DAVIS

This chronology lists the significant events in 2017 related to armaments, disarmament and international security. Keywords are indicated in the right-hand column.

Date	Event	Keywords
1 Jan.	A gunman kills 39 people at a nightclub in Istanbul, Turkey. The Islamic State (IS) claims responsibility.	Turkey; IS
1 Jan.	António Guterres becomes the ninth Secretary-General of the United Nations.	UN Secretary-General
3 Jan.	The Consultation Task Force, appointed by the Sri Lankan Government in Feb. 2016, publishes its final report on Sri Lankan citizens' aspirations for truth and justice.	Sri Lanka
7 Jan.	The Saudi Arabian-led coalition and aligned Yemeni troops launch a new military offensive against Houthi forces in the south-west of Yemen, bordering the Bab al-Mandeb strait.	Saudi Arabia; Yemen
18 Jan.	At least 47 people, including 5 suicide bombers from al-Qaeda in the Islamic Maghreb (AQIM), are killed by a car bomb at a military camp in the city of Gao in northern Mali.	Mali; AQIM
20 Jan.	Donald J. Trump is inaugurated as the 45th President of the United States, vowing to follow a policy based on 'America first'.	USA
20 Jan.	Following both diplomatic pressure and the threat of force by the Economic Community of West African States (ECOWAS), Gambian President Yahya Jammeh steps down, allowing election winner Adama Barrow to take up the presidency.	Gambia; ECOWAS
21 Jan.	Millions of people worldwide join the Women's March in response to the inauguration of Donald J. Trump as US President.	Women's March
23 Jan.	US President Trump withdraws the USA from the Trans-Pacific Partnership (TPP), a regional trade agreement among 11 Pacific rim countries.	USA; TPP
25 Jan.	At least 28 people are killed in an attack by al-Shabab on a hotel in Mogadishu, the capital of Somalia.	Somalia; al-Shabab
26 Jan.	The Northern Ireland Assembly, the devolved legislature set up under the Good Friday Agreement, is suspended and remains so throughout the year.	UK; Northern Ireland
8 Feb.	Former Prime Minister Mohamed Abdullahi Mohamed wins presidential elections in Somalia, defeating incumbent President Hassan Sheikh Mohamud.	Somalia

SIPRI Yearbook 2018: Armaments, Disarmament and International Security
www.sipriyearbook.org

9 Feb.	At least 34 people are reported killed and about 50 injured by a bomb detonated at a market in Somalia. Al-Shabab is believed to be responsible.	Somalia; al-Shabab
11 Feb.	North Korea prompts international condemnation by test firing an intermediate-range ballistic missile across the Sea of Japan.	North Korea; missile proliferation
13 Feb.	North Korean leader Kim Jong Un's estranged half-brother is assassinated at Malaysia's Kuala Lumpur international airport, reportedly with a highly toxic nerve agent.	North Korea; Malaysia; assassination
14–16 Feb.	The 2017 intersessional implementation meeting of the Australia Group (AG) is held in Buenos Aires, Argentina, including a meeting of experts on new and evolving technologies.	AG
16 Feb.	A suicide bombing at one of Pakistan's most prominent Sufi shrines in Sehwan Sharif, Sindh province, kills at least 88 people and injures more than 200.	Pakistan; Islamist extremism
16 Feb.	Prior to the opening of the UN Conference to Negotiate a Legally Binding Instrument to Prohibit Nuclear Weapons, a one-day organizational meeting is held in New York, USA, attended by more than 100 states.	Nuclear weapon ban treaty
20 Feb.	The UN declares a famine in South Sudan as a result of the ongoing war and a collapsing economy.	UN; South Sudan
22 Feb.	Pakistan announces a new nationwide counterterrorism operation, Radd-ul-Fasaad (End to Chaos), with a particular focus on Punjab, its largest province.	Pakistan; counter-terrorism
23 Feb.– 3 Mar.	UN-sponsored peace talks on Syria take place in Geneva, Switzerland, ending without a breakthrough.	Syria; UN
25 Feb.	Azerbaijan reports six of its soldiers killed during an exchange of fire on the southern section of the line of contact around Nagorno-Karabakh.	Azerbaijan; Armenia; Nagorno-Karabakh
28 Feb.	China and Russia veto a UN Security Council resolution that would have imposed sanctions against Syria for the use of chemical weapons (CWs), based on the findings of the Organisation for the Prohibition of Chemical Weapons (OPCW)–UN Joint Investigative Mechanism (JIM).	UN; Syria; CWs; JIM
28 Feb.	An international pledging conference for the implementation of the Anti-personnel Mine (APM) Convention is held in Geneva, Switzerland.	APM Convention
1 Mar.	Macedonia's political crisis deepens after President Gjorge Ivanov refuses to hand opposition leader Zoran Zaev of the Social Democrat party a mandate to form a new government, despite his majority support in parliament.	Macedonia; political crisis
2–3 Mar.	The high-level fissile material cut-off treaty (FMCT) expert preparatory group meets for informal consultations at the UN in New York.	FMCT
3 Mar.	The International Committee of the Red Cross (ICRC) condemns the use of CWs in the battle of Mosul, Iraq.	ICRC; Iraq; CWs

6 Mar.	The USA begins deploying the Terminal High Altitude Area Defence (THAAD) system in South Korea.	USA; South Korea; missile defence
8 Mar.	The Central African Convention for the Control of Small Arms and Light Weapons, Their Ammunition and All Parts and Components That Can Be Used for Their Manufacture, Repair and Assembly (Kinshasa Convention) enters into force.	Kinshasa Convention
10 Mar.	The UN warns that the world is facing the biggest humanitarian crisis since World War II, with up to 20 million people at risk of starvation and famine in Yemen, Somalia, South Sudan and Nigeria.	UN; Yemen; Somalia; South Sudan; Nigeria; humanitarian crisis
20 Mar.	The European Union (EU) imposes sanctions against four Syrian military officials for their role in the use of CWs.	EU; Syria; CWs; sanctions
21 Mar.	Ukraine imposes an economic blockade on territory held by Russian-backed separatists.	Ukraine
22 Mar.	Six people, including the attacker, are killed and 50 injured in a terrorist attack near the Houses of Parliament in the UK. The attacker drives into pedestrians on Westminster Bridge and stabs a police officer before being shot dead by police. IS claims responsibility.	UK; IS
24 Mar.	In the Democratic Republic of the Congo (DRC), 39 police officers are reportedly killed in an ambush by Kamwina Nsapu militiamen in Kamuesha, Kasai province.	DRC
27 Mar.–2 Apr.	The Conference of National Entente takes place in Mali, involving armed groups and opposition political parties.	Mali
27–31 Mar.	The opening session of the UN Conference to Negotiate a Legally Binding Instrument to Prohibit Nuclear Weapons takes place in New York. More than 130 states participate, along with representatives from international organizations and civil society groups.	Nuclear weapon ban treaty
29 Mar.	The British Government triggers Article 50 of the Lisbon Treaty, starting the process to leave the EU (Brexit).	UK; EU; Brexit
30 Mar.	Israel announces plans for its first new settlement in the West Bank in more than twenty years.	Israel; Palestine
30 Mar.	An alleged CW attack takes place in Ltamenah, in the Hama Governorate, Syria.	Syria; CWs
30 Mar.	US President Trump relaxes the US combat rules for Somalia, signing a directive that identifies parts of Somalia as an 'area of active hostilities', where war-zone targeting rules apply.	USA; Somalia
31 Mar.	Violent protests break out in Asunción, the capital of Paraguay. Protesters storm and set fire to the parliament building after senators vote to approve a bill amending the constitution to lift the one-term limit on the presidency.	Paraguay

31 Mar.	The UN Security Council recognizes the significance of the Lake Chad crisis and unanimously issues Resolution 2349 against terrorism and human rights violations in the region.	UN; Lake Chad Basin
4–7 Apr.	The USA, among others, holds President Bashar al-Assad's regime responsible for a CW attack on Khan Shaykhoun that kills at least 80. Three days later the USA launches a missile strike on the air base from which it believes the attack was launched.	Syria; USA; CWs
9 Apr.	Two separate suicide attacks by IS at Coptic churches in Egypt kill 48 people.	Egypt; IS
9 Apr.	During a by-election in Srinagar, Kashmir, Indian security forces open fire on protesters throwing stones and attacking polling stations, killing seven. Overall, eight people are killed and over 200 injured in election-day clashes.	India; Kashmir
10 Apr.	The UN Secretary-General, António Guterres, calls on Morocco and the Polisario movement to restart peace talks amid decades of territorial tensions over the sovereignty of Western Sahara.	UN; Morocco; Western Sahara
12 Apr.	The Atomic Energy Organization of Iran signs a contract with the China National Nuclear Corporation for the design concept of a new nuclear reactor.	Iran; China; nuclear cooperation
13 Apr.	The US military drops the largest non-nuclear bomb ever deployed in combat, targeting an IS base in Afghanistan. The GBU-43/B Massive Ordnance Air Blast bomb ('Mother of All Bombs') hit a tunnel complex in the Nangarhar province.	USA; Afghanistan: IS
16 Apr.	A referendum in Turkey adopts constitutional changes to establish a 'presidential system', although most of them are not due to take effect until after elections in 2019.	Turkey
21 Apr.	The Taliban infiltrate an army base in Mazar-e-Sharif city in the Balkh province of Afghanistan, killing at least 140 soldiers.	Taliban; Afghanistan
21 Apr.	Maoists ambush a police patrol in the Indian state of Chhattisgarh, killing at least 25, in what is reportedly the worst attack on security forces in the area since 2010.	India; terrorism
24 Apr.	The USA imposes sanctions on 271 Syrian officials and scientists in connection with the sarin attack on Khan Shaykhoun, Syria, on 4 Apr.	US; Syria; CWs; sanctions
25 Apr.	A suicide bombing by IS in Egypt's northern Sinai peninsula kills at least 40 people.	Egypt; IS
27 Apr.	Around 200 protesters storm Macedonia's parliament after an ethnic Albanian politician is voted in as Speaker. Clashes inside and outside the parliament injure over 70 people.	Macedonia
28 Apr.	Via Resolution 2351, the UN Security Council extends the UN Mission for the Referendum in Western Sahara (MINURSO) and calls for new negotiations between Morocco and the Polisario movement.	UN; Morocco; Western Sahara

2 May	Fayez Serraj, the head of Libya's internationally recognized government, meets General Khalifa Haftar, his major military opponent, for the first time in over a year.	Libya
2–12 May	The Preparatory Committee for the 2020 Review Conference of the Parties to the 1968 Non-Proliferation Treaty (NPT) holds the first of three planned sessions in Vienna, Austria.	NPT PrepCom
6 May	A partial ceasefire is agreed in the west of Syria, and de-escalation zones are created in an agreement between Iran, Russia, Syria and Turkey.	Syria; Russia; Iran; Turkey
7 May	Out of the 276 schoolgirls abducted by Boko Haram in Nigeria in 2014, 82 are freed in a prisoner exchange with the group.	Nigeria; Boko Haram
9 May	The USA decides to arm some Kurdish militias in Syria, principally the People's Protection Units (YPG), raising tensions between the USA and Turkey.	Syria; USA; Turkey, Kurds
9 May	A bomb at a department store in Pattani, southern Thailand, injures around 80 civilians. The main insurgent group, Barisan Revolusi Nasional, claims responsibility.	Thailand; terrorism
11 May	At the London Conference, Somalia agrees a security pact with international donors, in which Somalia's army and police will be trained to take over duties performed by the African Union (AU).	Somalia; AU
12 May	Computers around the world are hit by a large-scale ransomware cyberattack, which goes on to affect at least 150 countries.	Cybersecurity
18 May	EU member states endorse a Coordinated Annual Review on Defence (CARD) as a pilot activity to run for two years from the autumn of 2017.	EU; military cooperation
20 May	Hassan Rouhani is re-elected as the President of Iran, winning 57 per cent of the 41 million votes cast, as voters overwhelmingly back his reformists efforts.	Iran
22 May	At least 23 people are killed and more than 500 wounded in a suicide bomb attack at a concert in Manchester, UK. The bomber largely acts alone, although IS claims responsibility.	UK; IS
22 May	President Salva Kiir (South Sudan) declares a unilateral ceasefire and launches a national dialogue process.	South Sudan
23 May	President Rodrigo Duterte declares martial law in the southern island of Mindanao in the Philippines, after about 100 IS fighters take over large parts of Marawi City. Over 170 000 residents are forced to flee.	Philippines; IS
24 May	A roadside bomb hits the convoy of the Governor of Mandera County, Kenya, killing five bodyguards. From 8–25 May, al-Shabab attacks on security forces and civilians in the north-east of the country kill 18 people.	Kenya; al-Shabab
26 May	IS launches its first major attack in Upper Egypt, which leaves at least 29 dead. The Egyptian Government responds by carrying out airstrikes in Libya and intensifying repression at home.	Egypt; IS; Libya

31 May	A truck bomb explodes close to the heavily guarded diplomatic area of Kabul, Afghanistan, killing at least 150 people.	Afghanistan
31 May	Over five months after holding elections, under increasing international pressure, Macedonian President Ivanov finally agrees to offer the mandate to form a government to opposition leader Zoran Zaev of the Social Democrat SDSM party.	Macedonia
1 June	US President Trump announces that he is withdrawing the USA from the Paris Agreement on climate change, although this cannot be finalized until near the end of his term due to the accord's legal structure and language.	USA; the Paris Agreement
2 June	The UN Security Council unanimously adopts Resolution 2356 condemning North Korea's recent nuclear weapon and ballistic missile developments and extending the scope of sanctions.	UN; North Korea; sanctions
3 June	In the UK, an Islamic terrorist attack on London Bridge kills 8 people and injures 48.	UK; IS
5 June	Saudi Arabia, Bahrain, the United Arab Emirates, Egypt and Yemen break off diplomatic ties and close transport links with Qatar.	Qatar; Gulf states
5 June	Montenegro becomes the twenty-ninth member of the North Atlantic Treaty Organization (NATO).	Montenegro; NATO
6–7 June	The 16th annual meeting on the Hague Code of Conduct (HCOC) takes place in Vienna, Austria, with delegations from 64 of the 138 subscribing states attending.	HCOC
7 June	The European Commission launches the European Defence Fund (EDF) for military research and capabilities development.	EU; EDF
7 June	Two terrorist attacks by IS in Tehran kill 17 civilians and wound 43, marking the first IS attack in Iran.	Iran; IS
8 June	An attack by al-Shabab on a military base in Puntland, Somalia, leaves at least 70 people dead in what Somali officials call the deadliest attack in the country for years.	Somalia; al-Shabab
8 June	The EU agrees to establish a Brussels-based Military Planning and Conduct Capability (MPCC) to plan and conduct training and capacity-building missions.	EU; military cooperation
15 June	The European Parliament adopts a third resolution condemning airstrikes in Yemen by the Saudi Arabian-led coalition, including its use of cluster munitions.	EU; Saudi Arabia; Yemen; cluster munitions
15 June	The UN Conference to Negotiate a Legally Binding Instrument to Prohibit Nuclear Weapons resumes in New York, USA, with the aim of adopting a treaty before the talks end on 7 July.	Nuclear weapon ban treaty
18 June	A US strike aircraft shoots down a Syrian Government combat aircraft south-west of Raqqah, Syria, and US forces carry out several airstrikes on advancing pro-government forces.	Syria; USA

18 June	Five female Boko Haram suicide bombers kill 12 people in Kofa village near Maiduguri, Nigeria. Part of a series of attacks over several days in the north-eastern state of Borno, which leaves at least 80 civilians dead.	Nigeria; Boko Haram
18 June	In response to the terrorist attacks in Tehran earlier in the month, Iran's Islamic Revolutionary Guards Corps (IRGC) fires six surface-to-surface mid-range ballistic missiles from domestic bases targeting IS forces in Syria.	Iran; Syria; IS
19 June	As part of a merged peace process, a meeting with armed groups in Rome results in a 'political peace agreement' for the Central African Republic (CAR). However, the agreement is soon overtaken by a resumption of violence.	CAR
21 June	Prince Muhammed Bin Salman, the son of Saudi King Salman, is named heir to the throne as Crown Prince in a reshuffle that sidelines his older cousin, Prince Muhammed bin Nayef.	Saudi Arabia
21 June	The Great Mosque of al-Nuri in Mosul, Iraq, is destroyed by IS.	Iraq; IS
25 June	The World Health Organization (WHO) estimates that Yemen has over 200 000 cases of cholera.	WHO; Yemen
26 June	In Colombia, UN monitors report that FARC has completed the handover of their weapons to the UN mission a day ahead of the 27 June deadline, under the 2016 peace agreement.	Colombia; FARC; UN
27 June	A series of cyberattacks using the Petya malware begins, affecting organizations in Ukraine.	Ukraine; Cybersecurity
29–30 June	At the seventh round of High-Level Consultations on Maritime Affairs in Japan, among other things, China and Japan agree to launch an air and maritime contact mechanism as soon as possible.	China; Japan
30 June	The 20th anniversary of the entry into force of the Chemical Weapons Convention (CWC).	CWC
3 July	A series of accelerated North Korean missile tests in recent months culminate with the launch of an inter-continental ballistic missile (ICBM).	North Korea; missile proliferation
7 July	The UN Conference to Negotiate a Legally Binding Instrument to Prohibit Nuclear Weapons completes a final draft of the Treaty on the Prohibition of Nuclear Weapons (TPNW), which is adopted by a vote of 122 participating states in favour, 1 against (Netherlands) and 1 abstaining (Singapore).	Nuclear weapon ban treaty
7 July	The UN Secretary-General, António Guterres, announces the collapse of negotiations to reunify Cyprus after another round of talks between Greek and Turkish Cypriot leaders in Switzerland.	Cyprus
7 July	At least 23 soldiers are killed when IS suicide car bombs hit two military checkpoints in Egypt's northern Sinai peninsula.	Egypt; IS

22 July	Houthi forces in Yemen claim to have launched a ballistic missile into Saudi Arabia, the latest of many attempts to hit targets in Saudi territory with long-range ballistic missiles.	Yemen; Saudi Arabia; missile proliferation
27 July	Iran launches a satellite, prompting the US Congress to impose the first new US sanctions against Iran since the negotiation of the Joint Comprehensive Plan of Action (JCPOA).	Iran; USA; sanctions
28 July	North Korea carries out its second ICBM test launch this month.	North Korea; missile proliferation
30 July	The Venezuelan Government under President Nicolás Maduro pushes through a vote to elect a constituent assembly with the power to dissolve state institutions, including the opposition-led parliament, and rewrite the constitution. Opposition protests intensify.	Venezuela
2 Aug.	The UN Security Council adopts Resolution 2370, which calls for more stringent national measures to address the threat of improvised explosive devices (IEDs), including preventing the supply of weapons and explosive precursors to terrorists.	UN; IEDs
2 Aug.	The US Congress approves the Countering America's Adversaries Through Sanctions Act, which imposes new or expanded sanctions against North Korea, Iran and Russia.	Iran; North Korea; Russia; USA; sanctions
5 Aug.	The UN Security Council unanimously approves new sanctions on North Korean trade and investment, as part of Resolution 2371.	UN; North Korea; sanctions
7 Aug.	The UN Under-Secretary-General for Humanitarian Affairs and Emergency Relief Coordinator, Stephen O'Brien, tells the UN Security Council that the situation in CAR displays warning signs of genocide and calls for additional troops for the peacekeeping mission.	CAR
8 Aug.	Violence mars Kenya's general elections, with 37 deaths reported and a contested outcome in the presidential election.	Kenya
13–17 Aug.	Two suspected Islamist militants kill 19 people in Ouagadougou, the capital of Burkina Faso. Four days later, a military vehicle hits an IED in Inata in the north, killing 3 soldiers.	Burkina Faso
15 Aug.	Three Boko Haram female suicide bombers kill 27 people in north-eastern Nigeria.	Nigeria; Boko Haram
17 Aug.	Sixteen people are killed and over 130 wounded in two IS attacks in Barcelona, Spain.	Spain; IS
22 Aug.	US President Trump announces a new strategy for Afghanistan, with a shift from a time-based approach to a conditions-based approach and an increase of about 4000 deployed troops.	USA; Afghanistan
24 Aug.	In Yemen, former president Ali Abdullah Saleh stages a large rally in the capital Sana'a, leading to increases in Saudi Arabian-led coalition airstrikes.	Yemen

25 Aug.	Militants launch coordinated attacks on 30 police posts and an army base in Myanmar's northern Rakhine state. In response, the military conduct 'clearance operations' that set in motion an exodus of up to 38 000 Rohingyas towards Bangladesh.	Myanmar; Rohingya
25–30 Aug.	Hurricane Harvey strikes the USA and causes widespread damage to the Houston area, mostly due to record-breaking floods. At least 90 deaths are recorded and total damage reaches $198.6 billion, making Harvey the costliest natural disaster in US history.	USA; extreme weather
28 Aug.	Following diplomatic initiatives from both sides, a border confrontation between India and China ends after a 73-day standoff.	India; China
29 Aug.	North Korea launches an intermediate-range ballistic missile over northern Japan, triggering warning sirens in the area and prompting international condemnation.	North Korea; Japan
30 Aug.	A conciliatory move by President Paul Biya to release some jailed Anglophone leaders fails to stem unrest in Cameroon.	Cameroon
1 Sep.	Over 580 000 Rohingya civilians are estimated to have fled across the border into Bangladesh, prompting one of the fastest-growing refugee crises since World War II.	Myanmar; Bangladesh; Rohingya
1 Sep.	Kenya's Supreme Court annuls August's presidential election result, which gave victory to President Uhuru Kenyatta, and orders a rerun.	Kenya
1 Sep.	Russian President Vladimir Putin expels 755 US diplomats in response to US sanctions.	Russia; USA
3 Sep.	North Korea conducts its sixth and largest nuclear test, inflaming regional and international tensions.	North Korea; nuclear proliferation
4 Sep.	The Colombian Government and the National Liberation Army (ELN), the country's second main guerrilla group, announce a temporary ceasefire.	Colombia; ELN
4–6 Sep.	The Seventh Meeting of States Parties to the Convention on Cluster Munitions (CCM) takes place in Geneva, Switzerland.	CCM
5 Sep.	The UN Security Council unanimously adopts Resolution 2374 (2017), which establishes a sanctions regime against Mali, including a travel ban and assets freeze on individuals and entities impeding the implementation of the peace agreement.	UN; Mali
5 Sep.	Salvadorian rights groups present a report to the Inter-American Commission on Human Rights, chronicling alleged extrajudicial killings carried out by police elements within the Salvadorian National Police.	El Salvador
6–10 Sep.	The Caribbean and USA are struck by Hurricane Irma, the strongest hurricane ever recorded in the Atlantic basin outside the Caribbean and Gulf of Mexico. The storm causes at least 134 deaths and at least $63 billion in damage.	Caribbean; USA; extreme weather

11 Sep.	The UN Security Council unanimously approves Resolution 2375 in response to North Korea's sixth nuclear test explosion. The resolution contains several measures that strengthen sanctions on the North Korean economy.	UN; North Korea; sanctions
11–15 Sep.	The third conference of states parties (CSP3) to the Arms Trade Treaty (ATT) is held in Geneva, Switzerland.	ATT
19 Sep.	US President Trump tells the UN General Assembly that he would 'totally destroy' North Korea if it threatened the USA or its allies.	North Korea; USA; nuclear weapons
19–20 Sep.	Just two weeks after Hurricane Irma struck the Caribbean, Hurricane Maria strikes similar areas, causing at least 94 deaths and damage estimated in excess of $103 billion.	Caribbean; extreme weather
19–25 Sep.	Heads of state, foreign ministers and other high-level officials gather in New York, USA, for the UN General Assembly high-level debate to discuss urgent and emerging issues related to international peace and security.	UN
20 Sep.	Article XIV Conference on the Entry into Force of the Comprehensive Nuclear-Test-Ban Treaty (CTBT) takes place in New York, USA.	CTBT
20 Sep.	The TPNW opens for signature.	Nuclear weapon ban treaty
20 Sep.	The two main Tuareg coalitions of armed groups in Mali, the Platform (supporting national unity) and the separatist Coordination of Azawad Movements (CMA), reach an agreement that includes a ceasefire, release of prisoners and other confidence-building measures.	Mali
20 Sep.	The UN Security Council, the AU, the EU and the League of Arab States all endorse the UN Action Plan for Libya launched by the UN Support Mission in Libya (UNSMIL).	Libya; UN; EU; League of Arab States
23 Sep.	Forty murders in one day mark El Salvador's highest death toll in a single day this year. Nearly 200 people are reported killed that week in violence that police blame on fighting between criminal gangs.	El Salvador
25–29 Sep.	Iraqi Kurdistan holds a referendum on independence from Iraq in which over 92 per cent vote in favour, exacerbating tensions with the central government in Baghdad and within the region. Four days later the Iraqi Government bans international flights to and from Iraqi Kurdistan.	Iraq; Kurds
26 Sep.	The ban on women driving in Saudi Arabia is formally lifted (but the change does not come into effect until June 2018).	Saudi Arabia
27 Sep.	Russia completes the destruction of its CW stockpile.	Russia; CWs
27–28 Sep.	The high-level meeting to review the UN Global Plan of Action to Combat Trafficking in Persons takes place in New York, USA. It assesses achievements, gaps and challenges, including in the implementation of relevant legal instruments.	UN; human trafficking

1 Oct.	Over 800 people are injured as police try to block voting in an independence referendum organized by the regional government of Catalonia in north-east Spain, which the Spanish Government has declared illegal. The Catalan Government reports that 43 per cent of the electorate voted, 90 per cent of them favouring independence.	Spain; Catalonia
1 Oct.	The USA experiences the deadliest mass shooting in its modern history, with at least 58 people killed and over 500 wounded by a single gunman in Las Vegas.	USA; gun violence
1 Oct.	The confrontation between the Government of Cameroon and the Anglophone minority in the South West and North West regions continues to intensify as the Anglophone secessionists make a symbolic declaration of independence.	Cameroon
4 Oct.	In Niger, about 50 fighters from an IS-affiliated group ambush a Nigerien patrol and kill 4 US soldiers from a US Special Operations Task Force team that was accompanying the patrol.	Niger; USA; IS
5–11 Oct.	Reconciliation talks between the CMA and the Platform take place in Anéfis, Mali, and conclude with agreement on a road map for implementing the commitments reached during the talks.	Mali
6 Oct.	The International Campaign to Abolish Nuclear Weapons (ICAN) wins the Nobel Peace Prize.	Nobel peace prize; nuclear disarmament
12 Oct.	The USA announces its withdrawal from the UN Educational, Scientific and Cultural Organization (UNESCO) and is immediately followed by Israel.	USA; Israel; UNESCO
13 Oct.	US President Trump refuses to recertify the Iran nuclear agreement (JCPOA).	Iran; USA; JCPOA
14 Oct.	Two lorry bombs kill over 350 people, mostly civilians, in Mogadishu, Somalia, in the country's deadliest terrorist attack ever. The attack is suspected to have been carried out by al-Shabab.	Somalia; al-Shabab
16 Oct.	The Council of the EU adopts new autonomous EU sanctions to complement and reinforce those in UN Security Council Resolution 2375.	EU; North Korea; sanctions
16–20 Oct.	The Missile Technology Control Regime (MTCR) holds its 31st Plenary in Dublin, Ireland.	MTCR
17 Oct.	The head of UN peacekeeping operations in South Sudan warns the UN Security Council that the country is sliding into chaos and escalating violence.	South Sudan
17 Oct.	Over 70 people are killed in Afghanistan, mostly police, in Taliban attacks in the Paktia and Ghazni provinces.	Afghanistan; Taliban
17 Oct.	Raqqah, the de-facto IS capital, is declared fully liberated by the Syrian armed forces.	Syria; IS
19 Oct.	A Taliban attack on a military base in the province of Kandahar in southern Afghanistan kills over 40 soldiers.	Afghanistan; Taliban
20 Oct.	At least 56 people are killed in an attack by IS on a mosque in Kabul, the capital of Afghanistan.	Afghanistan; IS

25 Oct.	At the 19th National Congress of the Communist Party of China, Xi Jinping assumes his second term as General Secretary, and the political theory 'Xi Jinping Thought' is written into the party's constitution.	China
26 Oct.	A new global Women, Peace and Security Index is launched in New York, USA, at a side-event to the 2017 UN Security Council Open Debate on Women, Peace and Security. The index measures progress on women's inclusion, access to justice and security.	Women, peace and security
26 Oct.	A repeat presidential election is held in Kenya and is marked by further violence. President Kenyatta is declared the winner.	Kenya
27 Oct.	After Catalonia's parliament votes to declare independence, the Spanish Government dismisses the Catalan Government and calls new regional elections. Spain's Attorney General files charges against Catalan leaders for rebellion, sedition and misuse of public funds.	Spain; Catalonia
29 Oct.	The Iraqi Kurdistan president, Masoud Barzani, resigns after the Iraq Government forcibly takes back the disputed city of Kirkuk and its oil fields, as well as other parts of the disputed territories following the Kurdish region's earlier independence referendum.	Iraq; Kurds
31 Oct.	An individual claiming to act on behalf of IS drives a truck into people in New York, USA, killing 8 and injuring 11. It is the deadliest terrorist attack in the city since 11 September 2001.	USA; IS
3 Nov.	Both Deir Ez-Zor in Syria and Al-Qa'im in Iraq are declared liberated from IS.	Syria; Iraq; IS
4 Nov.	In response to the Houthis' foiled missile attack on Riyadh, Saudi Arabia, the Saudi Arabian-led coalition steps up its bombing campaign in Yemen.	Yemen; Saudi Arabia
5 Nov.	Saudi Arabia detains 11 princes, 4 ministers and dozens of former ministers as part of an alleged anti-corruption campaign.	Saudi Arabia
5 Nov.	Some of the details of the Paradise Papers, a set of 13.4 million confidential electronic documents relating to offshore investments that were leaked to a German newspaper, are made public.	Paradise Papers
6–17 Nov.	The 23rd annual Conference of the Parties (COP) under the UN Framework Convention on Climate Change (UNFCCC) takes place in Bonn, Germany. Agreement is reached on the foundations of a 'rule book' to chart progress in scaling back carbon emissions.	Climate change; Paris Agreement
13 Nov.	The Council of the EU imposes sanctions against Venezuela, including an embargo on the supply of arms and on material that might be used for internal repression.	EU; Venezuela; sanctions
13 Nov.	Airstrikes on a market in Atareb, northern Syria, kill at least 53 people. They are thought to have been carried out by either the Syrian Government or Russia.	Syria; Russia

13–14 Nov.	At the 31st Association of Southeast Asian Nations (ASEAN) Summit in Manila, Philippines, ASEAN and China formally announce the start of negotiations on the particulars of a code of conduct (COC) in the South China Sea.	ASEAN; China
13–17 Nov.	The Group of Governmental Experts on Lethal Autonomous Weapons Systems (LAWS) meets in Geneva, Switzerland, to discuss the technological, military and ethical/legal dimensions of emerging technologies in the area of LAWS.	LAWS
15 Nov.	Zimbabwean President Robert Mugabe is placed under house arrest as the military take control of the country.	Zimbabwe
16 Nov.	The mandate of the OPCW–UN Joint Investigative Mechanism (JIM) in Syria expires.	Syria; CWs; JIM
16 Nov.	Ahead of general elections scheduled for 2018, Cambodia's Supreme Court dissolves the Cambodia National Rescue Party, which is the main opposition to the Cambodian People's Party of the Prime Minister, Hun Sen, and bans more than a hundred of its members from politics for five years.	Cambodia
20 Nov.	The Eleventh Conference of the High Contracting Parties to Protocol V (on explosive remnants of war) to the Certain Conventional Weapons Convention (CCW) takes place in Geneva, Switzerland.	Protocol V; CCW
21 Nov.	The 19th Annual Conference of the High Contracting Parties to Amended Protocol II (on landmines and IEDs) to the CCW takes place in Geneva, Switzerland.	Protocol II; CCW
21 Nov.	A US airstrike in Somalia is reported to have killed over 100 al-Shabab militants.	Somalia; USA; al-Shabab
21 Nov.	Zimbabwean President Mugabe resigns following a 37-year rule, after being abandoned by the military and his own party.	Zimbabwe
22 Nov.	Ratko Mladic, former Bosnian Serbian commander, is sentenced to life imprisonment by the International Criminal Tribunal for the former Yugoslavia (ICTY), after being found guilty of genocide and war crimes in the Balkans conflicts over two decades ago.	Bosnia and Herzegovina; ICTY
22–24 Nov.	The Meeting of the High Contracting Parties to the CCW takes place in Geneva, Switzerland. The discussions focus on incendiary weapons, EWIPA and 'mines other than anti-personnel mines' (MOTAPM).	CCW
23 Nov.	Myanmar and Bangladesh sign a repatriation agreement, but the conditions necessary for the voluntary and safe repatriation of Rohingya refugees do not yet exist.	Myanmar; Bangladesh; Rohingya
24 Nov.	Islamic militants attack a mosque in Egypt's Sinai peninsula killing at least 305 people and wounding at least 128 in the deadliest terrorist attack in Egypt's modern history. No group claims responsibility, but IS is the main suspect.	Egypt; terrorism

26 Nov.	The general elections in Honduras trigger a crisis as the final vote count is postponed and the opposition alliance candidate, Salvador Nasralla, alleges fraud. Protests break out in several parts of the country when it becomes apparent that incumbent President Juan Orlanda Hernández will win by a small margin.	Honduras
27 Nov.	The Organization for Security and Co-operation in Europe (OSCE) reports substantial progress in talks held in Vienna, Austria, between leaders from Moldova and its breakaway region Transnistria.	Moldova; Transnistria
27–28 Nov.	A regional conference on the protection of civilians from the use of explosive weapons in populated areas (EWIPA) meets in Maputo, Mozambique.	EWIPA
27 Nov.– 1 Dec.	The 22nd Conference of the States Parties to the CWC meets in The Hague, Netherlands, to agree a 2018 programme and budget.	CWC
28–29 Nov.	North Korea test launches a new type of long-range ballistic missile. North Korean leader Kim Jong Un says that his country has completed its state nuclear force and achieved its goal of becoming a nuclear power.	North Korea; nuclear and missile proliferation
30 Nov.	The Government of Niger gives the USA permission to base and use armed unmanned aerial vehicles (UAVs, drones) from Niamey, the country's capital.	Niger; USA; UAVs
30 Nov.	Armed clashes break out in Sana'a, Yemen, between formerly allied Houthi and Saleh forces.	Yemen
2 Dec.	Former Yemeni president Saleh reaches out to the Saudi Arabian-led coalition battling the Houthis and offers peace talks if it lifts a blockade on Yemen.	Yemen; Saudi Arabia
4 Dec.	Former Yemeni president Saleh is killed by the Houthis, previously his alliance partners, initiating a new phase in the conflict that includes intensified airstrikes by the Saudi Arabian-led coalition.	Yemen; Saudi Arabia
4–8 Dec.	The annual Meeting of States Parties to the BTWC agrees a further intersessional process of annual meetings for the period 2018–20.	BTWC
5 Dec.	The United Arab Emirates (UAE) announces the formation of a new political and military alliance with Saudi Arabia, throwing into doubt the future of the 36-year old Gulf Cooperation Council (GCC).	UAE; Saudi Arabia; GCC
6 Dec.	US President Trump's declaration that the USA recognises Jerusalem as Israel's capital is condemned by the international community and Palestinians.	USA; Israel; Palestine
6–7 Dec.	The plenary of the Wassenaar Arrangement (WA) is held in Vienna, Austria. India is admitted as the 42nd participating state.	WA; India
7 Dec.	President Recep Tayyip Erdoğan makes the first visit to Greece by a Turkish head of state in 65 years.	Turkey; Greece
7 Dec.	The foreign ministers of the OSCE Minsk group co-chair countries issue a joint statement supporting resumed and intensified diplomacy in regard to Nagorno-Karabakh.	OSCE Minsk group; Nagorno-Karabakh

8 Dec.	The EU and the UK reach a deal on the terms of Brexit, after months of negotiations, and talks are opened on their future relationship.	UK; EU; Brexit
8 Dec.	On the 30th anniversary of the signing of the 1987 Treaty on the Elimination of Intermediate-Range and Shorter-Range Missiles (INF Treaty), the US State Department announces a new US strategy for resolving the INF Treaty dispute with Russia.	USA; INF Treaty
9 Dec.	Iraq declares victory in its war against IS. After lengthy assaults, an array of forces drove IS from its main stronghold in Iraq, the city of Mosul.	Iraq; IS
11 Dec.	EU member states formally activate the permanent structured cooperation (PESCO) on defence envisaged in the Lisbon Treaty.	EU; PESCO; military cooperation
11 Dec.	Russian President Putin visits Syria and announces a drawdown of Russian forces in the country, having declared victory over IS.	Syria; Russia; IS
12–14 Dec.	Delegations from the five parties to the INF Treaty (Belarus, Kazakhstan, Russia, Ukraine and the USA) hold a meeting of the treaty's dispute-resolution mechanism, the Special Verification Commission, in Geneva, Switzerland.	INF Treaty
13 Dec.	Martial law is extended for another year on Mindanao, Philippines.	Philippines
13 Dec.	Twelve members of a Congolese militia group are convicted of raping young girls in a landmark case in the fight against impunity for sexual violence crimes.	DRC; sexual violence
14 Dec.	Eighteen police officers are killed in an attack by al-Shabab on the Somalian police academy.	Somalia; al-Shabab
15 Dec.	The Mexican Congress passes a law strengthening the military's role in combating organized crime, authorizing the deployment of soldiers to areas controlled by drug gangs.	Mexico
17 Dec.	On the second anniversary of the 2015 Libyan Political Agreement, Field Marshal Khalifa Haftar announces that he considers the agreement to have expired and that related institutions are no longer valid.	Libya
18 Dec.	The USA uses its first UN Security Council veto in six years to block a resolution that would have indirectly criticized the Trump administration's decision to recognize Jerusalem as the capital of Israel.	USA; Israel; Palestine; UN
18–21 Dec.	The 16th Meeting of States Parties to the APM Convention takes place in Vienna.	APM Convention
19 Dec.	The Houthis in Yemen fire another missile at Riyadh, Saudi Arabia, which Saudi forces reportedly intercept over the city.	Yemen; Saudi Arabia
20 Dec.	The US special envoy to Ukraine, Kurt Volker, says 2017 is the most violent year so far in the conflict in Ukraine.	Ukraine
20 Dec.	The USA confirms that multiple ground operations involving US troops are taking place in Yemen.	USA; Yemen

21 Dec.	The South Sudanese Government and armed opposition groups sign a cessation of hostilities agreement.	South Sudan
21–22 Dec.	The eighth round of Russian, Iranian and Turkish-backed Syrian peace talks take place in Astana, Kazakhstan, and end with agreement to hold a peace congress for Syria in Sochi, Russia, in Jan. 2018.	Syria; Astana peace talks
22 Dec.	The UN Security Council unanimously approves Resolution 2397, which further tightens sanctions against North Korea, including measures to cut the country's petroleum imports by up to 90 per cent.	UN; North Korea; sanctions
24 Dec.	Guatemala follows the USA's lead by announcing that it will also move its Israeli embassy to Jerusalem; Honduras and Panama do the same two days later.	Israel; Palestine
28 Dec.	Anti-government protests start in the Iranian city of Mashhad and quickly spread to other towns and cities, where they also take on a political dimension.	Iran
29 Dec.	In a joint statement on the milestone of 1000 days of war in Yemen, the heads of three UN agencies reiterate calls for parties to the conflict to immediately allow full humanitarian access and stop the fighting.	Yemen; humanitarian crisis
29 Dec.	An attack on Coptic Christians outside Cairo, Egypt, kills at least nine people.	Egypt; IS
30 Dec.	Crowds attack state buildings in Tehran, the capital of Iran.	Iran

About the authors

José Alvarado Cóbar (Guatemala) is a Research Assistant in SIPRI's Peace and Development Programme, conducting research on gender and conflict. Prior to joining SIPRI, he completed his graduate thesis on the fragmentation of women's organizations during peace processes and the potential outcomes during post-conflict peacebuilding. He has also conducted research on human trafficking, gang violence and mining conflicts in the United States and Guatemala, as well as on the monitoring and evaluation of health and education projects in Jordan.

Dr Ian Anthony (United Kingdom) is the Director of SIPRI's European Security Programme. His recent publications include 'Våldets polarisering i svenska städer' [The polarization of violence in Swedish cities], *Våldsbejakande extremism* [Violent extremism] (SOU, Aug. 2017, co-author, in Swedish); 'Secure Cities: Inclusivity, resilience and safety', SIPRI Insights on Peace and Security no. 2017/3 (Aug. 2017); 'European Security after the INF Treaty', *Survival: Global Politics and Strategy* (Dec. 2017–Jan. 2018); 'Closing Sweden's military security deficit: The national debate on NATO membership' (NATO Defence College, Mar. 2018, co-author); and 'Military dimensions of a multipolar world: Implications for global governance', *Strategic Analysis* (May 2018).

Dr Sibylle Bauer (Germany) is the Director of Studies for Armament and Disarmament at SIPRI. Since 2018 she is also the Director of SIPRI's Disarmament, Arms Control and Non-proliferation Programme, having previously lead and established SIPRI's Dual-use and Arms Trade Control Programme. In that capacity, she designed and implemented capacity-building activities in Europe and South East Asia. Before joining SIPRI in 2003, she was a Researcher at the Institute for European Studies (ULB) in Brussels. Her recent publications include '3D printing and missile technology controls', SIPRI Background Paper (Nov. 2017, co-author); *Challenges and Good Practices in the Implementation of the EU's Arms and Dual-use Export Controls: A Cross-sector Analysis* (SIPRI, July 2017, co-author); and *Setting the Stage for Progress towards Nuclear Disarmament* (SIPRI, Apr. 2018, co-author).

Kolja Brockmann (Germany) is a Research Assistant in SIPRI's Dual-use and Arms Trade Control Programme. He conducts research in the field of non-proliferation and export control, focusing on compliance, transfers of technology, additive manufacturing and the Arms Trade Treaty. Previously, he did a European Union Non-Proliferation Consortium internship at SIPRI and an internship at the German Federal Office for Economic Affairs and

Export Control (BAFA). He received his MA in Non-Proliferation and International Security from King's College London. His recent publications include *The Challenge of Emerging Technologies to Export Controls: Controlling Additive Manufacturing and Intangible Transfers of Technology* (Apr. 2018, co-author) and *Challenges and Good Practices in the Implementation of the EU's Arms and Dual-use Export Controls: A Cross-sector Analysis* (July 2017, co-author).

Mark Bromley (United Kingdom) is the Director of SIPRI's Dual-use and Arms Trade Control Programme, where his work focuses on national, regional and international efforts to regulate the international arms trade. Previously, he was a Policy Analyst for the British American Security Information Council (BASIC). His recent publications include 'Export controls, human security and cyber-surveillance technology: Examining the proposed changes to the EU Dual-use Regulation' (SIPRI, Dec. 2017); 'Challenges and good practices in the implementation of the EU's arms and dual-use export controls: A cross-sector analysis' (SIPRI, 2017, co-author); and 'ATT-related outreach assistance in Latin America and the Caribbean: Identifying gaps and improving coordination', SIPRI Background Paper (Feb. 2017, co-author).

Dr Marina Caparini (Canada) is a Senior Researcher within Peace and Development at SIPRI. Her research focuses on peacebuilding and the nexus between security and development. She has conducted research on diverse aspects of security and justice governance in post-conflict and post-authoritarian contexts, including police development, intelligence oversight, civil-military relations, anti-corruption measures, and the regulation of private military and security companies. Recently, she has focused on police in peace support operations and capacity building, and policy responses to forced displacement, irregular migration, organized crime and violent extremism. Prior to joining SIPRI in December 2016, she held senior positions at the Norwegian Institute for International Affairs, the International Center for Transitional Justice and the Geneva Centre for the Democratic Control of Armed Forces.

Dr Ian Davis (United Kingdom) is the Executive Editor of the SIPRI Yearbook and an Associate Senior Fellow within Armament and Disarmament at SIPRI. From 2014–16 he was the Director of SIPRI's Editorial, Publications and Library Department, responsible for supervising a team of editors and managing the departmental budget and workflow. Prior to joining SIPRI, he held several senior positions and worked as an independent human security and arms-control consultant. He has a long record of research and publication on international and regional security issues and blogs on

NATO-related issues. His recent publications include *The British Bomb and NATO: Six Decades of Contributing to NATO's Strategic Nuclear Deterrent* (Nov. 2015).

Dr Tytti Erästö (Finland) is a Researcher in SIPRI's Nuclear Weapons Project, within the Disarmament, Arms Control and Non-proliferation Programme. Her recent and current research focuses on the Iran nuclear deal, the Treaty on the Prohibition of Nuclear Weapons, the United States/ NATO–Russia missile defence dispute, and the global disarmament and non-proliferation regime. Previously, she worked at the Ploughshares Fund in Washington, DC; the Belfer Center for Science and International Affairs, Harvard Kennedy School; the Vienna Center for Disarmament and Non-Proliferation; and the Tampere Peace Research Institute in Finland. Her recent publications include 'Time for Europe to put Iran's missile programme in context', SIPRI Topical Backgrounder (Oct. 2017) and 'Will the EU and the USA part ways on the Iran deal?', SIPRI Topical Backgrounder (Oct. 2017, co-author).

Vitaly Fedchenko (Russia) is a Senior Researcher in SIPRI's European Security Programme, responsible for nuclear security issues and the political, technological and educational dimensions of nuclear arms control and non-proliferation. Previously, he was a visiting researcher at SIPRI and worked at the Center for Policy Studies in Russia and the Institute for Applied International Research in Moscow. He is the author or co-author of several publications on nuclear forensics, nuclear security, international non-proliferation and disarmament assistance, nuclear forces and the international nuclear fuel cycle.

Dr Aude Fleurant (Canada/France) is the Director of SIPRI's Arms and Military Expenditure Programme. Her research interests focus on the transformation of the military market and analysis of the interaction of supply and demand dynamics. Previously, she was the Director of Arms and Defence Economics at the Military Academy Strategic Research Institute in Paris. She has authored many articles on the arms industry and military expenditure during her tenures at the Military Academy and at SIPRI. Her recent publications include 'Trends in world military expenditure, 2017', SIPRI Fact Sheet (May 2018, co-author) and 'Trends in international arms transfers, 2017', SIPRI Fact Sheet (Feb. 2018, co-author).

Richard Ghiasy (Netherlands) is a Researcher and Project Manager in SIPRI's China and Global Security Programme, where his overarching interest is the security–development nexus. He studies China's foreign and security policy, European Union–China and China–Central Asia relations, Europe and Asia's infrastructure and economic integration, and all affairs pertaining to Afghanistan's politics, development and security. Recently, his research has concentrated on European and Asian economic, infrastructure and security integration. This is primarily through analysis of the Belt and Road Initiative's security implications: *The Silk Road Economic Belt: Considering Security Implications and EU-China Cooperation Prospects* (SIPRI, Feb. 2017, co-author). Ghiasy has lived in China for extended periods and has conducted field research and presented his findings in more than 30 countries.

Zoë Gorman (United States) is a Research Assistant in SIPRI's Sahel/West Africa Programme. Her research interests include developing new methods for quantitative analysis of peace and security issues for policymaking and exploring the interplay of state conflict and violent extremism. She received a double major in political science and physics from Yale University and has written policy papers on security in Africa and the MENA region for the Center for Media and Peace Initiatives in New York, The Quilliam Foundation in London, and Innovations for Poverty Action in Accra. She also served as a Communications Coordinator at the United Nations General Assembly in 2015 and managed a successful political campaign in Alaska.

Dr John Hart (United States) is a Senior Researcher and the Head of the Chemical and Biological Security Project in SIPRI's Disarmament, Arms Control and Non-proliferation Programme. He has also worked as a Senior Consultant to the Comprehensive Nuclear-Test-Ban Treaty Organization (CTBTO).

Shannon N. Kile (United States) is a Senior Researcher and the Head of the Nuclear Weapons Project in SIPRI's Disarmament, Arms Control and Non-proliferation Programme. His principal areas of research are nuclear arms control and non-proliferation, with a special interest in the nuclear programmes of Iran and North Korea. His work also looks at regional security issues related to Iran and the Middle East. He has contributed to numerous SIPRI publications, including chapters on nuclear arms control and nuclear forces and weapon technology for the SIPRI Yearbook since 1994.

Dr Florian Krampe (Germany/Sweden) is a Researcher in SIPRI's Climate Change and Risk Programme, specializing in peace and conflict research, environmental and climate security, and international security. His primary academic interest is the foundations of peace and security, especially the processes of building peace after armed conflict. He is currently focusing on climate security and the post-conflict management of natural resources, with a specific interest in the ecological foundations for a socially, economically and politically resilient peace. Krampe is an Affiliated Researcher at the Research School for International Water Cooperation in the Department of Peace and Conflict Research, Uppsala University, and part of the UNESCO Centre on International Water Cooperation.

Hans M. Kristensen (Denmark) is the Director of the Nuclear Information Project at the Federation of American Scientists (FAS) and a SIPRI Associate Senior Fellow. He is a frequent consultant to the news media and institutes on nuclear weapon matters, and is co-author of the 'Nuclear notebook' column in the *Bulletin of the Atomic Scientists*. His recent publications include 'INF, New START and what really matters for US–Russian nuclear arms control', *Russia Matters* (Feb. 2017), 'The growing threat of nuclear war and the role of the health community', *World Medical Journal* (Oct. 2016), and 'Nuclear arsenals: current developments, trends and capabilities', *International Review of the Red Cross* (July 2016, co-author).

Alexandra Kuimova (Russia) is a Research Assistant in SIPRI's Arms and Military Expenditure Programme. Working with SIPRI's databases on military expenditure, the arms industry and arms transfers, she focuses on developments in the Middle East and North Africa region, and post-Soviet states. Before joining SIPRI, Kuimova was an Intern in the Department of New Challenges and Threats at the Ministry of Foreign Affairs of the Russian Federation. She has also completed summer internships at Abdelmalek Essaâdi University, Morocco, and Cairo State University. Her recent publications include 'Trends in international arms transfers, 2017', SIPRI Fact Sheet (Mar. 2018, co-author) and 'The SIPRI Top 100 arms-producing and military services companies, 2016', SIPRI Fact Sheet (Dec. 2017, co-author).

Dr Moritz Kütt (Germany) is a Postdoctoral Research Associate with the Program on Science and Global Security at Princeton University. His current research includes nuclear reactor simulations of fissile material production and elimination, and new nuclear warhead verification technologies for disarmament and arms control applications.

Dr Jaïr van der Lijn (Netherlands) is the Director of SIPRI's Peace Operations and Conflict Management Programme. He is also a Senior Research Fellow at the Netherlands Institute of International Relations 'Clingendael' and an Associate Fellow at the Radboud University in Nijmegen. His research interests include the future of peace operations, their evaluation and factors for success and failure, and comprehensive approaches in missions. His recent publications include *Peacebuilding and Friction: Global and Local*

Encounters in Post-conflict Societies (Routledge, 2016, co-editor); 'Peacekeepers under threat? Fatality trends in UN peace operations', SIPRI Policy Brief (Sep. 2015, co-author); *African Directions: Towards an Equitable Partnership in Peace Operations* (SIPRI, 2017, co-author); and 'Multilateral peace operations and the challenges of organized crime', SIPRI Background Paper (Feb. 2018).

Dr Diego Lopes da Silva (Brazil) is an Associate Researcher with SIPRI's Arms and Military Expenditure Programme. He holds a PhD in Peace, Defense and International Security Studies from São Paulo State University. His publications have mainly addressed issues of arms trade and transparency in military expenditure. Prior to SIPRI, he held research positions at the Group of Defense Studies and International Security (GEDES) and the Latin American Security and Defense Network (RESDAL).

Giovanna Maletta (Italy) is a Research Assistant in SIPRI's Dual-use and Arms Trade Control Programme. Her research on export control covers compliance and enforcement issues, with a particular focus on the dual-use and arms export control policies of European Union (EU) member states. She also works with activities related to SIPRI's role in the EU Non-proliferation and Disarmament Consortium. Her recent publications include *The Challenge of Software and Technology Transfers to Non-proliferation Efforts: Implementing and Complying with Export Controls* (SIPRI, Apr. 2018, co-author) and *Challenges and Good Practices in the Implementation of the EU's Arms and Dual-use Export Controls: A Cross-sector Analysis* (SIPRI, July 2017, co-author).

Dr Neil Melvin (United Kingdom) is the Director of SIPRI's Horn of Africa Peace and Security Project. Previously, he has held senior positions at the Organisation for Security and Co-operation in Europe, the Energy Charter Secretariat and the European Union. He has also held posts at the Centre for European Studies and the Royal Institute of International Affairs (Chatham House), as well as teaching positions at the London School of Economics, the University of Leeds and the Brussels School of International Studies. Melvin has been a Visiting Research Fellow at Harvard University, and he has a DPhil from the University of Oxford.

Dr Zia Mian (Pakistan/United Kingdom) is the Co-Director of the Programme on Science and Global Security at Princeton University, where he also directs the Project on Peace and Security in South Asia. His work focuses on nuclear weapons, arms control and disarmament, and nuclear energy issues in India and Pakistan. He is co-editor of the journal *Science & Global Security* and co-chair of the International Panel on Fissile Materials.

He is co-author of *Unmaking the Bomb: A Fissile Material Approach to Nuclear Disarmament and Nonproliferation* (MIT Press, 2014).

Dr Pavel Podvig (Russia) is a Researcher in the Program on Science and Global Security at Princeton University and a Senior Research Fellow at the United Nations Institute for Disarmament Research (UNIDIR). He began his work on security issues at the Center for Arms Control Studies at the Moscow Institute of Physics and Technology (MIPT), which was the first independent research organization in Russia dedicated to analysis of technical issues related to arms control and disarmament. Podvig directs his own research project, Russian Nuclear Forces (RussianForces.org). He is also a Co-editor of *Science & Global Security* and a member of the International Panel on Fissile Materials.

Timo Smit (Netherlands/Sweden) is a Researcher in SIPRI's Peace Operations and Conflict Management Programme. He is in charge of SIPRI's database on multilateral peace operations and conducts research on trends in peace operations and various related thematic issues. Prior to rejoining SIPRI in 2014, he worked for the European Union Institute for Security Studies (EUISS) and the North Atlantic Treaty Organization (NATO) Parliamentary Assembly. His recent publications include *African Directions: Towards an Equitable Partnership in Peace Operations* (SIPRI, 2017, co-author) and 'Multilateral peace operations and the challenges of terrorism and violent extremism', SIPRI Background Paper (Nov. 2017).

Dan Smith (United Kingdom) is the Director of SIPRI. He has a long record of research and publication on a wide range of conflict and peace issues. His current work focuses on the relationship between climate change and insecurity, on peace and security issues in the Middle East and on global conflict trends. He served four years in the United Nations Peacebuilding Fund Advisory Group, two of which (2010–11) were as the Chair. From 2014 to 2017 he was also a Professor of Peace & Conflict at the University of Manchester. He is the author of successive editions of atlases of politics, war and peace, and the Middle East, and of a blog on international politics.

Fei Su (China) is a Research Assistant in SIPRI's China and Global Security Programme, first joining in March 2015 as a Beijing-based representative. Her research interests focus on China's foreign and security policy, especially China's engagement with North Korea, South Korea and Japan. She is currently conducting research within the field of geo-economics in a project that analyses the security implications of China's Maritime Silk Road in the South China Sea and Indian Ocean Region. Prior to joining SIPRI, Su studied in Seoul for three years, where she strengthened her fluency in Korean. She holds an MA in Public Administration from the Graduate School of Public Administration at Seoul National University, focusing on governance. She wrote her Korean-language dissertation on the impact of government size on corruption in China.

Dr Nan Tian (South Africa) is a Researcher in SIPRI's Arms and Military Expenditure Programme, where he leads the Military Expenditure Project. His region of expertise is Africa and Latin America, with research interests focused on the causes and impact of military expenditure and civil conflict, and the issues relating to transparency and accountability in military budgeting, spending and procurement. Previously, he worked as an Economist on climate change at the World-Wide Fund for Nature (WWF) and was a Lecturer at the University of Cape Town. He has published in *Defence and Peace Economics*; *The Economics of Peace and Security Journal*; and *Peace Economics, Peace Science and Public Policy*.

Johanna Trittenbach (Germany) was an intern in SIPRI's Dual-use and Arms Trade Control Programme (Nov. 2017–Feb. 2018), where she worked on the challenges of emerging technologies to arms export controls, as well as on various databases. Her research interests focus on international and regional disarmament and arms control agreements, their implementation and their compliance. Prior to commencing her post-graduate studies in Public International Law, she is currently doing an internship at the United Nations Regional Centre for Peace and Disarmament in Asia and the Pacific (UNRCPD) in Kathmandu, working on implementing a pilot programme on small arms and light weapons (SALW) control from a gender perspective.

Maaike Verbruggen (Netherlands) is a PhD Researcher at the Institute for European Studies, Vrije Universiteit Brussel. From 2016–17 she worked as a Research Assistant at SIPRI, where she researched emerging military and security technologies. Her area of expertise is the challenges that emerging military technologies pose for arms control. Of special interest are the implications of the changing nature of science and technology for military innovation, and the potential synergies between arms control regimes to regulate emerging military technologies. She has an MPhil in Peace and Conflict Studies from the University of Oslo, and has done traineeships at the United Nations Office for Disarmament Affairs, and the Department for Non-Proliferation, Disarmament, Arms Control and Arms Export Controls at the Dutch Ministry of Foreign Affairs.

Pieter D. Wezeman (Netherlands/Sweden) is a Senior Researcher in SIPRI's Arms and Military Expenditure Programme. He has contributed to many SIPRI publications since 1994, including SIPRI's annual reviews of global trends in arms transfers, arms industry and military expenditure. Among other things, he has published on military expenditure and capabilities in the Middle East, multilateral arms embargoes, arms flows to Africa, and the European arms industry. In 2003–2006 he also worked as a Senior Analyst on arms proliferation for the Dutch Ministry of Defence, and in 2017 as a Technical Expert for the United Nations Group of Governmental Experts during a review of the UN Report on Military Expenditure.

Siemon T. Wezeman (Netherlands) is a Senior Researcher in SIPRI's Arms and Military Expenditure Programme. His areas of research include the monitoring of arms transfers, military spending and arms-producing companies, with a particular focus on the Asia–Pacific and the former Soviet regions, the use of weapons in conflicts, transparency in arms transfers, and the development of conventional military technologies. His recent publications include 'Military capabilities in the Arctic: A new cold war in the high North?', SIPRI Background Paper (Oct. 2016); 'Trends in world military expenditure, 2017', SIPRI Fact Sheet (May 2018, co-author); and 'Trends in international arms transfers, 2017', SIPRI Fact Sheet (Feb. 2018, co-author).

Errata

SIPRI Yearbook 2015: Armaments, Disarmament and International Security

Page 615	*For* 'The 2014 Arms Trade Treaty (ATT)' *read* 'The 2013 Arms Trade Treaty (ATT)'

SIPRI Yearbook 2017: Armaments, Disarmament and International Security

Page 74	*For* 'Section III provides an overview of military expenditures in and arms transfers to the countries of the Middle East' *read* 'countries of the MENA region'
Page 74	*For* 'Regional military spending increased by 50.5 per cent over the period 2006–15' *read* 'increased by 54 per cent'
Page 74	*For* 'Saudi Arabia is by far the largest military spender in the Middle East' *read* 'MENA region'
Pages 74, 106	*For* 'Arms imports to the region increased by 86 per cent between 2007–11 and 2012–16' *read* 'increased by 68 per cent'
Page 74	*For* 'The Middle East accounted for 29 per cent of global arms imports in 2012–16' *read* 'The region accounted for 34 per cent of global arms imports'
Page 366, figure 10.1	*For* the figure's y-axis labels '50 000, 40 000, 30 000, 20 000 and 10 000' *read* '50, 40, 30, 20 and 10'

SIPRI Yearbook 2018: Armaments, Disarmament and International Security

Errata for this printed version of SIPRI Yearbook 2018 will appear at <http://www.sipri.org/yearbook/> and in SIPRI Yearbook 2019. The online version of SIPRI Yearbook 2018 at <http://www.sipriyearbook.org/> will be updated as errors are discovered.

Index

Moise, Jovenel 133
Moldova:
JCC Peacekeeping Force 145
OSCE Mission to Moldova 145
peace operations 137, 145
peace process 521
Transnistria 521
unresolved conflict 60, 61–62
Mongolia: ATT signatory 410
Montano, Inocente Orlando 37–38
Montenegro: NATO membership 514
MONUSCO (UN Stabilization Mission
in the Democratic Republic of Congo)
102, 105, 106, 111, 123–25, 144
Morocco:
Arab Spring 66
arms imports 199, 201
MINURSO 122–23, 144, 512
Western Sahara conflict 512
Morsi, President Mohammed 68
Moscow Treaty (SORT, 2002) 4–5, 482
Mosisili, Pakalitha 126
MOTAPMs (mines other than anti-
personnel mines) 380, 392, 521
Mozambique:
arms imports from DPRK 418
cluster munitions 400
landmines and 380, 395
military expenditure 162
MTCR (Missile Technology Control
Regime) 404, 424, 425, 428–30, 438,
445, 506–507, 519
Mubarak, President Hosni 21
Mugabe, President Robert 83, 521
Mulet, Edmond 353, 357
Multinational Joint Task Force
(MNJTF) against Boko Haram 101, 139,
141–42
Myanmar:
armed conflict 48–52
arms embargoes 208
arms imports 208
ARSA 50
Australia Group and 427
ethnic minorities 48–52
EU arms embargo 421
Kachin Independence Army 49
landmines 393–94
military expenditure 165
MNDAA 49
peace conferences 49
Rohingya 30, 49–52, 208, 394, 421, 517,
521

Nagorno-Karabakh:
conflict 62–63, 510
Minsk Group 502, 522
OSCE PRCIO 145
peace operation 137, 145
Nairobi Protocol (2004) 478
Namibia: arms imports from DPRK 418
Naqou, Najmi al- 419
Nasralla, Salvador 522
National Intelligence and Space Center
(NASIC) 245, 266
NATO (North Atlantic Treaty
Organization) 499–501
Afghanistan 46, 104–106, 109, 135–36,
145
airbases: nuclear weapons 242
arms industry and 232
CFE Treaty and 5
enlargement 5
Euro-Atlantic Partnership Council 499
INF Treaty and 321–22, 323
Istanbul Cooperation Initiative 500
Mediterranean Dialogue 500
members 195, 514
military expenditure target 167, 170
NATO–Georgia Commission 500
NATO–Russia Council 500
NATO–Ukraine Commission 500–501
North Atlantic Council 323
nuclear weapons: modernization 243
peace operations 107, 145
ISAF 104–105
KFOR 107, 109, 137, 145
RSM 46, 106, 107, 109, 135–36, 145
Romanian membership 168
Russia and 12, 17, 248, 500
TPNW and 311, 312
Turkey and 15–17
Nayef, Muhammad bin 515
Nepal:
earthquakes (2015) 56
military expenditure 165
peace process 55–57
personnel contribution to peace
operations 109
poverty 56
Netherlands:
arms exports 195, 197, 206
arms imports from USA 195, 209
Syrian chemical weapons and 354
TPNW and 311, 314, 316, 515
uranium enrichment facilities 293
US nuclear weapons in 242